# FREEDOM FOR THEMSELVES

CIVIL WAR AMERICA
Gary W. Gallagher,
editor

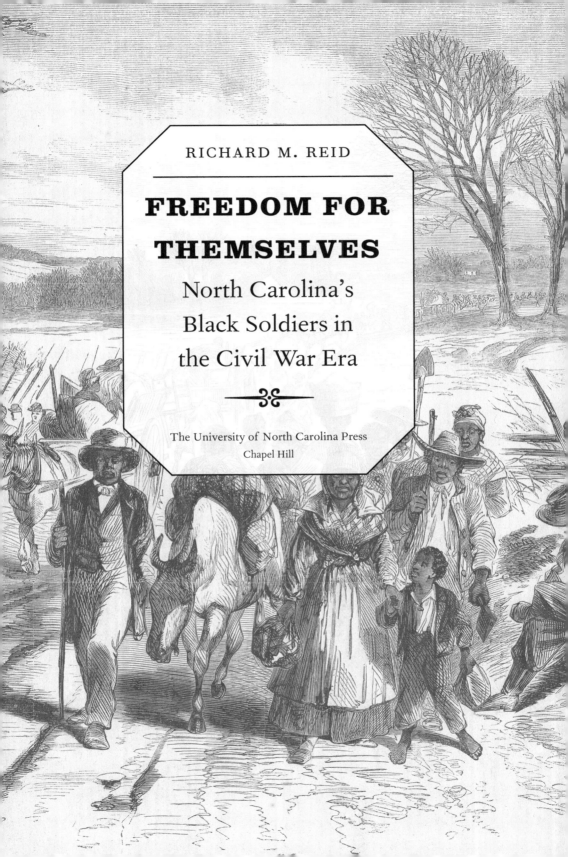

RICHARD M. REID

# FREEDOM FOR THEMSELVES

North Carolina's
Black Soldiers in
the Civil War Era

The University of North Carolina Press
Chapel Hill

—⸭—

This book was published with the assistance of
the Fred W. Morrison Fund for Southern Studies
of the University of North Carolina Press.
Designed by Heidi Perov
Set in Fournier and Clarendon
Manufactured in the United States of America
The paper in this book meets the guidelines for permanence
and durability of the Committee on Production Guidelines for
Book Longevity of the Council on Library Resources.

Library of Congress Cataloging-in-Publication Data
Reid, Richard M., 1943–
Freedom for themselves : North Carolina's Black soldiers
in the Civil War era / Richard M. Reid.
p. cm.—(Civil War America)
Includes bibliographical references and index.
ISBN 978-0-8078-3174-8 (cloth: alk. paper)
1. United States—History—Civil War, 1861–1865—Participation,
African American. 2. North Carolina—History—Civil War, 1861–1865—
Participation, African American. 3. African American soldiers—North
Carolina—History—19th century. 4. North Carolina—History—Civil War,
1861–1865—Regimental histories. 5. United States—History—Civil War,
1861–1865—Regimental histories. 6. United States. Army. Colored Infantry
Regiment, 35th (1864–1866) 7. United States. Army. Colored Infantry Regiment,
36th (1864–1866) 8. United States. Army. Colored Infantry Regiment,
37th (1864–1867) 9. United States. Army. Colored Heavy
Artillery Regiment, 14th (1864–1865) I. Title.
E540.N3R45 2008
973.7'415—dc22
2007029358

12 11 10 09 08   5 4 3 2 1

*For Susan,*
*who accepts me as a curmudgeon*

# CONTENTS

Preface  xi

Introduction  1

**ONE**
Raising and Training the Black Regiments  19

**TWO**
A Fine, Fighting Regiment  67

**THREE**
Issues of "Civilized" Warfare  111

**FOUR**
A Unit of Last Resort  153

**FIVE**
Black Workers in Blue Uniforms  187

**SIX**
Families of the Soldiers during the War  215

**SEVEN**
Service in the Postwar South  255

**EIGHT**
Black Veterans in a Gray State  297

Conclusion  323

Notes  329

Bibliography  389

Index  407

# MAPS AND ILLUSTRATIONS

MAPS

Eastern North Carolina, 1863  10

Battle of Olustee, Florida, February 1864  80

Richmond, Virginia, and Environs, 1864–1865  113

Roanoke Island, North Carolina, 1862–1865  225

Lower Rio Grande, Texas, 1865–1866  265


ILLUSTRATIONS

"Effects of the Proclamation, Freed Negroes Coming into
Our Lines at Newbern, North Carolina," 1863  12

Col. James C. Beecher  26

Sgt. Frank "Sergt. Bob" Roberts, 35th USCT  34

"The Steamer 'Escort' Running the Rebel Batteries
near Washington, North Carolina," 1863  60

Lt. Col. William N. Reed  77

"Battle of Olustee, Fla.," 1864  82

Surg. Henry O. Marcy  90

Maj. Archibald Bogle  96

Col. Alonzo Granville Draper  116

Lt. Col. Abial G. Chamberlain  156

"Recruiting Office for Contrabands on Market Street,
Wilmington, N.C.," 1865  183

"Recruiting at Newbern, N.C.," 1864  195

"The Campaign in North Carolina, Headquarters of Vincent Collyer,
Superintendent of the Poor at New Bern, Distribution of Clothing
to the Contraband," 1862  219

"Confederate Prisoners in Camp Georgia [at Weir Point],
Roanoke Island," 1862  229

"Wilmington Front Street, 1865"  283

USCT veterans from Washington County, N.C., ca. 1900  307

Civil War veteran William B. Gould and his six sons  326

# PREFACE

In late September 1864 Gen. Benjamin F. Butler wrote to his wife from his headquarters at the intersection of the Varina and New Market roads, just outside of Richmond, Virginia. The day before, the men of Gen. Charles J. Paine's all-black Third Division had taken part in an assault on Richmond's outer defenses. Butler had written the letter after riding across the battlefield where the black soldiers under his overall command had attacked the Confederate entrenchments on New Market Heights. He had moved slowly across the field of carnage. The hundreds of bodies still lying there left a lasting impression on the Union general. The bravery and sacrifice of the black soldiers seemed at odds with the treatment they had received from the Federal government. "Poor fellows," Butler observed to his wife, "they seem to have so little to fight for in this conflict, with the weight of prejudice loaded upon them, their lives given to a country which has given them not yet justice, not to say fostering care." He could better understand why white troops were willing to risk all in the conflict. "To us, there is patriotism, fame, love of country, pride, ambition, all to spur us on, but to the negro, none of these for his guerdon of honor. But there is one boon they love to fight for, freedom for themselves, and their race forever."[1] Although Butler had not begun the war as a supporter of black recruitment, by 1864 he was deeply angered that some Northern officials belittled the idea that black troops had the ability or the will to fight well.

Butler's growing respect for the contributions of black soldiers and his resentment of white Northern prejudice echoed the shifting attitudes toward race and slavery during the war years. Both the racial assumptions of white Americans and the Federal policies regarding African Americans underwent enormous change in the four bloody years after the firing on Fort Sumter. In 1861 the Federal government had refused the early offers of black men to enlist. Writers, ignoring historical precedents, argued that African Americans were unfit and unprepared for military service. According to President Abraham Lincoln, in response to the mere news in August 1861 that Gen. John C. Frémont (acting under his declaration of martial law) had freed the slaves of disloyal owners, "a whole company of our Volunteers threw down their arms and disbanded."[2] Many white soldiers—in North and South alike—shared the views expressed late in the war by the Confederacy's Maj. Gen. Howell Cobb to Secretary of War James A. Seddon. Cobb's opposition to black enlistment reflected earlier Northern feeling toward calls to enlist African Americans in the Union army. "I think that the proposition to make soldiers of our slaves is the most pernicious idea that has been suggested since the war began," Cobb told Seddon. "You cannot make soldiers of slaves, nor slaves of soldiers. . . . The day you make soldiers of them is the beginning of the end of the revolution. If slaves will make good soldiers, our whole theory of slavery is wrong— but they won't make good soldiers."[3]

The enlistment of blacks challenged not only Southern attitudes toward slavery, but also Northern views on what constituted proper race relations and the existence of discriminatory laws in the North. The majority of people in both sections of the nation did not believe that black soldiers could be the equal of white soldiers, and many of these doubters would cling to their prejudices even in the face of contradictory evidence.[4] Eventually, most white Northerners came to accept the practical need and even the desirability of enlisting black soldiers and sailors, but many did so only grudgingly as the war progressed. By the end of the conflict, some 179,000 black soldiers and 9,500 black sailors were in uniform. In the social climate of the era, how well they were perceived to have served depended both on how well they fought and on white America's willingness to recognize their achievements.

Once black troops entered combat, many of the white soldiers who had initially served alongside them only under protest and with much trepidation changed their minds. After black infantrymen had driven off an attack by Nathan Bedford Forrest's Rebel cavalry, their Union commander confessed: "I have been one of those men, who never had much confidence in colored troops fighting, but these doubts are now all removed, for they fought as bravely as any troops in the Fort."[5] Even Northern communities saw a shift in perspective. Eight months after white mobs had hunted black residents through the streets of New York City, the 20th Regiment of U.S. Colored Troops (20th USCT) paraded through the streets to the cheers of thousands of white citizens. The black soldiers received flattering speeches about their martial abilities and accepted a new stand of colors from "the first ladies of the City." The *New York Times* summed up the altered racial sentiment: "It is only by such occasions that we can all realize the prodigious revolution which the public mind everywhere is experiencing. Such developments are infallible signs of a new epoch."[6]

But for African Americans, it was not an entirely new epoch. At the same time that a growing number of white Northerners were altering their perceptions of black abilities, others firmly adhered to their existing prejudices. While many regarded the unsuccessful attack on Fort Wagner by the 54th Massachusetts, an African American regiment led by Col. Robert Gould Shaw, as a testimony to black bravery and discipline under fire, others did not. Maj. Henry L. Abbott, an equally prominent Massachusetts officer, felt that Shaw had been "sacrificed for an experiment." Abbott regarded the failure at Fort Wagner as proof that black soldiers "won't fight as they ought. For I am satisfied that they went back on their officers at the first shot."[7] Many senior officers in the Union army continued to hold similar views. Well into the fourth year of the war, Gen. William T. Sherman believed that blacks were of little use as soldiers and would be better employed as laborers. He opposed the recruitment of freed slaves to meet Northern draft quotas. "It is an insult to our Race to count them as part of the quota," he wrote. "A nigger is not a white man, and all the Psalm singing on earth won't make him so."[8] Such attitudes meant that black soldiers and their officers had to demonstrate their abilities and their courage over and over again.

The Civil War has long fascinated historians, in part by how it split or altered existing loyalties and ideologies. As the war intensified and as the fortunes of war shifted, policies and priorities of all governments involved in the struggle changed and re-formed. Union authorities who had earlier excluded African Americans from the war effort came to see them as a potentially useful ally. The changing views toward the institution of slavery, the use of black troops, and the perception of how black troops behaved all reflected the ambivalence of American thought in that time of crisis. Consequently, a study of black soldiers from even one state can reveal many things, including the spectrum of black military experiences and the changing white response. Years ago, when I first became interested in writing a book on black Union soldiers from North Carolina, I briefly considered spotlighting the history of one regiment. What drove my curiosity was the belief that the military service of these troops was both interesting and important—a story worth telling. The question was how to structure it. Examining one regiment had certain advantages because, by its very nature, a military organization generates large collections of documents that illuminate its membership and performance over time. The composition of the men filling the ranks or receiving commissions can often be drawn from these documents. In other words, a unit study provides both structure and sources. Yet at the same time, regimental biographies are prone to problems and limitations. Those concerns ultimately caused me to expand the project in order to illuminate a broader range of historical issues.

Some of the reasons for extending the focus were obvious. The process of selecting a regiment to study and the act of writing the subsequent history runs the risk of bias. It almost inevitably favors the regiments whose ranks teemed with heroes created at critical junctures of the Civil War and whose battle flags carried the names of the war's most famous engagements. Less studied are the units that broke at the first sound of musket fire or who saw little fighting and spent most of the war as provost marshal troops or on garrison duty around towns, well removed from the fighting. There is, understandably, a difficulty in constructing exciting stories from the boredom of war without combat or from the marginal contribution of units whose services were at best only average. Yet it seemed to me that there existed an obligation to a great many Civil War soldiers—black and white—to contributions made by the unexceptional soldiers, the ones who more frequently died from diseases or in forgotten skirmishes. In addition, the wartime experiences of African American soldiers could not, and should not, be isolated from their own communities. The bloody war, and the role played by black troops in it, had an enormous impact not only on the soldiers' lives during and after the war but also on the lives of their families and friends. How these men fought altered how their nation viewed them and their kin. Any study of black soldiers should try to capture some of that change. *Freedom for Themselves* was envisioned as fitting into the more recent studies of the impact of the war on all aspects of American society.

The African Americans who filled the ranks of the four Federal regiments raised in North Carolina seemed to offer an opportunity to speak to soldiers less often examined.[9] These men made up the vast majority of the approximately six thousand black recruits from the state, and most who survived the war returned to or remained in North Carolina during Reconstruction. These men reflect the diversity of the black military experience, from garrison troops to frontline soldiers. At least two of the regiments were involved in allegations of Confederate atrocities directed at black soldiers, an example of what Mark Grimsley refers to as racism's "very long shadow."[10] The real value of this study lies in the fact that the activities, abilities, and utilization of these four regiments were sufficiently varied to encompass the experiences of most black soldiers. Moreover, there were sufficient contradictions, demonstrations of extreme competence and total confusion, and acts of valor and timidity among these units to ensure that no simplistic image of the black soldier would dominate.

The first black infantry regiment recruited fought with considerable distinction, but in a lesser-known theater and in the shadow of other units whose officers were quicker to publish when the war ended. The men's conduct in battle raises issues of how black troops, particularly Southern black troops, were perceived to have performed. The second infantry regiment served as competently as most Civil War regiments when it had the chance. Before it became part of the Army of the James, this regiment experienced irregular warfare in the South and, as a camp guard of Confederate prisoners, became a powerful symbol of racial change. By contrast, the third—and final—black infantry regiment from North Carolina was treated by senior officers as a unit of last resort, one that was not entirely trustworthy. The fourth unit examined in this study, an artillery regiment, never engaged in combat and its men were used more as laborers than soldiers. All of its casualties were caused by diseases, ruptures from heavy lifting, or accidents involving heavy guns or careless musket handling. Nevertheless, this last regiment made an important contribution to the logistical buildup in the Carolina campaign. The relationship between white officers and black enlisted men also varied greatly among the regiments. The first infantry regiment, unlike the other units, completed its service without any sign of bitter animosity between officers and men. By contrast, the third infantry regiment would see one of its officers killed by rebellious soldiers in the ranks. Indeed, the attraction of these four regiments is that their variations and differences allow an examination of the full range of the black experience during the Civil War and its turbulent aftermath, when black troops policed a defeated South.

The title of the book, *Freedom for Themselves*, is meant to highlight the greatest accomplishment of these soldiers as a group, while at the same time hinting at other social gains that would be denied them despite all of their sacrifices. As Butler suggested, whereas black troops fought for freedom for themselves and their kin, what they achieved was a freedom that lacked so many of the privileges automatically extended to white veterans that it fell well short of their needs and dreams. And yet, in the military many blacks found a degree of equality they had not experienced in civilian life. The army, as an institution run by regulations and a delineated command structure, functioned most effectively and logically when race was not a determinant. It is true that the Federal government was slow to establish equal treatment in all areas. In June 1863 the U.S. War Department, acting on the advice of solicitor William Whitney, announced that it would pay black soldiers less than their white counterparts. It took Congress a year to redress the situation.[11] But on other issues, such as the handling of captured black soldiers, the Union army acted immediately and firmly to prevent them from being treated differently because of their race.

On the other hand, most of the officers who implemented Federal military regulations and orders had entered the service encumbered with the values, attitudes, and prejudices of the larger society. Between theory and implementation lay an ambivalent alliance between white officers and black enlisted men. This book points to some of the difficulties in assessing that relationship. As the war progressed, the Union army and African Americans became bound together by a common enemy, but that union was always ambiguous. When the first black regiments were formed, it was assumed that the officers and men, facing the same dangers, shared the same goals. That was only partly true. The vast majority of white officers assigned to the North Carolina regiments in the first year of recruitment deeply opposed the institution of slavery. Most of them also believed that black soldiers could and would fight effectively, and many accepted political equality as a black aspiration. Far fewer, however, would accept their social equality. White officers assumed that African Americans would need an extended period of paternal guidance before they would be ready for full independence. As a result of these attitudes, when the officers of North Carolina's black soldiers are compared, as a group, to other white officers at that time, they look racially progressive and sympathetic to black troops. But when their expectations of what the black soldiers wanted and needed are contrasted to the actual aspirations of these African Americans, a wide gulf emerges. At times, that gulf that could not be bridged.

It would be interesting if the soldiers themselves could be asked if their sacrifices had been worthwhile. As Butler suggested, what they fought for and what they received in return troubled more than just the black soldiers. Unlike many white veterans, when the war ended few of North Carolina's black veterans were able to translate their military career into a public or political career, and few came away from the conflict with the financial resources to achieve economic independence. Many were incapacitated in a host of ways. Only in their own communities could they expect to be seen and treated as heroes. For black Union veterans from Southern states realized at least as many liabilities as benefits from their service. And yet for all that, many were more than willing to pay the cost. How do you measure the intangibles expressed by one black soldier? "I felt like a man with a uniform and a gun in my hand."[12] It is hoped that this book will provide a measure of recognition long due these Civil War soldiers.

Recognition is also due of the many intellectual debts that a work of this nature accrues. Archivists and staff at the various institutions where I did my research invariably provided courteous treatment and patient guidance. I am particularly indebted to the National Archives and the U.S. Army Military History Institute for the always kind assistance I received. As anyone who has worked at these two institutions knows, Richard Sommers and Michael P. Musick have contributed enormously and in many ways to scholars of the American Civil War. Special thanks are also due the staff at the Massachusetts Historical Society, the Southern Historical Collection at the University of North Carolina, the archives at Duke University and East Carolina University, and the North Carolina Department of Archives and History. Much of the research for this book was funded by a Social Science and Humanities Research Council grant. I also benefited from being part of a USMA Summer Seminar at West Point. The instructors and my colleagues in the seminar had a significant impact on how I now approach military history. To them, I owe thanks.

Over the years I have sought help and advice from many friends and colleagues in order to distribute blame and to limit hostile reviews. I have been better served than I probably deserve. People giving valuable assistance, often after reading early chapters of the manuscript, include Dick Fuke, Jeff Prushankin, Joe Mobley, and John David Smith. In addition, my colleagues at the University of Guelph have always been ready and willing to give me advice and explain the errors and weaknesses in my arguments. Above all, I must thank my family, Susan, Chris, Andrew, and Jamie, for accepting me when I became preoccupied or too loquacious and for reading the bumpy parts of the manuscript. The good news is that I truly appreciate your support. The bad news is that I have a new project.

# FREEDOM FOR THEMSELVES

# Introduction

When the first engagements of the Civil War took place in the early summer of 1861, few young black men in North Carolina could have envisioned that in just over two years they would join the Union army and strike a blow against the Confederacy. For a variety of reasons, there seemed little likelihood that they would have the opportunity or, perhaps, the inclination to fight other Southerners. Many Southerners believed that the conflict would be over quickly, and, in any event, Union forces seemed far removed from North Carolina. In the first months of the war, local officials worked hard, if not always effectively, to make sure that the state would be ready to resist any Federal incursions, although few North Carolinians expected that the enemy could occupy a considerable part of their state. Moreover, any African American showing reluctance to support the Confederate war effort, let alone offering to help the Yankees, could anticipate swift retribution. With time, as the magnitude of the war became clear, many blacks understood that freedom was a possibility but that caution was necessary. Flight seemed a more successful strategy than insurrection, but either course required that the war come to North Carolina. Significant numbers of black North Carolinians would not find freedom or be able to join the Federal army until early 1862, when Maj. Gen. Ambrose E. Burnside's amphibious expedition managed to capture parts of eastern North Carolina. Only then was there any real opportunity for African Americans to aid the Union cause.

Even at the start of 1862, however, it was not clear how much black assistance, if any, would be encouraged by the Lincoln administration. In the early months of the war, as white volunteers surged forward, young black men in the North who tried to enlist in the U.S. Army were turned away. Although African Americans had served in both the American Revolution and the War of 1812, Federal authorities referred to a law passed in 1792 that prevented blacks from joining the army. Just two weeks after Fort Sumter surrendered, Secretary of War Simon Cameron announced that "this Department has no intention to call into the service of the Government any colored soldiers." In some places, as in Cincinnati, authorities were openly racist. "We want you damned niggers to keep out of this," a constable warned would-be black recruits. "This is a white man's war." Nevertheless, Northern blacks continued to organize and drill in the expectation that they would be allowed to fight at some point in the future.[1] Before the U.S. War Department would allow black soldiers into the Union army, however, a major adjustment in Northern attitudes as well as in the administration's policies had to occur. Given the slowness of changes in social attitudes, it was an enormous difficulty. In early 1861 only a small minority of white Americans in the North believed that the goal of the Civil War should be to end slavery; even fewer could envision that African Americans had an important role to play in the struggle. For most Northerners, the war was above all, as the Cincinnati policeman claimed, a white man's war to restore the Union to the way it had been before secession. The views of Gen. George B. McClellan, the military officer in whom Lincoln placed great hope during late 1861 and early 1862, mirrored this sentiment. As he confided to a friend in November 1861, "I am fighting to preserve the integrity of the Union . . . to gain that end we cannot afford to mix up the negro question."[2] It would require time and heavy casualties to alter such views.

In a number of ways, President Lincoln reflected the ambiguity felt by many Northerners. Slavery, he believed, was an unqualified evil to Americans, both white and black; as a Republican, he firmly opposed the spread of slavery to any U.S. territory as the first step toward its ultimate extinction. At the same time, he thought that the U.S. Constitution protected the institution in any state where the citizens wanted it protected. Moreover, because, he maintained, secession was unconstitutional, he saw the war as a rebellion of individuals against the legitimate Federal government. Given this argument, he felt, as president bound by the Constitution, his office compelled him to defend the existing right of loyal Southerners to hold slaves. With the fall of Fort Sumter, Lincoln came under increasing pressure from abolitionist groups to use the exigency of war to abolish slavery outright. His response to the conflicting demands was equivocal and fluid. The president's unwillingness to adopt a doctrinaire position only increased the widespread confusion about the government's actual policy.[3]

Of course, Lincoln's refusal to consider using black troops in the early stages of the war was also a result of his strategic and political concerns. He was convinced that only if the "loyal" slave states of Kentucky, Maryland, Missouri, and Delaware were held in the Union could the Confederate rebellion be crushed. Kentucky, in particular, was critical—the president was convinced that "to lose Kentucky is nearly the same as to lose the whole game."[4] Any action that could alienate the border states had to be discouraged, especially in the first year of the war. Perhaps because his roots were in Kentucky, Lincoln believed that he understood public opinion in the border states. A majority of citizens there would support the Union as long as the Federal government did not threaten slavery. Lincoln thus began the war willing to sacrifice black military aspirations in order to preserve the loyalty of the border states' slaveholders. It was only as the war dragged on, with escalating casualties and no clear signs of victory, that Lincoln, and Northern public opinion, would move, in graduated steps, to endorse emancipation and the widespread use of black troops. In the first year of the war, Lincoln tried to balance competing perspectives throughout the North and overrode commanders who either held more progressive views of the martial potential of African Americans or who wanted to appeal to the abolitionist emotions of the North and free Southern slaves.

The president's disparate responses to the actions of two Union generals highlighted his efforts to juggle the issues of emancipation and black military involvement. In May three fugitive slaves, who had been working on Confederate fortifications in Virginia, sought asylum within Union lines at Fort Monroe. The commanding general, Benjamin F. Butler, a man with little military experience but a keen political sense, refused to return the runaways to their owners, claiming that they were legitimate "contraband of war." Butler thus effectively both established their freedom and gained their labor while avoiding the issue of emancipation. Pragmatic officials, who were encouraged by the president's tacit approval, quickly followed Butler's example. In sharp contrast, Lincoln came under intense abolitionist criticism a few months later when he overruled the commander of the Western Department, Gen. John C. Frémont, also a man of limited military experience but with considerable political connections. At the end of August, after unsuccessfully grappling with the military and logistical problems facing him, Frémont had placed Missouri under martial law, ordered the death penalty for captured guerrillas, and issued an emancipation proclamation freeing the slaves of all Confederate sympathizers in the state. He later claimed: "As a war measure this, in my opinion was equal to winning a deciding battle."[5] Frémont's actions were popular in Northern circles but triggered cries of outrage in the border states. Lincoln first privately, then publicly, told the general to modify his proclamation. Frémont's refusal, his incompetence, and growing evidence of fraud and corruption among his staff finally led to his removal from command in October 1861.

Lincoln also faced pressure from within his administration to broaden black involvement in the war effort. By the early fall, Secretary of War Cameron, whose name was increasingly linked to stories of waste, corruption, and mismanagement, reversed his earlier position and began to endorse the possible arming of escaped slaves. He suggested to friends and associates that they might be used in combat and even tried to include authorization for their use in the War Department's annual report. In response to Cameron's action telling Gen. Thomas Sherman to use the freed slaves as he saw fit, Lincoln warned his general that under no circumstance should he consider "a general arming of them for military use."[6]

By the end of the first year of fighting, Northern opinion had begun to change. Military victory seemed no closer, and an increasing number of politicians and civilians had become convinced that there had to be an end, in some form, to Southern slavery. More Americans had come to accept the view of Gen. Ulysses S. Grant, whose own wife owned several slaves, that "if it is necessary that slavery should fall that the Republic might continue, let slavery go." The U.S. Congress, in passing the Second Confiscation Act and the Militia Act in July 1862, edged toward greater involvement of blacks in the war.[7] Despite these signs of change, Lincoln continued to believe that he had to proceed cautiously. As a result, when three of his generals began to recruit black soldiers in early 1862, the administration initially disallowed the actions, only to reverse its position in the months that followed. In Kansas, Brig. Gen. Jim Lane, a former senator from that state, recruited a regiment of black soldiers despite being twice informed by the War Department that he had no authority to do so. Lane simply ignored the notifications. In the first weeks of 1863, the 1st Kansas Colored Volunteers was formally mustered into service. Only then could the men be officially equipped and paid, even though many had already experienced battle.[8]

In South Carolina, Gen. David Hunter, a committed abolitionist who felt

that he had the support of Secretary of War Edwin Stanton, aggressively recruited a regiment of ex-slaves, often against their will, and, on 9 May 1863,
proclaimed all slaves in South Carolina, Georgia, and Florida forever free.
His actions triggered an angry debate in the U.S. House of Representatives,
where border politicians warned that arming African Americans was a violation of civilized conduct and could precipitate a slave war. Radicals ridiculed
their fears and called for greater use of armed blacks. Lincoln, who had to
chart a course between the two extremes, chose to revoke Hunter's proclamation while effectively turning a blind eye to his recruiting efforts. Nevertheless, it was not until late August, after Hunter had been replaced by Gen.
Rufus Saxon, that Secretary of War Stanton gave his first official authorization for the arming and equipping of up to five thousand black soldiers in
South Carolina.[9]

In Louisiana, events followed a slightly different path. There, Gen. John
W. Phelps, a career officer and antislavery advocate, clashed with his direct superior, General Butler, over the need to free slaves immediately and
to enlist black soldiers. After months of butting heads with Butler, Phelps
unilaterally decided in July 1862 to raise five black companies as a way of
forcing a decision from his superiors. In the absence of direction from the
War Department, Phelps asked Butler for arms and equipment for the men
he had recruited. Butler refused to provide the weapons, pointing out that
the president had not yet authorized the use of black soldiers and the arms
and equipment that he had for Louisiana volunteers was expressly limited to
white soldiers. His earlier order that Phelps use his recruits as a labor detail
enraged Phelps, who offered his resignation, refusing, in his words, to act as
a slave driver. His companies were never mustered in. Within a short time,
however, Butler, who was concerned about a Confederate threat to New
Orleans, reversed his position and accepted the need for black troops.[10] He
appealed to the free blacks of New Orleans to reconstitute the Louisiana Native Guard, promising them that they could keep their black officers. Butler
was astute enough to characterize them to authorities in Washington as all
being free, light-skinned blacks.[11] Moreover, because this group had been
originally organized under Confederate authority, Richmond could hardly
protest Butler's actions. Having forced Phelps out, Butler could then claim
credit for being the first Union general to have officially raised a black regiment.[12] Even if he began as a slow, and perhaps opportunistic, convert to the

need for black military service, Butler's willingness to use black officers was a radical position in 1862. The general remained an active champion of the black soldier until the end of the war.

Saxon and Butler had been able to take the actions they did in part because their conduct could be characterized as an ad hoc response to a critical but local problem. More important, however, they had more freedom in their decision making because, as the summer of 1862 progressed, Lincoln had come to accept the military necessity of involving blacks in the war effort. With the failure of McClellan's Peninsula campaign in Virginia and the lack of sustained success in the West, an end to the war seemed a long way off. Moreover, the apparent willingness of thousands of black men to serve stood in sharp contrast to the declining number of white volunteers. Despite all of his pragmatic arguments, the president was unable to persuade border state politicians and slaveholders to accept a program of gradual compensated emancipation. As a result, by August 1862 Lincoln was willing to overlook the action of some officers to enroll black troops even as he officially rejected an offer by the members of an Indiana delegation, including congressmen, to raise two black regiments from their state. His explanation to this group, and to a similar request from Chicago the next month, was that such a step would cost his army fifty thousand men from border states. The president was less than candid with the petitioners, however, because on 22 July he had already informed his cabinet that he intended to issue a proclamation as commander in chief freeing all slaves, for military reasons, in states engaged in war against the Union. Although his cabinet had agreed with his proposal, Secretary of State William H. Seward had persuaded Lincoln to hold off the announcement until after a Federal victory. The bloody battle of Antietam provided the opportunity, and on 22 September 1862 Lincoln proclaimed that as of 1 January 1863 "all persons held as slaves within any state . . . then . . . in rebellion against the United States shall be then, thenceforward, and forever free." By the time the Emancipation Proclamation went into effect, an additional paragraph had been added authorizing the use of the newly emancipated slaves by the army and navy in particular ways.[13]

As the president expected, the response to his proclamation and to the implications of employing black soldiers was diverse and emotional. He was, after all, making extraordinary use of the chief executive's war powers and was poised to erase millions of dollars of private property.[14] But many abolitionists and Northern blacks thought that his actions were too limited and should have been based on moral principles, not military necessity. Governor John A. Andrew of Massachusetts felt that it was "a poor document but a mighty act." George E. Stephens, who would serve in the 54th Massachusetts Regiment, labeled it "an abortion wrung from the Executive womb by necessity . . . the dogs laugh at it as they pass." Other Northerners felt that the president was moving too quickly and argued that freeing the slaves, to say nothing of using them as soldiers, would have a disastrous effect on slaves and free people alike. The *Chicago Times* called it "a wicked, atrocious and revolting deed," while the Illinois lower house adopted a series of resolutions condemning the Emancipation Proclamation and Lincoln's actions. In the legislature, Indiana politicians demanded that the proclamation be withdrawn. In the Army of the Potomac, many soldiers shared the views of Cpl. Felix Brannigan, who wrote his sister in New York: "We don't want to fight side by side with the nigger. . . . We think we are a too superior race for that." William Stoddard, one of the president's secretaries, reminisced that Lincoln's critics had been quick to warn that "the army will fight no more." Stoddard then quoted a soldier whose views he believed were more representative: "The Proclimashin? Well! Yes! I'm an old Hunker myself. Hardest kind of Hardshell Democrat. I ain't no Abolitionist. But then, if Old Abe kin get the niggers to quit work, it'd cut off the supplies of Lee's army. I'd thought of it myself, but I didn't think Linken'd hev the grit to up and do it. It's an all-fired good move, so far's the army's consarned."[15]

Even in the first months of 1863, after the proclamation had gone into effect, the Federal government encouraged black enlistment in an uneven fashion despite the escalating manpower needs generated by the bloody war. Although Secretary Stanton allowed the governors of Massachusetts, Connecticut, and Rhode Island to begin organizing black regiments, he refused a similar request from the Ohio governor. Northern blacks from Ohio and other states were expected to join the New England regiments. The black manpower pool in the North was clearly limited. Census officials informed the administration that the population of Northern free blacks of military age had been overestimated, claiming that only about forty thousand could be found.[16] If large numbers of African Americans were to be added to the army, recruitment would have to be encouraged in the occupied Southern states, where there were many more potential troops. Major recruiting efforts were soon begun in Louisiana under Gen. Daniel Ullmann, in the upper Mississippi Valley under Adj. Gen. Lorenzo Thomas, and in eastern North Carolina under Brig. Gen. Edward A. Wild. Although moving toward the large-scale utilization of Southern blacks in these areas, the War Department provided no uniform direction of recruiting activities for several months. It was not until May 1863 that the Federal government established a special branch to systematize and regulate the organization of black troops.

General Order No. 143, in establishing the Bureau of Colored Troops, centralized the process by which black regiments would be raised and staffed. Once it began operating, individuals could no longer do this "on a catch-as-catch-can basis with little or no control from Washington." The order stipulated that no longer could one person raise more than one regiment. All of the new regiments were to be numbered sequentially by the Adjutant General's Office as "—— Regiment of U.S. Colored Troops" (USCT).[17] To ensure that only qualified men were commissioned in these regiments, three screening boards were set up by the fall of 1863 in Washington, Cincinnati, and St. Louis to examine all potential officers who applied to the USCT and determine the rank at which the successful candidates would enter the service. The screening served a useful purpose because, as Stoddard satirized: "It was astonishing how large a number of second lieutenants of volunteers were willing to sacrifice themselves for the good of the service as majors and colonels."[18] This new procedure effectively limited the powers of a recruiter for a black regiment to select and appoint his own officers. However, because General Wild had been authorized to raise the first three North Carolina regiments before the Bureau of Colored Troops was established, he had few constraints on how he structured and staffed his regiments. Of course, other officers operating before the bureau was set up enjoyed many of the same powers. When General Saxon was authorized by Stanton "to arm, uniform, equip, and receive into the service of the United States" up to five thousand African Americans, he was allowed to appoint the officers to command them.[19] What would distinguish Wild's actions were not so much the exceptional powers that he had, but rather the way that he tried to use them to create a model brigade that would demonstrate black capacity.

—— ❦ ——

Although changes in Federal policy made possible the official utilization of black soldiers in the Union army by early 1863, a series of events in Washington and North Carolina had led to the Union's occupation of parts of eastern North Carolina. That occupation, in turn, opened up the possibility that black soldiers could be recruited from that state. By late 1861 General McClellan, who had reorganized the Army of the Potomac and had been appointed commander in chief of the army, was under increasing pressure to move on the Confederacy. When his friend and fellow West Point graduate, Ambrose Burnside, proposed creating a large joint land and sea force that could be used against the Confederate coast, McClellan seized on the idea as if it were his own and forwarded it to the secretary of war. Although McClellan had envisioned using the force in the Chesapeake Bay area, in the end the newly created division, under Burnside's command, was ordered to North Carolina, where another joint force led by flag officer Silas H. Stringham and General Butler had already captured the Rebel forts guarding Hatteras Inlet on the Outer Banks.

In early January Burnside's army, consisting of fourteen regiments of northeastern troops—about thirteen thousand men—was prepared to sail from Annapolis, Maryland. His first priority, McClellan had informed him, was to capture Roanoke Island, New Bern on the Neuse River, and Fort Macon on Bogue Banks. Possession of Roanoke would give Burnside control of the Albemarle and Currituck sounds, while from the latter two points he could seize part of the Atlantic and North Carolina Railroad and even threaten the Wilmington and Weldon Railroad supplying Richmond. Characteristically, McClellan cautioned Burnside against advancing too far inland. After a four-day trip, much of it in bad weather, the first of Burnside's motley flotilla of almost one hundred vessels reached Hatteras Inlet on 13 January 1862. Nevertheless, it was not until 3 February that the Federal fleet was inside the shelter of the Outer Banks and could prepare to move on Roanoke Island.[20]

Facing the Union invaders on the island were about 2,500 Confederate troops, many of them ill and all poorly equipped.[21] Although Brig. Gen. Henry A. Wise commanded the district, he remained at Nags Head while Col. Henry W. Shaw of the 8th North Carolina held field command on Roanoke Island. Late on 7 February, after Union gunboats had engaged the Confederate forts on the northwest end of the island, the first of Burnside's men landed at Ashby's Harbor, about half way up the west side of Roanoke. The next morning, as they started to advance, they encountered the defensive line thrown up by Colonel Shaw. With little more than 1,400 men and three pieces of artillery manned by untrained gunners, Shaw hoped that the natural

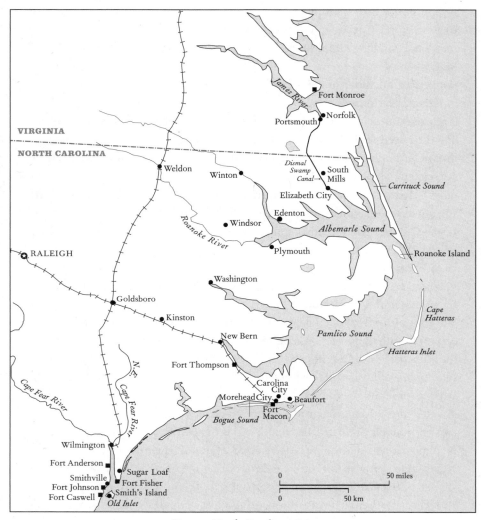

Eastern North Carolina, 1863

strength of his position, with swamps on both sides, would help him hold off the greater Federal numbers. For about five hours, Shaw's troops maintained their position until Northern soldiers fought their way through the swamps to turn both flanks of the Confederate line. With ammunition for the artillery exhausted and his flanks turned, Shaw ordered a retreat up the island. By the end of the day he had surrendered all remaining Confederate forces on the island. The "glorious" victory, in which his troops had captured more than 2,500 prisoners, made Burnside a national hero in the North. Confederate officers in North Carolina, by contrast, believed that his triumph would encourage greater resistance. An officer at New Bern claimed: "Since the Roanoke affair. . . . Our men are almost Crazy to Meet the Enemy."[22]

They had that opportunity a month later, when Burnside moved on New Bern, a position less vulnerable than Roanoke Island. Although the Confederate forces led by Brig. Gen. Lawrence O'Bryan Branch were half the number under Burnside's command, Rebel fortifications along the Neuse River were formidable.[23] Below the town were the mile-long Croatan breastworks near Otter Creek and another line of breastworks at the river battery, Fort Thompson. Because he was short of troops, Branch decided that the partially finished works at Fort Thompson provided his best defense. As a result, the Confederates manning the larger Croatan breastworks quickly abandoned them when threatened by a Federal landing above that position. After a day in which both sides endured heavy rain, mud, and cold weather, at dawn on 14 March the Union regiments attacked the Confederate lines at Fort Thompson while Federal gunboats shelled the river battery. Branch's brigade of six regiments was stretched over almost two and a half miles. In addition, the Rebel general had positioned a militia battalion at a critical point in the center where there was a brick kiln. After a short but fierce engagement, the militia gave way, opening a gap in the Confederate lines that the Federal soldiers were able to exploit. Branch's troops were driven back, and he was forced to order a general retreat.[24] After burning the bridges over the Trent River, most of the Confederates were able to withdraw toward Kinston.

Less than a week after capturing New Bern, Burnside moved troops toward his third objective: Fort Macon overlooking the Bogue Sound. The substantial casemated fort, completed in 1832, was the key to the deepwater ports of Beaufort and Morehead City, but it was vulnerable to a land attack. The fort had only four guns of long range, little ammunition, a depleted garrison, and no mortars to counter siege operations. By 12 April 1862 Federal forces had crossed over to Bogue Banks, pushed the defenders back into the fort, and begun siege operations. Although the commander of the fort's garrison, Col. Moses J. White, initially refused to surrender to Burnside on 24 April, an eleven-hour bombardment by heavy mortars and thirty-pound rifles reduced much of the fort and all of White's determination to resist. The fort, White, and almost four hundred Confederate prisoners passed into Union hands.

"Effects of the Proclamation, Freed Negroes Coming into Our Lines at Newbern,
North Carolina" (*Harper's Weekly*, 21 February 1863, Courtesy of North Carolina
Collection, University of North Carolina Library at Chapel Hill)

The captured soldiers were quickly paroled. Control of Fort Macon gave the
North Atlantic Blockading Squadron an important coaling station for ships
trying to seal off Wilmington and other Confederate ports. Within weeks,
schooners had begun to arrive from Philadelphia carrying coal to refuel the
Union ships that blockaded the Cape Fear River.[25]

The establishment of Union garrisons in parts of eastern North Carolina
opened up a large pool of potential black recruits that could be exploited once
the Lincoln administration had decided to actively recruit African Americans.
It was a manpower pool that was both valuable and growing. At all stages
of the Union occupation, significant help had been provided by black North
Carolinians. Typically, Burnside's decision to land his forces at Ashby's Harbor on Roanoke Island had been influenced by information provided by an
African American named Tom. Once the Union troops had arrived, the exis-

tence of Federal garrisons acted as magnets for slaves trying to escape their bondage. As black refugees flooded into Union-occupied towns, overworked Federal officials attempted to assess the actual numbers of African Americans clustered around New Bern and the contraband camps. In early 1863 Pvt. Henry A. Clapp of the 44th Massachusetts was assigned the task of compiling a census of the freed black population in the areas of North Carolina under Union control. The census, which was completed by March, indicated that there were at least 8,500 black refugees in New Bern and the three outlying camps.[26] Federal officers were quick to suggest various ways in which the freedmen might be used, working either for the army or in the army.

By the start of 1863, then, the occupation of parts of North Carolina and the new willingness of the Federal government to incorporate African Americans into the war effort made possible the recruitment of black North Carolinians. An important catalyst for such actions was provided by Massachusetts governor John Andrew, who had long been one of the most ardent advocates both of emancipation and of using black troops. Once the president had issued the Emancipation Proclamation, Andrew and a group of Massachusetts radicals traveled to Washington in early January to get permission from Lincoln and Stanton to raise black regiments in their state. Before the end of the month, the governor had authorization to recruit black soldiers and had begun to organize the 54th Massachusetts for "volunteers of African descent." With the help of white abolitionist George L. Stearns and black leaders and volunteers throughout the North, Andrew was able to fill the new regiment and to start raising a second unit, the 55th Massachusetts. Because of the opposition of many white Northerners to the use of black soldiers, Stanton had stipulated that Andrew handpick his white officers. To help him with the selection, Andrew turned to an experienced but disabled officer, Col. Edward A. Wild. As the two black Massachusetts regiments filled, the organizers considered other areas where black regiments might be raised. Because thirteen white Massachusetts regiments were serving in North Carolina in the aftermath of Burnside's expedition, Andrew had a special interest in that state. Moreover, many of the Massachusetts soldiers were commenting on the enthusiasm and aid for the Union cause demonstrated by the freedmen around New Bern. Col. Frank Lee, commander of the 44th Massachusetts, predicted that "a brigade of coloured men could be easily raised in North Carolina," which the results of Clapp's census seemed to confirm. Andrew had also been encouraged by letters from Col. Thomas Higginson in South Carolina describing the enthusiasm and determination of his black soldiers there.[27]

Although North Carolina contained many potential black recruits, Andrew understood that there would be considerable difficulties in persuading them to join a white-only Northern army, especially after the behavior of General Hunter in South Carolina. Selecting the right man for the job was very important. In addition, Andrew believed that African Americans, who might be suspicious of appeals from an all-white army, would react differently if they saw that black troops were a respected part of that army. The governor argued that it would "be comparatively easy to gain large numbers to join an army in part already composed of black troops." He recommended that Northern black troops be sent to the South to encourage recruiting among African Americans. As a result of Andrew's suggestions, the secretary of war made Wild a brigadier general and ordered him to raise a brigade of soldiers in North Carolina "from the freedmen of that state." Moreover, he was allowed to take the 55th Massachusetts with him to serve as "the nest egg of a brigade" and to show the black North Carolinians that the Union army was now biracial.[28] Wild believed that his challenge was to create a black brigade that would demonstrate to Northerners that a biracial army could be an effective army.

For most of North Carolina's black volunteers, the years after they joined the army would be difficult and dirty, often dangerous and sometimes deadly. They shared the boredom and terror that was common to most Civil War soldiers while they were expected to do much of the army's heavy lifting. Frequently their arms, clothing, tents, and rations were among the poorest in the army. Like all soldiers, they were required to follow orders without question and do whatever jobs they were given. The recent literature has fully demonstrated the disproportionate fatigue duties assigned to black troops and the reluctance to provide them with proper equipment. Nevertheless, all of this should not hide the fact that the military also provided an environment that was, in important ways, different and more egalitarian than what most blacks had experienced prior to 1860. This was especially true for ex-slaves or even most Southern "free" blacks, with the possible exception of New Orleans's "gens de couleur." Even Northern black recruits left behind a society steeped in prejudice that drastically restricted their social and political rights.[29] Once the War Department accepted African Americans into the Union army, it inevitably, if unevenly, extended to them an institutional safeguard and protection that guaranteed them, in theory if not always in practice, equality of treatment for men of equal rank. In an era of almost universal racial prejudice, the army treated them with a greater degree of equality than they could hope to experience in civilian society. Of course, the Northern armies were overwhelmingly made up of volunteers who brought with them all of the values, expectations, and biases that they had held as civilians, meaning that implementation of any color-blind policy was a contested event.

If the War Department's decision to allow the use of African Americans as combat soldiers did not immediately translate into equal treatment, the military moved inextricably in that direction. Despite early expectations that blacks would only garrison forts and posts and fill largely noncombat roles, the nature of the Civil War made such distinctions impossible.[30] No one could predict when a regiment might be called upon to serve in the front line. The experience of two years of fighting demonstrated that all men in uniform were potential combat soldiers and had to be treated as such. Nevertheless, as in all armies, some units were considered elite troops and received special treatment, while other units were seen as troops of last resort. Thus, when there were inadequate numbers of modern rifle muskets for all of the Federal regiments, and that was the case for most of the war, it was not surprising that perceptions of performance dictated which regiments received the best weapons. And yet, while racial attitudes might mean that black troops were slow to get new equipment, the army had a critical interest in ensuring that all units were properly armed. The army's measurement was military effectiveness, not profitability, and improperly armed or trained regiments could imperil the whole army.

If the Union army was to retain the loyalty of its members, as an institution it had to demand that all of its soldiers be treated equally. Of course, throughout the war many black troops received inequitable treatment. Nevertheless, once the Federal government had adopted the policy to use black troops, those soldiers gained an institutional safeguard that many had never known, and the army took the position, at least in theory, that black troops and white troops would be on an equal footing. Not surprisingly, many people both inside and outside the army were reluctant to accept such a position, but the inevitable logic of military necessity called for the equal treatment of anyone who wore a Union uniform. Efficiency, the strategic needs of the army, and any hope for a continued supply of black volunteers all worked in opposition to the social prejudices of the larger society.

—⚭—

In one critical area, the Lincoln administration forced the Confederacy to change its official policy and to treat black POWs as regular prisoners. In 1863 the very suggestion that the North might use black troops triggered angry threats from a broad spectrum of white Southerners that any African American captured in arms would not be accorded the status of a POW. Secretary of War James Seddon, speaking for the Confederate government, announced that black Union soldiers "cannot be recognized in any way as soldiers subject to the rules of war and to trial by military court." The *Richmond Examiner*, speaking for the wider Southern population, warned: "Should they be sent to the field, and be put in battle, none will be taken prisoners. Our troops understand what to do in such cases." In May 1863 the Confederate Congress resolved that all white officers leading black troops were guilty of inciting servile insurrection and, if captured, should "be put to death, or otherwise punished." Despite the bravado, however, Confederate officials were constrained by Lincoln's public threat to retaliate. In July the president issued General Order No. 252 declaring that the Federal government would protect all of its soldiers, black or white, who were captured. He gave notice that "for every soldier of the United States killed in violation of the laws of war a rebel soldier shall be executed, and for every one enslaved by the enemy or sold into slavery, a rebel soldier shall be placed in hard labor." Atrocities against black troops continued to occur until the war ended, but they were never authorized, at least officially, by the Confederate command.[31] The Confederate decision not to exchange black prisoners was largely responsible for the suspension of the exchange cartel. Although the Davis administration indicated that it would consider exchanging black soldiers from the North, the Federal government would accept nothing less than absolute equality for all black prisoners.[32]

Another example of the military's move toward equal treatment concerned, ironically, the issue of equal pay and bounties for black soldiers.[33] After the Emancipation Proclamation was issued, many Northern officials, including Stanton and Andrew, had assumed and promised that black recruits would receive the same pay as white soldiers: ten dollars per month and a three-dollar clothing allowance. But shortly after blacks began enlisting, the War Department solicitor, William Whiting, ruled that the legislation under which blacks were being accepted into the army—the Militia Act of July 1862—had set their pay at ten dollars per month, with three dollars withheld for clothing. When the act was drafted, Congress and most Northerners had assumed that blacks admitted under the provisions would serve as laborers, not combat soldiers. As a result of Whiting's ruling, some black soldiers, especially those from the North, and their allies felt betrayed. By June 1864, over Democratic and conservative opposition, Congress passed an act equalizing pay for all Union troops, although ex-slaves would receive retroactive pay only to the beginning of 1864. It was not until early 1865 that all soldiers who had been promised equal wages would receive full retroactive pay.[34] In the years after the war, when pensions were approved for men who had served in the army or navy, the policy applied equally to black and white veterans. While a series of systemic problems made it more difficult for many Southern black veterans to receive their pensions in a timely fashion, the payments were always based on disability and service—not color.

In one area the Union army did adopt a discriminatory policy in refusing to commission African Americans who might have to act as combat officers. The military was willing to allow black soldiers to command other black soldiers, but racial prejudice was too deeply embedded in American society for it to believe that white soldiers would accept orders from a black superior. Consequently, the army permitted blacks to become noncommissioned officers and lead troops within a black regiment, but it denied them commissions as line officers. Some exceptions were made for chaplains and assistant surgeons, both of whom would not be called upon to lead troops in battle. Of course, as in other areas, when the army began using black troops, there was some departure from military policy and experimentation. Initially, for instance, educated and cultured men from the free black community of New Orleans were allowed to staff the regiments of the Louisiana Native Guards before being forced out by Gen. Nathan P. Banks when he became the new department commander. The incident that precipitated Banks's action, and that spoke to the wider issue, occurred at Baton Rouge when a black captain reported for duty as officer of the day. Part of the guard was comprised of men from the 13th Maine who refused to acknowledge his authority; they even threatened to shoot him if he tried to force his control. An observer reported that the troops from Maine would "obey any order consistent with their manhood" but they would not "acknowledge a negro their superior, by virtue of any shoulder straps he might wear." Although Banks saw no need to punish the mutinous white soldiers, he began to purge the Native Guards of their black commissioned officers. By the summer of 1864, virtually all had resigned their commissions. Elsewhere, in January 1865, supporters of black officers were finally able to get Sgt. Stephen A. Swails, educated and light-skinned, commissioned as second lieutenant in the 54th Massachusetts.[35]

In North Carolina, of course, no comparable class of educated, prop-ertied, light-skinned mulattoes existed; in fact, there were less than fifteen thousand free black males in the entire state, only half of whom were of military age. Nor was there any evidence in the official records that when most black North Carolinians volunteered, they expected equal pay. What was clear, however, was that many black volunteers believed that enlistment transformed their status in a host of ways and demonstrated their manliness.[36] To encourage black enlistment, Frederick Douglass contended that when an African American joined the army and carried a musket, "then no one could deny that he had earned the rights of citizenship."[37] The black soldiers from North Carolina would test that assertion.

## CHAPTER ONE

# Raising and Training the Black Regiments

The four regiments of African American soldiers raised in North Carolina during the Civil War offer a range of insights into the ways in which black units were organized and trained over the course of the conflict.[1] In the case of the three infantry regiments, a progressive experiment begun in early 1863 to demonstrate the value and ability of black soldiers was overtaken by events and swallowed up in the larger war effort. At the same time, some of the abstract idealism of Northern white officers and the initial optimism of Southern black soldiers began to erode even while others, more skeptical about a biracial army, began to change their racial attitudes. As long as men like Brig. Gen. Edward A. Wild and Governor John Andrew of Massachusetts could influence their regiments, they used them as models of how black troops might be structured and used. But as the war progressed and attention was drawn elsewhere, and as the U.S. War Department increasingly institutionalized and systematized its control over the U.S. Colored Troops (USCT), the recruits from North Carolina were treated more like men in other black regiments. By contrast, the formation of North Carolina's black heavy artillery regiment in 1864 reflected, primarily, a mixture of local strategic needs and Northern opportunism. The creation of that unit had much less to do with any remaining progressive vision than it did with logistical requirements in the state. Indeed, the artillery regiment was never envisioned as participating in any real fighting. Because the four black regiments were raised over a considerable period of time, the recruitment, staffing, and training of the units were all influenced by shifting priorities at the national level and by altering battlefield needs. Taken together, these four regiments act as a prism to illustrate the wide spectrum of the black wartime experience.

Not surprisingly, the process by which the four units were created reflects, in many ways, the attitudes and practices involved in raising most Union regiments that served in the war. In significant ways, however, the soldiers in these North Carolina regiments were recruited, trained, and used differently from Northern black regiments or even other Southern black regiments. Of course, the patterns of recruitment and training in the North showed considerable variation over time and place, as well. The first Northern regiments were often formed through the actions of locally prominent, patriotic citizens who channeled the outpouring of support for the war by organizing rallies, encouraged volunteering, and becoming themselves the natural leaders of these recruits. Once they had gathered about a hundred men or enough for at least a company, they could offer its service to the Federal government. At rendezvous camps across the North, these companies would be organized into regiments. This process ensured that entire regiments were frequently created from the same county, city, or town. Regiments thus began with a sense of community that reinforced unit cohesiveness and military "esprit," whereas the terrible price paid for drawing most adult males from one locale only became clear in the bloody battles to follow. By contrast, a large number of black recruits for the North Carolina regiments had been dislocated by the war and were part of a growing pool of refugees in eastern North Carolina. Often the black companies were comprised of men who did not know one another when they first put on a blue uniform.[2] As a result, few soldiers were widely known and respected when the companies were first established. In white units, local leaders frequently became the commissioned and noncommissioned officers in the regiments. In black units, that did not happen, for the black enlisted men had little say in who was appointed to lead them.

Most of the first white regiments in the North adopted the militia's well-established volunteer tradition of electing not only the company officers but also the noncommissioned officers. The company officers could even elect senior regimental officers if there were vacancies. State governors, who officially appointed officers, generally accepted the results of the elections. Thus local leaders who had recruited companies or whole regiments could expect to gain a commission for their patriotic activities.[3] Enlisted men, on the other hand, could expect to be led by officers whom they knew and respected. In the black regiments, however, it was never envisioned that the enlisted men would be able to select their officers, and it was generally assumed that all officers would be white.[4] For these regiments, a more immediate question was whether or not the regiments' organizers would allow the senior noncommissioned officers to be black. Since sergeants usually were responsible for extensive paperwork and had substantial authority and independence, the decision by a white commander to appoint black senior sergeants indicated considerable faith in their potential. The efficiency of a good combat regiment was in large part dependent on the leadership abilities of its sergeants and corporals. There were obvious problems to overcome in appointing black noncommissioned officers in the summer of 1863, including the lack of leadership experience and low levels of literacy, but their selection sent a powerful message to the men. General Wild's initial decision to appoint only black company sergeants and corporals for the first regiment would be modified when the subsequent regiments were raised.

The formation of a typical Northern unit began when a body of volunteers arrived at an existing military camp, where they were provided shelter tents, blankets, and other camp equipment and organized into regiments. Until they were officially mustered in, the men did not receive uniforms. Since the volunteers technically remained civilians until they were mustered in, officers needed to act as quickly as possible to prevent anyone from changing his mind. Before they could be sworn in, the recruits stripped and were examined by a surgeon, who had to be convinced that they had no significant physical disability and were fit enough to serve. Lack of time, a large number of recruits, and a desperate need for manpower generally meant that the army surgeons were easily convinced. Once mustered in, the men could receive uniforms that might or might not fit and begin training. The instruction provided to all Civil War soldiers was at best haphazard. There was no prescribed number of weeks of basic training that all regiments had to undergo before they were considered combat ready, nor was there agreement on how much musket practice they should have. If there was consensus an anything, it was that regiments must drill relentlessly to be effective in the field.[5] A drill parade in the morning and afternoon was standard procedure whenever possible. Nevertheless, commanders differed on the purpose of drill. Some wanted their men to look good on the parade square, whereas others strove to get their troops as battle ready as possible. As a result, officers differed considerably on the importance of practical training at night or in broken terrain. In addition, how much training men received depended on their other duties and the demands of the conflict. Too much fatigue duty limited training, and imminent battle ensured that some units would be largely unprepared when they entered the field.

The end result was that some regiments found themselves in battle with little training, whereas others were as well prepared as raw troops could be. What type or amount of training a regiment or a brigade received depended mainly on the personality of the commander and on how soon the unit was needed in a campaign.[6] Often a unit did not trade in its camp equipment for arms issued by the quartermaster until the day it shipped out. In the early stages of the war, there were seldom enough new weapons for all the volunteers and some regiments were issued old, heavily modified muskets in poor condition. Some companies could not supply all of their men with the same weapons. Well into the war, few officers were concerned about the need for weapons instruction or regular musket practice. It was the exceptional Northern regiment that practiced live firing in close order.[7] Even for someone like General George B. McClellan, who specialized in organizing, if not using the Army of the Potomac, training "consisted primarily of drill with little emphasis placed on such essentials as rifle and musket practice."[8] Fortunately for the North Carolina regiments, when Wild's men began to train, their commander had a very different philosophy about musket practice.

When General Wild was assigned the task of forming an "African Brigade," the idea of raising black units was still a novelty and there was no established method as to how it should be done. Yet in the brief time between the authorization of Wild's brigade and his arrival in North Carolina to begin organizing his first regiment, the War Department had introduced a new policy for setting up the administrative framework to oversee future black enlistment. No longer would certain individuals or states be authorized to raise individual black units but rather, after May 1863, it would be the War Department's Bureau of Colored Troops, operating through officers such as Adj. Gen. Lorenzo Thomas, that would shape and direct the incorporation of black soldiers into the Union army. Although Wild saw himself as one of the first to organize black troops, he was in fact one of the last individuals to raise black regiments in what Dudley Cornish has called "a catch-as-catch-can basis with little or no control from Washington."[9] As a result, Wild possessed significant discretionary powers that few subsequent commanders would have. His most important prerogative, and the one with the greatest impact, was his right to select all of the officers for his brigade with few restrictions. Once the Bureau of Colored Troops was established, it began to regulate and supervise the appointment of all white officers to black regiments to make sure that they met certain criteria.[10] Although the African Brigade was never fully formed and Wild's command of the North Carolina regiments was brief, his legacy for these units was a group of officers selected for their experience and their sympathy for enslaved African Americans. In early 1863 Wild was well positioned to assemble a pool of competent and motivated officer candidates for his new regiments. A familiar figure in the New England abolitionist community, he drew on his connections in the Northeast to select the officers required to lead the black troops. Moreover, his service as captain in the 1st Massachusetts Volunteers and as colonel of the 34th Massachusetts Volunteers enabled him to personally assess the ability and character of many potential officers. Of even greater importance, he already had experience in selecting Northern officers for black regiments.

In the first months of 1863, while recuperating in Boston from wounds received at the Battle of South Mountain, Wild had been asked by Governor Andrew to help choose officers for black regiments then being formed in Massachusetts. His job was to "receive applications for commissions, to read and judge of their recommendations, to see and examine candidates, and to advise with Col. Robert G. Shaw and Lt. Col. N. P. Hallowell, commanders of the 54th and 55th Regiments respectively, in the selection of their officers."[11] That experience was immediately put to use when Wild began compiling a list of officers for his various regiments in North Carolina. He had to staff and fill his first regiment, the 1st North Carolina Colored Volunteers (NCCV), before submitting a list of officers for the next one, but the type of officer that he sought for each regiment was always the same.

Wild looked for officer candidates who combined military experience with an ardent commitment to both abolitionism and temperance.[12] In doing so, however, he was constrained by the requirement that he not draw men from the Army of the Potomac. He therefore looked for candidates stationed elsewhere in the eastern theater or who had been disabled or discharged. Wild turned first to the Massachusetts regiments that were still in New England or were just finishing their service in North Carolina. The general believed that the limitations on where he could get officers were more than balanced by the special privilege that he had been granted by the War Department in assigning commissions. Since its establishment in May 1863, the Bureau of Colored Troops, in an effort to standardize the process of black recruitment, evaluated and ranked all officers being offered commissions in black regiments to confirm that they satisfied the established criteria.[13] By contrast, Wild's officers, unlike those seeking commissions in other black regiments, did not have to appear before a board of examiners or be assigned a rank deemed suitable by the Bureau of Colored Troops. Instead, Wild not only selected whichever men he felt were qualified but also commissioned them at whatever rank he believed was appropriate. This freedom of operation, combined with his knowledge of the pool of candidates, enabled Wild to staff his first regiment quickly and effectively. It also allowed him to commission several African Americans despite official opposition to such a policy. Within three days of formally accepting his appointment to raise the brigade and being promoted to brigadier general, Wild had selected most of the officers of the 1st NCCV.[14]

The ability to select whom he wished was, he later wrote, "by far the most valuable privilege attached to my mission." It permitted him "to get the very best men for my particular work and to secure a unanimity of feeling and a harmony of action unparalleled, and unattainable otherwise." Wild insisted that his officers have military experience—even the few civilians whom he commissioned. "Not one man have I taken," he explained, "who has not seen service (chaplain excepted). Most are real *veterans*. Not a few were discharged from the ranks crippled by wounds, but not disabled from using the sword or pistol, and again facing the enemy in his bitter mood."[15] The general was more successful in his search for experienced soldiers than others who organized black regiments. In late 1863 the Supervisory Committee for Recruiting Colored Troops set up the Free Military School to evaluate and screen prospective officers for black regiments. During the ten months that it functioned, about 25 percent of its successful applicants had been civilians.[16]

Wild tried to find the commissioned officers that he needed among the soldiers who had already served for a time in North Carolina. He felt that these men would be at least somewhat familiar with the state and with the nature of black refugees in towns such as New Bern, Washington, and Plymouth. Seven of the new officers were drawn from the 17th, 23rd, and 25th Massachusetts Volunteers—all regiments that had been stationed in eastern North Carolina; most of the remaining officers had served in other Massachusetts regiments.[17] The case of Cpl. Leonard Lorenzo Billings of Cambridge, Massachusetts, provides an example of the political connections and personal convictions that influenced Wild in his selection of officers. Billings had served in the 29th Massachusetts Volunteers and had seen combat. Edward W. Kinsley, a close friend of Governor Andrew, recommended him to Wild. After an introduction that included the governor's warm greetings, Kinsley's letter summarized the corporal's qualifications. "He is Anti-Slavery, Temperance *ultra*—and a good soldier." Billings received a commission as a second lieutenant.[18] A month earlier another candidate, W. H. R. Brown, who was apparently equally qualified and came highly recommended, was turned down. Brown had served in the 39th Illinois Volunteers and claimed that he wanted to lead "African troops." A notation on his application that his wife objected "to seeing niggers with stripes on" perhaps explains his rejection.[19]

Four of the officers Wild selected for his first regiment, including the two senior officers, best reflected the kind of unit that he wanted to create. He had hoped to have Col. Edwin Upton of the 27th Massachusetts Volunteers lead the 1st NCCV, but Upton was unavailable. Wild's second choice was James Chaplin Beecher, son of the prominent minister Lyman Beecher and half brother of Harriet Beecher Stowe. Beecher had previously served first as chaplain in the 67th New York Infantry—the "Brooklyn phalanx"—and then as lieutenant colonel of the 141st New York Regiment before physical and probably mental disabilities forced him out of the regiment. Although his strong abolitionist credentials were known to Wild, the streak of mental instability that had led to his departure from the 141st and to his suicide after the war was not known. But in April 1863 Beecher felt that he had been given a second chance and that he was on "the threshold of a new life."[20] Wild thought that he was the best man to lead the regiment. The second senior officer, the new lieutenant colonel of the 1st NCCV, William N. Reed, was also a resident of New York and had been selected because of his abolitionist sentiment and military background. Reed had graduated from the military school at Kiel, Germany, and had reached the rank of état-major in the imperial army. He showed himself to be very competent and interested in the welfare of his men. There may have been another factor in Wild's selection. Some sources describe Reed as a mulatto, although the official records do not say this.[21]

Two other appointments reflect the belief of both Wild and Andrew that at least some of the new officers should be black despite opposition from the War Department. John V. De Grasse, commissioned assistant surgeon at the rank of major, was one of only a few black surgeons who were able to serve in a Union regiment. He had already proved himself an exceptional man. Born

Col. James C. Beecher, 35th USCT (Courtesy of Roger D.
Hunt Collection, U.S. Army Military History
Institute, Carlisle Barracks, Pa.)

in New York, where he received most of his early education, he attended
Aubuk College in Paris for two years before returning to New York to begin
the study of medicine under Samuel R. Childs. After receiving a medical degree from Bowdoin College in 1849 and spending more time studying in
French hospitals, De Grasse became the first black man admitted to a medical association when he joined the Massachusetts Medical Society in 1854.[22]
The American Colonization Society (ACS) had financed his education with
the expectation that he would practice medicine in Liberia, but De Grasse
did not leave the United States. Certainly by 1861, he had been influenced by
William Lloyd Garrison's opposition to the goals of the ACS. The implication was that De Grasse was committed to improvement through domestic
change, not foreign migration.[23] Although De Grasse was later stripped of his
commissions for allegedly being drunk on duty, it was obvious that his dismissal had as much to do with skin pigmentation as it did with intoxication.[24]

Wild, with the support of Governor Andrew, was also able to offer another African American a commission in the new regiment. He selected Rev.
John N. Mars to be the regiment's black chaplain, a policy that he would try
to continue for the other black regiments.[25] The position required that the
chaplain meet the spiritual and social demands of two distinct constituencies:
the white officers and the black enlisted men. The former group expected
him to encourage recruitment and to facilitate the men's social transition into
a military culture that met Northern expectations.[26] By contrast, the black
soldiers wanted him not only to provide religious guidance but also to act as
an advocate in their struggle for equal rights and treatment. It would have
been a difficult task for anyone, and it was an impossible one for Mars. At age
fifty-eight, the new chaplain was unequipped to meet the physical challenges
of active military service and he was frequently ill. When the 1st NCCV was
ordered to South Carolina, Mars remained in a North Carolina hospital, and
in early 1864 he resigned his commission for reasons of "chronic rheumatism
in the ankle joint, and old age."[27]

Wild was able to commission the two black officers only because they
were not line officers who might be placed in a situation where white soldiers
would have to follow their orders. As assistant surgeon and as chaplain, respectively, they would play no role in the leadership, training, or discipline of
the regiment. Rather, they were to look after the spiritual and physical health
of the regiment and act as prominent symbols to encourage recruitment.
Nevertheless, the selection of De Grasse and Mars (and possibly William
Reed) showed that on the issue of commissioning black officers, Wild was
ahead of most of the U.S. military establishment. The first attempts in 1862 to
commission black officers by Senator Jim Lane in Kansas and Gen. Benjamin
Butler in Louisiana had been rejected or effectively overturned.[28] At a time
when Nathaniel Banks was purging all black officers from the Louisiana Native Guards and Governor Andrew was unable to appoint a black officer in
the 54th or 55th Massachusetts, the 1st NCCV had at least two black officers.
The appointment of De Grasse was particularly noteworthy. In late 1863,
when the 20th USCT was being formed in New York, organizers had asked
the War Department if black chaplains and surgeons could be commissioned.
The department finally responded that while chaplains might "be appointed
without regard to color," surgeons were another matter. "The practice of the
department," wrote Asst. Adj. Gen. C. W. Foster, "has been to appoint white
men only." When the organizers persisted in their request to commission a

black assistant surgeon, they were told that "Colored medical officers will not be appointed."[29] The pressures of the war and widespread white hostility reinforced that policy in the North Carolina regiments, especially after Wild was posted away from the regiments. Following Reed's death at the Battle of Olustee, in Florida, both the black doctor and the black chaplain would be replaced by white officers. Those reversals, however, lay in the future.

Something else that lay in the future was how the Northern officers would interact with former slaves. Selecting officers to command the regiments who were against slavery no doubt prevented the extremely abusive treatment of African Americans that was evident in some black units, but it did not preclude the development of tension, conflict, and ill will between officers and enlisted men. The 1st NCCV saw few signs of discord until well into the war, although similar indications of stress had surfaced earlier in the other regiments. There was a cultural gulf between officers and men, and it would become clear that even abolitionists held preconceived racial stereotypes that influenced their treatment of black soldiers. Of course, conflicts between officers and enlisted men, who are almost always separated by class and culture, are common in most wars. To maintain discipline and authority, virtually all armies discourage fraternization between officers and men, so it was not just the black regiments that had to face these issues. On the other hand, the background of race relations in the United States created a different context in the black regiments that influenced how the separation of officers and men was perceived. Pejorative racial and regional attitudes and the legacies of slavery provided an ever-present backdrop for events within the black regiments from North Carolina.

Wild was aware of many of these challenges, and as soon as he had staffed his paper regiment, he set out for North Carolina. As he left Massachusetts, the war was about to enter a new phase. On 27 May 1863, a thousand black soldiers from the 1st and 3rd Louisiana Native Guards took part in the first major assault involving African American troops. Although the Union attack on the Confederate fortifications at Port Hudson failed due to poor organization and direction, the performance of the black soldiers was widely praised in Northern newspapers.[30] Stories of black heroism were credited with increasing black enlistments, and the reports may have also helped Wild's recruiting efforts. Ten days before the Union assault, Wild, Beecher, and thirteen other

officers in the 1st NCCV, including De Grasse, reached New Bern and immediately began to recruit from among the freedmen in the area. The presence
of De Grasse may have encouraged the town's young blacks to enlist, but it
also generated talk among the Union troops there. Thomas Hale of the 45th
Massachusetts wrote home about Wild's arrival and the response of many
white officers to his black surgeon, "who wears the uniform of a major and
is of course to be 'obeyed and respected accordingly.' I wonder," observed
Hale, "how the nice young men of Boston, the ladies' pets, the 'gallant' 44th,
will like the idea of presenting arms, the most respectful salute they can make,
to a negro?" Hale predicted that "it will come rather hard for some of them
but they will have to submit to it."[31] This response was a prelude to much of
what De Grasse and his comrades would face in the next year.

Once in New Bern, Wild was pressed to recruit enough men for his brigade and to find qualified noncommissioned officers for the new companies.
To achieve his first goal, he could tap into the widespread enthusiasm of local
blacks. Well before President Lincoln had authorized the use of black soldiers
in the Union army, African Americans in the New Bern area had reportedly
organized themselves into a militia.[32] Shortly after Wild's arrival, a Massachusetts corporal described the excitement in the black community: "Quite
a recruiting fever has seized the freedmen of Newbern. . . . Four thousand
colored soldiers are counted upon in this department." William P. Derby
of the 27th Massachusetts Volunteers was also impressed by this "recruiting
fever": "One can hardly forget the enthusiasm amongst the negroes of this
place, placards being posted around the city, calling for four thousand men
for 'Wild's colored Brigade.' Street processions of the most motley character
were the order of the day."[33] Wild knew that in staffing the 1st NCCV and in
filling its companies, he was setting a pattern for the upcoming regiments in
his brigade. He also understood that, regardless of the initial support for his
actions, he would have to overcome a good deal of skepticism among whites
and blacks alike. Although there was a large pool of potential recruits, these
men had to be convinced that it was in their best interest to volunteer for a
hazardous life in the army at a time when other economic opportunities existed for black workers.

The Union occupation in eastern North Carolina had created a growing
demand for black labor at wages as high as, or higher than, the army could
offer. Despite the persistent complaint from these workers that they were not
paid on time, a civilian job in a town like New Bern had many advantages. A

wide range of jobs offered fewer risks than military service, as well as permitting the workers to remain close to their families. In the future, if Confederate forces reestablished control in the east, there would be less chance of retaliation directed at civilian workers than at soldiers. In addition, the behavior of some of the Northern soldiers toward Southern blacks had left a sense of unease in the black community. While sexual assault by white soldiers was uncommon, other acts of discriminatory treatment were frequent.[34] One white soldier demonstrated his casual disdain for the rights of New Bern's black population in a letter to his parents concerning his collection of buttons. "I gain slowly," he wrote. "The other day I met a 'Shade' with a button on his coat which I wanted so I stopped him and cut it off, telling him, he was not allowed to wear that kind; he went on his way elated at not being taken to the guard house for the supposed offense, taking me for a Provost Guard."[35] It fell upon Wild to persuade black leaders to support his recruitment efforts despite such racist acts of Northern soldiers. To do so, he had to rely on more than just his presence or even that of his two black officers.

An incident just after Wild's arrival in New Bern is suggestive of the attitudes held by the black North Carolinians. Among several Northern civilians who had accompanied Wild and his officers to help with recruitment, Edward Kinsley was reputed to have played a major role in attracting black soldiers. Long after the war had ended, Albert W. Mann claimed that enlistments had been slow until Kinsley held a secret meeting in the middle of the night with influential New Bern blacks, headed by Abraham H. Galloway. At that meeting, as Mann described it, Kinsley agreed to certain demands in return for black support of Wild's recruiting efforts. Among the freedmen's demands were pay equal to that of the black Massachusetts troops, rations for the soldiers' families, schooling for their children, and a government commitment that captured African American troops would be treated as POWs by the Confederates.[36] The actual substance of the meeting may have differed from Mann's description, although his account does capture the freedmen's concerns and the fact that they had a range of options from which to choose. Individual freedmen could be persuaded to support the war, but they retained agency. Moreover, his behavior at the meeting reflected Galloway's defiant equalitarianism. Although Galloway was unquestionably influential in New Bern, he was characterized by Wild as "my special and confidential recruiting agent, a mulatto, originally sent to me by George L. Stearns." According to Wild, Galloway "has served his country well, since the commencement of the war—formerly as a spy—now as a recruiting emissary." Galloway's contacts in eastern North Carolina enabled him to have his mother—Hester Hankins, a slave in Wilmington—smuggled out of that city to New Bern.[37] As a black recruiter and a supporter of Wild, Galloway was probably a much more persuasive spokesman for the general than Kinsley.

A second black recruiter, an abolitionist from Pennsylvania by the name of Joseph E. Williams, was less effective.[38] Having traveled south with Wild, Williams had been very active in his recruiting efforts while volunteering was popular in New Bern. He became less interested and less persuasive as the initial pool of recruits was exhausted. Williams may have become a handicap for Wild, as he was described as "a restless intriguer [sic], and yet most imperious and overbearing to all below him, though obsequious to us; false and slippery, he put everything into a snarl wherever he went." Eventually, when given the choice of enlisting in the black regiment himself and staying in camp or leaving the state, he left North Carolina.[39]

Whatever the influence of any one individual accompanying Wild, the meeting described by Albert Mann and subsequent events revealed that significant black enlistment would occur only if there were general agreement to an implied contract between the government, as represented by Wild, and black recruits. If black men offered their services, then the government was morally obligated to protect them and their families while they served in the army. At the very least, it meant guaranteeing roughly equitable treatment to black soldiers, as well as food, clothing, schooling, and shelter for their families. Wild was convinced that he must give "much time and labor to the care and provision of negro families" if he hoped to fill his brigade.[40] For this reason he initiated a number of programs to aid the refugees, including one to locate the families of soldiers who joined his regiments on vacant land. It also explained why Wild often consulted with Northern teachers, such as Oscar Doolittle, "a number of times a day in regard to the establishment of Schools and other matters pertaining to them."[41] But before he could make provisions for the soldiers' families, he had to find the recruits.

Wild and the men helping him soon placed posters around New Bern calling for men to join the African Brigade. They also encouraged black leaders to hold recruiting rallies. Some of the most ardent supporters of enlistment were African American women, who encouraged their men to volunteer. William

Derby claimed that the women "seized every able-bodied man of their race, shouting' . . . you's look a heap better in de crowd dar!' at the same time shoving him by force into the ranks."[42] The search for recruits quickly spread beyond New Bern. Permanent recruiting stations were set up in Plymouth and Washington, and individual officers were sent out on sweeps through the surrounding counties. Wild himself spent several weeks visiting various parts of the Department of North Carolina to encourage enlistment. On one of these trips in mid-June, an officer stationed on Hatteras described the general's effectiveness as a recruiter. "A tall slim man with a reddish beard" and an empty sleeve dangling at his side, Wild appealed to the freedmen of the island, with impressive results. He "succeeded in getting about 150 men from the colored people on the bar, leaving only the old and decrepit."[43] In urging North Carolina's African Americans to enlist, Wild could not offer all the incentives provided to Northern blacks. Men joining the 54th Massachusetts could expect a bounty of one hundred dollars apiece, whereas the men enlisting in North Carolina in 1863 received no bounty at all.[44] Not until 1864 were black recruits in North Carolina and Virginia eligible for bounties. About all that Wild could offer his black recruits in 1863 was the opportunity to play a part in the bloody struggle for freedom.

The pace of enlistment in the 1st NCCV escalated in the last days of May 1863. Colonel Beecher had posted his first recruiting officer in New Bern on 21 May. A week later, on 28 May, Company A had 51 men. By 8 June that number had increased to 81, and the company was at its full complement of 100 men ten days later—though it was the slowest unit to fill.[45] Capt. James Croft had signed 87 men into Company D by 22 May, Company E had 89 recruits by 28 May, and Company G numbered 92 soldiers on 1 June. The other companies, organized in June, filled even more quickly when their books were opened. On 9 June Croft enrolled 97 men at Washington into Company C. Only 2 other men would be added to that company before the end of the war. Six days later, when Capt. Charles A. Jones began forming Company B, 87 men from New Bern signed on. Only one other recruit, Frank Harrison who joined on 13 July, was added to the company before early 1865.

Many years later, some veterans could still remember their medical examination, if not always the surgeon who had conducted it. Amos Mattick was twenty years old when he joined Company F in New Bern on 23 May. Decades later, he recounted: "I was stripped and thoroughly examined" by two surgeons whose names he could not remember. "They made me stoop down & use my hands & legs & walk off." Philip Wiggins, who had been a painter before he volunteered, brought his older friend into the same company. He remembered that Hannibal Sawyer "was stripped stark naked and carefully examined at New Berne [*sic*] by Dr. J. V. De Grasse."[46] Once the surgeons had approved the men, the recruits were ready to become soldiers. Capt. Thorndike Hodges recounted his first view of the troops in his new company. Colonel Beecher had "pointed to a long line of Dark-skinned tatterdemalions just arrived in camp, with the order: 'There's your company, captain: go and take command!' It was a far from attractive, indeed a formidable task, but before night these men were clean, soldierly-looking fellows in full uniform." Hodges remembered proudly that the men "afterward acquitted themselves bravely in the field."[47]

While the recruiting and medical examinations were going on and as the regimental officers took charge of their men, Beecher was busy laying out a camp and beginning the organization and training of the regiment. The 1st NCCV did not have an established training camp—enjoyed by many Northern regiments—awaiting the first recruits who arrived. Instead, Beecher selected a campsite in an uncleared section of the south bank of the Neuse River just outside of New Bern. Work began immediately. On the same day that he began enlisting men, the colonel took the first squad of recruits plus tents, equipment, and rations to the new campsite. The site was laid out, bush was cut down, hundreds of stumps were removed, and a parade ground was set up.[48] Adding to the recruits' adjustment to army routine and army food was the difficulty of learning a soldier's craft while filling a laborer's job. It would be an experience all too common for black soldiers while the war lasted. Despite all of the challenges, by 7 June seven companies of the 1st NCCV were in camp, two were already in uniform, and all had started to drill in the newly created parade square. Fortunately, the proximity of the camp of the 45th Massachusetts allowed some of the experienced and sympathetic white soldiers to help out with Beecher's new troops. "It was no unusual thing," wrote a soldier in the 45th Massachusetts, "for members of that regiment to go over to the camp of the First North Carolina Regiment and drill the 'raw recruits' in the manual of arms, and afterwards instruct them out of the primer."[49]

Military efficiency and literacy were essential, but not the only necessities of the new soldiers. Colonel Beecher reflected the attitude of most, if not all, of the officers in the African Brigade on the crucial role of religion. Camp grubbing and drill were important, but so too, he believed, was religious in-

Sgt. Frank "Sergt. Bob" Roberts, 35th USCT
(Courtesy of Tryon Palace Historic Sites
and Gardens, New Bern, N.C.)

struction. Because Chaplain Mars had been delayed, Beecher filled the role of
regimental chaplain as well as commanding officer during the first few weeks
at New Bern. He was very much moved by his own preaching. When the
nearly seven hundred newly uniformed men of the 1st NCCV knelt before him
and bowed their heads without instruction, "it affected me beyond measure,"
Beecher wrote, "and I prayed for them in faith . . . I know not that I ever
felt the reality of prayer more deeply."[50] Whatever reservations Beecher initially had about their quality, by the time the men had been in camp for a few
weeks, he was convinced that they would make excellent soldiers. He only
wished that "doubtful people at home could see my three week regiment.
They would talk less nonsense about negro inferiority. Our discipline is today

better than that of any regiment I know of, and I believe, by the blessing of God, our efficiency will be second to none."

The faith that Beecher and Wild shared in the new recruits was evident in their selection of the regiment's noncommissioned officers. If the unit was to be effective, sergeants and corporals had to be competent leaders at the company level, but both men rejected the argument used in other units that the senior noncommissioned officer in each company should be white. Wild had decided that black recruits would fill all of the noncommissioned officer positions, although this created problems. Selecting corporals and sergeants from the pool of black recruits precluded having anyone with formal military experience, since in May 1863 few freedmen in North Carolina had acted even as army scouts or in a quasi-military role. This group was clearly not large enough to supply the fifty sergeants and eighty corporals needed by the ten companies in the regiment. Moreover, few black volunteers had the literacy needed to do the paperwork expected of senior noncommissioned officers. Because of laws that prohibited the teaching of slaves, only a few black recruits had gained a rudimentary education. Given the amount of record keeping required of noncommissioned officers, there could be little hope that there would be a large enough pool of literate recruits to meet the regiment's needs.[51] Nevertheless, in early June 1863 each company commander was instructed to select "Two Sergeants and Eight Corporals from among the most promising" enlisted men in their company.[52] These individuals would then receive special instruction on regulations and record keeping from the hardpressed, overworked commissioned officers. Once the company officers had had a chance to evaluate the new corporals, they would select three more sergeants from among the most capable corporals and then fill those vacancies from the ranks.

Given the haste to staff these positions and the fact that relatively little was known about any individual recruit, it is remarkable how many of these newly created sergeants served long and well throughout the war. In the many months after the regiment was mustered in, only a few men were demoted. In mid-September 1863 Orderly Sgt. James Kimball of Company A was placed under arrest by his commanding officer. Although subsequently reduced to fifth sergeant on the grounds that he was "incompetent to act as Orderly Sergeant," he kept his stripes for two more years.[53] A week after Kimball was demoted, a regimental court-martial stripped Sgt. James Arnett of Company K of his stripes. Company D received a new first sergeant in late

October when Marcus Frazier, the original appointment, deserted and was replaced by 2nd Sgt. Henry Windham. Only one other sergeant was demoted before the end of 1863. Austin Sheppard of Company C was reduced to the ranks in November "on application of his company commander for inability to perform his duty."[54] In Sheppard's case, and perhaps in some of the others', the demotion may have been due as much to a lack of literacy as to objectionable character.

On the other hand, the fact that the other orderly sergeants retained their posts did not mean that their service was entirely satisfactory. A major problem for all of Wild's regiments that would require time and education to overcome was the initial illiteracy of so many noncommissioned officers. In November 1863 Colonel Beecher complained that there was "not an orderly sergeant or non-commissioned officer in the command who [could] write sufficiently well to be of any service and hence the whole duty [of maintaining records] has been thrown upon one or two commissioned officers in the command." In the long term, some soldiers were able to acquire both literacy and positions of authority in the regiment. By late 1865, for example, William Overton had been promoted out of Company D to the field and staff level as regimental sergeant major, while John Monroe became the unit's quartermaster sergeant. At least one other early recruit, Peter Camel of Company H, demonstrated the competence and literacy required for a similar promotion.[55]

In the short term, the lack of senior noncommissioned officers who could read and write forced the limited number of officers in camp to assume many duties normally performed by orderly sergeants in Northern regiments. Since a number of company officers were away on recruiting details, those left in camp were swamped with work. Not only did they have to drill and instruct the raw recruits and maintain the camp, but they also had to fill out endless returns of clothing and equipment, morning reports, sick calls, and muster rolls. As a result, the need for experienced and literate regimental noncommissioned officers to serve at the field and staff level was met by turning to a few white veterans in other regiments. Among them was James Elmsly, who became a regimental sergeant major in July 1863. A thirty-year-old native of Scotland, Elmsly had been a storehouse clerk in New York City before enlisting in the 132nd New York Volunteers. After more than a year of service, during which time he had been promoted to corporal, he accepted a transfer to the 1st NCCV and received the first $25 of his $100 bounty.[56] At the same time, two other Northerners were placed in similar positions. Charles A.

Clark, a twenty-year-old Brooklyn, New York, resident who had worked as a clerk, was appointed regimental commissary sergeant. He had joined the 17th Massachusetts Volunteers in July 1862 and served with the regiment in New Bern, North Carolina. He, too, was offered a bounty of $100 for joining the 1st NCCV. Delos Barber of Little Genesee, New York, filled the position of hospital steward. A twenty-four-year-old former carpenter, Barber had served in the 85th New York Volunteers since September 1861. The 85th had been stationed in Plymouth, North Carolina, before Barber accepted his promotion to the 1st NCCV. One other white noncommissioned officer was added to the regiment near the end of 1863. On 29 December Sgt. George Greene of the 112th New York Volunteers was honorably discharged so he could enlist in the 1st NCCV and become its quartermaster sergeant.[57]

The dates of these appointments suggest that initially Wild hoped to fill the positions with North Carolina freedmen and that only later did he decide to add a few white noncommissioned officers. All of the evidence indicates that Wild saw this as a stopgap measure and believed that black noncommissioned officers would ultimately fill these posts. It meant that in addition to being the only noncommissioned officers to receive bounties in 1863, these men differed from the black soldiers in another regard. The four white Northerners accepted their positions with the expectation of an officer's commission in the near future. In December 1863, for example, Barber told Wild that he had been "willing to enter the Brigade in a more humble capacity, and prove myself worthy of your confidence before asking further advancements" because he believed that merit would be rewarded. He was now three-quarters through his term of service and unless he received a commission in the next three months, he would return to school after discharge, convinced that he had done his duty and "also feeling that *others* (Perhaps) not more worthy have been advanced before me."[58]

While it is obvious why the white noncommissioned officers were appointed, it is less evident in the case of the black sergeants and corporals. From existing records, it is difficult to determine what qualities enabled some soldiers to be promoted, while others remained privates for their entire military service. Individual character and personality traits are seldom revealed by the military records. The extant data sometimes obscure as much as they clarify. There is, for instance, no evidence that sergeants in the 1st NCCV were appointed for their maturity or at least their age. Their average age, 24.3 years, was close to the regimental average, although fewer sergeants were under 20 or over 30. As in most armies, size was an advantage for promotion. Most senior noncommissioned officers were among the regiment's taller men, although small stature did not prevent Company B's Wilson Cox, 5' 3", or Company G's Alexander Gyan, 5' 4", from getting their three stripes.[59] One significant criterion for selection present in all four of North Carolina's black regiments related to complexion. According to the regimental description books, a full 25 percent of the sergeants of the 1st NCCV had a "light" complexion—well above the regimental average of 6.1 percent. Although this may have simply reflected a predisposition among white company commanders to choose noncommissioned officers with a lighter skin color, it might also indicate more important factors connected to the soldiers' prewar status. A high proportion of these light-skinned men were listed as having had special or skilled occupations and may have more frequently been literate. It is likely that a number of these sergeants were free men prior to 1861. Though it is reasonable that physical qualities such as height and complexion influenced some promotions, it is equally plausible that a more critical factor was an individual's prior experience and his ability to project a sense of leadership and authority.

Even while Beecher was selecting noncommissioned officers and carving a military camp out of the North Carolina bush, the process of training and disciplining the new recruits began. The transition from civilian to soldier in the 1st NCCV, as in all Civil War regiments, involved some painful readjustments to the code and patterns of military behavior and to the rhythm of army life. Given their slave backgrounds, most of the men would have been accustomed to rising at 5:00 A.M., the time of reveille. For the next forty-five minutes, the soldiers would be busy shaking out blankets, cleaning their tents and company streets, and hurrying down to the river, in squads, for their morning wash. Breakfast was followed at 6:45 by Surgeon's Call, and fifteen minutes later the companies began three hours of morning drill or fatigue duty. Given the amount of work necessary in the first few weeks to set up a military camp in the countryside, the time available for drilling whole companies was very limited. Following dinner at noon, most men could relax for a few hours in the heat of midday or look after their own personal needs. Another three hours of drill or fatigue began at 3:00 P.M. Supper at 7:00, tattoo at 8:30, and taps at 9:00 followed a dress parade at 6:20.[60]

Constant drilling was necessary because of the way Civil War armies fought. In addition to creating an esprit de corps, a well-drilled command had the ability to move and realign large numbers of men quickly and efficiently.[61] It ensured that in the confusion of battle, unit cohesion was still possible. Another part of training was designed to change ingrained patterns of civilian behavior and replace them with the stricter, formalized military code. To some extent the pattern of subordination may have seemed familiar to many ex-slaves, whose lives had been structured in ways unlike those of many Northern volunteers.[62] Nevertheless, for slaves and freedmen alike, the transition to army life meant change as the military demanded new modes of conduct. Near the end of June 1863, the number of soldiers who could receive daily passes was reduced to four. Their dress and deportment had to meet military standards. Colonel Beecher was adamant that no passes should be issued to "dirty Unsoldierly men." The army also underlined its control over the men's private lives. After 1 July, women were no longer allowed in camp after tattoo unless they were a "regularly appointed Laundress or Cook to some officers' mess." The acclimatization to army life was neither easy nor quick. Months later, senior Union officers were still unconvinced that many enlisted men fully understood the importance of following army regulations rather that their own personal preferences. Brig. Gen. Israel Vogdes had a list of complaints about the way some men in the 1st NCCV stood guard. Vogdes reprimanded sentries for swapping duties, for leaving their posts before they were formally relieved, for putting aside their guns, and for sitting down while on duty. They had to understand, he warned, how serious these offenses were and that they could be punishable by death.[63]

As the weeks passed, the regiment's military efficiency improved. Beecher was "amazed at the promptitude of these men to learn drill," and by mid-July the company commanders had their men training as skirmishers.[64] At the same time, a regimental stretcher corps with an attendant group of ambulance drivers was organized. In all of the companies, men had been detached to serve as teamsters, hospital aids, cooks, and pioneers. Occasionally, larger groups were detailed for special services away from the regiment.[65] Despite the various fatigue duties, both Beecher and Wild pushed the regiment hard in training to have it battle-ready as soon as possible. Through their efforts, the 1st NCCV was better prepared in very important ways than many other Civil War regiments, including those in North Carolina. Beecher's men received their weapons almost as soon as the companies were organized, and the soldiers practiced live firing frequently. As in most black—and many white—regiments, the equipment initially received was of poor quality. Beecher complained that the muskets "were all second hand, and of three different kinds," while Maj. Archibald Bogle declared that the guns, "Springfields, Enfields, & Swivel Bores," were "hardly suitable for Field Service."[66]

The weapons training of the 1st NCCV was probably better than that of most new white units in the North. It has been found that a Civil War soldier "usually lacked an adequate basis of target practice before he went into action, particularly in the type of sustained close-order firing which combat often required." The best study of black troops—Joseph Glatthaar's *Forged in Battle*—argues that whereas few commanders of white troops spent much time on live musket training, such was not the case in black regiments, where officers could not assume that the men had any familiarity with muskets.[67] Of course, because the black units were formed later in the war, the thinking on weapons training also reflected the experience of many regiments in battle. Its effectiveness was, in turn, a function of the type of instruction (individual versus mass firing), the frequency of practice, and the amount of ammunition that could be used.

Although Wild could not control the quality of the weapons issued, he could make sure that the men knew how to use them effectively before going into battle. The records of Company A, for which quartermaster returns still exist, give an indication of the rigorous training undertaken within the 1st NCCV. The company received ninety-six "Enfield rifled muskets, caliber .577," including accoutrements and cartridges, on 11 June 1863 and began using them immediately. Wild believed that his men should practice by actually firing their weapons. The last-quarter returns of 1863 for Company A, consisting of about one hundred men, show that they fired four thousand practice rounds, or about forty rounds per man.[68] During this period the regiment as a whole was assigned a disproportionate amount of fatigue duties and had seen its training time drastically reduced. The number of practice rounds recorded suggests that the 1st NCCV entered combat with much greater marksmanship training than most of the other new regiments, black or white.

Wild's emphasis on practical training and live firing soon involved the black soldiers of the 55th Massachusetts Volunteers. On 25 July 1863 the 55th arrived at Morehead City to join the African Brigade and was welcomed to New Bern by the 1st NCCV that evening. To the surprise of the men from Boston, Wild ordered a brigade drill for the following day that lasted until 8:00 P.M. For two days the regiments practiced brigade movements, firing blank cartridges by file, by company, and by battalion as they alternatively advanced and retreated.[69] Wild may have been driving his men especially hard because he planned to take them on a raid into the interior of the state in the next few days.[70] Just as the regiments were preparing for the expedition, however, orders came to move to South Carolina with all haste. Not only would that move end the period of intense training for the 1st NCCV, but it would also seriously disrupt the organization and preparation of Wild's next regiment.

---

The black units were ordered to join the Union forces at Charleston. The repeated failure of Gen. Quincy A. Gillmore to capture Fort Wagner and to open the way for a successful attack on Charleston had thrown the whole Union operation in South Carolina into question. When, after the failed attack on 18 July, Gillmore asked for an additional ten thousand soldiers to continue his offensive, an angry Maj. Gen. Henry W. Halleck considered refusing the request. Only after Secretary of the Navy Gideon Wells intervened with President Lincoln did Halleck grudgingly order another ten thousand men to Charleston Harbor. Half of the reinforcements would come from Maj. Gen. John G. Foster's command in North Carolina.[71] What existed of Wild's brigade was ordered to South Carolina as one of three brigades arriving from that state.

The move had serious consequences for the black soldiers. It effectively marked the end of the 1st NCCV's military training. Once in South Carolina, the regiment would face constant fatigue duty, which would leave little time to maintain even its existing level of drill. In addition, since it had only three hours' notice of the move and because the orders were to depart in light marching order, the regiment left behind most of its baggage, personal belongings, and even company books. Wild expected that before long his partially formed brigade would be transferred back to North Carolina. That assumption proved false, and the gear left behind was not forwarded to Wild's force in South Carolina until 28 September. By then, some equipment and personal property had been lost or stolen.[72] Of greater consequence, Wild had been instructed that "all men able to fight must go," but sickness requiring hospitalization forced him to leave behind 146 men and 2 officers from the 1st NCCV and the 55th Massachusetts Volunteers.[73] To fill the vacancies, Wild drew from the new recruits who had volunteered for the 2nd USCT. The 1st NCCV would carry these replacements even after the 2nd NCCV had been transferred from North Carolina to Virginia. To confuse matters further,

Wild also transferred a company under the command of Capt. John Wilder that had been seen as a possible start to the 3rd NCCV. Wilder's men would eventually be incorporated into another regiment, but not before leaving a record indicating that all three of Wild's infantry regiments were now in South Carolina.[74] But in fact, the 2nd NCCV was then struggling to organize itself in North Carolina.

———⚶———

Because Wild's original instructions were to raise his regiments sequentially, little could be done to organize the 2nd NCCV until the 1st NCCV was virtually complete. On 25 June 1863 Wild notified the War Department that his first regiment was full and that he had 125 recruits for the next one.[75] Only at this point could he submit a list of officers whom he wished to commission in the 2nd NCCV. It would take considerable time for the new officers to begin arriving in North Carolina. By the time the new commanding officer, Col. Alonzo G. Draper, could get to New Bern at the beginning of August, Wild had left for Folly Island, South Carolina, with the 150 recruits who belonged to the colonel's fledgling unit. In their place were the hospitalized troops from the 1st NCCV and the 55th Massachusetts for whom Draper was now responsible. Adding to the colonel's burden was the fact that he had to perform all of his new responsibilities—recruiting men, training the soldiers that were in camp, and looking after the sick—with the help of only a few officers. Draper's difficulties had one positive outcome. As a result of the challenges confronting Draper, Wild tried to commission the officers of the 3rd NCCV before the 2nd NCCV was complete so the third regiment would have enough officers when it began to organize.

Some of Draper's problems had stemmed from the fact that although Wild had submitted the list of officers to be commissioned in the 2nd NCCV by late June, few of them were available to the colonel on his arrival in New Bern. It took the army from four to ten weeks to inform the prospective officers that they had been offered commissions, to arrange the necessary releases from their original units, and to organize transportation to North Carolina. Thus when Draper assumed command of the 2nd NCCV, only four other officers had been mustered into the regiment. They had been in the district when they received their commissions, whereas many of the other officers had to travel considerable distances to join the unit. Until more officers arrived, it was impossible for Draper to conduct effective drill and weapons training.

As one might expect, the officers whom Wild selected for the 2nd NCCV were similar in background and experience to those commissioned in the first regiment. The general again looked for men expressing abolitionist and reform sentiments. Only seven of Draper's new officers had previously held commissions, and nine had served as privates. The vast majority of the men offered commissions, about twenty-nine, were from Massachusetts regiments. Moreover, at least sixteen of them had been serving in units stationed in North Carolina, and it was these officers who first reported for duty in July and August.[76] Understandably, those located outside of the state were much slower in reporting to New Bern. As he had done with the 1st NCCV, Wild commissioned a black chaplain, Rev. David Stevens, for the second regiment. Stevens, who was more than sixty years old at the time, said that he had been a drummer boy in the War of 1812.[77] Unlike Reverend Mars, however, Stevens had the physical stamina to withstand the hard life of military campaigns. Not only did he serve as the regiment's chaplain for the entire war, but he also would be the first black man to speak from the pulpit of Richmond's African Church soon after the fall of the Confederate capital. Stevens's commission was the last one that Wild was able to issue to an African American.

The newly appointed leader of the 2nd NCCV was an experienced officer who had previously served as captain, then major in the 1st Massachusetts Artillery. Draper was later described by another Union officer as "not a member of the regular army and . . . something of a fanatic," although a Richmond woman, expecting the worst, found him a "sleek, dapper, unmilitary man" who treated her politely.[78] As a twenty-seven-year-old resident of Lynn, Massachusetts, Alonzo Draper had been elected chairman of the Lynn Mechanics' Association when it was formed in 1859 and soon became editor of its newspaper, the *New England Mechanic*. In 1860 he had been one of the organizers of the Great Shoemakers' Strike. Town voters, angry at the way the police and militia had dealt with the strike, subsequently elected Draper assistant city marshal, and he used his power to replace the police chief and his deputies. In 1861 he organized a group of volunteers from Lynn who were mustered in as Company C of the 14th Massachusetts Infantry Regiment—later the 1st Massachusetts Heavy Artillery.[79] When it became clear that Massachusetts was going to raise black regiments, he wrote a series of letters to Governor Andrew outlining his qualifications to lead black soldiers. He had long been an antislavery man with "a sincere desire to assist in ameliorating the condition of the colored race, and in their enfranchisement from that social depression to which an ignorant popular prejudice has consigned them. This sentiment is not a novel one to me, but is consistent with the whole course of my life."[80] Although he may have been as sympathetic to the aspirations of the black soldiers as he professed, events would show that he could also be a harsh disciplinarian.

——⚬——

Within a week of reaching New Bern, Draper had made a start at raising and organizing the first five companies of the 2nd NCCV. He had almost 400 men on the regimental rolls, although that number included 150 absent soldiers, who had been detached to South Carolina. From the beginning, one of his most pressing problems was the shortage of officers. As late as 8 August, only ten officers had reported to the 2nd NCCV; one of them was on detached service on the orders of General Wild, while a second officer was with the detachment in South Carolina. Five of the remaining officers were recruiting in the field, leaving just two first lieutenants and one second lieutenant in camp with Draper. None of the three had held a commission before and only one, Joseph Hatlinger, had been a sergeant. These men were experiencing their own form of on-the-job training. Keeping up with the daily paperwork required as the regiment was forming was in itself a major task. Any serious military training of the new recruits was virtually impossible, especially given the lack of any experienced noncommissioned officers to assist the three officers. The problem was aggravated by the fact that the regiment's earliest recruits, and the men with the most military training, were the 150 detached enlisted men sent to South Carolina with the 1st NCCV. That transfer had removed an invaluable pool of potential sergeants and corporals to help the new regimental staff. Although seven more commissioned officers arrived in New Bern over the next two weeks, the 2nd NCCV would remain chronically short of experienced commissioned and noncommissioned officers, undermining the regiment's preparations.[81]

To speed up recruitment in North Carolina, Draper adopted a new tactic. He shifted some of his black noncommissioned officers, such as Sgt. William Johnson, into recruiting service along with his white officers.[82] Now when a recruiting party went out, there was clear and visible evidence of what a black volunteer might achieve by joining the regiment. Johnson's presence was clearly intended to serve as a dramatic reminder that the Union army was no longer white only. In addition to trying new ways to increase enlistment,

Draper used personal incentives to encourage the transformation of green recruits into reliable soldiers. To improve military appearance and to ensure that equipment was well maintained, the colonel devised a rewards system that offered daily passes to a limited number of soldiers "who shall come off guard and [have] the cleanest equipment." Draper's use of positive incentives was matched elsewhere among the black troops where officers believed that rewards were a more effective training tool than punishment.[83]

In addition to recruitment and training for the 2nd NCCV, Draper had assumed responsibility for the sick soldiers left behind from the 1st NCCV and the 55th Massachusetts Volunteers, although they were not under his formal command. This charge further stretched the resources of his limited staff, especially given the absence of a regimental surgeon until November 1863. All of these obligations together created logistical and bureaucratic problems for all concerned, including Brig. Gen. Innis N. Palmer, who took over the defenses of New Bern on 14 August. The general was concerned that the number of rations issued by the commissary at New Bern agreed with the morning reports from all of the units assigned to him. Lt. Sidney Phillips, acting quartermaster of the 2nd NCCV, predicted that unless the sick men were formally attached to Draper's regiment, he would have difficulty drawing rations for them. The bureaucratic solution adopted may have solved Palmer's problem, but it created more difficulties for Draper and Beecher. On 8 August 1863 the soldiers of the 1st NCCV and the 55th Massachusetts Volunteers who had been left behind in North Carolina because of illness were officially placed under Draper's command.[84] Consequently, when Draper was ordered out of North Carolina late in the month, they went with him.

These troops were of some benefit to Draper's regiment if only because, even before he had fully organized the unit, it was given a number of additional duties. The regiment's first official task was one familiar to black troops: garrison duty in the fortifications around New Bern to free up white troops. Draper was to select men to replace two companies of the 98th New York Volunteers occupying Forts Havelock and Croatan outside New Bern. He assigned a detachment of fifty men from the 1st NCCV under Capt. John M. Smith to garrison the first fort and another fifty men from the 55th Massachusetts Volunteers led by Lt. Hiram H. Allen to occupy the second fort.[85] In this way, Draper was able to minimize the disruption to the training of the 2nd NCCV's new recruits; he also may have been unsure that his own men were ready for such a task. Whatever his reasons, the assignment further depleted his small pool of officers. Before the forts could be fully occupied, however, the senior command in North Carolina was restructured and all of Draper's troops were pulled out of the state.

In mid-August 1863, Maj. Gen. John J. Peck assumed command of the District of North Carolina. The outgoing commander of the district, John G. Foster, had endorsed Wild's "enterprise with real zeal," whereas Peck seemed disinclined to support any effort to recruit black regiments in North Carolina.[86] On 28 August "all existing Brigades and Division Organization in this command" were ordered set aside, and the next day Draper was informed that his command was "destined (with all the other colored troops in NC) to Fortress Monroe [Virginia]." Unlike the earlier transfer of General Wild and his troops, this move was to be considered a permanent arrangement, and all of the property and the sick of the 2nd NCCV who could travel would have to go. The soldiers who could not be moved would be left under the care of Dr. Mansfield of the 92nd New York Volunteers. The regiment would immediately entrain for Morehead City, where transportation would take the men to Fort Monroe.[87] The move effectively ended the effort to raise a purely North Carolinian brigade of black troops and ensured that some companies of the 2nd NCCV would contain a significant number of Virginians. Although officers from the second regiment continued to recruit African Americans in North Carolina, the pressing need to fill the last companies caused Draper to seek black soldiers from southeastern Virginia. His efforts yielded only a limited number of recruits—probably due more to the actions of racially biased white officers than any want of black enthusiasm. Indeed, the challenges confronting Draper provide an insight into the ways in which some white officials attempted to manipulate or use the freedmen.

At a time when the 2nd NCCV had not been formally accepted into service and had not been armed, Draper's efforts to get volunteers from the Fort Monroe area were blocked by senior officers in the department who either disagreed with the enlistment of black troops, wanted to maintain a pool of black laborers, or were merely unwilling to bend the rules. In one case, Lt. Aaron Parker had gathered fourteen potential recruits at Yorktown and asked that Gen. Robert M. West provide rations for them until he could get them to the 2nd NCCV. His request was "refused on the grounds that the men were not entitled to rations until they were mustered into the U S service."[88] As a result, Parker lost his recruits.

Other officers in the 2nd NCCV grew bitter over the fierce competition for freedmen between the regiment and several government departments. At both Hampton and Yorktown, many blacks who were willing to join the army worked in the Engineering, Ordnance, or Quartermaster's departments. But General Foster refused to let the recruiting officers enlist any men employed in the Quartermaster's Department at Fort Monroe. The central issue was whether or not these departments had the right or the need to keep free men, working by the day, under their control. On 11 September 1863 Capt. Henry H. Miller was physically prevented from taking volunteer Jerome Johnson, a day laborer at Fort Monroe, back to Yorktown. On the same day Lt. James N. North in Hampton outlined his frustrations in a letter to Draper. There were, North reported, large numbers of men willing to enlist in the 2nd NCCV who had been blocked by Lt. Col. Hoffman, the assistant adjutant general, because they were employed by one of the three departments. Special Order No. 27, issued on 15 September, prohibited any further enlistment "by recruiting officers for colored troops from the Ordnance or Engineering Departments unless by consent of the Chief of the respective Departments."[89] Such consent was seldom forthcoming, perhaps because some officers in the Quartermaster's Department honestly believed that it was in the freedmen's best interest. Several officers told one of Draper's recruiters that Lieutenant Parker had "given the death blow to recruiting in this vicinity." They claimed that he had "taken some Cavalry men to the Contraband camp, and took some fourteen of them by force, and that since then the colored men had lost all confidence." There may have been some truth to the allegation, for Parker was discharged from the regiment in April 1864.[90]

Capt. Henry Miller was also angry at the restrictions imposed on him. When he had talked to the African Americans working on the fortifications at Yorktown, more than one hundred of them had indicated their intention to enlist. Then he had received Special Order No. 27. "The order is wrong in the sight of God and man," he raged in a letter to Draper. "These men are at work by the day," he argued, "and are just as free according to the laws of the U.S. as I am and consequently can choose for themselves." The tone of his protest, however, suggests that he was upset in part because he could not manipulate the freedmen as easily as General West could. If Miller had been able to enlist the men, he argued, West would merely have had to send a demand for more labor to the contraband camp. "The General did this very thing yesterday morning," Miller noted. "He made a demand for 23 men and obtained them in a very short time. But I cannot do this. I have to preach many a sermon."[91] Because the provost guards were seizing every freedman they could find and West was refusing to release black workers to the army, Miller would have to go into the countryside to have any chance of finding recruits.

Unfortunately for the regiment, Miller could not look for soldiers in the countryside at that time. Colonel Draper had already been denied permission to send a recruiting officer, accompanied by a small squad of soldiers for his protection, south through the counties of Princess Anne, Currituck, and Norfolk. General Foster's explanation reflected the prevalent attitude toward black troops. Draper's men could not go because "all of the force of the Colrd regiments are required either in Fatigue Duty, on the new fort, or in drilling." Moreover, "the discipline and drill should be quite perfect before sending the party through a section of the country where the opportunities for plunder often occur."[92] Nevertheless, Foster's subsequent actions indicate that he preferred to see the black soldiers engaged in manual labor rather than drill.

Instead of being allowed to plan recruiting expeditions that would also give his men some experience in the field, Draper was forced to assign them other duties that were, at the very least, unproductive. Just before Foster had turned down his request for a recruiting expedition, Draper had been ordered by Gen. Henry M. Naglee, in preparation for a troop review, to "detail a sufficient number of men to pull up all the weeds between the ambulance Camp and the rebel entrenchments."[93] Even when the work was not dangerous, it was often borne unequally by the black troops. Weeks later, Draper complained about the unfair amount of fatigue duty demanded of his men. His fatigue parties should "be permitted to quit work on the fortifications at 5 P.M. to enable them to prepare for Dress Parade. They are now obliged to work after dark. [A] considerable portion of them are raw recruits who require discipline and drill."[94] Draper needed to prepare his regiment for the combat that lay ahead, but the labor demands placed on his regiment by senior commanders made that task very difficult.

Throughout the early fall, the shortage of officers continued to hamper attempts to improve the regiment's military efficiency. Until all of the companies had most of their officers, they could not conduct effective drill and weapons training. Only slightly more than twenty officers had reported to

Draper by September, and some of them were unavailable for regimental ser-vice because of illness or special details.[95] The limited number of new recruits in Virginia had forced Draper to send officers such as Capt. G. M. Fletcher and Lt. George L. Seagraves back to North Carolina to staff recruiting sta-tions in Beaufort and New Bern.[96] At the same time, other officers were lost to the 2nd NCCV because of disability or dissipation. Lt. Joseph J. Hatlinger, one of Draper's first officers, had to resign due to ill health aggravated by a bout of typhoid fever, and Capt. George W. Ives's appointment was revoked be-cause of "intemperance and gross misconduct." Ives agreed to resign because "my habits which are intemperate render my usefulness of no effect." Still other company officers who were present but ill could provide only partial service.[97]

Nevertheless, by the first of October almost all of the officers were on board, even if they were not on duty with their own company. Draper now found that although his regiment had enough men, he could not get it offi-cially mustered in by the army. On 2 October he reported that the 2nd NCCV had 592 enlisted men stationed in Virginia plus several small squads of recruits in addition to the 150 men detached on Folly Island.[98] The total was 765 men, sufficient to fill the regiment. Draper pointed out the cost of the continued delay to his officers and men, some of whom had been serving for almost three months without compensation. "Both officers and men are greatly in need of their pay," Draper wrote; he pleaded that his regiment "be mustered in as an organization before next muster for payment." Captain Gould, assis-tant commander of muster at Norfolk, had informed the colonel that the 2nd NCCV could be mustered in despite the absent detachment in South Carolina if he submitted an affidavit affirming the correct number of absentees and if "the necessary authority be granted from Head Qrs Dept." Draper requested and received the necessary authorization. The 2nd NCCV was finally mustered in at Portsmouth, Virginia, for three years from 28 October 1863, almost three months after Draper had started to recruit its soldiers.[99]

Almost immediately changes in the command of the district allowed the men to act as soldiers instead of laborers. In early November General Wild was transferred to Norfolk to assume command of all black troops in the district.[100] He had argued, after he was ordered to Folly Island, that he would be more useful back in North Carolina raising the remainder of his brigade. By the time he was allowed to return to New Bern in mid-October, the 2nd NCCV was in Virginia. He was able to speed up organization of the 3rd NCCV but had to abandon plans for a fourth regiment. There was little left for him to do but settle brigade business and accounts in the state.[101] On the positive side, Wild's new command of the district of Norfolk and Portsmouth allowed Draper's regiment greater freedom of operation and more support for his attempts to ensure fair treatment of his black soldiers.

The case of one white officer, Lt. Joseph G. Langley, and his alleged abuse of men in Company F under his command, demonstrated the shared attitudes of the two senior officers, Wild and Draper, toward the rights of the enlisted men. Langley had previously served as a private in the 51st Massachusetts Volunteers before accepting a commission in the 2nd NCCV. Although detailed to recruit at Fort Monroe in early November, he had remained at Portsmouth settling his accounts and preparing for the muster service. His actions during this period caused Draper to believe "that he should be brought to trial for extorting his living from the enlisted men of his Company, maltreatment of his men, disobedience of orders, and other unmilitary behavior."[102] At a time when the officers were trying to earn the loyalty of the enlisted men, Langley threatened to undermine the regiment's cohesion. Wild's reaction, on the surface, was more moderate than Draper's, but Langley's appeal to the general during a personal interview had been largely unsuccessful. Apparently Langley and his servant had eaten at the company's expense, and for that Wild assessed him ten dollars, which he had to repay to the company. Of greater importance, Wild admonished Langley for the way he had treated his soldiers, concluding: "Although the specific injuries inflicted on any of the men are trivial in degree, yet his whole tone and manner are illy [*sic*] adapted to the treatment of African troops, and must be corrected in the future."[103] Wild was well aware that the lieutenant's behavior could jeopardize the whole recruiting effort. Langley's request for a second meeting with Wild was bluntly refused, and he was told that he could accept the fine and reprimand or face a court-martial or a court of inquiry. Although he accepted the fine, his days in the regiment were numbered. By 29 June 1864 Langley had been discharged from Draper's command.

Draper's efforts to get his regiment combat-ready were handicapped by more than just the occasional bad officer. For a number of reasons, the training of the second regiment had been slower than the first. Clearly, a conscientious and able regimental commander was necessary but not sufficient to ensure that the soldiers received proper training. The ongoing shortage of company officers hampered both the organization and the training of the unit, which had been further impeded by the move to Virginia. As soon as the 2nd NCCV arrived at Norfolk, Draper had been forced to detail the largely untrained recruits to numerous work parties. This left little time to drill the men as a unit. Like many black regiments, including those raised in North Carolina, the 2nd NCCV had to put up with poor or insufficient equipment. But unlike the 1st NCCV, which was armed almost immediately, Draper's command had to wait months before receiving all of its weapons. Indeed, as late as October 1863 the regiment still could not drill with weapons because none had been issued. It was not just the muskets—when they finally arrived—that were substandard. Other equipment, such as the tents for Company A, were unfit for use.[104]

Wild's transfer to Virginia made it somewhat easier to get guns and equipment. The regiment was largely armed and militarily functional by mid-November. An outside review of both the 2nd NCCV and the 1st USCT conducted by Capt. Hazard Stevens found them "in excellent order, considering how recent they have been organized and the fatigue they have been required to perform." The 2nd NCCV was specifically praised since "none of the companies have been armed over a few weeks. Some have not yet recd their arms and under these circumstances, the condition of the Regiment, the cleanliness of the arms and clothing, the proficiency in drill, and the general aspects and bearing of the Regt reflects the greatest credit on the officers." Nonetheless, there was some criticism. The entire camp "requires policing, the Hospital arrangements are good, but like the First, this Regt is suffering from an insufficient supply of medicine."[105] A medical examiner had been much more critical in September, when he reported that "the whole command shows strong evidence of a want of care and discipline." Draper felt that the report was unfair. From the moment that his command had reached Virginia, some 450 strong, he had been ordered to furnish 175 to 200 men daily to work on the fortifications. The remainder, still with little military training, spent much of their time drilling. In the first months, few men were available to finish stockading the camp and to construct a proper hospital. Draper maintained, however, that the current report of Captain Stevens indicated that his regiment was now in good shape.[106]

Only in late November was the 2nd NCCV adequately armed, supported by a sympathetic district commander, and thus able to undertake what Draper

and Wild had for so long advocated—an expedition into Confederate territory in search of recruits, refugees, and supplies. This would give the enlisted
men important field experience and provide a limited test of their military
readiness. How well the men handled themselves on the raid would reveal
much about the regiment's preparedness for battle. Unlike the 1st NCCV, the
second regiment was forced to enter the combat phase of its service with little
practice on the firing range. The long delay before the issuance of weapons and the heavy fatigue demands in camp had allowed no time for target
practice.

Two months before Draper received permission for his expedition into the
countryside, the last regiment that Wild would be able to raise in North Carolina had begun forming. This unit—the 3rd NCCV—faced an organizational
challenge unlike that of his first two regiments. With the departure of all black
troops from North Carolina, Norfolk became the new base of operations for the
fledgling regiment and the original plan of raising an all–North Carolinian
African Brigade was abandoned. Now recruiting parties in North Carolina
towns enlisted men and forwarded them to Norfolk. Distanced from its original source of recruits and without the guidance of General Wild, the 3rd NCCV
had even greater growing pains than the 2nd NCCV. The critical factor that
would undermine the unit's effectiveness, however, was the pressing demand
for more and more soldiers. The 3rd NCCV was forced to begin its formal existence in the winter of 1863–64 only partially complete, with just Companies
A, B, C, D, and E mustered into service. It would be months before the regiment, serving with the Third Division of the Eighteenth Army Corps, had all
of its companies mustered in. Companies F and G were added in May 1864,
after the 3rd NCCV had been redesignated the 37th USCT, and Company H was
organized and mustered into service in August at Point of Rocks, Virginia.
Companies K and I, which would complete the regiment's structure, were
not mustered in until November 1864, several months after the unit had been
battle tested. Fielding the partially complete regiment prematurely came at
a high price. In sharp contrast to the first two regiments, the third regiment
was continually beset with problems of organization, internal discord, and
military inefficiency.

The first steps to organize the unit had seemed promising. At the beginning
of September 1863, Wild had submitted to the War Department his proposed

roster of commissioned officers for the 3rd NCCV. The second regiment was still incomplete, he admitted, but he could justify issuing the new commissions. Before the new officers could reach North Carolina, Wild explained, the 2nd NCCV would have been completed and a start made on filling the third regiment. He wished to avoid the problems that Draper had encountered with a critical shortage of officers. In staffing the 3rd NCCV, Wild, once again, could select only a few men who were already commissioned, and, as before, he drew heavily from the ranks of the Massachusetts regiments. Thirty-three of the thirty-six names he submitted belonged to veterans, only two of whom were not from the Bay State. Many of these veterans were in the 1st Massachusetts Volunteers, where Wild had once served and which had been transferred from the Army of the Potomac to perform guard duty in Northern cities. Sixteen officers, including the first commander, Lt. Col. Abial G. Chamberlain, were promoted from that regiment, twelve of them from Company A. Company A was the unit that Wild had recruited and commanded at the start of the war.[107] Only a few of the men selected had held commissions, and only Chamberlain had commanded a company.[108]

The shortage of experienced officers compounded Wild's difficulty in trying to get one particular officer whom he had requested. That officer was Capt. John Wilder, a resident of Cambridge, Massachusetts, who had been transferred to Fort Monroe to recruit for the 54th Massachusetts. That plan was aborted, but Wilder was authorized to raise local companies of heavy artillery. The one company that he organized in 1863 was formally designated Company A, 2nd USCT, although it remained at Fort Monroe. When General Foster assumed command of the Department of Virginia and North Carolina and found the company still there, he ordered it to New Bern, expecting that it would be incorporated into Wild's brigade. Wild intended to make it Company A in the third regiment to provide a pool of relatively experienced soldiers for his new unit. However, before the transfer could be formalized, Wild and all of the armed men at his disposal had been ordered to Charleston. Wilder and his soldiers accompanied the general but were still officially designated as Company A, 2nd USCT. Wild's request in September that Wilder and his men be incorporated into his third regiment was denied, and Wilder and his company were ordered to rejoin the rest of the 2nd USCT.[109] It was an unfortunate loss for the 3rd NCCV, and it contributed to a new policy at the noncommissioned level.

The new policy, one followed by many other USCT regiments, was that each company's first sergeant must be white. Initially, field and staff noncommissioned officers in the 1st and 2nd NCCV were white veterans, but all of the company's noncommissioned officers were drawn from black recruits. The organizers assumed that black soldiers would be competent orderly sergeants. But when the first five companies of the 3rd NCCV were mustered in, white recruits were appointed orderly sergeants. There were two possible reasons for the change in policy. Abial Chamberlain may have felt that there were no qualified black candidates (that is, literate with leadership ability), yet that was hardly different from the first two regiments. Both Beecher and Draper believed that, despite their lack of education and military training, black enlisted men could fill the positions. By the time Chamberlain began to fill the noncommissioned positions, there had been a change of attitude.

Colonel Chamberlain assumed command of a detachment of twelve white men recruited in Boston in late January 1864 and took them to Virginia to serve as the senior company and staff sergeants in his regiment. Most of these men were between nineteen and twenty-five years of age, had seen military service, and had formerly worked as craftsmen and artisans. A few had been clerks, and it may have been their ability to help with some of the regimental paperwork that made them attractive to Chamberlain. Their willingness to serve in a black regiment may have originated in strongly held abolitionist sentiments and been encouraged by a three-hundred-dollar bonus, but it was also fueled by the expectation of receiving a commission before the war was over. Significantly, one of the few of these men denied a commission, Thomas B. N. Fitzpatrick, deserted while on furlough in Boston at the end of the conflict.[110]

One should not, however, underestimate the commitment of these noncommissioned officers to the Union's cause. Many had joined Massachusetts regiments as soon as the war began and had proved their resolve with blood and courage in numerous battles over the first two years. James H. Griggs provides one such example. After enlisting as a private in the 4th Massachusetts Volunteers on 1 April 1861, he was wounded four times at the Battle of Bull Run before his capture. For the next eleven months he lived as a POW at Richmond, Tuscaloosa, and Salisbury. On his release, he immediately reenlisted in the 33rd Massachusetts Volunteers but was discharged in March 1863 for disability caused by his former wounds. After a brief recuperation, he joined the 3rd NCCV on 18 January 1864 and became its commissary sergeant. James J. Sullivan, the youngest of the group at age nineteen, was equally committed to the war effort. A native of Ireland, he had been a bookbinder before joining the 11th Massachusetts Volunteers in June 1863. Sullivan fought in all of that regiment's engagements, and by the time he joined the 3rd NCCV, he had also been wounded four times.[111] Both men would be commissioned as lieutenants in Company I, and Sullivan was breveted as major before leaving the service.

Because the 3rd NCCV had been ordered to Virginia in late August 1863, its companies were mustered into service in various places in that state, even though most of the enlisted men continued to be recruited in North Carolina.[112] By the end of December, a start had been made to organize the regiment. Although its officers had not been appointed until 1 October, they joined their unit much faster than had been the case with the first two North Carolina regiments. On 19 October eleven officers, all formerly of the 1st Massachusetts Volunteers, arrived in Norfolk to join two others already at that post. By mid-November Colonel Chamberlain had arrived to take charge of twenty-five officers of the regiment. Unlike the 2nd NCCV, which initially lacked officers, the 3rd NCCV faced a shortage of enlisted men. The problem was compounded by the fact that at least six other regiments or battalions were trying to recruit African American soldiers in North Carolina. Not all of the recruiters were scrupulous. Some officers from other regiments, "availing themselves of the limited knowledge of some of the North Carolinians, have so worked upon their fears by threats of deeds of violence, which they have not the power to execute, as to compel men to enlist who preferred not to."[113] One effect of this approach was to make black civilians more skeptical about joining the Union army. Partly as a result of the increased competition for recruits and black caution in the face of unscrupulous officers, Chamberlain's regiment was slow in filling its ranks. By the end of December 1863 only one of the rudimentary units—Company C—had as many as forty soldiers. The others had only one to two dozen enlisted men in the ranks.[114]

Despite the limited number of men in uniform, beginning at the end of January 1864 the first five companies of the regiment were mustered into service over a two-month period. Most companies began operating at much less than full strength and were subsequently filled as contingents of new recruits were forwarded, generally from North Carolina. In an extreme case, Company E was mustered into service on 1 March with only 14 men, although within a month that number had climbed to 80. By the time Company E had reached its full complement, the regiment had almost 400 men on its rolls.[115]

As he struggled to get his new regiment combat-ready, many of the challenges that Chamberlain faced were familiar to virtually all commanders of black troops. His regiment was more fortunate than many in that it had sufficient officers for company and staff services even with some of the officers on detached recruiting duties. Still, his regiment, like most USCT units, was initially short of trained and literate noncommissioned officers despite the detachment that he had brought from Boston.[116] A more serious problem was that his men were allowed little opportunity to drill or train properly. General Foster had needed troops to finish the fortifications around Norfolk, which helps explain the regiment's transfer. When the 3rd NCCV arrived in Virginia, however, the men were so busy with regimental duties, including entrenching their own camp, and their ranks were so thin that they had few soldiers to spare for the general. With all the demands placed on their troops, the officers had little time even for company drill.

At the beginning of March 1864, Chamberlain was unable to meet a request for a fatigue detail of 50 men, although his regiment then numbered 300. His account of how his men were occupied explains why there was so little time to train new recruits. The men on guard that day, or assigned guard duty the next day, numbered 130. Another 20 were detailed as camp police or woodchoppers. Fourteen more were company cooks or had some other daily assignment. Twenty-five soldiers were sick, while another 72 were absent either as scouts or on a labor detail at Mise's Farm. One man was absent without leave. Excluding a handful of sergeants, this left only 30 troops for special detail. Besides depriving General Foster of the labor that he had requested, the heavy regimental details made company-size drilling extremely difficult and battalion exercises virtually impossible. Chamberlain's partial solution to the problem of inadequate training time seems to have been to push back reveille, first from 6:30 to 5:45, then to 5:00 A.M. The earlier start allowed one hour of drill from 6:00 to 7:00 A.M.[117] It was an attempt to provide at least rudimentary military instruction for new soldiers, but, for men engaged in hard physical work for much of the day, it meant that they had even less rest or time for themselves.

Insufficient hours in the day was not the only impediment to training. As late as March 1864, months after many men had enrolled, the soldiers of the 3rd NCCV had still received no training in musketry. They could not because they had yet to be issued weapons. The problem of obtaining usable muskets was one more example of the difficulties faced by a Southern black regiment competing for limited resources in a voracious army. On 5 March, in response to an official inquiry, Chamberlain explained that "the slowness in receiving guns that had just arrived, and the large details which have been made for fatigue and other duties elsewhere" had made it impossible to instruct his men in the use of weapons. Even after the armaments arrived, adequate training was problematic. The regiment had expected new Springfield rifled muskets but instead received a mixture of worn secondhand guns. Chamberlain soon asked that the weapons be inspected so they could be condemned. The regiment, which had been redesignated the 37th USCT on 8 February 1864, had received three different types of muskets—Springfields, Whitneys, and Enfields. In some cases "the springs in the locks [were] so weak that the hammers will not strike with sufficient force to explode the caps." Many of the ramrods and other equipment were defective as well. Chamberlain's attempts to exchange the faulty equipment with a minimum amount of time lost caused him frustration, but he did get his inspection. On 12 May the lieutenant colonel was able to report that 305 of his men's muskets had been ruled damaged by the examining committee.[118] The issue of defective and insufficient weapons, however, was never completely resolved. Even at the war's end, most of the regiment's companies lacked serviceable guns for all of their troops.[119]

In addition to excessive fatigue duties, poor equipment, and lack of training, Chamberlain's soldiers experienced acts of discrimination from white Federal troops that eroded military morale and created tensions in the regiment. Like black soldiers elsewhere, these men encountered prejudice from white troops wearing the same blue uniform. Sometimes the incidents were serious enough, or overt enough, to trigger official action. Near the end of February, Chamberlain had to caution the commander of the 7th New York Battery of Light Artillery to control his men. The 3rd NCCV had put up with a series of insults from the New York soldiers. In the most recent case, Chamberlain claimed, a fatigue party from his regiment had been at work when, without any provocation, an artilleryman from the 7th had hurled a piece of wood at the black soldiers. Chamberlain warned the New York commander that he had since instructed his officers "to defend themselves and men if assaulted." Furthermore, anyone guilty of assaulting or insulting the men of the 3rd NCCV "on account of their race or color, or any similar cause" would be arrested, confined in the guardhouse, and brought before a court-martial.[120]

Although the 3rd NCCV was, in many ways, plagued by more problems than North Carolina's first two black regiments, it did receive one benefit denied the soldiers who had enlisted earlier. Many of Chamberlain's men were able to take advantage of a small Federal bounty first offered in December 1863. The ten-dollar bonus was a concession that General Butler had squeezed out of the War Department after he took over the Department of Virginia and North Carolina. It had both practical and symbolic importance. Although the amount was small, it was official recognition that none of the black soldiers raised in the South had access to any state or Federal aid available to most Northern soldiers. Butler's order also included a commitment to "furnish suitable subsistence, under the direction of the Superintendent of Negro Affairs" for the soldiers' families.[121] Moreover, a two-dollar recruiting fee was paid to the person who brought in a new recruit.

Implementation of the new policy, though welcomed by the recruits, was not without its problems. As late as February 1864, there was uncertainty in the regiment as to how and from whom the payments should be made. Recruiting officers stationed in North Carolina, like Capt. H. L. Marvin at Plymouth, had to pay the two-dollar recruiting fee themselves and afterward apply to the disbursing officer in their district for reimbursement. If the disbursing officer denied the request, as in Marvin's case, then the recruiting officer had to apply directly to the chief mustering and disbursing officer of the department, a time-consuming process. Moreover, the ten-dollar bounty was not paid directly to all recruits, for in April Chamberlain had to send one of his officers to Fort Monroe to collect the outstanding bounties still owed some of his soldiers.[122]

A few of Chamberlain's soldiers never received the small bounties due them because by the end of May the regiment had suffered its first casualties from enemy fire. Although it was not yet fully formed or properly trained and equipped, the Union demand for more troops to man its new offensive meant that the regiment was swept up into the war in Virginia before it was ready for combat. As with the first two regiments, conduct in battle would be the test by which the unit's preparation and its soldiers' character would be measured.

———— ❧ ————

In contrast to the infantry regiments, the 1st North Carolina Colored Heavy Artillery (NCCHA), the last regiment raised from North Carolina blacks, was never properly conceived or trained for combat. The 1st NCCHA was first seen as an emergency force in a unique situation, then as a necessary labor force that could be utilized more easily than one composed of civilians. The African Brigade had been envisioned as a prototype military unit that would demonstrate to white Americans the capabilities of black soldiers. In contrast, the artillery unit was created to meet a series of local crises and later expanded in response to the practical needs of army bureaucrats. It was organized, at a time when Union control in eastern North Carolina was under Confederate threat, specifically to man permanent fortifications. After that danger had passed, the unit acted as an important manpower pool to handle the increasing logistical needs of the Federal army in North Carolina.[123] Because of this, the regiment was not a likely candidate for service outside the state. That fact, along with the sizable bounties that were offered late in the war, made the artillery regiment attractive to many recruits who wanted to stay close to friends and relatives. Even with the incentives of bounties and local service, however, the 1st NCCHA did not fill all of its companies until the last months of the war.

The actual organization of the 1st NCCHA, initially as a battalion, began in late February and early March 1864, and was a response to a succession of Confederate campaigns in North Carolina. In late January 1864 Maj. Gen. George E. Pickett, acting on Gen. Robert E. Lee's urging, led an army of 13,000 men against New Bern. Although the main assault was poorly handled and Pickett began to withdraw on 3 February, a diversionary raid against Newport Barracks, a Union railroad depot about twenty miles south of New Bern, had much better results. Southern troops operating out of Wilmington were able to destroy a large quantity of Union supplies before they were ordered to withdraw. This success and the continued Confederate threat posed by forces under Brig. Gen. Robert F. Hoke fueled Federal concerns about the region's security.[124] By 4 February, it was reported that the rail lines from Beaufort to New Bern had been cut off and Morehead City might have to be evacuated. During Pickett's attack, the Union gunboat *Underwriter* had been surprised and blown up near New Bern.[125] Butler informed Maj. Gen. Henry W. Halleck that he was trying to strengthen General Palmer's command there "by a company of heavy artillery, which is the arm they will need." As late as 20 February, Gen. John Peck believed that unless the Union forces were "immediately and heavily reinforced, both by army and navy, North Carolina is inevitably lost."[126] Those fears seemed to be confirmed when Hoke led a successful attack against the Federal garrison at Plymouth in early May.

It was in this climate of crisis that Maj. Thorndike C. Jameson of the 5th

"The Steamer 'Escort' Running the Rebel Batteries near Washington, North Carolina"
(*Harper's Weekly*, 9 May 1863, Courtesy of North Carolina Collection, University
of North Carolina Library at Chapel Hill)

Rhode Island Heavy Artillery had first received authorization to raise a black battalion of artillery and had begun to fill the first companies.[127] Initially, the response was good. By the beginning of May, however, the Confederate threat to New Bern and elsewhere was receding. With the retreat of the Confederate forces, Jameson stopped recruiting. During the eight months following Pickett's withdrawal, the 1st NCCHA functioned as a battalion of four companies before being expanded to full regimental size in response to growing manpower needs to handle supplies flowing into North Carolina. In the regiment's early organization, there was little sign of the excitement and idealism present at the raising of the African Brigade. The 1st NCCHA was merely one of a growing number of black units, one that might be used by a number of Northern state agents hustling for recruits in North Carolina.[128]

Once the decision had been made to raise the black heavy artillery unit, the next step had been to transfer officers and men from white regiments serving in the New Bern area so they could begin organizing the black recruits. Major Jameson had been temporarily transferred to coordinate the effort. Although he would command the new battalion for eight months, he remained a member of the 5th Rhode Island. In many ways, the major seemed like a good choice to establish a black artillery unit. A native of Providence, he had been a theological student at Brown University before preaching as a Baptist minister in both Connecticut and Massachusetts. Although he had not been formally connected to any antislavery society before the war, his antislavery sermons had won him the friendship and respect of William Lloyd Garrison.[129] When the Civil War began, Jameson was commissioned chaplain in the 2nd Rhode Island Regiment until promoted and transferred to the 5th Rhode Island Heavy Artillery unit.

Jameson had made himself a candidate for command of the new black artillery unit by his actions almost a year before the 1st NCCHA was authorized. When Gen. D. H. Hill and his Confederate troops had besieged Washington, North Carolina, in late March and early April 1863, Jameson had helped persuade General Palmer to let officers and men from the 5th Rhode Island run the blockade aboard the unarmed steamer *Escort*. On the evening of 13 April, Jameson was a member of the force that took the steamer, with hay bales protecting both men and machinery, up the Pamlico River, past the Confederate batteries that commanded the river at three points, and on to Washington. The forced passage of the blockade by the *Escort* and a gunboat, plus Lt. Gen. James Longstreet's need for Hill's men, effectively ended the siege.[130] In praising the action, Col. Henry T. Sisson noted the contribution "particularly of Lieutenant Colonel Tew and Major Jameson, whose advice and support materially aided me in the conception and execution of our undertaking."[131] Thus, when the time came to raise a black artillery unit in North Carolina, Jameson was perceived to possess the personal courage and antislavery sentiment that would make him an effective leader of black troops. A letter to the *Liberator* in the summer of 1864 claimed that Jameson observed "exact military discipline . . . tempered by the kindest regard for the comfort and well-being of the soldiers, whose intellectual and moral as well as physical conditions were evidently made the subject of Major Jameson's peculiar care."[132]

Several other members of the 5th Rhode Island were detached to assist the major, including Adj. James M. Wheaton and several noncommissioned officers. Wheaton served as acting quartermaster while two of the enlisted men sent as aides—Cpl. Thomas P. Maher and Cpl. James B. Babbitt—ultimately obtained commissions in the 1st NCCHA. Men were also detached from other regiments to help establish the battalion. Lt. Charles G. Allen, who would take command of the first company mustered in, had been drawn from the 99th New York Volunteers. Five enlisted men from different regiments were also transferred to assist in the recruiting. The appointment of one of them, Sgt. Barnes Griffith of the 2nd North Carolina Union Volunteers (NCUV) and a native of the state, began the practice of using white North Carolinians as commissioned officers in the 1st NCCHA.[133]

The activities of Barnes Griffith, and Butler's inquiries about him, reveal much about the early recruitment of the 1st NCCHA. By the end of the first week in April 1864, Sergeant Griffith had apparently assembled thirty black recruits for the new unit and, as he had hoped, was recommended for a commission. Butler had ordered Capt. James R. Shaffer, aide-de-camp at New Bern, to "see if Griffith is fit to be a Lieutenant," after which he could be offered a commission and his recruiting expenses would be paid. The thirty recruits were to be brought to New Bern and a list was to be made of their family members so they could be issued rations. The aide was also to report on how rations were distributed and whether either the quartermaster or the provost marshal in New Bern opposed black recruitment. Griffith was subsequently offered a commission, although he would be discharged from the regiment on 25 November 1864.[134]

As other officers were added to the artillery regiment, the pattern of appointing the new commissions differed significantly from the way the first three regiments had been staffed. The artillery officers, never a sufficient number for the regiment's needs, came from a wide range of state regiments; no more than ten were from Massachusetts. A considerable number of them had experience leading white North Carolinians. The white officers who joined the 1st NCCHA, like many of their counterparts in other black regiments, did so for numerous reasons. Still, at a time when "there seems to be a sort of epidemic desire throughout the whole department for commissions in colored regiments," few men sought a position in the 1st NCCHA specifically, and fewer still did so out of sympathy with black soldiers.[135] Lt. William Irving Bullis, for instance, obtained his commission in the artillery regiment through the efforts of a New York politician. Bullis's wife, backed by "some of our most prominent citizens," persuaded the representative from the 12th

Congressional District to appeal directly to Secretary of War Edwin Stanton. Although Bullis deserved promotion, they wrote, he had little chance for a commission in his present regiment, the 150th New York. He needed the promotion because of "the destitute condition of his family" and because "the small wages he now gets is nothing like sufficient for [their] maintenance." His supporters hoped that he would be offered a commission in any regiment in the USCT then being organized.[136] Bullis got the commission that he and his wife so badly wanted in the 1st NCCHA, but he was never promoted.

Frank H. Smith used the regiment to his benefit in a slightly different way. By early 1865, Smith, a private in the 2nd Massachusetts Heavy Artillery stationed in New Bern, had served for almost two years as clerk in the mustering office. General Palmer obtained a commission for him so he could serve as assistant commissary of muster. After receiving a commission in the 1st NCCHA, however, he was immediately detached from the regiment. Indeed, it was never envisioned that Smith would actually serve with that unit. Five months later, the colonel of the 1st NCCHA did not even know where Smith was stationed; no doubt he was also unaware that Smith had been breveted captain.[137] The use of commissions in the 1st NCCHA for purposes unconnected to the regiment only aggravated its chronic shortage of officers and lowered morale within the unit.

Jameson's few officers began to muster men into Companies A, B, C, and D in the first week of March 1864. Lt. James M. Wheaton in New Bern and Lt. Charles Allen in Washington, North Carolina, began to sign up recruits for three years' service and credited them to the state. In less than two months, each company had about eighty-three men who were hard at work, if not hard at drill, for the early recruits were immediately assigned general fatigue duties. After April, with a diminished Confederate threat, recruitment slowed to a trickle, and only a handful of new soldiers were added to the four companies in the next three months. Before then, in an earlier burst of recruiting, Jameson had detailed the five white enlisted men to recruiting stations at Roanoke Island, Beaufort, and other places.[138] These men probably assumed that their effectiveness as recruiters would quickly lead to a commission in the new regiment. By August 1864 they all did receive appointments, although Griffith's was delayed as a result of charges that he would confront in July 1864. Until these men were commissioned, at least one of them, Pvt. William Crombie, faced an awkward situation. When sent to Beaufort in early August to find recruits for the regiment, he took with him Cpl. John Godette, a black noncommissioned officer in Company B.[139] Despite their relative ranks, it was understood that while at this post the corporal would take his orders from the private even though Godette outranked him.

Even with the five new appointments, the regiment remained severely short of officers, reflecting a general disinterest among senior officers as to the fate of the 1st NCCHA. Consequently, most activities in the unit, including dealing with the army's all-important paperwork, were delayed due to the lack of commissioned officers or literate noncommissioned officers. Morning reports were not filled out in the first two companies until June and July respectively; even then, they showed that it would be weeks before either company would have a commissioned officer. Either these companies' black first sergeants—Jarvis Jackson and Benjamin Starkey of Company B, both of whom had joined in early March—were exceptional leaders, or little in the way of drill or organization was accomplished in the first months of their service.[140]

By August, however, the pace of recruitment picked up. The posting of Private Crombie to Beaufort was the start of a renewed effort to enlist men in the artillery regiment. Shortly after Crombie was sent to Beaufort, Sergeant Griffith was posted to Roanoke Island. He and the five enlisted men with him had been ordered to recruit not only on the island but also along the Chowan River and in adjacent counties.[141] The new emphasis on recruitment obviously reflected the growing need for manpower to handle the increased activities in the Federal-held port in eastern North Carolina. It was also part of a new scramble for black recruits throughout the South triggered by the actions of the U.S. Congress. On 4 July 1864 President Lincoln had signed into law a bill allowing agents for Northern states to enlist men in Southern states and credit them against their state's draft quota.

The new recruiting drive that followed the 4 July bill marked the end of the first stage of the artillery regiment's organization. The next stage would be influenced by a fierce competition among agents and Jameson to get credit for the new recruits and would be capped by the major's conviction in the spring of 1865 for stealing bounty money from his soldiers. In mid-August 1864, however, Jameson could inform Butler that his first four companies were armed and equipped and that "for the time they are well drilled and disciplined." He may have been right, but fortunately for the men of North Carolina's last regiment, they would never face Confederate troops in combat and they would never "see the elephant."[142]

Although the three black infantry regiments had been conceived of as a single brigade, selected and trained in the same standard, the fact that they had to be raised sequentially meant that their experiences and effectiveness varied considerably. Only the first regiment had received all of General Wild's attention, as well as the benefits of substantial training time. In all of the regiments, including the 1st NCCHA, Northern white officers, whether they saw themselves as sympathetic to the aspirations of African Americans or not, had to develop a practical relationship with their black enlisted men. For many it would be a stressful education, forged under fire.

## CHAPTER TWO

# A Fine, Fighting Regiment

In the summer of 1863, when the 1st North Carolina Colored Volunteers (NCCV) finally entered the combat phase of its service, the regiment was in many ways better prepared to fight than most other black regiments. It had a full complement of enlisted men, and its companies were almost completely staffed with experienced officers who, for the most part, were supportive of the use of black troops in combat. The soldiers were all armed, even if not with the best weapons, and they had received at least rudimentary training in their use. The 1st NCCV would prove to be both brave and reliable in battle, even in those cases where senior Union commanders did not serve the soldiers well.

When Gen. Edward A. Wild was given three hours' notice to begin moving every man that he could to South Carolina, he assumed that the transfer would be temporary. He expected that he would soon return to complete the task of raising a full brigade in North Carolina. This was not to be the case. The 1st NCCV, which left for Folly Island in late July, would never again serve in North Carolina. It would fight all of its battles and skirmishes in Florida and South Carolina before seeing Reconstruction service around Charleston. The men in the regiment who finally returned home to North Carolina would do so as veterans, not as soldiers.

As soon as he had received the orders for the transfer, Wild got his brigade on the move. He left behind men too ill to travel and much of the regiment's baggage. Most of the 1st NCCV went by train to Morehead City, where they embarked for South Carolina, while elements of the 55th Massachusetts sailed directly from New Bern. The passage was neither quick nor easy. It took some troops up to nine days to reach Charleston, during which time they experienced short, intense storms and longer periods of calm, flat, and windless seas. When the two black regiments finally disembarked at Folly Island, they "proceeded along the beach to the extreme northerly end of Folly Island, and bivouacked in the sand. So urgent was the call for men that heavy details for fatigue were made at once, and it was not until after five days that the camp vacated by the 47th New York, about four hundred yards south of Light-house Inlet . . . was assigned to the Fifty fifth, the First North Carolina going into camp directly north of them."[1]

By the time Wild's men arrived on the island, Gen. Quincy A. Gillmore, who was directing the operations against Charleston, had altered his strategy. His failure to take Battery Wagner despite two costly frontal attacks convinced him that it could be captured only by siege. Such an action, which involved the construction of a network of trenched and numerous batteries, demanded an enormous amount of labor.[2] Since Union officers for much of the war were predisposed to see African American soldiers as more suitable laborers than white troops, Wild's men were guaranteed to get a disproportionate share of fatigue duties. Their work began immediately.

The primary function of the 1st NCCV and 55th Massachusetts was made very clear from the start. On 2 August 1863 Gillmore informed Gen. Alfred H. Terry, commander of Morris Island, that a "colored brigade, 2,000 strong, will be encamped on the north end of Folly Island, for fatigue duty at the landing and on this island, on your requisition." In addition, Brig. Gen. Israel Vogdes, who commanded Folly Island, would "furnish 1,000 men for grand guard duty in the trenches every other day."[3] Wild's soldiers quickly settled into a routine that was always physically demanding, frequently boring, and occasionally deadly. In the evenings, men detailed under Terry would be ferried across Lighthouse Inlet to Morris Island, where they spent the next twenty-four hours. Unlike the white soldiers, or the newly respected 54th Massachusetts, these troops seldom were assigned guard duty. Instead, they normally worked—in eight-hour shifts supervised by an engineering officer—on the trenches that inched their way toward the Confederates at Battery Wagner or on gun batteries being constructed to batter the Confederate position. Although most of the work was done at night, sniper and artillery fire constantly harassed the fatigue parties.[4] The black soldiers also labored on Folly Island, where, for at least August and September, "General Vogdes required only the blacks to perform heavy fatigue duty."[5] That duty included maintaining the flow of supplies from the various transport vessels to the troops on shore. Supplies of all kinds were unloaded day and night. For Capt. Thorndike Hodges, one night stood out above all others. On that particular evening, his troops were scattered around the vessel they were unloading. Some were in the hold, loading munitions boxes into tackle to hoist up to other soldiers at the open hatchway above, who passed them on to men at the rail. On the pier was a long line of men with wheelbarrows who were in constant motion. Sometime around 4:00 A.M. the commanding officer had drifted into a brief sleep. When he awoke, he "saw a realization of the enchanted palace in fairy tales." All of the soldiers had also fallen asleep. "The poor, exhausted men had dropped to sleep, each at his particular post, almost in the attitude of active labor. In the hold, on the deck, at the rail, each slept, sitting or leaning against the nearest support." It was the same scene on shore. "All that was up the pier was a vanishing series of sleepers, each seated in his wheelbarrow, with the moonlight over all, to complete the illusion."[6]

The tired men might have drawn some comfort from the fact that in their new camp on Folly Island, the regiments faced one of the finest beaches that many of the men had ever seen.[7] It was one of the few positive features of their new location. Despite the fine scenery and the ability to bathe in the surf, both the 55th and the 1st NCCV were hard hit by illness. Part of it had to do with the timing of their arrival. "The sickly season," wrote one black Massachusetts soldier, "has now about commenced." The hot, humid weather, a poor water supply, and heavy fatigue duties took their toll. In the Massachusetts regiment, sick call saw turnouts of 140 men and more, most of whom suffered from diarrhea. Sickness within the 1st NCCV was almost as great. From August to December 1863, 34 men died and many others were disabled. Pvt. Gaston Davis in Company E later claimed that the bad water at Folly Island, obtained from shallow wells, had caused their contracting piles and diarrhea, leading to long-term disability. By August one Northern soldier complained that "the water here is worse than miserable—brackish and unhealthy."[8]

Two additional factors compounded the problems of the North Carolina troops. Many were sick even before the regiment had left New Bern. The approximately 150 men who stayed behind due to illness represented only the most serious cases. Many soldiers who were transferred to Folly Island had been in poor health when they left North Carolina. Moreover, when it arrived in South Carolina the regiment was short a medical officer. For the first month on the island, Dr. John De Grasse was the 1st NCCV's only surgeon, and part of that time he was ill himself. Dr. L. Mann, who had remained in New Bern with the sick soldiers, was slow to rejoin the unit. In fact, conditions soon grew so grave on Folly Island that the 55th Massachusetts was forced to transfer its junior surgeon, D. Babbitt, to help James Beecher's regiment.[9] Clearly disease badly hindered its ability to either drill or work effectively.

Yet illness was not the unit's greatest problem. The most serious obstacle to its military efficiency continued to be the heavy fatigue duty imposed on the 1st NCCV as soon as it arrived on Folly Island. The siege operations there were hard on all of the Union regiments involved but particularly for the black units. Senior officers continued to use them more as labor battalions than as line regiments. Colonel Beecher was incensed on hearing that his men on Morris Island had been assigned the task of "laying out and policing camps of white soldiers." A senior officer in a New York regiment had the black soldiers leveling ground, digging wells, and pitching tents for the New Yorkers. The officer's assumptions reflected the dual prejudice encountered by many Southern black recruits. The engineering officers in charge believed the black soldiers to be capable of a greater amount of work than white troops, although they were less skilled and "more timorous." Many Northern officers also felt that "the colored troops recruited from the free states are superior to those recruited from the slave states."[10] Southern black soldiers thus had to contend with this regional bias even from their Northern counterparts.[11] Regardless of where the men had been recruited, all black units were forced in these early months to perform far more than their share of fatigue duties, many of them on Morris Island under Confederate fire. As soon as the 1st NCCV and the 55th Massachusetts had arrived, they started "throwing up earthworks, digging trenches, mounting guns, etc., etc."; every available officer and man labored on fatigue duty continuously, often at night, through August and much of September 1863. The black soldiers—a minority of the troops present—performed over half of the fatigue duties. By the time the 1st NCCV reached Morris Island, the advanced Union trenches were only 540 yards from Battery Wagner and within range of the Confederate guns at Fort Sumter and James Island, as well as Southern sharpshooters. As the men at the front worked in the dark under enemy fire, they frequently made grisly discoveries that explained the island's nickname of "Coffin Island." In one night alone, troops working immediately in front of Wagner exhumed ten bodies from the sand. By the time the third parallel was begun, attitudes had become more calloused and the soldiers merely buried any corpses uncovered in the parapets of the works.[12]

In addition to fatigue duties on Morris and elsewhere, General Wild's soldiers also furnished pickets for the northern end of Folly Island. Frequently,
a majority of the men were available for company and battalion drill only at
night or early in the morning. At a time when most regimental commanders
had abandoned drill because of the heavy labor demands, Colonel Beecher
insisted that his regiment continue its military training. Drills were held on
the wide hard beach that bordered the camp. "For more than two months
during this period," Beecher wrote, "they did not once see their arms by day-
light."[13] Not only was normal military training virtually nonexistent, but also
the harsh pace of work left many soldiers sick and disabled. A few company
officers who could not, or would not, fulfil their duties exacerbated the labor
demands placed on the 1st NCCV. In early September 1863, for example, a
detachment formed in camp to work at Morris Island where Union trenches
were nearing Battery Wagner. When Company C's Lt. Levi G. Pratt failed
to appear, the noncommissioned officers took charge of the day's fatigue duties. Beecher later reprimanded Pratt, but such behavior left the black soldiers
vulnerable to "the abuse from irresponsible persons" and undercut the men's
confidence in their company's officers.[14] Weeks earlier, senior officers had
attributed the flight of some black soldiers from their trenches under heavy
cannon fire to the lack of white officers present.

Although the worst fatigue duties and the greatest danger to the men subsided with the fall of Battery Wagner on 6 September 1863, the failure to capture Fort Sumter left Charleston in Confederate hands. It also marked the effective end of the aggressive Union campaign against the city as troops were
redeployed. The 1st NCCV remained on Folly Island as part of a sizable force
left to threaten the city, to be used how and where senior officers wished. Although the levels of fatigue duties diminished, the regiment remained busy.
In October, Company B was detached to assist engineer Col. E. N. Serrell
on "Middle Island." Another 100 men were already serving on Long Island,
while another company moved to Botany Bay Island, thirty miles away, near
Edisto. It was not until December that these last two companies returned and
the regiment could drill as a whole. During this time, additional men were
assigned to assorted and brief labor details. In the second week of November,
for instance, Beecher sent 154 men from seven companies in the 1st NCCV to
Morris Island for ten days.[15] Even the soldiers remaining with the regiment
served continuously on day fatigue with no opportunity for drill or military
instructions. Officers also were called upon to satisfy equally exhaustive de-

mands on their time. In September Beecher had had to juggle his company officers. "The scarcity of officers present for duty," he explained, "makes it an imperative duty that they should be, as far as possible, equally distributed between the respective companies."[16] The returns from one company for November 1863 revealed just how difficult it was to drill soldiers, even at the company level. In Company E, over one half of the enlisted men—forty-nine out of ninety-seven—plus two of the three officers were absent. Thirteen of these soldiers had been left at New Bern and were now stationed, along with Second Lieutenant Barbough, in Virginia. Capt. Edward S. Daniels and twenty-seven troops were part of the regiment's larger detachment on fatigue duty at Long Island. Nine more enlisted men were detailed as teamsters, served as guards in the old camp, or were absent because of illness. Of the forty-eight men present in camp, ten were ill and a dozen more had been assigned extra or daily duties. As a result, the total number of enlisted men available for regular drill was down to twenty-six. Company E may have been an extreme case, but the pattern held for most other companies in the regiment. By November, however, the worst had passed. Fewer men were detailed away from camp. This left Beecher with more men available to drill and improve the regimental camp.[17]

The reduced fighting in the Charleston area was not the only reason for the drop in fatigue duties of the 1st NCCV in the late fall. It was also the result of a changing military policy that required, at least in principle, the more equitable assignment of black troops to fatigue duties. The initial assumption that manual labor was the appropriate role for most black troops had triggered a wave of complaints, both from black soldiers and from abolitionist officers, such as the men staffing Wild's regiments. At the same time, the performance of black soldiers at Fort Wagner, Port Hudson, and a dozen other engagements disproved claims that they were unsuitable for combat. Initially, it was theater commanders who took appropriate action. In the Department of the South, General Gillmore, accepting the testimony of Wild and Beecher, issued orders to prevent the discriminatory assignment of fatigue duties. Within a year, the Union army moved on this, as on other issues, toward a uniform policy for all soldiers. In June 1864 Adj. Gen. Lorenzo Thomas issued Order No. 21, which required an equitable division of fatigue duties for white and black soldiers alike.[18] Tensions continued, however, as some officers, many of whom remained convinced that black and white troops were not the same, reluctantly implemented new military regulations that were, at least in principle, color-blind.

———3⚏———

With the reduced fighting and fatigue duties around Charleston, the enlisted men in Beecher's regiment had more time to learn to read and write. The North Carolinians, as most black soldiers, eagerly seized the opportunity to become literate. Denied any formal education during slavery, many of these troops regarded such schooling as symbolic of their new status as soldiers and free men. Before they left North Carolina, volunteer teachers from Massachusetts regiments had helped the black recruits. Their appetite for learning continued even after they had entered combat. Despite almost constant demands on their time and the fact that sleep was precious, many blacks made heavy use of the few books available on Folly Island. They were sometimes assisted by off-duty officers in the 1st NCCV, as well as by white soldiers from other regiments posted nearby. By the start of 1864, Colonel Beecher claimed that three hundred men in his regiment had learned to read and write.[19]

As a unit, the 1st NCCV faced major setbacks as 1863 drew to a close. The heavy fatigue duty, the bad water, and the coastal climate swelled the unit's sick rolls. Morale was not helped by senior officers on Folly Island who believed that the men's ailments had less to do with ill health and more to do with malingering. General Vogdes maintained that many soldiers who had reported sick in the morning left their quarters as soon as the work details departed. Henceforth, he directed, any "sick in quarters" who did not confine themselves there would be promptly arrested and returned to duty. Asst. Surg. Burt Green Wilder of the 55th Massachusetts was incensed that Vogdes complained about the length of the sick list when he was assigning four hundred to five hundred men at a time to fatigue duties that might take them out four or five nights in succession.[20]

Within the 1st NCCV, the increased illness occurred during a period of growing conflict between assistant surgeons De Grasse and Mann regarding their relative seniority and duties. The problem may have originated in a clash of personalities, but it was not helped by the fact that De Grasse was one of the few African Americans in the army who held a commission. On Folly Island, Mann was responsible for all sick officers and men in camp and quarters, while De Grasse was in charge of the hospital and the scurvy camp.

Beecher, however, considered Mann to be the senior of the two and entrusted him with compiling final reports.[21] This may have been the colonel's attempt at conciliation, for Mann had complained almost as soon as he rejoined the regiment in mid-August 1863 that he had seniority over De Grasse. Mann argued that, in the absence of the regimental surgeon, Beecher did not have the authority to assign the respective duties of the assistant surgeons.[22] Ill feelings would continue to fester into the new year, but even before then, Mann found himself, albeit briefly, under arrest.[23]

In early November, both the 1st NCCV and the 55th Massachusetts moved to a new camp five miles south of their old one, in part to obtain a safer water supply. The shift initially involved at least two companies working for the better part of a week to prepare the site.[24] The new camp, located on the western slope of a wooded ridge, had the advantage, as winter began, of being at least partially protected by groves of large trees. It was a significant consideration, for the men had already felt the effects of cold nights and early morning duties in torrential rain. The troops did not receive overcoats until late November.[25] Meanwhile, the hospital department continued to complain about the difficulties of keeping patients warm. On the other hand, the cooler weather improved the health of most of the regiments on Folly Island. "The cold," one soldier suggested, "drives disease away." Of equal importance, the best water on the island was found in the sand ridges near the regiments' winter camp. Here the natural hydrology of large dunes allowed wells to tap clear water to depths of several times the height of the dunes.[26]

Given the problems confronting the officers and men of the two regiments, it was understandable that signs of intemperance had begun to surface by the late fall. In November, it became evident that some officers were illicitly drawing whiskey from the commissary stores. Whiskey was to be issued only to men returning from fatigue duty; general orders prohibited officers from purchasing the liquor. Although Beecher wanted to avoid unnecessary interference with the private affairs of his officers, he announced that "the discipline and reputation of the whole command demands that the utmost strictness should be observed in carrying out the provisions" of the orders. The colonel may have been reacting to the fact that on the previous night a number of the officers in the 55th Massachusetts, after a visit from "officers from another regiment," had become so intoxicated that four of them were placed under arrest. The next day, two of the officers resigned to avoid dismissal. Only a month later Capt. B. F. Oakes, who was in charge of the detachment of the 2nd NCCV that had been incorporated into the 1st NCCV during the move to Folly Island, showed up at the brigade headquarters drunk. Beecher publicly reprimanded him for conduct "grossly unbecoming an Officer"; he only regretted that the "exigency of the service" prevented a more severe punishment.[27]

Beecher did not feel that he asked for or expected the impossible from his officers, but, given the trying position of the regiment due to "constant separation, excessive fatigue and deprivation of opportunities for drill," he expected their "cordial co-operation."[28] Clearly he did not think he was receiving it. The behavior of the officers was a sharp contrast to what was perceived to be the behavior of the enlisted men. Regimental chaplain John Mars believed that "drunkenness was one of the few vices that was conspicuously absent from the black soldiers' camps."[29] Some of these problems decreased after November as the men's health improved throughout the island.

January 1864 saw signs of change in the 1st NCCV. When Beecher went north on leave, Lt. Col. William N. Reed assumed temporary command of the unit. Reed initially demanded greater discipline and stricter military behavior from the officers and enlisted men. Although he did not object to "cheerful and orderly merriment," Reed warned that he would not tolerate "riotous and disorderly conduct in the camp even before taps." If necessary, he would enforce the most rigorous discipline. He ordered all officers, as well as sergeants and corporals, not to "tolerate disorderly conduct and rude noise or any other improper disturbances in the Company streets."[30] Around this time, Reed had a corporal reduced to the ranks and a private given a three-day punishment detail for their disorderly conduct toward Lieutenant Redick.[31] Six other privates from six different companies were also punished for leaving their guard post without permission. Reed seemed intent on sending a message that any lack of discipline brought on by excessive fatigue duties or from details posted away from the regiment would not be tolerated.

By the end of January, the 1st NCCV had been, in large part, rearmed. After numerous complaints about substandard, secondhand weapons and appeals for replacements,[32] the regiment, on 26 January, was resupplied with armaments of one make. After handing in all of its Springfield and Enfield muskets, the unit received "smoothbore muskets altered to percussion, calibre 69."[33] These guns may have been an improvement, but, in any case, the regiment was now uniformly armed. Nevertheless, at the first real combat that the 1st NCCV would face, at the Battle of Olustee in Florida the following month, it became obvious that a large number of the new weapons were defective, "many bursting in action."[34] Only after that engagement did the army command take steps to arm the regiment with dependable weapons.

———— ✸ ————

In its last days on Folly Island, the 1st NCCV and the 55th Massachusetts experienced a series of significant events. On 8 February 1864, the 1st NCCV was redesignated the 35th U.S. Colored Troops (USCT), although many officers and men were slow to drop the regiment's original name. Two days later, the assistant inspector general presented an extremely critical picture of both regiments. The condition of their clothing was "poor," their military appearance was "indifferent," their military bearing was "unsoldierly," and their personal hygiene was "dirty." The 1st NCCV (now the 35th USCT) had "been neglected since last month on account of the absence of Field Officers, two of whom have been on special duty most of the time. The ill effects occasioned by it, were very perceptible on Inspection. The arms were reported dirty."[35] Clearly part of the problem was a result of the regiment's heavy fatigue duty on Folly and Morris islands. Both the men and their clothes were worn and dirty. The accuracy of the assessment of its military effectiveness, however, would soon be called into question.

The outbreak of smallpox within the 35th USCT in early February 1864 was probably more damaging to its combat readiness than the condition of its equipment. Physicians believed that a detachment of men returning from Norfolk had introduced the infection, and by 9 February several cases had been diagnosed. The danger to the camp was considerable because few men had been vaccinated against the disease. The threat increased when Dr. Mann, who was in charge of the regimental smallpox camp, seemed unable or unwilling to fulfil his responsibilities. Lieutenant Colonel Reed had to warn him that his repeated reluctance to obey the orders of the regiment's white surgeon, Dr. Henry O. Marcy, at this critical stage would not be tolerated. Only two days later, through the negligence of Mann or a junior officer, a patient infected with smallpox was allowed to go to the regimental hospital, "thereby jeopardizing the whole command." Reed was close to preferring charges against both men for incompetence.[36]

Reed instructed company commanders on how to combat the spread of the disease. They were to remove all clothes, blankets, and equipment of those stricken from the regimental camp and have them thoroughly fumigated. A

Lt. Col. William N. Reed, 35th USCT (Courtesy of
Massachusetts Commandery Military Order of the
Loyal Legion and U.S. Army Military History
Institute, Carlisle Barracks, Pa.)

disinfectant provided by Dr. Marcy was to be sprinkled on the company tents.
It was particularly important, Reed stressed, that none of the patients at the
smallpox camp be permitted to rejoin their comrades. This may have been
difficult given the concern of the enlisted men that the smallpox camp was a
death sentence. Finally, all men not yet vaccinated should immediately report
to Marcy for the injection.[37] Before the smallpox could be eradicated, the regiment received orders to move and, once again, was forced to leave some of
its sick behind.

———✤———

Just days before the outbreak of smallpox, the army ordered the 35th USCT
and the 55th Massachusetts to join the expeditionary force being organized
in Florida by General Gillmore, the recently appointed commander of the

Department of the South. The goal of the expedition, to be led by Brig. Gen. Truman B. Seymour, was to interrupt the supply of corn, cattle, and other foodstuffs from the state to the Confederate forces in the North and to open a new source of black recruitment. Two competing groups of Republicans promoted a secondary objective—to restore Florida to the Union—if Confederate forces could be driven from northern Florida.[38] Gillmore had originally planned to use only veteran troops, a large number of whom were to be mounted, but in the end he was forced to accept some inexperienced regiments. The small army of nine infantry regiments, including the 54th Massachusetts, one mounted infantry regiment, a cavalry battalion, and some artillery, had seized Jacksonville, Florida, on 7 February 1864 almost without firing a shot.[39] The Federal soldiers' rapid push inland along the Atlantic and Gulf Railroad promised great success and, on 14 February, the 35th USCT and 55th Massachusetts, along with a battery of artillery, were directed to move west from Jacksonville to reinforce Seymour's little army.

On the day that the two black regiments had received the order to proceed to Jacksonville, General Terry submitted a report of their medical condition: "In the two regiments . . . I found a considerable number of men sick with the small-pox, and a still larger number who had been exposed to contagion." He had kept all of those men behind "with one medical and one other officer from each regiment to command and care for them." In a postscript Terry noted that, on the assumption that the regiments were facing active service, he had "retained here also such men of them as were unfit to march."[40] The illnesses, compounded by Terry's actions, significantly reduced the effective strength of the regiments.

The arrival of the 35th USCT in Florida marked the beginning of the real combat phase of its service, for which it was only partly prepared. While serving on and around Folly Island, the regiment had occasionally found itself under fire, and some small units had participated in raids and ambushes. Detachments of the regiment acted, at least briefly, as "boat infantry." Although they may have inflicted casualties on the enemy, they suffered none themselves.[41] In one case, Lt. Henry L. Stone of Company F took twelve of his men and embarked at Pawnee Landing in a small boat. They pulled down the opposite side of Folly River to a small creek. Then they were to "go 100 to 150 yards up. Haul up boat and lie in wait for Enemy's boat or boats." If the enemy was too strong, they were to fall back to the picket reserves. Such actions, as well as short bouts of training, may explain why some companies had used up two thousand rounds of ammunition on Folly Island.[42] Nevertheless, these activities had done little to prepare the regiment to fight as an entire unit. Indeed, on balance, the time spent on Folly Island had reduced the regiment's overall military effectiveness. In addition to deficient training and equipment, on its arrival in Jacksonville on 15 February the 35th USCT still suffered from the effects of the smallpox outbreak plus other health problems. Ninety-nine men had been sick in January, and that number almost doubled to 171 soldiers on sick report during February. In all, 110 men in the 35th USCT were kept back in South Carolina in the care of two officers from the regiment. Another dozen men remained behind permanently in the brigade burial ground on Folly Island.[43]

The regiments arrived in Jacksonville with minimum baggage, only to find the weather wet and so cold that Assistant Surgeon Wilder "hardly slept after midnight; last night no sleep till 4 P.M." The town itself had a desolate appearance. The more affluent part of town had burned; only tall chimneys marked the location of former mansions.[44] Despite illness and thinned ranks, the North Carolina regiment, led by Lieutenant Colonel Reed, marched out of Jacksonville the next day to catch up with Union forces led by General Seymour that were moving west.[45] Although Seymour hoped to seize the railroad bridge over the Suwannee River at Columbus, he became increasingly concerned that, with an army of only about 5,500 men, he lacked the means to do so.[46] Nevertheless, in a controversial and precipitous move, the general pushed his strung-out forces up the Atlantic and Gulf Railroad toward Olustee with apparently little planning. In front of him was a hastily formed Confederate army put together by Brig. Gen. Joseph Finegan. In the days prior to the battle, Confederate officials had rushed a brigade of Georgia troops to Florida from South Carolina. Although the opposing armies had about the same number of men on each side, Finegan's army had more veterans and was more ably led.

Before 7:00 A.M. on the morning of 20 February, Seymour's troops began moving out of their overnight bivouac at Barber's Station, thirty-six miles west of Jacksonville. The 40th Massachusetts Mounted Infantry led the way. The long column of soldiers advanced about eighteen miles that day before making contact with the first Confederate positions near Olustee.[47] Seymour's tired and thirsty men extended along the line of march, with the 35th USCT and the 54th Massachusetts, comprising Col. James Montgomery's brigade, positioned as the rear guard. Both the speed of the advance and the

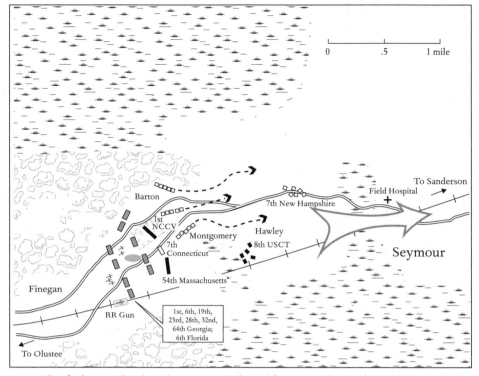

Battle of Olustee, Florida, February 1864 (adapted from a map by Noah Andre Trudeau).

lack of security on the flanks suggest that Seymour did not expect to encounter serious resistance before coming to Lake City or perhaps the bridge over the Suwannee River.[48] Before reaching the hastily constructed Confederate entrenchments near Olustee, the leading Union infantrymen had passed the 40th Massachusetts Mounted Infantry, apparently in bivouac. It was 2:00 P.M. and at a critical time in the advance, Seymour's little army no longer had a cavalry screen covering its movements. The men had been marching for about seven hours.

Once contact was made with the enemy, Seymour planned to pin down the Confederate center with artillery and two regiments—the 7th New Hampshire and the 8th USCT—while another Union brigade rolled up the Confederate left flank. Before the flanking movement could begin, however, the two Union regiments crumpled under Confederate fire and began to retreat in disorder. The 7th New Hampshire had received conflicting orders and quickly lost its cohesion, while the 8th USCT, with knapsacks on and weapons unloaded, double-timed to within two hundred yards of the Confederate lines before they stopped and tried to form a line of battle. Raked by Confederate fire, their ranks were shattered before the regiment could begin to fight. Seymour threw regiments piecemeal into the battle, while brigade commanders reverted to regimental leaders with the accompanying loss of control. As the battle progressed, the Confederates were able to extend their line of troops to achieve a concave line that overlapped both ends of the Union position.

At about 2:30 P.M., with the Union front in danger of collapse, Seymour ordered Montgomery's brigade forward on the double. Dropping knapsacks, haversacks, and all unnecessary gear by the wayside, the regiments hurried forward, passing wounded and demoralized soldiers who were falling back. Long after the war, Sgt. Alexander Griffin remembered the toll that the march had taken on some of his men. "While on the march from Jacksonville Fla. to Olustee Fla. on the day of the battle of Olustee [John Saunders] became disabled & fell in the ranks while the Regt. was on the Double Quick. . . . I did not stop to help him. . . . There was no time lost in the march[;] we went on for 6 or 7 miles till we reached the place of battle." Another comrade recalled that Saunders's fall caused some confusion in the ranks before the men re-formed and "went right on and left him." A third member saw "several men on the Road who were out of ranks. The claimant was one."[49] Leaving exhausted men in their wake, the regiments pressed on.

At about 4:00 P.M., the two black regiments reached the front. One white Union soldier who was present on the field that day described their arrival, "the First North Carolina passing between the Forty-seventh and Forty-eighth [New York] on the double-quick and cheered by those shattered regiments as it went into battle." The 35th USCT quickly formed on the right of the Union line and went "up into the field, halting and firing fiercely, with its right well forward, so as to form an angle of perhaps 120 degrees with the line of the Fifty-Fourth." This position opened the right side of the 35th USCT to a deadly enfilading from the overlapping Rebel soldiers. The Confederate advance, already short of ammunition, was checked but at a high cost. Seymour's apparent decision at this point to form a new line farther to the rear and to withdraw some units left the two black regiments terribly exposed. When the resupplied Confederates renewed their attack, both Union regiments were forced back.[50]

Although official reports indicate that Reed and his North Carolinians

"Battle of Olustee, Fla.," February 1864 (Courtesy of Anne S. K. Brown
Military Collection, Brown University Library)

acted "in the most brilliant manner," all that they and the men of the 54th
Massachusetts could do was to blunt the Confederate attack, then withdraw
slowly and in good order. Montgomery's brigade had, in large part, prevented
a rout, and Seymour praised the two regiments for behaving "like veterans."[51]
Another observer claimed that "no regiment went into action more gallantly,
or did better execution than the First North Carolina (colored) troops. Their
white comrades generally take pleasure in awarding them this honor." Their
performance was all the more remarkable given the recent outbreak of smallpox and the fact that, in the midst of battle, at least some of the companies had
found that their replacement muskets were unusable.[52] The North Carolinians,
of course, were not the only soldiers to enter this or other battles armed with

faulty weapons. While black regiments frequently complained, with justification, about their defective guns, some white regiments faced similar problems. Indeed, the poor weapons that had been distributed to about half of the men in the 7th New Hampshire just before Olustee, many without locks or ramrods, were blamed for that regiment's early collapse.[53] If, however, faulty muskets could explain the undoing of the 7th New Hampshire, then the conduct of the similarly armed 35th USCT was that much more extraordinary.

Another Federal regiment that performed poorly, the 8th USCT from Pennsylvania, also served as a foil for the North Carolinians' performance. Although Cpl. James Gooding might claim that "no regiment in the department can boast of a more healthy-looking, martial-bearing body of men" than the 8th USCT, they had little practice with their weapons and entered the battle in a fashion inviting disaster.[54] Only half of the men had loaded their muskets, and all of them still carried their knapsacks when they moved forward into battle. Before they could become an effective fighting force, the regiment suffered serious casualties and had lost much of its cohesion. The 8th USCT paid a heavy price for its inadequate training. The soldiers could march well, but they had not been instructed in rapid accurate shooting, despite their colonel's repeated request for permission to conduct target practice. Instead, they had "drilled too much for dress parade and too little for the field."[55] In sharp contrast to the 8th USCT, the 35th USCT received solid practical training under General Wild while still in North Carolina. The 35th USCT may have been less picturesque than some black Northern units, but it was well led and better prepared. The men's refusal to collapse in the face of superior numbers and a flanking fire helped prevent the Union army's retreat from becoming a rout. The North Carolinians deserved a great deal of credit that Seymour was able to draw off his forces without greater losses.

In many ways, the debate over the performance of Reed's troops at Olustee provides a microcosm of how black soldiers were perceived—by contemporaries and later commentators—to have fought during the Civil War. Some participants at Olustee praised the conduct of the 35th USCT, whereas white and black soldiers in other regiments often ignored or minimized it. They did so, in part, because of the tendency of most men to emphasize their own unit's contribution in an engagement or because few participants were aware of more than their own small sector of the battlefield. Typically, members of the

Rhode Island artillery later claimed that their batteries were well managed, "the men sticking to their guns like heroes and the officers displaying great gallantry." No mention was made of other Union troops, black or white, in the battle. Members of the 7th Connecticut would argue that their "brave little band stood like a stone wall in the center of the field" and repelled all attacks until their ammunition ran low. In this account, Seymour personally told the colonel of the 7th: "You will detach the Seventh Connecticut as a rear guard. I cannot trust any other regiment." By contrast, a letter in the *Liberator* in March maintained that only the actions of the 54th Massachusetts had prevented the whole Union army from being captured. "This was the only regiment that rallied, broke the rebel ranks, and saved us."[56] Some Northern black soldiers mixed their praise for the 54th Massachusetts with implicit or explicit criticism of the 35th USCT. Sgt. Maj. Rufus Jones of the 8th USCT claimed that the 54th Massachusetts fought the enemy all by itself; "had one more regiment come to its assistance," a defeat could have been averted. A private from the 54th was even more critical of the North Carolinians. "In they went, and fired a few rounds," he wrote, "but they soon cleared out; things were too warm for them." He continued: "When the 1st N.C. found out it was so warm they soon left and then there were none left to cover the retreat" but the 54th Massachusetts.[57]

It would be misleading, however, to imply that there existed clearcut attitudes toward the conduct of either the 35th USCT in particular or the black regiments generally. White and black soldiers held a spectrum of prewar biases and viewed the battle from different vantage points. Whereas supporters of African American troops praised the behavior of the black regiments, the *Philadelphia Ledger* ran a story under the title, "Bad Conduct of a Negro Regiment," that criticized black soldiers for breaking under fire and fleeing the field. Augusta's *Daily Chronicle and Sentinel* claimed that Union deserters captured after the battle were "very hostile to the Negro troops, and assert that they are not to be trusted in battle but will retreat on the first fire."[58] On the other hand, two soldiers in Georgia regiments had grudging praise for the African Americans, although they also echoed the Rebel bitterness about the use of black troops. Cpl. Henry Shackelford of the 19th Georgia Infantry wrote his mother that the "Yankees were giving back and on our pushing forward, pitched three Negro regiments against us, and all acknowledge that they fought well." A private in the 27th Georgia Infantry wrote, "We met with a more stubborn Negro Regt." But both Southerners indicated that little mercy was shown to their black adversaries. By contrast, a Union artillery-man wrote to a Northern newspaper that it was "our misfortune to have for support a Negro regiment, who, by running, caused us to lose our pieces."[59] Perhaps Col. Thomas Wentworth Higginson, commander of the 33rd USCT, presented, just days after the battle, the most balanced assessment of the black soldiers' performance at Olustee. He had heard from various officers that "the 54th Mass. and the 1st N.C. really saved the affair fr. being far worse than it was, by making a charge & driving back the enemy for a time under cover of which our troops retreated." Yet it was also said, he added, "that the 8th US Colored, being entirely raw, did not stand well." Higginson predicted that General Seymour's report would include criticism of the 8th USCT but maybe omit praise of the other two regiments. A few weeks later the colonel told his mother he had heard that Seymour "is now trying to throw the blame of his own folly on the colored troops."[60]

The various descriptions of the actions of the 35th USCT at Olustee un-derscore the difficulty in attempting to assess the roles and effectiveness of any group of men in combat. Blatant prejudice distorted some accounts, but more subtle factors influenced others. The officers who compiled such reports may have had incomplete information, little time, and many other things to do, while newspaper editors needed to fill columns that would satisfy their readers. Of course, observers were seldom impartial. All too often reports were prepared, as Colonel Higginson suggested, by participants who wished to present complicated events in a fashion that, while not entirely inaccurate, was self-serving or intended to reward some regiments and officers and pun-ish others. Moreover, other factors altered, in less detectable ways, how sol-diers remembered events of the day, especially when they involved Southern black troops. In the chaotic heat of battle, many participants were influenced by what cognitive psychologists call a "confirmation bias." According to this theory, people are more alert and responsive to evidence that conforms to previously held beliefs and more inclined to ignore evidence that might chal-lenge those beliefs. They do not consciously distort what they have seen, but their memory of events is influenced by their confirmation bias.[61] In an army that reflected the larger society's racial preconceptions, that influence perme-ated many after-battle reports.[62]

Region as well as race worked against Southern black regiments. As Sey-mour's army foundered, it is not surprising that some white soldiers remem-bered the collapse in ways that placed the blame more heavily on the black troops. A regiment like the 35th USCT was used, however, not just as a foil for the conduct of white units. At Olustee, the presence of a well-regarded Northern black regiment, the 54th Massachusetts, and the existence of various interest groups supporting and promoting that regiment, colored how some would depict the actions of the North Carolina soldiers. By the time it reached Florida, the 54th Massachusetts was famous for following Col. Robert Shaw onto the ramparts of Fort Wagner. In abolitionist groups, it had become a symbol of what free Northern blacks in uniform could do. For any Northerner who accepted the value of black soldiers, the 54th Massachusetts had earned its reputation in combat, a reputation used by abolitionists in what amounted to a national publicity campaign. As the various accounts of Olustee reveal, support for the 54th influenced how contemporaries viewed the actions of the 35th USCT.

Although some critics were predisposed to believe any story depicting the failure of black soldiers under fire, others demonstrated a new attitude toward African American troops after the Battle of Olustee. Though prejudices of race and region were slow to be erased, grudging admiration for fellow soldiers who had shared hardships, dangers, and death was evident in the aftermath of defeat. Dr. Ester Hill Hawks, who tended the wounded after their retreat to Jacksonville, was impressed that "many touching instances of friendliness occurred, among our patients, who were a mixed company of black and white, in very close quarters." She had already learned that "the black Regts. had borne the fiercest onslaught of the enemy, and the white soldiers were loud in their praise and when I saw white soldiers sharing their tobacco with the black ones, I concluded that the end of the war was near for the millennium had begun."[63]

The rearguard action of the 35th USCT that provided Dr. Hawks with some of her patients had extracted a high price from the regiment. Lieutenant Colonel Reed was mortally wounded "while managing his regiment with conspicuous skill," and the next ranking officer, Maj. Archibald Bogle, was severely injured and left behind in the retreat. Adjutant W. C. Manning, who had been incapacitated by a wound, managed to escape death or capture only because a friend, Lt. Andrew Leonard of the 54th Massachusetts, found him on the battlefield and carried the adjutant on his back to safety. Casualty rates among the rank and file were high. In the center of the fighting, a color sergeant went down, severely wounded, only to have other men take his place. An army correspondent recalled "one simple instance of cool bravery, that came under my observation—Color Sergeant Johnson of Company H, 1st N.C. (Colored) troops, while nobly facing the foe, had his right arm badly shattered by a minnie ball, nothing daunted, he knelt and held high 'the dear old flag' until he was reluctantly compelled to give it up." After the engagement, "of the eighty-six men composing the color company only thirty-four were left." Casualties were almost as high in other companies.[64] A number of the severely wounded lost their arms, most frequently the left, to amputation. Some men, like Sgt. George Johnson of Company K, survived several operations and lived to collect a pension, whereas others lingered on for weeks after surgery only to die of "exhaustion" or "haemorrhage."[65] Pvt. Henry Gregory of Company B was unusually fortunate. He had received a serious gunshot wound to the left ankle, but unlike others with severe leg wounds, he was not left behind.[66]

Although the armies that fought at Olustee were relatively small, the proportion of Union casualties was very high. The 26.5 percent of Federal soldiers killed, wounded, or missing made Olustee, proportionally, the Union's third bloodiest battle of the entire war. Losses in the 35th USCT were especially steep: 2 officers killed and 8 wounded, with 230 soldiers killed, wounded, or missing in action—three times more casualties than those suffered by the 54th Massachusetts. On the night of the battle, Samuel Johnson, who was escaping slavery in Florida, came across wounded black soldiers stretched out in a horse stable at Wellborn. "The sight of these wounded men," he recalled, "and the feeble medical attention given them by the Federals was so repulsive to him, that he decided that he didn't want to join the Federal Army."[67] The plight of these and other black Union soldiers may have shocked Johnson, but they were better off than the men who had been left behind. In Augusta, the *Daily Chronicle and Sentinel* claimed that "from seventy-five to one hundred Negroes all wounded, were captured and sent to Tallahassee" and a "Yankee major, who commanded a Negro regiment, was wounded in the thigh" and was being held at Lake City. In a melancholy footnote to the casualties, an advertisement appeared a month later in Jacksonville's *Peninsula* offering for sale a sorrel mare, formerly the property of Lieutenant Colonel Reed, and two horses that had belonged to Major Bogle.[68]

The 35th USCT lost in other ways as well. Much of its equipment—shelter tents, knapsacks, cooking utensils, and more—was abandoned when the regiment prepared to go into action and then "lost in the retreat for want of transportation." The men faced considerable hardships until it could be replaced.

This was the second, but not the last time that the men lost much of their basic equipment because of a rapid move. After Seymour's battered forces straggled back to Jacksonville, they hurriedly constructed fortifications and set out pickets in preparation for a Confederate attack that never came. Men slept with their shoes on and their equipment beside them and mustered in the very early morning.[69] For another month most of the soldiers did not know that the Confederate command was pulling almost all of its troops out of Florida.

The Battle of Olustee had clearly demonstrated the capabilities of the 35th USCT, but it also had highlighted the inadequacy of its armaments. Defective weapons and poor equipment had endangered the men and made their companies less effective. A month after Olustee Colonel Beecher, who had been in the North trying to obtain better weapons, complained bitterly about the snarl of paperwork that prevented his regiment from getting long-overdue guns. "An experience of eight months has forced the conviction upon me," he wrote, "that nothing is to be obtained from the Chief of Ordnance." In March 1864 Beecher sent Lt. James Ladd to Hilton Head, South Carolina, to secure "serviceable arms for three companies" without delay. The results of his trip are unclear. Shortly afterward Beecher requested that the assistant adjutant general inspect the regiment's ammunition and equipment so the unserviceable parts could be replaced. At the same time, the brigade commander ordered that all regiments were to conduct frequent target practice with the weapons that they had. "Attention will be given," Col. Benjamin Chew Tilghman ordered, "as far as possible, to the individual instructions of the men, both in firing as Skirmishers from behind trees or kneeling and also in line of battle."[70] The regimental commanders were to make sure that there were always sixty rounds of ammunition per man on hand and twenty rounds in reserve. It was a belated recognition that earlier preparations, especially of other regiments, had been inadequate.

But real improvement was slow in coming. Months after Olustee, Beecher was still asking for new Springfield rifled muskets to replace the mixture of Enfields and "Imitation Springfield" muskets used by his soldiers. An inspection had already condemned most of the smoothbore muskets in three of his companies.[71] As late as July 1864, Brig. Gen. William Birney, commander of the district, indicated that the 35th USCT had not yet received the new arms. According to him, "Colonel Beecher's regiment, the Thirty-fifth U.S. Colored Troops, numbered only a little over 320 men for active duty; of these 90 are without arms, and the rest have four kinds of arms, none of them fit for duty." On 2 July, when Birney received word of a Confederate move against a Union post at Yellow Bluff, Florida, he promised that "I shall attack them just as soon as Colonel Beecher's regiment gets its arms, which I trust will be by the next boat." Fortunately, the Confederate threat was as ephemeral as the prediction of new arms in a week. Even when new weapons finally reached the 35th USCT, Beecher's problems continued. The regiment received 308 new rifles in 16 arms chests just before 13 July. But, the colonel complained, 21 arms chests had been sent for his regiment and 5 of the chests were still missing. Furthermore, the equipment to go with the weapons had not yet arrived.[72]

It was also in the aftermath of the defeat at Olustee that the army accused the regiment's black surgeon, John De Grasse, of dereliction of duty and addiction to alcohol. De Grasse had carried much of the responsibility for the unit's health ever since it was raised in North Carolina. When the 55th Massachusetts had arrived in New Bern, it was De Grasse who met the troops and took charge of their sick. After the unit moved to Folly Island, he was once again its only surgeon. By September 1863, General Wild was concerned that something be done to relieve some of the strain on De Grasse, who had become quite ill. Consequently, Dr. Babbitt, the junior surgeon of the 55th Massachusetts, was temporarily detached to assist De Grasse until Dr. Mann rejoined the regiment in October. Within a week of Mann's arrival, however, there was friction between the two doctors. When the regiment moved to Florida, once again it was Mann who remained behind and De Grasse who, along with Henry Marcy, had to carry a larger share of the regimental duties. Neither Mann nor Marcy were abolitionists, and both were hostile toward De Grasse. Mann had complained to Surg. Horace R. Wirtz that De Grasse had been disputing his seniority and implied that the black surgeon wanted to gain control of the medical liquor supplies.[73] For a time, Lieutenant Colonel Reed had protected De Grasse from the prejudice of the other two doctors. But with Reed's death, De Grasse became more vulnerable.

His actions following the Battle of Olustee exposed him to renewed criticism, and months later he was court-martialed. In the early hours of 21 February 1864, the wounded had begun to arrive at Barber Station, where, on Marcy's orders, the hospital steward of the 35th USCT, Delos Barber, and the regimental nurse had built a large fire and established a crude field station. About sixty or seventy injured soldiers had preceded De Grasse to Barber

Surg. Henry O. Marcy, 35th USCT (Courtesy of Massachusetts
Commandery Military Order of the Loyal Legion and U.S.
Army Military History Institute, Carlisle Barracks, Pa.)

Station. On reaching the camp, the surgeon immediately pleaded "excessive
fatigue" and went to bed. Marcy, Barber, and Beecher all claimed that he was
too drunk to be of help or to be awakened after he had retired. On the other
hand, De Grasse maintained that during the battle, "having sent my horse
off the field, I devoted my entire time with the stretcher corps in bringing the
wounded off the field. Later still in the afternoon till dark I was untiring in
my efforts in caring for the wounded." Then without a horse, he was forced
to walk about twenty miles to Barber Station. He arrived, he claimed, "weary,
footsore, and completely exhausted, it was the greatest effort of mind that I

continued walking until I reached the Camp." De Grasse argued, with some justification, that if his actions had been as unprofessional as later alleged, then his superiors were also negligent for not rebuking him until eight months had passed. Nevertheless, as a result of charges orchestrated by Dr. Marcy, De Grasse was cashiered in November 1864.[74]

De Grasse's departure left the 35th USCT without a single black commissioned officer. Rev. John Mars, the black chaplain commissioned by General Wild when the regiment was raised in North Carolina, had already resigned because of disability. By this time a sea change had occurred in the attitude of the regiment's officers. A white minister, Thomas A. Hall of Otis, Massachusetts, was selected to replace Mars. The shift from a black chaplain for the soldiers to a white minister for the officers had occurred at "the expressed desire of the officers of [Beecher's] command." Since the regulations adopted in May 1861 called for the appointment of chaplains "on the vote of the field officers and the company commanders on duty with the regiment at the time of the appointment," there was little that Beecher could have done even if he had opposed Otis's selection.[75] Religious leadership for enlisted men would now have to come from the numerous lay preachers in the ranks.

The regiment suffered a further blow in late May 1864, when two officers and three dozen men were killed or captured aboard the *Columbine* in St. John's River. Not only did the loss render one company largely ineffective, but it also raised the specter of Confederate vengeance directed at Beecher's soldiers. The event typified the nature of the summer campaign waged by the 35th USCT. Urgent orders that the men be ready for immediate action were followed by long waits: exhausting, fruitless raids were mixed with small, brief, and occasionally deadly encounters. What the regiment did had little impact on the outcome of the war, but it could alter the lives of men in the unit, as the *Columbine* incident illustrates.

On 20 May Brig. Gen. George H. Gordon responded to exaggerated reports that about four hundred Confederate troops were pushing northward on the east side of St. John's River near the Union post at Volusia, Florida. In response, Gordon led out a combined force of some seven hundred soldiers from the 35th USCT and the 144th and 157th New York Volunteers.[76] His goal was to prevent a Confederate retreat across the river by capturing the enemy soldiers on the east side. Two companies of Beecher's men were assigned to the *Columbine*, a small, armed tug, and the *Ottawa*, a gunboat that had been assigned to guard four transport vessels. After a brief delay to sandbag the

*Columbine*, the tug with two officers and a detachment of men from the 35th USCT headed upstream to Volusia to support Union troops that were believed to be threatened by the Confederate raiders. While the two small vessels steamed up the river, Gordon and most of his soldiers proceeded by land to Volusia, where he found the garrison safe and no Confederate forces on that side of the river. Not until the day after he withdrew, he claimed, did he learn that the *Columbine* had been attacked on the night of 23 May.[77]

Survivors from the *Columbine* described what had happened. The tug had escorted some of the transports upriver toward Lake George. Hidden Confederate raiders let the vessels proceed and then, after briefly shelling the *Ottawa*, prepared an ambush for the *Columbine* as it returned downriver to support its consort. When the tug reached Horse Landing on St. John's River, a spot where it had to pass within sixty yards of the western shore, a Confederate artillery battery of two guns and sharpshooters concealed in the woods raked the little tug with fire. The black soldiers could not depress the vessel's rifled guns enough to bear on the Confederate position, and almost immediately Rebel fire disabled its rudder. In rapid succession shells destroyed the wheel chains, the men on the bridge came under heavy fire, and the pilot abandoned the wheel and jumped overboard before the tug ran aground on a mud bank. Immobilized, the *Columbine* was an easy target for the Confederate soldiers hidden on shore and surrendered after a forty-five minute exchange. The Confederate commander, Capt. John J. Dickison of the Second Florida Cavalry, then ordered the vessel to be burned and sunk. Only a few men of the 35th USCT on board when the tug ran aground managed to escape and make their way to Haw Creek, where they reported the loss to Union officials.[78] The fight, while brief, was costly to the regiment.

Captain Dickison, who had led both the raid toward Volusia and the attack on the *Columbine*, claimed that the boat carried 148 men, of whom only 66—many of them badly wounded—were found alive when his men boarded the vessel.[79] He initially reported capturing two officers and "47 enlisted negroes," most of whom "have owners in North Carolina and Florida"; another twenty-five were either killed or drowned while trying to escape.[80] Several weeks later Colonel Beecher asserted that two officers, Capt. Edward Daniels and Lt. James O. Ladd, and "thirty-nine men of this command were killed, wounded or missing." Company E was "now reduced to 22 enlisted men present for duty."[81] The muster rolls for Company E indicate that at one point after the loss of the vessel only one officer and thirteen men were present for duty.[82]

---

The defeat at Olustee and the loss of the *Columbine* left many officers and men of the 35th USCT in Confederate hands and once more raised concerns about the treatment of black prisoners. The men captured by the Confederates left ambiguous records that do not permit a clear assessment of their fate. There is no doubt that individual Southern soldiers committed acts of cruelty and savagery, but these were never officially authorized although they may have been condoned by officers. After Olustee, a member of the 54th Massachusetts informed a Northern paper that he could "learn nothing of the colored prisoners. It is reported that they were killed on the field." He also claimed that a party sent out under a flag of truce to inquire about the fate of the officers and men was told that the Confederates "will hang every d——d Negro officer we catch." The men of the 8th USCT feared that their captured comrades had been killed, although weeks after the battle they received "a list of our wounded in the enemy's hands and find quite a number supposed and reported to be dead are alive." Yet there was reason for concern. Numerous reports indicated that vindictive Confederate troops shot unarmed black prisoners as a personal vendetta if not as military policy.[83]

A New York sergeant who lay wounded on the battlefield said that he had heard the cursing of "some marauding soldiers who were ill-treating wounded Negroes."[84] Confederate Henry Shackelford, whose 19th Georgia Infantry faced the 54th Massachusetts, boasted: "How our boys did walk into the niggers, they would beg and pray but it did no good." A private in the 27th Georgia, which engaged the 35th USCT, wrote that the "Negroes were badly cut up and killed. Our men killed some of them after they fell in our hands wounded." According to one Virginian, "If it had not been for the officers their would not one of them been spaired." Certainly some Confederates expected to show the black soldiers no quarter. A trooper testified that before the 2nd Florida Cavalry went into combat, the commander told his men: "General Seamore's [*sic*] army is made up largely of Negroes from Georgia and South Carolina, who come here to steal, pillage, run over the state and murder, kill and rape our wives, daughters, and sweethearts. Let's teach them a lesson. I shall not take any Negro prisoners in this fight."[85]

After the fight at Olustee, seventy-seven soldiers of the 35th USCT were reported missing in action. No doubt some of them died during the fight or shortly afterward, but many more were taken prisoner. Confederates captured Maj. Archibald Bogle after a serious leg wound left him crippled and unable to retreat. He and about two hundred black enlisted men from the 54th Massachusetts, 8th USCT, and 35th USCT were initially sent to Tallahassee for several weeks. Then, as the seriously wounded recovered some mobility, the soldiers who were taken at Olustee traveled in small groups to the new Confederate POW camp at Andersonville. Residents of that small Georgia town saw the first black prisoners unloaded from boxcars during the second week of March 1864. After some initial uncertainty, the commander of the post, Gen. John Winder, ordered them to be held like other POWs pending further instructions from Richmond. They were marched into the prison, where they formed a small settlement near the south gate that grew as more black soldiers trickled in. Despite Winder's orders, other white prisoners indicated that the black soldiers were dealt with more harshly and given even less medical attention than other inmates. By midsummer there were still fewer than seventy black prisoners at Andersonville; the maximum number of African Americans held there was only about one hundred.[86]

Postwar testimony from other white Union prisoners indicate that many black POWs were badly treated. "Scarcely any of them," wrote Warren Lee Goss, "but were victims of atrocious amputations performed by rebel surgeons." They were, John McElroy concurred, "treated as badly as possible. The wounded were turned into the Stockade without having their hurts attended to."[87] The descriptive books for the various companies of the 35th USCT yield information on only about one-third of the soldiers missing or captured at Olustee. Of these, only six—Jacob Newberry in Company D, Starking Northcott in Company F, James Perkins in Company K, and Frank Mattox, Aaron Oberman, and Frank Williams in Company E—left any records that they were released or returned after the war.[88] Obviously, some of their comrades died at Andersonville. Ironically, the treatment of black POWs may have saved some of their lives. Assuming that the African Americans were the logical inmates to work on labor details outside the stockade, prison authorities organized a "Negro Squad" to unload lumber delivered to the camp. (Guards whipped those who refused to work.) The forced exercise and additional rations that the black POWs received partly explain their lower mortality rate: 12 percent for blacks as opposed to 30 percent for white POWs.[89]

The lower mortality for blacks only adds to the confusion about the fate of captured black soldiers. Several hundred black POWs may have been taken at Olustee, but only half of them are recorded as having reached Andersonville. Although the reported mortality rate for these men was, by the prison's standards, extremely low, few of the captured men of the 35th USCT ever reappear in the regiment's records. Some of the missing soldiers may have simply been lost to sloppy record keeping. Others were likely casualties of vindictive Southern troops immediately after the battle, although the official, if grudging, Confederate position was to treat them all as POWs. And some may have escaped as control of the camp deteriorated at the end of 1864. Henry Wirz, Andersonville's commandant, had kept the black prisoners as long as possible to serve on fatigue and burial details. By mid-November there were only several hundred prisoners left, and the few remaining guards were demoralized. Some POWs simply walked away. Another fate is also suggested, however. After the Battle of Olustee, some of the captured enlisted men were recognized, General W. M. Gordon reported, "by intelligent and reliable gentlemen [as] negroes known to have been the property of friends in North Carolina, and who are reported to belong to a North Carolina regiment now on this coast." Confederate officials may have surreptitiously shipped these men back to North Carolina. In October 1864 Secretary of War James A. Seddon ordered at least two black prisoners to be turned over to a man claiming to be their former owner, although there is no record that the exchange took place.[90]

Pension and military service records of the few returned prisoners from the 35th USCT give insight into the experience of black POWs. One such man was Frank Mattox, a private in Company E and a friend of POW Gaston Davis. "He and I and a number of others," wrote Mattox, "were captured and carried from there to Tallahassee as prisoners of war." He remembered little of this time, as he had received a severe injury in the hip "and was too bad off to remember anything." Several weeks later they were transported to Andersonville, where "we had no treatment . . . and we suffered the tortures of death, we were half naked and half starved."[91] Although Aaron Oberman had been seriously wounded in the left side and ankle, there was "no record of treatment at Confed Hospl." Confederate officials, however, left the men at the Tallahassee hospital for several weeks. Oberman's company commander, Edward S. Daniels, explained that "such of our wounded who could be taken no further, on account of their wounds, were left in a Confederate hospital

Maj. Archibald Bogle, 35th USCT (Courtesy of Massachusetts
Commandery Military Order of the Loyal Legion and U.S.
Army Military History Institute, Carlisle Barracks, Pa.)

where Oberman remained several weeks until he was able to be conveyed to
Andersonville." Starking Northcott of Company F, also wounded at Olustee,
received medical treatment at Tallahassee before continuing on to Andersonville, where he and his comrades entered the stockade, "suffering all kinds of
Brutal Treatment."[92] Company E's Frank Williams, who suffered four gunshot wounds at Olustee, also recorded harsh treatment at Andersonville.

The limited records of the surviving black soldiers taken prisoner in Florida suggest several things. All of these men had been so seriously wounded,
or suffered such debilitating leg wounds, that retreat with the regiment was
impossible.[93] Black soldiers avoided capture at all cost. Despite the claims
of Warren Lee Goss, no amputations were recorded, although a number of
soldiers had serious leg injuries that could have provided an excuse for any

malicious Confederate surgeon.[94] Instead, the common attitude of both the guards and the prison's surgical staff, and perhaps even white POWs, seemed to be one of callous indifference to the suffering of black prisoners.

Major Bogle fared no better than the black soldiers in his command. His captors sent him to Andersonville despite his wounds and despite the fact that that prison was intended only for enlisted men. He was the only commissioned officer deliberately placed in Andersonville to underline Southern refusal to acknowledge him as an officer.[95] After his capture and during his confinement at Andersonville, Confederate officers denied Bogle medical treatment. Union POWs working as hospital stewards provided the only medical aid that he received at the prison. Even before reaching Andersonville, the major suffered sadistic treatment. By one account, while he lay wounded in a boxcar long after his capture, a Confederate soldier repeatedly shot at Bogle, missing every time. The incident may have been simply a demonstration of one soldier's grisly sense of humor, but it reflected the bitter feelings toward white officers who commanded black soldiers. Once at Andersonville, Bogle faced insults and gestures of contempt from both Confederates and hostile Union soldiers. Nevertheless, prison officials did not deliberately mistreat the major, except in denying him early medical treatment. Conditions at Andersonville were so bad that by the summer Bogle's weight had dropped from 170 to less than 80 pounds. Although Wirz attempted to get Bogle exchanged or transferred to another prison, the major was one of the last Union prisoners to leave the camp. In November 1864 he was removed from Andersonville and sent to another military prison at Millen, where once again Confederate authorities refused to recognize him as an officer. Despite his ordeal, Bogle survived. In May 1865 he finally returned to his regiment and was breveted lieutenant colonel.[96]

The officers and men captured on the *Columbine* a few months after Olustee received similar treatment. Southern officials were uncertain how to handle the two Union officers taken when the tug was captured. The Confederate captain in charge of the officers' prison at Macon, George C. Gibbs, was aware that Major Bogle had been, "and I think very properly, confined with the negro prisoners at Andersonville." He wanted "to obtain permission to send to the same place, Lieut. J. O. Ladd, of Company E, Thirty-fifth U.S. Negro Regiment, who is now a prisoner here, and who also was captured in Florida on board steamer *Columbine*." Gibbs made no mention of the other officer from the tug, although that man, Capt. Edward Daniels, had survived the ordeal. The assistant secretary of the Confederate War Department authorized Gibbs to send Lieutenant Ladd to Andersonville to join the major, but there is no record that he was actually transferred there. Ladd was eventually exchanged at Annapolis, Maryland, on 17 December 1864, after being "confined in several Confederate prisons." He rejoined the 35th USCT shortly after Major Bogle.[97]

The record suggests that the black soldiers from the *Columbine* were only slightly more fortunate than their comrades taken at Olustee. Thirty-nine men from Company E, including two sergeants and two corporals, were listed as missing in action following the tug's seizure. Union authorities did not believe that all the men had been captured, and they assumed that a number had died: "Many of the men were wounded badly. Some are supposed to have drowned in trying to swim to shore."[98] Although it is not known exactly how many men were taken prisoner and held by the Confederates, one corporal and six privates withstood the privations of black POWs and rejoined their regiment in June 1865.

In addition to the loss of men killed and captured, as well as inadequate and missing equipment, other factors diminished the efficiency of the 35th USCT in the summer of 1864. The problem of detached service, which reduced Beecher's command to six companies by May, had long impaired the unit's ability to train and function as an effective line regiment. On Folly Island, the regiment frequently was called upon to provide large detachments of soldiers, most often as laborers, for extended service away from the regiment. This practice continued in Florida—indeed, it was common within many regiments in that theater. Near the end of April, however, the district command detailed three companies of the 35th USCT for special service as mounted infantry. The posting reflected General Seymour's belief that he suffered a critical shortage of cavalry. Having tried to turn the 40th Massachusetts Mounted Infantry into cavalry, he now ordered Companies F, G, and K of the 35th USCT to provide "66 officers and serviceable men" apiece. Because, in the aftermath of Olustee and the smallpox outbreak, the average number of men present for duty in each of those companies had fallen below forty, vacancies were filled by details from the remaining companies, further disrupting Beecher's command. The colonel placed Capt. William Emerson, who had briefly commanded the regiment following the battle, in charge of the three detached companies to be stationed in Jacksonville. There they remained for the entire summer, although they were always handicapped by a shortage of serviceable mounts. In June their commander reported that the three companies "had less than 100 horses fit for service and this number will be greatly reduced unless there is a supply of hay and small forage within a week."[99]

Throughout the summer, members of the regiment took part in a number of raids into the interior of the state. The raids involved much marching but little fighting. Some of the officers and men doubted the usefulness of such ventures. In April the disgruntled regimental surgeon, Dr. Marcy, told Dr. Ester Hawks that the regiment, minus the three mounted companies, was to undertake a ten-day march across country "merely *to take observations*, and anything else to be taken!" The next day Hawks recorded a conversation she had with Colonel Beecher: "He is not very sanguine of the success of this expedition and feels a little depressed." In fact, the trek was a response to reports of a Confederate cavalry raid, although contact was never made and the march was uneventful. A month later it was the turn of the three mounted companies to participate in an expedition that was more successful in finding the enemy, although equally frustrating to the black soldiers involved. Colonel Shaw of the 7th USCT had led a combined force toward Camp Finegan, about fourteen miles west of Jacksonville. Finding more Confederate soldiers than he had anticipated, he hesitated to attack and ordered his men into bivouac. When his pickets were fired on early in the evening, Shaw ordered the troops to withdraw. He and his men were back in Jacksonville about twelve hours after they had marched out of the town.[100]

The value of these raids was open to the interpretation of both sides. In June, 504 officers and men of the 35th USCT took part in an attempt to capture Camp Milton, a Confederate entrenchment on the Jacksonville and Tallahassee Railroad about twelve miles from Jacksonville. The North Carolinians were part of one column of 1,400 men led by Col. William H. Noble that planned to flank the Confederate position. At the same time, a second column of 1,000 soldiers threatened the Rebels from the front. Confederate cavalrymen evacuated the log and earth fortifications as the Union soldiers approached their position. Gen. George Gordon emphasized the strength and size of the works and how "solidly constructed and beautifully finished" they were. He then had them 'fired and completely demolished." The next day he received reports of approaching enemy soldiers. "Although I believed the force and the intentions of the enemy had been exaggerated and misunderstood, I did not feel that it would have been prudent to totally disbelieve it." Gordon quickly declared that he had "accomplished my purpose" and ordered his men back to Jacksonville. The report of Confederate general Patton Anderson was very different. He wrote that his cavalry had met the enemy's advance guard and "drove him back to Jacksonville. Our lines are the same as they were before the movements. It was probably a reconnaissance by the enemy. Our loss trifling." The black soldiers who landed at Cedar Creek at 3:00 A.M. and marched ten miles in the dark to capture Camp Milton may have been more inclined to accept Anderson's assessment. Dr. Marcy was convinced that Gordon had simply become frightened; he estimated that "about a hundred mounted men drove back our brave *3,000*."[101] Everyone was exhausted by the hard march and excessive heat, and many soldiers fell out along the way. The ambulances were full by the time the troops returned to Jacksonville.

In July, two other raids underscored the frustrations of black soldiers during their campaign in the South. On 2 July, Gen. William Birney led the 7th USCT and the 34th USCT, strengthened by four companies from the 35th USCT, on a raid into South Carolina. The morning after they landed at White Point, the 1,200 Union soldiers moved out and began skirmishing with a small number of Confederate soldiers. The Rebels drove the Yankees back until the advancing Union troops reached a bridge over a small creek. Because an enemy battery guarded the bridge and the creek was wide and marshy, Birney decided not to press the attack. Birney had a few rounds fired from his howitzers and then ordered a retreat. All of the Union forces, including 241 men of the 35th USCT, withdrew from South Carolina. Although the action may have served as "an excellent drill for them preparatory to real fighting," as Birney argued, Colonel Beecher lost almost half of his regiment for over two weeks. Just after the four companies returned to Jacksonville, the regiment received new orders to be prepared, within twenty-four hours, to move out with minimum equipment and rations for six days. Extra arms were assembled and stored with the regimental quartermaster. Despite an initial flurry of activity, the 35th USCT was still in camp a week later, still being held in readiness to march on twenty-four hours' notice with a minimum of gear. When the soldiers finally left camp, it was as part of a largely unopposed march on Baldwin and the railroad junction there. Only at the crossing of the South Fork of Black Creek did they encounter Confederate troops. The regiment quickly drove off the dismounted Rebel skirmishers with only one serious casualty.

Some enlisted men were frustrated at not encountering a major Confederate force because, as General Birney testified, "these colored troops were burning with a desire to avenge Olustee."[102] If Birney was correct, then the last thing they wanted was timid leadership.

In late August, Beecher detached an additional two companies for an extended period, ordering Company A "detailed as an additional guard to Fort Foster" and sending Company I to Fort Hatch. He instructed the men to take all of their camp and "Garrison Equipage" and informed the company commanders that they would be under the authority of the officers in charge of the two forts. Companies A and I would not rejoin the regiment until it prepared to leave Florida in November. It was a discouraging period for the soldiers. A majority of the army, including the white regiments with whom they had served, had been moved north. Birney's raids, or "cow-hunting expeditions," as some men described them, only confirmed the belief of many troops that their commander suffered from "the St. Vitas' dance, in a military point of view."[103]

Colonel Beecher was concerned about the scattered deployment of his companies. For many months, he had attempted to reunite them so he would have a fully functioning unit. He wanted the 4 officers and 175 enlisted men still posted at Jacksonville returned to his regiment. "The excessive drafts from the command by reasons of details and other causes," he wrote in March 1865, "have reduced the Command from thirty-three officers and seven hundred eighty-seven enlisted men down [to] twenty officers and four hundred & sixty enlisted men."[104]

—— ❧ ——

The 35th USCT's experience in Florida was similar to that of many Civil War regiments. It fought in only one major battle but was seldom inactive. The companies still under Beecher's control were constantly involved in large and small raids, forced marches, and false alarms. Officers and men were convinced that the generals who led them did not know what they were doing. For four months, Beecher claimed, his troops were never in camp for more than five days. They were worn down and casualties rose. The constant activity and the oppressive climate swelled the numbers on the sick list. During a month-long posting at the railroad junction at Baldwin, for example, the soldiers began "sickening at the rate of twenty a day from exposure day and night on swampy ground." Worst of all, the colonel wrote, while his command was "pretty well ragged and worn down," they "have accomplished nothing."[105] The enlisted men shared Beecher's frustrations by the army's seemingly ineffective leadership, but additional factors added to their stress.

The number of permanently disabled enlisted men being carried by the 35th USCT was a reflection of the strain placed on the military effectiveness of the regiment and the health of the troops. During the summer of 1864, the regiment carried from thirty to forty physically incapacitated soldiers, most of whom suffered from chronic rheumatism or "ruptures." These men had been unable to undertake any duty for six months, the surgeon had pronounced them incapable of marching, and yet Beecher was unable to obtain their discharge. Ultimately, his efforts were, at best, partially successful. None of his disabled soldiers was released in August, and only twenty-one were discharged for various disabilities in the two months following 10 September. Many enlisted men grew bitter over what they saw as the callousness or indifference of their officers and the willingness of Surgeon Marcy to rule sick troops fit for duty. Necessity forced some officers to assign them work. Men who were "nor Abel to march three mild [sic]" were called out for normal duty, a black soldier fumed.[106] The removal of Asst. Surg. John De Grasse, the last black officer, compounded their sense of grievance.

Many enlisted men in the 35th USCT had difficulty sending money safely to relatives back home. The army had promised to provide for the families of black recruits, but stories coming out of North Carolina suggested that many family members were enduring severe hardships. After the regiment had moved to Folly Island and had been paid back wages, some troops sent funds to their wives in New Bern and Washington, North Carolina. They had entrusted their money to Edward Kinsley, of Boston, who then gave it to William Doolittle for distribution. The money never arrived, and Beecher could not find out what had happened to it. Meanwhile, other soldiers saw large deductions from their wages for clothing allowances that had been overdrawn. Many were being charged between ten and forty dollars for extra clothes. These charges seemed unfair, as some of the clothing they had been ordered to leave behind when the regiment was transferred to South Carolina had been lost or stolen. Moreover, the men had been assigned heavy fatigue duties at Charleston, were constantly on the march in Florida, and in at least three engagements were forced, through no fault of their own, to abandon much of their personal baggage. Eventually a board of survey, composed of three officers of the 35th USCT, established the amount of clothing that had been lost due to marching and other orders.[107] Both enlisted men and officers in the unit believed that it was unfair to penalize black soldiers, who were receiving lower wages than white enlisted men, for actions over which they had no control.

⁂

The combination of all of these factors produced demoralization and unrest in the 35th USCT by the late summer of 1864. During the Fourth of July celebrations in Jacksonville, men from the regiment clashed with soldiers of the 3rd USCT, a black Pennsylvania regiment. Although General Birney appeared to blame the Pennsylvanians, the North Carolina soldiers did not escape criticism. Beecher was disturbed by the "invidious and possibly malicious reports" that were circulating about the military condition of the 35th USCT, and he wanted a general's inspection of "a Battalion Drill of the portion of the command left in my charge." Beecher was particularly upset because he took great pride in his regiment's deportment and appearance. The camp of the 35th USCT presented a sharp contrast to some of the other regiments. Ester Hawks wrote in her diary that the 34th USCT's camp "more resembled an irregular grouping together of *pig and chicken pens* than anything to which I could liken it." Another regiment, "the 2nd S.C. was close by and no better in appearance." On the other hand, Beecher's camp "was laid out regularly, with Co. streets regularly laid cleared out and graded—and the unsightly huts which serve instead of tents entirely hidden from view. . . . The men exhibit great skill in making their cook house and dining-rooms attractive."[108]

More serious than rumors of the regiment's military inefficiency or the condition of its camp was the apparent increase in conflicts among the officers and between the officers and the enlisted men. Before the summer of 1864, incompetence, neglect of duty, or incapacity of some kind were the most frequent reasons for a noncommissioned officer being reduced to the ranks.[109] After that time, demotions were increasingly linked to insubordination. In August 1864 Beecher downgraded Sgt. George Duffee to corporal "for disorderly conduct and using insulting language to his superior officer"; Cpl. David Bowen lost his stripes "for disobedience of orders." When Capt. Henry McIntire took it upon himself to demote Sgt. Jack Brinckly in Company F, Brinckly complained that he had been unfairly treated. Since only the sentence of a court-martial or the order of the regimental commander on recommendation of a company officer could reduce a noncommissioned officer, Brinckly remained a sergeant. His case was helped by the fact that Captain McIntire had already displayed incompetence and contempt for his enlisted men.[110] Perhaps more troubling was the regimental surgeon's suggestion that Colonel Beecher's "influence on his officers was really *pernicious*, and that they did not respect him as they otherwise would but for certain habits."[111] The fact that Marcy was apparently referring to card playing may reveal more about the character of the doctor than of the commander.

In a case with complex interracial overtones, a white officer accused Sgt. Lewis Bryant of Company D and five privates, while in St. Augustine, of making "insulting proposals to a certain unmarried white woman, name unknown." When ordered to leave by the guard, they refused and were charged with being "guilty of insubordination." The white officer subsequently withdrew the charges against the privates but not against Bryant. On the sergeant's behalf, Colonel Beecher wrote that this was the only negative mark in the sergeant's entire military career.[112] Bryant was able to keep his stripes and the privates were not punished. These men were fortunate, indeed. Earlier in the summer, three men in the 55th Massachusetts had been charged with "committing an outrage on a white woman." Arrested shortly after midnight, the black soldiers were taken directly before Col. M. S. Littlefield, the acting commander, and tried, convicted, and ordered hanged at 3:00 P.M. the same day. After the execution, General Seymour told the officers and men: "Served them right, now let any other man try it if he dares." Ester Hawks confided in her diary that had the same punishment been meted out to white soldiers who treated black women in a similar way, then Seymour "might have grown hoarse in repeating his remarks."[113]

In September 1864 a court-martial tried and convicted Pvt. Albert Hassel of the 35th USCT's Company I for a serious breakdown in discipline. While on guard duty at Orange Mills on 23 May of that year, Hassel had quit his station in the early evening without permission and was absent without leave until 31 May. He had been ordered by Capt. Benjamin F. Pierce, the commandant of the post, to help "in quelling a mutiny, at said Post . . . and did fail to obey said orders." When challenged by Pierce, Hassel had not only given his name as Jack Jones, but also had conducted himself "with contempt and disrespect towards said Captain Pierce" before he went absent. Hassel was found guilty of all charges and sentenced to hard labor at Fort Clinch, Florida. He would not be released until late October 1865. Shortly after his conviction, another private in the 35th, Maby Todd, received a similar sentence. His case stood in contrast to that involving the three soldiers of the 55th Massachusetts who were executed. While on guard, eighteen-year-old Todd had left his post, broken into a house, and entered the room of two black women with "malicious intent."[114] Perhaps because of the race of his victims, his sentence was not as severe as it might have been. During the same month a number of other soldiers were also convicted of being absent without leave. Most were absent for a period of hours, rather than days, and the violations seem to have been related to the proximity of the camp to Jacksonville and the soldiers' growing friendships there. Most privates were fined ten dollars and denied leave for one month, while noncommissioned officers were reduced one rank. Orderly Sgt. Jesse Lynch, accused of "Disobedience of orders," was only downgraded to second sergeant.[115] The disposition of Lynch's case might have been the bellwether of attitudes in the regiment, because earlier that year he had been so well regarded that he had been appointed acting sergeant major of the 35th USCT.

Colonel Beecher was obviously concerned about what was happening within his command. During the summer he issued orders to prevent men leaving camp or lounging around the mess houses. He was also disturbed by irregularities in roll calls, where certain men who failed to appear were not being reported absent. By September, he admitted that earlier efforts "to prevent indiscriminate straggling from camp" had been ineffective and announced tougher measures. In addition, Beecher felt the need to curb the growing practice of enlisted men carrying pistols and revolvers on their persons.[116] An anonymous letter sent by a black noncommissioned officer in mid-October summed up many of the problems engulfing the regiment. A large number of enlisted men, the writer declared, endured ailments ranging from lameness to broken bones and blindness. "It is a pitty to see," the letter continued, "how the offices are treeting those men as are Sick." Dr. Marcy, in particular, was indifferent to their pain and judged fit for service men who were seriously incapacitated. The officers generally were unsympathetic to the sufferings of the rank and file. "It seem like the officers want to kill those men," the anonymous soldier argued. The handicapped troops included those who had been wounded at Olustee and were not yet fully recovered. On the other hand, the letter had been dictated to at least one sympathetic white officer, and the anonymous writer still considered the 35th USCT to be "the Best regiment that we have in our army."[117] If some of the original optimism of both officers and recruits had eroded, men of the regiment were still proud of what they had created.

There may have been a sense of relief for some of the officers when the army ordered the 35th USCT back to South Carolina on 25 November 1864 and Beecher directed the various detached companies to rejoin the regiment. The whole operation was to be kept as quiet as possible. The move came about as a result of a telegraph message from Gen. William T. Sherman in Atlanta to Gen. Henry W. Halleck, chief of staff of the U.S. Army. Sherman had informed Halleck that his army was starting for the coast and asked that Gen. John G. Foster be ordered to "break the Savannah and Charleston [rail]road about Pocotaligo about December 1." The proposed raid was intended to reduce Confederate resistance to Sherman's army as well as to create a supply base for its operation. The transfer of the 35th USCT from Florida to South Carolina was part of the troop buildup for the expedition.[118]

Once at Hilton Head, the regiment joined Brig. Gen. Edward E. Potter's First Brigade, which was part of the Coast Division commanded by Brig. Gen. John P. Hatch. The theater commander, General Foster, planned to use the Coast Division as the expeditionary force that would cut the Charleston and Savannah Railroad in the vicinity of Grahamville, about fifteen miles from Pocotaligo, and stop Confederate reinforcements from being sent by rail to oppose Sherman.[119] On 28 November 1864 five thousand soldiers and five hundred sailors embarked on Federal gunboats at Hilton Head Island. The expedition was delayed first by heavy fog and poor seamanship, then by faulty maps and incompetent guides, and finally by poorer leadership. Some of the transport vessels lost their way in the fog and had to be rerouted, while other boats ran aground. Once the Union troops had landed at Boyd's Neck on the morning of 29 November, Grahamville and the railroad lay just seven miles to the west. Confused directions led to further delays. Troops took the wrong roads, no effective overall control was provided by senior officers, and the expedition had to camp for the night at Bolan Church. A vital day was lost while Grahamville remained undefended. These mistakes allowed the Confederates to concentrate troops just outside of Grahamville on a fifteen- to twenty-foot rise of land called "Honey Hill." Here recently fortified positions looked down on a swampy creek bordered by dense undergrowth that could only be approached on a single road running through thick woods.

As the Union units arrived on the field on the morning of 30 November, they were thrown forward in a series of unconnected and unsuccessful attacks. The delays of the previous day proved critical, for the bulk of the Confederate defenders were just reaching Honey Hill as the Federal soldiers began to advance. A majority of the Confederate reinforcements, led by Maj. Gen. Gustavus W. Smith and transported by train from Georgia, did not reach Grahamville until 9:00 A.M. Although at the critical point of the Federal attack, Confederate officers feared that their positions would be overrun, all of the Union assaults were thrown back. Foster and Hatch were quick to blame the failure not on any lack of gallantry or courage of their own troops, but rather on the strong defensive position occupied by the Confederates. The 35th USCT arrived after the initial Union attacks had been repulsed and formed on the right center of the Union line. Although the soldiers quickly attacked the fortifications, the "heavy fire of the enemy and the difficulty of the ground compelled them to withdraw." Colonel Beecher was wounded twice, once severely, but resisted being carried from the field despite "acting in a dazed sort of way." Capt. Luis F. Emilio of the 54th Massachusetts, who later described the terrible gunfire confronting the 35th USCT, witnessed the heavy losses that the North Carolinians suffered before they withdrew and supported the artillery.[120] At dusk the Federal troops broke off the action and retreated without opposition to Boyd's Neck.

General Potter, who praised almost all of his men, wrote that the 35th USCT was "also deserving of great credit." Lt. Col. Amiel J. Willard, who assumed command of the regiment after Beecher was wounded, was singled out for particular mention. A measure of the strength of the Southern defensive position and the ineffectiveness of the Federal leadership can be seen in the disproportionate casualties suffered by the two sides. Foster's command had 88 killed, 623 wounded, and 44 missing, whereas the Confederate forces under Gen. G. W. Smith lost only 8 dead and 42 wounded. Early casualty reports indicated that although the 35th USCT had suffered only 6 men killed during the engagement, 4 officers and 73 men had been wounded. Significantly, the casualties among the noncommissioned officers of the regiment, men who led the attack, were particularly high during this engagement: 12 sergeants and 15 corporals were among the wounded.[121]

For a week after the action at Honey Hill, General Hatch's Coast Division sporadically skirmished with Confederate troops, threatened the Charleston and Savannah Railroad, and dug fortifications. On 6 December, Potter's brigade, still trying to cut the railroad line, landed in force at Devaux's Neck and threw out skirmishers. The following day, after both sides had received reinforcements, the Confederates attacked. For the next three hours, the Rebels launched a series of unsuccessful assaults before the engagement finally petered out. Despite throwing back the Rebel attacks, the Yankees were unable to reach and cut the railroad line. During the fighting, the 35th USCT had participated in an attempt to open a gap in the woods so Union artillery could shell the rail line. This unsuccessful maneuver, which cost Company D two men killed, marked the end of the regiment's serious fighting.[122] From then until the end of the year, the 35th USCT spent its time "doing Picket Duty in front of the enemy." The danger that this could entail was demonstrated on 18 December, when Lt. Marshall N. Rice was "captured by Guerrillas." Maj. Thomas Ward Osborn, a Union artilleryman serving with Sherman, added a fitting, if inadvertent, postscript to this phase of the 35th USCT's service. Men from Sherman's Seventeenth Corps had seized the railroad in January 1865 with the loss of only a dozen men. Osborn wrote: "I am told here that at one time and another 6,000 men have been lost in attempts to occupy the railroad from this point. Of course, we have more men than has at any other time been employed and the enemy are in less confident spirit than at any time before. Yet I am disposed to think that the success with so slight a loss is more owing to good military judgement than any other cause."[123]

The year 1864 had been a hard one for the 35th USCT. The regiment had done more than its share of hard marching and heavy fighting without any of the exhilaration of victory to sustain it. Over the previous twelve months, it had lost 153 enlisted men. At least 44 soldiers had broken down under the physical stress of military service and had been discharged for various disabilities. Another 10 had deserted. The majority of the losses, however, were men who had died. Over 50 had been killed in action, died of wounds, or were missing in action; 43 more succumbed to "ordinary" causes such as smallpox and fever. Dozens of other men still in the ranks had broken down physically. That other Civil War regiments may have suffered more should not mask the sacrifices endured by the 35th USCT. Over the entire year, the regiment obtained only eight new soldiers to fill its depleted ranks. Six were new recruits, and two transferred into the unit from other regiments. Three soldiers who had been reported as missing in action were able to rejoin their companies. By contrast, four officers had been killed or were missing in action, and another eight had been dropped, transferred, dismissed, or had resigned.[124] Their loss had been only partly compensated by the addition of five new officers to the regiment. Several of the new officers were, in fact, the result of internal promotions. Two white noncommissioned officers received commissions for their service in the ranks. In October 1864 Beecher had recommended both George H. Green, the quartermaster sergeant, and Harlan P. Loomis, the commissary sergeant, to be commissioned as second lieutenants.

—⚬—

When January 1865 began, the 35th USCT continued to perform picket duty at Devaux's Neck, South Carolina, under General Hatch. From mid-January through February, the regiment participated in the advance on Charleston and the destruction of "all property that could prolong the War." In early March it took part in a raid from Charleston to the Santee River. The division drove scattered Confederate forces before it, while destroying or capturing Rebel property. The 35th USCT played only a minor role in this raid, perhaps because the Union commander accepted as real the white Southern hysteria concerning black vengeance.[125] The end of the war found the regiment posted at Mt. Pleasant, outside of Charleston.

# CHAPTER THREE

# Issues of "Civilized" Warfare

The second regiment formed as part of the African Brigade, the 2nd North Carolina Colored Volunteers (NCCV), encountered many of the same problems experienced by Col. James Beecher's regiment as well as some unique to the second regiment. The transfer to South Carolina of Gen. Edward Wild's command, including the first men recruited for the 2nd NCCV, effectively split the regiment in two for several months. The subsequent relocation of the 2nd NCCV to Virginia in late August effectively ended any hope of organizing a black North Carolina brigade and removed the men from proximity to their friends and families. The move also made it harder to tap the pool of recruits in North Carolina and greatly impaired General Wild's ability to help mobilize and safeguard the regiment. The 2nd NCCV now had to rely almost solely on its new commander, Col. Alonzo G. Draper, who was also committed to the task of raising and leading black troops. In Wild's absence, Draper quickly became a protégé of Gen. Benjamin Butler. Although the colonel had few of the debilitating personal problems plaguing Beecher and would rise to the rank of brigadier general, he had flaws of his own. On his appointment as commander of the 2nd NCCV, fellow officers raised questions about his standards of discipline, and his leadership style precipitated at least one crisis among the commissioned officers in his regiment. Moreover, by the summer of 1864 Draper was increasingly willing to tolerate the use of harsh discipline for his enlisted men.

Like Beecher's regiment, Draper's command would face hard fighting in the months ahead. Nevertheless, in a number of important ways its experiences differed from those of the unit sent to South Carolina and Florida. Early in their service and in a reversal of traditional Southern authority, Draper's troops—most of them former slaves—would find themselves at Point Lookout Prison Camp, in Maryland, guarding Confederate POWs, many of whom were or had been slaveholders. Later these soldiers would participate in raids intended to stamp out guerrilla activity in northeastern North Carolina. Since many of the men had families and friends in the area who were especially vulnerable to attack by the guerrillas, they responded eagerly to the chance to liberate loved ones. Finally, in the last months of the war, the 2nd NCCV would experience trench warfare around Petersburg and Richmond, Virginia, as the nature of combat in the East altered dramatically. Before that, however, like many other black units, the 2nd NCCV encountered the repeated reluctance of regional commanders to use black troops for much more than garrison and fatigue duties or to believe that a black regiment was as militarily capable as a white unit. Once placed under a senior commander who was a strong advocate of African American soldiers, the enlisted men of the 2nd NCCV showed their abilities, winning Congressional Medals of Honor as they fought in the Army of the James. At the end of the war, when the senior command in Virginia accepted the argument of Southern civilians that black troops were not sufficiently disciplined for peacetime service in the East, the regiment, as part of the Twenty-fifth Army Corps, was transferred from Virginia to the Texas-Mexico border. After seventeen difficult months performing garrison duty along the Rio Grande River, the regiment was mustered out in October 1866.

---

Following the transfer of Draper's partially raised regiment to Virginia at the end of August 1863, the unit's officers spent the first months filling the ranks and trying to find enough time to adequately drill all of the men. Draper set up his headquarters outside the town of Portsmouth, across the Elizabeth River from Norfolk and just above the northern entrance to the Dismal Swamp Canal. Because Gen. John Foster believed in using black soldiers for fatigue and garrison duties and because he distrusted their behavior if they were turned loose in the countryside, he refused to let Draper lead any expeditions outside the Union enclave. Instead, the men built fortifications and worked on general fatigue details. Despite these problems, by the end of December the colonel could report a troop strength of eight hundred men.[1] Not until General Wild arrived in Norfolk in October to assume command of all of the black troops in Norfolk and Plymouth did Draper have freedom of action.

On 17 November, Draper received permission to lead a party south from Norfolk through Virginia and North Carolina in search of recruits and refu-

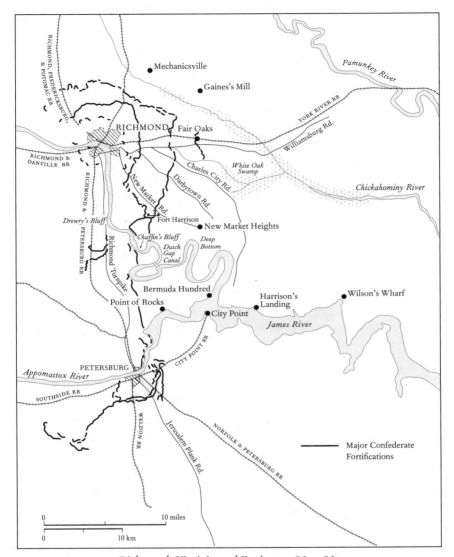

Richmond, Virginia, and Environs, 1864–1865

gees in the states' Confederate-controlled counties. It was a military exercise that provided both the enlisted men and officers with valuable training. Wild's aide gave the colonel clear instructions. Draper was to carry rations for three days. If he had to extend the expedition pursuing guerrillas, his troops could confiscate supplies "from the farms of disloyal men," but he was not to allow any plundering. All black refugees who wanted to escape to Union lines should be assisted and the able-bodied men turned over to Capt. James N. Croft for enlistment.[2] Wild's harsh attitude toward guerrillas was unequivocal. Draper was told that if his men were fired on, "you will *at once*, hang the man who fired" and label the body according to the crime. "Guerrillas are not to be taken alive."[3]

Recent historiography has placed raids such as the one authorized by Wild, and the events that precipitated them, into a more informed context. Authors like Phillip Paludan, Michael Fellman, and Stephen Ash have underlined the fact that guerrilla activities not only influenced Federal and Confederate military policies and played a significant role in the outcome of the war but also impacted on the lives of thousands of combatants and noncombatants across the South.[4] By late 1862 bands of guerrillas, or "irregulars," flourished on the fringes of much of the occupied South, especially in the no-man's-land adjacent to towns and forts.[5] Although not always recognized as a potent force by Civil War historians, this low-level conflict was widespread and lethal. Federal authorities were forced to alter their stand on the conduct of irregular warfare, and their new mood of retaliation helped to shape the emerging policy of total or hard war.[6] What was happening in eastern North Carolina and southeastern Virginia mirrored partisan activities elsewhere in the South and stiffened the Union's determination to end local support of guerrilla bands. Small Federal patrols and small-scale raids had not diminished partisan activities in the eastern counties. The 2nd NCCV was now part of a new and larger Federal attempt to crush the guerrillas. The enlisted men saw these raids as much more than just another military expedition. Many African Americans had joined the Union army with the hope of liberating family members and friends still held in bondage.[7] The raids enabled some men to actually achieve this goal and others to bring the hard war to their former owners.

Over a nine-day period, Draper led his detachment of 118 officers and men of the 2nd NCCV some 250 miles through disputed territory and brought back to Norfolk 475 black refugees, plus livestock, carriages, and wagons. During the expedition, several Confederate companies that operated with what Draper referred to as "Major Burroughs Guerrilla Forces" threatened to attack his men. In response, the black troops captured Burroughs when he attempted to visit his family. Under questioning, the Confederate officer claimed that he commanded a battalion of partisan rangers and acted with the authority of a legitimate government. His testimony and other evidence,

Draper argued, revealed the extent of the assistance that local citizens provided these irregulars. Although he accepted Wild's position on guerrillas, Draper refused to be as punitive as his orders had specified. Nevertheless, the expedition's actions touched off a growing hostility between Draper and Col. Frederick F. Wead of the 98th New York Volunteers. For the nine days that Draper's soldiers were on the march, his regiment always worried about attacks by partisan or irregular Confederate forces assisted by local civilians. Some of the enlisted men had come from that area and knew the planters personally. Their prior knowledge of the behavior and sympathies of local whites partly explains Draper's harsh treatment of a few of the planters he encountered. Colonel Wead was outraged by Draper's conduct.[8] He unhesitatingly accepted all reports and rumors that soldiers of the 2nd NCCV had committed "the grossest outrages, taking the last morsel of food from destitute families, grossly assaulting defenseless women, destroying school books, stealing horses, and otherwise disgracing their color and cause." He cited a report by Capt. J. Ebbs that detailed some of the complaints of offended citizens. Based on this report, Wead believed that Draper had led "a marauding and plundering expedition." It struck at one of Wead's basic values. Since he himself would severely punish any man in his command "who interferes in any degree with the rights of private property," the New Yorker was appalled by Draper's attitude toward the possessions of Southern civilians.[9]

The clash between Draper and Wead illustrates fundamentally different perceptions of the war being fought and the range of attitudes among Union officers. Draper saw northeastern North Carolina and southeastern Virginia as a region harboring guerrillas just waiting to ambush any and all Union troops, but with a particular vengeance for black soldiers. These irregulars could function as they did only with the widespread support of the white civilian population. As long as the guerrillas operated effectively, most of the local whites should be considered disloyal to the Union. For Draper, the only Southerners whom he knew for certain to be loyal were black. In many ways, Draper's views reflected the growing acceptance among Northerners of a hard war policy. By contrast, Wead's posting in Currituck County and his interactions with white citizens had convinced him that most whites in the area had taken, or would take, the oath of allegiance to the United States. Any ill treatment of them threatened that renewed loyalty. Wead's belief in the effectiveness of a policy of leniency and suasion was predicated on the assumption that large numbers of white North Carolinians were really Unionist at heart.

Col. Alonzo Granville Draper, 36th USCT (Courtesy of Massachusetts
Commandery Military Order of the Loyal Legion and U.S. Army
Military History Institute, Carlisle Barracks, Pa.)

Not surprisingly, Wead and Draper disagreed on the extent to which partisan
activities depended on support from the white community.

Union officers who had come to believe that they were fighting not just
hostile armies but also a hostile people were more willing to support black independence. Draper encouraged slaves to find their own freedom by leaving
their owners. Moreover, he felt that ex-slaves had an inherent right to some
of the wealth that their former masters, now in active rebellion against the
national government, had amassed by exploiting them over the years. Therefore, he urged them to provide their own transportation by taking their former owners' livestock and wagons. Wead, on the other hand, was committed
to the sanctity of private property, even if that property was in human form

and owned by men and women who sympathized with the Confederacy. The two officers differed in their views of the discipline, control, and courage of the black troops, just as they disagreed on the issue of the equality of black soldiers to other troops. Draper did not question claims that certain slave-holders had "kicked" to death some of their chattel and transported others to more secure areas. Wead, however, was predisposed to focus on any atrocities that blacks might have committed or planned against white Southerners. He thus took at face value Captain Ebbs's assertion that "a large share of the women. . . . were so badly frightened by the Negro troops that they were rather confused in their statements."[10]

The case of one citizen, Edmund Simmons of Currituck County, exemplifies the gulf between Wead and Draper. Simmons had submitted a claim for damages that resulted from the actions of Draper's soldiers; he presented himself to Ebbs and Wead as a loyal citizen of the United States who had taken the oath of allegiance. His was typical of the declarations made by persons of ambiguous loyalty across the occupied South. Draper did not believe him because a number of his soldiers who knew Simmons personally had described him as an active traitor. Pvt. Peter Furby and Pvt. Brister Foreman of Company A "both say that Edmund Simmons used to send provisions to the rebels at Roanoke Island. Corp. Robt. Frost, Co. A, has lived with Simmons. Says he used to feed Belcher's Rebel Cavalry without pay, from sympathy." Other members of the 2nd NCCV supported these claims.[11] Moreover, Draper had searched the provost marshal's records and failed to find evidence of any loyalty oath taken by Simmons. Given Draper's belief in his men and his distrust of people like Simmons, conflict with Wead was almost inevitable.

In fact, that enmity nearly precipitated fighting between their respective regiments the following month. When Draper's first raid had proved relatively successful, General Wild quickly planned another one, on a larger scale. Men from Draper's regiment joined a 2,000-man force that Wild led into northeastern North Carolina in early December. The general was particularly concerned about guerrilla activity in the regions bordering the Dismal Swamp Canal—an important transportation link to eastern North Carolina. Besides soldiers of the 2nd NCCV, the expedition included members of the 1st NCCV and 55th Massachusetts who had still not rejoined their regiments, the 1st USCT, and the 5th USCT. The raid took many enlisted men of the 2nd NCCV into counties where they had formerly lived—Currituck, Camden, Pasquotank, Perquimans, and Gates. On 5 December, the expedition left in two columns from Portsmouth and Norfolk, moved south through the Dismal Swamp, and reunited at South Mills in Camden County. Draper, who had been absent when the four hundred troops from his regiment had departed under the command of Lt. Col. Benjamin F. Pratt, rode through the night with a few aides to rejoin his men.[12]

The northeastern counties of North Carolina into which the troops were moving represented a bitterly contested area, with enough hiding places and local support to provide sanctuary for Confederate irregulars. Whether these armed men were a legitimate home defense force or uncontrolled guerrillas was a matter of angry debate between Union and Confederate authorities. While these officials quarreled, irregular forces killed. Repeatedly, Federal soldiers in the northeast had come under fire from hidden marksmen while trying to rescue Union supporters or arrest Confederate sympathizers. When pursued, the irregulars fled into the swamps. Two clashes had occurred in the month before Wild's soldiers reached South Mills. On 17 October "guerrillas concealed in the swamp" had fired on a small detachment of Pennsylvania cavalry on its way to Camden Court House, killing two cavalrymen and wounding several others. Although the Union commander had heard that fifteen armed men had been seen in the area, his soldiers were unaware of the enemy's presence until they took fire from the rear. The hidden gunmen were never found. At almost the same time, another group of soldiers aboard the steamer *Fawn* bound for Currituck Court House via the Dismal Swamp Canal came under attack. As the vessel passed Pungo Bridge, "a citizen appeared with a white flag, calling to us to stop the boat." The *Fawn* had begun to slow before soldiers on board saw men hiding on the shore. As the captain tried to get the boat back up to speed, an officer reported, "we received a volley from about 30 men, at very short range, delivering in all about four rounds for each man." The captain was badly wounded, and the boat was "riddled with ball." Once the *Fawn* reached Currituck Court House, Federal officers there organized an expedition and returned to Pungo Bridge, but they could find no guerrillas.[13] These two incidents typified the irregular warfare that Wild hoped to stamp out with his expedition.

After Wild had regrouped his forces at South Mills, he led the main body of the expedition across the Pasquotank River and occupied Elizabeth City. Along the way, guerrillas "pestered" his column and hidden marksmen fired on detached groups of Union soldiers. At night, the Federal pickets were under constant threat. Once Wild reached Elizabeth City, he sent out parties of soldiers, some going as far as the Chowan River, to raise recruits and to free black families. Still other detachments attempted to locate and attack Confederate home defense forces, or "guerrillas" as Wild consistently labeled them. Once under Union protection, the refugee families, their baggage, horses, and carts boarded steamers to be shuttled to Roanoke Island. In less than two weeks, Wild's men relocated several thousand newly freed African Americans on the island.

The general's policy toward anyone perceived to be a Rebel sympathizer was exactly the same as outlined in his orders to Draper in November. Indeed, as his men faced increasing harassment from irregular Confederates who refused to fight in the open, Wild resorted to "a more rigorous style of warfare." He ordered that the houses and barns of many suspected Rebels be burned and much of their remaining property seized. In the most extreme case, he had the prisoner Daniel Bright executed as a guerrilla and a sign placed on his body that read: "This guerrilla hanged by the orders of Brigadier-General Wild." Bright, originally from Pasquotank County, though he served as a private in the 62nd Georgia Cavalry, had been charged with "carrying on robbery and pillage in the peaceable counties of Camden and Pasquotank" and convicted in a "drum-head court martial."[14] Although Wild's actions precipitated an outburst of protests from within North Carolina and in Richmond, the general was acting well within established Federal policy. According to General Order No. 100, published in April 1863, Federal authorities did not regard as soldiers those who committed hostile acts but who were not part of an organized enemy army, who were not continuously in the war, who did not wear uniforms, and who lived part of the time at home. Such men, "if captured are not entitled to the privileges of prisoners of war, but shall be treated summarily as highway robbers or pirates." Acting under that general order, some Union commanders executed Southern guerrillas as soon as they were captured, whereas others granted them a trial by a military commission. Field commanders were allowed considerable latitude in applying the army's instructions.[15] There was little that Wild ordered during this raid that had not been done elsewhere in the South by other Union commanders when facing equally serious threats.

While Wild was trying to eradicate the guerrillas in Elizabeth City, Draper led his men south to Shiloh in Camden County. At Shiloh, the 2nd NCCV met a strong night attack from Confederate regulars. Fortunately, the colonel had expected such a strike and had withdrawn most of his soldiers from their bivouac to sleep in a nearby church for the protection that it offered. His pickets, warned and hidden, maintained the campfires and the illusion of normal camp life. When the assault came, the pickets fought off the Confederates before Draper and the regiment could go to their assistance. The following day, a little to the east at Sandy Hook, a Rebel force of about two hundred men attempted to ambush Draper's troops, but the black soldiers outflanked and routed their attackers with a bayonet charge. The Confederates lost at least thirteen soldiers killed or wounded, while the 2nd NCCV suffered four dead and seven wounded. That day the regiment engaged in one further skirmish with Confederates, at the Indiantown bridge, before destroying an enemy camp in the Great Swamp. The soldiers then rejoined Wild's main force. The next day the combined Union force returned to the Indiantown area and chased the enemy into the swamp. This time, the Federal troops were able to find the guerrillas' camp. After burning the deserted camp and "the neighboring houses," and removing all of the captured equipment, the Federals marched on to Currituck Court House.[16] A day later, Draper and 170 men found and destroyed the camp of guerrilla leader Captain Grundy at Crab's Island.

On 21 December 1863, as Wild began to organize the return to Virginia, Draper's troops—now numbering 250—moved by steamer from Currituck Court House to Knott's Island. Following Wild's instructions, the colonel ordered the houses of "Henry White, Lt. in Capt. Caffey's Guerrilla Co. and of Caleb White, 1st Serg.," to be burned. In addition, he arrested "Miss White, daughter of Henry White as hostage for two of my men who had been captured by the guerrillas." The next day, after Draper learned that a combined Confederate party of infantry, cavalry, and artillery threatened Wild's reduced and tired force, the 2nd NCCV marched to the general's aid. At Pungo Bridge, Colonel Wead invited Draper and his prisoner into his quarters to warm themselves.[17] When Miss White informed Wead that she wanted a white guard to take her to Norfolk, a dispute broke out between the two colonels. Angry talk led to physical blows, with Wead knocking Draper down and seizing his sword and hat. A pitched battle between the men of the 2nd NCCV and Wead's 98th New York Volunteers assisted by two companies of the 3rd New York Cavalry was narrowly averted when Draper returned with his full regiment. Despite Draper's explicit threat to have his troops fire on Wead, another New York colonel intervened to calm the dangerous situation.[18] Wild angrily protested the "personal violence inflicted upon Colonel Draper and Lieutenant Conant" by the white soldiers. Luckily, the delay occasioned by

Draper's confrontation was not crucial, as the expected Confederate attack on Wild and his troops failed to materialize. The exhausted and footsore Union forces, some of whom were suffering from mumps and smallpox, then marched back to their camps in Virginia without further incident. The last soldier was back in bivouac by Christmas Eve.[19]

---

Wild's expedition was instructive. The black troops had performed well, protests of men such as Wead notwithstanding. Wild reported that they "marched wonderfully, never grumbled, were watchful on picket, and always ready for a fight. They are most reliable soldiers." General Butler pointed out that although several civilians complained about Wild's harsh treatment of planters, even the protesters agreed that "the negro soldiers conducted themselves with propriety." A Northern newspaperman with the Union troops confirmed that positive impression. The troops had done well in all aspects of soldiering and "the question of their efficiency in any branch of the service has been practically set at rest."[20] It was clear that the national attention given the raid was due primarily to the soldiers' skin color. Months before, Federal troops had conducted a raid in Martin County and plundered the town of Williamston. Most of the livestock in the area had been slaughtered except for the horses and mules used to draw off the confiscated wagons and buggies. Despite considerable local bitterness and suffering caused by the action, it received little notice outside the area, largely because the soldiers were white. In another case, when the Union commander at Gallatin, Tennessee, arrested several civilians, including the wife of a suspected guerrilla, as hostages for the safe release of a kidnapped Unionist, there was no demand for an investigation in the Confederate Congress, as there had been following the seizure of Miss White.[21]

All of the parties involved interpreted the raid into eastern North Carolina in ways that supported their assumptions about black soldiers. Wild and Draper had high praise for their men, whereas Wead saw the raids as ill-disguised attacks on peaceful and possibly loyal citizens by troops often out of control. Wead placed much of the blame on the white abolitionist officers who had led the black soldiers. At the other extreme, Confederate officer Col. Joel R. Griffin, representing the perspective of white Southerners, told Wild that no other incursion in the war had "been attended with more disregard for the long-established usages of civilization or the dictates of humanity, than your late raid." Moreover, his soldiers "[had] fired on confederates after they had surrendered, and they were only saved by the exertions of the more humane of your white officers."[22]

A report submitted to Colonel Draper by Lt. Owen A. Hendrick in early January 1864 captured the differing views on the conduct of the black troops. Hendrick was responding to a list of their alleged outrages that had been sent to Colonel Wead. One accusation concerned the search of citizen Soloman W. Caffrey's home. When Caffrey opened the door, it was charged, men of the 2nd NCCV pointed their bayonets at him and threatened to "stick him if he opened his mouth." When his daughter protested their actions, especially the search of her room, "one of the Negro soldiers told her that if she did not keep still, that he would take her into her bed room and use her." Lieutenant Hendrick's version was very different. The house had been surrounded prior to a search for weapons. Caffrey had been stopped as he came out "by bayonet," but Hendrick did not hear the alleged comment and he was right beside the soldier. The lieutenant had then searched the house. The one soldier with him stayed at the door to each room while he went inside. The daughter had tried to stop him from searching her room, but he had opened the door and looked in. He was adamant that no insulting remarks had been made to the young woman. In a second case, the house of a widow, Judith M. Dyer, was searched but, despite her allegations, there had been no destruction of property and a pistol had been found. The six slaves—a mother and her five children—who left the Dyer house had done so voluntarily, taking a horse and cart for transportation. The youngest two were crying, but Hendrick suggested that they were "tears of joy not sorrow."[23] In contested accounts like these, individuals believed what they were predisposed to believe.

The raid into eastern North Carolina also confirmed the existence of a sizable contraband trade entering Elizabeth City from Roanoke Island and the Outer Banks. Wild seized four large boats so engaged. The trade "has been connived at," wrote Wild, "by the authorities of Roanoke Island, probably for gain. Sutlers' stores changed hands largely. The post sutler of Roanoke Island was implicated." These illegal operations, he believed, had been going on for months and could be stopped only if Union troops established the Dismal Swamp Canal and Pasquotank as the frontier and used gunboats to patrol the Chowan River. Certainly, General Butler had been concerned by reports that the provost marshal on Roanoke had been granting passes to merchants "for trading beyond our lines with the enemy's country." In a rhetorical question, he asked General Peck, commander of the District of North Carolina, "What is the use of blockading Wilmington and supplying the rebels through Roanoke Island?" Trade with the enemy, either from North Carolina or Norfolk, would remain an ongoing problem. Rumors of illegal trade out of Roanoke continued.[24] Neither military action nor congressional compromise could effectively end it.

Various incidents during the December expedition offered further proof of the hostility toward officers and men of black regiments shown by other Union officers. Indeed, Wead was not the only officer in blue to interfere with Wild's objectives. Col. John Ward of the 8th Connecticut sent cavalry outriders ahead of Wild's troops to warn Confederate planters and farmers that the general's "nigger-stealers were coming to plunder them of everything." Actions such as these supported Butler's claims of the existence in "some of the officers in this department in command of white soldiers, of a considerable degree of prejudice against the colored troops, and in some cases impediments have been thrown in the way of their recruiting, and they interfered [sic] with on their expeditions."[25] Most damaging, such actions outside the regiment eroded the rapport that other officers were trying to build with their black soldiers and came at a time when the regiment was facing other internal problems.

Although the 2nd NCCV, or the 36th USCT, as it was designated by the War Department on 8 February 1864, had demonstrated its military capabilities during the November and December expeditions, tensions were growing within the regiment because of Draper's leadership style. The new year began with a crisis among the regimental officers over orders that Draper had issued governing their behavior. The problem was rooted in Draper's approach to discipline. In the summer of 1863, when he was being considered to lead the 2nd NCCV, his commander, Col. Thomas B. Tannatt, warned Governor John Andrew of Massachusetts that Draper was "a too severe disciplinarian" to handle new black soldiers. In response, Draper had claimed that he "should no more think of applying to [black] recruits the discipline suitable for old soldiers, than I should of feeding an infant on diet proper for an adult." Many officers in his regiment, however, came to accept Tannatt's assessment and later testified to Draper's capricious temper and arbitrary orders. His clash with Wead perhaps revealed a good deal about the colonel's reaction to anyone who opposed him.[26]

As events revealed in early 1864, a number of commissioned officers had developed a deep-seated and visceral resentment of Draper's policies and actions. In April the colonel showed Butler the resignation applications from nine of his officers, five of them company commanders, who had submitted their notice in a block. According to Draper, they were reacting to his ban on intoxicating liquor in the officers' tents and his warning not to be seen drinking in front of the enlisted men. Draper also required each company commander to personally examine all of the soldiers in his unit to ensure that they had been vaccinated and to compel those who had not received the vaccine to obtain it. If he failed to do so and his men developed the virus after 11 March, the officer would be "placed in arrest and charged with disobedience of orders."[27] In addition, the nine officers objected to a ban on the punishment of enlisted men by company officers without reporting the offenses to regimental headquarters and to the prohibition of any types of discipline that did not apply to the whole regiment and that he not approve. The final complaint of the officers was that Draper required that they be in the company streets at "taps" to make sure that lights were out and quiet restored.[28] The officers protested that they would get less than seven hours sleep every night if they had to police at taps and rise half an hour before reveille.[29]

Butler held a meeting to examine the behavior of Draper and his officers. Present were Gen. Edward W. Hinks, General Wild, and most, but not all, of the named officers. During the examination, the officers of the 36th USCT admitted that they had accepted their commissions with the understanding that they must submit to any regulations on temperance that their brigade general might set. They also acknowledged, with one exception, that Colonel Draper had treated them with respect.[30] Butler then decided that the alleged reason for the resignations was groundless and frivolous, and it "was evidence of a combination to force some action upon their colonel, and was a very grave breach of military subordination and discipline." He believed that the officers' grievances had existed for some time and were only being brought forward "when the spring campaign was to begin." As a result, he issued General Order No. 46, which revoked the commissions issued to the nine men and their mustering out of their original regiment. Butler ordered them to return to the regiments from which they had been promoted and to serve out their original terms of enlistment.[31] Moreover, Draper directed them to leave the camp within twenty-four hours and from Point Lookout, where the regiment was based, within two days. He would only give them travel passes "as enlisted men of the 25th Mass. Vols." Since President Lincoln had not yet approved Butler's orders, the nine discharged officers refused to accept passes as enlisted men and were ultimately placed under arrest.[32]

In their long, unsuccessful attempt to get redress for what they thought was unfair treatment, these nine men portrayed Draper as "hasty, excitable, vacillating and we consider rash." Twelve men, not nine, had actually submitted resignations between 6 and 18 April. Two had been accepted and one rejected, while the other nine officers were presented to Butler, inaccurately, as acting in "combination." Since they had all resigned for much the same reason, why should Draper have treated them differently? In addition, when Butler questioned them, he did not allow the officers "to make any statements which were to be, & could be proved by third persons, present and absent; statements which were of great influence in prompting us to resign." The men gave a detailed defense of every charge laid against them. In doing so, they painted an ugly picture of Draper. "The Colonel has repeatedly ordered us to shoot down and cut down men for any disobedience of order or insolence, threatening to punish officers if they did not."[33] It is not surprising that Col. Josiah Pickett, who commanded their former regiment, praised their character and courage. But it is unusual that both Lt. Col. Benjamin Pratt and Maj. Daniel Preston of the 36th USCT testified that they "cheerfully concur" in Pickett's assessment. Indeed, Pratt and Preston considered the nine men to be "good, reliable, faithful officers, always ready to do their Duty, Brave and fearless at all times." They were "men of good principles and character, and of strict integrity," and regarded "as honorable and upright in their intentions and motives, actuated by the spirit of Patriotism, and with a desire to do all they can for the Country."[34]

Perhaps because so many officers vouched for their good character, Butler did not treat them as severely as he did other officers in a similar position. When officers in a New York regiment had resigned en masse, citing what Butler considered to be frivolous complaints, the general ordered that they be released from the army. But before they could leave, he charged them with loitering in a combat area in noncombatant status. Quickly found guilty, they were set to work as prisoners on Federal fortifications within Confederate artillery range. It was only after Ulysses S. Grant objected to their treatment that Butler suspended their sentences.[35]

On 23 February 1864, while the nine dismissed officers were appealing their case, the 36th USCT pulled out of Portsmouth and relocated to Point Lookout Prison, where it would remain on Federal guard duty until the first of July. Established in August 1863, following the Battle of Gettysburg, to house captured Confederates, the prison camp was situated on a finger of level land bordering the Potomac River and the Chesapeake Bay. None of its approximately thirty acres was more than five feet above sea level. As the largest Union prison, Point Lookout held more than 15,000 Confederates by June 1864.[36] Before the war, Point Lookout had been a popular resort hotel and summer vacation spot. In 1863, however, existing buildings were converted into a prison and stockades and outbuildings added. During its two years of operation, the stockades held over fifty thousand Confederate soldiers, most of whom found life there extremely unpleasant. The conditions were primitive; rations and accommodations were never enough; and malaria, fevers, and smallpox were common. Prisoners were housed in dilapidated old Sibley tents with insufficient blankets and inadequate sanitary facilities. As more and more POWs were sent to the camp, its resources became increasingly incapable of serving the swelling population. Conditions deteriorated even further. The clearest measure of overcrowding was the fact that approximately four thousand Southerners died at Point Lookout. Contributing to the high disease rate was the lack of sanitation. The prisoners' latrines were built over the bay on the east side of the very crowded camp, and tubs or wooden boxes were provided for nighttime use. A number of inmates chose not to use the tubs. After inspecting the facility, one member of the U.S. Sanitary Commission reported that the prisoners "void their excrement in the most convenient place to them, regardless of the comfort of others."[37] Their behavior became a contentious issue for the soldiers who guarded them.

When Draper's regiment moved to Point Lookout, the colonel became its commander in chief. The regiment's transfer to the prison increased the potential for social conflict as black soldiers on duty guarded white POWs and off duty dealt with a hostile but supposedly loyal civilian population, exacerbating an already volatile situation. In November 1863 guards from the 5th New Hampshire had shot four prisoners trying to escape, killing two.[38] In two separate incidents in late December, more inmates were shot and killed by white Federal sentries. Just after the 36th USCT arrived, "too of the Rebs got kild the nite of the 24th attempting to get away." The regiment's appearance shocked and angered the POWs, many of whom had never seen black troops before. "For the first time in my life," wrote Charles Warren Hutt, "I have seen a Regt. of Negro troops in full uniform and with arms." The next day he angrily recorded: "Negro soldiers were put on post to guards us. Was there ever such a thing in civilized warfare?"[39]

Three months later Col. W. Hoffman, commissary general of prisoners, inspected the camp under orders from Secretary of War Edwin Stanton. The 36th USCT, with a total of 753 officers and enlisted men combined, made up the largest single component of the 1,654 soldiers available for duty. Hoffman found the guards "to be in a state of discipline, their camps are in excellent condition, and the duty of the post is satisfactorily performed." But he felt that if the number of prisoners, then almost 11,000, increased by an expected 5,000 or more, at least one more Union regiment should be sent to the Point. There was always the possibility, he warned, of an external attack from Virginia to free the prisoners or by an organized attempt from within the camp to break out. Hoffman's findings suggest that the Federal guards were themselves increasingly concerned about the large number of prisoners they controlled and the potential danger if the camp's security eroded. Initially, the black soldiers stood guard on the perimeter while white Union soldiers patrolled inside the camp during the night. Only later did African Americans work inside the camp at night.[40]

The events that would transpire at Point Lookout both underscored the social transformation that had occurred when black soldiers joined the Union army and the difficulties most white Southerners perceived in that change. Formerly slaves, the men of the 36th USCT were now soldiers, and soldiers had both rights and responsibilities. Guard duty, an essential part of military life and discipline, was crucial and clearly regulated. The guards at Point Lookout—white and black alike—were consistently reminded to be strict, and they could be provoked. A soldier on guard duty was to be obeyed by anyone, regardless of their rank or status. In assigning authority to a guard, the army was color blind and unambiguous. A guard's legitimate orders were to be obeyed; violators must accept the consequences. Many Southern prisoners, however, did not consider the guards legitimate symbols of military authority but rather continued to think of them as slaves masquerading as soldiers. The tragic outcome of this attitude soon followed.

Hoffman's inspection was indirectly related to a board of inquiry convened at almost the same time to investigate the shooting of two POWs back in April and May. Hoffman may have been aware of the allegations, but his primary focus was the conduct of the black troops as they wielded their authority over hostile and rebellious POWs. New rights and old assumptions provided a potentially explosive mix. Lt. John Owen, a new officer in the 36th USCT, described the attitude of many officers and men in his regiment. They were, Owen wrote home, "well armed and prepared to shoot the first who lifts his arm or voice against the black—one prisoner was fearfully sabred yesterday for insulting a negro—by the field officer of the day." The problem was aggravated, he suggested, by the fact that some of the black soldiers were guarding their former owners. Tensions were also heightened by Confederate prisoners who baited their white guards with taunts that "the negro was superior to the Yankee" or that a white guard was "a fit subject to associate with [the black soldiers]."[41]

In the first case that Hoffman examined, Irving Williams, a twenty-year-old private in Company D of the 36th USCT, had fatally wounded Pvt. Mark Lisk of the 60th Tennessee Infantry, in an episode that underscored the clash of old and new relations among white and black Southerners. All of the Union soldiers on guard the night that Lisk was shot had been instructed not to allow prisoners to cluster around the cookhouse or "to do their business anywhere on the grounds except at the portable sinks built for that purpose." Any prisoner who violated these rules and ignored three warnings could be shot. The overcrowding of the prison, the refusal of some POWs to use the seaside latrines or the tubs, and the strict discipline established by earlier camp commanders all created a climate that would not tolerate disobedience. In the early morning of 21 April, Private Williams was on sentry duty when POW Lisk left his tent and stooped down to relieve himself by the side of the kitchen. Williams testified that when he told the prisoner to get up, Lisk moved to "between his tent and the officers' to do his business." He was again warned to move but refused, saying that "he would do his business first." After three warnings, Williams fired. Lisk was hit in the right foot and subsequently died of the wound.[42] No other guards witnessed the incident. One can easily imagine the response of Lisk and his fellow POWs to the fundamental clash of authority over something so personal and private as relieving themselves and perhaps understand their indignity at having to obey a black private. The Confederate prisoner acting as the sergeant major of the camp's POWs, William H. Laird, claimed that the attack was unprovoked. Although he had not seen the shooting, he believed that "both the conduct and conversation of the colored men evidence that there is a sort of rivalry among them to distinguish themselves by shooting some of us." The guards were "animated frequently by vindictive feelings" toward the prisoners, often "tantalizing them with threats."[43]

Cpl. Miles James, who posted Williams on guard, arrived four minutes after the shooting. He later testified that when he reached the scene, he saw no sign of a tub (one of the portable sinks that the POWs were to use) and that sometime afterward, but before morning, other prisoners placed a tub in front of the tent where Lisk had been killed. Lt. W. M. Tilcomb, the senior officer on guard, had not appeared until forty-five minutes after the shooting. He had waited until the officer of the day and four enlisted men arrived before he would venture into the camp.[44] He also reported seeing no tub. They went to the hospital where Lisk had been moved but did not speak to him before he died. Although members of the board of inquiry visited the camp, they did not find any new evidence bearing on the case. Despite a disagreement as to exactly when the shooting occurred, the board found that Williams had "acted in strict conformity to the orders he received" and was justified in shooting Lisk. The Union surgeon who had treated Lisk, however, accepted the other prisoners' claim that he had been asleep in his tent. The doctor hoped that measures would be taken "to prevent further reckless shooting by the guard."[45]

A second incident occurred the day before the board met. On 23 May 1864 Pvt. Miles Holloway, in Company F of the 36th USCT, had killed William Jones of the 2nd Virginia Regiment and wounded several other POWs. The next day Hoffman wrote that as the prisoners were coming from dinner, Holloway, "without justification, fired at one of them, wounding him mortally, of which he died last night, wounding another seriously and two others slightly." The board was empowered to look into this action as well. After an initial inquiry, however, the case was discontinued by Maj. Gen. Silas Casey, who was authorized to investigate it.[46]

Although the black soldiers had been exonerated, or at least had not been found guilty, Hoffman was gravely concerned about conditions at Point Lookout. New instructions were issued immediately to reduce the chances of further violence. The guards could use their weapons only if attacked, if a group of prisoners gathered at night and refused to disband, or if prisoners tried to escape. If a POW ignored the order of a guard for any other reason, the guard was to arrest him and turn him over to the commander of the guard for punishment. Prison authorities also changed camp policy to ensure a greater presence of company officers. But over the next few months the guards' dif-

ficulties escalated as more prisoners were squeezed in, straining the Point's
supplies, especially the limited safe water and fresh vegetables. The camp
hospital became increasingly crowded at a time when Hoffman was demanding that "the closest economy must be studied."[47] The diaries of POWs give
the Confederate version of the ongoing clashes between black soldiers and
white prisoners. Just days before Williams shot Lisk, Sgt. Bartlett Malone
of the 6th North Carolina had claimed that "a negrow Senternel shot one
of our men wounded him very bad threw the sholdier. The nite of the 21st
[April] a Negro shot in a tent wounded two of our men." On 24 May, Malone
recorded in his diary that "a Negro Senternel Shot a mung our men kild one
and wounded three it is thought that one of the wounded will die." Although
POWs like Laird and Malone blamed the shooting on black vindictiveness,
there were clearly other factors. In March, Charles Hutt noted, "one negro
sentry shot another and killed him dead."[48] A single black sentry, alone in a
dark camp with thousands of Confederate prisoners and aware of rumors that
some of the Rebels had obtained guns, might well have been nervous enough
to shoot at the first thing that threatened him. Hoffman's instruction that the
sentry should arrest a defiant prisoner and remove him from his comrades
without using his weapon may not have been seen as enforceable. That tension and fear help explain why at least one soldier in the 36th USCT took his
own life. On 29 April, Sergeant Malone had reported that "a nother Neagro
kild him Self. Shot him Self in the mouth with his gun." Regimental records,
by contrast, indicate that Pvt. John Green of Company I died on 29 April,
"killed by an accidental discharge from his gun."[49]

In the month before Williams shot Lisk, several incidents outside Point
Lookout reflect the social violence and bitterness that confronted the 36th
USCT even from Northern soldiers. Such events surely affected some actions
of black soldiers inside the camp. It certainly influenced many black soldiers'
views of their white "comrades." On the afternoon of 7 April, Private Williams and four other soldiers from Company D were returning to their camp
from the Point when three Union cavalrymen and a civilian approached
them. After ordering the enlisted men out of the road, the riders charged and
attempted to run them down. According to Draper, "then [the calvarymen]
turned back and one, drawing his sabre, ordered one of the colored soldiers to
fall on his knees; at the same time cutting and thrusting at him with his sabre."
Sutler Henry B. Walker, of the 36th USCT, who witnessed the attack, believed
that at least one of the riders was drunk; he followed them far enough to

see them head toward district headquarters. With Walker's help, the attackers were identified as three privates in the 2nd New Hampshire Volunteers and a local civilian named William Uncle.[50]

At almost the same time Pvt. Larry Griffin, a seventeen-year-old drummer in Company H, experienced a similar attack. Griffin was returning from the store with several other soldiers when he encountered a mounted civilian, Frank Smith, who lived about a mile and a half from camp. Smith turned his horse, spurred his mount, and tried to run Griffin down. He knocked the soldier unconscious with a kick to the stomach, yelling: "Get out of the way, you damn black son of a bitch." Although there were nine witnesses, all of them soldiers, and despite Draper's demand that Smith be arrested, records do not indicate that he was ever charged. A month later tensions were still high between the 36th USCT and local farmers, who believed that the black soldiers were augmenting their diet at the farmers' expense.[51] The farmers complained to the regiment's acting commander, Lieutenant Colonel Pratt, who seemed to accept at least some of their accusations. Pratt issued a circular "informing the Regiment that insults and depredations committed by men in this command on citizens will be severely punished." Such behavior was a disgrace to the uniform, and any soldier found offending them or stealing their property would "receive the severest punishment such conduct deserves." The bad feelings between the soldiers and the local population may explain the increasingly common practice of enlisted men and servants arming themselves with pistols despite their commander's objections.[52]

Relations between black soldiers and both white civilians and the district commander were also colored by the events that led to the exodus of most refugees from a contraband camp outside Point Lookout. Even before the facility had been constructed, a small Federal outpost at the site of the future prison attracted black refugees from Virginia and Maryland. By the time a military hospital had been set up at the Point in mid-1862, a small contraband camp had taken shape and a steady stream of fugitive slaves continued to arrive. Assistance for the refugees had come first from Northern aid societies and then, first informally and later officially, from the district commander, Gen. Henry H. Lockwood, who authorized the distribution of tents and other material to the refugees. Although Lockwood was disposed to help blacks fleeing from Virginia's slaveholders, he was not willing to assist Maryland blacks who were trying to escape from their "loyal" owners. Well before the 36th USCT had arrived at Point Lookout, Lockwood announced that slaves from Maryland would not be admitted and, if found, "placed without the lines." Many black Marylanders tried to pass themselves off as Virginians, but that did not protect them from pursuing owners or sheriffs with warrants. Many fugitives in the camp were seized and returned to bondage. Sympathetic Northerners helped many more vulnerable blacks to move north, and by the time the 36th USCT arrived at the Point, the contraband camp contained only a few hundred residents. The people who did remain were in contact with the black soldiers and would have recounted how the unfortunate slaves had been treated. Although the new district commander, Gen. Gilman Marston, rejected Lockwood's policies, a good deal of suspicion remained.[53]

Life at Point Lookout was hard on the Federal guards. Food was limited and monotonous; even the officers complained of having to live on hardtack and little else. Moreover, rumors circulated that soldiers of the 5th New Hampshire had sold guns and civilian clothing to prisoners and an attempted escape was likely.[54] Union soldiers walking guard at night had reason to be apprehensive. New prisoners arrived continually, swelling the inmate population. Not surprisingly, a surgeon's report in early April 1864 indicated that the camp was dirty and unhealthy. The winter had been cold and wet, while the summer, on the shadeless peninsula, promised to be a furnace. Prison authorities tried to improve conditions by imposing new regulations ranging from required bathing and mandatory changes of underwear to the cleaning and airing of tents and the disposal of human refuse in the sea.[55] Despite these attempted improvements, by the next month the camp contained about twelve thousand prisoners and "the place [was] miserably crowded." In the 36th USCT, there was discord between Draper and many of his officers. A few enlisted men complained about the behavior of certain officers, causing Draper to warn that "the practice of striking enlisted men must be discontinued."[56]

On the other hand, during this period black soldiers saw gains in their personal lives. Although Draper imposed a general ban on the presence of women in camp overnight, he allowed wives to stay with their husbands and at least a few took advantage of the opportunity. This was one of the first signs of official recognition of marriage among former slaves, and it stood in stark contrast to the experience of black soldiers in other regiments.[57] The colonel also responded to educational aspirations of the African Americans and the army's need for literate noncommissioned officers by establishing a school for the enlisted men. There were two sessions in the morning, from 7:30 to 8:00 and from 9:00 to 11:00, for all men excused from duties and company drill. An evening session from 6:30 until tattoo, generally 8:00, was only for noncommissioned officers, who were required to attend on the grounds that one of the army's objectives "in providing teachers [was] to promote the good of the service by obtaining non-commissioned officers able to read and write."[58]

Colonel Hoffman, who was always concerned with prison security, worried about the shortage of guards. Nevertheless, in May 1864, at the request of Capt. Edward Hooker, Draper received permission to lead an expedition of three hundred men to the mouth of the Rappahannock River to assist the navy in seizing or destroying torpedoes that Confederates had placed there. On the morning of 12 May, the black soldiers landed at Mill Creek, where they found and destroyed five torpedoes. During a subsequent search for more weapons, and the men building them, a small party of five or six enlisted men led by Sgt. Sylvester Price of Company H encountered and attacked nine Confederate marines and cavalrymen.[59] They killed five and captured three of them. One black soldier was killed and three were wounded. It was the first combat experience of these black troops on Virginia soil, and it occurred without a white Union officer present. It was an emotional event for the African Americans who had endured so much. "The colored soldiers," Draper reported, "would have killed all the prisoners had they not been restrained by Sergeant Price, who is also colored." Two days later the party was back at Point Lookout, having destroyed nine torpedoes, killed five of the enemy, and captured five more. The expedition had also seized a good deal of livestock and wagons destined for the contraband farms on the Patuxent River that had replaced the earlier contraband camp at the Point.[60]

Draper was more than satisfied with the results of the expedition. Two weeks later he requested permission to conduct a second raid in Virginia, as horses and "other property [are] much needed in the quartermaster's department and on our contraband farms on the Patuxent." Some delay ensued. General Butler thought, incorrectly, that Draper already had authority to raid whenever he wished. Then, after that misunderstanding had been sorted out, the colonel had to await reinforcements for the camp guard and some last-minute improvements at the Point. Extra gunboats were brought in to protect the causeway leading to the prisoners' camp, and ten pieces of artillery were repositioned to dominate the Point. With the prison secure, Draper and 475 men from the 36th USCT—along with 50 troops from the 2nd and 5th U.S. Cavalry—finally boarded four steamers in the late afternoon of 11 June.

The next morning, after some problems with their transport vessels, the men landed at Pope's Creek on Virginia's Northern Neck. Soon after their departure, rumors began to circulate among the POWs at Point Lookout that the troops had left "for the Neck with orders to burn all public buildings."[61]

For ten days, Draper's expedition marched across the Neck through Westmoreland and Richmond counties, while detachments scoured the countryside for cattle and horses, as well as guerrillas. After hearing that horses were abundant south of the Rappahannock, the party crossed the river to forage deep into Essex County. Then, as a major Confederate force moved against them, the Federal soldiers reboarded the steamers and returned to Point Lookout by way of the Rappahannock. The raid was a successful test of the colonel and his men, who had demonstrated their ability to use information from plantation slaves to avoid the enemy. Moreover, Draper repeatedly displayed his personal courage and willingness to run extreme risks. On the night of 13 June, for instance, accompanied by only a few staff members, he crossed the northern neck to contact Union gunboats. Three days later, after his white cavalrymen had fled at the sight of a large body of Confederate troopers, the colonel attacked the Rebels with just his assistant adjutant and a few orderlies. Only after two men had been captured at his side as they fought to secure time for a dismounted man to escape did the colonel retreat.[62]

The raid also confirmed Draper's faith in his soldiers' discipline under fire. On 16 June his infantry had dispersed a small group of Confederate soldiers after the Union cavalrymen had refused to attack.[63] The following day, near Union Wharf, Draper led 150 soldiers of the 36th USCT and 36 cavalrymen against a combined Confederate force reportedly consisting of 150 members of the 9th Virginia Cavalry and 450 infantrymen, largely of the home guard. Draper's troops advanced to within five hundred yards of the Confederate barricade and fired a half-dozen carefully aimed volleys before the enemy appeared to be in disarray. Despite the long range, the colonel observed that when his men got off their first volley, "several of the enemy were seen to fall, and heard to scream." Draper then ordered an attack across open fields, during which his own men had to halt to allow the Union cavalry, moving at a walk, to catch up. In contrast to the behavior of the cavalrymen, "the gallantry of the colored troops," their colonel wrote, "on this occasion could not be excelled. They were as steady under fire and accurate in their movements as if they were on drill." Nevertheless, Draper was critical of his own Capt. Joseph J. Hatlinger, whom he described as "an inefficient officer" who had been slow to execute orders during an earlier skirmish. Draper's report implied that Hatlinger's failure to attack immediately had cost the expedition a chance to capture a number of Confederates.[64]

Back at Point Lookout, the Southern POWs believed that Draper's soldiers were "devastating the country," and the triumphant return of the black soldiers "bringing several prisoners" was a matter of regret. The Richmond press charged that members of the expedition had raped a Confederate officer's wife.[65] There may have been some truth to the accusation. Much later, one of the officers dismissed from the 36th USCT claimed that "while in command of an expedition, some of the men committed *rape* & Col. D. never endevored [*sic*] to ferret out the person." In contrast to the Confederate accounts, Union observers portrayed the raid as "one of the most successful of the war." The expedition had freed about 600 African Americans, including about 60 to 70 potential recruits. In addition, the soldiers seized 375 cattle, 160 horses and mules, plows, harrows, cultivators, wheat drills, corn shellers, and other equipment desperately needed at the contraband farms. In early July, however, St. Mary's District was removed from General Butler's control, and the new district commander prohibited all further expeditions of a similar nature.[66]

By the end of June 1864, the 36th USCT's days at Point Lookout were numbered. Even before Draper's latest raid, Benjamin Butler had made at least two requests to use the regiment in the Petersburg campaign.[67] In early July the unit joined Butler's Army of the James, marking the end of Draper's command of the regiment. When the 5th Massachusetts Dismounted Cavalry arrived at Point Lookout to replace the approximately nine hundred men of the 36th USCT, it carried orders that Draper was to remain at the post until relieved by Brig. Gen. Edward W. Hinks.[68] In the meantime, Lieutenant Colonel Pratt assumed interim command of the regiment. What was to be a temporary delay dragged on when Brig. Gen. James Barnes replaced Hinks at Point Lookout.[69] Butler, who had initially ordered Hinks to the Point, believed that leaving Draper at the POW camp was wasting "a valuable officer." While Draper impatiently waited at Point Lookout, the 36th USCT went into camp at Bermuda Hundred. When Barnes finally assumed command of the prison, the War Department ordered Draper to take charge of recruiting duties at Fort Monroe rather than rejoining the 36th USCT. Butler again protested the misuse of "one of my very best officers." Lt. Gen. Ulysses S. Grant agreed to Butler's suggestion that General Wild would be more suitable than Draper for the recruitment post.[70] Butler felt strongly that the colonel would make too good a brigadier general to be passed up. In the fall, he recommended that Alonzo Draper be breveted to that rank and given command of a brigade.[71]

During this period the 36th USCT, led by Benjamin Pratt, was sent to a training camp after military authorities questioned its readiness for battle. Under Gen. Charles J. Paine, the men drilled until 3 August, when they marched to the trenches in front of Petersburg.[72] There the regiment formed part of the Second Brigade, Third Division, Eighteenth Army Corps. At the same time, the newly promoted Draper was placed in charge of the brigade. The move to the trenches may initially have come as a relief to the 36th USCT, for life at the training camp was far more rigorous than it had been at Point Lookout. Reveille was at 4:30, and the first battalion drill, which lasted three hours, commenced at 6:00. There was a roll call at every drill, reveille, dinner, and the 8:30 tattoo. Paine stopped all music such as band playing, drumming, or even bugle calls, and word of mouth was used to assemble the men. The camp's emphasis was on live firing and practices to prepare the troops to fight effectively. Paine wanted each regiment to form a unit of sharpshooters, using interregimental competition as an incentive. Each regimental commander would select, using the records from target practice, the fifty best marksmen in his regiment. He, or a senior officer, would then take the men to the firing grounds, where they would fire off five rounds each. On the basis of their scores, the officer would select the twenty best marksmen, including not more than two sergeants and three corporals. The chosen group from each regiment would then, under Paine's supervision, "shoot a match—regt against regt" over a distance of 125 yards. By the end of the month, the general had selected the regimental corps of sharpshooters. These men drilled hard to perfect loading and firing their weapons while lying down or kneeling.[73]

By the time the regiment moved into position outside Petersburg, all men on details, the pioneers, and even the cooks received arms and equipment to ensure the maximum number of combatants.[74] Pratt needed all of the men, because the 36th USCT formed one small section of Grant's massive autumn offensive aimed at seizing both Petersburg and Richmond. If the troops expected they would be called upon to spearhead the opening campaign, they were disappointed. Many of their tasks were familiar and mundane to all soldiers, but especially to black troops. Part of the 36th USCT moved into the trenches around Petersburg and were assigned as pickets when they were not digging and repairing trenches.

At the same time, a detachment of the regiment, including Asst. Surg. Mortimer Sampson, went to work on the Dutch Gap Canal. General Butler had begun the canal in August 1864 to allow Federal gunboats to bypass Confederate batteries and Federal obstructions that blocked the James River at Trent's Reach.[75] A few miles below Trent's Reach the river doubled back on itself, and at Dutch Gap about 175 yards separated the upper and lower river. The canal, begun here on 10 August, would provide a waterway fifteen feet deep and twenty-seven yards wide for Union vessels. That required excavating nearly 67,000 cubic feet of dirt and mud. Almost from the start, the workers—both black laborers brought in for the project and soldiers detailed from black regiments—were exposed to Confederate sniper fire and artillery shelling. Many were wounded, and at least one soldier in Company C was killed.[76] While African Americans did most of the hard, dirty work, approximately one hundred Confederate prisoners, guarded by black soldiers, also labored on the canal. Butler used these POWs to force Confederate officials to stop using captured black soldiers in the trenches around Richmond. Despite the concentrated drive to finish it, the canal was completed too late to assist the final assault on Richmond, in part because Union naval officers were afraid that the canal might allow Confederate rams to get at Grant's supply base.[77]

---

While part of the 36th USCT was at Dutch Gap, the rest of the regiment confronted life in the trenches. Dirt, tedium, and bad food were constants; death and maiming were occasional visitors. A black sergeant in another regiment clearly remembered "those long, dreary days and nights spent in the trenches . . . the tedium being relieved by occasional brilliant displays of pyrotechnics, gotten up at their expense by the enemy, though more ornamental than useful." The fireworks were not always ornamental. On 13 August Company F was manning the second line of breastworks on an otherwise uneventful day when a shell struck. Seven men were wounded, and two—Henry Jones and Hardy Ebon—had legs amputated. Jones and Ebon were moved to Philadelphia's Summit House Hospital, where they eventually died from their wounds. Three days after the shelling, Pvt. Lawrence Midget, also of Company F, was "killed by a bullet from enemy's S. Shooters."[78]

The regiment's problems, however, went beyond enemy shell fire and snipers. Increasingly, signs of discontent and conflict appeared in the ranks.

Authorities began to question the stability of the regiment and to identify incidents of insubordination. On 22 August the corps officer of the day reported that the 36th USCT seemed "unsteady and unreliable." He ordered half of the 4th Massachusetts Cavalry to be "stationed among the men and restore confidence by their presence and by keeping down the enemy's fire." The change in behavior had occurred after a serious clash between the officers and enlisted men. It began when Lt. Francis A. Bicknell shot and wounded Pvt. Silas Hollis of Company G "for alleged stubbornness, disobedience of orders, and manifesting a mutinous spirit."[79]

Bicknell's action was the kind of ruthless discipline that Draper had earlier advocated in the 36th USCT. Whether justified or not, the shooting sparked anger and resentment among the enlisted men. At almost the same time, James Williams accidentally shot another member of the regiment, John Williams. Williams was expected to die.[80] Only days later Sgt. Thomas Artis, a member of Hollis's company, disobeyed an order of Lt. Michael Sullivan. Sullivan had directed Artis to quiet down noisy soldiers, but he refused. Artis apparently told the lieutenant, "Oh! Let the men go to hell—I'll have nothing more to do with them." Allegedly he then said, "I cannot stand by and see the men shot down like dogs by anybody." Company A's Cpl. Alexander Gregory was reported to have exclaimed: "The son of a bitch! He had better be careful how he shoots our men; he may get shot himself when he goes into a fight."[81]

When Lt. Edwin C. Gaskill, the officer of the day, attempted to intercede, Pvt. Edward Roby of Company A ignored the lieutenant's command to go to his quarters. When Gaskill threatened Roby with his pistol, the private told him to "shoot and be damned." Roby then left but returned armed with a musket to confront Gaskill. Only the arrival of Lt. Jose Robinson, who helped Gaskill restore order, ended the conflict. All three enlisted men faced charges, although Corporal Gregory escaped with only a severe reprimand because he had not been given an opportunity to respond to the accusation. The other two men were found guilty. Sergeant Artis was sentenced on 21 December 1864 "to be reduced to the Ranks and confined one year at hard labor & wear a ball and chain." He returned to the regiment in time to be mustered out in Texas in September 1866, but Roby was still "absent—in confinement at the time of muster out of the Co."[82]

A short time later, Lieutenant Gaskill himself had a physical encounter with an enlisted man in Company I. Pvt. John Wesley, a twenty-one-year-old mulatto from Canal Bridge, North Carolina, who had been confined for disorderly conduct, allegedly warned Sgt. Miles Sheppard that if he ever got out, "there are two men in Company I that I will kill. If I had been in the company all the time, I would have killed them before." When the sergeant informed Gaskill, who was again officer of the day, of the threats, Gaskill confronted Wesley and they ended up in a fight. In December 1864 a court sentenced Wesley to forfeiture of all pay and allowance due him and "to hard labor during his term Enlistment & C. with a 12lb Ball & chain attached to his right leg." Wesley managed to desert in April 1866 while still serving his sentence in Norfolk.[83]

Whereas some enlisted men in the 36th USCT openly defied authority, a few others tried to quietly slip off. Although the regiment suffered only a handful of deserters during the war, this was a time when several enlisted men walked away from Company G. Perhaps they were still angry about the shooting of Silas Hollis. One deserter, Pvt. Alonzo Marshall, later enlisted—under the name Alonzo Brooks—in 38th USCT, where he was arrested. Marshall, an eighteen-year-old from Mathews County, Virginia, may have thought that desertion was a way of transferring to a Virginia regiment. Another soldier from Virginia who abandoned the company was Pvt. James Smith. On 9 September, while on picket duty at Deep Bottom, Smith—leaving his musket and cartridge box behind—tried to cross over to Confederate lines but was caught in the act by guards. Acknowledging that he had a wife in Confederate territory, he said that he would have probably been better off if he were fighting for "the rebels than the Yankees." It is likely that Smith was one of the refugees brought back by Draper's June raid, for he was from Essex County and had enlisted at Point Lookout on 18 June 1864. But he was not the only black Union soldier who attempted to desert to the enemy that September.[84]

The turmoil in the regiment came at a bad time, for the men of the 36th USCT were about to see their first major battle. The coming days would tell whether or not the discord within the unit had undermined its military effectiveness. The Second Brigade, containing the 36th USCT and part of General Paine's all-black Third Division of Gen. Edward O. C. Ord's Eighteenth Corps, was one of eighteen brigades that Butler planned to use to smash north of the James River in a two-pronged attack at the fortified lines blocking his route to Richmond.[85] On the left, most of Ord's corps would cross the James at Aiken's Landing, move up the Varina road, and attack Richmond's defenses at Fort Harrison. On the right, Gen. David B. Birney's Tenth Corps, including Paine's Third Division and the 36th USCT, would cross the James at Deep Bottom. The initial targets of Birney's assault were the Confederate entrenchments around New Market Heights, just north of Deep Bottom. Success would open the door to Richmond and draw off troops from around Petersburg. Secrecy was crucial. By shifting troops at the last moment from south of the James River, Butler hoped to find entrenchments only lightly guarded by Confederate troops. His plan, however, required a long march, much of it after dark, before the black regiments could cross the James and be ready, after a short night's rest, to attack New Market Heights. Paine's black regiments were in position in time, but the Tenth Corps, having farther to march, was late in reaching its jumping-off point. Soldiers, in the hundreds if not thousands, had dropped from the ranks exhausted. Although more white troops fell out, the black soldiers also found the march difficult and would remember it years later. Orderly Sgt. Peter Furby of Company C believed that the illnesses many of his comrades suffered after the war could be traced to that march. "We had a very hard march from Dutch Gap, Va. . . . when many of the men were taken sick with diarrhoea from the exposure and exhaustion and hardship."[86]

In the early hours of 29 September, the men of the 36th USCT, carrying only arms, ammunition, a haversack, and a blanket, joined the other troops moving out to attack the Confederate position along New Market Heights. The Union troops advanced in three columns, with Paine's soldiers on the extreme left. Although the Confederates defending this line were greatly outnumbered, they occupied formidable defenses that had broken several Union attacks in August. Some 1,800 Texan and Arkansas soldiers of Brig. Gen. John Gregg's brigade manned the section targeted for the assault by the black troops from Paine's division. Natural obstacles, such as a creek and marshland fronting part of the Confederate line, strengthened the fortifications. The enemy's position, a correspondent noted, was "rendered doubly formidable by the almost impenetrable slashing that covered the slopes."[87] In this attack on New Market Heights, Union planners used the soldiers on the right to occupy Rebel defenders while the black soldiers on the left smashed through the Confederate lines and cut their route of retreat.

Because both Birney and Paine threw their units in piecemeal during the battle that followed, Draper's brigade found itself largely unsupported in its assault on the right side of the Confederate line. The 36th USCT waited in the early morning while one attack led by Col. Samuel Duncan was beaten back with savage losses; at about 7:30 A.M. Paine ordered the regiment forward.

The soldiers crossed Four Mile Creek in front of the Confederate lines as the mist rose, then struggled through the swampy east bank of the creek, where they were slowed by the first line of the abatis, some thirty yards short of the enemy line. Order broke down as the black soldiers fought and died below New Market Heights, unable to force their way forward and unwilling to retreat in the face of the fire from the Texas and Arkansas regiments above them. As the African Americans began returning fire, the noise and confusion was so great that Draper and his officers could not be heard, or were not listened to, as they urged their men to attack. For half an hour Draper's brigade took terrible punishment before the Confederate fire slackened enough to permit the commissioned and noncommissioned officers to lead a renewed and successful charge through the abatis and over the entrenchments. The Heights were taken that day but at enormous cost. The 36th USCT lost 22 men killed and 5 officers and 102 enlisted men wounded; the brigade lost 16 officers and 537 men.[88] But the 36th USCT had proved that doubts about the regiment's soundness the previous summer were unfounded. Moreover, any tensions existing between officers and enlisted men were left behind when the regiment went into battle.

Indeed, so many officers went down under the Confederate fire that at least four companies of the 36th USCT were led in the final assault by sergeants. Although the regiment's commanding officer, Lieutenant Colonel Pratt, "did not particularly notice their conduct and management of their companies," General Paine later identified the men. The sergeants who assumed the leadership of their companies were Jeremiah Gray of Company C, William Davis of Company E, Miles Sheppard of Company I, and Samuel Gilchrist of Company K. Gray, Davis, and Sheppard had been first sergeants for six months, while Gilchrist was a second sergeant. Pratt praised another noncommissioned officer, Sgt. Maj. Richard Adkins, for having "distinguished himself by his gallantry in urging on the men." Besides the enlisted men, senior officers singled out many of the regiment's commissioned officers, especially the junior ones, for displaying exceptional bravery on a day when courage was as commonplace as death. Lt. Edwin Gaskill, who had been the center of so much controversy only a short time before, led the regiment in the last charge and, "waving his sword, [he] called on the men to follow" before he was shot down twenty yards from the Confederate trenches. He would later be promoted for his actions that day. Lt. Richard F. Andrews, who had been so sick with fever that he had been excused from duty for two months prior to the battle, volunteered for service though he could barely walk. Riding horseback most of the way, he dismounted—just before the charge across the creek and into the swamp—where he fell, shot through the leg. Lt. James B. Backup, an officer "excused from duty for lameness, one leg being partially shrunk so that he could walk but short distances, volunteered, hobbled in as far as the swamp, and was shot through the breast."[89] All three men were subsequently promoted to captain, and Andrews was breveted major early the next year.

Despite the tensions in the regiment in the weeks leading up to the attack on New Market Heights, the soldiers had performed gallantly. A junior officer in Draper's brigade, Lt. Joseph J. Scroggs, whose men attacked along with the 36th USCT, described the horror of the battle at a time when success looked impossible. As Draper's regiments bogged down in the swampy ground below the heights, "the utter hopelessness of succeeding pervaded the mind of every one when they had time to think. I did not lie down as that position offered no security, and I seen [sic] companies one by one commencing on the left rise to their feet, run a few yards and then as if recollecting themselves, *walk* from the field." Scroggs was particularly impressed by the courage of the men. "I seen a Sergeant who had received three different wounds crying because the battalion would not go farther. I seen men tenderly and slowly carry their wounded captain (Walker) off that field of death, and also their wounded comrades, from where to delay was almost madness. . . . I seen all this and more, and no man dare hereafter say aught in my presence against the bravery and soldierly quality of the colored soldiers."[90]

Although most troops responded to combat courageously, a few showed fear or insubordination. Draper's acting aide-de-camp, Lt. Samuel S. Simmons, abandoned his colonel at the ravine in front of New Market Heights and skulked back to Deep Bottom without his knowledge.[91] Several enlisted men did not even make it across the James River and were placed on charges. One such man was Sgt. Willard H. Johnson, of Company F, who was confined on 29 September "for mutiny," or disobedience of orders and disrespect to his superior officer, as the charges later read. Johnson was subsequently demoted to private.[92]

But the actions of a few shirkers did not detract from the perceived heroism of the vast majority of black troops. Thomas M. Cook of the *New York Herald*, who had been impressed with their formidable defense, reported that the charge against New Market Heights "was one of the grand features of the day's operation. . . . They never halted or faltered, though their ranks were sadly thinned by the charge." The reporter from the *New York Times* claimed that it was "a wonderful, a sublime sight to see those black men stand up to the rack."[93] Whereas Northern observers praised the black soldiers and regarded the attack as proof of their martial abilities, Southern reports stressed the orderly withdrawal of the outnumbered Confederate defenders who were running short of ammunition. In fact, the fighting at New Market Heights was another example of how Union and Confederate observers present on the field could view the actions of black soldiers in the same battle in opposite ways. The attack by Paine's division had not been well planned or implemented by its senior officers. Against the strong Confederate position, all that the black soldiers could do initially was to demonstrate how bravely they could die. Only as Confederate fire slackened did they renew the assault. For the men in blue, the Heights were taken because of their bravery and determination. For Gen. John Bell Hood's Texans, all black attackers had been easily shattered and driven back. The Heights were not taken; rather, they were abandoned only after the Confederate troops were ordered to leave the line. Confederate general Edward Porter Alexander would remember Birney's advance up the New Market road as a minor event, "driving in our pickets & taking our Exterior Line where it crossed that road and was practically without any garrison."[94]

It was after the black regiments had captured New Market Heights and after General Butler had ridden across the grisly battlefield that he perceptively commented to his wife on the courage and commitment of the African Americans on the field. "The man who says the negro will not fight is a coward, and his liver is white, and that is all there is truly white about him. His soul is blacker than the dead faces of these dead negroes, upturned to heaven in solemn protest against him and his prejudice. I have not been so much moved during this war as I was by this sight." He believed that he must publicly acknowledge the soldiers' bravery during the battle and, in some small way, reward them for their sacrifice.[95]

The capture of New Market Heights, accomplished by mid-morning, marked the end of the fighting for the 36th USCT on that day, but it did not mean the regiment could rest. Butler's original plan called for Birney's wing to drive up the New Market road toward Richmond. Considerable time was taken up in reorganizing the brigades that had done the bulk of the fighting and mobilizing the divisions of the right wing, but after 9:30 P.M. Draper's

men were again on the move. Fortunately for them, when Birney's wing attacked westward against the Confederates' intermediate line, they were held
back in reserve, while a Federal assault on Fort Gilmer was mowed down by
Confederate fire. At the end of the long hard day, the men of the 36th USCT
were among the Union forces who dug in around Fort Harrison in the expectation of a Confederate counterattack. When that assault came on the afternoon of 30 September, the black North Carolinians helped to repel it. The
regiment then occupied a section of the line of fortifications running from
Fort Harrison to the James River until late October.

———※———

Most officers and enlisted men of the 36th USCT, like their counterparts in the
Army of the James, were very conscious of what they had accomplished and
proud of their conduct in battle. Missed opportunities in the campaign were
largely ignored. General Butler, having seen firsthand the sacrifices in front
of New Market Heights, decided to award his black soldiers medals as official recognition of their valor. He created a medal modeled after the Victoria
Cross that was marked "US Colored Troops. . . . Distinguished for Courage,
Campaign before Richmond."[96] In part because of his efforts, four enlisted
men in the 36th USCT were among the black soldiers who received the North's
highest awards. Miles James and James Gardner received a Congressional
Medal of Honor, and William Davis and Samuel Gilchrist were awarded a
medal for gallantry. As is often the case in war, these men were recognized
not because their considerable courage and remarkable achievements had
been unmatched by soldiers in other units. Rather, it was because they had
come to the attention of senior officers—in this case, General Butler—who
wanted to use them, as heroes are often used, to symbolize the courage of a
larger group. In important ways the four soldiers reflected diverse military
stereotypes. One seemed to be a model soldier, one achieved a brief moment
of glory in battle, and two soldiered quietly and competently throughout the
war, leaving few records behind.

By the summer of 1864 Miles James had become the image of the ideal
noncommissioned officer. A thirty-four-year-old farmer when he joined the
36th USCT at Norfolk in November 1863, he was made corporal in Company
B three months later. At New Market Heights he prominently led the attack,
although he had been severely wounded. "Having had his arm mutilated,
making immediate amputation necessary, he loaded and discharged his piece

with one hand and urged his men forward; this within 30 yards of the enemy's works." After surgeons at a field station amputated his shattered left arm above the elbow, he was hospitalized for months. While recuperating in York Hospital, and having been promoted to sergeant for his actions on 29 September, he wrote to Colonel Draper, pleading not to be discharged for his disability. Draper then appealed to the surgeon in charge. "He is one of the bravest men I ever saw," wrote the colonel, "and is in every respect a model soldier. He is worth more with his single arm than half a dozen ordinary men." If Sergeant James were detailed to the provost guard or the headquarters' guard, he "could do a full duty in many ways."[97] Authorities acted on Draper's request. When James left the hospital in April 1865, he was assigned to the headquarters of the First Brigade, First Division, Twenty-fifth Army Corps. He went west when his regiment, as part of the Twenty-fifth Corps, was ordered to Texas. James was finally discharged for disability at Brazos Santiago on 13 October 1865.

Pvt. James Gardner represented a very different type of soldier. He had been an oysterman before enlisting in the 36th USCT at Yorktown before his twentieth birthday. Few records survive of his military service before his actions at New Market Heights brought him to Draper's attention. The colonel praised him in dispatches for having rushed in advance of the brigade, shooting a Confederate officer who was rallying his men, then running "the bayonet through his body to the muzzel." As a result, Gardner was "promoted to sergeant for heroic conduct to date Sept. 30, 1864." Whereas Gardner had found his potential in combat, he fared poorly as a noncommissioned officer in peacetime. Less than a year after his promotion, while his regiment was on frontier duty in Texas, Gardner lost his stripes and was reduced to the ranks "for incompetence and for being slovenly and dirty in his habits." The following year authorities reported him in confinement during part of March and April before he was mustered out in Brazos Santiago in late September 1866 at the expiration of his term of service.[98]

The third soldier in the 36th USCT to receive a medal for gallantry was Sgt. Samuel Gilchrist, a twenty-four-year-old carpenter in Surrey County, Virginia, before signing on to the regiment at Portsmouth on 28 October 1863. Within four months he made corporal, and in early May 1864 he became a sergeant in Company K. Gilchrist filled his office quietly and competently in the months before the autumn offensive. During the fighting of 29 and 30 September, he was one of the sergeants recognized by General Paine for taking command of his company after all of its officers had become casualties. During the attack he had been shot in the right side. The wound was serious but he survived. After recurring periods of illness, he was discharged in June 1865 because of "weakness of right lung and extensive debilitation of side, the result of Hospital gangrene in a gun shot wound."[99]

Sgt. William Davis, the fourth man decorated in the 36th USCT, was also praised for taking command of his company in the absence of its officers. Davis had been a slave in Halifax County, North Carolina, before enlisting, at age twenty-seven, at Norfolk on 15 August 1863. He received his sergeant's stripes only three days later and was made orderly sergeant of Company E in early February 1864. He remained first sergeant after his heroics at New Market Heights, but by early 1865 he was frequently in the hospital—due partly to bouts of diarrhea and, later, to a back injury. But much of the time from the fall of 1865 to the early summer of 1866 his hospitalization was the result of syphilis. Despite his physical ailments, Davis remained with his company until mustered out in Texas in August 1866.[100]

After the heavy fighting at New Market Heights and Fort Harrison, the 36th USCT returned to the tedium of life in the trenches around Richmond. On 21 October 1864 a general review of the black brigades in the Third Division of the Eighteenth Corps broke the day-to-day routine. As the 36th USCT paraded past its division commander, the effects of the hard fighting of the previous month were evident. T. Morris Chester reported that "there were but three white officers present, the companies being commanded by the colored sergeants. . . . There is no lack of qualifications in these sergeants to command their companies." Those qualifications were needed only days later when the regiment took part in a movement of troops under Maj. Gen. Godfrey Weitzel toward the Williamsburg road leading into Richmond. Senior officers planned a major Union attack south of the James River, and Weitzel's thrust at Richmond was designed to tie down Confederate units that might otherwise be sent south. With luck and surprise, Weitzel's troops might be able to flank the Confederate defenses and open up the way into Richmond. Early on 26 October, Draper's brigade was pulled out of the line and assembled with the division's other brigades near corps headquarters on the Varina road. Because Lieutenant Colonel Pratt had just been admitted to the hospital at Point of Rocks, Maj. William Hart, who had recently been promoted for meritorious conduct, took command of the 36th USCT.[101] At

5:00 A.M. the next day, the regiment began moving north. By the early afternoon, after eight hours of hard marching on slippery, muddy roads, the lead elements had reached the Williamsburg road, hoping to find an unguarded Confederate flank. As they formed up and waited for orders to attack, Rebel soldiers from Maj. Gen. Charles William Field's division were hurried north to oppose them. Not until 3:30 P.M. did the first Union brigades attempt to force the rapidly reinforced Confederate line.

During the subsequent attack, the 36th USCT acted as a reserve. It could only wait as Union regiments launched a series of separate assaults across hundreds of yards of open ground into the effective fire of Southern artillery and infantry. Many of the Union soldiers were tired, discouraged, and uncertain even before the fighting began. Although most of the attacks were turned back well short of the Confederate defenses, on the extreme right Col. John H. Holman's First Brigade of black soldiers initially made substantial gains. Without reinforcements, however, they were forced back. By about 5:00 P.M. Weitzel decided that he had carried out his first assignment of tying down the Confederate units, so he called off the attack and ordered a general retreat. The Federal assault had been repulsed with considerable casualties, and, in the confusion of a retreat conducted at dark in a driving thunderstorm, hundreds of men were cut off from their units and straggled across the Virginia countryside, discarding equipment as they went. Although the 36th USCT was not involved in any fighting, two of its enlisted men were lost in the chaos. Weitzel wrote: "This march, in this very dark night and through such country and over such roads, has had an awful effect on the organization of my troops." In fact, the retreat was so disorganized that the 38th USCT and four companies of the 36th USCT were not aware of the brigade's withdrawal until the next morning, when they discovered that the other regiments were gone. It was with some alarm they realized that they were the only Federal troops facing the enemy. Fortunately, they were able to withdraw through the heavy woods and regain their command without being attacked. By the end of the month, the entire 36th USCT was back in its old position on the line west of Fort Harrison. There they spent the next four months manning batteries and serving as pickets, free of battles or marches. While they kept guard in the winter rains, Butler's recommendation that Draper be promoted to brigadier general was finally acted upon.[102]

——⅜——

The winter spent in the trenches around Richmond lacked drama or comfort. For much of the time, it was quiet along the lines except for persistent shelling in the vicinity of the Dutch Gap. Nevertheless, the men of the 36th USCT endured privation, disease, shortages of supplies, hard work, and, occasionally, sudden danger. Picket duty in front of Richmond may have been less dangerous than in front of Petersburg, but that could change quickly.[103] In late November 1864, a Union shell hit a Confederate picket post and the Rebels retaliated. The counterfire hit a post manned by soldiers of the 6th and 36th USCT in a part of the line called the "graveyard." Two soldiers were literally blown to pieces. Andrew Newbern, a thirty-seven-year-old from Currituck County who had enlisted the year before, was killed instantly. Silas Hollis, who had been shot by his own company officer in August, suffered a severe injury on the left hand and was discharged four months later.[104] That such an occurrence was rare did not make the men less apprehensive. Yet, for most of the soldiers, army life during the late fall and winter was more about dirt and work and less about danger and fighting.

Only occasionally was the monotony broken. At Thanksgiving, for example, the black soldiers received turkeys and other donations from the North, and for a brief time the smell of turkeys being cooked over campfires and the music from regimental bands and groups of singers triumphed over the background roar of Confederate mortars firing away at troops still laboring on the Dutch Gap Canal. Men took the opportunity to visit friends in other units and renew their ties. The regiment's acting commander, Major Hart, put on a Thanksgiving dinner for all of his officers, who were joined by General Wild. The notes of an observer indicate that some of the biracial ideals present on the regiment's founding remained intact. The role played at the dinner by the regiment's black chaplain, David Stevens, and the way that his fellow officers behaved in his presence, suggested "that the guests were not at all afraid of his color rubbing off by association."[105] Unlike those of the 35th USCT, the officers of the 36th USCT seemed content to have Stevens remain at his post.

In early February the now General Draper excused his old regiment from a routine inspection because the men had been on continuous fatigue duty for an extended period and needed Sunday for the simple basics of washing clothes and maintaining equipment. He was concerned that "the amount of Fatigue and guard duty now required of the 36th, as the entire brigade, is so great as to preclude the possibility of drilling." During the same period, General Wild, now in charge of the Second Division, complained that soldiers in his command "for some time past have been poorly supplied with clothing, etc., and that it had been quite impossible to obtain any supplies from the City Point Depot." Union officials quickly denied that the failure lay in their logistics system, declaring: "If the proper officers of General Wild's command attended to their duties as prescribed, there should be no good cause for complaint."[106] Unfortunately for the soldiers, whether it was the overtaxed officers, incompetent administrators, or inflexible supply system, they were the ones who suffered.

The men and, by extension, their families also experienced delays in receiving their back wages. The last regimental payment to the 36th USCT had been at the end of August 1864, and by February 1865 some of the soldiers' families faced serious privation because of the lack of cash. Major Hart investigated the extent of the problem in his unit. Although no officer claimed to have a family in trouble because of the issue of back pay, eighty-six enlisted men, or about 15 percent of the regiment, reported that their families were seriously affected by the delay. Twenty-four of these families, Hart wrote, were "in an extreme destitute condition." Indeed, "many of the men are constantly receiving letters containing heart rendering accounts of misery and suffering among those who are dependent upon them for support." The problem was even more acute for men with families on Roanoke Island, who worried that rations there were being cut back.[107]

The hardships of the soldiers' dependents may explain another problem that confronted Hart at this time. He could not understand nor accept why his enlisted men could be found "ragged and almost shoeless" given the amount of clothing issued to his command every month. Some consumption could be explained by heavy fatigue duty or loss due to carelessness. But many of the missing articles may have been passed on to dependents living in or near the regimental camp. Hart became convinced that the men were irresponsible or, even worse, were destroying shoes in an attempt to avoid duties. He thus ordered all company officers to make every effort to impress upon the troops that "to waste or destroy their clothing [was] a criminal offense, punishable by a Court-martial."[108]

During the winter, two organizational changes affected the black soldiers serving in Virginia. By early December, senior officers had decided that combining white and black units in an army corps did not work. The result was the creation of the all-white Twenty-fourth Corps commanded by Gen. Edward

Ord and the all-black Twenty-fifth Corps under Gen. Godfrey Weitzel.[109] In January 1865, after the failure of the first attack on Fort Fisher, General Grant forced Butler's removal as commander of the Army of the James and replaced him with General Ord, who was seen as a "Grant man." Although an effective general, Ord was a conservative Democrat who as late as the early 1850s had supported slavery; many viewed him as a bigot who would deprive black soldiers of much of the glory of Robert E. Lee's defeat. As commander of the Army of the James, he removed, when he could, officers whom he identified as protégés of Butler, and he remained convinced that black soldiers were useful only as auxiliaries. Gen. William Birney, whom Ord regarded as a "Butler man," claimed that Ord discriminated against black troops, giving them the hardest work with restricted supplies, the poorest camp sites, and few positions of military importance.[110] Certainly, in the final campaigning around Petersburg Ord used few black units in critical situations.

Ord's attitude and actions restricting the use of black troops in pursuing Lee's battered army help explain the fierce desire of officers and enlisted men of the U.S. Colored Troops to be first into the Confederate capital. In the early hours of 3 April 1865, the sound of explosions and the sight of flames behind Confederate lines indicated that the enemy was destroying what it could not take away. Well before dawn, elements of the Army of the James began to move northward, and in the vanguard were General Draper and the 36th USCT. Someone, perhaps Gen. Charles Devens, later complained anonymously of Draper's haste to be first. "He started his whole Brigade for Richmond—without any baggage whatever—all others had tents, blankets, knapsacks, and everything. In his haste to be there first, he did not break camp. He ran his Staff through the midst of my advance guard to break them up and get the 36th there first!!!" The black soldiers moved slowly through the Confederate fortifications, in part because of the dark and in part because of the torpedoes set out by the retreating forces. As soon as the troops reached the Osborne Turnpike, however, their pace accelerated and the real race to enter Richmond began. After discovering that the 36th USCT was well up the turnpike, officers from General Devens's Third Division, Twenty-fourth Corps, sought to slow down the black soldiers. When the 36th USCT was about three miles from the city limits, Draper received orders from Maj. Gen. August V. Kautz to move his soldiers to the left of the road so white soldiers could pass. Draper obeyed the letter of the order by moving his men to the left side of the road, but he also put his entire brigade on a double-quick pace, effectively preventing Devens's soldiers from overtaking them. Once inside the city limits, the 36th USCT, the first infantry regiment to enter Richmond, stacked arms while its drum band played "Yankee Doodle" and "Shouting the Battle Cry of Freedom."[111]

When Devens's white soldiers finally caught up and marched past the black troops, a correspondent reported, "they were loudly cheered by the colored troops, and they failed to respond, either from exhaustion or a want of courtesy." Military custom dictated that the first units into a city should constitute the provost guard, but in this case that would have been unacceptable to many Richmond residents, as well as to General Ord. Men of the all-white Twenty-fourth Corps became the provost guard, while the black troops manned the fortifications on the city's perimeter. Indeed, as soon as Ord reached Richmond, he wanted all of the black soldiers removed quickly—even from the outskirts of the city. General Wild claimed that when Ord first met him in the city, he snapped, "You must get these damned niggers of yours out of Richmond as fast as you can!" Consequently, on 12 April all of the black troops marched down to Petersburg, through that city in a triumphal procession, and on to the south side. There the black soldiers settled into the old, crowded, and unsanitary camps abandoned by the white troops.[112] Three days before they left, however, many of the African Americans had the satisfaction of seeing their black chaplain, as part of a jubilee held in Richmond's African church, give the very first address by a black man from the pulpit.[113]

While the 36th USCT camped outside Petersburg waiting for further orders, a black draftee from Pennsylvania, Lorenzo Gould, joined the regiment. Gould's posting reflected a new trend of using literate Northern black soldiers as noncommissioned soldiers in regiments composed primarily of Southern blacks who possessed little education. Some of his diary entries describe their duties. During the summer Gould was "helping the Lt. make out pay rolls and muster rolls." These entries give a sense of both the hardships and the boredom of army life at this time and the ways that men sought relief from the tedium. Any soldier—black or white, North or South—would have understood them. A constant theme was the concern with the quality and frequent scarcity of rations. The army's apparent indecisiveness or confusion also frustrated Gould. Several times the regiment marched from Petersburg to City Point and took a boat to Fort Monroe, only to return to their starting point within a few days. The spring was a time of hurried activity followed by longer periods of inactivity and boredom. Some men found ways to pass the time, and some men got into trouble. A typical diary entry in early May gives a flavor of what camp life was like. "The boys are amusing themselves," Gould wrote, "by playing ball[.] I washed a shirt[.] I saw a man tide up by the hands[.] I have read from 14 chapter to the 25 of Mathew[.] we laid on the ground day and night[.] it is hot in the day and cold at night." While Gould himself passed the time reading the Bible, writing to his relatives in New Jersey, and listening to the camp preacher, other soldiers spent their free periods playing ball or cards, working on puzzles, dancing, or merely lounging around.[114] As the men filled their leisure time with various activities, they looked forward to peace, but many months would pass before they could again experience civilian life. First, they would be called upon to do Reconstruction service in Texas.

## CHAPTER FOUR

# A Unit of Last Resort

Because Gen. Edward Wild could not complete his African Brigade, the 3rd North Carolina Colored Volunteers (NCCV) turned out to be the last black infantry regiment organized in the state.[1] The transfer in late July 1863 of Wild and his partially completed brigade to South Carolina and the removal a month later of all other black soldiers from North Carolina to Virginia not only ended Wild's dream for the African Brigade, but it also deprived the fledgling regiment of an energetic organizer and a senior officer with significant allies in the North. The support of influential connections to shield a unit from decision makers who disagreed with the use of African Americans benefited both Col. James Beecher's 1st NCCV and Col. (later Gen.) Alonzo Draper's 2nd NCCV. Had Wild been in the state when Gen. John Peck took over the district of North Carolina, he might have been able to persuade Peck to leave some black troops behind. As it was, the enforced move, ordered by Peck, shifted the partially formed 3rd NCCV's base of operations to Norfolk and, in many ways, left it an orphaned unit.

Despite its new headquarters in Virginia, the 3rd NCCV, like the 2nd NCCV, continued to maintain recruiting stations in North Carolina that sought and forwarded volunteers to the regimental camp in Norfolk. The experience of the third regiment, however, differed in a significant way from that of the first two regiments. Although the 1st and the 2nd NCCV had encountered problems in their incorporation and early service and the 2nd NCCV had received only limited training before its first battle, both regiments were completely formed on entering combat, even if some personnel were on detached duty. By contrast, the 3rd NCCV had begun its formal existence at the end of January 1864 with just four companies mustered into service. When it joined the First Brigade of the Eighteenth Corps' Third Division three months later as the redesignated 37th U.S. Colored Troops (USCT), it still had only five fully organized companies. The next two companies were not added until the last week of May, after the regiment had already seen arduous service around Petersburg.

The performance of this unit in combat also differed significantly from that of the first two regiments. Those units fought well and were praised by military authorities. But at New Market Heights and Fort Harrison, as well as in the attempt to flank the Richmond defenses on the Williamsburg road—all before the last company was mustered in during November 1863—observers did not believe that the 37th USCT had performed well. More than many other black regiments, this unit was beset with organizational problems, internal discord, military inefficiency, and the memory of an atrocity involving its early recruits. Because of the regiment's limited role in combat, senior officers were reluctant to entrust it with an important military role. Instead, it was used in the campaign around Petersburg and Richmond only when combat troops were desperately needed and other units were unavailable. Fortunately for many of its soldiers, when the war ended the third regiment was campaigning in North Carolina. As a result, the unit remained in its home state until mustered out of service in February 1867.

Given the regiment's incomplete status and its lack of weapons in the first months of 1864, there was no question of using troops from the 3rd NCCV in the type of extended raids led by Wild and Draper in late 1863 and early 1864. Local military authorities showed little interest in facilitating the unit's formation but considerable regard for its muscle power. In fact, the army called on the partially developed regiment to provide continuous labor for construction projects around Norfolk, a task that made any effective military training impossible. Adding to its many problems, the limited number of staff officers appointed to the regiment were slow in actually joining the 3rd NCCV. The unit's first commander, Lt. Col. Abial G. Chamberlain, appeared a month after it had moved to Norfolk. Chamberlain had been a captain in the 1st Massachusetts Volunteers before suffering a near-fatal head wound in 1862. Although he rejoined his regiment after recuperating from the injury, Chamberlain was soon transferred to the North. When commissioned lieutenant colonel in the North Carolina regiment, he was acting as provost marshal at Riker's Island in New York Harbor. His duties on the island might explain his delay in reaching his new regiment. The next ranking officer, Maj. James N. Croft, did not join the regiment until February 1864 and received his discharge papers five months later.[2] For several months, Chamberlain had only a few junior staff officers to help him with the mound of paperwork generated by the still-developing regiment. He did, however, have a surgeon, Arthur H. Cowdry, and a chaplain, William A. Green, to assist him as he tried to organize his new regiment and meet the army's demand for workers.

In addition to the numerous problems that Beecher, Draper, and other commanders had encountered in setting up a new regiment, Chamberlain had a more difficult time finding recruits since, by the start of 1864, the competition for African American volunteers was fierce among the new black units. Recruiters from numerous Federal regiments were combing North Carolina and Virginia; any young black man willing to sign up had a range of options to consider. Thus it was no easy task to persuade North Carolinians to enlist in the 3rd NCCV, especially now that it was based in Virginia. Increasingly, Chamberlain and his officers tried to add men from around Norfolk. Douglass James, a private in Company D, was one such soldier. Although often vague about specific aspects of his service, James remembered enlisting at Fort Monroe in the late fall of 1863 and being "brought over here to the entrenched camp where we drilled for about six months. Was stripped and physically examined at enlistment." Interestingly, he recalled that Cpl. Abraim Reed (or Abel Read) "who was a corporal of my company was our recruiting officer."[3] The fact that he made no mention of a white officer being involved suggests that what was memorable about his recruitment was the authority exercised by the black noncommissioned officer.

Because the regiment was drawing men from both North Carolina and Virginia, with a sprinkling of volunteers from Maryland and the District of Columbia, there may have been less concern, especially among non–North Carolinians, when, on 8 February 1864, the unit's name was officially changed from the 3rd NCCV to the 37th USCT. Of much greater importance was the fact that before the regiment took the field in Virginia, it had suffered its first casualties in North Carolina in a manner that all black regiments feared. A Confederate attack on Plymouth, a major recruiting station for the 37th USCT, raised the specter that the enlisted men from the regiment captured in battle had not been treated as POWs, but had either been shot outright or dealt with as slaves apprehended for insurrection. On 20 April 1864 a Confederate force of about 7,000 men under Gen. Robert F. Hoke seized Plymouth after a four-day siege. Among the some 3,000 defenders of the Union garrison were 166 "Buffaloes" (white North Carolina Unionists) and about 200 black soldiers and sailors, many of whom had just enlisted. Some of the African Americans

Lt. Col. Abial G. Chamberlain, 37th USCT (Courtesy of Massachusetts
Commandery Military Order of the Loyal Legion and U.S. Army
Military History Institute, Carlisle Barracks, Pa.)

were part of a recruiting detachment of enlisted men from the 37th USCT who
had assembled an unknown number of new recruits. In addition to the Federal soldiers, there were about 1,000 black refugees of all ages in the town.
Soon after Plymouth was taken, stories began to circulate about a massacre
of Buffaloes and black prisoners—both soldiers and civilians. Coming only
eight days after the tragedy at Fort Pillow, the rumors raised the prospect of
no quarter given or asked for the black soldiers. Whether the actual massacre
was condoned by high-ranking Confederate officers, or whether the killing
of prisoners or soldiers trying to surrender was the savage response of a few

soldiers acting as individuals and facing blacks in arms for the first time, is still fiercely debated. Even the exact number of casualties remains uncertain.[4] What is clear is that events in Plymouth held out to all black soldiers the stark reality of what combat and capture might bring.

The attack on Plymouth was an especially bitter blow to the 37th USCT. For months Plymouth had been an important source of new recruits. In December 1863 and January 1864, Company B alone had enlisted ninety-five men and Company C twenty-nine from the town.[5] Many of these soldiers left behind family in Plymouth and the vicinity. It was inevitable that some of these relatives were among the one thousand black civilians clustered in the town when the Confederates overran the defense. When Southern victory seemed inevitable, a large number of Buffaloes and blacks fled to sanctuary in the swamps around the town although many, including women and children, were captured or killed in the process. Estimates of the civilians captured vary considerably, but at least several hundred women and children were taken prisoner by the Confederate troops. Some of the captives were presumably returned to slavery.[6] It was a reminder for many Southern black soldiers that their families were also vulnerable to reprisals if they fell into Confederate hands.

More than just family members were caught up in the fall of Plymouth. When the Confederates launched their attack in April, at least fifty members of the 37th USCT were in the town. Capt. Hiram L. Marvin of Company B had been in charge of the recruiting station at Plymouth since January. With him were ten enlisted men, including Pvt. George Burden (or Berden) of Company D and Pvt. John Ward, Pvt. John Berden (or Berdan), and Pvt. Jackson Miller of Company F, as well as new recruits who had not yet been sent on to the regiment. A month later, Chamberlain reported that Marvin and a number of recruits were captured, although he could not give the names or exact number of the privates as their enlistment papers had not been forwarded before the town fell. Marvin himself had reported having forty-one recruits at the end of March 1864, three weeks before the Confederate strike, and there is no record that these men ever reached Norfolk. By the time Plymouth was captured, he may have had more. Moreover, there were other recruits in town belonging to the 2nd Colored Cavalry.[7] When Plymouth was threatened, all of these soldiers were incorporated into the Union defense. On the morning of the final attack, Captain Marvin and the men under his command manned the breastworks guarding the western part of town. Within hours, however, the combination of the Confederate ram *Albemarle*, firing into the Union position from the river, and an assault by Brig. Gen. Matt W. Ransom's brigade on the town's eastern defenses compelled Brig. Gen. Henry W. Wessells to capitulate. Ominously, when Wessells first offered to surrender Plymouth "if the negroes and North Carolina soldiers would be treated as 'prisoners of war,'" his proposal was refused. At 10:00 A.M. the Union commander was forced to surrender unconditionally, although several groups of Union soldiers, including some of the black soldiers, continued to resist for a short period.[8] The continued resistance of the black soldiers was used, at least unofficially, to justify subsequent Confederate retaliation.

Once organized resistance ended, it was unclear what happened to all of the black soldiers. Among the returns of the Union troops killed, wounded, and missing at Plymouth was listed one detached officer in charge of 244 unattached black recruits. The officer was undoubtedly Captain Marvin, but only a portion of these 244 soldiers would have been destined for the 37th USCT.[9] On the other hand, there may have been more black recruits caught up in the fall of Plymouth than would show up on the Union casualty reports. Initial Confederate reports listed the number of black prisoners as between 300 and 400. Although Marvin was exchanged and discharged in June 1865, the fate of most of the enlisted men in his command is difficult to determine. At least one captured soldier from the 37th USCT—George Burden—was held by the Confederates but later rejoined the regiment in August 1865. Although Burden, and some others with him, had not been shot despite rumors circulating after the fall of Plymouth, neither had he been treated as a normal prisoner of war. Testimony in his widow's pension application decades later referred to the treatment he had received. For at least part, if not all, of the time that Burden was held, he was not in a POW camp but rather was forced to work on Confederate fortifications. When he rejoined his regiment in 1865, he told his comrades that his captors "would hitch him up with others to pull heavy logs to build their, the rebel, breastworks & in that way he strained himself." He did not mention by name any black soldiers captured with him, nor did he suggest that any were killed. He had claimed, however, that "while a prisoner of war, the rebels made all the colored soldiers they took there work to build fortifications." A fellow soldier who was with him regularly at sick call after his release, described him as being "pretty bad off." Another soldier remembered Burden's accounts of how "the rebels had treated him very cruel."[10]

Some soldiers from the 37th USCT were less fortunate than Burden. Pvt. Anderson Reddick and Pvt. Peter Ruffin were killed either during the defense of Plymouth or immediately after it fell. Other soldiers, though lost initially, were able to rejoin the regiment days later. The *Miami*, one of the Federal gunboats operating at the mouth of the Roanoke River, picked up Pvt. Jackson Miller of Company F after he had spent three days hiding in the swamps. John Ward, another survivor who managed to make it back to Federal territory, described and perhaps embellished his escape many years later. He had been wounded in the head and chest and only escaped capture by feigning death. He was able to slip away in the dark and make his way to Little Washington.[11] Some of the enlisted men who had been staffing the recruiting station seem to have returned to their companies, although they left few records describing how they did so. Their stories would suggest that many of the more recently recruited soldiers might also have escaped, although some were probably shot after they surrendered.

Many accounts that began to circulate after the capture of Plymouth spoke of atrocities committed against the black soldiers. Sgt. Samuel Johnson of the 2nd U.S. Colored Cavalry testified that he had eluded capture by donning civilian clothes but witnessed the savage killing of many prisoners. He claimed that over the next day, all of the blacks captured in uniform were hung, shot, or bludgeoned to death. Other witnesses supported the charges, which the Confederates denied, that surrendered black prisoners were murdered.[12] Those blacks captured but not killed were placed in the custody of Governor Zebulon B. Vance to determine who might be escaped slaves from North Carolina. Such fugitives were to be returned to their owners. Vance was warned that in order to "avoid as far as possible all complications with the military authorities of the United States in regard to the disposition which will be made of this class of prisoners," he should "take the necessary steps to have the matter of such disposition kept out of the newspapers of the State, and in every way to shun its obtaining any publicity as far as consistent with the proposed restoration."[13]

It may never be known whether most black soldiers captured at Plymouth were returned to slavery, shot, or held prisoner. On one level, what actually happened to the black prisoners mattered less to the regiment than what the soldiers believed had happened. The enlisted men quickly became aware of the rumors, and, in the case of Captain Marvin, even Chamberlain suspected the worst. In June the lieutenant colonel had heard unofficially that after Marvin was captured, he "was compelled to dig his own grave, and was then shot and buried by the rebels." There was little reason to believe that any enlisted man received kinder treatment. Thus, when the regiment went into combat that summer, the men believed that they were in a fight without quarter. Certainly, the fate of the captured soldiers at Plymouth was the subject of emotional speculation in the other black North Carolina regiments. From Point Lookout Prison Camp, Maryland, Lt. John Owen, in Company H of the 36th USCT, wrote his aunt in Massachusetts that he and his comrades had heard "fearful accounts of the barbarity of the rebels at Plymouth & Fort Pillow towards the colored troops. I think our boys will either come off successful or fight to the death. Better to be killed fighting to the last man than tortured to death after surrendering."[14]

Ironically, the day after Plymouth fell and Marvin and his recruits were captured, Lieutenant Colonel Chamberlain had decided to reduce the number of enlisted men that each recruiting officer could retain at a station to assist him. The new policy would have meant fewer men from the 37th USCT at Plymouth. Chamberlain's decision was, in large part, a response to concerns of senior officers that too many regiments had too many soldiers recruiting in North Carolina. Although some military recruiters were very effective, many others appeared to be idle much of the time. All men who were not essential to the recruiting effort were needed in their regiments in Virginia as the new campaign season began. As a result, recruiting officers like Marvin would henceforth have only two soldiers with them, not the ten who had been at Plymouth. Recruiters were also to forward the newly recruited men more quickly to the regiment. For at least some of the soldiers at Plymouth, the new policy came a little too late.[15]

Chamberlain issued his new orders after Maj. Gen. John J. Peck had disseminated a very critical assessment of how recruiting was conducted in North Carolina. Recruiting stations, Peck noted, had been established at New Bern, Washington, Plymouth, Beaufort, and Morehead City. At least three white regiments and seven black ones had officers and men operating in the various subdistricts, often without proper authorization or much apparent organization. Although some recruitment teams had been efficient and effective, Peck worried that many more were ineffectual or inactive. The recruiting detachments were often much too large, leaving many of the soldiers with little to do. Of even greater concern to Peck were reported cases of what amounted to virtual impressment or fraudulent recruitment. Some recruiting officers had intimidated young men by threats of what would happen if they did not sign up. Sometimes—and here Peck pointed a finger at the black cavalry units—"mere boys, children, some of them weak, puny, scrofulous, have been enlisted, passed by the surgeon, and mustered in by the mustering officer." In still other cases, old men—incapable of service—had been enlisted, fed, and clothed before the examining surgeon or the mustering officer rejected them. Indeed, one of Peck's greatest misgivings had to do with the amount of wasted clothing. He perhaps misunderstood the motives of some officers who enlisted men who were clearly incapable of passing a medical examination, but who were immediately given a uniform. When the surgeon or mustering officers later turned them down, they were allowed to leave with the now used clothing.[16] At a time when many friends and kin of recruits were desperately short of all necessities, it is not surprising that the black soldiers seemed to consume more clothing than senior officers expected. In addition, Peck may not have understood, or considered, the new choices offered to young black men by recruiters in North Carolina. These African Americans could hope to work as civilian laborers for a branch of the military, or they could decide, if wanting to volunteer, in what arm of the service they wanted to serve. Certainly, for the 37th USCT, operating outside the state, these factors made recruiting North Carolina men much more difficult.

At almost the same time that Plymouth fell, what remained of Wild's original African Brigade was broken up in the general reorganization of General Butler's forces in Virginia in preparation for his thrust up the James River. In the early months of 1864, the 37th USCT, along with the 36th USCT and the 1st USCT, was still designated as the African Brigade under the command of Col. John H. Holman.[17] But on 24 April, the African Brigade ceased to exist, and the 37th USCT was merged with the 1st USCT, 10th USCT, and 22nd USCT to form the First Brigade in Gen. Edward Hinks's Third Division. At least for a short time, Wild would remain in command of the First Brigade. His troops would join the new Army of the James, which Butler was building to operate against Richmond by way of the James River. In this army the U.S. Colored Troops not only would comprise 40 percent of the officers and enlisted men, but they also would be made to feel an integral part of the command. No longer would they be assigned fatigue duties and worn-out equipment. In the Army of the James, black soldiers would be treated as equal to white soldiers. Black regiments would serve on the front line and lead assaults, and the army expected them to perform as well as white units. Indeed, Butler made the commitment that "every enlisted colored man shall have the same uniform, clothing, arms, equipments, camp equipment, rations, medical and hospital treatment, as are furnished to the United States soldiers of a like arm of the service."[18] For all his faults, Butler demanded that the military treat its black soldiers just like all other men in uniform. When the Army of the James advanced on Richmond, the First Brigade—made up solely of black regiments and now under the command of General Wild—was selected to lead the way up the James and to seize and fortify key positions dominating the river. The men's behavior would justify Butler's faith in them.

The movement by Butler's forces was part of a series of coordinated assaults by all of the Union armies. Butler planned to lead thirty thousand men up the James and land midway between Richmond and Petersburg, where they would be opposed by only about five thousand Confederate soldiers plus whatever Confederate militia that could be hastily scraped together. With luck and daring, the army would be able to seize the Southern capital.[19] At the very least, it would cut the Richmond and Petersburg Railroad and threaten Petersburg. Butler's primary objectives were to establish a base well up the river from which his army could interrupt the flow of Confederate supplies into Richmond, draw off forces from General Lee's army, and threaten the Southern capital itself. To ensure safe lines of supply and communication, Butler believed, key strategic positions on the James River below Bermuda Hundred, the focal point of Butler's landing, had to be secured quickly. That was the assignment of the First Brigade.

By the end of April, the 37th USCT had left its camp at Norfolk; every man had been issued one hundred rounds of ammunition and four rations. On the morning of 4 May, the regiment, along with the rest of the Army of the James, began to board the transport ships that would take them upriver. All day the ships' officers loaded men and equipment; then, one by one, the transports moved into the James River and anchored off Fort Monroe. By the time the sun rose on 5 May, the first of the fleet's 120 vessels had begun to head upriver. The "first fleet," comprised of a flotilla of wooden army gunboats, formed the vanguard, followed by the transports carrying Wild's brigade. The brigade's major task was to seize certain strategic positions along the James to protect the army's supply lines. The first position, Wilson's Wharf, was a high bluff on the north bank of the James commanding that section of the river. Here the Confederates had built Fort Pocahontas, but they had abandoned the works by the time the Union forces moved up the river. Squads from the

1st USCT and 22nd USCT, plus two sections of Choate's battery, seized the position without opposition, established a signal station, and began to entrench.

The remainder of the brigade continued seven miles farther upriver to the south shore, where another unoccupied Confederate garrison, Fort Powhatan, dominated that stretch of the James. This site was secured, again without resistance, by the 10th USCT and 37th USCT supported by two sections of Howell's battery. Records of the 10th USCT indicate that at noon the regiments "debarked & proceeded to occupy the place, meeting with no opposition & seeing no enemy except a party of four horsemen who immediately made off." Small detachments were directed to scout the immediate area, "while the main body were [sic] engaged in throwing up defenses & cutting away the covering woods." Adm. S. Phillips Lee detached three ships from the Federal fleet to remain behind to provide supporting fire from the river if necessary. The ironclad *Atlanta* and the lightly armed screw steamer *Young America* stationed themselves off Fort Powhatan, while another gunboat, the *Dawn*, stood ready to cover the men at Wilson's Wharf.[20]

Three days later, the 37th USCT moved upriver to City Point, located at the mouth of the Appomattox River, where General Hinks's Second Brigade had landed, to help man the fortifications there. Here, as elsewhere, the unprepared Confederates put up limited initial resistance and a bold Union advance might have yielded great success.[21] Yet Butler and his subordinates squandered the potential opportunity. On 9 May Hinks made what he described as a reconnaissance toward Petersburg. His force, composed of 1,800 infantrymen, one battery, and a company of cavalry, pushed to within four miles of the city before coming under fire from Confederate artillery and withdrawing. By 11:00 P.M. Hinks's men were back at City Point.[22]

While at City Point, Chamberlain took advantage of the growing number of refugees crossing the Union lines to try to recruit two more companies for his incomplete regiment. The loss of Plymouth had cut off a major source of potential enlistees from North Carolina and had made recruitment in Virginia an even greater necessity. On 9 and 10 May 1864 officers of the 37th USCT enrolled the first freedmen at City Point. By 25 May, two dozen recruits from that town, more from both Wilson's Wharf and Norfolk, and three dozen men previously admitted in Plymouth, Washington, and Roanoke Island were combined to form Company F. Company G signed on fifty-five men at City Point in one day and became the regiment's seventh company by the end of the month. Company G was an exception in the North Carolina regiment, for it contained a minority of enlisted men from the state. Once the company mustered in the City Point recruits, it added only two soldiers from North Carolina—Gilbert Joiner and John Lewis—for the rest of the year. In November, eighteen men, some draftees, were enrolled from the District of Columbia. It would be another five months before a little over two dozen North Carolinians joined the company from Wilmington.[23] Perhaps because Company G was so short-staffed, when the 37th USCT left City Point, Chamberlain directed Chaplain Green, rather than a regular officer, to remain there "and gather up such men as are suitable for enlistment in this regiment."[24] Regimental records suggest that the chaplain was not very successful.

The 37th USCT was perhaps fortunate that in the following weeks of the Bermuda Hundred campaign it was not involved in the heavy fighting when Butler's tardy advance was thrown back at Drewry's Bluff. With green recruits and poor weapons, the regiment was ill-prepared to face veteran Confederate troops. Nevertheless, the 37th USCT did its share of strenuous work, and General Wild held it as a mobile reserve. On 24 May Hinks rushed the regiment to Wilson's Wharf, where Confederate cavalry led by Gen. William Henry Fitzhugh Lee threatened to overrun Wild's black soldiers. By the time the 37th USCT arrived, Wild's men had driven off Lee's attackers. In the following days, the army shuttled Chamberlain's men back and forth between Wilson's Wharf and Fort Powhatan, although the expected strike never materialized. The regiment's only casualties during the occupation of the James had occurred a week earlier. On 16 May Lt. Charles N. W. Cunningham led an unauthorized foraging party of about twenty men out from City Point and was attacked by a much larger Rebel force. One Union soldier, Pvt. David Miller of Company D, was killed, four were wounded, and two were captured.[25] A military commission met to investigate the incident. Even before the commission had reached a conclusion, General Hinks expressed severe criticism of Cunningham's conduct, contrasting the white officer's behavior with the courageous example of a black sergeant.[26]

Hinks did not use the 37th USCT more actively in Butler's assault on the Petersburg-Richmond line because of grave concerns about the unit's military fitness, especially the lack of training for combat. Most of its companies had not had the opportunity for sufficient drill and target practice before the campaign began. Furthermore, the soldiers were still armed with the muskets condemned only months before. As late as 12 May, Chamberlain complained that over three hundred muskets were damaged in some way. One gun had burst at the breach, many of the locks were too weak to explode a cap, and some of the cones on the firing mechanisms were broken. The regiment could simply not be expected to fight effectively with the weapons the men had been given. In addition, the unit was still well under full strength. Even with the latest recruits added at City Point and along the James, the 37th USCT had only 506 enlisted men on its rolls and 23 commissioned officers. Even more disturbing than the limited manpower, lack of training, and poor equipment was the dissension within the regiment.[27]

One serious conflict involved both commissioned and noncommissioned officers. In June 1864 Chamberlain chided Capt. George A. Bailey, who commanded Company H, for his inability to handle one of his sergeants, Andrew Marshall, and for cautioning Lt. A. C. Rembaugh to obey all orders that he received from Bailey "without remonstrance." The evidence suggests that the problem had less to do with racial tension and more to do with Bailey's incompetence. The captain wanted to exchange Sergeant Marshall for another sergeant, but Chamberlain told him either to manage Marshall or to jail him. The episode was resolved only when Bailey resigned his commission on 14 August 1864. Two months later Rembaugh transferred to Company C and became its captain, while Sgt. Andrew Marshall would rise to the rank of regimental quartermaster sergeant.[28] In another case, Chamberlain refused to accept the recommendation of one of his senior captains to demote a corporal in Company A. There was, the lieutenant colonel believed, insufficient cause. Since "the man says that he will do better," Chamberlain ordered Captain Nitzsche to "try him once more."[29] The incident hinted at more serious issues in the black regiment. Should the commander consider the social or cultural background of the newly recruited ex-slaves in imposing military regulations, or should he provide greater latitude than he might use with white recruits?[30] If he did, and it appeared that Chamberlain had done so in this case, would he undermine the legitimate authority of his subordinate officers? A more disturbing series of events led to the court-martial of Pvt. Silas Miller of Company B on 28 May. Miller was charged with disobeying orders and striking Lt. Owen A. Hendrick. "The offense was so glaring, and committed in the presence of so many enlisted men," wrote Chamberlain, "that it would be injurious to the service and discipline of the regt to pass it over lightly." He had been deeply angered by the private's conduct, in part because had "it not been for the assistance rendered by Capt. Cutler, Lt. Hendrick would have been overpowered and probably injured seriously by the accused."[31] The records do not show what caused Miller to attack the lieutenant, but it was a bad sign for the company. Taken collectively, the incidents revealed that the regiment was handicapped by problems involving discipline.

A further sign of discord were the number of men who were absent without leave or who deserted the regiment at this time. The largest wave of desertions would occur while the 37th USCT was serving in North Carolina during Reconstruction, but even in 1864 the rate was higher than that of the other black units. Significantly, these desertions tended to occur when the regiment was not actively campaigning. The commander of Company A later explained that "owing to the strict discipline by the officers in command of the Company, several desertions have occurred" but only three individuals had been court-martialed. A private from Roanoke Island who deserted from Company E in late August 1864 maintained, years later, that "I was forced to Leave my regiment on account of being unable to Serve after my officers refuse given me a leaf of absence." Desertion was not restricted to enlisted men. The records of Company D indicate that at the end of October 1864, Lt. William P. Chase "Deserted from Regt." Chase had been a private in the 1st Massachusetts Infantry Volunteers when he accepted a commission in the 37th USCT the previous year. Before being charged with desertion, he had been in and out of the hospital with fevers and diarrhea. Whether his illness played a role in his subsequent departure is unclear from the records, but he soon returned to his regiment. Within months he was up on charges again, this time for "Drunkeness on duty." The army cashiered Chase on 20 February 1865.[32]

Adding to Chamberlain's personnel problems was his increasing concern about the character of his assistant surgeon, William A. Crouse. The complaints that he received about Crouse echoed those laid against the assistant surgeon of the 35th USCT, John De Grasse. If the charges were similar, however, the outcome was strikingly different. Less than a month after Crouse joined the regiment in late March 1864, Chamberlain reported that he "was in the habit of getting intoxicated while in the performance of his duties." Crouse was warned by Chamberlain and put on a month's probation. A short time after his probation ended, and while in charge of the sick of the 7th New York Battery, Crouse "was found in the Dispensary of the Battery, in a *beastly state of intoxication*." Military authorities placed him under arrest. Once again, Crouse promised Chamberlain under oath that he would drink no more. His sobriety lasted until 4 July, when the regiment camped at Point of Rocks.

Crouse's alcoholism and negligence was more clear-cut than De Grasse's, but, unlike De Grasse, Crouse was released from confinement and ordered to report to Surgeon Dubois of the 38th USCT for service in that regiment.[33]

General Hinks and other senior officers were well aware of the problems in the 37th USCT. Certainly Hinks did not believe that the regiment measured up to the readiness of most of his other black units and thus assigned it more often than the others to labor details. When a brigade commander in a different division needed a "working party of 200 or 300 men daily" on fortifications, the commander of the Twentieth Corps, Gen. W. T. H. Brooks, asked Hinks, "Can't you send him the Thirty-seventh Colored Troops?"[34] Even fatigue duty could be dangerous. One private of the 37th USCT recalled that while unloading big guns from steamboats at City Point, the lifting caused "a rupture of my entrails." Fatigue detail may have injured other soldiers as well. It obviously hindered Chamberlain's ability to prepare his men for battle. The regiment was caught in a vicious circle. Because Hinks distrusted its fighting ability, the 37th USCT received a disproportionate share of fatigue duties, ensuring that Chamberlain would have even greater difficulty properly training his soldiers. The test came in June 1864. While much of the division took part in an engagement in front of Petersburg on 15 June, Hinks kept back the 37th USCT at Point of Rocks; on 28 June, he detached the regiment from the First Brigade with orders to report to Eighteenth Army Corps headquarters. Hinks informed the headquarters that the move was necessary because the 37th USCT was "largely composed of new recruits, and but partially organized." Because this regiment and four others were unfit for duty in line of battle, he had not used them in the recent fighting. "Justice to these troops" and the good of the service required "that these five regiments . . . be sent to a camp of instruction, and prepared for effective service. As they now are I am unwilling to risk them in battle."[35] The length of the sick list and the large number of daily casualties within the division, however, meant that Hinks could not release the 37th USCT immediately. Instead, the regiment remained where it was for a few more days and was assigned picket duty along the river. Whereas Gen. W. F. Smith had "been most unreasonably alarmed" by the condition of the regiments, Hinks was more balanced. He cited other black regiments in his division that had performed very well and attributed the 37th USCT's inefficiency primarily to the fact that it had "had little or no opportunity for drill."[36]

The attitude of Hinks merely reflected the concerns already voiced by

Chamberlain. The lieutenant colonel had previously asked headquarters to relieve the regiment of its duties in the field so it could be sent to a training camp. He explained that the "events of the last two months have convinced me that it is impossible to properly drill and discipline a new organization in the field." Compounding the problem that he outlined, the three companies recruited since leaving Hampton had "not had the opportunity to drill since they were organized as the regt. has been constantly employed on works day and night." Chamberlain did not believe that the men had enough confidence in themselves or in their arms to make a stand under fire in the open field. Properly trained, he argued, they would do credit to themselves and their flag in future combat. Senior officials agreed with Hinks and Chamberlain and on 4 July transferred the regiment to a training camp under Gen. Charles J. Paine "for purposes of discipline and drill."[37]

The time in the training camp not only allowed the 37th USCT to improve its military effectiveness, but also enabled it to reach its full complement of companies. Chamberlain partially filled Company H by enrolling men from various places along the James River and by sending Captain Bailey to look for recruits at Point Lookout and along the eastern shore. When the company was finally mustered in on 13 August 1864, it had relatively few North Carolinians, and the Virginian conscripts had been drawn from at least nine different locations within the state. The company's first sergeant, Henry S. White, and several other noncommissioned officers, however, were from Washington, North Carolina, perhaps reflecting their seniority in the company.[38] In November Company H added thirteen recruits from the District of Columbia and in the next year enlisted over twenty men at Wilmington, North Carolina. By contrast, the last two companies to be mustered into the regiment were drawn entirely from North Carolina. The Confederate withdrawal from the state to help protect the threatened Petersburg-Richmond line may have increased the opportunities for slaves in North Carolina to flee to Union-held territories in the eastern part of the state. But many of these fugitives discovered that they now faced the risk of being impressed to serve as laborers in Virginia. On 22 August 1864 Ulysses S. Grant had telegraphed Butler from City Point. Grant had seen a newspaper report that there were "a large number of negro men at Newbern who will not enlist." The Quartermaster's Department in Virginia needed one thousand laborers to replace black enlisted men who had moved into the field. Butler replied that he believed the accounts to be at least partially true. He promised that he would "send an energetic Staff officer to investigate the report and bring up the Negros."[39]

In the face of this threat, some freedmen may have chosen to enlist in the 37th USCT, or other regiments, rather than to be impressed as laborers and sent out of North Carolina. Nevertheless, Lieutenant Rembaugh was able to tap considerable black manpower at New Bern in late August and early September. In less than three weeks, Rembaugh enrolled ninety-one men at New Bern and a handful from Roanoke Island. By the first week in September, he had filled Company I with well over one hundred men and had started on the last company. When Company K was mustered into service at Chafin's Farm on 27 November, it contained only one soldier who was not from North Carolina, as Rembaugh found enough men in New Bern during the first two weeks of September to form the bulk of the company. It was not until 20 January 1865 that any soldiers were added from outside the state.[40]

While the 37th USCT drilled at the training camp, the remainder of the First Brigade was occupying trenches in front of Petersburg and suffering a slow drain of casualties. During that time, six of its soldiers were killed and another twenty-seven were wounded in scattered skirmishes. In early August, after the 37th USCT had completed its training and while the bulk of the First Brigade was still stationed near Petersburg, the regiment received orders to perform picket duty across the Appomattox River. Through part of this period, the 37th USCT and the 36th USCT were close enough for their officers, if not their enlisted men, to exchange visits.[41] Not until late in the month did Chamberlain receive orders to move his men back to Wilson's Wharf to replace the troops stationed there. At the end of August the regiment was finally ordered to rejoin the reorganized brigade prior to attacking the Richmond defenses. The First Brigade of the Third Division, Eighteenth Army Corps, now consisting of the 37th USCT, 1st USCT, and 22nd USCT, was commanded by Gen. Charles Paine.[42] In preparation for casualties that would result from the assault, Chamberlain requested the return of the regimental surgeon, Arthur H. Cowdry, from the brigade hospital.[43]

On 28 September 1864 the 37th USCT joined the 1st USCT at Harrison Landing, and together they marched to their divisional headquarters at Deep Bottom. When they arrived early the next morning, the 22nd USCT and their brigade commander, Colonel Holman, were waiting for them. General Butler was concentrating troops for an attack across the James River, hoping to smash through the Confederate defenses around Richmond and capture the capital. Even if the assault failed, it would draw off Confederate troops from Petersburg and allow the Army of the Potomac to defeat Confederate forces south of the James.[44] It was a complex plan. In total, over 26,000 men made up a two-pronged attempt to punch through the exterior line. While Gen. Edward Ord attacked the Confederate defenses on the Varina road with seven brigades, Gen. David Birney led the Twentieth Corps and a division of the Eighteenth Corps against the Confederate entrenchments on New Market Heights. Like the 36th USCT, Chamberlain's regiment was part of General Paine's all-black division that had been added to Birney's right wing of the Union attack. While the two infantry columns moved against the southern fortifications, Butler sent Gen. August Kautz's cavalry to sweep north around the upper flank of the Southern defense.

During the subsequent assault on New Market Heights, Holman's brigade was held in reserve directly behind the initial line of attack, but, unlike the other two brigades in Paine's division, it did not take part in the battle.[45] When Colonel Draper's brigade attacked the Confederate line, Holman used the men of the 22nd USCT as skirmishers to cover Draper's left flank, but he did not move forward either the 37th USCT or the 1st USCT. Clearly, he still had concerns about the preparedness of the two regiments. In the afternoon, after the Heights had been captured, the 37th USCT endured hard marching but little fighting in an unsuccessful advance on Laurel Hill Church. By evening the whole brigade "was ordered to the left [of the line] and worked all night, throwing up works in the rear of the fort on Chaffin's [sic] Farm." The next day the 37th USCT took part in a Union defense that broke a Confederate counterattack. Holman's three regiments held the Union line just to the right of Fort Harrison, however, and did not face the brunt of the Confederate onslaught. Significantly, when the enemy was driven back, the 22nd USCT was the regiment Holman directed out of the trenches to seize a small lunette in front of their position. Although the 37th USCT lost Capt. Daniel Foster in the fighting around Fort Harrison, the regiment suffered only three enlisted men killed and sixteen wounded—considerably fewer losses than those of the other units involved in the fighting.[46]

Most of October saw the 37th USCT manning trenches on the lines southeast of Richmond, but late in the month the regiment took part in an expedition toward the Williamsburg road in an attempt to break through the northern flank of the Richmond defenses, or at least pin down Confederate defenders. Grant had ordered Butler to demonstrate against the left flank of the Confederate lines in front of Richmond. The primary goal of the strike was to prevent Robert E. Lee from sending Southern reinforcements south to Petersburg, where Grant had called for an attack in force. Acting on what he believed to be the Confederate positions, Butler directed Gen. Alfred H. Terry's Twentieth Corps to extend northward, probing and putting pressure on the Confederate line from the New Market road to the Charles City road. At the same time, Gen. Godfrey Weitzel's Eighteenth Corps, screened by August Kautz's cavalry, was to swing around behind Terry's men, drive north, and then turn the Confederate flank, which Butler believed ended at the Williamsburg road. On the evening of 26 October, as the soldiers prepared for the next day's action, spirits were high. Black reporter Thomas M. Chester described that night as "a lively one, particularly among the colored troops under Col. Holman" during which the men sang tunes such as "John Brown," "Rally Round the Flag," and the "Colored Volunteer." According to Chester, "never was an army in better spirits, or more confident of a victory."[47]

The first Federal troops began their march at 4:00 A.M., but the difficult terrain and a breakdown in communications between Federal units slowed the advance of Weitzel's soldiers. Weitzel, who had assumed command of the Eighteenth Corps after General Ord was wounded at Fort Harrison, was a very cautious man, and his leadership reflected that trait. Lt. Gen. James Longstreet, who was in charge of the Confederate defenses around Richmond, correctly guessed the Union objective sufficiently early to realize that Weitzel's thrust was the real danger. He began pulling regiments out of his line and rushing them north to the Williamsburg road to reinforce Gen. Charles W. Fields. Despite Longstreet's action, Weitzel's first units reached the road at about 1:00 P.M., behind schedule but well ahead of most of the Confederate reinforcements. But the opportunity for a successful Federal thrust was lost as Weitzel hesitated, refusing to launch an assault for two and a half hours. By the time his forces moved forward, there were enough Confederates defending the existing fortifications to smash the attack.[48]

The 37th USCT, with the rest of Holman's First Brigade, did not move out until 5:00 A.M., bringing up the rear of the Union column as a reserve. When they reached the Williamsburg road, the Union regiments were already attacking the Confederate position astride the road. During this engagement, Maj. Philip Weinmann, newly promoted to the 37th USCT and commanding the division's company of sharpshooters, led his men out as skirmishers but the rest of Holman's brigade was not engaged. Holman soon received orders to move the brigade farther to the north, across the York River Railroad and up the Nine Mile road, "until he should come within sight of the enemy's line, and then to halt and report to corps headquarters."[49] It was a recipe for inactivity. Once in contact with the enemy, Colonel Holman, like Weitzel, hesitated before attacking the Confederate position. As the Union soldiers began to advance, Confederate cavalrymen were sighted, "estimated by Lieutenant-Colonel Chamberlain to be about 1,500 to 2,000 strong." Holman apparently accepted Chamberlain's exaggerated figures because he ordered the 37th USCT, in open ground to the right of the road, to form a square in preparation for a cavalry strike. Positioning men in a square was an anachronism by 1864, but it still appeared in most infantry manuals used by Civil War officers.[50] Less excusable was Chamberlain's inflated estimate of the enemy. The only cavalry facing the Union sweep around the Confederate flank was Maj. Gen. Martin W. Gary's under-strength brigade—about a thousand men —and only a small part of that command was at the Nine Mile road. Just after the battle, General Longstreet reported that Gary had only a "small squadron," or a "small force," picketing the road. Although by the time he wrote his memoirs the defenders had become "a strong picket force," they never came close to the numbers Chamberlain claimed, raising doubts about his command abilities.[51]

Shortly after issuing his instructions to Chamberlain, Holman ordered the 1st and 22nd USCT to attack the Confederate defenses, which consisted of lightly manned earthworks. This assault, Longstreet would recall, "was so well executed . . . that the guard was taken by surprise and pushed away from its post by the first attack, losing its field-works and a piece of artillery." The 1st USCT, striking across open ground, managed to capture part of the enemy's work and two cannons, but the 22nd USCT became entangled in heavy brush and, under heavy fire, lost all cohesion. Gary's brigade of dismounted South Carolina cavalrymen was able to drive back the isolated 1st USCT. The 22nd USCT failed to effectively support the 1st USCT for a number of reasons. It had to attack through woods and heavy undergrowth that broke up the regiment's formation. More confusion resulted from an instruction to change marching by the right flank to marching by the left flank. Before order could be restored, the regimental commander, Colonel Kiddoo, was seriously wounded and some of the new recruits broke in panic. Another officer of the 22nd USCT later explained: "Had the regiment left its recruits behind I think we could have gone in. They kept firing their muskets while advancing and in the midst of the excitement broke and ran, causing the worst of confusion."[52] Regardless of what caused the collapse of the 22nd USCT, Holman could have ordered the 37th USCT to support the gains made by the 1st USCT. His refusal to put Chamberlain's regiment into the fight ensured the Federal defeat, just as it suggested a serious lack of confidence in the regiment.

By the time the assault had been thrown back, Holman was wounded and Chamberlain assumed command of the brigade. At this point, Weitzel recalled the black soldiers, having made the decision that their gains were "too late in the day to be of any service." Squads of soldiers collected all of the wounded who could be found, a strong rear guard of skirmishers from the 37th USCT moved out, and the brigade rejoined Weitzel's troops. At dark, the entire Eighteenth Corps began a retreat to its original camp. A New Hampshire soldier described the withdrawal. "Everything is mixed together," he wrote. "Utter confusion reigns; teams, artillery, ambulances and infantry all jumbled together, and all heavily loaded; mud and water in many places knee-deep in the roads, the night pitchy dark, the rain pouring in torrents." An officer in the 5th USCT summed it up concisely: "The move was a grand fizzle."[53] One of his sergeants recalled: "Rain had fallen during the day and the road was flooded with water, this together with the darkness, rendered it almost impossible to get along. And as the column wound slowly down the road, doubtless, we presented quite a forelorne [sic] appearance, as one after another, missing their footing would fall full length in the mud, and then call piteously for a comrade to lend a helping hand, but we bore it patiently."[54] Even soldiers in the 37th USCT who had not fired a shot all day did not escape unscathed. In the darkness Pvt. Martin Wilkirk of Company C stepped into a "stump hole," wrenching his left leg and hip.[55] It was one small example of the suffering exacted by the retreat. Union attempts—both north and south of the James River—to flank the Confederate lines had failed. Despite their initial surprise, Southern reinforcements arrived just in time. Then, as Confederate general Alexander wrote, "during the whole of that black & rainy night, great columns of defeated troops were floundering back home through mud & darkness."[56] It was a sad end to a promising attack.

Although the new divisional commander, Alonzo Draper, praised the determined efforts of Major Weinmann in leading the sharpshooters in this action, no one else in the 37th USCT was cited when Butler summarized the achievements of his army. A large number of black soldiers and white officers in other regiments were singled out for commendation, but none from the

37th. In part this reflected the frequent use of the regiment as a reserve force. More significantly, however, it indicated that the senior command and even the brigade commander had little faith in the unit's military preparedness. Weinmann had just been promoted and transferred after distinguishing himself as leader of the division's sharpshooters against New Market Heights.[57] His transfer to Chamberlain's regiment may have been an attempt to improve its performance.

—⁂—

As the assaults of Confederate fortifications north of the James subsided in a temporary stalemate behind ever-expanding trenches, the 37th USCT had the opportunity to address some pressing regimental concerns. Foremost were problems with the noncommissioned officers. Most of the cases involved the contempt of senior noncommissioned officers for commissioned officers. For "disrespectful and mutinous language to his superior officer," for example, Sgt. John Crawford of Company C was paraded in front of his unit and stripped of his sergeant's chevrons in late October 1864. On 4 November Sgt. Charles Nelson and Cpl. Nicholas Lammerson, both in Company B, were reduced for "disobedience of orders and contemptuous language towards their Co. commander." Less than two weeks later, two more sergeants were demoted: Sgt. Abel Reed of Company D, who once served as a recruiting officer, was charged "for being intoxicated," and Sgt. Henry Harrison of Company C faced punishment "for Abusing men of his company."[58] The fact that these incidents took place in some of the longest-serving companies indicates the severity of discipline problems in the regiment.

Another difficulty was presented by Sgt. Thomas B. N. Fitzpatrick, a white noncommissioned officer. Fitzpatrick had been a member of the twelve-man detachment recruited in Boston by Chamberlain in early January 1864. Born in Massachusetts, he was a twenty-four-year-old porter when he enlisted in the 37th USCT. Unlike most of the other Boston recruits, Fitzpatrick was not a veteran. On 8 February 1864 he became first sergeant of Company A, but sometime around the attack at Fort Harrison, Captain Nitzsche had placed him under arrest. Nitzsche had requested that he be demoted and transferred to a white regiment for obvious reasons. Chamberlain disagreed with the action. The sergeant had been under arrest for six weeks, possible court-martial charges were pending, and his services were needed in the company. "I see no reason," Chamberlain wrote, "why this should interfere with the discipline of

Capt. Nitzsche's company as the Sergeant has already been severely punished by being so long under arrest." Fitzpatrick was released on 9 November. In February he was once again under arrest, and this time the new commander, Col. Nathan Goff, reduced him to the ranks and tried unsuccessfully to get him transferred to the 4th Massachusetts Cavalry Regiment.[59] Fitzpatrick remained in the regiment as an anomaly, a white private who had to take orders from black noncommissioned officers. He finally solved the company's problem by deserting in Boston while on a furlough.

William A. Green, the regimental chaplain, also tried to use the lull in the fighting to take up a pressing concern of the black soldiers who had left families behind. Green was the third chaplain appointed by General Wild and the first who was white. Although he may not have provided the type of spiritual guidance that some of the men wanted, he worked hard for their general welfare. "Faithful and conscientious," Green spent a great deal of time teaching the enlisted men to read and write. In addition, he served as a critical link between the soldiers and their families in North Carolina and Virginia. By July 1864, the regiment had not been paid in more than four months. The lack of wages inconvenienced many officers, but it created enormous hardship for most families of the enlisted men. At the same time, nearly every man in the regiment owed the government money for extra clothing, due in large part to their heavy fatigue duties and arduous work in the trenches. A large percentage of the men's back pay would be required to keep them decently clothed for the next six months. Consequently, those soldiers with families would likely have little to send home. Even when the regiment was finally paid, the men faced the very real problem of getting what money they could spare safely to their families. Chaplain Green's solution was to request permission for a twenty-day trip to Norfolk, Portsmouth, New Bern, and Roanoke Island to personally deliver the funds to the families. "The money cannot be sent by express," he explained, "on account of the families not being known; and at Roanoke Island there is no Express office." If the chaplain shared the soldiers' distrust of officials at these places, he was prudent enough not to voice it in his letter. Nevertheless, his postwar experiences as assistant superintendent on Roanoke Island would convince him of the extreme exploitation of both the soldiers and their families by some Federal officials.[60]

Although active campaigning in Virginia had ended for the year, the physical hardships of the 37th USCT had not. Company K, in particular, suffered badly at this time. Perhaps because it had only recently joined the regiment (at

Chafin's Farm in November 1864), the men were not prepared or equipped for what they experienced in the trenches around Richmond. Many years later, a number of them remembered their service around Chafin's Farm with bitterness. In a pension application on behalf of former Pvt. John Whitfield, former Pvt. Willis Elliot testified that Whitfield had been "a well and hearty man from all appearances till after the march from Harrison's Landing to Chapins [*sic*] Farm. We lay out in snow & ice. He was taken with cough bleeding at Lungs & complained of back & breast also had diarrhoea & piles & was sick all through service." Sgt. Thomas Kelly remembered that several men became ill after they "had to lay out in snow & sleet without tents." Long after the war was over, the daughter of Charles Oats learned from his comrades that her father's extensive postwar mental problems were, they believed, the result of an illness contracted from exposure and cold at Chafin's Farm.[61]

While Company K suffered through a Virginia winter, most of the 37th USCT left the state. In early December, when the company was held back to receive extra training, the rest of the regiment—as part of General Paine's division, along with Gen. Adelbert Ames's division of white soldiers—was detached from the Army of the James to participate in the first expedition against Fort Fisher.[62] By the fall of 1864, the U.S. War Department, under growing pressure from the navy, had grudgingly concluded that a joint operation was needed to close the mouth of the Cape Fear River and thus cut off the flow of supplies shipped through Wilmington to the Confederacy. Capturing the river would also seal up the Southern commerce raiders using the port. General Grant, who did not place great importance on the capture of Fort Fisher at this time, although he understood the pressures confronting President Lincoln, was unwilling to send more than the minimum complement of men and materiel that would be needed. As a result, success would depend on the navy's ability to reduce the fort from the sea before any land attack.[63] The navy ordered Rear Adm. David D. Porter east from the Mississippi in September to command the operation, but it was still unprepared when Grant, after months of lending minor support, abruptly gave his approval for the expedition on 2 December and directed the combined forces to move "without a moment's delay." Grant had just received reports that Gen. Braxton Bragg had left Wilmington with eight thousand Confederate troops to oppose William T. Sherman in Georgia, and the Federal commander wanted to attack Fort Fisher before they could return. Grant's decision to send little more than five thousand men, however, made it clear that he, like Porter, expected that the navy would destroy the fort.[64] Their assumption was based on the belief that a naval bombardment, aided by the explosion of a powder ship just offshore, could reduce the huge earthwork to rubble, or at least render the garrison unable to effectively resist. Events would prove them wrong.

The Union soldiers chosen to attack Fort Fisher, including eight companies of the 37th USCT as part of Col. Elias Wright's Third Brigade, began to hurriedly embark on transports on 8 December.[65] Once on board, the men were stuck on the cramped ships for five days waiting for the fleet to leave due to poor coordination between the army and the navy. On the morning of 13 December, Porter's fleet and the powder ship were finally ready.[66] Only after their departure did they learn that their overall army commander would be not General Weitzel but rather General Butler, who as commander of the Department of Virginia and North Carolina had the right and the seniority to assume control of land operations.[67] Once at sea, the vessels steamed out of the James into the Chesapeake Bay; then, in an attempt to confuse any Confederate spies that might be watching, turned up the Potomac River. Once darkness fell, they reversed course and headed for open water. The weather was good and the winds light for their transit to the vicinity of Cape Fear. The transports arrived by 15 December, but Porter and his fleet were delayed until 18 December, when the weather had begun to deteriorate. Butler took the army transports back to Beaufort, North Carolina, to ride out the storm and to resupply some of the vessels with coal and water. He would not, however, let any of the troops disembark. Only after the storm was over did he lead the vessels, some now damaged, back to Cape Fear, where Porter was collecting his scattered fleet. Because of the delays, Butler's transports did not get back to the waters off Fort Fisher until Christmas Eve. Conditions on the ships during the two-week transit must have been dreadful for the black soldiers. The four-day gale that struck on 20 December was so severe that on some ships all regimental horses had to be shot and dumped overboard. To make matters worse, in addition to the general seasickness and discomfort caused by rough weather, two soldiers in the 37th USCT died of an unspecified disease.[68] Then, in what must have been growing frustration, the men could only watch the assault on Fort Fisher from their transports.

The first attempt to take the massive earthworks, which dominated the entrance to the Cape Fear River, depended on the partial destruction or silencing of the fortification by exploding the powder ship *Louisiana* near its walls. The fort would be further reduced by the bombardment of the fleet, then occupied by the army. The actual assault consisted of a series of disjointed, ineffective actions that reflected the lack of cooperation between Butler and Porter. At 1:40 A.M., in the darkness of 24 December, Cmdr. Alexander C. Rhind and fourteen sailors grounded the powder ship, carrying too few explosives too far out from the beach. The explosion had no serious effect on the fort.[69] The only enemy soldiers disoriented by the blast were some North Carolina Junior Reserves who were camping on the beach nearby. They were shaken from their blankets "like popcorn from a popper," but those inside the fort were unaffected. Shortly before noon, even before the army transports had arrived, Porter's fleet began to shell the earthworks. The sailors inflicted only minor damage despite the fact that they fired off almost half of their munitions, but the clouds of smoke hanging over the fort and his faith in naval bombardment convinced Porter otherwise.[70] He assumed that Fort Fisher had been seriously damaged and that the army would have an easy task. Not until Christmas Day, after the admiral had landed the white soldiers of Ames's division and a small group of black soldiers on the beach, did the invaders realize that the fort was largely untouched. On the beach, the Federal soldiers advanced to within fifty yards of the earthworks before they pulled back and hesitated. Weitzel believed that it "would be butchery to order an attack" and that even to leave them on the beach overnight could be disastrous. Despite Porter's frustration, Butler quickly agreed. The first attempt was over and the soldiers reembarked, although not before seven hundred New York troops spent two nerve-racking nights on the beach. Once everyone was on board, the transports steamed back to Virginia and the recriminations began. The 37th USCT had not even put foot on North Carolina soil. On the evening of 29 December, after three uncomfortable weeks on the cramped transports, the regiment rejoined the two companies left behind in Virginia.[71]

A renewed attempt to reduce Fort Fisher was launched early in 1865. Grant had changed his mind about the importance of seizing both the fortification and the port of Wilmington. With Sherman's army moving north through the Carolinas, a Federal-held Wilmington would guarantee him a critical supply line and expedite his advance toward Virginia. Grant decided to use the same troops that had constituted the first expedition, plus an additional brigade of white soldiers under Col. Joseph C. Abbot, despite Admiral Porter's hostility to the use of black troops. "We want white men here—not niggers," Porter told his aide. On 2 January 1865 Paine's black soldiers were ordered from the line and marched down to Bermuda Hundred. Three days later they once

again boarded transports for Fort Fisher, but this time under the overall command of General Terry. Now that the plan had the full support of Grant and
Henry Halleck, the expedition had everything that it might possibly need to
capture Fort Fisher. Unlike the first venture, the army provided siege equipment and related supplies, several batteries of rifled guns and plenty of ammunition, and extra coal for the fleet. With the additional brigade, Terry had
almost nine thousand men in his transports. Moreover, Grant ordered Gen.
Philip H. Sheridan to send an additional division of troops to Baltimore to be
held there in case Terry needed reinforcements.[72]

Once again the soldiers, most of whom were crowded into decrepit old
crafts, were battered by storms at sea. The conditions for both white and
black troops were miserable. Rufus Noble, a white soldier from Pennsylvania, wrote his family: "We got on the 'Triton,' a dirty lousy old hulk as
could be found looked like a hog pen just shovelled out got 2 or 3 bales of
straw in & got it tramped dry as if you had wintered a lot of Pigs in it." Even
some of the pilots and crew were concerned about the fitness of the vessels
and put to sea only because they were ordered to do so. On Noble's transport,
with the hatches lashed down and cracks hastily caulked, life below deck became ghastly. When the storm peaked off Cape Hatteras, "all crowded below
that could get & between tobacco juices, heaving stomachs, stench of a lot of
dutch, swearing & black guarding it was next to Pandemonium."[73] Conditions on the vessel carrying the 37th USCT were no better.

On 8 January, after a battering that forced some boats to limp back to Fort
Monroe, the remaining transports rendezvoused with Porter's fleet off Beaufort. Five days later, after waiting for the rough water to subside, the first
soldiers of General Ames's division began to disembark. Paine's black soldiers had all reached the beach by midafternoon. The landing was wet, difficult, and dangerous. The commander of Paine's First Brigade, Col. J. W.
Ames, described the technique used to land the men. As the landing boats
approached the surf, they dropped small anchors and let the boats ride in
on the surf. As the surf receded, sailors leaped overboard and steadied the
boats while the soldiers "climbed over the sides into knee-deep water, carrying knapsacks and the sacred ammunition high up on fixed bayonets, and ran
for the shore, chased by the crested advance of the succeeding billow." It took
about five hours to get all of the black soldiers on the beach. An officer in one
black regiment summed it up: "High surf, all got wet, but none hurt."[74] Once
ashore, rather than attacking Fort Fisher, the primary task assigned to Paine

and Abbot was the creation of a defensive line from the ocean to the river facing north toward Wilmington to prevent Southern reinforcements from reaching the fortification.

That task became more critical when Terry learned, after the troops had landed, that the six thousand Confederate soldiers of General Hoke's division had not left to fight Sherman. Instead, they were still posted in Wilmington and at the fortifications below the city, where they presented a threat to Terry's land operations. Establishing a defensive line across the peninsula was crucial to protect the vulnerable landing area and to prevent Hoke from going to the fort's aid. The 37th USCT and 5th USCT, in line of battle, led the advance across the peninsula, marching much of the way through swamp and marshy thickets. Shortly after dark, the advanced units reached the Cape Fear River and the black soldiers immediately began fortifying a line. After surveying the area and reviewing scouting reports, General Terry chose a defensive line closer to the fort and relocated the regiments, and the work began again. Two miles north of Fort Fisher, Paine's division began to build fortifications from the Cape Fear River shore across the peninsula to join the line that Abbot's men were constructing on the ocean side. Spades were issued, brush was cleared, and throughout the night the men constructed a line of breastworks fronted by abatis across the entire peninsula.[75] With little rest, the job continued through the following day until a strong continuous line had been established.

On 15 January, while Gen. Braxton Bragg held back Hoke's men in a defensive line anchored on Sugar Loaf Hill, about six miles above the landing site, the Union forces attacked Fort Fisher. A combined assault by Federal soldiers, sailors, and marines eventually overwhelmed the remaining Southern soldiers in the earthworks after they had suffered another massive shelling from the fleet. Although the sailors and marines were driven back in their attempt to break into the fort on the ocean side, the soldiers fought their way into the western gun emplacements gun chamber by gun chamber. After a savage six-hour engagement, the Rebels finally surrendered. Several times the Confederate defenders had fought the attackers to a standstill, and Terry had had to order new brigades into the fight. Only after the Federal assault on Fort Fisher had begun did General Bragg finally direct Hoke's Confederate infantry to attack the Union defensive lines held by the regiments of Paine and Abbott. Hoke's soldiers were able to push Abbott's white pickets back, but on the west side of the line Paine's black troops held firm and skirmished with the Confederate attackers. Before the fighting could become severe, Bragg recalled his brigades. Hoke's men reluctantly obeyed, for many of them believed that their strike would succeed "because the troops in front were blacks." Gen. W. H. C. Whiting, the Confederate commander at Wilmington whom Bragg had replaced, declared on his deathbed that "Bragg was held in check by two negro brigades while the rest of the enemy assaulted and, he didn't even fire a musket."[76]

There was considerable truth to Whiting's accusation, for the Federal line facing Hoke had become depleted during the battle.[77] As the fighting reached a climax, Terry had decided to weaken his rear lines in order to send fresh troops into the fort. Late in the day, all of the sailors and marines who could be found from the repulsed attack on the works were rounded up to replace Abbot's brigade in the defensive line. After Abbot's men were thrown into the fight, Terry considered using Paine's black soldiers. When he finally told Paine to send in "one of the strongest regiments in his division," it was not the 37th USCT that Paine called up but rather another regiment in Colonel Wright's brigade, the 27th USCT. The rest of Wright's brigade, including the 37th USCT, was finally pulled out of Paine's defensive line, leaving only four regiments of Paine's Second Brigade plus the sailors and marines facing the inactive Bragg. Although the 27th USCT was present in the fort when the Confederates surrendered, Wright's other regiments, who were moved too late to take part in the fighting, were soon back in their original positions.[78] Because they were in the fort, it is possible that some troops in the 27th USCT witnessed the surrender of four Confederate artillerymen who would have been highly visible among the defeated soldiers. Pvts. Charles Demsey, Henry Demsey, and Daniel Herring of Company F, 2nd Regiment, North Carolina Artillery, plus Pvt. J. Doyle of the 3rd North Carolina Artillery, who surrendered that day, were all carried on their regimental rolls as "Negro."[79] It was a war of complex alliances.

The fall of Fort Fisher made untenable all of the Southern positions in the Cape Fear estuary. The day after being driven from the earthworks, Bragg directed the Confederate soldiers on the west side of the river to blow up Fort Caswell after disabling all of its heavy guns. They then destroyed the outlying posts at the mouth of the Cape Fear River and retreated upriver to Fort Anderson, across the river from Hoke's defensive line at Sugar Loaf Hill. The way to Wilmington was now open for the Union army to attack, but Terry, advised by Porter to be cautious, probed Hoke's defenses and then waited for the arrival of Gen. John M. Schofield with the Twenty-third Corps from Tennessee before starting to move his army north.[80] As a result, Paine's men remained entrenched at Federal Point until 11 February 1865. On that day, Schofield, the new Federal commander, ordered an advance on Hoke's line at Sugar Loaf Hill, six miles north of the Federal position. The final move on Wilmington had begun.

While the Confederates were pinned down by a demonstration on their front, Schofield planned to land Federal soldiers behind Hoke's position. Paine's soldiers, led by the Second Brigade under Col. J. W. Ames, drove the Rebels from the entrenched picket line back to their main fortification. Then the black soldiers dug in. Continuous skirmishing cost Paine's division two officers and fourteen men killed and seventy-six wounded but achieved little because the Federal troops could not be landed behind the Confederate position. Unable to get his men behind Hoke from the ocean side, Schofield ordered a joint army-navy advance up the west bank of the Cape Fear River. The terrain there caused considerable difficulties, but by 19 February the Federal troops had captured Fort Anderson and were west of Hoke's fortification and heading upriver for Wilmington. In response, Bragg instructed Hoke to abandon his position at Sugar Loaf and retreat northward. While Federal soldiers moved up the west side of the river, Terry ordered an advance on the east side. This time the Third Brigade, with Wright still in command, led the way up the Telegraph road toward Wilmington. For a day and a half the march was unopposed. But five miles from the city the brigade ran into another Confederate entrenchment near Forks Road. Assuming that the position was lightly defended, General Terry directed the 5th USCT, supported by the 1st and 27th USCT, to lead an assault on the line. In fact, the black soldiers faced a full Confederate brigade, and the attack cost the 5th USCT two dead and fifty-one officers and men wounded, including Colonel Wright. Among the injured was Sgt. William Thomas, who had received a musket ball in the right arm. As with many similar wounds, the low velocity musket ball had shattered the bone and resulted in amputation and a long recuperation.[81] Once again, the 37th USCT had been held back and thus largely uninvolved in the skirmish.

Faced with the two-pronged advance, General Bragg, never eager to engage Federal troops, accepted the inevitable and, on the night of 21 February, gave the order to abandon Wilmington. Confederate soldiers led by Generals Hoke and Johnson C. Hagood withdrew from the city's fortifications and

"Recruiting Office for Contrabands on Market Street, Wilmington, N.C.," 1865.
Recruiting was carried on even as the war came to an end. (*Frank Leslie's
Illustrated Newspaper*, 1 April 1865, Courtesy of North Carolina Collection,
University of North Carolina Library at Chapel Hill)

began retreating north. As this was happening, other Rebel soldiers set fire
to all military and naval stores, as well as cotton and tobacco supplies that
could not be transported, rather than have them fall into Union hands. They
also scuttled a Confederate gunboat upriver and burned other ships at the
dock. During the night, the Southern soldiers abandoned their defenses and
at 9:00 A.M. on the morning of 22 February, as a dense pall of smoke hung
over the city, Paine's division entered Wilmington. Residents were deeply divided in their response to the arrival of Union troops. Few white citizens were
seen as the first soldiers entered the city, but African Americans were out in
numbers. Federal soldiers recalled the joy shown by black spectators. Some
were sitting and crying, while others "were shouting and singing, dancing
and hugging each other, and showing the gladness of their hearts." In sharp

contrast, one white resident wrote: "I am completely heartbroken, can't eat, or sleep. God have mercy on me, I feel it will kill me." White anxieties were generally unnecessary, for the occupying army was under strict control. Capt. Charles A. Hill, in Wright's brigade of black soldiers, recalled that both black and white troops "passed thro with the utmost order—no pillaging or plundering of any kind that I saw." These men must have been doubly gratified by the response of the black residents. Hill wrote his wife: "The darkies were indeed jubilant—they line the streets giving tobacco to our men and utterance to the strongest expression of delight."[82]

After a few hours' delay, the Union advance continued—hard on the heels of Bragg's retreating army—toward Northeast Station. A Confederate rear guard skirmished briskly with the Union forces until late in the day before abandoning the bridge over Northeast River. Bragg was allowed to withdraw toward Goldsboro while the Federal troops celebrated their success.[83] The 37th USCT could now go into camp long enough to permit its two companies left at Chafin's Farm in Virginia to rejoin the regiment. In early March the regiment took part in the Union advance to Kinston and Goldsboro. Just south of Kinston, at Wyse Fork, Confederate troops under General Bragg's command tried unsuccessfully for several days to stop the Union advance before retreating and allowing Kinston to be captured. On 16 March Paine's men crossed the Northeast River and reached Cox's Bridge on the Neuse River five days later. Following another skirmish with Southern forces, the brigade pulled back and camped at Faison's Depot along the Wilmington and Weldon Railroad. It remained there until 10 April, when it proceeded to Raleigh in three easy marches and camped about a mile south of the city. The division expected to enter Raleigh and pass in review before General Sherman at 9:00 on the morning of 15 April, but instead the men received the order to stay where they were. They spent all of that day and the next shifting their camps "to better ground."[84] Only on 20 April did officials allow the troops to parade through Raleigh for inspection by Sherman and the townspeople. The division then moved first to the Neuse River and, after General Johnston's surrender of Confederate forces in the Carolinas, relocated to Goldsboro, where it stayed from 1 May to 4 June. On 5 June the Third Brigade, including the 37th USCT, traveled by rail back to Wilmington and went into camp.[85]

The 37th USCT had not proved itself an effective fighting regiment. Both in Virginia and in North Carolina, brigade and division commanders depended on other black regiments wherever possible rather than using the 37th USCT in combat. It remained to be seen how the unit would perform in its new role of provost guard. Although the regiment could not claim to have been battle-hardened, it had suffered numerous casualties and its commander, given the uncertainty of what lay ahead, wanted to begin his new tasks with the ranks full.

During the first three months that the regiment was in North Carolina and while it was actively campaigning, Colonel Goff continued to fill his compa-nies' rolls. In January and February 1865 he mustered recruits into the regi-ment at Newport News and Norfolk, Virginia. Company E added 29 enlist-ees, more than any other company, but overall the 37 USCT grew by more than 80 enlisted men in these two months. The fall of Wilmington allowed large numbers of freedmen the opportunity to volunteer. In the first nine days of March, the regiment acquired 166 new soldiers, almost entirely from the occupied city.[86] Only 5 more men joined the 37th USCT that year. Most of its companies had, by the middle of March, reached their upper strength of 98 en-listed men. That number began to gradually erode over the next few months. By the end of the summer, death, desertion, and disability had significantly cut into the regiment's size. Well over 50 men had died, almost entirely of diseases, and 40 more seized the chance to desert while stationed in North Carolina. A smaller number of soldiers had received medical discharges for physical disabilities. In spite of these losses, when peace came, the regiment still contained 832 enlisted men.[87]

Nevertheless, Major Weinmann requested permission to fill the regiment to its maximum level. He explained that another sixty men were about to be discharged on the surgeon's authority as "entirely unfit for military service." Twenty more, who had been enrolled for one year's service, were due to leave over the next two months, although, Weinmann believed, they "would be only too glad to re-enlist again as they are entirely unable to obtain any employment within the State and their funds are already exhausted."[88] The major was turned down. The 37th USCT added only a few more men before the end of the year, and by the early spring of 1866 the regiment was down to 755 enlisted men. Eight slots for commissioned officers were also unfilled.[89]

## CHAPTER FIVE

# Black Workers in Blue Uniforms

The history of the 1st North Carolina Colored Heavy Artillery (NCCHA), or the 14th U.S. Colored Heavy Artillery (USCHA) as it became in early 1865, presents a sharp contrast to that of the three black infantry regiments previously raised in the state. These artillerymen fought no battles and won little praise. In many ways, however, their experiences reflected those encountered in the other black units that saw little combat and that historians have largely ignored. North Carolina's black artillery regiment was established in early 1864, when Confederate forces threatened New Bern and other Union positions. When the threat passed, the future role of the artillery regiment was uncertain. The official but seldom used term for "heavy" artillery was "foot" artillery, and these units were established to man permanent coastal or river fortifications of which there were few in eastern North Carolina. As well, such regiments had limited use in any future Union campaigns. Unlike field artillery, the men in "heavy" regiments were not trained to handle batteries of mobile guns, although they were drilled and trained to use muskets. While garrison troops seldom catch the attention of historians or artists, the experience of the 1st NCCHA was far from unique among black regiments, especially artillery units, which were frequently assigned this task. The 1st NCCHA never fought off a Confederate attack, and it was never fully officered. The work that it did, though mundane, was essential enough to ensure the regiment's continuation. By the summer of 1864 the growing logistical importance of the Union ports in North Carolina raised the value to the army of a large and regulated labor force. Heavy artillery regiments, when established, had a complement of twelve companies instead of ten companies in an infantry regiment. When all the companies were full, an artillery regiment would number twelve hundred men who could be used in a number of ways. The artillerymen were easier to manipulate and control than black civilians doing the same work, and, if the Rebels launched another offensive, the soldiers could man forts or be added to the infantry reserves. When, in the summer of 1864, the new law authorized Northern agents to recruit in the South for the benefit of their home state, the 1st NCCHA was a major beneficiary.

The measure, introduced by Senator Henry Wilson, was controversial and had triggered considerable opposition in Congress among politicians who felt that the legislation would unfairly allow eastern states, such as Massachusetts, to fill their draft quotas using Southern black recruits. Under this act, any soldiers, white or black, enlisted in the South by these newly appointed agents would be credited against the quotas of the agents' home state. It was the outcome of a prolonged campaign by New England and New York that had been fueled by an uneven blend of altruism and self-interest.[1] Western politicians had correctly predicted that agents would come predominantly from the East. Five days after the bill had passed, the War Department issued General Order No. 227 outlining the regulations to implement the part of the new law that applied to recruiting in Southern states. This directive laid out the terms under which Northern recruiting agents, enrolling Southern freedmen and crediting them to the Northern District, could operate. Agents, with letters of appointment from their governors specifying the "particular field of a State" in which they would operate, were required to report to the commanding officer of the military district and file a copy of their appointment. The number of agents was to be limited. The order also suggested that, to avoid fraudulent practices, the agents be paid a fixed salary for their work rather than a cash payment for each recruit. Commanding officers had the power to arrest or send back to their home state any agent who violated the terms of the general order. Agents were not allowed to recruit anyone already in the military or employed by a military official as teamster, laborer, or guide. In North Carolina, the recruits enrolled by the agents were to be delivered to the rendezvous camp at New Bern, where they would be examined and mustered into service. The men would then be "sent to the regiments for which they may have been enlisted or assigned."[2]

The act to regulate recruitment in the Southern states was, in large part, a response to existing pressures within parts of the North to exploit Southern recruitment in order to meet Northern quotas. Governor James Y. Smith of Rhode Island informed Secretary of War Stanton that "before Maj. Jamison [*sic*] commenced raising the men referred to, he called upon me requesting my assistance. At that time, I assured him of my willingness to pay our bounties to such recruits as he might raise provided he could have the men credited on the quota of the State." The governor indicated that if his state received the credit, Rhode Island would pay the bounties for the balance of the regiment as fast as it was raised. Smith maintained that such action was not an attempt to avoid furnishing more men from his state; Rhode Island, he claimed, had more than met all calls for recruits. Rather, it was "because I desire that Major Jamison [sic] should receive every assistance that Rhode Island can offer him in filling up his regiment."[3] Smith might only have been motivated by a desire to help Maj. Thorndike Jameson, but the agents who quickly moved into North Carolina to find men for units such as the 1st NCCHA were there to get recruits credited to their home state and to make money.

Although the new law and General Order No. 227 provided the opportunity for Governor Smith to get additional men credited to his state, agents from Massachusetts acted first. During the first week of August, at least three Massachusetts agents—N. S. Ellis, W. H. Wrigley, and William R. Black— signed men into the 1st NCCHA. For the first time, recruits were enrolled by Northern agents, promised state bounties, and credited to a Northern state. Since all three of the Massachusetts agents operated out of New Bern, it was unlikely that they were drawing from any new pool of potential recruits. Instead, their success depended on their ability to offer prospective enlistees a three-hundred-dollar bonus, with the promise of a first installment of one hundred dollars. The offer was sufficiently attractive, especially if the regiment was designated for state service, to tempt many African Americans to come forward. In doing so, the young blacks around New Bern were assessing the range of options available to them and choosing what was in their best interest. In fact, the willingness of African Americans to join the 14th USCHA as long as it did not entail service outside their state was remarkably similar to that of the white North Carolinians who enlisted in the 1st and 2nd North Carolina Union Volunteers in 1862.[4] For many, but not all, black men in New Bern in 1864, enlistment in the artillery regiment was the best option available. Thus in the town and the surrounding area, recruiting picked up. Whereas Company A had been able to find only one new soldier since April, the three Massachusetts agents recruited an additional nineteen men for the company during the first nine days of August. The muster rolls of the other companies show a similar pattern of recruitment. The state agents' success perhaps helped fuel the speculation among senior officers that New Bern held a large pool of potential black soldiers. Certain newspaper articles had caused

General Ulysses S. Grant to believe that there were "a large number of negro men at Newbern who would not enlist." Benjamin Butler concurred. He wrote Grant that he had "reason to believe that there is truth in the report. I will send an energetic Staff officer to investigate and bring up the Negroes."[5] Both men were concerned with maximizing the war effort, and both assumed that that was in the best interest of African Americans. If there were available black men in eastern North Carolina, then Butler was ready to decide for these men how their talents and their lives could best be used.

The implicit threat presented by Butler's staff officer may have encouraged some men with dependents in North Carolina to accept the offer—and the bounty—of state recruiting agents to join the 1st NCCHA rather than risk being removed by force to Virginia without any financial benefit. In early September 1864, John W. Francis, Rhode Island's superintendent for recruiting in North Carolina, was able to enlist a considerable number of men at New Bern and have them credited to his state. His efforts were helped by the fact that he was working with the approval and support of Major Jameson. At the end of August, Jameson had written to senior officials requesting that the mustering officer for the District of North Carolina be directed to accredit such recruits "to the State of Rhode Island upon the condition that the Agents of that State pay down the State bounty of three hundred dollars ($300), Two hundred directly to the Recruit, and one hundred to the Mustering Officer, in accordance with General Butler's Order No. 90."[6]

The order to which Jameson referred had been issued by Butler in early August and reflected common attitudes about both the vulnerability of black soldiers and, implicitly, their relative lack of responsibility. Up to this time, the Federal government had provided the only institutional support to the dependent parents, spouses, and children of the black soldiers who enlisted in the South. If Northern states were to get credit toward their quotas for these men, then it was only equitable that the states pick up part of the burden of supporting the soldiers' families. Furthermore, the experience of Northern white soldiers revealed that many recruits had been swindled of part, if not all, of their bounty at the time of their enlistment. In New York, for example, "bounty-brokers" were keeping two hundred dollars or more of the bounties being offered to recruits. Would black soldiers, having fewer powerful advocates, fare any better? Butler had thought not. He also had concerns about the willingness or ability of black soldiers to look after their own kin. As a result, he laid out a series of stipulations in his General Order No. 90. On the enlistment of a black soldier in the army for three years by any state agent, and before the soldier could be credited to any Northern state, one-third of his bounty, usually one hundred dollars, would be placed in the care of the superintendent of recruiting. At the end of the month, those funds would be turned over "to the superintendent of Negro affairs to be expended in aid of the families of Negro soldiers in this department."[7] The order may have been based on the belief that the government could distribute the funds more efficiently than individuals, but it smacked of paternalism and the belief that black soldiers would likely not care for their own dependents. It also meant, effectively, that individual black recruits received only two-thirds of the bounty that white troops from the same state had received.

Despite the attempts by senior officers such as Butler to protect the financial interests of the recruits, inequities continued to occur. Gen. George H. Gordon recalled information that had come out in the court-martial of an officer charged with selling black recruits to a Massachusetts agent. The agent was a copartner in a New Bern–based venture to "buy up Negroes to fill the requisition made upon Massachusetts." A paymaster from the state, who had been allotted $425 for each recruit, had accompanied the agent south. Of that sum, $325 was the state's bounty to recruits and $100 was "hand money" that had been raised by private subscription from towns to assist in meeting their quotas. The agent paid any new recruit that he had signed $200 of the state bounty and kept at least $125 as profit for himself. Although "as sharp a bargain as could be was generally driven with the poor ebony emblems of patriotism," the Massachusetts agent still paid much more than many agents from other states.[8] How much money due the recruits was siphoned off to others? The exact amount will likely never be known. But clearly it was a large amount, because this one particular recruiting agent had reportedly "made ten thousand dollars as his share."[9]

In addition to the problems encountered in regulating unscrupulous state agents, Butler and his subordinates also had to deal with the difficulties of earlier recruiters who had had less money to work with. The availability of Northern bounties might help future volunteers, or at least the Federal government, but it was cold comfort to a commander like Jameson who claimed that he had already incurred a sizable personal debt enlisting soldiers. In September 1864 he requested that the Recruiting Fund reinburse him for expenses he had been forced to cover from his own purse. "Besides the numerous incidental expenses," he wrote, "I have paid three hundred and four dollars ($304) in premiums for one hundred and fifty one [*sic*] Recruits as authorized by an Order from the Provost Marshal General's Office date Jany 11, 1864." Since there was no disbursing officer at New Bern, he asked that the paymaster be directed to reimburse him for these expenses.[10]

Jameson's second challenge, especially in the face of the competing state agents, was to get the men he had previously enlisted retroactively credited to Rhode Island. If he could do that, these recruits would be eligible for Rhode Island's bounty. The Rhode Island state agent was more than willing to assist him. On 22 August, John Francis asked the major to give his opinion "as to the interest and expediency of the General Government having the soldiers accredited to the quota of the State." Three days later Jameson gave Francis the response that he had sought. The four companies Jameson had raised had cost the government no expense other than for rations and clothing, nor had the soldiers received bounties or been credited to any state other than North Carolina.[11]

Jameson summarized the benefits to his men if they could be credited to a Northern state and allowed bounties. It would be an act of fairness, since any future recruits would receive a bounty and the soldiers already enrolled desperately needed financial help. "Both the men and their families," he wrote of the soldiers in his four companies, "are extremely destitute, and are in painful want of this bounty." His troops were the best, the brightest, and the most patriotic of the freedmen, and it would be unfair to reward fresh recruits only now coming forward and not compensate the earliest volunteers. There was a danger that they would blame the officers or, at the very least, that their unhappiness would erode their military efficiency. "To give these men this bounty," Jameson advised, "would not only be an act of mercy and justice, and secure the union and efficacy of the organization—but give interest and enthusiasm to the whole recruited operation." Unwisely, Jameson went beyond recommending bounties and proposed that "the raising of this regiment could once be placed under the patronage of the state of Rhode Island."[12] Since senior commanders were already concerned with limiting state control of black troops, nothing came of Jameson's suggestions.

———⸓⸓———

Historians have generally depicted the recruiting agents as both ineffective in their own jobs and prejudicial to military effectiveness. Driven by personal motives, agents soon antagonized local military authorities and hindered recruiting efforts as much as they helped. In North Carolina, however, the agents seemed to have been very active, if not ethical. Indeed, the role that various state agents played in the development of the 1st NCCHA differs from the standard view of recruiting agents. Historians for the most part conclude that the Northern agents, who operated for about a six-month period before new legislation rescinded their powers, enrolled few blacks. According to the official record, 1,050 agents were able to draw only 5,052 recruits. To get even this number, they had to resort to a wide range of fraudulent and unethical activities. Wherever they went, as one observer noted, "they created embarrassment, struggle, strife, and contention."[13] In the Department of North Carolina, these agents spawned problems, bitterness, and a sense of betrayal. Jameson and other officers came to believe that the actions of some were creating ill will in the African American community. Unlike their counterparts elsewhere, however, the agents in North Carolina secured, or at least received credit for securing, a large number of recruits for the 1st NCCHA. Although not all of the Compiled Military Service Records for the artillerymen indicate to what state the recruit was credited, a sample study of individual soldiers' service records for whom a credit is listed suggested that about 44 percent of enlisted men in the 1st NCCHA were credited to the Northern states. The credits covered about five hundred men. Agents from six northeastern states actively sought black recruits in North Carolina. The most successful operators came from New York and Massachusetts. Agents from New York recruited 41 percent of all of North Carolina artillerymen credited to the Northern states, while those from Massachusetts claimed 36 percent. The next most active state, Rhode Island, was given credit for only 11 percent of the recruits, despite the sympathies of Jameson.[14]

The estimated number of men recruited by state agents may, in fact, be too low. Records indicate that the heaviest recruitment by agents occurred in the first three months of 1865. The surviving lists in the muster rolls indicate that during this period, the nine different agents acting for New York, Massachusetts, Maine, and Connecticut were credited with enlisting 419 men. One agent, E. Wardle, who acted for the County of Albany, New York, recruited the largest single group—43 men—on 14 March 1865. The most productive agent, however, was Isaac McDougal, acting for the Twentieth and Twenty-first District of New York, who enlisted 126 men during February and March.[15] Moreover, these figures underestimate the numbers credited to the agents. Because there are no records for the outcome of their efforts during the last two months of 1864, the actual numbers may have been significantly higher.

The renewed recruitment in the artillery unit, which began in August 1864, created an opportunity for Jameson to expand his battalion. But it also presented him with serious organizational problems, for his companies continued to remain short of line officers. Nevertheless, he welcomed new recruits. Within a month, most of the companies had increased their rosters to about 110 men. On 17 August, Jameson was able to inform General Butler that his first four companies were armed and equipped and that "for the first time they are well drilled and disciplined." With almost enough soldiers for a fifth company, he requested permission to organize it as well as additional companies. Jameson claimed that recruits could be readily found for his regiment "who cannot be induced to go into any other Organization." Butler had wanted him to fill the existing companies to their maximum before attempting to organize new ones. Jameson's solution was to supply the ones in place well beyond their normal complement. Then, when he was ready to organize a new company, he would be able to transfer large numbers of men with some rudimentary training from the old companies to the new one.[16]

The expansion that Jameson desired occurred despite the difficulties he continued to have in staffing his original companies with enough line officers. His attempts to address the problem were only partly successful. After conferring with the commander of the District of North Carolina, General Palmer, Jameson recommended nine officers for commissions in the 1st NCCHA. Four were junior officers in various white infantry regiments, four were enlisted men in the 2nd Massachusetts Heavy Artillery, and the ninth man was a hospital steward. Four of the white enlisted men who had originally been detailed to help in the organization and drill of the regiment were also recommended for commissions at this time. The desperate shortage of officers in Jameson's command was aggravated in August, when he detailed Lts. Charles G. Allen and William E. Moses on special duty. Jameson was left with "but two (2) officers, Lieut. Hubbard who is constantly involved with Quarter Master and Recruiting business and Lieut. [James M.] Wheaton, 5th R I Arty who is left in charge of Camp and to manage the three remaining Companies of the Battalion in the best way he can." The new commissions that the major had requested would alleviate some of the staffing problems, but those gains would be offset by the loss of Lieutenant Wheaton, one of the few experienced of-

"Recruiting at Newbern, N.C." The cartoon captures popular stereotypes
of Southern blacks and recruiting agents. (*Harper's Weekly*,
3 September 1864, Author's collection)

ficers in the artillery unit, who requested, in early November 1864, to return
to his original regiment.[17]

While Jameson struggled with the staffing dilemma, he and two of his senior noncommissioned officers in Company B became embroiled in a bitter
dispute with some state recruiting agents and the Union officers who supported their unethical practices. The major had previously told his superiors
that many blacks in and around New Bern were willing to enlist if they could
join the 1st NCCHA, which would enable them to remain in the state and stay
relatively close to their families. They were less inclined to join units that
might be shipped out of North Carolina for unknown lengths of time. State

agents who wished to enlist men for other regiments simply lied to the new recruits in collusion with Union officers. The men were told that they would be mustered into the artillery regiment, but, once in the army, they were sent to different regiments. General Order No. 227 clearly stated that the recruits would be "sent to the regiments for which they may have been enlisted or assigned," but the language was subject to very different interpretations.[18]

At the beginning of September 1864, while serving as post guard at the recruiting center in New Bern, Sgt. Warren Hill and 1st Sgt. Benjamin Starkey of Company B tried to assist new recruits who felt they had been deceived or misled by state agents about which units they would enter. Apparently angered by their interference, post commander Lt. Col. Rodgers—in two separate incidents—tried unsuccessfully to have both men stripped of their rank.

A week later, on 10 September, Rodgers arrived at the post and summoned Starkey. In an obvious rant, he told the sergeant that he was "guilty of mutiny," that he "ought to be shot to death by musketry," and that "the paper was all a lie." He then ordered that Starkey's stripes be removed and that he be placed in close confinement. "The paper" to which Rodgers referred was a letter that the sergeant had drafted at the request of nearly two hundred recruits "who claimed that they had enlisted to go in the Heavy Artillery." After they had been sworn in, they discovered that they were to be sent off to another regiment. Starkey's letter outlined their claim "that they had been falsely enlisted." The new soldiers, Major Jameson later wrote, were "thus taking the proper steps to have their just rights." Furthermore, Starkey "has always performed his duties as a good soldier and non-commissioned Officer as well" and had Jameson's full confidence. The major asked that the district commander undertake an investigation so "a seemingly innocent man may not be disgraced and that the claims of a large number of the petitioners may be heard." Starkey was more fortunate than the recruits. Three days after Jameson's appeal, the sergeant was ordered released and restored to his duties as first sergeant.[19] Jameson was less successful in helping the recruits.

In a letter to the secretary of war almost two weeks later, Jameson protested that his recruiting operations "have been interrupted by the recruiting agents from the States and I respectfully ask that the colored recruits about one hundred and thirty (130) now at the Rendezvous near this city" be sent to his camp. He should receive them, he argued, both because they were needed in the 1st NCCHA and because "the men were enlisted and mustered in, under the distinct promise by the recruiting Agents that they should be so assigned." The next month saw a swirl of accusations by Jameson and denials by Rodgers. Jameson's frustration was reflected in his last letter on the issue. He had been told that he would have to place beside the name of each man who had signed the original complaint "the name and State of the Agent whom he states made these promises." That was impractical, he maintained. "All of the men who have signed the paper, with the exception of Barber, have been sent away and are not now in the district." He wanted his letter sent forward to General Butler as soon as possible. Rodgers's reply, which Jameson could not satisfy, was that the major should show "what evidence he has that such promises as he refers to in his first endorsement of the 11th inst were ever made to these soldiers." There was no further indication in the records of what became of these men, but Jameson managed to get his company removed from Rodgers's recruitment post. The major's fear, as he told Butler, was that events such as this one would leave "a most unfavourable impression with regards to the justice of our Government . . . upon the minds of the whole colored population of this District."[20]

The incident involving Starkey and Hill had not been the only conflict between the 1st NCCHA and unscrupulous state agents. Jameson had complained about New York agents operating in the New Bern area in mid-September. One of his enlisted men, Pvt. Alfred Powers, had admitted under questioning "that the agents claiming the eight (8) men for New York State had offered him, the said Powers, $200 two hundred dollars if he would take the men to their office." Jameson's protest and Power's testimony were ignored, and two days later a special order transferred the recruits. Lt. James M. Wheaton, who was in charge of the regimental camp, was ordered "to deliver to *W. F. Fields* (8) eight men now under Guard at said Camp being Recruits belonging to the State of New York."[21] Despite Jameson's complaints, Fields, who was agent for the Twenty-first District in New York, was still recruiting in North Carolina six months later.

The new recruits not only resented being manipulated, short-changed, and lied to by the agents, but they also were offended by the actions of abusive officers from other Union regiments stationed in the area. Sometimes these officers were merely supporting the practices of the recruiting agents. At other times, the officers openly demonstrated their disdain and dislike of the black soldiers. Such an attitude caused Jameson, in September 1864, to criticize a lieutenant from the 2nd Massachusetts Heavy Artillery working at the New Bern recruiting station. The major claimed that because of "the abuse received from this man, the Company doing Guard duty at the Post Rectg Rendezvous has been brought to a state bordering on mutiny."[22] Jameson requested that the officer be removed and tried before a court-martial, although his fate is unknown.

During August and September, Jameson frequently contended that his regiment was filling an important utilitarian role in the district and that for the good of the service and the efficiency of the department, he needed more recruits to increase the size of his unit. A good deal of what his soldiers did was menial work, but their labor was important, at least in the eyes of white officers, because it freed up white soldiers for other tasks. Although Company B of the 1st NCCHA acted as a guard for the recruitment station at New Bern, the other soldiers spent most of their time working on the surrounding fortifications and on general fatigue duties. Jameson never had enough men to meet all of the requests for labor. At the end of September, he explained, "more men than we are able to furnish are called for daily for important duties connected with the Military and Sanitary condition of this District."[23] Implicitly, Jameson accepted the assumption that assigning black regiments to do a majority of the fatigue duties was a reasonable use of the existing manpower.

The regiment's resources had been stretched to the limit a few weeks earlier when the local commander ordered Jameson to provide a detachment for day duty in the forts around New Bern. Although the withdrawal in May of the Confederate troops under Gen. Robert F. Hoke marked the last actual assault of New Bern, the presence of the Confederate ram *Albemarle*, safely moored at Plymouth, represented a continuing threat to the town. That threat, and the Union concerns about any weakness in the New Bern forts, did not end until the ram was destroyed at the end of October. In the meantime, the 1st NCCHA was called upon to help man the fort and strengthen the town's defenses. A total of 133 enlisted men in three parties were detailed for duty at Forts Dutton, Stevenson, and Totton. Their presence was needed because of an "unprecedented amount of sickness in the 2nd Massachusetts Artillery." Thirty-four soldiers were ordered to report in fatigue dress for police duty while the rest were to present themselves fully armed and equipped. Twenty noncommissioned officers, but no commissioned officers, accompanied the men.[24] This illustrates, once again, the important role that noncommissioned officers played in the artillery unit. The lack of officers in the 14th USCHA meant that many black artillerymen would serve, during fatigue and guard duties, under white officers from other white regiments. It was a situation that commonly produced complaints from the enlisted men about abusive treatment at the hands of these officers.

The troops in the detachment ate breakfast in camp and brought their dinners with them to the forts. When members of the 2nd Massachusetts Heavy Artillery relieved them at retreat, the black soldiers could return to their own camp for supper and the night. Although the men were initially to report to the forts at 8:00 A.M., the time was soon pushed back to 7:00 A.M., and they were also required to provide a guard for Fort Rowan. The detachment rose early and returned late. Palmer ordered the commander of the Massachusetts regiment to make every effort "to instruct them in heavy artillery drill," but it is unclear whether the drill took place.[25] It was an onerous enough duty for black soldiers with little time for training even before an epidemic hit New Bern.

In the fall of 1864, Jameson's men, as all the inhabitants of New Bern, faced a threat much more deadly than the Confederate ram at Plymouth. The yellow fever outbreak that ran from September to November killed hundreds of people. Yellow fever had probably claimed its first victim in the town as early as June 1864, but senior medical officers, worried about the panic that would ensue, refused to accept that yellow fever was the cause of the first deaths. It was not until a sergeant in the 15th Connecticut Volunteer Infantry died in early September that the presence of yellow fever in New Bern became widely known.[26] The disease was especially terrifying to the town's inhabitants because no one knew the exact cause or any preventative or cure. Although medical opinion by 1860 generally held that yellow fever was noncontagious, it was believed that it was "transportable" and could be passed on by certain things such as clothing, soiled linen, and so forth. It would be almost another half century before the correct vector, the *Aedes aegypti* mosquito, was identified as the agent of transmission. Until then, doctors practiced a wide range of equally ineffective cures ranging from doses of quinine or calomel to hot baths and blistering.

As soon as it was accepted that yellow fever was present in New Bern, the army moved all military personnel who were still healthy and who could be stationed elsewhere to places such as Morehead City, Beaufort, Hatteras, Roanoke Island, and coastal forts. Because it was believed that strenuous exercise left people more vulnerable to the disease, Gen. Edward Harland, who was commanding the defenses of New Bern, District of North Carolina, Department of Virginia and North Carolina, agreed to cancel all unnecessary activities. One regiment that could not benefit from these precautions was the 15th Connecticut Volunteer Infantry, which was on provost duty when the epidemic broke out. Even in good times the assignments of the provost guard were burdensome. The soldiers not only acted as the town's police force to keep order, but also made sure that the military headquarters and hospitals had water. In addition, the soldiers on provost duty had to provide at least minimum sanitation services within New Bern. The appearance of yellow fever made what was always an unpleasant assignment much worse. Because doctors feared that a miasma in the air played a role in the epidemic, the 15th Connecticut took on the additional responsibility of keeping barrels of tar, turpentine, and rosin burning throughout the town so the smoke might somehow purify the air. The soldiers also broadcast lime, in an unsuccessful attempt to achieve the same end. In addition to all of the other tasks, the troops collected the dead in New Bern and hauled them outside the town for burial. While the 15th Connecticut served as provost guard, man after man in the regiment contracted the fever. By late September, perhaps half of its troops were sick and many had died. One soldier recalled that from 28 September to 31 October, "there was scarcely a day in which one or more members (frequently four or five) of the 15th did not give up their lives to the terrible scourge."[27]

When the 15th Connecticut no longer had enough men to carry out all of their duties, the district commander selected the 1st NCCHA to replace it as provost guard. The black regiment was available and, perhaps in the eyes of some senior officers, more expendable than other units. Moreover, because it was widely believed by white officers and doctors that African Americans were less susceptible to yellow fever, there was a certain logic to using the artillerymen to police the town.[28] Once reassigned, the black soldiers quickly took up their duties. In early October Jameson directed Lieutenant Wheaton to detail ten men to Foster General Hospital. In an order that revealed wider social attitudes, the major told Wheaton to select a detail "made up of the most rugged men of the Command and also full-blooded blacks." These troops brought their blankets with them, for they would not return to camp until further orders. The Foster General Hospital was a complex of buildings in the center of New Bern where the most serious cases were taken. Any patient who was well enough to travel was evacuated to the Mansfield Hospital in Morehead City or the hospital at Beaufort.[29] Those who were too ill to move and remained behind would either recover or be buried.

The epidemic struck the artillery regiment while it was not yet fully organized. The 1st NCCHA still had no regimental surgeon on its staff although, given the lack of medical knowledge about yellow fever, there was a limited amount that any surgeon could have done. More important, the additional demands placed on the regiment came at a time when it was neither adequately trained nor officered. As the regiment struggled to meet all of its responsibilities during the crisis, the black soldiers came under criticism of their future commander. Lt. Col. Walter S. Poor, who was then provost marshal general of the district, condemned both the appearance of the regimental camp and the behavior of the men. He also criticized the leadership of Major Jameson, for he believed that the major knew that the camp was unsanitary and had done nothing to improve matters. In late October Poor issued a general order to Jameson to make the camp as clean as possible and to keep it that way. His men were to wash the latrines and to clear away all of the brush. The directive warned that "neglect of this order will be deemed wilful disobedience of orders." Few improvements could be made, however, while the regiment was trying to cope with the effects of yellow fever on New Bern. Ten days later Poor wrote Jameson that frequent complaints had been "made to these Hd Qrs of the unsoldierly conduct of the men of Major Jameson's Command. Maj. J. must take some measures to keep his men in Camp and under control."[30] There is no evidence that Jameson was able to take any steps to remedy conditions in the camp or promote discipline among his men. Improvement would come only with the next commander.

Lt. Col. Poor believed that the tiny size of the camp guard set by Jameson was a prime example of improper control of his men. The guard, which consisted of only one corporal and three privates, was much too small to control all of the black soldiers, let alone ensure that no one left the camp without authority. Viewing the matter in a different light, Jameson angrily protested the unfairness of Poor's criticisms. He was trying to accomplish with four companies what the 15th Connecticut had done with ten. The small size of the camp guard reflected the large number of men who were detailed for provost guard duty or assigned other important duties. Jameson pointed out that he had been merely acting on the advice of the man he replaced, Col. Charles L. Upham, of the 15th Connecticut, who had been in charge of the subdistrict

of New Bern before his regiment had become too depleted to meet its responsibilities. Upham had recommended that Jameson keep a skeleton camp
guard so he would have more men for the other essential functions needed
to combat yellow fever. "During the prevalence of the epidemic," the major
wrote, "my men have been kept on duty about the Streets, Dead Houses,
Burial Ground, and as the Provost Guard of the City."[31] In the emergency,
Jameson had recalled virtually all of his men from recruiting services, reduced his camp guard, and did his utmost to supply all of the men requested
from his regiment. For a large portion of the time, many of his soldiers had
to serve double duty.

If his men seemed unsoldierly or undisciplined, it was not solely their
fault. "Those detailed for Provost Guard were placed in the charge of Officers of Another Regiment, and if the men have become demoralized, it is
because they have in these various ways been removed from our supervision." Jameson felt compelled to protest Poor's unjustified criticism from a
"sense of justice to my Officers and Men who in order to save the lives of
others, have cheerfully remained at the post of danger and who feel keenly
the censure." The danger to which Jameson referred was very real, although
other white officers did not always agree. Capt. M. A. Butricks of the 15th
Connecticut had remained in New Bern after the bulk of the regiment had
left the town, and he supervised some of 1st NCCHA troops during the crisis.
He later claimed that "so far as I know, not a single man of the [black] provost guard was attacked by the fever, and it was remarked that the colored
people seem to be proof against its attack."[32] Butricks was able to maintain his
racial stereotyping only by ignoring what was happening in the 1st NCCHA. In
Company B alone, seven artillerymen died of yellow fever during October.
In Company C, six men died of "disease" during October, and it is probable
that they were yellow fever victims. Many other men were seriously ill but
recovered.[33] Although the 1st NCCHA did not lose as many men to the fever as
the 15th Connecticut, they still paid a heavy price for their service as provost
guard in the stricken town.

Even soldiers who were on detached duties elsewhere were not immune
from the disease. Yellow fever claimed the life of one exceptional black artilleryman on Roanoke Island. Sgt. Robert A. Morrow had entered the Union
lines when New Bern was under attack. Previously, he had been the personal
servant of Confederate general James Johnson Pettigrew, whom he had accompanied to West Point and the University of North Carolina in Chapel

Hill. In March 1864 he enlisted in Company B, 1st NCCHA, as a private. Morrow had managed to obtain a good education as a result of his experiences with Pettigrew, which explains his rapid promotion within the regiment. In September 1864 he was detailed to organize a recruiting station on Roanoke Island under the command of Sgt. Barnes Griffith. When he left New Bern, he would not have known that he was already infected with yellow fever. During his short stay on the island as a recruiter and before the disease became evident, Morrow also opened a school for blacks under the auspices of the National Freedmen's Relief Association. The school was not open long, for Morrow died on 10 October 1864.[34]

In early November the weather in North Carolina turned colder, and the epidemic began to subside.[35] New cases stopped appearing in New Bern and on 9 November, the 15th Connecticut resumed its provost duties, replacing the 1st NCCHA. The army command was willing to use the black soldiers as a provost guard during the epidemic, but it was not ready to challenge white sensibilities after the crisis had passed. It was also in the aftermath of the yellow fever epidemic that the regiment's commander was arrested for fraud and for abusing his authority. Long after the war, one of the enlisted soldiers, Cherry Wright, remembered joining the army in 1864. "At that time," he recounted, the "Regiment was commanded by Maj. T. C. Jameson who was afterwards court marshalled and reduced to ranks, when Col. [sic] Walter S. Poor took the command." Wright, however, was not in a position to know why an apparent supporter of the black soldiers would be replaced by an officer who had been so critical of the regiment. Jameson may well have been guilty of the charges that he faced, but his friends believed that other factors were involved. Military authorities arrested Jameson in December 1864 at Fort Monroe on his return from the North.[36] They charged him with "fraudulent and dishonest conduct to the prejudice of the service," as well as "employing a private soldier as a servant and failing to make the proper deductions from his pay, in violation of the Act of Congress July 17th, 1862." He was also accused of appropriating for his own use at least some of the bounty paid to his soldiers and of misusing money they had given him for safekeeping. The court subsequently found Jameson guilty of the charges and ordered him dishonorably dismissed from the army. In addition, he was fined eight thousand dollars and sentenced to three years' hard labor at Norfolk.[37]

Jameson had the good luck to have an effective and persuasive champion in William Lloyd Garrison. In one of a series of letters written on Jameson's behalf, Garrison raised with General Butler the motives of some of Jameson's accusers. The abolitionist was concerned that "Major Jamison [*sic*] may have unfortunately subjected himself to the ill-will and personal dislike of some others whose hostility to the negro would be gratified to see him cashiered and who would not be scrupulous in regards to their testimony against him." In a letter to Governor John Andrew, Garrison again suggested that the major was "the victim of mean and selfish accusers," while his letter to Abraham Lincoln assured the president that Jameson was unlikely to have committed the acts of which he was accused. Garrison begged Lincoln to see that Jameson was "not sacrificed to personal malice, or on account of his antislavery principles and sentiment."[38]

Lincoln ordered Jameson's case to be reopened, and the charges against him were reexamined. One result of the president's actions was an inquiry, in January 1865, from the office of Gen. I. N. Palmer to newly promoted Capt. Charles G. Allen, the temporary commander of the 1st NCCHA. Palmer claimed that "enlisted men of the 1st NCC Hy Arty have complained of depositing money with Major Jameson for safe keeping," and he wanted to know what had become of it. In mid-February Allen replied that, although he had conducted "a thorough investigation, I can find no men of the command who have deposited money with Maj. Jameson." Partly because of Allen's findings and the weakness of the case against the major, and perhaps partly because of the political pressure being brought to bear, Jameson was pardoned by Lincoln and ordered released.[39] He would, however, never regain command of the regiment or serve in any other unit. In his absence, from 15 November until a new commander was appointed, Captain Allen served as acting commander of the regiment.

The new officer who took over the 1st NCCHA in early 1865 was a very different man from Jameson in both temperament and background. Walter Stone Poor was born in Andover, Maine, in 1836 to a large family of modest means. By 1860 he had graduated from Bowdoin College but only by interrupting his education periodically while he taught school to save enough money to return to the college. When the Civil War broke out, he was teaching at Mount Pleasant Academy, a private military school in New York. He quickly decided to volunteer in one of the new regiments being organized. Poor first enlisted in the 10th New York Volunteers, but by the summer of 1862 he had become captain in the 1st New York Mounted Rifles. Although others may have doubted his commitment to antislavery, Poor did not. Writing home to his sister in the early months of the war, he assured her: "What-ever people may say, I am an abolitionist." In the summer of 1863 he wrote home that he hoped he might command a regiment of black cavalry. Instead, on 30 March 1864 he received a commission as lieutenant colonel and took command of the five companies of the 2nd North Carolina Union Volunteers (NCUV), a white regiment, that were slowly being raised in and around Beau-fort. Here he commanded the post and served as both provost marshal and treasury agent. Poor may have enjoyed his new rank, but he must have dis-liked his new regiment. The 2nd NCUV was made up of desperately poor men from the eastern part of the state. Almost a third of them had served in the Confederate army, and all of them were despised and scorned by Confederate and Union officers alike. Only five companies were raised, and they served in scattered parts of the state. The execution, by Confederate authorities, of men captured from this regiment had led, by late 1864, to a rapid decline in morale and effectiveness.[40]

When the provost marshal general of the district, Maj. Henry T. Lawson, died of yellow fever, General Palmer selected Poor to replace him. The New Yorker must have been relieved to distance himself from the 2nd NCUV. Once in New Bern, the new provost marshal general soon became very critical of the African Americans that he would later command. An incident that oc-curred shortly after the yellow fever epidemic ended revealed something about his character and his handling of people. In November, while Poor was in charge of affairs in New Bern, a fire broke out in the town and spread rapidly. A number of African Americans had gathered to watch the blaze, but they refused to help the military. When Poor ordered them to assist the soldiers, they told him "that it being Sunday they did not propose to break God's law by working." Poor was enraged. His response was "the repeated command coupled with the discharge of his revolver into their very faces. One man was severely wounded, after which, in the language of Lieutenant W. Griffin of the 15th Connecticut, 'the colored troops fought nobly' and the fire was subdued."[41] The event seems to have been symptomatic of his at-titude toward African Americans. Poor remained in New Bern until the start of 1865, when a consolidation of the 1st and 2nd NCUV rendered the lieuten-ant colonel supernumerary. He needed a new command, and by then the 1st NCCHA needed a new commander.

Even before Poor took command of the 1st NCCHA on 28 February 1865, the regiment had been relocated and had undergone a series of changes in function as well as leadership. Until the fall of 1864, the army had used the artillery regiment primarily as a garrison unit, policing the town and working on fortifications. The military command now assigned the regiment a new role in the state. As part of the Carolina campaign, the ports of eastern North Carolina became critical logistic centers through which massive amounts of supplies and munitions began to flow. The 1st NCCHA would act to ensure the continuity of that flow. The temporary commanding officer of the regiment, Captain Allen, was determined that the regiment would be up to the task. While Major Jameson was on furlough in the North, and just after the 1st NCCHA had relinquished its provost duties to the 15th Connecticut, the regiment had been ordered to Carolina City, near Morehead City, and Allen took over as the acting commanding officer. By 11 November, the regiment reached its new camp and starting the next day, Allen issued a series of general orders aimed at improving the appearance and discipline of the regiment.[42] His actions were in part a response to Jameson's leadership style and perhaps in part an effort to respond to the criticisms of Colonel Poor, but they were also typical of a new, albeit temporary, commander's attempt to stamp his own personality on his command. The move away from New Bern freed the regiment from its demanding duties and allowed Allen to improve the appearance and effectiveness of his troops. The captain wanted to ensure a uniform, proper dress of all of his soldiers, and he was particularly concerned that men not be able to slip out of camp at night, past a guard who would turn a blind eye. To tighten up the perimeter of the camp, Allen ordered that all sentries must now carry loaded muskets and that they were to use them on anyone who ignored their challenges.

The stricter discipline came at a time when the regiment was struggling with the repercussions of its recent move. Decades later, many of the soldiers remembered the hard times that they endured when they first arrived at Carolina City. At the most basic level, many did not have access to safe, clean drinking water. Chester Amieny of Company A claimed that he had contracted diarrhea "by drinking bad water at Carolina City and was treated in Rgt hospital." He was not alone. Sgt. Israel Harget and Pvt. Benjamin Heston of the same company both testified to the harmful effects of the water at that camp. Sgt. Gordon Wiggins had been healthy until the move, but he began to suffer a range of problems afterward. "I was first taken sick at Carolina City in the first part of the winter of 1865 about Jan. I had the yellow jaundice. I did not get clear of it all winter, before I did get over it I was taken with a running off of the bowels." The men also complained about other aspects of their new camp. The rapid relocation of the regiment after it had been ordered to Carolina City left the men without tents and sufficient blankets for an extended period. Parker W. Smith of Company D believed that the rheumatism developed by his messmate, Henry Hill, "came from exposure as we had no tents and it was bad wet cold weather." Another member of the company, John Franklin, remembered "when at Carolina City, N.C. Nov. 1864 we were exposed to the weather, night & day, some two weeks—no shelter except brush."[43]

Faced with these hardships and a growing sick list, improvements in the appearance of the regiment were slow in coming. A month after the move, Allen was still upset by "the filthy conditions of their Company Streets in consequence of allowing the men to cook oysters, etc., at will, and also by a neglect of ordinary police measures." He ended the casual dining practices, demanded a rigorous policing of the camp, and ordered that all garbage be dumped far enough out on the beach that it would be removed by the ebb tide. Blankets and tents were to be aired, and men were to bathe at least once a week. Although the soldiers in the regimental camp could be held responsible for their own general cleanliness, some men on detached service could not be. The company that was detached to Fort Heckman at Morehead City had been forced to move without knapsacks or any extra clothes. Because of their heavy fatigue duties and their shortage of clothes, the artillerymen at the fort were "very filthy from want of change of clothing."[44] Their commander had to arrange to have the knapsacks and clothes sent over before the men's appearance and hygiene could be improved.

In the final months of the war, the 14th USCHA guarded the forts around Morehead City, built docks and wharves, and helped off-load the supplies flowing into North Carolina. The work was hard, boring, and occasionally dangerous. Men who were careless or just unlucky could be seriously hurt. Isaac Bryant claimed that he had wrenched his back and abdomen badly lifting boxes, "resulting in rupture in both sides." He later testified that "his guts came down so that he is not able to do anything." Richard Faircloth of Company I also suffered serious injuries to his back and right side "while unloading vessels and boats at Morehead City." A member of Lewis Bass's company described how the heavy manual labor left its mark on Bass: "We were unloading subsistence near Beaufort . . . in lifting barrels and bags out of the Steamers & vessels he kind of strained his back; near the small of his back." The injury was aggravated by a woodcutting detail and other fatigue work. Indeed, as Israel Hardy, a companion of Bass, had testified, "Nearly all the work we had to do at Beaufort & Morehead City N.C. was heavy work, lifting heavy guns." Windsor Ormond explained that he had hurt his left shoulder, side, and foot "while unloading Boat at Fort Macon by a box falling on him which smashed him down and hurt his hip and heel and that his shoulder has never been in a sound condition." After he had partially recovered from those injuries, Ormond's foot was reinjured by a falling box. Some accidents gave new meaning to the term "pork barreling." A comrade of Thomas Morris of Company H remembered seeing "him at the time he received the Injury to his arm [and chest] by a Pork Bbl falling from the Tackle Block when he was helping to unload a Boat."[45]

Less frequent but potentially more serious injuries resulted from the careless handling of the big guns. Benjamin Heston in Company A was helping to dismount a cannon from its carriage when the skid on which it rested broke. Heston was using a pole as a lever to move the cannon when the skid gave way, smashing the heavy gun into his shoulder. In another accident, Henry Hill was blinded in the left eye by an exploding gun. According to Hill, in 1865 "we were trying to jar down a wall to the fort that had been cracked—so a cannon on top of said wall was heavily charged & fired & as a result of over charging it burst." A small piece of the gun, plus fine particles of dust and dirt flew into his eye. "My eye was badly hurt but I did not go in the hospital." Another soldier who had heard the explosion and came running, remembered that "Hill was holding his face with both hands, blood was coming out of his face. . . . He said then he believed his eye was gone." As serious as Hill's injuries were, he was still more fortunate than Thomas Bayman, who died a few months later from "shell wounds." Sometimes even the claims of veterans to injuries that were discounted by Federal authorities are suggestive. George Taylor, who had served as a private in Company H, argued in his pension application that he had suffered permanent injury from a cannon that had exploded. As the pension official described the case as presented, while "George Taylor was with a gun crew in August, 1865, firing to stop a passing vessel the gun exploded killing several men, . . . causing injury to [the applicant's] back and chest." The skeptical official concluded that it was improbable "that in

August 1865, long after the termination of active hostilities in eastern North Carolina that a cannon was fired at Morehead City, N.C., to stop a passing vessel." Taylor's claims were rejected.[46] The pension official may have been correct that Taylor lied about being injured by the cannon, but his description of the accident has the ring of truth. But if a veteran lied about being disabled by an exploding gun, he did so only because those accidents occurred frequently enough that such a claim would be plausible.

The heavy cannons created a dangerous environment and could still leave left their mark on the men who fired them, even when they did not explode. Years later, numerous men from the 14th USCHA complained of having to live with "ringing in the ears," "roaring in the head," and either partial or complete deafness caused by the guns.[47] Of course, old men lose their hearing, and some of the infantry veterans were growing deaf. But the number of veteran artillerymen who complained about this disability was much larger, suggesting the long-term detrimental effects of operating the heavy guns. Even drilling with muskets, a part of the regiment's training, involved risk of injury. Pvt. Israel Harget was shot through the left hand, and William Moore of Company C "was shot in both legs on drill ground at New Port River. Rheumatism resulting."[48]

The regiment also faced a range of problems common in many Civil War units. At the end of 1864, a series of disputes over whiskey rations and the abuse of alcohol revealed another aspect of life in the regiment. A daily allotment of whiskey was provided to all soldiers on heavy duty, as the army considered the drink a necessary stimulant to support their work. The 1st NCCHA had more than its share of strenuous labor. Through much of December, over 150 men from the regiment worked on the fortifications and docks around Morehead City and Beaufort. Another 50-odd soldiers performed assorted guard duties each day. Although the experience of the artillerymen was not unique, the number of men detailed from the relatively new and untrained regiment reflected the difficulties in improving, no less maintaining, regimental drill and discipline. Moreover, the work was exhausting, and most men saw the whiskey as both necessary and a right that they had earned. Nevertheless, the regimental correspondence indicates that many of the enlisted men never received their authorized rations of whiskey despite all of Allen's protests. That provided the men with a legitimate and ongoing grievance that some viewed as part of a larger pattern of inequitable treatment of black regiments.

They and their officers could only grumble. The real source of the whiskey rations problem, Allen believed, lay in corruption or mismanagement within the Commissary Department, but it was not an issue that he could resolve.[49]

A few months later, evidence of further impropriety surfaced concerning the regiment's two civilian sutlers. On 10 February 1865 Willis and Wheeler were placed under arrest and sent to district headquarters to face charges. Another case involving alcohol resulted in Pvt. James McCabe being sentenced to 18 months of hard labor for smuggling whiskey on board a schooner into the post at New Bern and selling it to the soldiers. McCabe had not only sold five or six gallons to enlisted men but also had been "proven guilty of mutinous conduct refusing duty while on the voyage threatening the life of the Captain." Maj. W. P. Briggs, the chief provost marshal, dismissed McCabe's subsequent claims of ill treatment on the part of the captain and ruled that the soldier "richly deserves his sentence." Actually, Briggs felt that the private deserved a harsher punishment since "several soldiers were arrested for crimes committed while under the influence of the vile stuff this man peddled out to them." Of course, this type of problem was not uncommon in other regiments—white and black. Nor did it just involve enlisted men. Some of the newer officers in the 1st NCCHA assumed that they could leave camp and visit New Bern whenever they wished. The regiment's new surgeon, Isaac W. Sitler, who had been transferred from the 158th New York Infantry, was chastised for "the very irregular way in which you have heretofore visited New Bern without first receiving permission from these Hd. Qrs."[50]

At the beginning of 1865, senior officers approved plans to expand the 1st NCCHA from the four companies that were in service to twelve companies— the normal complement of a heavy artillery regiment. In part, the expansion reflected the new manpower demands created by the need to prepare Morehead City as a trans-shipment base to supply General Sherman's army when it reached North Carolina. Much more labor would be needed to expand and protect the wharves at Morehead City and to handle the supplies flowing through the port. A larger artillery regiment would provide some of that needed manpower. Through the final months of 1864 and into early 1865, new recruits had been added to the four existing companies. On 11 January 1865 Captain Allen reported that the four companies contained 486 men and requested that another company be mustered in, especially since there was "no record of any order that the Battalion should be filled to its maximum before forming new companies."[51] By February, Companies A, B, and C were carrying over 140 enlisted men on each of their rosters, while Company D's ranks had reached 161, for a total of almost 600 troops. The increase forced Allen to renew his efforts to obtain more company officers for his unit, drawing some of them from experienced noncommissioned officers serving in Northern regiments stationed around New Bern. If Allen hoped that his efforts to enlarge the unit would lead to his promotion, he was mistaken, for by the end of February 1865 Walter Poor had assumed command of the regiment.[52]

During March and April, Poor completed Allen's work. Eight new companies were organized and mustered into the regiment that was redesignated the 14th USCHA. Poor used Allen's tactic of transferring large groups of enlisted men from the existing four companies to the new organizations. As Poor transferred men, the enrollment figures in the four original companies dropped back to the mid-eighties and remained at that level for the rest of the regiment's service. Noncommissioned officers were also transferred from the established companies to the new ones in order to provide a core of leadership and experience. Although the transfer of soldiers with previous military service benefited the new companies, they continued to face problems of leadership. Given the chronic shortage of company officers that had always hampered the regiment, black noncommissioned officers would be forced to play a critical role if the 14th USCHA was to become a functioning, effective unit.

The new companies consisted, in large part, of men who had been stockpiled in the original four companies. On 4 March 1865 2nd Lt. William Crombie was assigned to Company E and directed to proceed with its organization. The commanding officers of Companies A, B, and C were to send Crombie all surplus men in their companies; that is, in excess of eighty-six. The commander of Company D was to transfer the nineteen recruits that he had just received from the recruiting depot. The first sergeant of the new Company E was John Wallace, formerly a sergeant in Company A. On 8 March, the day before Crombie's command was transferred from Carolina City to Morehead City as part of a larger move, the newly established company had eighty-seven men on its rolls. On 10 March the next company was begun. Lt. Edwin A. Kenney was ordered to form Company F, and sixty-seven soldiers were sent to him from Companies B, C, and D. A month later Cpl. William H. Peoples of Company D transferred in as first sergeant. A short time after Kenney began to raise his company, Lt. John B. Willet took charge of organizing Company G.[53] Within a few days Sgt. William H. Hendrick, formerly of the 2nd NCUV, was brought in as Company G's drill instructor. Hendrick's expectation in leaving the white regiment was that he would receive a commission in the artillery unit within six months.

Hendrick was not the only white enlisted man from the 2nd NCUV to join the 14th USCHA. On 23 March Pvt. Robert B. Hayes was assigned to Company D, where he assumed command in the absence of Captain Allen. To overcome the obvious problems resulting from putting in positions of authority enlisted men lacking command experience, the drill instructors were obliged to take part in the regular officers' school conducted at 7:00 A.M. on Monday, Wednesday, and Friday, where *Casey's Tactics* formed the basis of instruction. Allen ordered that not only must every officer attend, but also "the enlisted men attached to the Regiment as drill Officers will be required to attend."[54]

Two items in early April spoke to the conditions in 14th USCHA. As the regiment increased in size and as the labor demands placed on it decreased, Lieutenant Colonel Poor had an opportunity to actually train his men as soldiers. On 1 April he informed the enlisted men and officers that "Company and Squad drills will take the place of fatigue duty so long as the present reduction of the fatigue detail shall continue." All enlisted men would be drilled, and the companies that were equipped with muskets would be instructed in the manual of arms.[55] Now that the war was ending, the regiment was to be trained to fight. The troops were grateful to be putting aside their labor duties. The settlement of a deceased soldier's estate in the first week of April revealed just how demanding the fatigue duties had been on the men and their equipment. Pvt. Samuel Stone, a thirty-one-year-old native of Duplin County who had served in Company B for slightly less than four months, died of "disease unknown." Although he was due $100 in unpaid bounty, he "was indebted to the US for clothing over drawn to the amount of $305." Stone had been drawing about $70 a month for clothing, well in excess of his monthly pay. It is possible, of course, that some of these items went to Stone's dependents—despite official regulations—and did not reflect loss due to heavy fatigue duties.[56]

Poor and Allen had greater success in getting enlisted men than they did officers. By 13 April 1865 Poor reported that he had 930 enlisted men in his command but only ten company officers. Another fourteen officers had been recommended, but it was unclear when, or if, they would arrive. At a time when many Union officers and soldiers thought first and foremost about demobilization, a commission in a mediocre black regiment was not particularly attractive. Obviously the army placed a higher priority in filling the regiment's rank and file than it did in providing officer leadership for the enlisted men. As long as most of the regiment was assigned to fatigue duties, often under the supervision of other, outside authorities, the unit did not need a full complement of officers. Nevertheless, in early May, when he had over a thousand men in uniform and twelve complete companies, Poor requested but failed to be promoted to colonel of the regiment. He also was unsuccessful in getting a promotion for many of his other officers. Despite the fact that the companies's ranks were full, the regiment still had only thirteen commissioned officers.[57]

The perpetual shortage of officers was the most obvious limitation on the regimental command system, but there was another, less obvious one. Unlike the officer corps in the three black infantry regiments from North Carolina, in the 14th USCHA there were few common bonds uniting the officers. Indeed, the artillery regiment acts as an interesting foil by which to judge the other three regiments. Gen. Edward A. Wild had used his powers to select officers from a common pool of men in the Massachusetts regiments who shared similar values. He had sought veterans who were committed to abolitionism and temperance. As a result, the officers of the three North Carolina infantry regiments enjoyed a strong cohesion. Those bonds did not exist in the artillery regiment. Since there were so few officers and so much to do, there was little time for off-duty social interaction to strengthen a sense of command unity. Moreover, many officers had little in common with their fellow officers. Lt. Albert Weideman, for instance, had emigrated from Prussia and joined the regular army in 1840. When the Civil War began, he was acting as Gen. Joseph Roberts's orderly. Although he held a commission during the conflict, he returned to life as a sergeant in the regular army at the end of hostilities. Capt. William Hendrick, by contrast, was twice a sergeant, but in two different armies. A resident of Forsyth County, North Carolina, he had joined the 21st Regiment North Carolina Troops in May 1861. Hendrick was captured at Winchester by Federal troops and then exchanged. Returning to his regiment, he was wounded at both Fredericksburg and Chancellorsville before deserting the Confederate army in early 1864. He then enlisted in the Union army at New Bern and served as sergeant in Company C, 2nd NCUV, until transferred to the artillery regiment, commissioned, and promoted. Such men shared little in common with Lt. William H. Willey, who had come from an abolitionist environment to enlist first as a lieutenant in the 26th Regiment Massachusetts Volunteers and then, after mustering out for disabilities, as a sergeant in the 2nd Massachusetts Heavy Artillery. By the time he accepted a commission in the 14th USCHA, Willey was suffering badly from malaria. Albert Weideman, William Hendrick, and William Willey were reflective of the differences within the 14th USCHA's staff of officers.[58]

Although a few new officers were added to the regiment in early 1865, the new appointments just matched the resignation of the regiment's original officers. The only way that the regiment could function effectively was by using eleven white non-commissioned officers and privates who were acting as drill officers. Indeed, some of these men had to take command of companies. Poor's orders in May to stop any further recruiting activities freed up only two second lieutenants to rejoin the 14th USCHA. As the regiment faced an uncertain service in post-war North Carolina, it was not clear the unit would ever be able to achieve a proper level of drill and discipline without the proper number of commissioned officers.

## CHAPTER SIX

# Families of the Soldiers during the War

For many African Americans who volunteered to serve in North Carolina's Union regiments, enlistment was a time fraught with worries about the families, friends, and dependents they were leaving behind to an uncertain fate. As black Union soldiers from Southern states, not only did they face higher risks if captured by Confederate troops, but also their families, either at home or in refugee camps, could find themselves in equally perilous situations. The Union's white soldiers from the North could expect that, in their absence, their families would receive support and assistance from their local community, their state government, and Federal agencies. If they were killed or seriously wounded in battle, some aid would be provided for those left behind. At the very least, family members would enjoy the respect of their society for the sacrifice their men were making. Moreover, many of these men and their families had financial resources that would help buffer dependents from privation while the war lasted. The African American soldiers from North Carolina and elsewhere in the South had no such assurances. As a group, they had few financial resources to support their immediate families in their absence. Moreover, their dependents could expect few benefits from the state or the Federal government and, in the worst case, their families might face retaliation from Confederate supporters for the actions of the black soldiers.

Not surprisingly, the wartime experiences of the families of black soldiers from across the South varied enormously. In many parts of North Carolina, young African American males of military age who wanted to enlist had been able to escape from Confederate territory only by leaving their families and friends behind. After they entered the Union army, their fears for dependents who remained in bondage must have been great, especially when owners reportedly were relocating their slaves to less threatened parts of the Confederacy.[1] Certainly some of these soldiers made many attempts to return and retrieve their loved ones. Others had been fortunate enough to escape with their family members but only by becoming refugees. Still other African Americans were effectively freed after 1862, as Union forces occupied vital areas in eastern North Carolina. While life for them continued to be hard, at least it was slightly more stable than for the refugees. For all blacks in Union-occupied territory, the war created a wider range of occupational choices than had existed previously. Some families remained in the cities and towns held by Federal troops, sustaining themselves through employment opportunities opened up by the military presence. Many black entrepreneurs managed to become relatively well off and, by the end of the war, some of these tradesmen and businessmen earned hundreds of dollars.[2] They were the fortunate minority. Often black laborers worked long and hard for wages that were never paid. Other ex-slaves, however, took advantage of the Federal army's encouragement of black recruitment in North Carolina. When Gen. Edward Wild began to enlist black recruits from the Union-occupied area, he promised the soldiers that their dependents would receive support during the war.[3] The result was a refugee settlement on Roanoke Island specifically established for the families of the soldiers he would recruit. Although it presented a full range of problems, the dependents who moved there were far better off than the black families in camps that grew up around army posts in other states. As the war drew to an end, however, the government's commitment to these families was eroded by issues of retrenchment. Even when conditions in the Roanoke colony were good, soldiers serving at a distance worried about their families' welfare. Only a very few men were able to have their immediate family members travel with their unit, or at least live in close proximity to the regimental camp.

Of course, for the first part of the war, escaped slaves of all ages who managed to reach Union lines were considered, at best, refugees who should fend for themselves. In eastern North Carolina, Union officials managing the war effort offered little relief and assistance. There, the swelling black population would have to rely, first and foremost, on their own initiative. Some support came from Northern associations involved with the welfare of freedmen, but that aid was sporadic and limited. Although agencies such as the New England Freedmen's Aid Society, the National Freedmen's Relief Association, and the American Missionary Association donated some supplies, they had limited resources and focused mainly on providing teachers for freedmen.[4] Moreover, the clothing and rations that were made available by Northern benefactors were never sufficient to meet the needs of all of the black refugees. Nevertheless, the Union military presence soon opened a wide range of economic opportunities for enterprising African Americans.

Once Federal troops under Maj. Gen. Ambrose E. Burnside had captured Roanoke Island in February 1862 and New Bern the following month, black refugees, or "contrabands" as they became known, began entering the Union lines. Uncertain of their future, they hoped for greater freedom than they had known. As elsewhere, the Union response was halting, inconsistent, and overshadowed by other aspects of the war effort. A coherent response was some time in coming and emerged most fully in conjunction with Union recruitment concerns. In the interim, waves of black refugees were dealt with in an ad hoc manner. By late 1862, a policy had been cobbled together that placed the contraband camps that were growing up around Union posts in the occupied South under the authority of the Federal Quartermaster's Department, since it was assumed that able-bodied black men could be best used by that branch of the military. At the same time, regional Federal commanders appointed superintendents whose duties were initially to supervise the swelling numbers of refugees—black and white. Most of the officers assigned to this task were selected from the pool of army chaplains. Their background ensured that most superintendents were sincerely concerned about the welfare of the refugees, although they understood that the camps were subordinate to military exigencies.

Vincent Colyer, an early superintendent, described the arrival of the first group of fifteen or twenty refugees in the days immediately after Roanoke was captured. "They came from up the Chowan River, and as they were passing they had been shot at by their rebel masters from the banks of the river." Some had traveled considerable distances and, occasionally, with unexpected assistance. In early March 1862 boats were left at the mouth of the Scuppernong River in Washington County by three white Unionists for slaves who were trying to flee to Roanoke Island. It was in sharp contrast to the harsh treatment that fugitives received from some Union officials and soldiers who were sympathetic to the institution of slavery.[5] Yet despite the behavior of some racist officers and the uncertainty of the Federal treatment they would receive, runaways continued to move east, often hiding in the woods during the day and traveling at night. In June 1862 two escaped slaves arrived from northern Alabama, a distance of about 750 miles. It took two other refugees six weeks to make their way up from South Carolina. Confederate planters responded by moving their slaves farther inland and by attempting to intercept the fugitives.[6] When Union general Edward Potter's cavalrymen raided Greenville in July 1863, they reportedly released twenty-five African Americans from jail "who had been imprisoned in attempting to get inside our lines, in order to join the colored regiment at Newbern." The conditions encountered by the runaways were so hazardous that often only men made it to safety. When Hattie Rogers and other slaves on an Onslow County plantation learned that they were to be moved to Franklin County "to keep them [the Yankees] from setting us free," only a few of the men were able to swim the White Oak River to Jones County and walk to New Bern. In another case, George Harris, with family members who had not been sold, escaped from Jones County to New Bern, where he spent part of the war working for a Union officer. A more remarkable case was that of Mary Barbour, whose father transported his whole family by wagon from McDowell County, in western North Carolina, to Roanoke Island, traveling by night and hiding by day. The exodus of slaves increased during the early summer. The soldiers in every Union raid into disputed territory were accompanied on their return by black refugees.[7] By July 1862 about ten thousand African Americans were within Federal lines, and by early 1863, according to a military census, there were almost six thousand in New Bern alone.[8]

The refugees who found shelter around Federal garrisons represented only a small part of North Carolina's African American community, but their numbers were sufficient to create acute problems for Federal officers who increasingly had to find them food, clothing, and shelter. Union officials took the first steps to provide assistance to the blacks clustering around the various Union posts. Just after the capture of New Bern in February 1862, General Burnside appointed Vincent Colyer, then a member of the Christian Commission, as superintendent of the poor in North Carolina. Colyer devoted much of his time seeing to the needs of white soldiers and destitute white civilians and only a portion of it to black refugees. Indeed, the supervisor stressed in his report that the poor African Americans under his care were far less dependent on Federal support than the poor whites. In part, that was because the various branches of the army employed large numbers of black men.[9] Burnside directed Colyer to hire as many as five thousand to work on the Union fortifications. Although he was never able to meet that target, black

"The Campaign in North Carolina, Headquarters of Vincent Collyer, Superintendent
of the Poor at New Bern, Distribution of Clothing to the Contraband," 1862
(*Frank Leslie's Illustrated Newspaper*, 14 June 1862, Courtesy of North Carolina
Collection, University of North Carolina Library at Chapel Hill)

labor built many of the forts in eastern North Carolina. Much of the aid and
employment offered to Southern blacks reflected the ambiguous attitude of
Northern authorities. Colyer's assessment of Burnside was equally applicable
to many Federal officers. While the general was "by no means an abolitionist," he "had too much sagacity to despise the service of the blacks."[10]

During his four months as superintendent, Colyer not only supervised relief and distributed supplies but he also established schools for both whites
and blacks. This brought him into conflict with military governor Edward
Stanly, who objected to the creation of black schools and who was willing, at
least initially, to return black refugees to North Carolina planters. Although
President Lincoln ultimately supported the superintendent, the dispute probably hastened Colyer's resignation in July 1862. His successor, the Reverend

James Means, took on more limited duties before his death in April 1863, but those duties focused entirely on the problems of black refugees. Just six weeks before he succumbed to typhoid, Means convinced Gen. John G. Foster of the need to undertake a census of all African Americans in the New Bern area as a preliminary step in addressing their needs and assessing their potential usefulness.[11] Because the census was completed before General Wild started to enlist black soldiers, he used the information in his recruiting efforts.

James Means went to North Carolina to serve as a chaplain in the military hospitals around New Bern. He had also begun preaching in the African Baptist Church, where he had opened a school. As the new "Superintendent of Blacks in North Carolina," he recorded and disbursed wages, rations, and clothing to all black laborers employed by the army. He also tried to address the moral and social needs of the black refugees at a time when his health was declining. By February 1863, Reverend Horace James and others took over some of Means's preaching duties for they realized that he was physically exhausted. His death two months later persuaded General Foster that Means had been burdened with too many responsibilities. Thus, when Foster appointed Horace James, chaplain of the 25th Massachusetts, as superintendent of blacks on 24 April, certain duties were left in the hands of army officers to reduce the superintendent's workload.[12]

Even with fewer obligations, James was entrusted with a wide range of activities. He continued to track the demographics of black refugees; supervised the distribution of clothes, rations, and medicine to those in need; helped the freedmen find employment; and oversaw "the making of contracts between former slaves and whites and to ensure that those agreements were faithfully executed by both parties." At the same time, he worked hard to increase the literacy of the black population. James also introduced to North Carolina the policy of creating refugee camps on abandoned or confiscated land, a measure that was being implemented elsewhere in the South. He would have preferred to locate the ex-slaves on government-sponsored farms, but the amount of available land in the Federally controlled areas was simply insufficient. Nevertheless, his goal was to achieve self-sufficiency in these camps through programs of education, vocational training, and the establishment of small industries that would draw on the abilities and skills of freedmen. Ultimately, half a dozen such quarters were set up in Union-occupied North Carolina.[13] The largest and most permanent camp was just outside of New Bern, but it was at Roanoke that Federal officials would be most active.

Across the South, officers like James had become concerned about the problems manifested by the clustering of black refugees around Union posts. In part, they worried that their close proximity to army camps would undermine military discipline and increase fraternization between displaced blacks and soldiers. Moreover, the crowded, and unsanitary conditions in the rapidly growing refugee camps created health problems that threatened to spill over into the army camps. Thus, as the winter of 1862 approached, the Federal government established a new policy that assigned responsibility for the contraband camps to the Quartermaster's Department.[14] Department commanders were to select supervisors, who, as in the past, would most often be army chaplains. Although contraband camps were established near Union posts throughout the South, the nature of these camps varied considerably from region to region. But common to all was the attempt to take advantage of black labor. In early 1862 military authorities in Louisiana began to oversee the leasing of black workers to white employers under wage contracts, and within two years such programs existed in virtually all occupied regions.[15] In other areas, such as the Sea Islands of South Carolina, the camps were organized primarily as appendages to free labor schemes that focused on established plantations. In the Mississippi Valley, by contrast, most camps were temporary places to hold women, children, and the elderly while the able-bodied men were employed elsewhere by the military. Just across the Potomac River from Washington, on property owned by Robert E. Lee, Federal officials opened "Freedman's Village," a public relations showcase to which they could bring foreign dignitaries. By contrast, the camp at nearby Mason Island, Maryland, was established "to make it a general depot for hireing [sic] out Contrabands." In some cases, camps were intended to provide for those who could not care for themselves. In early 1864 the provost marshal in New Bern designated a thirty-acre farm, dubbed the "U.S. House of Refuge," on the outskirts of town "to house and support widows, orphans, and other indigents."[16]

In North Carolina, the camps around New Bern and the smaller port towns most closely resembled camps elsewhere in the South. New Bern was a magnet for most black refugees. A majority of the African Americans found places to stay in the town, but three camps were established on the outskirts to house several thousand more freedmen who were not as fortunate. After Maj. Gen. George E. Pickett attacked New Bern in late 1864, Confederate soldiers captured or killed some of the refugees in the two most exposed camps before the rest could flee to safety behind Union lines. After the Confederates withdrew, all of the black refugees were consolidated into one settlement on the Trent River just across from New Bern. The Trent River camp had the security of being within the Federal fortifications. It had one other advantage. The confiscated property had belonged to Confederate colonel Peter G. Evans, who, at the start of the war, had allowed the land to be used as a camp for Confederate soldiers.

Horace James, acting on the orders of Gen. John J. Peck, quickly designed the new camp on the Trent River. Soldiers surveyed the streets and laid out fifty- by sixty-foot lots that allowed for a garden with each structure. Before long, the settlement had almost eight hundred small cabins. James reported that by the end of 1864, 6,560 freedmen were living in New Bern and another 2,798 in the camp, of whom 1,226 were receiving some help from the government. A majority of these refugees supported themselves through civilian or government jobs. The families of black soldiers were scattered through the town and the camp. All were eligible for government rations; James recorded that 660 adults and 691 children were receiving rations at the end of 1864. All adults were supposed to get "10 oz. of pork or bacon, or 1 lb. of fresh or salt beef. In addition, they got a pound of flour or soft bread, or 12 oz. of hard bread twice a week. For every 100 rations, they were given 10 lb. of beans, peas, or hominy, 8 lb. of sugar, 2 qt. Of vinegar, 8 oz. of candles, 2 lb. of soap, and 15 lb. of potatoes when practical." Women and children could also claim ten pounds of coffee or fifteen ounces of tea for every one hundred rations. Half rations were given to children under fourteen.[17] Military dependents in any of the camps could expect this level of support.

By staying in New Bern, the refugees, including many soldiers' families, could not only claim rations but also find a variety of ways to augment their income. A larger number of the men and older boys found civilian jobs with the military, while others provided laundry and personal services. Black seamen crewed over twenty steamers in the waters around New Bern, while tradesmen, porters, and stevedores could also hope to find jobs in the busy port. Some of the more courageous freedmen performed farming chores at surrounding plantations or found work in the turpentine woods.[18] Although towns such as New Bern and even Beaufort offered new opportunities for the freedmen, old problems often resurfaced. Black workers did not always receive the wages and rations due them. And there was always the possibility that local authorities would arbitrarily draft them to work on projects without compensation or even impress and ship them outside the department. This occurred in September 1864, when two hundred black men in and around New Bern were rounded up and transported to Virginia to work as laborers for the army.[19] Moreover, the Confederate attack on the town in February 1864 highlighted the perilous position of freedmen in this area.

Of course, some families of black soldiers were longtime residents of New Bern, and, for them, leaving the town would have represented the greater hardship. This was true of Mary Elizabeth (Bess) Kent and her husband Henry, a sergeant in Company M of the 14th U.S. Colored Heavy Artillery (USCHA), who had both been free before the war began. Her parents, also free, lived in New Bern. Henry Kent, who worked as a wheelwright, had moved there three or four years earlier. Henry and Bess were married in June 1860 in the home of her parents, where Bess remained after Henry enlisted in the artillery regiment. The only time she left New Bern was when she occasionally traveled down to Morehead City to visit Henry while he was stationed at Fort Macon.[20] For Bess Kent, it was logical to stay in New Bern—close to family, friends, and her husband's business interests. Since Henry had not joined a regiment in the African Brigade, she had little incentive to move to Roanoke Island.

The factors that led another soldier's wife to stay in New Bern are not as obvious. Harriet Winn had been a slave in Onslow County before the war but managed to make her way to New Bern by August 1862. Her husband Archibald had been a slave in Bertie and Washington counties, and, after a series of sales while he was a teenager, he had ended up in Plymouth, where "he remained until after the emancipation proclamation." He moved first to Roanoke Island and later to New Bern. After working as a laborer on Fort Totten and then as a cook for the army teamsters, as well as serving as a preacher, Archibald Winn enlisted in Company F of the 35th USCT on 23 May 1863. By that time he and Harriet were living in James City as husband and wife. Several of his comrades testified that Harriet "used to come to camp to see Archibald, who claimed her as his wife then." Harriet remained in James City while Archibald was in the army. When he returned, they, like many other black couples, "went to the Court House in New Bern and got the 25[-cent] marriage license the same as all the colored people did."[21] Why Harriet decided not to join the other soldiers' wives on Roanoke Island is not documented.

Other dependents helped to create a distinct settlement on Roanoke Island—one unlike the other refugee camps in North Carolina. Once General Wild began recruiting African Americans in the early summer of 1863, it became clear that in order to attract large numbers of blacks, the Federal government would have to guarantee substantial aid to their families while the men were under arms. Rations were only part of this assistance. Security was another. Such a policy was important for both moral and practical reasons. When white civilians enlisted in the army, Federal and Northern state governments had acknowledged their obligation to support the soldiers' dependents. That policy was gradually extended to Southern black families, albeit in a halting and ambivalent fashion. Ultimately, the commitment would entail making the Federal bounty system available to black soldiers and their dependents. Wild understood that without such material and financial support, the number of African Americans willing to enlist would be considerably reduced. But the first priority in a state like North Carolina was the physical safety of the black families. Thus it was a logical extension of the policy introduced by Superintendent James to dedicate the most secure camp—the one on Roanoke Island—to the families of the soldiers whom Wild had begun recruiting. This experiment was intended to establish a community that was significantly different from the "regimental villages" that were sometimes tolerated around garrison towns elsewhere in the South.[22]

Unlike the other camps in North Carolina and elsewhere, Roanoke was frequently described as a "colony." Thus, for example, whereas the Trent River site was intended to serve only as a temporary home for the freedpeople, Roanoke was to be more durable. The officials involved in setting up and overseeing the colony may have been ambivalent about their expectations, but most believed the experiment to be both long-lasting and self-sustaining. Unfortunately, the differing visions of the island community conflicted. For Wild, it was a refuge for military dependents needing support. For others, it was a means of regenerating a class of people scarred by the effects of slavery. Certainly Horace James, the most influential force in the island's development, saw the colony as a chance to create a model black community that, through education and Northern guidance, could achieve a free and independent social unit imbued with middle-class values. Whereas he referred to the "temporary camps or settlements" housing black refugees around towns like New Bern, Beaufort, and Washington, he always talked of "colonizing" the former slaves on Roanoke Island.[23]

Roanoke Island officially became a settlement to receive the families of

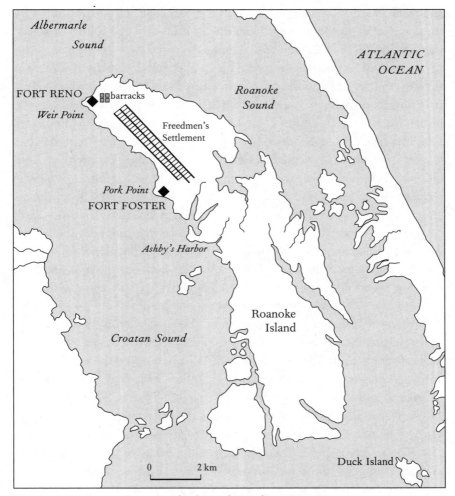

Roanoke Island, North Carolina, 1862–1865

soldiers recruited by Wild in July 1863. Secretary of War Edwin M. Stanton had cautioned General Foster that his predecessor had neglected to encourage black enlistment and "that you [Foster] will not fall into that error." Stanton wanted him to do all he could to "encourage and stimulate the incoming of colored men from the rebels, and cause them to be enrolled and armed." Prompt action could increase the general's military effectiveness and, at the very least, guarantee a larger labor force. Foster immediately replied, indicating the steps that he had taken to enlist black soldiers, to impress black labor, and to facilitate Wild's efforts. As a central part of his efforts, he "intended to carry out the colonization schemes as a nucleus for the colored soldiers' families, and to make Roanoke Island the key-point."[24]

The colony on Roanoke Island makes an interesting study for a number of reasons. It provided critical aid and a dedicated safe haven for many families of Wild's recruits. Such security for the dependents of black soldiers was rare in the South. During much of the war, most, but not all, of the families on Roanoke Island were considerably better off than their counterparts elsewhere. In western Tennessee and the Mississippi Valley in particular, conditions for black refugees were extremely harsh. Most contraband camps in these areas had few resources and little government protection from the exploitation of white soldiers and civilians.[25] When black dependents, out of necessity and anxiety, tried to find security near army camps, senior officers became alarmed by their potentially adverse effect on the discipline and morale of the troops. Some tried to restrict access between the men and their families and to discourage a satellite community.[26] Other commanders attempted to relocate the families to distant contraband camps. Few shared the conviction of Wild and James concerning the need for and the benefit of a well-supported community for black soldiers' dependents. Despite the numerous problems that arose on Roanoke Island, the existence of the colony encouraged many men to enlist who might otherwise have remained civilians in order to look after their families.

The way in which the settlement was run demonstrates the limitations and restrictions of progressive white support to African Americans during the war. The efforts made on Roanoke Island, the behavior of various officials in charge, and how the black soldiers perceived that their families were being treated all offer useful insights into Civil War race relations. The settlement also illustrates the ways concerned, sympathetic Northern soldiers and civilians attempted to better the lot of the newly freed slaves and the ways in which unsympathetic or racist Northerners undermined those actions. The most basic assumptions about the nature of the island community varied among the military officials who worked on the island, although the attitudes of many changed significantly over time. Indeed, the fading optimism of the colony's earliest white supporters, something that was apparent by the start of 1865, was representative of changes elsewhere in the South.

In addition, many structural and institutional difficulties confronted the freedpeople on Roanoke Island as they struggled for autonomy and economic independence during the war. By the last months of the conflict, the range of problems on the island was becoming increasingly evident. Government assistance to the blacks at Roanoke, and elsewhere in the state, had often been sacrificed to broader war issues. The differing extent of support for the refugees reflected the conflicting white views of what was best for Southern blacks in both the short and the long term. Black workers on the island were expected to support themselves and their families even though their wages were paid infrequently, if at all. When Federal officials decided, as the war ended, that too much aid was creating dependency, rations were cut even to the families that had been promised support. Equally detrimental, the ways in which the settlement was administered opened the door to fraud, financial abuse, and cultural misunderstandings that created unnecessary hardships for the black residents. The colony also suffered from trying to be both a haven for army dependents and a settlement for diverse black refugees. Even at the peak of its operation, the island community could never accommodate all of the family members of every recruit. At the same time, a significant portion of the population—both long-term residents and some of the later refugees—were not related to black recruits. In fact, by the summer of 1862, so many ex-slaves had settled there that Federal officials, looking for more labor, had begun transferring able-bodied men from the island to New Bern. Even after Foster had given the settlement its special designation, some Federal officials regarded Roanoke as just another camp to be exploited.[27]

When Foster first authorized the colony, he envisioned that Wild and James would share responsibility for looking after the infantrymen's families. Their joint control reflected the overlapping motives for the experiment. The chaplain was concerned with religious and social matters, and he was to handle the distribution of all donations sent to Roanoke from Northern states. In June 1863 Foster had sent him to the Northeast to raise money and supplies for the envisioned settlement to augment what the government could provide. In just a few weeks James was able to collect between eight and nine thousand dollars, primarily from the freedmen's associations in Boston and New York. In his absence, Wild was in charge of distributing food and clothing to the settlement's residents, as well as paying the black employees.[28] In addition, Wild was to take possession of all unoccupied lands on the island, to lay them out, and, at his own discretion, to assign them to the families of his soldiers, to invalids, and to blacks working for the government.

One problem that hindered effective supervision of the settlement stemmed from the fact that both James and Wild were overburdened with other responsibilities, and Roanoke could receive only part of their attention. Moreover, Wild felt that he had to organize the colony and support the early refugees despite the hostility of other Federal officials. Some officials thought that too much assistance would undermine the perceived necessity of creating black self-sufficiency through a degree of hardship, but the general disagreed. In addition, "between the military general business, the military recruiting business, the colonization scheme, and the endless appeals of the oppressed for protection," Wild believed that he had too many jobs to do them all well. "At times," he wrote, "when I see the weak, or the false and rotten course pursued by different provost marshals, it exasperates me so." Horace James may also have exasperated Wild, for the men differed philosophically on how to treat the refugees. James contended that refugees should not be given free aid and supplies. This view reflected his commitment to a free labor ideology: that is, for a man to be truly free, he must have the chance to achieve economic independence by his own efforts. It was far better, James wrote, to provide essential goods to the freedmen of North Carolina "at prices within their reach, putting it in their power to live within their scanty means," than to give them goods free of charge. An inexpensive store, rather than donations, "promotes their *manhood*, instead of inviting them to be mendicants." Wild, on the other hand, was more concerned with the immediate needs of his soldiers' families and less with a theory of social regeneration. Whatever disagreement might have existed between the men was resolved in September 1863, when Wild and his regiments left for South Carolina, and James was given sole power over Roanoke Island.[29]

By this time, the process of laying out the colony was well under way. Although it did not escape many of the social and financial problems faced by refugee camps elsewhere, it was, as its planners envisioned, far less vulnerable to Confederate threats. That had been the major reason the site had been selected, with General Foster's approval, to act as the primary refuge for the dependents of Wild's men. Roanoke, located just inside the Outer Banks, was well suited for this purpose. Moreover, the island had other advantages. At a time when Union forces held little secure land in North Carolina, the northern and western part of the island contained hundreds of acres that the army could put to good use. In addition, existing structures could be converted to house families. When black refugees, as well as a small number of white refugees, began arriving after February 1862, some of the barracks that had previ-

"Confederate Prisoners in Camp Georgia [at Weir Point], Roanoke Island," 1862.
The barracks in the background were used to house the black refugees as they arrived
at Roanoke Island. (*Illustrated London News*, 29 March 1862, Courtesy of North
Carolina Collection, University of North Carolina Library at Chapel Hill)

ously housed Confederate and Union troops were turned into the receiving
quarters for the freedmen. Pvt. John Henry Byrd, of the 9th New York Volunteers, who had stayed in one of these structures at that time, described them
in a letter to his father. "The barracks are between seventy and eighty ft. long
[and] thirty ft. wide. There is a partition through the center of the building so
that each Comp'y. are separated and then our part of the building is separated
into seven rooms." The room that housed Byrd's company was about sixteen
by seventeen feet. "Each room have a fireplace," he told his father, "which
make them very comfortable." Although a Pennsylvania soldier agreed that
they were "first rate Barracks" and must have been made at "a tremendous
expense," the buildings would deteriorate badly over the next few years.[30]
Whatever their state of comfort, they provided the first, and sometimes the
only, home on the island for the arriving refugees.

The barracks included "about twenty-four long gabled buildings, with
chimneys and out-houses," capable of housing several thousand people. In
the largest buildings the room partitions consisted only of palings that did not

reach the ceiling, "giving smoke the freedom to run from room to room, and making it cold and cheerless" as well as limiting privacy. With a continuous inflow of refugees, the barracks were never empty. It was expected that most of these people could be quickly resettled in their own small homes, but that did not occur. The structures remained occupied throughout the war; while some black families could live in comfort in their own homes, others endured an unpleasant existence in the barracks. That, however, lay in the future. In late 1863 the plan was to lay out a village with surveyed roads forming a large regular grid that contained sizable lots on which most people could build their homes. Sgt. George O. Sanderson was released from the 43rd Massachusetts to act as assistant superintendent and began surveying the limited land available.[31]

Three wide avenues were laid out, 1,200 feet apart, running approximately between Weir's Point and Pork Point on the northwest side of the island, while twenty-six smaller streets 400 feet apart intersected the avenues at a right angle. The blocks created held twelve one-acre lots, each fronting a street or an avenue. The lots, sufficient for a cabin and a garden, allowed the black families partial self-sufficiency.[32] Despite the lack of tools and limited resources, the freedpeople immediately began clearing their lots and building crude houses. According to H. E. Rockwell, an assistant of Sanderson, the homes were built "of logs or poles, covered with a kind of board or shingle simply rived from the pines or cypress, making a tolerably comfortable house for fair weather." At the same time, the new lot holders began cultivating small gardens to help meet their food needs. Officials never intended to give farms to the freedmen. Unoccupied land on the island was limited and not rich enough for profitable farming. With most able-bodied men in the army, their wives and other dependents could not be expected to clear and plant much more than an acre.[33]

As one might expect, rations, materials, and shelter of all kinds were constantly in short supply. For this reason, and perhaps because James believed that necessity could best stimulate Southern refugees, black and white, to emulate Northern workers, he consistently tried to reduce the number of rations that he distributed. The soldiers in the black regiments might draw some consolation that their families were receiving full rations at a time when others were given only enough "to prevent positive suffering."[34] There was always the danger, however, that James or other authorities would, in their attempt to minimize the rations, shortchange the families. When 35th USCT was transferred to South Carolina in 1863, not only did its soldiers lose the comfort of proximity to their families, but they also lost the active supervision of General Wild. Although Wild retained an interest in events on the island and was concerned about conditions there, in fact, full responsibility for the Roanoke settlement lay in the hands of Horace James and his assistants.

James's first official report, delivered in early September 1863 after a brief visit to the island, indicated that considerable progress had been made. He claimed to have found "the eleven or twelve hundred negroes now here in a very comfortable condition, happy and content," except that many had not been paid for their work for the government. Sergeant Sanderson had been busy, and the grid of streets and avenues had been laid out. It had all been done without encroaching on anyone's improved or occupied land. James explained that, once they had selected their lot, almost all of the refugees had begun building rough log houses and getting ready for the coming winter. The island appeared to be very healthy, and, "on the whole, the colony is doing well."[35] There were, however, two significant problems. The lack of draft animals of any sort put an extra burden on the residents. James hoped that any broken-down mules or horses in the vicinity of New Bern could be sent to the island, where they could recover and be put to work.

An even more pressing problem was that many blacks who had been employed by the Federal government for more than a year had never been paid. There was certainly plenty of work for able-bodied laborers on the island. A large number had been hired to work on the fortifications. Others were required to support the provisioning trade. Roanoke Island became a depot for resupplying the Union ships that policed the sounds. Captains anchored colliers off Roanoke with coal for the fleet. Workmen completed a 500-foot wharf to off-load the hundreds of pounds of potatoes, onions, tomatoes, and beef needed each week to keep the ships and the army supplied. The problem was never a shortage of work. Rather, it was the long delay in paying the black workers, which caused hardship and perpetuated a sense of injustice. If they were only paid, James reported while on the island, the men could support themselves and their dependents in relative comfort.[36] His brief visit over, the chaplain returned to New Bern.

On 10 September 1863 General Foster, in General Order No. 12, officially transferred overall responsibility for Roanoke Island from General Wild to Horace James. As the colony's new leader, James was to take charge of the unoccupied lands, lay them out, and assign them, "according to his own discretions," not only to the families of black soldiers, but also to "invalids and other blacks in the employ of the Government." James's authority was to be respected "in all matters relating to the welfare of the colony." Early in October, General Peck visited the island to see how the work was coming along. The general was impressed. "My expectations in respect to the colony," he wrote after returning to New Bern, "were more than realized by my visit to Roanoke Island. No better place could have been selected, and I see no permanent cause for apprehension on the score of health." He noted that James had been very active in laying out the settlement. In response to James's request, Peck reported that "mules, horses wagons, etc., have been condemned and ordered turned over to the colony. He expected that the settlement could be self-supporting after the first year.[37]

A few weeks later James submitted another optimistic report. He was particularly pleased by the growing support within the black community. The settlement had become "increasingly popular among the Negroes, and the drift of (black) sentiment is decidedly towards the enterprise." While he could draw much comfort from the motivation displayed by the freedpeople, he reiterated his concerns that black workers had still not been paid. And the lack of a quartermaster on the island ensured that they would not receive the money owed them anytime soon. Moreover, it meant that James could not guarantee wages to men who could "put up rude houses for the wives and children of the colored soldiers, whom we have *pledged ourselves* to care for, and cover from the cold weather of the coming winter." The chief medical officer at New Bern was planning to send nearly one thousand more freedpeople to Roanoke before the end of the year. They could be easily accommodated, James argued, but only if he had the means to pay men to do the work.[38]

James soon had the authority to do just that. In November 1863 General Butler replaced General Foster as commander of the Department of Virginia and North Carolina. Butler immediately demonstrated greater concern for the welfare of the black soldiers and their families. Among the numerous policies he introduced was one that made all military dependents in any camp in the department eligible for subsistence rations. Although the new policy merely confirmed what was already happening on Roanoke, two other actions had significant implications for the island's inhabitants. First, Butler placed full responsibility for the freedpeople in a new Department of Negro Affairs, with James as the superintendent of the District of North Carolina. And second, while most of the superintendent's duties were merely a continuation of his earlier responsibilities, in mid-December 1863 James was appointed quartermaster, at the rank of captain, enabling him to receive and disperse military funds. Black laborers employed on Roanoke Island by the Quartermaster's Department at last had the means to be paid.[39]

The settlement's apparent progress came when James was increasingly busy soliciting aid from the North. The hidden cost, however, was that he had much less time to personally monitor conditions on the island. Northern aid societies in general and the New England Freedmen's Aid Society in particular saw a greater opportunity to help African Americans in North Carolina with the departure of Governor Stanly. James traveled to Massachusetts, New York, and Pennsylvania several times in search of money and supplies. He spent much of his time, both then and later, recruiting and overseeing Northern teachers who were willing to work with the refugees in North Carolina. He was able to attract teachers like Oscar E. Doolittle, who had previously run a successful school for African Americans in Boston, as well as instructors who were experienced and highly recommended. In at least one case, he persuaded private individuals in Massachusetts to pay the salaries of teachers in North Carolina. James found his time taken up in juggling the different priorities of the Northern aid societies, obtaining rations and a schoolhouse for teachers at Morehead City, and responding to requests by Northern newspapers for detailed information about North Carolina. All of these activities drew his attention away from the Roanoke settlement. Nevertheless, James planned to establish six schools on the island. One of the persons employed to teach there, at least briefly, was Sgt. Robert Morrow, of the 14th USCHA, who had been detailed to recruit on Roanoke. Morrow had acquired a "decent education" as the personal servant of James J. Pettigrew while Pettigrew attended West Point and the University of North Carolina. After he had been posted to Roanoke, the National Freedmen's Relief Association commissioned him as a teacher. But "he died suddenly, and in his bed, having retired at night as well as usual."[40]

Despite the superintendent's optimistic reports, there were signs by the end of 1863 that conditions on the island, at least for many inhabitants, were deteriorating. This was due, in part, to the influx of more than a thousand refugees following the Union raids through northeastern North Carolina in December. Wild had planned and led the expedition both to raise new recruits and to free black families. He also used the opportunity to send badly needed supplies to Roanoke. By 12 December Wild had ordered a steamer to

Roanoke "with a load of contrabands, including horses and carts" and sent more soldiers into Hertford County to help slaves escape. By the time the expedition was over, Wild reported that he had secured the release of perhaps 2,500 people, although both the actual number and the destination of the refugees were difficult to establish. What was clear, however, was that most of the people freed were not able-bodied young men.[41]

The arrival of this group at the onset of winter put an extra strain on the island community. Only a few weeks later, D. W. Hand, medical director of the district, was extremely critical of conditions there. Hand had inspected "the Negro camps and quarters on Roanoke Island" and found them "in a very unsatisfactory condition." Although he realized that over a thousand black refugees had arrived since 1 December, Hand felt that the management of the colony had been "almost wholly neglected." He placed much of the blame for the lack of proper supervision on "the other duties imposed on *Chaplain James*." In late January 1864 more than five hundred refugees were living in huts made of brush and earth—seven to ten in each hut—and suffering terribly from the weather. Conditions in the barracks were almost as bad. One barrack, thirty feet by twenty feet and lacking both flooring and chimneys, "had fifty-four people living in it." In others, people were trying to keep warm by building fires where there were no fireplaces. The consequence was sore eyes for many and blindness for some. Mortality was high. Many had died without the doctors having been notified that they were sick, and some corpses had begun to decompose before they were placed in coffins. At the same time, scurvy had broken out. Steps were only just being taken to build a new hospital to accommodate the new arrivals. Hand also warned that the burial place for the colony was so near the main camp that it should expect an outbreak of disease in the summer.[42]

At a time when numerous refugees were facing severe privation, Sergeant Sanderson told Surgeon Hand that as many as five hundred adult men were idle on the island, enough, if organized, to build cabins to house everyone and remedy the worst conditions. The inability to pay them wages and put them to work meant that any improvements took place slowly. James, in contrast, took a more positive view. He acknowledged that the influx of refugees after Wild's expedition put a good deal of strain on the island's resources and that the new arrivals "suffered somewhat in the stress of weather which we experienced early in January, having come in so large numbers, before we had suitable accommodation." Nevertheless, he felt that all of the arrivals had been provided for and that there was room for more. A month later, James wrote to Wild to reassure him about conditions on the island. The colony was becoming more established, and a majority of the freedpeople would be able "to sustain themselves this season with the aid the govt allows the soldier's families."[43]

In his letter to Wild, James did not mention the rumors circulating throughout New Bern and Roanoke in early 1864 that the Confederates were planning to attack the island as part of their larger campaign in eastern North Carolina. In late January and early February, General Pickett led a poorly coordinated strike on New Bern that failed. The very threat of the assault had prompted the military to order a "portion of the contrabands now living outside the lines" around New Bern to be transferred to Roanoke Island, along with their movable possessions. When Picket was recalled to Virginia, Gen. Robert F. Hoke assumed command of the Confederate forces and ultimately led a successful assault against the Union base at Plymouth. It was the uncertainty of Hoke's intentions that had fueled the rumors that the Roanoke colony was in danger, though New Bern was perceived to be the Confederates' main target. In late February, Federal authorities warned Gen. Henry W. Wessells, who commanded the subdistrict of the Albemarle, that the "Negroes on Roanoke Island should be prepared to resist a boat raid against the island." General Peck had told Wessells that he had "reliable information that the taking of Roanoke Island is a part of the plan ordered to be executed at Richmond." Peck was sufficiently concerned that in early March, when other garrisons were asking for reinforcements, he transferred the 99th New York Volunteers to the island to help defend it. He also sent three hundred muskets so all able-bodied African Americans could be organized and armed. As Peck wrote, "intimations of a boat attack at night on the island have been made of late, and I cannot risk anything now."[44]

The islanders feared not just Confederate regulars. In various parts of the South, guerrilla groups angered by the effective end of slavery in Union-occupied territory turned their fury on the newly freed blacks, particularly those employed by the army or living in contraband camps.[45] It is not surprising that Federal officials on Roanoke may have felt vulnerable. As it turned out, the island was never attacked, but the fall of Plymouth in April triggered a flood of black and white refugees that soon reached the island. Just before the final Confederate assault on Plymouth, the families of Union officers and Buffaloes were evacuated to Roanoke, followed the next day by another boatload of African American women and children. They were the lucky ones. Others had managed to escape only by crossing the river and seeking safety in the swamp. After the battle had ended, some of these refugees managed to reach Roanoke Island. Once again the colony was faced with the challenge of finding accommodations for a new wave of displaced persons.[46]

Although the impoverished refugees who constantly arrived always dominated the black population on Roanoke, the island's African American community was never homogeneous. Amid the large number of transients, there were some blacks who had been born there and who, like Richard Etheridge, had close ties to the white island society. In addition, some black residents were comfortable financially or even well off. When Lucy Chase went to Roanoke Island in January 1865 for a brief stint of teaching, she stayed with "a very genteel colored family from Plymouth." Although she said little about the family or how it got to Roanoke, her accommodations included "a carpeted room with a stove and a luxurious bed." Perhaps closer to the norm was the success story of Mingo Obman, as related by Rev. Elinathan Davis, of Massachusetts, to a Northern audience. According to Davis, who had visited Roanoke in December 1864, Obman had managed to reach the island colony in May 1863 with virtually no money. Soon afterward, his wife also escaped and joined him, and together they built a small cabin in the settlement. Davis found that the couple had "plenty of provisions for themselves and to give a meal to anyone who was hungry." In addition, they had managed to build up "a hundred dollars in cash, besides two hundred and fifty due him from the government." The Obmans represented one side of a stark contrast that existed on the island. Refugees who had arrived when the colony was being organized had managed by 1864 to carve out a new life for themselves. They had received lots, constructed simple houses, and cultivated garden plots. Some of them worked for the government. These residents made up the scenes that missionaries liked to describe in letters home. But hundreds of other freedpeople lived in more primitive conditions when they first arrived on the island. One missionary recorded: "I see sights, *often*, *often*, that make my heart ache, & which I have no power to relieve."[47] A measure of how crowded, cold, and uncomfortable the barracks could be was that some refugees chose to live instead in the huts of brush and earth, as reported by the district's medical director.

Black residents, whether recently arrived and desperately poor or comfortably established in a village plot, all faced a wide spectrum of treatment from the white soldiers and officials with whom they came in contact. They encountered blatant, hostile racists and sympathetic, helpful supporters, although the majority of whites they met probably fell in between these two extremes. Two local officials who held considerable power over the lives of the African Americans reflected the two extremes. Both the white missionary teachers and the black residents regarded Amasa W. Stevens, superintendent of the island sawmill, as a friend. Indeed, his willingness to protest the treatment of the refugees in June 1865 would contribute to the termination of his position at the sawmill. By contrast, most freedpeople and missionaries believed that Holland Streeter, assistant superintendent on the island and director of the shad fisheries, was unprincipled and corrupt. Horace James had hired Streeter, a butcher from Lowell, Massachusetts, to manage the fisheries. While some officials questioned Streeter's efficiency, James and senior officials would continue to defend him.[48]

In early 1864 an attempt was made to establish a degree of local black autonomy. A "council" of fifteen of the leading freedmen on the island had been appointed to act for the common good of the refugees and to "be the germ of a civil government." But officials soon considered the venture a failure. Superintendent James claimed that the members were "too ignorant to keep records, or make and receive written communications, were jealous of one another, and too little raised in culture above the common people to command their respect." Only education, James argued, would fit them for republican self-government. White officials ignored several other factors that might explain why the "council" had difficulty gaining the respect and support of the island society generally. The black population of the island was primarily made up of refugees recently brought together and thus lacking the established patterns of leadership and consensus that form over time. Perhaps more important, people like James envisioned the council as "a medium through which the rules and orders of the Superintendent of Negro Affairs and of the military authorities might be communicated and enforced."[49] In other words, Federal officials who saw the council as a means of enforcing their decisions envisioned little local autonomy. This may have doomed the experiment in black self-government.

There was also the danger, both at Roanoke Island and in New Bern, that black aspirations could at any time be sacrificed to white interests. Two incidents underlined this possibility. The first case concerned the use of condemned military horses on the island. In early 1864 General Order No. 177

had authorized the transfer of horses that had been inspected and condemned for military use to James's control "for the advantage of the negroes," as the superintendent had requested months earlier. Nevertheless, although the original idea was that the freedmen would have the use of the animals, James had changed his mind and now wanted his assistants to have the horses while carrying out their duties of supervising and teaching the black inhabitants. Since army officers were prohibited from using these animals for either official or private purposes without the adjutant general's authorization, James put in a special request. The assistant adjutant general agreed with James, and the horses were diverted from the black residents of Roanoke to James's staff.[50]

A second case underscoring the vulnerability of African Americans developed during 1863 and early 1864. Initially a struggle in eastern North Carolina for control of black membership in the Methodist church, it quickly became enmeshed in Union war priorities. The conflict began as a contest between a black minister, Reverend J. W. Hood, and a young white Massachusetts Congregationalist, Edward S. Fitz, whose goals were supported by Horace James. Despite attempts allegedly orchestrated by Fitz to use the military to remove Hood as leader of the church, the black minister won over most of the black congregation and retained control of the church. Hood's resistance of the white attempts to take over, as well as his success in obtaining approval for the congregation to choose its own minister, elevated his status among the freedmen. The repercussions of this dispute, however, affected many freedmen throughout the east. Through James, Fitz used the ever-present Union need for black labor to try to undermine his opponent. Fitz passed on to General Butler a report that there were "thousands of idle Negroes in New Berne who might be profitably employed on the Dutch Gap Canal."[51] He then produced a list of the men whom he suggested might be sent to Virginia. Most of them supported Hood, most were employed, and some were old and infirm.

The military's need for black laborers who could be used in Virginia on projects such as the Dutch Gap was sufficiently great that officers were willing to overlook advanced age and infirmities. Only by appealing directly to Gen. Innis Palmer was Hood able to secure the release of some of his church officials. In one case, he persuaded Palmer to check a boat that was about to leave for Virginia. James, who was supervising the loading of the vessel, assured the general that the man in question was not on board. When the man called out and begged to be taken off, Palmer turned on James "and gave him such a tongue-lashing that Zion's members were safe from that time till the war closed."[52] Hood's recollection of the incident may well have been one-sided and perhaps not entirely accurate, but it does suggest that even James, a man frequently described as an ardent friend of the freedmen, functioned under conflicting motives. It also demonstrates how Union officials were willing to use black labor in ways they would never consider for white labor. For instance, there was never a suggestion that unemployed whites might be sent to Virginia.

Military necessity and racial prejudice combined to ensure that Union officials put manpower requirements ahead of the equitable treatment of African Americans. The primary concern in the fall of 1864 was to get labor from North Carolina to meet Butler's needs in Virginia. In September, a group of forty-five black workers who had been impressed from Roanoke Island to work on the Dutch Gap Canal petitioned General Butler about their treatment. The men had been building fortifications on Roanoke for four months when, near the end of August, they received orders to report to the island headquarters to be paid. When they got there, an armed guard put them on a steamer and they were shipped to Virginia. At the same time, white soldiers scoured the island for more laborers, even if they were young or sick. Although there were conflicting allegations as to whether the men had been promised their wages or had been given certificates of indebtedness by which they could draw clothes, one thing was clear. Laborers were urgently needed in Virginia, and Federal officials were sent to North Carolina to get them as quickly as possible, using force if necessary. The impressed workers claimed that many of them would have gone voluntarily, but they protested the methods used by the Federal officials. They had been given no chance to prepare for the trip or to speak to their families. James had not paid many of the workers since early in the year, and some of them were the sole support of women with young children.[53]

The workers who protested their removal to the Dutch Gap stated that there were other serious problems with how the freedpeople on the island were treated. They claimed that white soldiers plundered their gardens with impunity, and anyone who complained ran the risk of ending up in the guardhouse. In addition, they believed that Sanderson, in his capacity as assistant supervisor, allowed rations designated for the soldiers' dependents and the infirm, as well as clothing donated by Northern aid associations, to be sold to "the white secesh citizens" on the island.[54] Moreover, in the absence of

Horace James, Sanderson was engaged in illegal trade. There was a ring of truth to their charges. Several months earlier, General Wild had deplored the extent of the contraband trade. He reported that there had been a great deal of it "connived at by the authorities at Roanoke Island, probably for gain. Sutlers' stores changed hands largely." Wild believed that the post sutler was implicated but did not accuse anyone else.[55]

In addition to their complaints about the illegal trade, the petitioners worried that the island women, including the wives of absent soldiers, might be subjected to a fate similar to that of the impressed men. There were rumors that they might be shipped off the island against their will. Sanderson had apparently talked about sending two hundred women away. Certainly Federal officials, including James, had encouraged and assisted women to go north to work as household servants. In 1864 there was a big demand for black domestic servants in northeastern cities. Northern relief societies advocated shipping hundreds of black women to places like Boston and New Haven, where they could find good homes and fair wages. Many societies set up employment bureaus to help move black servants to Northern states.[56] It is understandable why women on Roanoke Island feared they might be forcibly moved.

Those fears, and stories of hardship and privation, were passed on, in various ways, to black troops serving in the field. Missionaries and sympathetic white soldiers on the island frequently wrote letters on behalf of dependents who could not write themselves but who desperately wanted to communicate with loved ones in uniform. Recruits from the island population brought disquieting news of events on Roanoke that left many black soldiers concerned about the welfare of their families. The regiments were paid infrequently, and there was no assurance that the money sent home was reaching those who so badly needed it. A few enlisted men, such as Pvt. Leon Bemberg, who had joined the 36th USCT at Roanoke Island in August 1863, were fortunate. Bemberg received a furlough from Company F so he could return to the island to check on his family. Pvt. William L Benson, in Company E of the 37th USCT, was not so lucky. He left his regiment on 27 August 1864, probably in an attempt to visit his family on the island. Years later he explained that he had been compelled to desert after his commanding officer had refused him a leave of absence. His action would later cost him and his family a pension.[57]

By late 1864 Roanoke Island reflected the ambiguities and contradictions in the minds and policies of the various Union officials as to what the colony should be. For General Wild, the island was primarily a safe haven where the dependents of his black soldiers could wait out the war, supported by the Federal government for as long as the men were in uniform. The soldiers themselves expected the government to honor its promise. Officials like Horace James, on the other hand, envisioned the island as a self-supporting, permanent community of freedmen imbued with Northern values of industry and thrift. For James, it was a long-term experiment designed to fundamentally alter black attitudes toward work and independence and to regenerate a people scarred by slavery. Men like James initially ignored the fact that the island was really a small, not very fertile area, and that only a part of it had been allotted to the black refugees. Since all of these families had been granted less than one acre, it was unreasonable to expect them to support themselves wholly by farming. Indeed, the problem of too little land undermined not just the objectives of Roanoke Island but also other attempts to establish family settlements.[58] The colony could become self-supporting only through the development of small-scale industries and activities, but even that was countered by the shifts in government policies. The Federal government, concerned that it was creating dependency, wanted blacks to become self-supporting but then paid those whom they employed irregularly and inadequately. When officials decided that the colony would or could not be self-sustaining, they reduced government support in an attempt to force self-reliance, even if it meant breaking their promise to the soldiers and their families.

If at times Federal officials promoted the growth of diverse enterprises, their constant removal of able-bodied men and boys effectively doomed the projects. Indeed, the very success of Union recruiters and the black commitment to the ongoing war effort ensured a constant drain on the number of male workers. As a result, during the war years most of the colony's inhabitants were females, young boys, old men, or invalids. For instance, John Dail, like many recruits from Roanoke Island, served in Company F of the 37th USCT. In the summer of 1864 he was detailed to work at Dutch Gap, where he "received an injury of the eyes by the explosion of a shell and . . . was treated for loss of vision by the Regimental Surgeon." After his discharge, he returned to Roanoke but there was little productive work that he could do. Indeed, on the first day of 1865, out of a total black population of 3,091, only 217 residents were men between the ages of eighteen and forty-five.[59]

It is likely that the island never held the large numbers of available healthy black workmen suggested in the reports turned in to General Butler and other Federal bureaucrats.

Even if Roanoke had been much larger and offered a greater agricultural potential and a more stable labor force, its residents would have had to accumulate at least a small pool of private capital before achieving economic self-sufficiency. That might have been possible, in the best of situations, through the careful saving of wages or through special payments such as bounties. But while some may have hoped to use government earnings to generate private capital, this was impossible when wages were either not paid or, if paid, did not reach the workers themselves. The frequent turnover of military command meant that some accounts were lost or misplaced. Sometimes the confusion was due to bureaucratic bungling, but more often it was the result of fraud. In all, overdue and unpaid wages to laborers on Roanoke Island at the start of 1865 totaled at least $18,570, most of which James felt would never be paid. Eighteen months later, officials in Washington were still trying to get payrolls from James in order to sort out unpaid wages to former government employees.[60]

The loss of these funds and the limited economic potential of the island made government support even more essential for the families of soldiers. Federal officials, however, alternated in viewing the black population as either a refugee problem to be managed within the priorities of war or a handy labor pool to be exploited on behalf of the war effort. Horace James was never inclined to be liberal with government assistance. While most of his subordinates, as well as the freedmen's aid societies, testified to James's hard work and efficiencies, the superintendent had become convinced that a certain degree of deprivation would spur self-reliance. Although he was totally committed to the success of his operations in North Carolina, it was only in the context of his vision for the freedpeople, whom he wished to imbue with Northern values. As part of that vision, he was convinced that the Department of Negro Affairs in the North Carolina District should be self-supporting. This was one reason why he had sought to have a sawmill constructed on Roanoke Island and had encouraged the freedmen to pursue economic ventures. The goal of economic independence may have reflected a larger plan for the entire Department of Negro Affairs, or it may have revealed James's fear that if his operations could not pay for themselves, they would be taken over by the U.S. Treasury Department. For whatever reasons, surviving accounts suggest that of the three district superintendents in the Department of Virginia and North Carolina, James was the most reluctant to disperse government funds. Although the District of North Carolina had the second largest population of freedmen, it received less in spending than the other two districts.[61]

By the end of 1864 there were ominous signs that government officials like James believed that the level of support offered to Southern blacks should be substantially reduced, even for the families of soldiers still in the army. Conditions, they maintained, had altered from the time that promises had been made to recruits, and experience had convinced them that too much aid was counterproductive. James's report in January 1865 illustrates this change in attitude. The superintendent proposed decreasing the rations issued to the black soldiers' families, now that these troops were being paid at the same rate as white soldiers. Moreover, he argued, many "wives of soldiers are well able to support themselves by their own labor." In addition, they "now receive supplies of money from their husbands in the field." To give them "full rations without regard to their circumstances is teaching them to be indolent, saucy, and unchaste." Although James admitted that many husbands were supporting their wives, he went on to depict their marital bonds as weak. "Slender as is the marriage ties between them, strong as are their passions, is it not strange that they often prove unfaithful to their husbands in the field?" He therefore proposed to give local officials the power to decide who were actually needy or to support only children and the elderly. On the island, the effects of the official policy of retrenchment were compounded by the apparent dishonesty of the man in charge of distributing aid, Holland Streeter. When Gen. John M. Schofield, commander of the Department of North Carolina, ordered a further reduction of rations in the contraband camps, James was quick to concur. He reported that he had "ceased giving rations to any on account of their being members of soldiers families" and that he would issue rations only to orphans, the infirm, and the indigent.[62]

Retrenchment led to protests by both whites and blacks on the island and by soldiers in the field who had been told about deteriorating conditions at Roanoke. In March 1865, at the request of island residents, a black schoolteacher named Richard Boyle drafted a petition addressed to the U.S. president and secretary of war. The document began by outlining the conflicting messages conveyed by Federal officials. Initially, they had been told that no able-bodied man could draw rations unless he worked for the government. The petitioners claimed that they had willingly taken on government jobs, although they seldom saw the ten-dollar monthly wage that they were due. Next they had been told "to work and get our living as White men and not apply to the Government." Men who had followed that advice suddenly found themselves vulnerable to the type of impressment that sent islanders to Virginia to work on the Dutch Gap Canal. Some of these men had been killed or had died of disease, but more than six months later, none of them had returned to the island.[63]

Actions such as these fed a growing sense of injustice in the colony. Residents felt that they had tried to comply with the government's demands, but that their efforts had not been appreciated. They had built houses and cultivated gardens. They "have Tried to be less exspence [sic] to the Government as we Possible Could be and we are yet trying to help the Government all we Can for our lives." In return, they were charged exorbitant amounts to use the sawmill, their wives and daughters were harassed by the white troops, and their minister was threatened when he criticized the behavior of white soldiers in church. According to the petitioners, "those head men have done every thing to us that our masters have done except by and sell us and now they are Trying to starve the women & children to death cutting off they ration." At times it would appear that black residents' sense of mistreatment represented a clash of cultural differences. The freedmen claimed that the government "wont Give them no meat to eat, every ration day beef & a little fish." Moreover, officials had been deceptive. In one case, a group of about twenty adolescent boys had been shipped to New Bern. The government had decided to cut off rations to boys fourteen years and older in order to make them look for jobs. Many black parents preferred to have them in school, even if it meant less food on the table. In this particular incident, island officials directed the white schoolteachers to tell the boys to get their rations near the superintendent's headquarters. When the boys arrived, they were given the rations but then marched under armed guard to the dock and sent to New Bern. Some of the teenagers among them were the main source of support for the wives of black soldiers.[64]

Although the petition prompted an investigation, little came of it. James's report to Federal authorities was accepted at face value. He maintained that the government had supported many of the petitioners for more than three years and that a reasonable attempt to force boys aged fourteen and older to work had generated cries of anger and outrage.[65] "When beef and fish are given them instead of *bacon*," James wrote, "they complain of 'no meat' and speak of starvation." There had never been evidence of starvation, he argued. Indeed, the fact that 50,000 to 80,000 rations had been issued each month when the black population never exceeded 3,000 was proof that the residents had been given too much. What was needed was a "wholesome *retrenchment*." He felt that the best policy for the island at the end of the war was "to *put two thirds of its people upon plantations on the main land*." Col. Eliphalet Whittlesey, assistant commissioner of the North Carolina Freedmen's Bureau, agreed with James. He believed that too much had been done for the islanders, and too many able-bodied men and boys were idle. Whittlesey shared James's view that the best incentive for self-sufficiency was to cut back rations as quickly as possible.[66]

The soldiers of these families were understandably bitter. Men of the 36th USCT, who were then based in Virginia but about to be shipped to Texas, had petitioned Maj. Gen. Oliver O. Howard, commissioner of the Freedmen's Bureau, for redress sometime in May 1865. They had heard, the soldiers wrote, that the rations to their families at Roanoke had been cut in half and that wives and children were going hungry. Also, Assistant Supervisor Holland Streeter was stealing and making a profit from the sale of their families' rations. Streeter, they continued, was a Copperhead; he was hostile to abolitionism and cared little for the suffering of black refugees. Furthermore, although both Horace James and Col. Theodore F. Lehmann, the officer in charge of Roanoke, had been informed of these allegations, they had ignored them. James's tardiness in paying freedmen their long-overdue wages exacerbated conditions on the island. Adding to all these problems, the soldiers contended, were the thefts of poultry and produce by white soldiers. Streeter had made little or no effort to stop them from stealing from the cabins of the refugees. The petitioners claimed that they could prove all of these charges and urged Howard to contact Chaplain William A. Green, assistant superintendent of the colony, for information that would verify their story. Although protests like this one could not remove Streeter, complaints by Gen. Alonzo Draper did prompt General Howard to order that rations be restored to the soldiers' families.[67]

Howard may have acted because, at almost the same time, he had received complaints about conditions from Green and others on Roanoke Island. Although Green was chaplain of the 36th USCT, at the end of 1864 Draper sent him to Roanoke to act as assistant superintendent of the refugees. Green's accusations transmitted to Howard in early June 1865 were supported by eight missionary teachers and the superintendent of the sawmill. They were concerned about many of the colony's African American families. Most of the approximately 3,500 black residents were old and infirm, orphans, or soldiers' wives and children. They had planted and tilled the garden plots to the best of their abilities, but the output was not sufficient to feed them without support, especially since most of the able-bodied men had left the island. Some 2,700 residents had previously been given rations, but now only 1,500 received any government support. Although the men in the black regiments had been promised at enlistment that their families would be supported as long as the men were in the army, this pledge was being broken. Green and the teachers agreed that the government should not support anyone who could work, nor should it encourage idleness, but they had witnessed firsthand the suffering of orphans, the sick and disabled, and wives and dependents of soldiers. Both justice and humanity, they argued, demanded action. Green was frustrated because, although he was the assistant superintendent, Streeter had not let him assist in the distribution of rations and had only recently allowed him to be present in the ration house while the rations were being given out. Green was convinced that the black islanders were getting little more than half of their allotted supply, while Streeter was selling the rest on and off the island.[68]

Because of the growing pressure, Howard ordered an investigation of Streeter's conduct, and Capt. John McMurray of the 6th USCT was sent on a fact-finding mission to the island. After interviewing residents such as Green and examining how rations had been distributed, McMurray concluded that Streeter had not just been reducing rations as ordered, but that he had been profiting from illegal sales and "had not faithfully performed the duty assigned him." He then arrested Streeter and transferred him to New Bern for trial.[69] In the first week of June, while McMurray was still conducting his investigation, Col. John Holman arrived with the 1st USCT to assume command of Roanoke Island. Shortly afterward, he, too, launched an inquiry into conditions on Roanoke. Holman's findings, though not surprising, were discouraging. There were too many people on an island with very limited resources. The freedpeople were "in a deplorable condition," and the reductions in rations had caused tremendous suffering. Black laborers had not been paid for work on government projects or at the sawmill; some were owed more than two hundred dollars. The people "had been very badly treated" either because of dishonesty or through gross mismanagement. Holman determined that many refugees should be moved from the island to places where they could find work. Those who remained should have access to real, paid employment. On reporting his findings to General Howard, Holman emphasized that the residents had lost faith in the officials in charge.[70]

The refusal of the Union government to grant the freedmen title to their homesteads on Roanoke Island guaranteed the settlement's ultimate failure. Both General Butler and Superintendent James had lobbied in late 1863 and 1864 to clear up the ambiguity about the possession of lots. Their tentative, sporadic attempts to get clear ownership for the colonists, at least for their lifetime, all failed. Any hope of a transfer of land ended with President Andrew Johnson's proclamation of amnesty and restitution of property. Moreover, the experiment at Roanoke had never enjoyed the economic success that its supporters had envisioned. With so many heads of family absent during the war and with island resources so limited, the colony's demise was probably inevitable. No significant industries had been established, and the steam sawmill, which had seemed to promise so much, was by mid-1865 merely grinding small amounts of corn for the inhabitants.[71]

The appointment of Eliphalet Whittlesey as assistant commissioner of the state Freedmen's Bureau did nothing to reverse the settlement's decline. Whittlesey, a close associate of General Howard, had been a Congregational minister in Maine before joining the 19th Maine Volunteers as chaplain. After serving as Howard's judge advocate for the Army of the Tennessee, he had accepted the post in North Carolina. Although active and energetic, Whittlesey possessed "a troubling lack of sensitivity" to minority groups, a strong sense of Anglo-Saxon superiority, and a belief that a certain degree of suffering among the freedmen would be an educational and toughening experience.[72] He thought that James, who had become the Freedmen's Bureau superintendent for the eastern district, had done all that he could for the islanders. Indeed, Whittlesey and James developed a strong friendship based, in part, on shared perceptions of the freedmen. Like James, Whittlesey felt that perhaps too much had been done, which had prompted some refugees to live in idleness. He soon accepted James's argument that the real solution was to use encouragement if possible and force if necessary to transfer most freedpeople to the mainland. Less than a month after taking over in North Carolina, Whittlesey ordered James to begin moving the freedmen from the island as quickly as they could be relocated on the mainland. It would be a slow process despite the growing pressure from pardoned Confederates to get their land back.

The freedpeople sought to remain at Roanoke for several reasons. Bad as things were on the island, there was no assurance that the mainland would offer better living conditions, more humane treatment, or more certain payment of wages. For others, the island was home. Moreover, the ambiguity of the Federal government's policy toward abandoned or confiscated property led some freedpeople to hope that clear title to their own land might still be forthcoming.[73] It was a sad irony that black soldiers began returning to Roanoke just when most of their families were being forced to relocate on the mainland. Some of the men who had served in Texas during Reconstruction reached the island in the fall of 1866. In December, a number of troops from the 36th USCT who had been born and raised on Roanoke petitioned Whittlesey to be allowed to rent or buy the lots on which their families were living. A year later, a larger group of veterans who had been fishermen on the island were among sixty-seven blacks who petitioned Col. Charles Benzoni to stay on the land until May or June 1868.[74] The man responsible for moving the freedpeople, Isaac Meekins, was advised to let them remain until June, but the final outcome is unclear. At least some of these veterans were among those who collectively bought two hundred acres on the west side of the island for five hundred dollars.

Of course, some relatives of the black soldiers never reached the security of Union-controlled areas, and these people left the fewest records. Frequently, family members simply remained behind on the farms of Confederate planters. Did they suffer reprisals for the actions of the volunteers? There is no clear answer. Certainly many slaves who remained behind were relocated elsewhere in North Carolina after early 1863, but that was probably as much due to the fear of Union proximity as it was to any retaliation for the behavior of the young men.[75] When bondsmen enlisted in the "loyal" slave states, there is evidence that other family members frequently paid a high price. The testimony of a Missouri slave woman was typical. She wrote her husband that after he enlisted, her owners "abuse me because you went & do nothing but quarrel with me all the time and beat me scandalously." It would have been surprising if some North Carolina slaveholders had not turned their anger and hostility against the families of young men who had run off to join the Union army. However, the case of Drew Smith represents another recurring pattern of behavior in the complex relationship of planter and slave. Smith had been born and lived on the farm of William Smith near Scotland Neck in Halifax County until he bolted to join the 14th USCHA in February 1865. After his discharge, he returned to Smith's farm, married Janis Smith who had also been born there, and worked on the property until his death in 1876. If there was anger or resentment for his actions, there is no record of it. Years later, the son of his former owner, Peter Smith, wrote in support of Janis's pension application: "I have known Janis Smith and Drew from their childhood being slaves of my father, Wm. R. Smith, and that they lived with him till the death of Drew Smith except the time of Drew's enlistment in the army."[76] Often the pension records of black veterans, which frequently hide as much as they reveal, merely indicate that a soldier went off, enlisted in the Union army, and returned home when the war was over, apparently picking up the pattern of his life. Some soldiers left their wives with family or friends and sent money home for their support. Chester Amieny of Company A, 14th USCHA, was one of these. When he enlisted in March 1864, his wife Frances Reddick, whom he had married with the consent of their owners, stayed with a close friend and church member, Daniel Weeks. Until his discharge in 1865, Chester sent money to Daniel for his wife's subsistence. Oliver Blount, who served in Company A, 37th USCT, was less fortunate. After enlisting in December 1863, he had sent his wife money until his death. Blount contracted frostbite and "his toes rotted from his feet from the effects of cold and exposure in the army." He died on the way home.[77]

Throughout the Civil War, as in most wars, a small group of determined women sought to accompany their husbands or lovers into the field. The most unconventional way was for a woman to pretend she was a man and enlist. Perhaps as many as four hundred women performed as male soldiers in various regiments, and at least a few of them were black. None of the existing records indicate that any of the women passing as men served in North Carolina's black regiments.[78] For women who did not wear the blue uniform, there were only a few ways to stay with a regiment. Occasionally a woman was fortunate enough to have important connections that made it possible for her to join her husband when his regiment was not actively campaigning. These women were almost always the wives of staff officers and could hope to spend periods of the war with their husbands. After March 1864, while the 35th USCT was in Florida, the opportunity arose for some women to join the senior officers of the regiment. Because the army's role in the state had been reduced largely to garrison duties following the Battle of Olustee, several wives of staff officers received special exemptions to join their husbands in Jacksonville. That summer Frances Johnson received permission to visit her fiancé, Col. James Beecher. Their marriage had already been postponed several times when he failed to get a leave of absence to travel north. Because a general order had "been issued, excluding women in general from the department of the South, lest their presence should interfere with the stern duties of war," Frances had arranged a personal meeting with Secretary of War Stanton to explain why an exception should be made in her case.[79]

Frances succeeded in getting her pass after having been turned down a month earlier. The day following her arrival in Jacksonville, she and Beecher were married, and Frances was able to spend the last year of the war close to her new husband. Periodically they were separated while the colonel led his men out on raids, but Frances, who kept busy helping the soldiers, remembered her time in the South very fondly. Most of her mornings "were spent in teaching the men of our regiment to read and write." She was proud that, although only a few soldiers were literate on enlistment, "when the men came to be mustered out each one of them could proudly sign his name to the pay-roll in a good legible hand." Frances Beecher was impressed by the importance the men gave to learning to read and write. After her husband and many of his troops had been wounded at Honey Hill, Frances managed to get transportation to Beaufort, South Carolina, where she worked briefly as a nurse. For much of her time in Florida, her only female companions were missionary teachers. But in December 1864, she was joined by at least one other woman, the wife of Lt. Col. Amiel J. Willard. Mrs. Willard quickly established herself in Jacksonville, where her home became a center of entertainment for the senior officers.[80]

The wives of the enlisted men did not fare as well. A lucky few managed to stay with their husband's regiment as contract employees, while others remained in more informal ways. For regimental commanders, however, the presence of women and dependents in camp, unless exempted for specific reasons, was universally viewed as harmful to discipline and efficiency. Exceptions were made for a limited number of women who could serve as cooks or laundresses. In the 14th USCHA, the most sedentary North Carolina regiment, incomplete records indicate that most companies employed from one to four laundresses on a permanent basis. Nevertheless, the unauthorized presence of women in the camps was a constant source of controversy. Despite talk of rebuilding the black family, officers, aware of what was occurring in many regiments, felt that unsanctioned women would likely be prostitutes, not wives.[81] These concerns escalated when a regiment was not actively campaigning. The difficulty in distinguishing legitimate family relationships from the activities of prostitutes help explain the general order issued by Colonel Beecher when the 35th USCT was garrisoning the Citadel in Charleston. His directive, entitled "Scandal to the Regiment," barred women from entering enlisted men's quarters or from being in the Citadel's vicinity after tattoo. Even if a regimental commander wanted to allow his men some leeway, he faced pressure from superiors. Col. Walter Poor, in charge of the 14th USCHA, received a reprimand from his regional commander, who understood that "the wives of Soldiers are in the habit of visiting Camp & remaining over night. This must stop."[82]

Despite the reservations of senior officers, some women, though not formally attached to the regiment, managed to remain close to their men. Frequently these were women from outside North Carolina who had decided to follow their husbands and leave behind the world they had known. In one such case, Celia Mariner had married her husband Eli in May 1864, while the 36th USCT was stationed at Point Lookout, Maryland. When the regiment was posted to Virginia, the fifteen-year-old bride was left behind, but she rejoined Eli at Chafin's Farm after he had been detailed with a wagon team. A month later he was sent to Wilmington, and she returned to Hampton. In June 1865, when the regiment went to Texas, Celia stayed with her husband until he was mustered out in June 1866. The quarters of married couples were sometimes just a row of tents, and the soldiers' wives did their best to support one another. While in Texas, Celia helped a soldier's wife, Lucy Crocker, in the birthing of her child. When the regiment was finally mustered out, these wives traveled with their husbands, first by steamer to New Orleans and then by train to North Carolina and the soldiers' homes.[83] In the case of the 14th USCHA, which never left the state, it was possible for the women to live at home but have short visits with their men in camp.

The example of Alice Mullen, who married Pvt. Lamb Baxter of Company H, 35th USCT, underscores the complexity of these relationships. In the spring of 1865 Baxter and his regiment had been stationed at Summerville, South Carolina, where he met Mullen. The couple soon fell in love, and Alice eventually accompanied Lamb back to North Carolina. Charles C. Wilson, who served alongside Baxter, later gave his account of their relationship in testimony supporting Alice's claim for a pension. Lamb Baxter had taken Alice Mullen "as his wife (Slave Union). . . . Soldier rented a place for claimant near Camp, so that he could be with her when off duty." Wilson also testified that while the regiment was at Summerville, the couple had lived together "as man and wife." When the 35th USCT moved to Charleston in preparation for mustering out, the "Soldier took her on to Charleston with him. Soldier & claimant then started for Currituck, N.C., after our discharge. I accompanied them as far as New Bern."[84]

In her pension application, Alice explained that she and Lamb were formally married only after they had returned to the home of Lamb's parents in Currituck. "I staid [sic] with the soldier while he was in the army, washed and done for him, done his mending and patching," she testified. "I never took his name while he was in the army, and was not recognized as his wife until after he married me." The pension official who examined the case shed light on the couple's rapid marriage after they had arrived in Currituck. Following his review of all the evidence, the official concluded "that said legal and ceremonial marriage was brought about so soon after his return from the army to his home by reason of the fact that his association with the appellant at the time was regarded as immoral and scandalous by his relatives and others in the community."[85]

Clearly the war disrupted the lives of families all over the United States. In the case of African American families, the degree of disruption is difficult to assess. In addition to the lack of surviving records that might help us, the absence of legally defined marriages for so many Southern blacks meant that a legitimate "marriage" was understood more by the partners than by the wider community. During and after the war many black couples wanted recognition that their "slave marriages" involved a true commitment to each other and reenacted their vows as part of a legally recognized ceremony. Other couples perceived their "slave marriages" as a relationship imposed on them by white slaveowners. Because of this, it is impossible to measure just how disruptive the war was to black relationships in North Carolina. Some couples, or entire families, were able to maintain contact or resume their former alliances despite the turmoil of war. They were perhaps atypical. The families most disrupted were among those most likely not to have left records of the disruption. Some pension records, however, offer glimpses of the ways in which families were pulled apart or, less often, were able to find ways to remain united after the war ended. Nevertheless, it is easier to identify families that were broken up during the war than it is to determine what caused the breakup.

Such was the case of Lewis Bass and his widow, Frances. In April 1864, at age twenty-six, Lewis had enlisted in Company C of the 14th USCHA after escaping to New Bern. Left behind in Wilson County, where he had grown up, were his "slave wife"—"he never returned to her"—and a young daughter named Benzona. When the war was over, Lewis moved to Currituck County, where he met Frances Wiggins. Frances also had a previous family. Born and raised in Martin County, she explained that "I had a slave husband named Isaac Wiggins. Morris Gardner read the book to us. He was a magistrate." Isaac's mother had been free but had apparently bound out her son to white farmers. While Frances could not be precise about the date, she knew that she and Isaac "were married so long before the war that we had a son who was large enough to go in the army. His name was Daniel Wiggins and he was a flag bearer in his father's company."[86]

After Union forces occupied eastern North Carolina, the father, mother, son, and a daughter managed to get out of Martin County and reach Plymouth. Sometime later, they went by steamer to New Bern, where the family had little time together. Frances testified that shortly "after I got there my husband and son left saying that they intended to join the Northern Army and that was my last sight of either one of them." Pension records indicate that father and son enlisted in Company F, "1 U.S.C. Vol. Inf.," but there was little other evidence to support such a claim.[87] What was clear was that they had disappeared from Frances Wiggins's life forever. She moved to Roanoke Island and, after hearing that Isaac Wiggins had died in the army, married Lewis Bass perhaps in late 1866. It may have been a fortuitous match for her because her name had turned up on a list of "Freedmen Living on Roanoke Island Likely to Become Destitute during the Winter of 1866–67."[88] Whatever the reasons behind the union, it was a stable one. The couple lived together in apparent happiness until Lewis's death in 1902. Their lives, like those of so many other blacks in North Carolina, had been shaped and scarred by the war. Both husband and wife had an earlier relationship with a spouse and child that had been dissolved during the war; both had lost close family members. It remains less clear whether those relationships ended because of the war.

## CHAPTER SEVEN

# Service in the Postwar South

——— 3·8 ———

Once the last Confederate armies had surrendered, the U.S. War Department and the Federal government generally faced a new series of difficult issues. Conditions in the Southern states guaranteed that Union troops would be needed for some time to establish and enforce the yet-to-be-determined Federal policy. It was clear to most Americans that the social and economic fabric of the South was confronting fundamental changes, and any gains for the black community would be fiercely contested by the white majority. An occupation force would be required to ensure some degree of Federal control. At the same time, most soldiers wanted a quick demobilization, and they represented tens of thousands of voters. Therefore, Union policy was to begin demobilizing, as rapidly as possible, most of its huge volunteer army, while retaining enough troops to police Southern states and to intimidate any Confederates who might want to resume the war. Union regiments were generally released according to their length of service, with the first to join being the first to leave. As Northern white units were mustered out, the army became blacker.

At the war's end, black soldiers comprised about 10 percent of the army, but by the fall of 1865 slightly over one-third of the Federal occupying army was composed of African Americans.[1] Any military occupation was bound to trigger a resentment fed by centuries of British-American concerns about the general threat of a standing army to civil liberties. When the occupying soldiers were black, they became an even more powerful symbol of the Confederate defeat. Many white Southerners perceived their role as a deliberate, premeditated insult.[2] Although most grudgingly accepted that slavery had been destroyed by the war, the racial attitudes and values associated with the system still existed in much of the South. Racial violence in the postwar era resulted, in large part, from the clash of conflicting attitudes over what constituted legitimate behavior of African Americans—civilians and soldiers alike. As white Southerners struggled to regain control of their society, some of their first victories came when they were able to force the Federal government to alter how it would use black soldiers in different parts of the former Confederacy. Immediately after the fall of Richmond, Washington began receiving demands, requests, and pleas that black troops be removed from various Southern states, only some of which would be honored. At the same time, concerns were raised at the prospect of thousands of Southern black veterans, battle-hardened and perhaps armed, entering the civilian population. The competing priorities forced the new administration in Washington to make difficult and frequently inconsistent decisions.

After some uncertainty in the early summer, both Lt. Gen. Ulysses S. Grant and President Andrew Johnson reached a similar conclusion about the use of black troops, although perhaps for different reasons. The very presence of black soldiers in Southern cities had provoked a violent response by whites at a time when increasing numbers of Northerners were focusing on reconciliation. While Grant still saw the importance of employing black soldiers to protect freedmen and enforce Federal policy, he, like Johnson, accepted the argument that they should be stationed away from major urban areas to avoid unrest. Then, as disturbances continued in Southern cities and Southern anxieties were manifested in fear of insurrection, the majority of black regiments were either mustered out, transferred to coastal forts, or shipped to the western frontier. This change in Federal policy was matched within many black units by greater discord between officers and enlisted men as African American soldiers worried that their priorities were being ignored. At the very least, they feared that Federal officers were more willing to support the interests of white Southerners than of their own men.

The Reconstruction service of the four North Carolina black regiments reflects not only the diversity of the black soldiers' experience but also the evolving Federal policing policy in Southern states. The rapid demobilization of the 14th U.S. Colored Heavy Artillery (USCHA) in 1865 placed it among the first black units to be mustered out. By contrast, the 36th U.S. Colored Troops (USCT), which was stationed briefly in Virginia after the war, was sent, as part of the black Twenty-fifth Corps, to Texas in an action that had as much to do with purging Virginia of black troops as it did with frontier security. Despite complaints of Carolina planters, who were less successful than their Virginian counterparts, the 35th USCT remained in South Carolina as a provost guard in

Charleston before being transferred to the countryside, where it performed valuable work for the Freedmen's Bureau. Of all the black regiments, the 35th USCT was the most involved in efforts to help Southern blacks in the transition from slavery to free labor. The 37th USCT continued to serve in North Carolina for almost two years, although it soon was moved, in part due to Southern anxieties, from urban areas and was dispersed among the state's coastal forts.

The North Carolina artillery unit was one of many black regiments mustered out in late 1865. Although a disproportionate number of these units had been raised in the North, the 14th USCHA may have been among the first selected for demobilization because it had never been fully officered or trained for the duties now required.[3] Nevertheless, during its limited peacetime service, the regiment experienced many of the problems and tensions that troubled other black regiments in the South. Late April and early May 1865 had seen the last spurt of recruiting activity in the Union army, but, for the artillery unit, new recruits only compounded the perennial problem of too few officers. In a two-week period during mid-April, the 14th USCHA enlisted well over 100 African Americans, bringing its total troop strength to 1,050 men at a time when it had only 10 officers, many of whom were eager to leave the army. By the first week in May, after all recruitment had been suspended, the regiment reached a peak of 1,085 men in the ranks. Its commander, Lt. Col. Walter Poor, used that fact, plus his four years of service, to request that he be appointed a full colonel.[4] Despite his self-promotion, Poor remained in his rank. He was equally unsuccessful in getting badly needed commissioned officers for his regiment. During the late spring and summer he pleaded, begged, or demanded that the army give him more commissioned officers. Most of the candidates recommended were never approved. The regiment's complement of officers in the late spring mirrored the ongoing problem. Although the 14th USCHA had twelve full companies, the only officers available for duty were a lieutenant colonel, a major, two captains, four first lieutenants, and four second lieutenants. Thirteen officers were not enough to run the regiment effectively, so Poor turned to white enlisted men from other regiments. He reported that "eleven worthy non-commissioned officers and privates had been detailed as Drill Officers for the Reg't and are now acting as such." Indeed, some of the eleven had to take command of the various companies.[5] During the ensuing months, some of these noncommissioned officers would receive commissions but those promotions only compensated for the loss of original officers who had resigned. The reason for the shortage of officers was obvious. While the war was ongoing, a black heavy artillery regiment in eastern North Carolina had neither sufficient priority in the War Department nor much attraction to men hoping for a commission that would advance their fortunes. Once the war ended, the Federal government was much more concerned with winding down the military than issuing commissions, and most officer candidates were eager to return to civilian life.

Like other black regiments, the 14th USCHA experienced greater discontent in its ranks during the summer of 1865. As other volunteer regiments were mustered out, certain disciplinary measures, appropriate during a war, seemed less legitimate in peacetime. The artillery regiment had always had more deserters, or at least more men absent without leave, than the other three black regiments from North Carolina. In the fall of 1864, during the yellow fever epidemic in New Bern, the desertion rate had increased, but in the spring/summer of 1865, it soared. From May to July, thirty enlisted men deserted, even though most were still owed upward of three hundred dollars in bounties.[6] Clearly the men were willing to forgo bounty money for the chance to get back to their families and civilian life. Lieutenant Colonel Poor believed that many of the soldiers who were absent without leave were living around New Bern and Goldsboro. He ordered Capt. Thomas Maher to take some enlisted men and search for the deserters, but these efforts were largely unsuccessful. As the desertion rate rose, so did the number of men facing court-martials. While some of the charges, such as those against Pvt. Bryant Collins and Pvt. Lofton Chance, were for theft or for being absent without leave, increasingly the cases involved challenges to the authority of white officers. In the case of Sgt. Nathan Andrews, who had "threatened to break down the Cook House door & take what he wanted," his refusal to obey an officer's warning and to follow orders led to his conviction.[7]

Such challenges to white authority may have been fueled by the hostility of whites to the idea of blacks in uniform. Although there is scant documentation of white-on-black violence involving black soldiers in the Bogue Sound area, that may have more to do with a bias in record keeping and law enforcement.[8] At least one black soldier in Morehead City was killed shortly after two additional black regiments were moved to the city in June 1865. The *New Bern Times* reported that the soldier, possibly a member of the 14th USCHA, was killed for taking "rather more liberty than an Anglo-Saxon . . . likes to submit to."[9] Black soldiers, on the other hand, believed that their service in the Union army entitled them to many of those liberties as well as to respect. The conflicting values virtually ensured such incidents in the future.

Peacetime service also saw serious tensions among the officers of the 14th USCHA. One case revealed the bitter feelings between company officers. In late May 1865 Capt. Fred A. Nourse had preferred charges against Lt. Henry Hallam in what may have been rooted in a domestic dispute. Poor refused to proceed, partly on the grounds that a "wife cannot be a witness against her husband. Some of the witnesses know nothing of the complaint. The charges can scarcely be sustained before any Court Martial." He concluded that it would be "better to let this matter rest." The incident was complicated by an earlier argument between Nourse and Poor over whether captains could be forced to perform fatigue duty with their companies. The next month Poor turned down Nourse's request for a leave of absence, even though he was due for a leave. Poor said that he based his decision on the limited number of officers available in the regiment and on the duties that had to be covered. Furthermore, Nourse was the only officer with his company, and others had a greater claim to a leave. Within two weeks Poor indicated which officer he felt had the greater claim. He recommended a leave for Henry Hallam, now a captain, because "no other officer in the regiment has served more faithfully" and "none more fairly earned a leave." For the first and perhaps only time, Poor suggested that there were enough officers and that Hallam could be spared.[10] Poor's favoritism must have left Nourse grinding his teeth.

In the months following Robert E. Lee's surrender, the 14th USCHA remained at its base in Morehead City, where it continued to provide logistical services. In August, as pressure built to remove all black troops from urban areas, the regiment shifted across the Bogue Sound to Fort Macon. A month later, pairs of its companies were detached and posted to such places as Fort Hatteras and Fort Totten. For most of the soldiers, their last months of service would be in relatively isolated posts before the regiment was mustered out on 11 December 1865. For a few men, however, there were more interesting duties. In October a detachment from Company L, under the command of Lt. S. F. Braley, went to Beaufort with orders to arrest four freedmen who were "charged with beginning, causing, and exciting a riot in said town." Braley was to take the accused to New Bern, using as many men as he deemed necessary. Just a few weeks later, another officer from the regiment, Raleigh-born Lt. William H. Eddins, led an investigation "to collect evidence of the execution of certain U.S. Soldiers by the Rebels in February, 1864 near Kinston,

NC." It is unclear what evidence, if any, he found, but by early December all of the detachments returned to the regimental headquarters, handed in their arms, and were mustered out of the army.[11]

The black soldiers stationed in Virginia when the Confederate army surrendered at Appomattox faced a very different Reconstruction service. These men would play no part in any attempt to create a new postwar society in the commonwealth, because white Virginians, unlike advocates for other regions, were able to get the black troops of the Twenty-fifth Corps removed from their state and replaced by an all-white corps.[12] Peace found the men of the 36th USCT camped just outside of Petersburg awaiting further orders and speculating about what would happen to them in the coming months. Like other black units, the 36th had been promptly removed from urban areas to placate white Virginian sensibilities. Maj. Gen. Edward Ord, who had ordered Brig. Gen. Edward Wild to "get these damned niggers of yours out of Richmond as fast as you can," later explained that he had done so to facilitate the city's occupation by reducing white hostility. Yet another Federal official claimed that the action was taken due to bad discipline and criminal behavior in the black regiments. While the men waited in camps outside Petersburg, rumors—as in all armies—took on a life of their own. In late April it was said that a general order had been issued indicating that all recruits in the rendezvous stations would soon receive an honorable discharge. This news triggered a flurry of excitement in the barracks and spread among the ranks.[13] Quickly, however, that hope vanished with stories of the regiment going to Texas. This time, the rumors proved to be true.

The transfer of the black troops in Virginia to Texas was the result of several factors. Gen. Edmund Kirby Smith's army in the Trans-Mississippi Department of the Confederacy had not yet surrendered, and Washington feared that he might receive aid from the French imperial forces in Mexico. In response to this threat, Ulysses S. Grant, who envisioned possible conflict with Mexico, ordered Gen. Philip H. Sheridan, in mid-May, to proceed immediately to Texas with sufficient forces to pacify the state and to cut off any possible Confederate retreat to Mexico.[14] Sheridan could have as many troops as he needed, but Grant did recommend that the Twenty-fifth Corps be included. After assessing the situation in Texas, Sheridan predicted that he would require at least three full corps for his Army of Observation. He received Maj. Gen. Gordon Granger's Thirteenth Corps, which quickly moved to Galveston, Brownsville, and Shreveport; the Twenty-fifth Corps led by Maj. Gen. Godfrey Weitzel; and the Fourth Corps under Maj. Gen. David Stanley. By the time Sheridan set himself up in the Southwest, Kirby Smith's surrender on 26 May, the collapse of all Confederate authority in Texas, and the presence of roaming armed gangs ensured that chaos would become a greater problem than an organized Confederate military. Because many Southern soldiers, "armed and unrepentant," had gone home before receiving parole, Sheridan feared that the surrender was a "swindle" and that more fighting lay ahead.[15] Based on these concerns, he ordered the Fourth Corps to occupy a line north from Victoria. In the meantime, however, Gen. Frederick Steele, with a division from the Thirteenth Corps and the bulk of Weitzel's Twenty-fifth Corps, moved to seal off the Rio Grande border to Southern fugitives.[16] Grant was convinced that regardless of Kirby Smith's surrender, a large body of Union troops had to be stationed along the Rio Grande River to intimidate Maximilian's forces in Mexico and to encourage the Mexican nationalists. Ultimately, one-half of all soldiers sent to Texas would see service along the river. In total, some 111 volunteer regiments served in Texas, 30 of which were black units.[17]

The other reasons that Weitzel's black soldiers were available for service in Texas were the conciliatory policy adopted by the military toward Virginia and unrest among white soldiers. At a time when all volunteer units expected to be demobilized and sent home, further military service in the Southwest met with a sullen response from most soldiers.[18] If units of the black troops were detailed to Texas, more white Northern regiments could muster out. Equally as important, sending the black troops was seen as a gesture to encourage the loyalty of Virginia's white population. Indeed, the decision to send the Twenty-fifth Corps west was anticipated by some senior Federal officers who were more sympathetic to white Virginians than to African Americans, even though the latter wore Union blue. General Weitzel had begun the policy of conciliation toward Richmond's white population, and it was maintained by the military triumvirate of General Ord, commander of the Army of the James; Gen. M. R. Patrick, provost marshal general of the Army of the Potomac; and Maj. Gen. Henry W. Halleck, senior military officer for the Department of Virginia and North Carolina. After the capture of Richmond, Weitzel had kept his black soldiers in the forts surrounding the city to allay white apprehensions. When Ord took over from Weitzel, he ordered Weitzel to move his black troops south toward Petersburg. At the time that Halleck replaced Ord as military commander of Richmond, he accepted Ord's claim that the black soldiers in Virginia were poorly disciplined and badly officered and that they constituted "a very improper force for the preservation of order" in Virginia.[19] More important, he continued Ord's lenient policies toward Confederates and supported his view that the Twenty-fifth Corps should be removed from Virginia. Soon after taking command, Halleck began to petition for the removal of the black soldiers to either Texas or, at the very least, coastal forts in the South. On 30 April 1865, the day after he had told Grant that "the rebel feeling in Virginia is utterly Dead," Halleck telegraphed his commander, without elaboration, that "on further consultation with Genl Ord, I am more fully convinced of the policy of withdrawal of the twenty-fifth corps from Virginia. Their conduct recently has been even worse than I had supposed yesterday."[20] The combination of military need in the West and political expediency in Virginia plus, perhaps, Sheridan's view that "Texas has not yet suffered from the war," all explain Grant's decision to send the corps to Texas. Ironically, when Weitzel heard the complaints leveled against his troops, he defended their "most excellent" behavior. By that time, however, Halleck had already decided to send the Twenty-fifth Corps to Texas and Weitzel had received orders to move west. The overall commander of the expedition, General Steele, was told that, unless directed by Sheridan to the contrary, he was to proceed to the Rio Grande and "occupy as high up the river as your forces and means of supplying will allow." But he was to maintain a "strict neutrality towards Mexico, in the French and English sense of the word," while operating along the river.[21]

A dramatic illustration of the changing attitude within the black regiments occurred as the troops left Virginia. As word got out that the Twenty-fifth Corps was going to leave the state, rumors about what lay in store for the enlisted men spread rapidly. One story that gained credibility was that the black soldiers were to be sent south to work on cotton plantations and help pay off the government debt. Although white officers tried to reassure the men, they were only partly successful, and many soldiers became "sullen and disobedient." A lieutenant in the 1st U.S. Colored Cavalry recounted the events that led up to his unit's mutiny. Part of his regiment, while being transported down the James River, began firing at something or someone on shore. From the top deck, Lt. Frederick Browne, brandishing his revolver, raced down the steps to stop the firing. "I had got but half way down when a dozen carbines were put to my head and breast and I was told that I could kill one man, but it would be the last one I ever would kill." Intimidated, Browne withdrew and the firing gradually ended. When the regiment reassembled on a troopship at Hampton Roads, the black soldiers discussed what had occurred. "They just went wild, and refused to obey all orders," recorded Browne. The next morning, when the regiment disembarked at Fort Monroe, many of the soldiers assumed that they had won. They were wrong. Instead, in the presence of the fort's garrison, the troopers were stripped of their arms and sent back to their ship. That afternoon, many of the men broke into the ship's stores and got drunk. For a brief period, the sixteen armed officers confronted hundreds of soldiers armed with axes, hand spikes, and clubs, yelling, "Kill them: throw them overboard." Faced with a mutiny, the officers shot the ringleader. Order was restored and a bloody confrontation only narrowly averted. For the remainder of the voyage, the officers kept a thirty-pound Parrott gun loaded with canister trained on the forward deck where the enlisted men were crowded. Browne believed that of all of the fights that he had been in, this was his most perilous moment.[22]

Although the actions of the 1st U.S. Colored Cavalry represented an extreme case of breakdown in discipline, the underlying factors that had caused the unrest were present in other black units. The 36th USCT never experienced the same level of disaffection, but there were other signs of stress in the unit. Black enlisted men and white officers no longer could assume that they had a common cause. In fact, desertion and individual acts of disobedience became much more common in all of the black regiments.

During the last week in May, the 36th USCT prepared to depart for Texas despite rumors that Kirby Smith's defeat would reverse the order to move west. Concern that some soldiers would try to avoid the transfer caused regimental commanders such as Lt. Col. Benjamin F. Pratt to take extra precautions to prevent last-minute desertions.[23] Pratt had reason to expect that some of the men would try to leave, for many of them faced a cruel choice: either to be sent far from home at a time when other soldiers were being discharged, or to desert and try to return home to help their families, whose living conditions were growing markedly worse. One surviving document captures their dilemma. Just before the 36th USCT left City Point, soldiers petitioned Maj. Gen. Oliver O. Howard, commissioner of the Freedmen's Bureau in North Carolina. They had heard that food rations to their wives and families had been cut in half and that the assistant supervisor of African American affairs at Roanoke Island, Holland Streeter, was selling their rations. The men felt betrayed, as they had been promised at enlistment that their families would receive rations as long as they were in the army. In addition, discharged soldiers and men wounded while working on the Dutch Gap Canal who were back on Roanoke Island were denied rations. Superintendent Horace James had been informed of their charges, but apparently, the soldiers believed, he had taken no action. A few days later, Cpl. Frank James of Company C complained to his colonel that rations to his family at Roanoke had been stopped.[24] When the complaints finally reached him, General Howard ordered the assistant commissioner in North Carolina to continue to issue rations to the soldiers' families until further notice.

The troops being shipped west could only hope that their protests might help their families, since they had little prospect of returning home anytime soon. As they left City Point, they must have felt that the most fortunate men in the regiment were the fifteen soldiers in Companies B, C, and H who remained behind on detached duty in Virginia and North Carolina as teamsters and ambulance personnel. Indeed, a small number of men did prefer to desert rather than go west with their regiment. Pvt. George E. Poole of Company K was one such person. Left in late April to guard the company baggage, Poole "deserted when ordered to join the Regiment" after it had received news of the move west. Pvt. Alfred Bray of Company C deserted at the very last moment. He had "received a pass to visit Norfolk for 12 hours while the Regt. was on board the U.S.S. Turnsporte off Fortress Monroe & never returned." A third man, James Parker, on detached duty in Norfolk, deserted in June 1865.[25] Yet these soldiers were the exception. In fact, during its entire service the 36th USCT lost only two or three men per company through desertion.

On 31 May 1865, after several days aboard crowded transports, the 36th USCT put to sea. Because of the vessels' limited space, half of all the unit's wagons and three-quarters of its mules were left in Virginia. After a week of seasickness, cramped quarters, and restricted water rations, the regiment rendezvoused with the rest of the Twenty-fifth Corps at Mobile Bay, where it was to report to General Steele. The men disembarked for several days while the steamers were cleaned and restocked with water and coal. On 10 June the regiment cleared Mobile Bay and headed for the island of Brazos Santiago. Although the 36th USCT reached the mouth of the Rio Grande within three

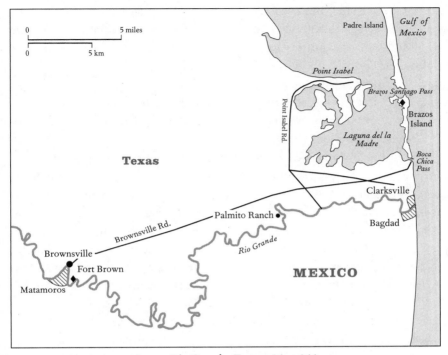

Lower Rio Grande, Texas, 1865–1866

days, a shortage of shallow-draft boats caused a further three-day delay, at anchor off the river, before the men could begin to disembark. Well before then, some rations had become "so musty" that they were virtually inedible. Nevertheless, however unpleasant the voyage had been for the men of the 36th USCT, other soldiers had faced much worse. The 115th USCT had lost up to twelve men a day during the trip—the result of bad food, poor sanitation, and fever. Other regiments had suffered the effects of improper and insufficient rations even before they boarded the transports.[26]

Their arrival in Texas did not end the men's suffering. Difficulties in landing the troops at Brazos Santiago's shallow harbor caused a lengthy delay in disembarking. The island was a narrow strip of sand about ten miles long at the mouth of the Rio Grande, and little had been done to prepare for the large number of troops who would soon occupy Brazos. At the northern end was a small cluster of wooden buildings that constituted the village and the military headquarters. Across a narrow strait of water was a longer, though equally barren, sand island, Isla del Padre. A shallow bar guarded the entrance and prevented vessels that drew more than seven feet from crossing. Even for the small lighters, passage was hazardous, especially in rough seas. Two years before, an English officer who had crossed in good weather described the bar: "It is often impassable for ten or twelve days together: the depth of water varying from 2 to 5 feet. It is very dangerous, from the heavy surf and undercurrent; sharks also abound. Boats are frequently capsized in crossing it."[27]

Because of the obstructions, the transports carrying the Twenty-fifth Corps had to anchor offshore and unload their cargoes into the small sloops for the perilous voyage across the bar. A constant shortage of the small boats created chronic delays. When the 36th USCT began to disembark, some men were nearly killed when the schooner carrying them ashore was staved in. All night the men manned pumps to keep the vessel from foundering. It was not until 7:00 A.M. that the crew managed to get a line to the beach and began to transfer the men to land. Four hours later the schooner went down. This experience was not unique to the black soldiers from North Carolina. A week later, when men from the 8th USCT were landing, one of their schooners also foundered trying to cross the bar. Troop landings all along the Texas coast faced similar difficulties and at times involved "the necessity of lightering" for up to twenty miles. Just after the first troops arrived, a series of bad storms kept all vessels from crossing the bar at Brazos, Galveston, and Indianola for four or five days at a time.[28]

Given the isolation of the Rio Grande frontier, the postwar service of the 36th USCT in the Army of Observation had little to do with assisting freedmen in their transition to wage laborers or supporting the activities of the Freedmen's Bureau by enforcing labor contracts. Rather, the U.S. Army's primary mission in the summer of 1865 was to ensure the military pacification of Texas and to intimidate Maximilian and the Mexican imperialists in a largely passive role, as well as the French and ex-Confederate supporters of Maximilian who had crossed the Rio Grande. U.S. officials, sympathetic to the efforts of Benito Juárez's republican revolutionary forces, frequently turned a blind eye to the arms and equipment that were being smuggled to his supporters. Indeed, General Sherman was proud of the weapons and ammunition that he ensured would reach the Liberals under Gen. Mariano Escobedo. By contrast, any transition assistance from slave to free labor was a minor concern for the

Army of Observation. Moreover, the part of Texas bordering the Rio Grande
was a lightly inhabited region with few black residents.[29] Because the 36th
USCT served only on the Rio Grande, primarily at the isolated post at Brazos
Santiago, it experienced relatively little of the virulent white violence directed
at freedmen that dominated other parts of the state. The regiment was also
not in a position to assist former slaves when the Freedmen's Bureau began
to play a more active role in the fall of 1865.[30] For the soldiers of the Twenty-
fifth Corps, the greatest enemies in the last months of the year were loneli-
ness, isolation, illness, harsh living conditions, and constant worries about
what was happening to their families back home.

The black troops soon found that conditions on Brazos Santiago were little
better than those on the transports. The island, where the 36th USCT would
spend much of its time over the next sixteen months, lacked a sufficient supply
of water, fresh food, and wood. All that they had in abundance were sand and
sand flies. Especially in the summer of 1865, it was a very unhealthy posting.
By mid-June, Lorenzo Gould reported, "the soldiers [were] dieing here every
day." Gould himself became ill, although he recovered and described what
happened to the unlucky ones: "The mode of burying is to put the boddy in a
six muels wagon and a band of music marches a head and a company behind
the wagon their is tow or three buryed every day." Even as the number of
sick increased, the water rations were cut back from three pints to one pint
per man per day and what they received came hot from the condenser. Partly
because of the shortage of water, fresh food, and the harsh conditions on the
island, in late June several regiments, including the 36th USCT, were ordered
up the Rio Grande, where the water, if not much better in quality, at least was
more plentiful. A soldier at Twenty-fifth Corps headquarters was skeptical of
the improvement. "This water is good," he wrote, "when you have not tasted
any for 50 hours. . . . The water of the Mississippi is crystal compared to it,
and what is worse, is that all of the sediment seems to be alive."[31] Although
the orders to the 36th USCT to march to Brownsville may have promised better water, the march itself must have been agony for the men who were ill or
endured the symptoms of scurvy.

After fording the channel to the mainland, the first part of the march took
the men across a broad prairie. Soon they encountered stretches of mesquite
chaparral, where the vegetation consisted of impenetrable thickets of scrubby,
thorny trees—too small for shade and too thick to allow any breeze. For miles
and miles, there was no water and very little grass. Maj. William Hart com-

plained that, despite the use of a strong rear guard under a watchful officer to prevent stragglers, many men dropped out of the march. He believed that they managed to slip into the chaparral bordering the road and outflank the rear guard. Hart blamed the unusually high numbers on "the bad conditions of the roads and the weak and exhausted condition of the men." (Other regiments would also experience much straggling; many officers found it hard to blame the men, "for it was impossible to march under such a sun.")[32] Adding to the misery, the 36th USCT was forced to repeat the march and return to Brazos Santiago within two weeks. Brazos remained its base camp for the rest of the regiment's service in Texas, although, at any point in time, large numbers of men were detailed elsewhere.

Conditions for all troops serving on the Rio Grande were particularly hard when they first arrived. In October 1865 the chaplain of another black regiment serving along the river looked back at the summer and claimed that no "set of men in any country ever suffered more severely than we in Texas. Death has made festful gaps in every regiment." Part of the problem was that many soldiers had been in bad health to begin with. Some troops exhibited signs of scurvy even while the regiments were still in Virginia, and the movement west exacerbated the problem. During the summer, more than half the men in the Twenty-fifth Corps suffered from the ailment. In August, General Weitzel described to Benjamin Butler the conditions confronting his troops. "All the officers, myself included," he complained, "have had the bone-break fever, and many the chronic diarrhoea. The men are dying fast with scurvy, and not a vegetable to be had. I have to-day nearly 2,500 cases of scurvy in the corps." Before his men left City Point, Weitzel had begun "to preach anti-scorbutics, knowing that scurvy would be the worst enemy." Despite all of his requests, no vegetables had been sent to him. Fortunately, he had brought a sufficient supply of seeds and, as he informed Butler, "my whole command is planting their own gardens now."[33] Only at the end of August did adequate amounts of fresh fruits and vegetables begin to reach the soldiers on the frontier. By fall 1865, many of the worst physical conditions at Brazos were becoming less severe. In 1866 there were fewer recorded deaths from "chronic diarrhoea" and none from scurvy. Nevertheless, service in Texas was always hot, dirty, tiresome, and lonely. For most soldiers, the day they would muster out could not come soon enough.

Before the physical conditions had begun to improve or disease rates drop, tragedy struck the regiment when a senior officer died under suspicious circumstances.[34] Late in the afternoon of 30 August 1865, Brig. Gen. Alonzo G. Draper was shot while riding through the camp of the 36th USCT, his former unit. The bullet struck him from behind, entering his spine and knocking him from his horse. For several days the general clung to life while officers tried to decide why he had been shot and who had fired the fatal bullet. Officers made every effort to determine if the shooting had been the result of carelessness or a deliberate attempt at murder. Given the obvious anger of many volunteer regiments that were forced to serve in the West, the intent to assassinate was a real possibility, but the investigators could not establish motivation or responsibility. There had been few signs in the 36th USCT of the kind of unrest evident within the ranks of many other black regiments. On 3 September, as the inquiry continued, Draper died. Eventually it was concluded that a stray bullet from a firing party practicing on the beach had killed the general. No charges could be brought, and no individual was ever held responsible for his death.[35] By then, Capt. A. Draper, a brother, and Capt. R. F. Andrew, a brother-in-law, had accompanied the body back to Massachusetts.

Draper's death aside, the relative harmony in the regiment was striking given the numerous signs of stress and conflict displayed in other regiments—black and white—that resented their postwar service in Texas. Soldiers in the volunteer regiments, who had thought that they were enlisting for only as long as the war lasted, grew increasingly angry when others were mustered out while their units remained in service. Officers crushed a mutiny in the cavalry brigade of the Twenty-fifth Corps when it was originally ordered west, and in March 1866 the 48th Ohio Infantry Battalion stacked arms and refused to do further service. Another potential mutiny met a similar fate in San Antonio, and in Austin soldiers from a departing volunteer regiment apparently attempted to ambush their commander, Gen. George A. Custer. Custer's frequent use of the lash, his withholding of rations, and his assignment of soldiers as "nursemaids" for his wife had all earned him the loathing of his Midwestern troops.[36]

The very isolation of Brazos Santiago protected the 36th USCT from the white hostility that faced African Americans, freedmen, and soldiers elsewhere in Texas and in other parts of the South. To that extent, it may have reduced social and physiological grievances within the regiment. By contrast, the black soldiers posted farther up the Rio Grande, at Brownsville, encountered repeated acts of racial enmity. They risked severe punishment for threatening to shoot businessmen who refused to serve them. (In 1867 angry soldiers killed a policeman and a barkeeper after the white men had fired on them.)[37] In the late spring of 1866 Major Hart wrote from Brazos that, because he had "no official intercourse with the civil inhabitants of this island and no social intercourse with any of them except a few northern men (traders)," he was unable to report on the allegiance of the residents. He could say, however, that he had "never heard of any disloyalty on the part of the people, or any imenical [sic] feelings towards northern men, refugees or Freedmen."[38]

If the 36th USCT managed to avoid some of the discord present in other units, it also may have reflected a change in the command style of the new senior officer. Lt. Col. Pratt, who had replaced Draper as acting commander, had not accompanied the regiment to Texas and had been absent due to illness since May 1865. William Hart's long de facto command of the 36th USCT had been considered temporary only because Pratt kept insisting that he would soon be able to rejoin the regiment. Not until October did Pratt accept the inevitable and resign his commission. The formal transfer of command to Hart seems to have had a positive effect on his behavior. In Virginia, he had used his temporary powers harshly. In November 1864, when Hart first led the 36th USCT, he demoted several noncommissioned officers for disregarding orders and for incompetence. The major warned, in a general order, that "the carelessness and inattention so often displayed by some of the non-commissioned officers of this Regt will be tolerated no longer." A month later he was outraged by what he saw as the soldiers' refusal to use the latrines. "The men of this command," he declared, "having displayed a total disregard for the cleanliness of the Camp, and the sanitary Conditions of the regiment by committing gross nuisances all along the line, and in some places within ten (10) feet of their quarters, it becomes necessary to place a strong guard in rear of the Camp, to prevent the men from making beasts of themselves."[39] In future, any man convicted of such an offense would be mounted on the horizontal pole at the guardhouse for forty-eight hours. This apparently unbending leadership style began to change after the regiment reached Texas. By midsummer, Hart had softened his management approach and increasingly used noncommissioned officers of the day to police the camp, trusting them to ensure that the camp was "in the best possible condition as regards cleanliness, order, and so forth."[40]

A month later Hart was using incentives, rather than threats, to gain the men's cooperation in producing the most orderly camp in the division—with white washed woodwork, uniformly structured tents, clean streets, and an enlarged cookhouse. The regiment was given one week to make all of the necessary improvements, after which each company would be inspected. The company with the best quarters, which turned out to be Company F, was excused from fatigue duties for one week. For the next half year, Hart encouraged the intercompany competition, commending a series of companies over this time. By early 1866 he was pleased to report that "the camp and its surrounding presents a very fine appearance." In June General Sheridan, during his tour of the frontier, found the troops at Brazos Santiago well quartered, comfortable, healthy.[41] Certainly, the food supply was better. Hart had taken steps to improve and diversify what the soldiers had to eat. Included on the menu was fresh fish, caught by a party of enlisted men under Sgt. Richard Etheridge, a Roanoke Islander familiar with the sea. But other critical shortages continued to exist. Wood was issued to the regiment in such limited amounts that had it not been for the driftwood salvaged from the beaches, it would have been "impossible to cook sufficient food to sustain life." Moreover, as long as the regiment was stationed at Brazos, the men faced periodic epidemics of deadly contagious diseases ranging from yellow fever to cholera. Nevertheless, there was little sign of the abusive treatment and angry response that occurred in other black regiments.[42]

The 36th USCT thus seemed to accept its postwar service with fewer complaints than many other volunteer regiments. It was all the more surprising because the North Carolina soldiers had to watch as other white and black regiments were discharged and sent home. By the start of 1866, forty-seven white volunteer regiments and twelve black regiments serving in Texas had been mustered out. The remaining eight white units and another nine black ones would be gone by June.[43] Even with the discharge of other black regiments, there were no signs of dissent within the 36th USCT. Although, inevitably, a few noncommissioned officers were demoted, these cases were relatively rare. So too were desertions, although the regiment's island post in a scarcely populated area would by itself inhibit flight. The commander of the French forces in Mexico, François-Achille Bazaine, believed that black soldiers had been transferred to the border specifically so they could desert by the thousands to Mexico. He was clearly mistaken, for reports confirm that only one soldier deserted the 36th USCT while in Texas.[44] Cpl. Charles Cadwell, a fisherman from Currituck County, left the unit on 26 March 1866 while it was in Brazos. Conditions in the regiment supported Sheridan's impression, formed after he had visited the region, that the "officers of the colored troops are desirous of being mustered out, but the men are not, and are content and happy." Significantly, by the summer of 1866 the inspection report for the 36th USCT recorded discipline, not as the widely used "good," but rather as "excellent."[45]

———❧———

In the summer of 1866 the regiment was gradually moving toward demobilization. By late June, 68 enlisted men had been discharged because their term of service had expired. The vast majority, nevertheless, had to wait another four months. In July the 36th USCT had a total strength of 705 men, down from 806 in January, but more than half of them were still on detached service. These soldiers rejoined the regiment over the next two months. When it came, demobilization would be too late for some of the troops. During August and September, while the men waited for their orders, an outbreak of cholera struck the army, killing at least twenty men. Finally, on 28 October 1866 the regiment was mustered out of service at Brazos Santiago. It was one of the last volunteer regiments in the Army of Observation to be discharged.[46] The black soldiers believed that they knew why they had been kept in service even while "Our Corps is pretty much gone home." The last regiments mustered out, a Kentucky sergeant major claimed, were all "slave state troops." The army would furnish transportation and subsistence for all officers and men to take them back to Portsmouth, Virginia. The men, of course, had the option of remaining in Texas. In the summer of 1866, Texas planters in numerous areas were desperately short of labor; many of them appealed to the assistant commissioner of the Texas Freedmen's Bureau for help in importing workers from the east. Indeed, groups of eastern freedmen, including some in New Bern, sent representatives to Texas to assess their opportunities. How many ultimately decided to immigrate to Texas is unclear. What is known is that nearly all of the soldiers in the 36th USCT chose to head east. They may well have agreed with Maj. Gen. Oliver O. Howard, who was "very hesitant to encourage negroes to go to Texas, as long as it is reported that they are killed and outraged, and have so little show of justice."[47] They may also have decided that one taste of Texas was enough.

———❧———

The other two North Carolina regiments—the 35th USCT (formerly the 1st NCCV) and the 37th USCT (formerly the 3rd NCCV)—played very different roles during Reconstruction because military officials were less concerned about white sensibilities in North Carolina and South Carolina than in Virginia. In South Carolina, in particular, black troops formed a large part of the occupation forces. Of the 14,000 Federal soldiers serving there in the late summer, 11,500 were black. Perhaps because it was one of the most experienced black regiments then stationed in the state, the 35th USCT had been transferred from its post at Mount Pleasant on the coast to serve as the provost guard at the Citadel in Charleston from April to early June 1865. The move to Charleston placed the regiment in a highly volatile social climate, for white South Carolinians, perhaps more than other Southerners, were determined not to lose control of the society that slavery had produced. Their resolve would lead to what some historians have called a "people's war."[48]

The war's end had thrown Charleston's traditional hierarchy of social and racial groups into chaos, and the city quickly became the scene of bitterly contested claims of new rights and old privileges. Here, as elsewhere in the South, rumors circulating among the white population predicted insurrections by the freedmen to exact bloody revenge or to seize property. The introduction of black soldiers, who were expected to support the freedmen and to encourage their demands for equality, further inflamed the situation, heightened fears of black violence, and provoked a hostile white response. As Charleston's freedmen began to assert themselves in both words and deeds, the white community was quick to blame the presence and influence of the black soldiers. In the summer, one urban resident declared: "If the Negro troops were only removed we could get on very well. They demoralize and excite the Negroes who have been slaves and will not allow them to remain with their owners." In the countryside, attitudes were much the same. Dr. Benjamin Huger warned that although "I am not an alarmist, it seems to me, that if the Negro troops are not removed & our own Negroes made to submit to the civil law, massacre of white or black must soon come."[49]

Not surprisingly, throughout 1865 and 1866 violent clashes between white and black civilians frequently involved soldiers. Moreover, the racial attitudes of white and black Charlestonians were reflected in the tension seen among white and black Union soldiers. The 35th USCT was thus caught up in the city's social conflicts as well as disputes with other Union regiments. Some of the black troops were disciplined for entering private homes and removing both guns and the whites who owned them, while others faced punishment or reprimands for actions ranging from being absent without leave to using profane language on city streets. Tensions escalated as the summer progressed. According to the *New York Times*, "Robbing, clubbing, stabbing, and shooting were freely indulged in by the white soldiers, colored soldiers, and, in many instances, colored citizens." In mid-June a guard from the 127th New York Volunteers, while on duty in the Battery, fought with members of the 35th USCT in a skirmish that left several soldiers and some civilians injured.[50] The cause of the fight was not documented, but Maj. Gen. Quincy A. Gillmore, after investigating the incident, criticized the 127th New York. "The regiment was carefully chosen for its good discipline," he later wrote, "but street quarrels have taken place, in some cases, arising from insolence and brutality of soldiers towards the Negroes," adding that sometimes the blacks had been the aggressors. Gillmore's first response to the incident was to ship the 127th New York north to be demobilized. He soon transferred most of the 35th USCT to Branchville, some sixty miles northwest of Charleston. But these actions did little to solve the fundamental problem. The next month a bloodier clash broke out between the 165th New York Regiment and the 21st USCT, as well as some troops from the 54th Massachusetts. An initial confrontation between freedmen and white troops soon expanded to involve black soldiers rushing to help the freedmen. A twenty-minute firefight ensued between the combatants, and for several days the sporadic sounds of musket fire could be heard in the city. Both the number of casualties and the exact cause of the conflict were debated, but the 165th New York was promptly isolated on Morris Island while the 21st USCT received a transfer to Hilton Head, South Carolina.[51]

Clashes between white Southerners and Northern soldiers were a continuing problem that the 35th USCT shared with many other black units. Acts of violence were widespread during Reconstruction, but some of them may have been fueled less by racial or regional antagonisms and more by another issue. Few Americans, black or white, wanted to be professional soldiers, especially in a society traditionally hostile to a standing army. As it became clear that black soldiers might have to remain in uniform much longer than most of their white counterparts, some men decided that they would no longer serve. Desertion rates in the 35th USCT, though never high, increased in 1865. Still, it would be inaccurate to stereotype the whole regiment on the basis of the occasional fights involving some of its soldiers or the sporadic desertion of a few privates and noncommissioned officers. Just before the regiment left Charleston, Col. James C. Beecher praised his regiment for the "excellent reputation gained by the command while in the city." Certainly, relations between the white and black troops in Charleston were no better after the 35th USCT was transferred.[52]

---

By the early summer of 1865, the regiment had begun to establish programs of military instruction for both its commissioned and noncommissioned offi-cers. These schools were, in part, a means of tightening discipline, which had slackened by the end of the war, and, in part, a response to claims that black troops were unrestrained, badly trained, and poorly led. They were also an at-tempt to develop greater professionalism and improve leadership skills in the regiment at all levels. Maj. Archibald Bogle, having just rejoined his troops, taught tactics and regulations to all commissioned officers not on duty, while a parallel school operated for noncommissioned officers and privates who had demonstrated leadership potential.[53] Beecher's aggressive recruitment efforts among South Carolina freedmen heightened the need for expanded training. Along with the commanders of black regiments, the colonel sought to increase his numbers as a precaution against troops mustering out. The establishment of the school for noncommissioned officers was thus influenced by rumors then circulating that qualified black soldiers might soon be receiv-ing commissions.

During the early summer of 1865, Colonel Beecher directed most of his efforts at obtaining new recruits. In March, while still at Mount Pleasant, Beecher had complained about the need for more soldiers. His demand im-plicitly recognized that for the 35th USCT, a potentially long and dangerous ar-mistice had just begun. He believed that his request for 223 additional enlisted men was justified given that his regiment had brought in over 500 recruits who were now in other regiments. Initially unsuccessful, Beecher persisted after the 35th USCT was transferred to Charleston. By early May, he outlined a new recruitment problem. Promises had been made, he wrote, "that the 105th U.S. Colored Regiment now organizing in this city, shall be partially of-ficered by Commissioned Colored Officers." The response among the city's young black males was striking: what potential recruits there were all wanted to serve in a unit that had black officers. As a result, other black regiments found few men willing to join their ranks. Yet, despite all of his attempts to expand his regiment, Beecher enrolled only 31 recruits in April. The failure to establish the 105th USCT, and the release of about 250 men earmarked for that regiment, improved matters only a little. In the first week of May, the

35th USCT added another 60 new soldiers, well short of the total that Beecher had looked for.[54]

The time for training and recruiting in Charleston was limited. In late June, following the clash at the Battery, the bulk of the regiment moved from the Citadel to posts along the railroad northwest of Charleston. Three companies and the operational headquarters were based at Branchville, an important railroad junction about sixty miles from the coast. The other companies, excluding Company C, which remained in Charleston, were posted at various sites along the railroad line. Each company commander was to organize his pickets to provide "the most efficient guard of the R.R. and vicinity." They were to be ready to move quickly and, reflecting concern that they might encounter some form of irregular warfare, each man was to carry sixty rounds of ammunition. Station commanders were emphatically instructed to inspect their portion of the railroad and to position guards at "exposed points such as culverts, trestles, etc." that could easily be sabotaged. In addition to their guard duties along the railroad, the black soldiers had to impose order in the coastal areas under their control at a time when roaming bands of outlaws, driven both by destitution and antipathy toward the Union victory, threatened retribution against the freedmen and anyone who had taken the oath of allegiance to the Federal government.[55] It was a role that allowed the members of the 35th USCT to act as the protectors of freedmen.

Although the anticipated guerrilla warfare never developed, the enlisted men still faced enormous hostility from rural white South Carolinians.[56] Dr. Ben Huger, writing from his plantation near Charleston, typified the whites' stereotype of the black soldier: "The licentious & ferocious Negro is encouraged to insult us, & no atrocity which he may commit meets with punishment." That attitude partly explains a clash on 28 July at Georges Station between civilians and soldiers from Company G. Huger and other whites ignored or dismissed orders such as those given by Beecher to his company commanders that they must "exercise the strictest discipline over your own men and avoid all unnecessary collisions with the people." Moreover, when someone was killed, it was usually not a white civilian. For instance, on 1 August 1865 William Jackson, a twenty-two-year-old private from Pasquotank County, "died from Gun Shot wound by a Rebell," an aftermath of the clash at Georges Station. By contrast, there are no records of civilian deaths during this incident. Nevertheless, impoverished white planters would remember events that involved black soldiers very differently. Elizabeth Jamison, whose Burwood plantation in the Barnwell District had been burned by Union troops, would record: "Col. Beecher and his coloured troops were stationed some six miles above and some ten miles below us. They were constantly about trying to excite those who would otherwise have been quiet, to insubordination. Murders and other outrages were committed, but no inquiries were made." But white hostility toward the 35th USCT never reached the level encountered by the 33rd USCT (the former 1st South Carolina Volunteers) in the western part of the state. Not only was Lt. J. T. Furman of that regiment shot down in cold blood in Walhalla, but also unrepentant Rebels tried to ambush and destroy the train carrying the 33rd to Charleston, where it was to be mustered out. Only the quick action of a black sergeant prevented multiple casualties.[57]

By the summer of 1865 it had become obvious that guarding the railroad was a secondary responsibility of the 35th USCT. The district in which the regiment operated was in the territory covered by General Sherman's Special Field Order No. 15.[58] The unit's primary tasks would now be to supervise relations between planters and freedmen, to ensure peace and good order in the rural countryside, and to mediate rival claims on the land. The presence of the 35th USCT on the mainland helped to limit the violence directed at freedmen, but it also introduced a new regularization of labor on the rice and cotton plantations. Initially, company commanders were ordered first to survey all plantations within ten to twelve miles of their stations and to report on conditions on the farms. The officers would then oversee the preparation of labor contracts to be signed by both owners and freedmen, and resolve any subsequent disputes that arose. Sherman requested that they pay special attention "to the detection and capture of any men who have been guilty of robbing or abusing freedmen." At this stage, he recommended an uncompromising policy toward such individuals since the "hanging of two or three offenders will greatly simplify the provost duty of the whole District."[59]

Soon the officers received more detailed instructions. Armed with blank contracts, they were to visit as many plantations as possible within a wide area. When an officer arrived at a farm, he would call together all the adults and explain to them the nature of the contracts. Then he would make an inventory of all stock and equipment and list the principal crops. Once both parties understood the contract, the officer would select the most reliable freedman to act for the others, who would sign over their power of attorney to him. The proportion of the crop contracted to the freedmen would depend on two factors: (1) the greater the amount of stock, the less produce assigned to the freedmen, and (2) the larger the number of children or infirm adults, the greater the amount left to the planter who must support them. In practice, this meant that the freedmen got one-half to one-fifth of the crops.[60]

During this period, several officers of the 35th USCT were detached to serve on a special commission to draft and supervise labor contracts in the areas around Bamberg and Branchville. The two men assigned to Bamberg were Lt. James Elmsley and Lt. H. P. Loomis, both of whom had been noncommissioned officers in the regiment for the better part of a year. Because they had served in the ranks, Elmsley and Loomis were the only officers in the 35th USCT who had lived in such intimate contact with the enlisted men. This may have played a part in their selection, and it certainly seems to have made them more empathetic to the freedmen's concerns. The officer detailed to Branchville was Capt. Edward Daniels, who had recently rejoined the regiment after spending more than a year as a prisoner of war.[61]

After the summer of 1865, Federal officials appeared to be more permissive toward white Southerners. In part, this could be attributed to the establishment of a provisional civilian government, but, in addition, there was a marked change in the military's role in the district. Increasingly, officers were called upon to act as arbiters as planters and former slaves disputed not only ownership of the land but also of food, clothing, and the rudiments of daily life. The widespread deprivation of whites and blacks alike only made claims to limited resources all the more hotly contested. As ex-slaves tried to acquire the means of subsistence and cultivation, white planters, and more frequently white army officers, saw their efforts as plundering. In July, Colonel Beecher became concerned about what he regarded as an illegal trade in goods— including cattle, arms, and agricultural supplies—that were being removed from mainland plantations and taken to the Sea Islands. Lax supervision by the Freedmen's Bureau allowed island freedmen and "a low class" of white mainland residents to conduct the trade. Beecher was also upset that radical freedmen from St. Helena and Chisholm had taken over a plantation in lower Colleton. These freedmen had driven off the owner, beat up the black foreman, and declared that no white person could enter the plantation.[62] Beecher's partial solution to both problems was to try to limit black mobility and to keep black labor on the mainland plantations.

In late August, after the time limit for contracts had expired, company officers in the 35th USCT received orders "that careful attention be made to enforcing Contracts already made." Where freed persons were working without a contract, the officers were to ensure that "from ⅓ to ½ the proceeds of such crops or produce of any and every kind shall be secured to the working hands for labor." At the same time, the officers were to continue disarming the civilian population, white and black, and bring all lawless individuals to justice. Beecher took several steps to lower the political profile of his black soldiers. When elections were held in the early fall, the officers were instructed to "take all necessary precautions to avoid or prevent disturbances on the day of election." Moreover, "all troops are to be kept at quarters and in no case to be out or away from the same unless required to keep the peace or upon application of respectable citizens." Such actions convinced some white South Carolinians that "the Administration and the Military are altogether in favor of doing what is reasonable & possible for the planters. . . . Time and patience will probably set matters, not straight, but straighter a great deal." They had reason to be hopeful, for the commander of the 35th USCT, under the stress of the competing factions, had become less sympathetic to the goals of the freedmen. By October 1865, friends of Beecher were denying rumors circulating in Charleston that he "had turned against the colored people and that he was becoming dissipated" until they had received more reliable evidence.[63]

When the local commandants of the various stations received their new orders for the crop year of 1866, the instructions included significant modifications. Officers were again to make returns for all plantations and to include the owners' names, total acreage and acres under cultivation, and principal crops, along with their observations on the behavior and general treatment of the freedmen. This time, however, there was less emphasis on verification in the field. Rather, much of the information was to be collected "in the office from parties coming on business," a practice that had obvious advantages for the plantation owners.[64] Late in the year, a circular from headquarters noted further changes. Noncommissioned officers were to make sure that all freedmen knew of, and understood, the terms for the next year. On or before 15 December 1865, every man and woman must have decided whether to remain where they were or to go elsewhere. They must understand that they were free to go or to stay, but that they must have made arrangements to be located somewhere. After 1 January 1866, each proprietor would have sole charge of his place, and any freed person not under contract would be obliged to leave the property. Although Federal authorities required no particular form of agreement, the expectation was that each individual would sign a year's contract specifying a wage of so many dollars per month. However, if both parties to the contract preferred a lease or working for shares, it was their right to agree to such terms. After 1 January 1866, any able-bodied person without property or visible means of support was subject to arrest as a vagrant and would be forced to work by the military authorities.[65]

Clarification of these instructions made it clear that "in the manner of making contracts, the Freedmen's Bureau or Military Forces are to interfere as little as possible." Their only role was to prevent dishonesty and deceit. Although freed persons could choose the nature of their contracts, they were encouraged to sign for wages at a suggested monthly rate of twelve dollars for men and eight dollars for women. A further clarification stated that while every able-bodied man and woman without "visible means for an honest living" might be arrested as a vagrant, evidence that the person was trying to find employment would be considered an adequate defense. Officers like Colonel Beecher found it difficult to understand why freedmen would smuggle themselves to the Sea Islands, "preferring to starve upon 40 acres of land which they have no means of working rather than to lay up from $100 to $200 by working for fair wages on land restored to its former owner."[66]

In early 1866 events on a plantation on the Combahee River mirrored the tensions between local commanders and senior officers who were distant from the freedmen. Specifically, some of Beecher's most junior officers, the ones who had the greatest interaction with black soldiers, seemed more sympathetic to the concerns of former slaves than their colonel. Lt. H. P. Loomis, the post commander at Combahee Ferry, had refused to approve contracts drawn up on Mrs. W. Mason Smith's Smithfield plantation, apparently because he felt that the workers were underpaid and lacked sufficient provisions "to carry them through." Loomis also denied the request of Mrs. Smith's agent, D. E. Huger Smith, to vacate a house occupied by a teacher of the freedmen, also named Smith and supported by the Northern Freedmen's Aid Association of New York. Loomis was first informed that Gen. Rufus Saxton's restoration did not permit any exceptions and that Thomas Smith, the teacher, must leave. Beecher then told him that in his opinion, since the workers had signed the contracts and had done part of the work, the contract would remain in force. Although Beecher soon changed his mind, Loomis approved the contracts with only slight modification of the ones he had initially found unacceptable.[67]

The enlisted men soon found themselves in situations very different from their initial role of protectors of the freedmen. By the start of the 1866 planting season, military officials and the Freedmen's Bureau staff had, retroactively, come up with a framework to judge the validity of black land claims. For a claim to have legitimacy, the freedmen usually had to show a certificate stating the number of acres. In addition, the property must have been measured and staked out, and occupied by the claimant or his family. Beecher interpreted the guidelines strictly for the four thousand settlers on certain Sea Islands. He identified only eleven valid titles of possession, and in February 1866 he began to restore island land to former planters despite contrary claims by black settlers who failed to meet all of Beecher's requirements. By the end of the month, detachments from the 35th USCT had forcibly removed from the islands freedmen whose claims were ruled invalid and who refused to sign contracts. Many black workers were taken under guard to regimental headquarters at Summerville, where Beecher operated an employment bureau for the local white planters.[68] Thus Beecher's men were now being used to evict black squatters rather than protecting them from white retribution.

Fortunately for those soldiers who resented this new role, the 35th USCT had little time left for Reconstruction service. The regiment was paid off and discharged on 1 June 1866. Before that date, Beecher had canvassed all of the enlisted men as to where they wished to be discharged: New Bern or Charleston. It was a test of their feelings for their home state and a measure of the extent to which wartime experiences had expanded the men's horizons or given them different priorities. Initially, Beecher found the men almost evenly split, and he recommended disbanding the regiment at Charleston. By 21 May, however, those preferring New Bern were in the majority (396 to 217), although, as Beecher noted, "there seems to be considerable vacillation as the time approaches and the results might be different every day it was [sic] taken."[69] By the end of May, the scattered companies of the 35th USCT had been consolidated at Charleston in preparation for mustering out. On 1 June, the men handed in their equipment and received their pay along with three days' rations. They were not, as a regiment, provided transportation back to North Carolina. The soldiers were now civilians and could go where they wished. How many of them still had their primary ties to their home state remained to be seen.

In North Carolina, more than in South Carolina, Federal officials were willing to listen to white complaints. As a result, black soldiers there only briefly performed the Reconstruction services done by the men of the 35th USCT in South Carolina. The 37th USCT avoided such work in Texas because, in December 1864, it took part in the Fort Fisher campaign in North Carolina. But returning to its home state did not mean that the regiment's postwar service would be free of conflict and dissent. Indeed, of all North Carolina's black regiments, the 37th USCT exhibited the greatest animosity between the enlisted men and their officers during this period. The regiment's postwar service took place entirely in North Carolina and was divided into two stages. The first, and shortest, consisted of duty in Wilmington and along the Wilmington and Weldon Railroad. Then, in late November 1865, after a series of racially motivated conflicts and at a time when rumors of a black insurrection were rampant in the Carolinas, the regiment moved away from the populated areas of the district.[70] For the remainder of its service, the unit garrisoned the various coastal fortifications from the Cape Fear River to Fort Hatteras. In some forts, it replaced the 14th USCHA before the latter regiment was mustered out, but reassignment of the 37th USCT had more to do with bitter strains between that unit and the larger white community than it did with coastal security. From the start of their occupational duties, the black soldiers clashed with white civilians and other Union troops. The 37th USCT provides a case study of why, by the fall of 1865, the senior Union command wanted to move most of the remaining black regiments into seacoast garrisons. Moreover, racial hostility toward the enlisted men of the 37th USCT by other Union troops, as well as internal altercations between officers and men, reveal just how fragile was the bond between white and black Union soldiers and how circumscribed was any new respect for the military contributions of African Americans.

At the war's end, the Department of North Carolina was under the immediate command of Gen. John A. Schofield. A West Point graduate with moderate Republican views, Schofield had assumed the post in February 1865. As in the case of other department commanders, the instructions under which he operated were general rather than specific. Consequently, these officers "were left to fill in the details, local condition might require." In May Schofield presented General Grant with a plan for Reconstruction that expressed the philosophy under which the army would function in North Carolina. Schofield believed that events of the war had effectively freed all slaves in

"Wilmington Front Street, 1865," showing released Union prisoners on their way to the transports. (*Frank Leslie's Illustrated Newspaper*, Courtesy of New Hanover Public Library, Wilmington, N.C.)

the state and that slavery would be constitutionally abolished. The freedman must be protected but should not be given the franchise immediately because of the "absolute unfitness of the Negroes, as a class, for any such responsibility." Schofield argued against giving the freedmen the vote partly because of his pejorative view of African Americans and partly because he felt that only the state should make that decision. The use of the prewar constitution under the guidance of a military governor would open the way for a convention that would abolish slavery, repeal secession, and elect a loyal governor and legislators.[71] The issue of suffrage would be left for the state's electors. For such a commander, the role of the army in the state was limited to actions that would not alienate potential white Republicans. Although the War Department replaced Schofield in June 1865 and Congress and the new provisional governor dismissed his plan, the army's role in North Carolina remained circumscribed.[72]

During the first week in June, when the 37th USCT moved to Wilmington, one of its first assignments was to help police the area and to guard the transportation links. It was a role that the regiment would play for only a short time. Even as the men took up their duties, an important change in leadership took place in the town. The district and town had been under the command of Gen. Joseph R. Hawley, who had been an active Free-Soiler and then a Republican Party organizer in Connecticut.[73] Hawley, a North Carolinian by birth, had little time to implement his ideas of greater racial equality before Brig. Gen. John W. Ames replaced him. The change in leadership reflected the policy of conciliation toward white Southerners. Although Ames had commanded the 6th USCT for part of the war, in 1865 he was sympatico with President Andrew Johnson's desire to return control of state and local governments to white civilian leaders. Agreeing with the president's policies and the plans articulated by General Schofield, and having no desire to implement radical social change, Ames restored the government of Wilmington to its former officials.[74]

As soon as the 37th USCT arrived in Wilmington, a small detachment of soldiers deployed for guard duty at the railroad depot. Seemingly, the men were soon forgotten. By late July, neither the town guard nor another detachment from the regiment had relieved them. No officer supervised them, nor did they receive regular supplies. Maj. Philip Weinmann sought to intervene on their behalf, since several of the men had begun to "suffer greatly from Chills and Fever they being compelled every two days to go on guard." He finally succeeded. Another detachment of eight privates and a sergeant received orders to report to the depot, and relief squads rotated at regular intervals. During this time, each company of the 37th USCT provided seven or eight men, including a noncommissioned officer, for the daily provost guard at Wilmington. In an action that Southern whites must have viewed as a highly symbolic role reversal, the Federals formed a squad of twenty privates and noncommissioned officers into a permanent mounted patrol.[75]

The white response to such actions frequently revealed a hardening of social attitudes during this period of rapid legal and social change. White Southerners had developed a series of complex responses to black behavior, but none had prepared them for African Americans' possession of significant authority. Before the war, North Carolina law justified a white physical response to signs of black "insolence." In State v. Joiner (1850), the court equated the use of "insolent language" by either a slave or a free black "to a blow by a white man."[76] As a result, the white response to blacks exercising their new independence was frequently violent and commonly condoned by white society.

In fact, the mere presence of black soldiers on town or city streets, much less their attempt to enforce Federal regulations, was an affront to many white North Carolinians. In less than a year of Union occupation, Wilmington witnessed at least five incidents of racial violence involving black soldiers. The first occurred in July 1865, when a provost guard demanded that an ex-Confederate soldier remove his gray jacket and brass buttons. The *Wilmington Herald* described the soldier as "saucy" and claimed that a white officer, who had overheard the exchange, grabbed the enlisted man by his coat, proceeded to kick him across the street, then forced him back to his regiment. This was just one of many "frequent . . . collisions between blacks and whites," the paper observed, and warned that black emancipation had not made whites the slaves of freedmen. The *Herald* believed that the white officer had shown the correct response to the demonstration of black authority. In August, a white city policeman and a black soldier, whom the *Herald* accused of being drunk, got into a fight and both men were injured. The soldier was likely Pvt. Edward Pierce, in Company E, who, on 9 August, had been "severely wounded at Wilmington, by a rebel while on patrol."[77]

During the summer, as the black soldiers increasingly clashed with the wider white community, Lt. Col. Abial G. Chamberlain received complaints from civilians about their behavior. General Ames told him that "good reliable citizens" had protested the conduct of troops guarding the railroad. The citizens reported that the soldiers were leaving their posts and pilfering from whites in the surrounding area. To the extent that such acts took place, they could be attributed in part to the fact that early detachments guarding the railroad were not properly supervised or supplied. Even worse in the minds of white Southerners, black civilians approached the soldiers for assistance when they felt ill-treated by whites. The soldiers had then assumed "the responsibility of redressing their wrongs, and administering justice between the Freedman and his former master, an assumption of authority entirely unwarranted."[78] Such complaints had been made before, Chamberlain was told, and officers had been issued instructions designed to end the problem. The difficulty, of course, was that it was the presence, not the behavior, of black soldiers that lay at the root of Southern concerns. White protests would continue until Federal officials decided to move black soldiers out of urban areas.

The enlisted men's problems were not limited to clashes with hostile whites within and outside Wilmington, for conditions within the regiment itself began to decline. Starting in June 1865 and for the first time since they had mustered in, some companies of the 37th USCT began to note in their monthly inspection reports that the condition of the soldiers' clothing was not "good" but rather "Very Poor." Regimental reports reveal that other supplies were also insufficient to meet the men's basic needs. Food became a pressing concern for many of the soldiers. Lt. McKendree Shaw of Company B reported during the summer that although his men's health was good, they had "been poorly fed and poorly clothed." Several other company commanders complained of insufficient or underweight rations for their men.[79] Stories began to circulate in the 37th USCT, as they did in other units, that profiteers were siphoning off food designated for the regiment. Before many months had passed, enlisted men began to accuse their officers of selling the soldiers' rations to the navy.[80]

A shortage of officers in many companies compounded the regiment's problems and contributed to an overall loss of esprit de corps among the men. This decline started at the top. Despite the recommendations of General Wild in April 1864, Chamberlain had remained a lieutenant colonel. Chamberlain felt that he deserved a promotion, and in October 1864, when Nathan Goff was appointed colonel of the 37th USCT, Chamberlain submitted his resignation.[81] Any ill will at the field and staff levels would ultimately filter down to the company level, especially when the companies were suffering from a lack of officers. During this period, various officers had been detached for service at division headquarters or, in the case of Lt. R. W. Drinker, at the Freedmen's Bureau in North Carolina. For months at a time Companies G and F were commanded by lieutenants, while Company I and its ninety-five enlisted men never had a captain. By August 1865, the number of officers discharged or on detached service forced some lieutenants to assume temporary command of two companies simultaneously.[82] One way to handle the dearth of company officers was through promotion from within the ranks, and Goff made the attempt. In early April 1865, Quartermaster Sgt. Charles Drayton, who had previously served in the 13th Massachusetts Volunteers, was commissioned second lieutenant in Company C based on Goff's recommendation. By the next spring, after he had "proved a very effective Officer," Drayton earned a brevet to captain and for a short time served on the staff of General Ames as assistant provost marshal for the District of Wilmington. First Sgt. Edward Williams also received a commission, although his career was not as successful as Drayton's.[83] Both of these men were part of the original complement of white noncommissioned officers recruited in Boston by Chamberlain.

A much more controversial recommendation involved 1st Sgt. John L. R. Hodges of Company F. In June 1865 Colonel Goff endorsed the promotion of Hodges to lieutenant in Company G to replace a discharged officer, Lt. James M. Munroe. Hodges had served previously in the 5th Rhode Island Heavy Artillery from July 1863 to March 1864, when he joined the 37th USCT as first sergeant in Company F. Goff considered him "well qualified for the position and deserving of promotion."[84] Less than two months later, Major Weinmann put Hodges forward again, and this time headquarters approved the commission. Only later did General Ames find out that Hodges was not white. Ames then reversed himself and changed his endorsement in "deference to the previous practice and supposed policy of the Government." Although Hodges was serving as regimental quartermaster sergeant during this time, the enlisted men of the 37th USCT must have recognized that his rejection as officer material was a statement about all of them. They may even have been aware that a limited number of black soldiers were receiving commissions in other units, and if so, that could have fueled discontent. Hodges's personal response was not recorded, but less than a year later he had lost his sergeant's stripes.[85]

The ongoing shortage of officers also forced the recall of Chaplain William A. Green from Roanoke Island. Green had been detached from the 37th USCT to serve as assistant supervisor of Negro affairs in the Freedmen's Bureau in November 1864. However, there had been so little knowledge of his activities that at one point he was listed as absent without leave. His return to the regiment was now seen as more urgent by Goff because the soldiers were being increasingly restricted from leaving camp. Since General Order No. 7 prohibited passes for the men to attend religious services off base, it became essential for a chaplain to be available to hold services in camp. The creation of a regimental hospital also required the presence of a chaplain, especially since the 37th USCT was then short a medical officer.[86] Although Green provided an important function for the regiment, men with families still on Roanoke worried about their welfare in his absence.

On the evening of 23 September 1865, tensions within the 37th USCT exploded into mutiny at Camp Hilton. The spark that triggered the violence was the method used to discipline an enlisted man in Company D who was hung by the thumbs with his feet just touching the ground. Such punishments occurred throughout the army, but officers used them more frequently on black troops, who were growing more and more hostile to punishment that was reminiscent of slave discipline. Moreover, disciplinary actions that might have been accepted as necessary during the war were increasingly seen as unacceptable and humiliating in peacetime.[87] In at least two other black regiments, the 109th USCT and the 115th USCT, the use of hanging by the thumbs had touched off violent protests. When some soldiers in the 37th USCT attempted to release the prisoner, violence erupted and shots were exchanged. During the riot that followed, Lt. James M. Mellon was shot through the body and died. Mellon, who had been recommended for promotion to captain, had been described by Chamberlain as "a very effective and capable officer." Four men in Company D—Samuel Alderman, Manuel (or Rowan) Davis, Isaac Moore, and George Smallwood—were charged with the actual shooting. A court found them guilty, although the specifications alleged the killing of Lieutenant Mellon an act "which [was] not established by the evidence." The court then indicated that it intended to reconsider its decision, and there is no evidence that the men were punished. Isaac Moore, in fact, was promoted corporal on 15 December 1865; Smallwood served with Company D until his death in late 1866 of "Chronic Diarrhoea."[88]

In the aftermath of the mutiny, many soldiers felt that the enlisted men were not to blame for the incident, but were actually the victims of the white officers. One event that reflected the depth of some men's bitterness occurred the day after the riot. Pvt. Henry Portlock of Company H allegedly asserted "that all white men in the regiment ought to be shot" and was charged with using mutinous language.[89] Despite evidence to support the charge, Portlock was acquitted. Nevertheless, the behavior of several officers on the night of 23 September suggests that they did not believe that threats such as the one allegedly made by Portlock were idle warnings.

An investigation led to the court-martial of two officers in the regiment as a result of their inaction that evening. After the first shot, Lt. Edward Williams of Company E allegedly "did leave his Company and run to the dwelling-house, hiding his sword and revolver in the upper storey, and after that secreted himself somewhere near the river bank." Although acquitted, Williams submitted his resignation and left the army within a few months.[90] The other officer charged in the incident, Lt. Samuel Edgar, was one of the former white noncommissioned officers recruited in Boston. A native of Nova Scotia, Edgar had been first recommended for promotion in June 1864 and was commissioned in October. He was charged with having "made no endeavor to suppress the mutiny, but cowardly ran away and left the officers of the regiment without his assistance." The court found him guilty of the specifications, with the word "cowardly" excluded, but attached no criminality. The assistant adjutant general, Brig. Gen. J. A. Campbell, disapproved of all of the proceedings, findings, and acquittal. According to Campbell, the evidence showed "that at the time of the mutiny, 2nd Lieutenant Edgar was physically able to attempt the performance of the duties of adjutant at dress parade" and "he did not remain and make all possible exertions to quell the mutiny."[91] Nevertheless, the army returned Edgar to active duty.

The events of 23 September suggest that the enlisted men were less willing to accept treatment in ways that they felt were inappropriate for soldiers and free men. At the same time, some officers were growing increasingly anxious about controlling their companies and about their personal safety. Boards of inquiry that handled disputes between the men and their officers frequently found it difficult to balance the needs of command with the legitimate concerns of the black soldiers. Sometime after the mutiny at Camp Hilton, Capt. John Farnsworth preferred new charges of mutiny against a corporal and four privates in Company E. The accusations were not acted upon. When Farnsworth inquired whether the assistant adjutant general had received his complaint, the captain was informed that it had been received but had not been forwarded for trial. It had been found "that the whole company were more or less engaged in the disturbance and that *these* men were no more guilty than the rest. The ringleaders of the disturbance were arrested and had been tried by Court Martial."[92]

The November ballot in North Carolina offered an insight on what the army viewed as its proper role in the state. Throughout the South the question of how the army should act during an election was one of great difficulty and delicacy. It was both prudent and politically expedient to have troops nearby in the event that there was trouble at the polls. On the other hand, it was unwise to create the impression that the troops were there to intimidate voters. Commanders of the various departments established policy as they saw fit given the local conditions. In Arkansas and Virginia, officers and men were ordered to avoid polling stations unless the civil authorities called them in to suppress violence. In contrast, soldiers were sent into western and central

Tennessee to ensure that ex-Confederates did not disturb the voting in July 1865, a move that may have helped the conservatives win the election. In North Carolina, General Schofield took firm action to prevent any soldier from being involved in the gubernatorial election of November 1865 between Jonathan Worth and William Holden. Colonel Goff relayed the order from department headquarters to his men that, on 9 November, "no com. officer or enlisted man shall upon any pretense whatever, be within the limits of the city of Wilmington, N.C., unless he be regularly detailed for duty there." Any officer violating the order would be immediately arrested and charged, and enlisted men would be placed "in the military prison and used for labor duty."[93] Worth won the election, largely because of support from the pro-secessionist east.

Shortly after the election the district commander sent the 37th USCT to man coastal installations. The move was based on a new Federal policy put out in response to pressure from white Southerners. By September, General Grant was convinced that black troops should be used on the Atlantic coast primarily to garrison seacoast forts. He may have been influenced by the mutiny at Camp Hilton, but he was certainly affected by reports of the soldiers' incendiary behavior in Southern cities and towns. There was growing white anxiety that these troops, at best, encouraged independence among the freedmen and, at worst, might help lead a widely rumored Christmas insurrection in December 1865. Even the troops' symbolic presence antagonized the white population and retarded "reconciliation." Complicating matters, a mustering out of Southern black soldiers would do little to mediate conditions, for the presence of black veterans, trained and perhaps armed, also fed white hysteria. In the face of conflicting pressures, Grant compromised. On 6 October, he composed the following memorandum that would lie dormant for almost two months: "Order four regiments of colored troops from N.C. to Dept. of Washington. Direct all Seacoast Garrisons south of Ft. Monroe, exc[ept] Ft. Taylor and Dry Tortugas, to be garrisoned by colored troops." The 37th USCT remained in North Carolina, but its companies were dispersed. Four companies went to Fort Fisher, two across the river to Fort Caswell, and one to Fort Johnson, although by the beginning of 1866, the first two forts each had three companies. The three remaining companies were detached from the regiment at Wilmington and detailed for service in the district of New Bern. Company F occupied Fort Hatteras on Roanoke Island, while Companies I and K garrisoned Fort Macon.[94]

Although the regiment would occupy these forts for well over a year, the officers and men had initially hoped for demobilization in early 1866. In the spring of that year, Nathan Goff, who had been recently breveted brigadier general, explained that he had interpreted the delay following his much earlier request for new weapons as evidence that the 37th USCT was among the black regiments scheduled for release. He had not made new requests to replace the badly worn or missing arms because "it was expected that my Reg't would be mustered out."[95] When it became clear that the unit would remain in service for the foreseeable future, Goff resubmitted the paperwork. He felt that the requisition was necessary because most companies were short not just of muskets in good condition, but of an adequate number of guns for all of the enlisted men. In early March, there were 144 men in the two companies at Fort Caswell but only 116 serviceable guns. At Fort Fisher, 261 soldiers had to share 208 muskets. On Roanoke Island, the company whose strength was normally 61 men had 55 guns, while at Fort Macon, the two occupying companies had 95 muskets for 114 men.[96] Chronically short of officers and supplies, both the men and the weapons were worn down in numbers and quality.

Despite the removal to the coastal forts, troubles continued between black troops and white citizens. A few soldiers still had duties in the towns, while other men on leave visited family and friends there. On 16 December, Pvt. Henry Cotanch was shot at Morehead City by a Southerner for whom the war was not over. Near the end of March 1866, Wilmington's mayor, A. H. Van Brokkelen, complained about disturbances caused by soldiers stationed in the town or visiting from posts in the vicinity. He cited one case of two enlisted men from the 37th USCT who had arrived on 21 March and subsequently had been arrested for "creating a disturbance in the most public part of the City where they resisted the police and came very near causing a riot." Although the two men ended up in police headquarters, they were ultimately released into the custody of two officers from the regiment who, the mayor noted, were not on duty. The mayor was annoyed that the two soldiers were back on the streets early the next morning with no charges preferred. Van Brokkelen believed that the current state of affairs, covered by General Order No. 3 of 12 January 1866, had given unlimited license to black soldiers for that kind of immunity.[97]

The dispersal of the companies in November may have pleased some whites, but it hurt regimental morale. In early January, Lt. G. W. Singer warned Major Weinmann "that the troops of your command are so utterly demoralized, but it is nothing more than can be expected where all the officers or nearly all (*over* 18) are on detached service or absent with or without leave." Singer may have been correct about the mood of the soldiers, but his explanation—that over the past year one officer often had to command two or even three companies—was incomplete. He may have been closer to the real cause when he commented on how some officers used their authority. There are, he wrote, "some officers place[d] here in emaginary [*sic*] Power and there is no end to the road they travel." Less than a month later, the men were again challenging military authority. In early February, two corporals and a private forcibly released a soldier from punishment at Fort Fisher. They were charged with violating the 7th Article of War, convicted, and sentenced to five years at hard labor and forfeiture of all pay and allowance. The sentence was reduced to one year in November 1866. In February 1867, when the regiment was mustered out, the prisoners were released and dishonorably discharged, although they received transportation to their homes.[98]

When the behavior of their officers or the military courts seemed unfair or overly harsh to the enlisted men, some soldiers tried to help the accused even if it meant a risk to themselves. In one case, Cpl. Henry Holeman, while acting as sergeant of the guard over prisoners confined at Fort Caswell in late January 1866, helped two convicted soldiers get away through his own inaction. Charged with neglect of duty, the noncommissioned officer allegedly "did fail to report immediately, but allowed ten or twelve hours to pass" before he notified the commander that the prisoners had fled the post. The extra time allowed the prisoners to make good their escape. Holeman was found guilty as charged, sentenced to two months of hard labor without pay, and reduced to the ranks.[99]

The abuse of power by officers was not always related to race. One such example took place in the summer of 1866, when two officers of the 37th USCT each independently assaulted hospital steward Benjamin F. Allen. To justify his actions, Maj. William A. Cutler claimed that, "in view of the mutinous conduct of the Steward," he had "'twitched' him down, to use his expression, and then choked him until he became quiet." But nothing in Cutler's report proved that those measures were appropriate at the time. If force had been necessary, Gen. J. C. Robinson pointed out, Cutler should have called upon the guards who were present instead of using it himself. The conduct of the second officer, Lt. O. H. P. Howard, was even more unprofessional. Howard admitted "having used a sling-shot upon the person of the steward," though he did not show just cause for his action. Again, guards were at hand, and, Robinson noted, "If physical force was necessary, the bayonet was the proper weapon." The general directed that Cutler receive an official reprimand "for his unofficer-like treatment to Hospital Steward Allen, and cause charges to be preferred against Lt. O. H. P. Howard, for his cruel and illegal treatment of the same person."[100] Despite their conduct, both officers were subsequently promoted. Cutler was breveted a lieutenant colonel while Howard was made captain of Company E in June 1866.[101]

It may very well be that these officers were treated less harshly because Allen was facing serious charges relating to the misuse of government supplies. Both he and commissary sergeant Nelson Miller were to be tried by a military court in June 1866. The sutler's clerk at Fort Fisher, who had allegedly received stolen supplies, was also implicated. On 23 August, Allen, who had joined the regiment only in September 1865, was dishonorably discharged from the army, lost half of his pay, and was sentenced to one year at hard labor. Soon after, Miller was reduced to the ranks for the remainder of his term of enlistment and lost half of his pay for four months.[102] The career of both men reflected the regiment's difficulty in finding effective and honest senior noncommissioned officers.

Throughout 1866 the 37th USCT continued to garrison forts in eastern North Carolina while the army mustered out other volunteer units. It was an equally hard time for the dependents of the regiment's enlisted men. Records suggest that some officers, aware of the soldiers' difficulties, attempted to temper the full severity of the military law, at least for men who deserved special consideration. For instance, Pvt. Madison Miller, who had volunteered in February 1864, was convicted of mutinous conduct and, as part of his sentence, lost twenty-two months' back pay. When Miller sought leniency from the court, Major Cutler tried to help him out so his family would not suffer unnecessarily. "This man having always been a good soldier previous to his arrest for Mutinous Conduct," wrote the major, "I recommend that his request [that the loss of pay be dropped from his sentence] be granted for the benefit of his family." The court approved Cutler's recommendation.[103]

The major also understood that some of the men's troubles were aggravated by white antagonism. In Smithsville, where the regiment made its headquarters, problems surfaced between the soldiers and civilians. The major issue, and a timeless issue of most armies, was the willingness of some local citizens to sell liquor to the troops. It was the source of much disturbance in the regiment, Major Cutler argued. Attempts to end the trade in liquor seldom succeeded. A more specific concern arose from anonymous complaints about the honesty and character of the commander, General Goff, and his quartermaster. Apparently persons in Smithsville had written to the War Department in May or June questioning Goff's behavior. The department then referred the matter back to North Carolina and ordered an investigation. The general claimed that he was well aware that the presence of his regiment in the state was "very obnoxious to our Southern brethren," but he was surprised by an anonymous personal attack. Goff requested the original correspondence so he could "feret [sic] out the guilty parties,"[104] but there is no indication that he was ever able to identify the party or parties who made the allegations.

As more regiments were mustered out, the 37th USCT was expected to take on additional responsibilities. In July 1866 the unit sent three companies to Charleston, South Carolina, at a time when it was the only black regiment left in North Carolina and the total Union troop strength had dropped below 2,000.[105] Companies C and H were told to prepare to embark from Fort Caswell on 2 October, while Company E was sent by boat from Smithsville to accompany them. Just five officers were available for service with the three companies. That left only five officers in the four companies on Cape Fear until later in the month.[106] The transfer of Companies C, E, and H created new problems for Goff. A serious consequence of the wide dispersion of Federal troops in the South, as well as of the chronic shortage of officers, was the difficulty in holding courts-martial. A general court-martial required a minimum of three officers, and preferably six or seven. In October 1866 Goff wrote that it was "useless to order a Court at this place, as there will not be officers enough." Indeed, he was unclear as to what he should do with the five prisoners just arrived from Fort Macon. Should he send them to a court-martial in Raleigh or back to the jail at Fort Macon?[107]

There was little sign in North Carolina that whites had become accustomed to the presence of black troops or that their level of hostility had declined two years after the war had ended. In the last months of its service, the 37th USCT experienced more violence from whites, especially from other soldiers. In early January 1867, after the regiment had been ordered to concentrate all companies at Raleigh in preparation for mustering out, clashes between the black soldiers and antagonistic whites began to recur. In late January, as Chaplain Green and several enlisted men walked in town near the military prison, "two Inf. soldiers (white) who can be identified by the above mentioned, met them armed with clubs; one of them without the slightest provocation, struck Sergeant Moses Turner over the head with his club and knocked him senseless to the ground." Major Cutler demanded "that measures be taken to prevent such occurrences in the future."[108] This attack may have been retaliation for an attempt, on 22 January, by some of Goff's soldiers in Raleigh to arrest several men of the 5th Cavalry. Gen. E. A. Carr, commander of the cavalry regiment, had accused enlisted men in the 37th USCT of using "violent and improper language towards them." Such conduct, especially since no white officer had authorized it, had to be stopped, Carr warned, "as [it is] likely to lead to serious trouble."[109] It is probable that the cavalrymen wanted more direct action.

The clashes continued. A week later, Sgt. William McDonnell attempted to arrest a private from Company A who entered a store to buy bread. A white cavalryman intervened, ordered McDonnell to halt, and threatened force if the sergeant did not recognize his white authority. The white private "told the Sergt that he would not only order him, but would do something else, and called him a black son of a b——h." Maj. Charles Whitney, in temporary command of the 37th USCT, insisted that it "was an interference on the part of Pvt Read uncalled for and unsoldierly, [and] that instances are occurring daily of insult and abuse towards the colored soldiers from the white."[110] Whitney hoped, perhaps unrealistically, that the guilty parties would be punished promptly by military officials and that enlisted men would not seek their own revenge.

By the time the regiment finally was mustered out on 11 February 1867, all weapons had been boxed up. As a result, the guard around the camp had been unarmed for several days. Now the enlisted men were far more willing to risk sneaking out of camp, and there was increased "danger of a collision between them and the citizens."[111] After 11 February, any such "collision" would find the new black civilians even more vulnerable than they had been in the army.

## CHAPTER EIGHT

# Black Veterans in a Gray State

The arrival of the black regiments in Wilmington in February 1865 triggered an emotional response from all of its inhabitants. For African Americans, the soldiers came as liberators, while for most white citizens, they represented a frightening specter of the changes confronting Southern society. All recognized that the black men in the ranks had themselves been changed. One private, recognized and embraced by his mother, was described in a letter of a fellow soldier from the 4th U.S. Colored Troops (USCT) in a way that would have resonated with many black enlisted men across the South: "He had left his home a slave, but he returned in the garb of a union soldier, free, a man."[1] Both mother and son were aware of the soldiers' new aspirations and their expectations of equal treatment that were formed as part of their service experience. Many black veterans had achieved literacy, while black noncommissioned officers had developed leadership abilities and learned to handle a range of new responsibilities. Some of the men, frugal with their wages and bounties, left the army with enough capital to start a new life. All of the soldiers had their personal worlds broadened as they tramped through areas of the nation they had never seen before. Above all, these veterans believed that they had earned the right to be treated like men. Most would have agreed with Frederick Douglass that when a black man could "get an eagle on his button, and a musket on his shoulder, and bullets in his pocket," no one could deny him the rights of citizenship.[2]

Yet as black veterans eagerly looked forward to change, much of Southern white society clung to the values and attitudes of the past. One of the black soldiers occupying Kinston, North Carolina, in the summer of 1865 described the anger and frustration of the townspeople. He wrote of them "calling in all manner of names that were never applied to the Deity, to deliver them from the hands of the *smoked Yankees*." When God did not respond promptly enough, some ex-Confederates took matters into their own hands and murdered at least one black soldier in Kinston. That killing was not an isolated event. A few months later, Pvt. Henry Cotanch of the 37th USCT was shot at Morehead City by a vindictive white Southerner. About the same time, Bill Jones, who had served in the 14th USCHA, was lynched in Greene County.[3] These events involved attitudes and conflicts that framed the veterans' experiences for decades after the war. Few of them had left the army without undergoing fundamental changes, some positive and some not. The world they carved out for themselves was in the midst of a larger society that clung to older values.

Although recent scholarship has increasingly examined the Reconstruction experiences of Southern African Americans, little of it has focused on the postwar readjustment of the region's black Union veterans.[4] Indeed, some recent studies of Civil War soldiers in war and peace give limited coverage to the experiences of Southern black veterans. Interesting new studies have been completed on individual black regiments, but they have not followed the soldiers' careers after discharge.[5] When broader studies have made passing references to the impact of Union military service on Southern blacks, they have tended to portray that service as a positive force in the veterans' lives. According to some historians, their years in the military served, at least for a select group, as a means of achieving successful postwar careers. Other writers have seen little evidence of what a later generation would call postcombat or post-traumatic stress disorder. Thus Eric Foner has argued that "for black soldiers, military service meant more than an opportunity to help save the Union, even more than their own freedom and the destruction of slavery as an institution. For men of talent and ambition, the army flung open a door to advancement and respectability. From the army would come many of the political leaders of Reconstruction." Joseph T. Glatthaar also believes that military service acted for black veterans, as it has for so many others, as a springboard into politics or other careers. In addition, he has argued that although their postwar experiences were diverse and some, like a large number of their officers, suffered personal and emotional problems after the war, "for most black soldiers, psychological adaptation to a peacetime environment seems to have gone quite smoothly." Glatthaar cites as evidence their low divorce rate and few cases of opium addiction or mental illness. But he does acknowledge that there is limited reliable information by which to accurately judge the veterans' peacetime readjustments. One implication of his argument is that the ease of transition back to civilian life was helped by the support of the local black community. Larry Logue's study of postwar readjustment of both black and white soldiers deals with only a few specific issues concerning Southern black veterans. Regional studies, however, suggest that, in addition to suffering from the endemic white violence that affected all African Americans in various parts of the South, newly mustered-out veterans had difficulty competing for jobs with black civilians who had not been in the war.[6] This problem was exacerbated by the late discharge of most Southern black regiments. Whereas most Northern black regiments were demobilized in 1865, Southern black regiments remained in service as late as 1867.

Virtually all historians agree that the experience of black veterans differed enormously depending on where they had been recruited, what their prewar situation had been, and what kind of military experience they had during the war. Black veterans returning to a victorious and prosperous Northern state could expect a response very much different from the one encountered by those discharged in a Southern state crippled economically and in the throes of social readjustment. Wartime experiences altered the veterans in many ways. Some black units had traveled extensively across the nation and had developed an esprit de corps as the results of successful military service. Others had served only locally, functioning more as a uniformed labor force.

Because the black veterans from North Carolina had served in different theaters of operation and experienced the spectrum of military duties, they provide a useful example of how one group of Southern black ex-servicemen created new lives following the war.[7] Among the four regiments were men who had been the first blacks to volunteer for service and others who had entered the ranks only after the shooting had stopped. Although many had died of wounds and disease, almost 4,100 survived the war.[8] These soldiers could persuasively claim that they, more than others in their state, had played an important part in the struggle to end slavery. Moreover, during their Reconstruction service they had frequently been the only force preventing or limiting white abuse of freedpeople. Did those credentials translate into personal success for the veterans after they were discharged? Did their lives differ significantly from the lives of men who had not volunteered?

The soldiers who made up the regiments from North Carolina shared a number of qualities with black troops recruited elsewhere in the South. The vast majority of the North Carolinians had been illiterate slaves, had worked as agricultural laborers, and were between eighteen and twenty-eight years of age when they joined the service. Many had enlisted after fleeing from their owners. Once in the army, they shared other common experiences as well. Virtually all of their commissioned officers were white, with most of them from Massachusetts.[9] These enlisted men, like all other black soldiers, initially received lower wages than their white counterparts and were more often equipped with substandard material. In addition, as other black troops, the North Carolinians spent more time performing fatigue or garrison duties than in combat and they were more likely to suffer a higher mortality rate because of disease.[10] In other ways, these men had experiences common to all Civil War soldiers, including long periods of boredom and privation, as well as shorter periods of intense elation or terror. Campaigning was physically stressful, and some black troops, like some white troops, broke under the strain. On the other hand, military service allowed others to develop and hone a range of skills in their roles as noncommissioned officers, and it enabled even more to take their first steps toward literacy. Moreover, for the infantrymen, service outside of North Carolina changed their worldviews and gave them experience in the wider black community.

With the end of the war and the beginnings of demobilization, the black veterans had to make complex decisions as to where they wished to live as a precondition to what they wanted to do. Where they chose to live revealed much about their expectations and values and what kind of life they hoped to have. Many of these men had spent years outside their home state and had served alongside African Americans born in other Southern states as well as white officers from the North. It would seem reasonable that the broader the men's wartime experience, the broader the range of possibilities they would envision for their future. Demobilization meant immediate decisions for many. U.S. War Department regulations stipulated that white regiments to be mustered out would go "generally to that point in the State where mustered in" and be paid off and disbanded. Policy for the U.S. Colored Troops differed. Often the regiments were mustered out in the locale where they were serving, although, for those who wished it, transportation was provided to where they had been mustered in. Thus the men mustered out in Texas and South Carolina had to decide whether to accept government assistance to return to North Carolina or to remain where they were. This may have been relatively easy for the men in Texas, for service along the border had been very hard. An officer in one black regiment claimed that no "set of men in any country ever suffered more severely than we did in Texas." Few soldiers wanted to remain on the Mexican border. Deciding whether to return to their home state was clearly a more onerous choice for the men who had served in South Carolina, where some had married local women and many had made friends. Although the commander of the 35th USCT, Col. James Beecher, polled his men to see where a majority of the soldiers wished to be discharged, he found no clear consensus. The final decision to muster them out at New Bern came after considerable vacillation among the men.[11] A different option was open to the black veterans demobilized in North Carolina. They had to decide whether to stay in familiar surroundings, close to family and friends, or to explore new opportunities outside of the state.

It is possible to get some sense of their decisions by locating the veterans at later points in time. In the case of ex-soldiers who left the state, that can be an extremely difficult task. But for those who remained, later censuses allow significant numbers of veterans to be tracked down. Various methodological problems, however, make it impossible for even the most diligent researcher to find all of the veterans. One of the standard sources available to historians, the 1870 national census, turns out to be one of the least accurate tallies for the South. It probably underenumerated all blacks living in North Carolina by as much as 20 percent.[12] Moreover, an attempt to link individuals through both their military service records and later census information presents additional problems. Many veterans used aliases after they had been discharged from the army. Of course, researchers familiar with nineteenth-century records who are tracking someone named Pierce will, as a matter of course, also check for Pearse, Peirce, or Peerse. Further complicating the matter, most African Americans had chosen surnames as one of their first acts of freedom. How they picked their names and their willingness to replace their first choices varied enormously. Many followed the course selected by Daniel Hill, who wrote, "I took the name after my owner." Others may have simply been recorded that way by Union recruiters, thus ensuring that at least some would later wish for new surnames. Some ex-soldiers who changed their names did so for the same reason that prompted former private Jeremiah Gray of the 36th USCT to become Jeremiah Walker: "I enlisted under [the] name Jeremiah Gray, my master's name," he wrote. "Since I came out of the war I changed my name to that of my father and now I vote and pay taxes under [the] name of Jeremiah Walker."[13]

Sometimes veterans continued to be known by both names. Thus the son of one veteran who had served in the 35th USCT wrote that his father had "enlisted under the name of America Etheridge or America Baum, his real name being Etheridge, but was owned by Mr. Baum, either name being correct." The same son later wrote of "my father America Etheridge (real name America Baum)." In other cases, names that seemed appropriate when selected in 1863 were altered over time (thus Allen Newborn later was called Allen Newton). Moreover, because these names were recorded by regimental clerks and census enumerators whose level of literacy was sometimes only slightly higher than that of the enlistees, wide variations in spelling were inevitable. Other soldiers may have had an experience similar to that of Lewis Creech, who explained that his name at the start of the war was Lucas Barrow, after his owner Reuben Barrow. When asked why he had enlisted in the 14th USCHA as Lucas Bond, the veteran explained: "I gave my name as I recollect as Lucas Barrow, and they put it down as Lucas Bond, and I served under that name."[14]

Despite the methodological problems involved in tracking down black veterans, an insight into the postwar mobility of these soldiers can be gained by selecting a representative sample of the troops from each regiment and locating as many as possible who still resided in North Carolina in 1870 and 1890.[15] By contrasting the postwar experiences of the different groups, it is possible to measure what influence out-of-state service may have had on the soldiers' later lives. Of the veterans in the sample, some had died, some were living outside the state, and some could not be found. Nevertheless, about 40 to 50 percent of the veterans from the four North Carolina regiments could be located in 1870 and between 15 to 25 percent in 1890. Assuming an equal mortality rate for all ex-soldiers after 1865 and similar difficulties in locating veterans from any unit, the differing numbers should reflect the percentage of veterans from each regiment who were living outside North Carolina after the war.[16]

When a comparison is made of the postwar residences of different groups of these black veterans, several patterns emerge. The more extensive their service outside the state, the less likely they can be located in North Carolina in their later years.[17] The regiment with the fewest veterans living in postwar North Carolina, the 35th USCT, had operated entirely outside the state during the war and mustered out in Charleston. The largest percentage of veterans that could be located in North Carolina had served in the artillery regiment, which never left the eastern part of the state.[18] Almost 25 percent fewer members of the 35th USCT could be found in North Carolina than artillery veterans. Nevertheless, ties to the home state were strong, because even a large majority of soldiers from the 35th USCT returned to their home state and remained there. Twenty years later, after death had thinned the ranks of veterans, the pattern remained unchanged. Indeed, the men of the 35th USCT made up an even smaller percentage of North Carolina's black veterans alive in 1890 than they did in 1870.[19] Clearly, some of the men who had served outside the state during the war chose to remain where they were demobilized or to return to locales outside North Carolina where they had served and had developed close personal ties. Service outside the state may have made them more receptive to new opportunities beyond North Carolina. In the decades after the war, veterans who had traveled extensively outside their state seemed more open to relocation and may have been more inclined to join the various migration schemes and economic incentives offered to North Carolina blacks to leave the state. Taken as a group, the soldiers who had never left North Carolina appear to have been more cautious about starting anew in regions unknown to them.[20]

Although many of the veterans who chose to live outside the state left few records to trace them, case studies of the small number who can be tracked reveal a wide spectrum of options available to North Carolina's black veterans.[21] Some of the soldiers mustered out in Texas and South Carolina never returned to their state of enlistment, and most of these men simply disappeared from government records; only a small number can be traced. Veterans like Pvt. Louis Belk (Belt, then Williams), who had served in the 14th USCHA, chose to reenlist in the new black regiments that were established in the regular army. Belk was not typical, however, for by the time he had been discharged from the 10th U.S. Cavalry and applied for a pension, he was living in Alabama and had lost contact with all of his old comrades, who, he wrote, had "scatered [sic] like the chaff before the wind."[22]

More commonly, the men who did not return to North Carolina maintained contact with other veterans, and these ties help explain why they had not gone back to their home state. Pension records, compiled decades after the war, show a cluster of men from the 35th USCT living around Summerville, South Carolina, in a region where the regiment had served during the first year of Reconstruction. Several of them, while still in the army, had married local women. Similarly, a number of veterans from the 36th USCT settled in and around Norfolk, Virginia, where the regiment had been stationed during the war and from where it had recruited some of its soldiers. Returning to Norfolk allowed Henry Clarke, a former musician who had grown up in Plymouth, North Carolina, to stay in contact with some of his Virginia-based comrades while maintaining his ties with North Carolina. It also allowed him to sign on to serve with the U.S. Navy for several years.[23]

The records suggest that men who left North Carolina did so because of the influence of friends or kin, to pursue employment of a limited term, or just to satisfy a sense of adventure. Some left almost as soon as they were mustered out of the service, only to return after a few years. Still others stayed in the state through part of Reconstruction before they left. For Simon McIver (Bostic), formerly of the 14th USCHA, who had enlisted at New Bern but who had been born in Marlboro County, South Carolina, leaving North Carolina meant going home. For John Jack, who had served in the 37th USCT, out-of-state migration was a short-term employment strategy. Pvt. Abram Bissel left North Carolina in search of seasonal labor and never returned, living the remainder of his life first in Georgia and then in Florida. Other veterans traveled outside North Carolina only for brief periods after they left the army. George Gaylord, a private in the 35th USCT, was seriously injured at the Battle of Olustee and was discharged in the fall of 1864 after losing the sight in one eye. On being paid off, he took a steamer to New York, stayed there for two weeks, then returned to Hyde County and never left.[24] A few veterans left North Carolina as a matter of necessity. Nathan Joyner, who had served in the 14th USCHA, fled after becoming involved with the law. One of his former comrades recounted that after the war he "got into a scrape, was accused of helping or assisting a white man Bryant Field of burning a house in Kinston and had to leave the state."[25]

A few veterans, perhaps influenced by their officers, moved north immediately following demobilization, whereas others left only as the political climate in North Carolina changed. Nicholas Clairborne of the 37th USCT departed for Boston as soon as he had been mustered out. Nathaniel Spellman, a former artilleryman, waited until 1874 before he followed one of his friends—Henry E. Dewell (Duert), formerly of the 14th USCHA—to take up residence in Brooklyn, New York; Dewell had been influenced by his sister, Annie, who left Roanoke Island for New York late in the war. She met him while visiting Elizabeth City in 1867 or 1868 and told him about opportunities in the North. It is likely that other veterans moved north to try to rejoin loved ones. During the war, Union officials had repeatedly tried to persuade black women on Roanoke to take domestic service jobs in the Northern states. Because the island had been a designated settlement for the families and dependents of Gen. Edward Wild's soldiers, some of the women who had moved north from the island, like Annie, very likely were the wives or relatives of these troops.[26]

As some African Americans became pessimistic about life in the reconstructed South, migration to another country became an increasingly attractive option. A few Southern blacks dreamed of a life free of oppression and sorrow in Africa.[27] By the late 1860s, interest in the American Colonization Society (ACS) and its activities in Liberia generated a response in northeastern North Carolina among at least some Civil War veterans. But the limited surviving records offer only tantalizing clues as to how many veterans were involved in the migration movement. Two hundred freedmen from Martin County headed by A. W. Powers, likely a former private in the 35th USCT, told the ACS that they would be ready to immigrate to Africa by May 1870.[28] Another veteran of the 35th USCT, Pvt. Peter Mountain, headed a group of 163 African Americans who left Windsor, North Carolina, in November 1871 for Liberia. John F. Shepherd, who had served in Company B of that regiment, had led an even larger group that departed from Windsor the previous year.[29] Because only the leaders of these groups were identified in their correspondence with the ACS, it is impossible to estimate how many other veterans may have gone. It is also unclear from ACS records whether the people who asked for passage actually left North Carolina or, if they left, whether they remained in Africa.

In early 1877, for instance, Samuel Wiggins, formerly of the 14th USCHA, applied to move his family from Plymouth to Liberia. His application was one of sixteen the ACS received from North Carolina that year. The records do not show whether Wiggins went to Africa and then returned or whether he ever left the state. But he nonetheless resided in Plymouth in 1890. As interest in migrating to Liberia waned in North Carolina, it was replaced by plans to resettle blacks hoping to escape oppression in other states such as Kansas and Indiana. In 1879 approximately one thousand African Americans left North Carolina for the West, with an unknown number following in later years. Although no veterans were among the organizers who can be identified, the migrants were recruited from an area of the state where numerous veterans resided, and the migrants may have included some ex-soldiers.[30]

Given the wide dispersion of black veterans who left the state, the residence pattern of those who remained in North Carolina is striking. The majority of the veterans who appear in the 1870 census had returned either to their county of recorded birth or to an adjoining county. Twenty-five years after the war, virtually all of the almost 700 ex-soldiers found in the Civil War Veterans Census of 1890 lived in the easternmost areas of the state, close to where they had been born and where they had enlisted. Just over half of these veterans—some 360 men—resided in six counties near or on the coast: Beaufort, Bertie, Craven, Halifax, Pasquotank, and Washington.[31] Indeed, the 1890 residencies were more closely clustered in the eastern counties than the pre-1860 residencies had been. No more than two or three veterans lived west of the eastern fringe of the Piedmont.[32] And few veterans had even returned to the counties along the Piedmont's eastern edge, which had supplied significant numbers of recruits during the war.[33] Instead, large numbers of these elderly ex-soldiers lived in the Tidewater region, especially in or close to coastal towns and cities like New Bern, Elizabeth City, and Wilmington.[34] In the countryside where many of these veterans still resided, they were frequently found in close proximity to other members of their old units.

For example, in 1890 more than three dozen black veterans, including twenty-five from the 14th USCHA, gave their postal address as the small town of Windsor. This clustering was common throughout the northeastern counties. As numerous pension records confirm, such grouping allowed many black veterans to remain in close contact with old comrades whom they could see on a weekly basis and from whom they could draw various forms of assistance. Besides the potential support network it offered, this residential pattern testified to the importance of kinship, friendship, and local attachment to these men. William Thomas summed up the way that the war had forged bonds among black veterans that would last for the rest of their lives. The loss of mutual friends, shared suffering, and wartime dangers overcome had cemented their relationships. They had been changed, Thomas wrote, by "the horrors of war, and with it the loss of friends." Their common experience created "a bond of union that pervaded the entire ranks of the regiment." The war had made them "a *fraternal* band"—a band of brothers.[35] Moreover, the presence of a large number of black veterans, especially if in close proximity

A reunion of USCT veterans from Washington County, N.C., ca. 1900. The man of light complexion standing prominently in front is Samuel Wiggins, the first black judge in Plymouth after the war. (Courtesy of Port O'Plymouth Museum)

to each other, created a sense of security lacked by African Americans elsewhere in the state.

Soldiers who had developed bonds of comradeship during the war sought to maintain those ties in peacetime. After the Grand Army of the Republic (GAR), a fraternal organization of Union veterans, was established in 1866, chapters were quickly set up in North Carolina. By 1871, at least eighteen GAR posts had been opened in the state. A few posts appeared across the Piedmont in cities such as Raleigh and Charlotte, and a cluster of posts sprang up in the western section of the state, but the majority of posts were in the east—in places like Elizabeth City, Wilmington, New Bern, and Washington.[36] The little town of Windsor, with its cluster of black veterans, was home to General Reynolds Post 58, while J. C. Abbott Post 15 at Wilmington was formed as a black organization. New Bern had two posts in 1871, one of which, J. C. Beecher Post 22, was named after the commander of the 35th USCT.[37] Elizabeth City had four posts.[38] These posts were supported by veterans for the rest of the century and became an important institution in the lives of many African Americans in North Carolina. They have also become the focus of a historical debate.

Stuart McConnell has argued that by the 1880s, almost all of the GAR posts were segregated and black veterans organized their own posts and held their own parades. Within the GAR, black veterans "were accorded separate and unequal status." Other historians believe that although both black and white veterans joined the GAR, they remembered the war in fundamentally different ways that negatively impacted African Americans. Black veterans were marginalized within the organization. More recently, however, historians such as Barbara Gannon and Andre Fleche have argued that black and white veterans, unlike the wider white community, were unwilling to sacrifice the memory of black military agency to the "whitewashed road to reunion." Although all-white and all-black posts did exist more commonly in the South, the GAR had no official policy of segregation and prided itself on being color blind. Indeed, the fact that GAR records, for all intents and purposes, ignore the issue of race makes it difficult even to establish which posts were integrated and which were not. Furthermore, regional department meetings were inclusive and the GAR's official paper, the *National Tribune*, carried dozens of articles about black military accomplishments, some as late as the 1920s. Certainly black veterans believed the GAR to be inclusive. Jacob Hector, a popular black speaker at Pennsylvania GAR meetings, declared that the GAR was "the only association . . . where black men and white men mingle on a foot of equality." Hector contrasted the GAR's openness with the segregation exhibited by the Masons, the Oddfellows, and the Knights of Pythias.[39]

Although black veterans in North Carolina may have gathered at all-black posts, the segregated post was, Gannon persuasively argues, "an autonomous social organization within a larger interracial group." It was a choice taken by the black veterans, and it was a world that they made. Certainly, veterans of the state's four black regiments who moved to the North often joined mixed-race posts. William Keyes and William Singleton, who had both served in the 35th USCT, became members of Admiral Foote Post in New Haven, Connecticut. The Foote Post counted as many as sixty-five African Americans among its hundreds of members. At least one other veteran of the 35th USCT joined Taylor Post in Hartford, Connecticut, and Wallace George, a former lieutenant in Company E of the 37th USCT, was a longtime member of the mixed-race Major How Post in Haverhill, Massachusetts. In 1891, when the efforts of delegates from Louisiana and Mississippi to establish racially separated departments were rejected by the GAR's National Committee, former commander in chief William Warner summarized the majority position. "During that fierce struggle for the life of the Nation," he declared, "we stood shoulder to shoulder as comrades tried. It is too late to divide now on the color line. A man who is good enough to stand between the flag and those who would destroy it when the fate of the Nation was trembling in the balance is good enough to be a comrade in any Department of the Grand Army of the Republic. No different rule has been, or ever shall be, recognized."[40]

By January 1868, Emancipation Day was widely celebrated in North Carolina's black communities, and GAR posts were in the center of the activities. In that year "General Allan Rutherford presented a flag to the Grand Army of the Republic Post No. 3. The banner was received by William McLaurin," a black naval veteran.[41] More than a decade later, the *New York Age* reported that the all-black "Fletcher post No. 20 GAR and Afro-Americans generally" were observing Memorial Day in Elizabeth City. The article implied that here, as in many places in the South, it was primarily the African American community that celebrated the day and honored the Union army's dead of both races.[42]

In 1879, during the second wave of GAR expansion, black veterans in Wilmington began organizing a new post, holding meetings that were closed to outsiders. As in the case of all GAR posts, this post was created only after a group of veterans petitioned the state GAR for a charter. In 1884 they formed J. C. Abbott Post 15 and elected a slate of officers that included George Mabson as president and John Eagles as vice president.[43] Establishing and supporting the GAR posts was no small act for many black veterans. They paid a muster fee to join as well as annual dues. Although they varied, most annual dues were between one and two dollars, with a muster fee of perhaps four dollars. This was no small financial burden for many black veterans, who also had to purchase a GAR uniform as specified by the state organization.[44]

For many black veterans, the GAR provided comfort and a final support. The posts used their limited finances to aid sick members, to bury their dead comrades, and to help surviving family members. The aging veterans were also assisted by the Women's Relief Corps (WRC), the official women's auxiliary of the GAR, organized in 1883. All that the WRC asked of its members was that they be "loyal" women, committed to the welfare of the veterans and to the Union. In North Carolina and elsewhere, they offered important charity and relief to ex-soldiers. In 1891 an inspection report of the national WRC praised the all-black James Beecher Corps of New Bern. It was "a bright smart corps. . . . [The women] have good attendance at their meetings though they live miles apart." The report also commended "another good corp," the black unit at Elizabeth City. "They take good care of their sick and needy ones and walk in perfect harmony with their post." For many veterans, the GAR was a key part of their lives to the very end. When George Burden died in Wilmington in 1885, he "was buried by J C Abbott GAR post at the National Cemetery" near the city. Although Burden had been ill for some time, he "was at the post the night before he died, complaining of not being well." He was not the only North Carolina veteran to spend his last hours with other GAR members. In 1938 William Singleton, then aged ninety-eight, attended the seventy-fifth reunion at Gettysburg and three weeks later marched in the grand parade at the national encampment. It was virtually his final act, for he died of a heart attack a few hours after the parade.[45]

Ex-soldiers, whether organized or not, were less easily intimidated than many freedmen. Gun ownership, especially of pistols and shotguns, was common among the veterans, and local white militia units or police forces seem to have had less success disarming them than they did other African Americans. When militiamen confiscated pistols and shotguns from black veterans returning to Hertford County in December 1865, the ex-soldiers appealed to the Freedmen's Bureau assistant commissioner for assistance. The weapons, which the veterans had purchased when they were being discharged, were returned.[46] Owning weapons and demonstrating a willingness to use them offered these former soldiers a security not available to others. In some places, Confederate veterans had taken over the newly formed county police force in order to intimidate blacks and Unionists through violence; if arrested by U.S. soldiers, the perpetrators found county courts sympathetic and country jails porous. That was less frequently the case in areas where black veterans were numerous. In Wilmington, for example, veterans were involved in both the police force and militia units. In August 1868 the town's Board of Aldermen organized a police force and stipulated that 50 percent of its privates would be black. At least three of the twelve policemen—Samuel Nixon, George Burden, and John Wright—had served in the 37th USCT. Moreover, John Eagles was the police sergeant while the corporal, William Brook, had served in the 35th USCT.[47] Black policemen served on the Wilmington police force until 1898.

African American veterans were also instrumental in establishing several militia units in the Lower Cape Fear region. David Cooper, the first commander of "Cooper's Military Company," organized in December 1872, was a veteran of the 37th USCT. At virtually the same time, John Eagles became captain of the Wilmington Rifle Guard; David Chadwick, a veteran of the 35th USCT, was his first sergeant. Within two years the Rifles had created two companies that drilled every Wednesday night. Members were warned that unless they attended regularly, they could not take part in the annual Emancipation parade. The black militia maintained a public presence in the city. In 1874 Company A celebrated the unit's anniversary by holding a parade on 20 April through the streets of Wilmington, followed by a target competition on Summer Hill.[48]

Black veterans organized themselves in other ways elsewhere in North Carolina. In the northeastern counties, they helped counter white intimidation by an open display of their military preparedness. For instance, on 4 July 1866 Horace James, the former superintendent at Roanoke Island, invited three hundred to four hundred blacks to his plantation in Pitt County for fireworks, food, and a public demonstration of the martial readiness of local veterans. James described the events that followed dinner: "Target practice with Springfield rifles and ball cartridges elicited spirited competition, in which exercise the two best shots were made by colored men. An extempore organization of infantry and of cavalry (mule-mounted) drilled, fired, charged, and marched, to their own intense delight." Although white-on-black violence was widespread in the state, it was more frequent and more visible in the central and western counties than it was in the northeast.[49] While local demographics, conflicts in the white community, and political struggles explain some of the variation, the presence of large numbers of black veterans in close proximity no doubt discouraged at least some white violence.[50]

The location of so many veterans in northeastern North Carolina offered them the potential of strong political influence and leadership in the postwar period. Blacks began to organize within months of the official end of hostilities, and some of their rising leaders had been members of USCT regiments. Moreover, the areas with the most political activity—the coastal region and eastern cities and towns—were precisely those counties where black recruitment had been the greatest. In May 1865 a group of black veterans met to demand—among other civic changes—the right to vote. As former soldiers who "had the privilege of fighting for our country," they had become anxious "to show our countrymen that we can and will fit ourselves for the creditable discharge of the duties of citizenship. We want the privilege of voting." By the summer of 1865, Equal Rights Leagues or Union Leagues had emerged in Wilmington, Beaufort, New Bern, and Kinston. In fact, the strongest supporters of the first freedmen's convention in the state, convened in Raleigh on 29 September 1865, were the black residents of New Bern, a city that had supplied so many African American recruits.[51] And yet, when that convention met, as was true of the one that followed a year later, only a very few of the North Carolina veterans were delegates.

Of course, in the summer and fall of 1865, only a minority of North Carolina's black soldiers were in a position to participate in the political activities of the black community. When the freedmen's convention was called in the fall of 1865, none of the regiments had been mustered out, although two units, the 14th USCHA and the 37th USCT, were serving in the state. When the next convention was called one year later, only the veterans of the artillery regiment had reentered civilian life. The 37th USCT continued to serve in North Carolina, and the 35th and 36th USCT had just been mustered out; many soldiers in the latter two units had not yet returned to North Carolina.[52] At the first convention, out of over one hundred delegates, many of whom remain anonymous, only Sgt. Hezekiah Foster of the 14th USCHA can be identified from among the black troops at the meeting. Because he was described merely as a man "of few words and careful deeds," it is reasonable to assume that his role at the convention was limited.[53] Present, however, were more prominent men who had military credentials and would provide greater leadership.

One of the most radical individuals behind the convention movement was Abraham H. Galloway, a mulatto who had escaped the state in 1857 and moved first to Philadelphia, then to Ohio, and finally to Canada. He returned to North Carolina as soon as Union troops occupied the eastern part of the state and became a major force in encouraging recruits for General Wild's brigade. Although he did not enlist, Galloway may have been involved in intelligence work for the Union army. He later became the most influential black politician before his sudden death 1870.[54] A more moderate member of the convention was its chaplain, Rev. George A. Rue, who had ministered for six years in Massachusetts before becoming chaplain of the 32nd USCT, a unit formed in Pennsylvania. The actual leader during the convention, according to reporter Sidney Andrews, was James H. Harris, a free mulatto from Granville County who had moved first to Ohio and then to Canada at the start of the war. In 1863 Harris had helped to raise men in Indiana for the 28th USCT, although he had not joined that regiment. Two other eastern delegates who played important roles in the convention and who had encouraged black recruitment were Rev. James W. Hood and John P. Sampson. Hood had moved from Pennsylvania to New Bern in 1863 to take over the city's African Methodist Episcopal Zion church. Although he had assisted in the recruitment of African Americans, he had also protected his congregation from unscrupulous white officers.[55] Hood was elected president of the convention. Sampson, a free mulatto from Wilmington, had moved north, was educated in Ohio, and published the *Cincinnati Colored Citizen*. He was almost as radical and influential as Galloway.

Both the first and second freedmen's conventions are interesting because they operated at two seemingly conflicting levels. The delegates debated radical issues but afterward issued cautiously worded public statements. Thus the first convention's address to the Constitutional Convention of North Carolina, following several days of radical debate, was moderate to the point of being almost apologetic. Then the convention resolved itself, upon adjournment, into a state Equal Rights League. Public notice of the next convention in 1866, however, referred to the meeting as a "Colored Educational Convention."[56] Certainly the second gathering, which took on a more militant tone in many of its debates, showed no significant increase in the number of veterans among its delegates, even though three of the North Carolina regiments had been discharged and the fourth was then serving in the state.

The lack of direct political involvement by the veterans became clearer in the years following the state election of 1868. Although the ex-soldiers provided little political leadership, other blacks in North Carolina filled a number of important roles. At least 60 African Americans were elected to state and local offices during the Reconstruction era. Another 55 state and national representatives won seats from 1877 to 1900. Yet among the 115 successful candidates, only one man, John S. W. Eagles, a former first sergeant in the 37th USCT, was a veteran of the North Carolina regiments, and he only served out a partial term after a member elected in 1868 resigned.[57] A few more veterans from these regiments were appointed to positions such magistrate, justice of the peace, or election registrar. But that is all. In contrast, twice as many black elected officials had spent part of the war as servants of white Southerners in North Carolina military units.[58]

In addition to Eagles, however, at least ten more black North Carolina elected officials had fought for the Union, two in the navy and eight in the army. But they were recruited outside North Carolina and for a time had lived in the North. Among the ex-soldiers, George M. Arnold was a reporter for the African Methodist Episcopal Church's *Christian Recorder* before joining the 4th USCT, a regiment raised in Baltimore. George L. Mabson, the slave son of a prominent white Wilmington citizen, was sent to Boston in 1854 for an education and there joined the 5th Massachusetts Cavalry. Benjamin Morris, born in New Bern, was also educated in the North before enlisting. Henry E. Scott was born in Ohio and educated in Wisconsin before he joined the Union army, and John A. White, a native of Virginia, served in a Pennsylvania regiment. Parker Robbins and his brother Augustus, property-owning mulattoes in Bertie County before the Civil War, joined the 2nd U.S. Colored Cavalry. After the war, both men represented Bertie in the state assembly.[59]

The military service records of these politicians may have won them some votes. More likely, what their electoral success reveals is the political advantage of having some Northern credentials. Victory at the polls, of course, depends foremost on the character of the candidate (or perhaps the weakness of the opponent), but it was not coincidental that among the most influential of the early black politicians were men who carried with them a Northern cachet. Such a group would include Galloway, George L. and William P. Mabson, and North Carolina's leading black politician, James H. Harris, who was elected to the U.S. Congress in 1882.

Why were the veterans of the four black regiments raised in North Carolina underrepresented among the elected and appointed political black leadership? It may have had as much to do with their personal characteristics as with voter preference. Certainly the profile of the "average" soldier differed from that of the successful black Reconstruction politician. Both the current historical literature and the data from postwar North Carolina indicate that the early black leadership was lighter-skinned, wealthier, more literate, and more inclined to have been free and to have resided in urban centers than the bulk of the black population. Although there were a significant number of mulattoes among the first soldiers recruited, only a tiny percentage of North Carolina's veterans had the credentials that the voters desired.[60] Most of North Carolina's USCT veterans were rural, black, and poor.

In addition, military service did not automatically guarantee white Republican support for black veterans. When white political appointments were made in Reconstruction North Carolina, or when white Republicans voted, the chief concern generally was the "loyalty" of the candidate. When the same appointments were made among blacks, loyalty was assumed, and the greatest concern often was literacy. This can be seen in the appointment of white and black election registrars in 1867. The search for white registrars focused on "northern men" or men from North Carolina's white Union regiments. The "loyalty" of the black population never was an issue. Instead, the primary concern was to find men who could "read or write sufficiently to be of any use to the Board of Registration." Even though the black registrars who were appointed included some USCT veterans, the search by white officials frequently seems to have been restricted to ministers and teachers.[61]

The fact that veterans did not hold numerous offices, however, did not mean that they were politically unimportant. The bulk of the former soldiers lived in the state's famous "Black Second" Congressional District, which would continue to elect Republican candidates until the end of the century.[62] Conservatives had gerrymandered this district in an attempt to minimize black voting power. The veterans in the Black Second helped elect three important black politicians, O'Hara, Henry Plummer Cheatham, and George H. White.[63] But even in the Black Second," success depended on attracting white as well as black votes. Local black veterans were not the best candidates to draw votes from the white electorate.

The limited political success of black veterans was mirrored in other aspects of their postwar careers. Just as the army had not provided a springboard into politics, neither did it open financial doors for most of the ex-soldiers. The limited funds they had received in bounties and wages during the war did not give black veterans, as a class, much financial independence. Of course, few enlisted men, black or white, came out of the war financially enriched. Indeed, North Carolina's veterans seemed to have been quite similar to their black counterparts from Ohio, who "returned to virtually the same conditions from which they had left."[64]

Many veterans emerged from the war physically, if not psychologically, disabled. A considerable number were unable to take care of themselves, let alone launch successful business or political careers. Although pension records are full of accounts of their disabilities, white contemporaries often viewed the cries for assistance with considerable skepticism. Nevertheless, regimental records show that even before the war ended, many soldiers had become sufficiently disabled to be discharged; many would remain permanently impaired and limited to doing whatever work they could obtain.[65] Some had been disabled from wounds, whereas others had contracted diseases that left them with permanent physical disabilities. Even soldiers who had never seen the enemy experienced such problems. For example, Isaac Bryant of the 14th USCHA spent more of his service as a stevedore than he did firing ordnance, but he did not escape injury. In December 1864, while unloading ammunition boxes, his comrades slipped and the full weight of the box they were handling fell on him. Bryant suffered a "rupture of both sides laying him up two or three weeks at a time. . . . His guts came down so that he is not able to do anything like work having to wear truses [*sic*] to keep up." In July 1865 Allen Smith, a member of the same regiment, suffered a debilitating groin injury "by means of lifting heavy T iron for R.R. and while unloading boats at Morehead City, caused him to become what is generally termed hurting of privates. He was taken down and sent to Hospital where he remained about two months." The company clerk described him as "feeble" on his discharge in December 1865.[66] Smith would wear a truss for the rest of his life.

Many USCT enlisted men suffered serious but less identifiable personal damage. Glatthaar has argued that the psychological adjustment of black veterans seems to have been relatively easier than that of white officers—at least by such measures as psychological problems and divorce. In part, this speaks to the fact that few whites cared enough or were in a position to record black psychological problems or to see them as similar to those that afflicted white veterans. The best documented case of a mental disorder among men who had served in the USCT regiments was, not surprisingly, that of the prominent white officer, Col. James C. Beecher, who both before and after his service in the 35th USCT suffered mental breakdowns. After years of anguish and periods in asylums, he committed suicide. The U.S. Pension Office agreed that his being "exposed to all of the vicissitudes of army life" had exacerbated Beecher's condition.[67]

Pension officials, however, tended to be less sympathetic to black veterans who claimed that an ailment, especially diminished mental competence, was the result of their military service. When the daughter of Charles Oats, formerly of the 37th USCT, applied for a pension, she stated that she had "learned from comrades of the Regt. that her father contracted a disease of [the] head by exposure and cold at Chaplin [Chafin's] Farm causing him to be very lightheaded and to act as if he were not very bright—would at times wander away from camp."[68] James H. Moore claimed in his application that severe sunstroke, which afflicted him while he was serving in the 14th USCHA, had left him a wreck. After the war, he "would be giddy and weak headed and at times crazy and have fits." Sometimes, "he would be out of his mind" for over a month. Yet neither Oats nor Moore received a disability pension. George Burden applied for and obtained a pension based on physical injuries suffered after he had been captured at Plymouth and forced to work "like a horse" dragging logs for Confederate fortifications. Again, pension officials gave no monetary consideration to his mental problems, even though another soldier testified that he had "known him to be out of his head for several minutes while we were at Fort Casnell [*sic*] and here at Wilmington." His "fits," however, were infrequent—even his wife Eliza "never knew he had fits until about three months after my marriage, then he had a fit."[69]

In extreme cases, black veterans who, like Colonel Beecher, were driven by their own private demons, later committed suicide. Washington Newby left far fewer records to make his actions understandable than did the New England colonel, but he also took his own life. After a long period of hospitalization, Newby was discharged from the 36th USCT in June 1865 and returned to North Carolina. Years later his mental health declined, and the veteran began to suffer from a series of physical ailments. His widow explained that "we had to watch him constantly and one night we fell asleep and he got out and we could not find him." By the time that they located Newby, he had drowned himself. "It was said," his widow wrote, "that he went crazy from the roaring of the guns in the war."[70]

According to their correspondence with government officials, the war had as deleterious an impact on the domestic lives of North Carolina's USCT veterans as it had on many Northern white veterans. Assessing those postwar problems, however, was complicated by contemporary social perceptions of black marriages and by the legal difficulties involved with understanding relationships that the soldiers had begun before the war. Although not legally recognized, stable slave marriages clearly existed, usually with the consent of owners and the recognition of the black community. There were also common-law relationships enforced by slaveowners and perceived as transitory by African Americans. Moreover, there is a good deal of evidence that the influence of slave marriage customs led some black veterans to leave their spouses and remarry without first obtaining a divorce.[71]

Of course, some relationships were remarkably durable. When Chester Amieny enlisted in the 14th USCHA in February 1864, he arranged for his wife

Frances to live with a friend, Daniel Weeks, and his family. When he could, Chester sent part of his pay for his wife's support. After the war, Weeks testified that "we all belong to the same church and a rule came in the church for us to be remarried under special act of Legislature and my wife and I and Chester Amieny and his wife Frances Amieny and about sixty other couples got married by Rev. Hull Grimes."[72] This long and stable marriage thus was unaffected by the wartime transitions of black life.

A more complex and troubled relationship was that of John Banks and his wife Julia, who had married in 1866 while the 35th USCT was stationed in South Carolina. Despite conflicting accusations, it appears that some years later, after Julia "took up with" her deceased daughter's husband, John left his wife. Although a friend of his testified that John had left "because Gaddes was too intimate with his wife," Julia claimed that she had tried unsuccessfully to get him back. His reply, she testified, had been "that he was too old to work for me, that he wanted to live off his pension." In another case Peter Downing, who had been discharged from the 36th USCT after losing his right arm in the fighting around Deep Bottom, Virginia, had returned to Plymouth, North Carolina, "after first going to Roanoke Island to [visit] my folks." Downing was not just a man whose bad judgment led to marital problems. His postwar experiences reveal how susceptible some uneducated and aging black veterans were to exploitation by people who were quick to overcharge or defraud the gullible ex-soldiers. When Downing first applied for a disability pension in 1867, the man who drafted his application charged him ten dollars, while his "attorney at Washington" deducted twenty-five dollars for his services— more than Downing's monthly check. Decades later strangers were still taking advantage of him. After receiving his pension check in 1901, he allowed a Mrs. Pickens to cash it. "And when she came back she gave me what was left after she took out her charges" and the charges of a man who had signed the voucher. Downing explained that "I am ignorant and did not know enough to keep away from her until I found out that she was robbing me." He was equally unlucky in his choice of wives. By 1870, he had married twice. Following the death of his second wife, he wed Eliza Garrick, and that union was a disaster. Eventually Downing moved out of their home because she treated him "so mean"; he also noted that "she has not a good character and used to go away and remain away for days and when I would ask her where she had been, she would say that it was none of my business." Downing was clearly intimidated by Garrick, for he failed to contest her initial demand that she receive half of his pension. Years later, when he contested her right to it, he testified that he had already given her property worth one thousand dollars to live on. The old veteran bitterly complained that his wife "is untrue to me and She gets one half of my Bounty and I am obliged to go very short in my Dealings and after She gets ½ of my Money She puts it on other men. . . . She is a very bad woman." The agent investigating the claim had trouble deciding whom to believe. His uncertainty was understandable in view of the conflicting accounts, but ultimately Eliza received a widow's pension.[73] She was fortunate. Numerous other African American women had great difficulty in obtaining widows' pensions because of their clouded legal status, which also attests to the inherent problems in assessing the stability of the marriages of North Carolina's USCT veterans.

A case that reflected a problem facing female applicants involved two women, Roena Creech and Mymia Creech, both of whom claimed to be the widow of Lewis Creech, a veteran of the 14th USCHA. Pension officials who reviewed their applications found that Lewis "took up" with Roena some years after the war and after "a desultory cohabitation, resulting in the birth of two children, he left her." On one of his subsequent visits, Lewis's relatives persuaded him to marry her, which he did in November 1889. Shortly after, he left Roena permanently and "took up with the claimant Mymia," with whom he was living at the time of his death. Mymia stated that they married in May 1894. After extensive investigation, however, officials discovered that Lewis had had two earlier marriages: the first, to Annie Hammond, ended with her death in 1878, and the second, which took place in 1881, to Penelope Paxton, whom he never divorced. A special examiner also found that a fifth woman, Philis Cox, claimed to have married the soldier at Kinston in 1867, but there were no surviving records to document her assertion. In his earlier pension application, the veteran admitted his marriage to Paxton. She had "deserted" him and was, to the best of his knowledge, still living in Baltimore. They "were never divorced." He had been sent to prison for a year "and then she went off." Lewis also recounted his subsequent two marriages. The Bureau of Pensions ruled that he had not been "legally competent to contract a marriage with either claimant," and neither Roena nor Mymia received a pension.[74]

In addition to the physical and emotional problems that the veterans may have experienced, other factors constricted their financial fortunes. The fact that they had to reenter the workforce months, and sometimes years, after the Confederate surrender put them at a disadvantage compared to men of both races whose businesses were already established. A year before the war ended, at least eighteen black businessmen, turpentine farmers, and grocers working in areas under Union control reported annual incomes of one thousand dollars or more.[75] Thus they began the postwar years with a significant advantage over the men just leaving the service. Moreover, black veterans in Southern states generally were poorly positioned to succeed in business enterprises that depended on the goodwill and patronage of the surrounding white community.[76]

Blacks were able to leave the Union army with some financial benefits if they had been frugal and had enlisted late in the war. But few soldiers could save much from their wages, especially if they were sending money home to dependents. The men who had enlisted first were the least fortunate, for Southern black soldiers received no bounties until the summer of 1865. Only soldiers who had enlisted late in the war qualified for bounties of up to three hundred dollars. For some men, a bounty could be the start of modest property ownership. On the other hand, many veterans who were owed money by the government for bounties or back wages were at the mercy of the agents and lawyers who handled their applications. At best, they could expect to pay these agents $10 to $25 plus expenses in order to obtain relatively small amounts of money. At worst, they might lose most or all of what they were entitled to. One black veteran, William Latham, who used an unscrupulous attorney found that after various fees, expenses, and stationery were deducted from his $100 check, he received only $19.20.[77] Even when legal fees were reasonable, few veterans achieved a secure financial future from the money they received for their military service.

This does not mean that black veterans emerged from the war without any benefits. What it does suggest is that their benefits were limited or intangible. By the end of the war, black soldiers received not only the same pay as whites but also, in some instances, bounties of almost equal value.[78] The money allowed some veterans who managed to avoid fraudulent practices to buy a modest property or enter a trade. Moreover, increasing numbers of soldiers became eligible for veterans' pensions in the decades after the war. Before 1890, ex-soldiers had to demonstrate that their disabilities were war-related in order to receive a pension. In those years, periodic acts of Congress increased the size of the awards for disabilities and expanded the categories of ailments for which there would be compensation. The Arrears of Pension Act, passed in 1879, made Union veterans or their dependents eligible to receive their pension from the date of discharge rather than from the date of the pension application. In addition, veterans who applied for the payment before July 1880 would receive the whole arrears payment in one lump sum. After the passage of the Disability Pension Act of 1890, however, any veteran who had served for ninety days and had been honorably discharged was eligible for a pension even if his disabilities were not war-related as long as they were not due to "vicious habits or gross carelessness." The number of pensions granted and government expenditures rose rapidly after the measure went into effect. By 1907, with the encouragement of President Theodore Roosevelt, the original legislation had become a service-and-age pension law.[79] While many voters across the nation believed that the legislation opened the door to widespread pension fraud, many black veterans received critical financial support. Regrettably, the popular concern that fraudulent pension applications were common often focused on black veterans.

For the former members of the 37th USCT, the publication of the regiment's history created even greater skepticism among pension officials. Noah Willis, a former member of Company C, was one veteran who had great difficulty getting his application approved, in part because he possessed a copy of the *History of the Thirty-seventh USCT*. The Pension Bureau noted that in the years immediately after the book appeared, there were "considerably in excess of 100 claims based on service in said company." The bureau believed that many of these claims were submitted by men who had never been in the regiment but who used the information in the publication to create a bogus application. In addition, the bureau investigator who examined Willis was dubious of his testimony, as he seemed "to be nervous and uneasy, and to be greatly relieved when his disposition was finished." Adding to the inspector's suspicions, War Department records listed Willis as being 5' 9½" at one time and 5' 3½" at another. He ruled against Willis's claim. The following year a special investigator, Dow McLain, interviewed Willis at New Bern. McLain then brought in three members of Company C for identification purposes, and "the recognition was mutual and immediate in each case." Also reporting that none of his questions cast any doubt on the veteran's claim, McClain concluded that Willis was "a nervous man and easily excited." When the old veteran died in 1920, he was receiving fifty dollars a month. A number of factors in addition to nervousness made other applicants vulnerable to accusations of abusing the system. Many of the ex-soldiers were illiterate and vague about their exact age or specific details of their service; most no longer had their discharge papers. The records that did exist were, as in Willis's case, contradictory. Moreover, many of the agents presenting their cases used "'ready made' affidavits" that generated doubt among pension officials.[80]

For many veterans, the difficulties encountered in applying for their pensions were worth it. Even the limited veteran pensions, which varied from only a few dollars to, by 1912, perhaps twelve dollars a month, proved important to elderly ex-soldiers. The pensions may have let some of them enter into a tacit understanding with a young woman that involved the exchange of support in their old age for the benefits of a widow's pension. The fact that the amount of money was small did not mean that it was not desperately needed by many impoverished veterans.

In a few cases, veterans like Sgt. Richard Etheridge were able to translate their military careers into long-term government appointments. Etheridge, a free black from Roanoke Island, had served during the war as regimental commissary sergeant in the 36th USCT. After the conflict, he worked first as a fisherman and then as a surfman at the lifesaving station at Bodie Island. In 1879 the former sergeant was appointed the first black commander of a station in the history of the U.S. Lifesaving Service. At his death in 1900, Etheridge was earning $900 a year, but after a long and distinguished career he was able to leave only a modest estate of $1,055. The case of John S. W. Eagles perhaps suggests that the veterans' success should not just be measured in the short term. As significant as his role was in helping to establish the Republican Party in New Hanover County and in serving as a policeman and registrar there, perhaps Eagle's career should be measured by the achievements of his offspring. His son, Dr. John Eagles, a graduate of the Leonard School of Pharmacy at Raleigh's Shaw University, established one of the major black drugstores in the state and became a member of the black elite.[81]

Etheridge and Eagles were the exceptions, however. Financial or political success among North Carolina's USCT veterans was uncommon.[82] Although they may have been insulated and supported by their local community, few became wealthy. They could draw great comfort from knowing that they had played a major role in ending slavery and launching the freedom generation. Like the soldier at the fall of Wilmington, they emerged from the war not only with their freedom but also with their manhood. Having served their race and their country, most returned to friends and kin, perhaps moving to coastal towns as their health declined and living quiet lives of destitution.

# Conclusion

In 1884 Oliver Wendell Holmes delivered what would become perhaps the most famous Memorial Day address in American history.[1] In his speech, Holmes tried to give meaning to the sacrifices of the Civil War soldiers who had served on both sides of the conflict, as well as to their families and to later generations. In doing so, he tried to bridge the complexities of a conflict that involved millions of men and their dependents and to speak to shared experiences. Most of all, he wanted to show that the war had allowed the participants to be part of something larger than themselves. While much of his speech would have resonated deeply with North Carolina's black veterans, other aspects of his address would have stood out as describing someone else's war.

Holmes understood that for the men who had gone into battle, regardless of their race or the color of their uniforms, Memorial Day needed little justification. For many veterans, the war was never so far away that a sound or a smell could not trigger a vivid recollection. Memories of war's bitter moments, of comrades lost or of friendships made, came back to the veterans, including the North Carolinians, all too easily. Holmes spoke of soldiers that he had known and loved during the conflict, men of courage, kindness, determination, and youth. He spoke of them, he said, not because they were his friends but because they were types that all soldiers would have known and recognized, and, in the passing of years, keenly remembered. They should be remembered, not because they were great, but because they were normal men with common flaws who achieved greatness through their willingness to gamble everything for an idea. Holmes was correct when he said that the men who had "carried on the war had been set apart by its experience." The Southern black veterans, more than others, had been marked in this way, whether the wider society recognized it or not. It was not just because they had faced greater risks than white troops or suffered more from inadequate supplies and support. Almost overnight, most black Southern soldiers had changed, in the words of a member of the 4th USCT, from a slave to "a Union soldier, free, a man."[2] White veterans were more inclined to recognize that transformation, an attitude that explains why the Grand Army of the Republic (GAR) was a more color-blind institution than other American fraternal organizations.

The experience of war marked the families of all soldiers, black and white, as they worried about absent sons and husbands and prayed for their safe return. Children who had lost a father, or a mother her son, or a wife her soul mate, all bore the scars of the conflict long after the armies had been mustered out. In many ways, however, the war and its aftermath were harder on the families of Southern black soldiers than on Northern families. For the former, there was little approval and support from the wider society around them, which all too often viewed black military service as a betrayal. Dependents left behind when a black North Carolinian slipped away to join the Union army often faced savage retaliation from his angry owner. Even when the families were safe in Union-controlled territory, their economic condition was always precarious and they could hope for none of the state aid provided to Northern soldiers. Even what constituted a true black family was a contested issue. Although Federal authorities provided limited support to black soldiers' dependents, because they often gave less legitimacy to black family bonds, officials were more willing to suspend that assistance as the war drew to a close. Even where Union officials made a special effort to allow black dependents to begin a new life, as in the case of the Roanoke Islanders, government concerns about the sanctity of private property and the need to combat dependency trumped the justice of rewarding loyalty and service to the Union.

Although there was much in Holmes's speech to stir the memories of black veterans, issues central to the black North Carolinians' war were absent, while other aspects spoke more to the white experience than to the black. African Americans had gained much from the war. However despairing they may have been at the end of the nineteenth century by the slowness of change, the war had triggered a transformation in attitudes toward racial policies and African Americans. Black men who had been denied the right to join Northern regiments in 1861 were praised by many white Americans only four years later for their critical role in the Union army's ultimate success. Millions of African Americans had won their freedom and challenged, even if they did not fully overcome, the spectrum of social prejudices facing them. North Carolina's veterans could claim much of the credit for what the black soldiers had achieved. Nothing symbolized the change in white Southerners' perception of black martial abilities more than the decision of the Confederate Congress in March 1865 to enlist African Americans in the Confederate army.[3] It was recognition of the black soldiers' value to the Union army. Moreover, at a fundamental level, it was also recognition that they had disproved Howell Cobb's prediction that slaves would not make good soldiers. The men had worn eagles on their buttons, demonstrated their manliness, and established a justifiable claim for equal treatment even if much of society would soon ignore or forget their lesson. Their lives were a complex balance of gains and frustrations. William Thomas spoke for many black soldiers when he declared: "We are no longer the football for Southern autocrats . . . but we are *men*, standing upon the broad platform of Universal Freedom and with that dignity, compatible with self-respect, demanding such recognition from all classes." He was proud of what black troops had achieved. He had formed a bond with some white soldiers, but he was embittered by "the injustice and ingratitude of the American people."[4]

Thomas, other black soldiers, and their white supporters all assumed that a continued display of black courage and abilities would change the minds of most Americans. After battles from Port Hudson to Petersburg and from Fort Wagner to Olustee, observers repeatedly proclaimed that no longer could anyone doubt the martial ability of the black soldier. They were, of course, wrong. Some white Americans remained skeptical of black recruitment. It was not just that it took so long to dispel social prejudice. The very diverse experience of black soldiers, as the four North Carolina regiments demonstrated, allowed white Americans to remember and interpret events in ways that reinforced and confirmed their preexisting biases. While the rear guard action of the 35th USCT and the 54th Massachusetts regiments at Olustee was praised by observers and remembered by participants, elsewhere white soldiers and civilians used the questionable abilities of the 37th USCT to confirm their existing doubts about black troops. If standing guard over Confederate prisoners, as soldiers of the 36th USCT did at Point Lookout, seemed to threaten the traditional social order, then the manual labor assigned to the black artillerymen at Morehead City reassured social conservatives that this was the proper contribution of the African Americans in uniform. The large volunteer army, in many ways, reflected the values of civilian society.

Civil War veteran William B. Gould and his six sons, all of whom served in the army in the Spanish-American War, were symbolic of the black commitment to the nation. (Courtesy of William B. Gould IV and New Hanover Public Library, Wilmington, N.C.)

Nevertheless, most black soldiers found in the army an organization that offered them a less unequal treatment than they had, or would, receive in civilian society. The very fact that they were accepted into the army, as Frederick Douglass had predicted, carried implications about their manliness and their rights as citizens. At the very least, military service radically changed the ways in which they viewed themselves. Moreover, once the Union army had accepted black soldiers, senior officers took steps that forced Confederate officials and white civilians to reverse their initial policy and to accept black Union soldiers, at least theoretically, as a legitimate part of the Federal military who therefore must be treated the same as white soldiers. Of course, initially the black soldiers were paid less than their white counterparts, an issue that provoked widespread protests among black soldiers and their abolitionist allies. It is easy to overlook the fact that within a year, the unfair policy had been reversed, giving black troops equal pay, as well as similar bounties and other benefits. The arguments used by the soldiers to justify equal pay—arguments accepted by the government—were that they wore the same uniforms, faced the same risks, were answerable to the same military code, bore the same hardships, and served similar functions. In other words, soldiers of equal rank, whether white or black, must be treated equally. As the Federal pension system expanded after the war, there was never any suggestion that black veterans should not receive exactly the same benefits as white veterans. The degree of equality conferred on them by the army would be matched within the GAR, where black veterans enjoyed greater acceptance than they could find in any other American fraternal society in the second half of the nineteenth century.

---

By the turn of the century, Memorial Day had come to mean different things to white and black veterans. Holmes's speech was part of wider efforts at reconciliation within the nation. For him, the vast majority of soldiers on both sides were never motivated by personal animosity; rather, they were willing to sacrifice themselves for an abstract ideal. Soldiers in both blue and gray respected their opponents and recognized their courage. But when Holmes referred to "brotherhood for the enemy," a concept that appealed to much of white America after the actual fighting ended, he spoke of a different war from the one that many African Americans had fought. The black recruits and civilians who fled Plymouth, North Carolina, as the Confederates seized the town in April 1864 fully understood the fate that might await them if they were captured. The men of the 36th USCT, standing guard in the night at Point Lookout, understood the social values and power relationships they were challenging. For Southern black soldiers, the possibility that the war would devolve into atrocities or that they or their families could be reenslaved was always with them. Their war was always a personal one, and they seldom felt fully respected as men or men-of-war.

The problems of discrimination that black Civil War soldiers faced because of race, exacerbated by class, are well documented. In addition to the widespread racism of the time, however, Southern black soldiers also encountered a prejudice based on region. Northerners in the Union army, and that included black as well as white soldiers, were quick to undervalue the black Southerners' contribution to the war effort. Perhaps interunit rivalry influenced Charles Fox, an officer in the 55th Massachusetts, when he described his soldiers as superior to the recruits from North Carolina. But Col. George H. Gordon of the 2nd Massachusetts reflected a common Northern attitude when he later wrote that he was "not impressed with the negroes as soldiers; but there was a difference between the colored men from Massachusetts and those from North Carolina. Those from the former State were well made and intelligent, while those from the latter were dwarfed and ill formed."[5] Even Northern abolitionists who believed that slavery scarred its victims presupposed that black Southerners would make inferior soldiers.

Southern black troops were not always able to alter long-held biases, but in the face of the racism and regionalism, the black regiments, through their actions and achievements, created images, symbols, and memories of black courage and commitment to the nation that could not easily be ignored. While many white Americans in the postwar years were willing to sacrifice African American aspirations for national reconciliation, those images made forgetting more difficult than they otherwise would have been.

———— ❧ ————

As the veterans looked back on their role in the costly struggle for black freedom, they could take pride in what they had achieved for their community. They had paid a high physical and emotional price, and few had come out of the conflict with anything like financial security. The safer course would have been to remain a civilian and work for the Quartermaster's Department or to set up a small business to supply Union forces. Instead, North Carolina's black volunteers learned how profound, passionate, and perilous life could be when a total commitment was made to an ideal. As the veterans lived out their final years in a society that increasingly defined a successful life in financial terms, they could draw solace from Holmes's words. In their youth, their hearts too were filled with fire.

# NOTES

## ABBREVIATIONS

| | |
|---|---|
| ACSP | American Colonization Society Papers, Library of Congress, Washington, D.C. |
| AGO | Adjutant General's Office |
| CMSR | Compiled Military Service Records, RG 94, National Archives, Washington, D.C. |
| CU | Kroch Library Rare and Manuscript Collections, Cornell University, Ithaca, N.Y. |
| CWPF | Civil War Pension Files, RG 15, National Archives, Washington, D.C. |
| DOCLEM | Description, Orders, Circulars, Letters, Endorsements, and Morning Report Book |
| DU | Special Collections, William R. Perkins Library, Duke University, Durham, N.C. |
| ECU | Joyner Archives, East Carolina University, Greenville, N.C. |
| HC | Dinand Library, College of the Holy Cross, Worcester, Mass. |
| LC | Library of Congress, Washington, D.C. |
| LEOB | Letters, Endorsements, and Order Book |
| MA | Massachusetts Archives, Boston |
| MHS | Massachusetts Historical Society, Boston |
| MOLLUS | Military Order of the Loyal Legion of the United States |
| NARA | National Archives and Records Administration, Washington, D.C. |
| OR | *War of the Rebellion: A Compilation of the Official Records of the Union and Confederate Armies.* 128 vols. Washington, D.C.: GPO, 1880–1901. *OR* citations take the following form: volume number(part number):page number. Unless otherwise noted, all citations are to series 1. |
| RG | Record Group |
| SHC | Southern Historical Collection, University of North Carolina, Chapel Hill |
| TP | Tryon Palace Historic Sites and Gardens, New Bern, N.C. |
| USAMHI | U.S. Army Military History Institute, Carlisle Barracks, Carlisle, Pa. |

## PREFACE

1. Gen. Butler to Mrs. Butler, 29 September 1864, *Private and Official Correspondence of . . .*, 5:192.

2. Donald, Baker, and Holt, *Civil War and Reconstruction*, 328.

3. Cobb to Seddon, 8 January 1865, *OR*, ser. 4, 3:1009.

4. Of course, only a relatively small number of white Americans actually saw black soldiers in combat. Most perceptions of black martial abilities came from second- or third-hand accounts passed on most frequently by critics or supporters. It was a process that allowed contemporaries, or later generations, to exaggerate or diminish black accomplishments according to the existing climate of opinion.

5. Boritt, *Why the Confederacy Lost*, 156–57.

6. *New York Times*, 7 March 1864.

7. Robert Garth Scott, *Fallen Leaves*, 198–99. Abbott, a Democrat, was a member of the "Harvard Regiment," as the 20th Massachusetts was known.

8. Marszalek, *Sherman*, 271.

9. A fifth black regiment, the 135th USCT, was mustered into service at Page Station, N.C., on 28 March 1865 and demobilized at Louisville, Ky., in October 1865. Because it served for only seven months and consisted largely of refugees who followed Sherman's army into North Carolina, the 135th USCT was not included in this study. Manarin, *Guide to Military Organizations*, 3.

10. Grimsley, "'A Very Long Shadow,'" 241.

11. On the other hand, it could also be said that, in the face of widespread protest from both officers and men, it *only* took a year to establish the principle of equal pay for black and white soldiers. On the issue of unequal pay, see Glatthaar, *Forged in Battle*, 169–75, and Westwood, "Causes and Consequences."

12. Freehling, *South vs. the South*, 195.

## INTRODUCTION

1. Trudeau, *Like Men of War*, 8 (Cameron, Cincinnati constable); Horton and Horton, *In Hope of Liberty*, 269. Early in the war, black petitioners raised arguments that would resonate in the months ahead. They would supplement white losses and loyally support the Lincoln administration, they were better able to withstand extended service in an unhealthy South, and they would balance the Confederacy's use of Southern blacks. Some of the groups offering their services, such as the Fort Pitt Cadets, had been drilling for two years and could take over auxiliary duties and occupying forts almost immediately. Berlin, Reidy, and Rowland, *Black Military Experience*, 78–86.

2. Paludan, *Presidency of Abraham Lincoln*, 103.

3. Historians have long debated whether Lincoln was a "reluctant Emancipator" or an adept leader who understood the social and political constraints that he faced while moving aggres-

sively toward emancipation. For a recent thoughtful discussion of this question, see Paludan, "Lincoln and the Greeley Letter," 79–98.

4. Basler, *Collected Works of Abraham Lincoln*, 4:533.

5. Butler, *Butler's Book*, 256–58; *OR*, ser. 2, 1:752, 754–55; McPherson, *Ordeal by Fire*, 159–60; Edward A. Miller Jr., *Lincoln's Abolitionist General*, 73 (Frémont).

6. Klingaman, *Abraham Lincoln*, 83–84.

7. Simon, *Papers of Ulysses S. Grant*, 4:227. The Second Confiscation Act freed the slaves of all disloyal citizens and gave the president wide powers on how they could be used. The Militia Act allowed the Federal government to employ African Americans "for . . . any military or naval service for which they may be found competent." But it was a power that the president was not yet willing to wield. Significantly, the Militia Act established a pay rate for blacks hired by the army of ten dollars per month and permitted one ration. It also specified that three dollars of the pay could be in clothing.

8. Glatthaar, *Forged in Battle*, 122. For a full discussion of Lane's actions, see Cornish, *Sable Arm*, 69–78.

9. Klingaman, *Abraham Lincoln*, 25–27; Edward A. Miller Jr., *Lincoln's Abolitionist General*, 107–15; John David Smith, "Let Us All Be Grateful," 10–11; Paludan, *Presidency of Abraham Lincoln*, 130, 152–53.

10. Hollandsworth, *Louisiana Native Guards*, 13–14. In part, Butler was reacting to a Confederate offensive that forced the Union's abandonment of Baton Rouge, as well as the apparent shortage of troops in his command due to the reluctance of "loyal" Irish and German immigrants in the city to volunteer as civilian wages rose. Butler was also sensitive to the changing Federal policy on black recruitment.

11. Butler, *Butler's Book*, 491–93. Butler could then ignore the fact that a majority of the regiments' rank and file were darker-skinned fugitive slaves. Hollandsworth, *Louisiana Native Guards*, 16–18.

12. Berlin, Reidy, and Rowland, *Black Military Experience*, 42–44.

13. Basler, *Collected Works of Abraham Lincoln*, 5:356–57, 423, 434. The new authorization envisioned that the freed slaves would garrison forts and military establishments and man a range of naval vessels. This limited role, essentially freeing up white troops for combat, was in keeping with what even early advocates had envisioned might be the function of black troops. Berlin, Reidy, and Rowland, *Black Military Experience*, 82–83, 85.

14. For the contemporary view of the law of war, see Farber, *Lincoln's Constitution*, 152–58.

15. Hesseltine, *Lincoln and the War Governors*, 256 (Andrew); Yacovone, *Voice of Thunder*, 324 (Stephens); Voegeli, *Free but Not Equal*, 76–77 (*Chicago Times*); Quarles, *The Negro in the Civil War*, 31 (Brannigan); Stoddard, *Inside the White House*, 97.

16. Berlin, Reidy, and Rowland, *Black Military Experience*, 9, 87–88.

17. Dudley T. Cornish, "African American Troops in the Union Army," in Current, *Encyclopedia of the Confederacy*, 1:11 (first quotation). As a result, units such as the four North Carolina regiments under study—first formed under a state designation—were redesignated

in early 1864 as a numbered USCT. Only a few Northern black regiments—including the 54th and 55th Massachusetts, the 5th Massachusetts Cavalry, and the 29th Connecticut—were excluded from this policy.

18. Stoddard, *Inside the White House*, 174.

19. Edward A. Miller Jr., *Lincoln's Abolitionist General*, 113–14.

20. Barrett, *Civil War*, 68–69, 75; Marvel, *Burnside*, 37, 41–50.

21. Barrett, *Civil War*, 74.

22. Marvel, *Burnside*, 60; Robert Garth Scott, *Fallen Leaves*, 102; Hardy, *Thirty-seventh North Carolina Troops*, 37 (quotation).

23. The timing of the Union attack favored Burnside's troops. One part of the Conscription Act passed by the Confederate Congress on 16 April 1862 offered, as an incentive, a furlough for soldiers who reenlisted in their current regiments. The number of men taking advantage of this offer, Michael Hardy estimates, reduced Branch's army of 8,000–10,000 men to less than 4,000. Hardy, *Thirty-seventh North Carolina Troops*, 44–45.

24. Glenn Tucker, *Zeb Vance*, 122–25; Hardy, *Thirty-seventh North Carolina Troops*, 41–43.

25. *OR* 4:682; Barrett, *Civil War*, 10, 113–14; Barrett, *Civil War*, 118–20; Dan Blair, "'One Good Port,'" 302.

26. Marvel, *Burnside*, 55; Pvt. Henry A. Clapp to "Dear Willie," 27 February 1863; H. A. Clapp to "Dear Father," 1 March 1863; H. A. Clapp to "Dear Mother," 14 March 1863; H. A. Clapp to Helen Clapp, 20 March 1863, and H. A. Clapp to Louise Clapp, 26 March 1863—all in Clapp Letter Book, TP.

27. Hesseltine, *Lincoln and the War Governors*, 202; Magdol, *Owen Lovejoy*, 337; Berlin, Reidy, and Rowland, *Black Military Experience*, 75 ("volunteers of African descent"); Duncan, *Blue-Eyed Child of Fortune*, 320; Keith Wilson, "In the Shadow of John Brown," 314.

28. *OR*, ser. 3, 3:110 (Andrew): Governor Andrew to Maj. Gen. Foster, 14 May 1863, Wild Papers, USAMHI ("from the freedmen of that state"). Andrew was willing to spare the 55th Massachusetts, but he wanted the 54th Massachusetts to be used in an active theater where it would demonstrate the martial abilities of the black soldiers.

29. Although conditions varied considerably across the North, most states restricted the rights of black residents. Ten Northern states prevented blacks from voting, while another three placed severe restrictions on voting rights. Midwestern states such as Michigan, Ohio, Illinois, and Indiana banned interracial marriage, and many school systems were segregated. Horton and Horton, *In Hope of Liberty*, 168–70; Voegeli, *Free but Not Equal*, 172; Cook, "The Fight for Black Suffrage," 218–21.

30. Berlin, Reidy, and Rowland, *Black Military Experience*, 83–85.

31. Speer, *Portals to Hell*, 108–9 (Seddon, *Richmond Examiner*); Hollandsworth, "Execution of White Officers," 52 (Confederate Congress); John David Smith, *Black Soldiers in Blue*, 47 (Lincoln). The extent of these atrocities is well covered in Urwin, *Black Flag over Dixie*.

32. This Northern resolve was seen by white Southerners as mere pretense for a Federal decision that any prisoner exchange benefited the South more than the North. Ulysses S.

Grant, in particular, has been accused of undermining the exchange of prisoners for strategic reasons.

33. It is ironic in the sense that most writers use this issue to illustrate the discriminatory treatment of black soldiers. The argument offered here is that, in an age of widespread discrimination, it took the military slightly over a year to adopt an equal-pay-for-equal-work policy and to make it retroactive for most black soldiers.

34. John David Smith, *Black Soldiers in Blue*, 49–52. In May 1865 Congress authorized bounties for all black soldiers who had enlisted after July 1864.

35. Hollandsworth, *Louisiana Native Guards*, 43 (quotation); Berlin, Reidy, and Rowland, *Black Military Experience*, 305–7, 345, 377.

36. One symbolic incident, captured by one of the black soldiers entering Wilmington in 1865, was the reunion of another black soldier and his mother. She had last seen her son as a slave. He had returned now "free, a man." The correspondent noted that similar incidents were happening in other black regiments. Redkey, *Grand Army of Black Men*, 167.

37. Frederick Douglass, "Address for the Promotion of Colored Enlistments" (6 July 1863), *Douglass' Monthly*, August 1863, as cited in Philip Foner, *Life and Writings of Frederick Douglass*, 3:365.

## CHAPTER ONE

1. For a fifth black regiment raised in North Carolina, the 135th USCT, see n. 1 of the Preface.

2. One exception to this pattern was the mass enlistment of 150 men from Hatteras when Gen. Wild visited the island.

3. McPherson, *Ordeal by Fire*, 165. The recruitment, organization, and training of regiments are extensively covered in William J. Miller, *Training of an Army*.

4. The exceptions to this were the regiments of the Louisiana Native Guards organized by Gen. Butler in September 1862. The captains, lieutenants, and one major in these regiments were black. Butler claimed—not quite accurately—that they were all freed men and mulattoes, and that he planned to use them only for garrison and fatigue duties. Nevertheless, his replacement, Gen. Nathaniel P. Banks, systematically drove the black officers out of the service. Glatthaar, *Forged in Battle*, 8–9; Hollandsworth, *Louisiana Native Guards*, 16–22, 43–45, 71–83.

5. In some cases, especially in the first year of the war, colonels saw little purpose in drilling their men and spent very limited time on such training. For an excellent discussion of the values and practice of drill, see Griffith, *Battle Tactics*, 91–115.

6. For one officer's view of the importance of providing training to any unit as soon as it came under his command, see Hattaway, *General Stephen D. Lee*, 29–32.

7. Griffith, *Battle Tactics*, 87.

8. Kreidberg and Henry, *History of Military Mobilization*, 121.

9. Dudley T. Cornish, "African American Troops in the Union Army," in Current, *Encyclopedia of the Confederacy*, 1:11.

10. John David Smith, "Let Us All Be Grateful," 26.

11. Gen. E. A. Wild to Calvin Cutter, 13 March 1863, Wild Papers, USAMHI.

12. By contrast, Capt. T. W. Higginson in South Carolina and Brig. Gen. Daniel Ullmann, raising the Corps d'Afrique in Louisiana, wanted men of good character but were not concerned about previous military service. Adj. Gen. Lorenzo Thomas, in recruiting black regiments in the West, selected his officers entirely from within the military structure and took at face value their assurances of sympathy for African Americans. Glatthaar, *Forged in Battle*, 35–39.

13. John David Smith, "Let Us All Be Grateful," 26.

14. "Appointment of Col. Edward A. Wild," Personnel File, RG 94, NARA. Twenty-six officers were appointed on 28 April 1863, although the colonel and lieutenant colonel were not appointed until 1 June, reflecting, perhaps, Wild's unsuccessful search for senior Massachusetts officers to lead his regiments. "Roster, First North Carolina African Volunteers," Wild Papers, USAMHI.

15. Gen. E. A. Wild to Maj. Thomas M. Vincent, 4 September 1863, ibid.

16. The majority of the successful applicants, approximately 67 percent, had been privates or noncommissioned officers. Wild also seems to have obtained many more officers who had previously held a commission. Only 9 percent of the successful candidates screened by the Free Military School had been officers. Berlin, Reidy, and Rowland, *Black Military Experience*, 408; Keith P. Wilson, *Campfires of Freedom*, 5.

17. Thirteen officers came directly from Massachusetts units, and eighteen others were residents of that state. "North Carolina Volunteers, Wild's African Brigade," Letters Received, Colored Troops Division, RG 94, NARA.

18. Edward W. Kinsley to Gen. E. A. Wild, 9 September 1863, Wild Papers, USAMHI.

19. W. H. R. Brown to Gen. E. A. Wild, 9 August 1863, ibid.

20. Rugoff, *The Beechers*, 455–66; Glatthaar, *Forged in Battle*, 240–41. Beecher's first wife's long battle with alcoholism and her behavior when drunk partly explain his near nervous breakdown and his renewed commitment to temperance (Rugoff, 454–57).

21. Various official military records give no indication that Reed was not white, but other records do. In late 1863 Surg. Horace R. Wirtz claimed that he was a "mulatto," whereas years later George W. Williams wrote that Reed was "bound to both races by the ties of consanguinity." H. R. Wirtz to ——, 29 September 1863, Personal Papers of Medical Officers and Physicians, RG 94, NARA; Williams, *History of the Negro Troops*, 207–8.

22. De Grasse's father had been born in Calcutta, and his mother, Maria Van Surly, was German. Logan and Winston, *Dictionary of American Negro Biography*, 69; *North Star* (Rochester, N.Y.), 8 June 1849; *Frederick Douglass' Paper* (Rochester, N.Y.), 22 September 1854.

23. De Grasse was one of several people who sought out Garrison's views of the offer made by the president of Haiti, Nicholas Geffrard, to have African Americans migrate to the island

republic. Although Garrison refused to criticize such migration, he argued against it. Merrill, *Letters of William Lloyd Garrison*, 5:24–26.

24. Asst. Surg. John De Grasse, Proceedings of General Court-Martial, RG 153, NARA.

25. Gen. E. A. Wild to Maj. Thomas M. Vincent, 12 May 1863, Letters Received, AGO, RG 94, NARA.

26. For the role played by black chaplains in the Civil War, see Berlin, Reidy, and Rowland, *Black Military Experience*, 309–11, 348–54, 358–61; Redkey, "Black Chaplains in the Union Army"; and Edward A. Miller Jr., "Garland A. White." For a general study of Civil War chaplains, see Armstrong, *For Courageous Fighting*.

27. "John N. Mars," CMSR.

28. For a discussion of this issue, see Berlin, Reidy, and Rowland, *Black Military Experience*, 18–26.

29. George Bliss Jr. to Col. C. W. Foster, Asst. Adj. Gen., 14 December 1863; Foster to Bliss, 15 December 1863; Bliss to Foster, 17 December 1863; and Foster to Bliss, 19 December 1863—all in Letters Received, Colored Troops Division, RG 94, NARA.

30. Abolitionists in Philadelphia who sponsored a recruiting poster depicting the heroism of the black soldiers at Port Hudson believed that the valor of the 1st and 3rd Louisiana Native Guards had been responsible for thousands of new black recruits in the summer of 1863. For a full discussion of the role played by the two black regiments in the attack and the differing perceptions of their performance, see Hewitt, "Ironic Route to Glory," 78–106.

31. Thomas Hale to "Dear Mother," 19 May 1863, Hale Papers, SHC.

32. Singleton, *Recollections*, 8–9.

33. "Corporal" [Zenas T. Haines], *Letters from the Forty-fourth Regiment M.V.M.*, 109 (Massachusetts corporal); Derby, *Bearing Arms in the Twenty-seventh*, 192.

34. The slaves on Josiah Collins's plantation in Washington County were told in mid-February 1863 that they had been freed by the U.S. army commander at Plymouth, but at almost the same time a white soldier raped one of the black women. Another ex-slave, Jim, found work in Plymouth but soon left his Northern employers, claiming that they "made him work very hard and fed him badly." Durrill, *War of Another Kind*, 120, 140. In other states there were numerous examples of similar mistreatment. Glatthaar, *Forged in Battle*, 66–67.

35. Carl to "Dear Parents," 6 April 1863, Federal Soldiers Letters, SHC.

36. Mann, *History of the Forty-fifth Regiment*, 300–302; Cecelski, "Abraham H. Galloway," 44–45.

37. Gen. E. A. Wild to Edward W. Kinsley, 30 November 1863, Kinsley Papers, DU.

38. Williams had acquired a reputation as an antislavery speaker in parts of the North. Redkey, *Grand Army of Black Men*, 90.

39. Several months later, Williams had been employed to recruit black soldiers from the Vicksburg region. Gen. E. A. Wild to Edward W. Kinsley, 28 July 1863, and Joseph E. Williams to Kinsley, 19 August 1863, Kinsley Papers, DU.

40. "Military Life of Edward A. Wild," Massachusetts MOLLUS Collection, USAMHI.

41. Oscar Doolittle to J. W. Sullivan, 22 July 1863, Kinsley Papers, DU.

42. Derby, *Bearing Arms in the Twenty-seventh*, 192.

43. Roe, *Fifth Regiment Massachusetts Volunteer Infantry*, 244.

44. O'Connor, *Civil War Boston*, 130.

45. The numbers and dates of enlistment are drawn from Regimental Descriptive Books, 35th USCT, RG 94, NARA.

46. Aging veterans who were applying for government pensions, of course, had reason to show that they had been in excellent health when they entered the service. See also "Amos Mattick" and "Hannibal Sawyer," CWPF (Wiggins's quotation).

47. Hodges, "Scattering Fire, 1863," *Personal Recollections*, 72.

48. *The History of a Gallant Regiment*, Massachusetts MOLLUS Collection, USAMHI.

49. Mann, *History of the Forty-fifth Regiment*, 302.

50. *The History of a Gallant Regiment*, Massachusetts MOLLUS Collection, USAMHI.

51. About 5 to 10 percent of the black population—slave and free—had at least partial literacy by 1861. But the actual percentage of black soldiers who could read and write effectively varied widely by state and region. Keith P. Wilson, *Campfires of Freedom*, 83.

52. Regimental Order Book, 35th USCT, RG 94, NARA. The sergeants would be numbered, in order of seniority, from first to fifth sergeant, with the first sergeant sometimes referred to as the "orderly sergeant."

53. Special Order No. 31, 11 September 1863, Regimental Order Book, 35th USCT, RG 94, NARA. On 15 July 1865, after two years of service, Kimball was reduced to the ranks "for Drunkenness on Duty." CMSR.

54. Special Order No. 70, 31 October 1863, Regimental Order Book, 35th USCT, RG 94, NARA.

55. Col. J. C. Beecher to Lt. Thomas Robinson, 1 November 1863, Regimental Letter Book, ibid. (quotation). The most fundamental measure of the literacy of these men was their ability to sign, with fluid penmanship, for receipt of payment. Muster Rolls, 35th USCT, DU.

56. Special Order No. 195, 10 July 1863, Regimental Order Book, 35th USCT, RG 94, NARA; "James Elmsly," CMSR.

57. Special Orders No. 195, 10 July 1863, and No. 576, 29 December 1863, Regimental Order Book, 35th USCT, RG 94, NARA.

58. Delos Barber to Gen. E. A. Wild, 14 December 1863, Wild Papers, USAMHI.

59. At 5' 1", William Woodward in Company K and Peleg Moore in Company C may have been the smallest sergeants. It is also possible that for these men a recording error may have been made, and their real size might have been 5' 10" or 5' 11". A height is recorded for all of the soldiers in the Regimental Descriptive Books, 35th USCT, RG 94, NARA.

60. General Order No. 1, 17 June 1863, Regimental Order Book, ibid.

61. The creation of a "tactical articulation in the period leading up to close combat" is discussed in Griffith, *Battle Tactics*, 105–15.

62. The very subordination that had been forced on the men as slaves could, however,

jeopardize relations in a regiment. The danger that some Union commanders ignored was that insensitive or abusive officers could make the black soldiers feel that they had just exchanged an old master for a new one.

63. Special Order No. 3, 22 June 1863 (Beecher), and General Orders No. 5, 1 July 1863 (women in camp), and No. 17, 29 September 1863 (Vogdes)—all in Regimental Order Book, 35th USCT, RG 94, NARA.

64. *The History of a Gallant Regiment*, Massachusetts MOLLUS Collection, USAMHI.

65. On 18 June Capt. E. S. Daniels took a detachment of 27 fully armed and equipped troops to Beaufort. In mid-July 44 men were detached to serve under Capt. Wilson, an engineer, on a raid into eastern North Carolina to try to cut Confederate railroads. About a week later, 20 men in civilian dress led by Sgts. Jackson and Edward Williams were detached for special but undisclosed service. Special Orders No. 2, 18 June 1863; No. 200, 15 July 1863; and No. 11, 20 July 1863—all in Regimental Order Book, 35th USCT, RG 94, NARA.

66. *History of a Gallant Regiment*, Massachusetts MOLLUS Collection, USAMHI; Maj. Archibald Bogle to Lt. Thomas Robinson, 30 December 1863, Regimental Order Book, 35th USCT, RG 94, NARA. Although poor-quality weapons of various types were common in black regiments, they could also be found in many white regiments. Many Michigan infantry regiments, for example, were armed at this time with a variety of weapons. In June 1863 companies in the 23rd Michigan Volunteer Regiment were using converted 1816 smoothbore muskets, Springfields, Enfields, and 1842 U.S. muskets. In early 1863 probably half of the regiments had at least two different types of weapons. Genco, *Arming Michigan's Regiments*, 38, 52, 55, 57–59.

67. Griffith, *Battle Tactics*, 91 (quotation); Glatthaar, *Forged in Battle*, 105.

68. Quartermaster Returns for the 1st NCCV, Remick Papers, DU. They also fired two thousand rounds in action during the same period.

69. Wilder Diaries, 28 July 1863, CU; Fox, *Service of the Fifty-fifth Regiment*, 9–10.

70. In the late summer, rumors circulated among Confederate soldiers in the 25th Regiment North Carolina Troops that they would soon be fighting black Federal troops below Weldon. One soldier predicted, "If they do we will give them a lesson long remembered." Sgt. William England to "Dear Father," Alfred England Papers, North Carolina Department of Archives and History, Raleigh.

71. Wise, *Gate of Hell*, 119, 137–38.

72. Maj. Bogle to Lt. F. W. Taggart, 10 January 1864, Regimental Letter Book, 35th USCT, RG 94, NARA.

73. Annual Returns of the 1st NCCV for 1863, Muster Rolls and Returns, and General Order No. 6, 30 July 1863, Regimental Order Book, ibid.

74. *OR* 28(2):75.

75. Gen. E. A. Wild to Maj. Thomas M. Vincent, 25 June 1863, Letters Received, Colored Troops Division, W9 CT 1863, RG 94, NARA.

76. Special Order No. 302, 8 July 1863, LEOB, 36th USCT, RG 94, NARA.

77. Redkey, "Black Chaplains in the Union Army," 338.

78. Emma Mordecai Diary, April 1865, SHC, as cited in Patrick, *The Fall of Richmond*, 122.

79. Philip S. Foner, *History of the Labor Movement*, 1:241–45; Faler, *Mechanics and Manufacturers*, 199, 230; Dawley, *Class and Community*, 78–80, 191; *Massachusetts Soldiers, Sailors*, 296; Bryant, "A Model Regiment," 19–20.

80. Maj. Alonzo G. Draper to Governor John Andrew, 2 March 1863, Executive Letters, vol. 14, no. 50, and 28 April 1863, Executive Letters, vol. 102, no. 58, MA.

81. "Roster, Wild's African Brigade," Letters Received, Colored Troops Division, W9 CT 1863, RG 94, NARA.

82. Special Order No. 7, 2 August 1863, LEOB, 36th USCT, RG 94, NARA.

83. Circular, 15 August 1863, ibid. (quotation); Glatthaar, *Forged in Battle*, 100–102.

84. Special Order No. 228, 13 August 1863, LEOB, 36th USCT, RG 94, NARA.

85. Special Orders No. 8, 21 August 1863, and No. 9, 24 August 1863, ibid.

86. Gen. E. A. Wild to Maj. Thomas M. Vincent, 25 May 1863, Letters Received, Colored Troops Division, W9 CT 1863, RG 94, NARA. Gen. Peck, a graduate of West Point in 1843 before going into banking and railroads, had been active in Democratic politics before the war.

87. General Order No. 8, 28 August 1863; Maj. Gen. Peck to Col. Draper, 29 August 1863; and Asst. Adj. Gen. J. A. Judson to Draper, 29 August 1863—all in LEOB, 36th USCT, RG 94, NARA.

88. Lt. Aaron Parker to Adj. C. D. Griggs, 2[?] September 1863, ibid.

89. Special Order No. 53, 11 September 1863; Capt. Henry H. Miller to Col. Draper, 11 September 1863; Lt. James N. North to Col. Draper, 11 September 1863; and Special Order No. 27, 15 September 1863—all in LEOB, 36th USCT, RG 94, NARA.

90. Capt. Henry H. Miller to Col. Draper, 18 September 1863, ibid. (quotation); *Massachusetts Soldiers, Sailors*, 306.

91. Capt. Henry H. Miller to Col. Draper, 18 September 1863, LEOB, 36th USCT, RG 94, NARA.

92. Col. Draper to Capt. George H. Johnson, 14 September 1863, and [endorsement] Gen. J. G. Foster, ibid.

93. Capt. George H. Johnson to Col. Draper, 12 September 1863, ibid.

94. Col. Draper to Capt. H. Stevens, 16 October 1863, ibid.

95. One such officer, Lt. B. F. Kinsley, had been appointed to the 2nd NCCV on 22 July but had been ill in the hospital at New Bern. By 16 September he still had not rejoined his regiment, although he planned to reach Fort Monroe by the next week. B. F. Kinsley to Edward W. Kinsley, 16 September 1863, Kinsley Papers, DU.

96. Col. Draper to Lt. Col. Hoffman, 18 September 1863, LEOB, 36th USCT, RG 94, NARA.

97. Lt. James L. Hatlinger to Lt. Col. Hoffman, 19 October 1863; Gen. E. A. Wild to Capt. George W. Ives, 15 October 1863; and Ives to Hoffman, 23 October 1863—all in ibid. In late

September, Capt. George Bradbury had requested a thirty-day leave of absence due partly to illness in his family and partly to his own disability. In denying the request, Draper stated that Bradbury had been seen out in the company streets apparently in no worse physical condition than certain other officers who were able to continue their duties. Moreover, Draper wrote, "My command is very short of officers." Bradbury to Lt. Col. Hoffman, 29 September 1863; [endorsement] Col. Draper, LEOB, 36th USCT, RG 94, NARA.

98. In fact, the number of men from the 2nd NCCV then serving on Folly Island was 118.

99. Col. Draper to Lt. W. Schroeder, 2 October 1863, and Draper to Lt. Col. Hoffman, 14 October 1863 (quotations), LEOB, 36th USCT, RG 94, NARA. Company H, the detached unit, was mustered in at Norfolk, Va., on 25 January 1864. Manarin, *Guide to Military Organizations*, 3.

100. General Order No. 1, 4 November 1863, LEOB, 36th USCT, RG 94, NARA.

101. Gen. E. A. Wild to Maj. Thomas M. Vincent, 3 September 1863, Letters Received, Colored Troops Division, RG 94, NARA; *OR* 24(2):290. Wild was upset by a number of things, including the amount of government and private property left behind at the lightly guarded camp of the 55th and the 1st NCCV. He implicitly chastised Col. Draper. Wild to Draper, 14 September 1863, LEOB, 36th USCT, RG 94, NARA.

102. Col. Draper to Lt. Col. Hoffman, n.d. [1–10 November 1863], LEOB, 36th USCT, RG 94, NARA.

103. Lt. Joseph G. Langley to Gen. E. A. Wild, 10 November 1863, and [endorsement] Wild, ibid.

104. Capt. J. M. Smith to Col. Draper, 7 October 1863, ibid.

105. "Report of Capt. Hazard Stevens," 13 November 1863, ibid.

106. Col. Draper to Maj. R. S. Davis, 14 November 1863, ibid.

107. Gen. E. A. Wild to Maj. Thomas M. Vincent, 4 September 1863, and "3rd Regt N.C. Vols., Proposed Roster," Letters Received, Colored Troops Division, W9 CT 1863, RG 94, NARA.

108. Wild's proposed quartermaster, Lt. Frank Stone, had been recently commissioned a second lieutenant in the 1st NCCV from the ranks, and a proposed captain had been chaplain in the 33rd Massachusetts Volunteers.

109. Gen. J. G. Foster to Gen. E. A. Wild, 2 October 1863, Letters Received, Colored Troops Division, W9 CT 1863, RG 94, NARA; *Massachusetts Soldiers, Sailors*, 314. Adding to the confusion, in the official report of troops on Folly Island Wilder's company was designated "3d North Carolina, colored (one company)." *OR* 28(2):75.

110. For Fitzpatrick, a more important factor in his desertion may have been his reduction to the ranks, which stripped him of power and status within the company.

111. "Detachment Recruited by 3rd NCCV," Muster Rolls and Records, and General Order No. 3, LEOB, 37th USCT, RG 94, NARA; *History of the Thirty-seventh Regiment*, 113–14.

112. There were some exceptions. Company H, organized and mustered in at Point of Rocks, Va., drew just over 60 percent of its recruits from Virginia. By contrast, Companies I

and K had 228 recruits from North Carolina and only 19 from Virginia, although both companies were mustered in at Chafin's Farm, Va.

113. *OR* 33:870.

114. For example, at the end of 1863 Company B had about eighteen men, almost all of them enlisted at Plymouth, N.C. In a two-week period in mid-January, it received an additional sixty-three men recruited from Plymouth, allowing the company to be mustered in on 4 February 1864.

115. Morning Report Book, Companies A to E, and Lt. Col. Chamberlain to Capt. George H. Johnson, 3 March 1864, LEOB, 37th USCT, RG 94, NARA.

116. A majority of the regiments on both sides of the conflict may have voiced the same complaint.

117. Lt. Col. Chamberlain to Capt. George H. Johnson, 3 March 1864, and General Order No. 8, 13 April 1864, LEOB, 37th USCT, RG 94, NARA.

118. Lt. Col. Chamberlain to Lt. H. W. Allen, 5 March, 2 May (quotation) 1864, and Chamberlain to Brig. Gen. George D. Ramsay, 12 May 1864, ibid.

119. Not until the summer of 1865 did companies begin to record the number and condition of their weapons in their morning reports. In all cases, there were fewer guns than men. Company E, for example, had 100 enlisted men in May 1865, but only 71 guns. Several months later, Company G listed 1 unserviceable gun and 41 serviceable guns for its complement of 96 men, 56 of whom were present. By the last year of service, Company C listed almost 30 percent of its weapons as unserviceable. There were only 50 effective muskets for the 75 enlisted men. Morning Report Books, Companies A to E and F to K, 37th USCT, RG 94, NARA. Although white regiments in the Union army could also be found with old, defective weapons or fewer serviceable guns than men, this problem was much more common among black troops.

120. Lt. Col. Chamberlain to "Comdg Officer of the 7th N.Y. Battery, Lt. Arty.," 27 February 1864, LEOB, 37th USCT, RG 94, NARA.

121. *Private and Official Correspondence of . . . Butler*, 3:183–90.

122. Lt. Col. Chamberlain to Capt. Fred Martin, 18 February 1864; Lt. Calvin S. Mixter to Capt. H. L. Marvin, 19 April 1864; Chamberlain to Maj. R. S. Usher, 20 April 1864; and Mixter to Lt. J. A. Monroe, 20 April 1864—all in LEOB, 37th USCT, RG 94, NARA.

123. Heavy artillery regiments were made up of twelve companies and therefore had a larger complement of men. They were also given some training as infantry soldiers in case they had to be used as such in times of crisis.

124. Barrett, *Civil War*, 202–12.

125. A Confederate boarding party led by Cmdr. John Taylor Wood had seized the vessel in an attempt to use it against the defenses of New Bern. A lack of steam in the boilers and increasingly heavy Union fire forced Wood to burn his prize. Browning, *From Cape Charles to Cape Fear*, 98–99.

126. *Private and Official Correspondence of . . . Butler*, 3:369, 4:2.

127. Burlingame, *History of the Fifth Regiment*, 197; *OR* 33:870.

128. In the spring of 1864, at least seven black regiments were trying to enlist men in North Carolina. Gen. Peck complained that whereas some recruiting officers were energetic and efficient, others were "zealous without knowledge" and "others labor to labor as little as possible." *OR* 33:870–71.

129. *Private and Official Correspondence of . . . Butler*, 5:424.

130. Barrett, *Civil War*, 156–61.

131. Burlingame, *History of the Fifth Regiment*, 347–48. In fact, Gen. Hoke probably ended his siege of Washington and retired when it was clear that the Federals were evacuating the town. Welcher, *Union Army*, 1:150.

132. "A Letter from New Bern," signed A. G., *Liberator*, 22 July 1864.

133. Special Orders No. 8, 14 July 1864, and No. 9, 21 July 1864, DOCLEM, and "Detachment on Recruiting Service," Muster Rolls, 14th USCHA, RG 94, NARA.

134. *Private and Official Correspondence of . . . Butler*, 4:29–30; *Official Army Register*, 164. On the other hand, William H. Hendrick, formerly of the 1st NCUV, rose to the rank of captain in the 1st NCCHA.

135. Burlingame, *History of the Fifth Regiment*, 198. For the range of motives for seeking a commission in a black regiment, see Glatthaar, *Forged in Battle*, 28–30, 39–41.

136. "We the Undersigned Citizens of Poughkeepsie," 28 January 1864; Mrs. Bullis to H. A. Nelson, 5 February 1864; and Nelson to Hon. E. M. Stanton, 7 February 1864—all in Letters Received, Colored Troops Division, B232 CT 65, RG 94, NARA.

137. Gen. Palmer to Brig. Gen. L. Thomas, 31 March 1865, and "Roster of Commissioned Officers in the 14th Reg.," 13 September 1865, Letters Received, Colored Troops Division, P523, RG 94, NARA.

138. The five white recruiters were Sgt. William E. Moses, 58th Pennsylvania Volunteers; Sgt. Barnes Griffith, 2nd NCUV; Cpl. Fred A. Nourse, 17th Massachusetts Volunteers; Pvt. Albert J. Brown, 9th Vermont Volunteers; and Pvt. William Crombie, 2nd Massachusetts Volunteers. Muster Rolls, 14th USCHA, RG 94, NARA.

139. Special Orders No. 10, 23 July 1864, No. 14, 4 August 1864, No. 15, 5 August 1864, and No. 17, 16 August 1864, DOCLEM, 14th USCHA, RG 94, NARA.

140. Jackson and perhaps Starkey were literate, which may explain why their companies' morning reports began to be filled out relatively quickly. Companies C and D did not fill out morning reports until October and September, respectively. By September 1864 commissioned officers were listed in most company reports, although at least one was on detached service. Morning Reports, Companies A to M, 14th, ibid.

141. Special Order No. 17, 16 August 1864, ibid.

142. Maj. Jameson to Maj. R. S. Davis, 17 August 1864, DOCLEM, 14th USCHA, RG 94, NARA.

## CHAPTER TWO

1. Fox, *Service of the Fifty-fifth Regiment*, 11.

2. Wise, *Gate of Hell*, 119–20; Hagy, *To Take Charleston*, 42–45.

3. *OR* 28(2):35.

4. Wise, *Gate of Hell*, 139–41.

5. Hagy, *To Take Charleston*, 48–49.

6. Hodges, "Scattering Fire, 1863," *Personal Recollections*, 73.

7. Burt Green Wilder, assistant surgeon in the 55th Massachusetts Volunteers, left a detailed description of both the passage to Folly Island and conditions in the camp. Although there is no equally good account of life in the 1st NCCV, since the two camps adjoined and they were both under Wild, one can assume that their experiences were similar. Wilder Diaries, 9–14, CU.

8. Adams, *On the Altar of Freedom*, 47 (first quotation); Wilder Diaries, 15, CU; Annual Returns of the 1st NCCV for 1863, Muster Rolls and Returns, 35th USCT, RG 94, NARA; Pension Application of Gaston Davis, Harper Collection, ECU; Longacre, "Many a Day before Charleston Falls," 116 (last quotation).

9. Wilder Diaries, 28, CU.

10. Berlin, Reidy, and Rowland, *Black Military Experience*, 493 (first quotation); *OR* 28(1):329 (second and third quotations).

11. In a letter to President Lincoln, Cpl. James H. Gooding of the 54th Massachusetts emphasized that the men in his regiment "were not enlisted under any 'contraband' act." He agreed that the ex-slaves needed the government to act as a temporary guardian, whereas Northern free blacks were able by birth and education to think and act for themselves. Adams, *On the Altar of Freedom*, 120.

12. Annual Returns of the 1st NCCV for 1863, Muster Rolls and Returns, 35th USCT, RG 94, NARA (quotation); Wise, *Gate of Hell*, 140; *OR* 28(1):279.

13. *The History of a Gallant Regiment*, Massachusetts MOLLUS Collection, USAMHI.

14. Special Order No. 32, 11 September 1863, Regimental Order Book, 35th USCT, RG 94, NARA.

15. Special Order No. 44, 25 October 1863, ibid. ("Middle Island"); Annual Returns of the 1st NCCV for 1863, Muster Rolls and Returns, and Special Order No. 69, 8 October 1863, Regimental Order Book—all in 35th USCT, RG 94, NARA.

16. Special Order No. 35, 18 September 1863, Regimental Order Book, ibid.

17. "Returns of Company E," November 1863, Muster Rolls, ibid.; Fox, *Service of the Fifty-fifth Regiment*, 13.

18. Keith P. Wilson, *Campfires of Freedom*, 41; Berlin, Reidy, and Rowland, *Black Military Experience*, 486.

19. *The History of a Gallant Regiment*, Massachusetts MOLLUS Collection, USAMHI.

20. Special Order No. 53, 19 October 1863, Regimental Order Book, 35th USCT, RG 94, NARA; Wilder Diaries, 16, CU.

21. Special Order No. 56, 22 October 1863, Regimental Order Book, 35th USCT, RG 94, NARA.

22. When Mann had called upon the surgeons of the 55th Massachusetts to resolve this issue, they had advised him to consult the chief medical officer on the island. Wilder Diaries, 39, CU.

23. General Order No. 66, 5 November 1863, Regimental Order Book, 35th USCT, RG 94, NARA.

24. Special Order No. 52, 5 November 1863, ibid.

25. When overcoats were finally issued on 21 November, four companies of the 1st NCCV were on detached service at the "White Howse [sic]" and would have to wait longer to get the clothing. Special Order No. 36, 21 November 1863, ibid.

26. Fox, *Service of the Fifty-fifth Regiment*, 18; Longacre, "Many a Day before Charleston Falls," 121 (quotation); Steven D. Smith, *Whom We Would Never More See*, 30–31.

27. General Order No. 16, 16 November 1863, Regimental Order Book, 35th USCT, RG 94, NARA (first quotation); Wilder Diaries, 44, CU (second quotation); General Order No. 15, 17 December 1863—all in Regimental Order Book, 35th USCT, RG 94, NARA (last two quotations).

28. Special Order No. 27, 2 December 1863, ibid.

29. Keith P. Wilson, *Campfires of Freedom*, 66.

30. Regimental General Order No. 17, 21 January 1864, Regimental Order Book, 35th USCT, RG 94, NARA.

31. This case crossed the lines of company authority, for Lt. Redick commanded Company A while the two enlisted men who had been found guilty of misconduct, Cpl. A. Cherry and Pvt. D. Spencer, were from Companies E and G, respectively.

32. The mixture of weapons used by Maj. Archibald Bogle's soldiers were "mostly second hand and many of them more or less imperfect." Bogle to Lt. Thomas Robinson, 30 December 1863, Regimental Order Book, 35th USCT, RG 94, NARA. See also Chapter 1.

33. Special Order No. 29, 26 January 1864, Regimental Order Book, ibid. These guns were most likely either the Model 1822 or Model 1842 .69-caliber smoothbore muskets that were converted to percussion. The Model 1842 was also rifled with long-range sights.

34. A notation on the muster rolls of Company I for February 1864 reported this problem. Muster Rolls, Company I, 35th Regiment, RG 94, NARA. At least one white Union regiment in the battle had similar problems.

35. Significantly, all subsequent inspections (April 1864 to May 1866) rated the regiment as "good" in all categories (except that "arms" was assessed "well kept" in April 1864). "Inspection Report of the 1st NCCV," 10 February 1864, Regimental Order Book, and Muster Rolls and Returns, 35th USCT, RG 94, NARA.

36. Lt. Col. Reed to Dr. D. Mann, 10 February 1864, and D. C. Manning to Lieutenant [Pratt], 12 February 1864, Regimental Letter Book, 35th USCT, RG 94, NARA.

37. Special Order No. 16, [12] February 1864, Regimental Order Book, 35th USCT, RG 94, NARA.

38. Because 1864 was an election year, supporters of both Treasury Secretary Salmon P. Chase and the president hoped that a reconstructed and loyal Florida might yield compliant delegates for the presidential nomination convention. Coles, "'Shooting Niggers Sir,'" 65–66; Nulty, *Confederate Florida*, viii–ix, 72–74.

39. Nulty, *Confederate Florida*, 76–82.

40. *OR* 35(1):480–81.

41. The use of "boat infantry" is described in Emilio, *A Brave Black Regiment*, 119–20, 188. After the southern end of Morris Island had been captured, the 7th Connecticut began sending out boats with armed men to patrol the waters around the island. That practice was maintained, by various commanders, for the entire siege of Charleston.

42. Special Order No. 98, 29 December 1863, Regimental Order Book, 35th USCT, RG 94, NARA (quotation); Quartermaster Returns for the 1st NCCV, Remick Papers, DU.

43. Muster Rolls, January–February 1864 and September 1863–February 1864, Muster Rolls and Returns, 35th USCT, RG 94, NARA; *OR* 35(1):481; Col. J. C. Beecher to Lt. Col. E. W. Smith, 8 April 1864, Regimental Letter Book, 35th USCT, RG 94, NARA; Steven D. Smith, *Whom We Would Never More See*, 25.

44. Wilder Diaries, 18 February 1864, CU; Schwartz, *A Woman Doctor's Civil War*, 59.

45. Col. Beecher had received leave to return north and, to his regret, missed the battle.

46. The record shows that Seymour oscillated from extreme pessimism about the expedition's likelihood for success to supreme confidence in his ability to defeat the enemy in front of him. His advance would take place despite Gillmore's understanding to the contrary. Coles, "'Shooting Niggers Sir,'" 68–69.

47. Schmidt, *Civil War in Florida*, 179.

48. The comments of observers suggest that the advancing Union troops had become used to only token resistance from the enemy, or that Seymour had received new information that caused him to push forward so quickly. In his official report, Seymour claimed that he had expected to encounter a Confederate force of about 4,000 to 5,000 men at or in the vicinity of Lake City. Nulty, *Confederate Florida*, 124–26.

49. "John Saunders," CWPF.

50. Palmer, *History of the Forty-eighth Regiment*, 133 (first quotation); *OR* 35(1):308 (second quotation); Nulty, *Confederate Florida*, 162–66.

51. *OR* 35(1):305.

52. Moore, *Rebellion Records*, 8:410; Muster Rolls, February 1864, Company I, 35th USCT, RG 94, NARA.

53. About half of the seven-shot Spencer repeating rifles belonging to the 7th New Hampshire had been transferred to the 40th Massachusetts Mounted Infantry. In return, the infan-

trymen received the mounted soldiers' old Springfield and Bridesburg muskets. The regiment also had a large number of new recruits. *Boston Journal*, 4 March 1864; *OR* 35(1):305; Nulty, *Confederate Florida*, 206–7.

54. Adams, *On the Altar of Freedom*, 109–10.

55. Norton, *Army Letters*, 202.

56. Denison, *Shot and Shell*, 225–27 (first quotation); Walkly, *History of the Seventh Connecticut*, 121–22 (second quotation); Adams, *On the Altar of Freedom*, 115 (last quotation).

57. Redkey, *Grand Army of Black Men*, 41, 47–48.

58. Yacovone, *Voice of Thunder*, 69 (*Philadelphia Ledger*); *Daily Chronicle and Sentinel*, 24 February 1864.

59. *Atlanta Intelligencer*, 2 March 1864, as cited in http://extlab7.entnem.ufl.edu/olustee/letters/Hshackelford.html. (Shackelford); James Matt Jordan to Louisa, 21 February 1864, *Letters from Confederate Soldiers*, vol. 2, Georgia State Archives, as cited in http://extlab7.entnem.ufl.edu/olustee/letters/Jjordan.html (19th Ga. Infantry private); *Boston Herald*, 1 March 1864 (Union artilleryman).

60. Looby, *Journal and Selected Letters of Thomas Wentworth Higginson*, 200, 361.

61. For this concept, see Reisberg, *Cognition*, 392–93, 412–13, 440–41. Given that both white and black Northern-born soldiers considered Southern culture and slavery to have had a retarding effect on the region's inhabitants, many were predisposed to see Northern black troops as better, in a number of ways, than Southern black troops.

62. Of course, a confirmation bias also affected how later commentators who were supportive of black troops evaluated records.

63. Schwartz, *A Woman Doctor's Civil War*, 63.

64. Emilio, *A Brave Black Regiment*, 169 (first quotation); *Worcester Aegis and Transcript*, 2 April 1864, as cited in http://extlab1.entnem.ufl.edu/olustee/letters/1stnclet.html (second quotation); Perkins, "Two Years with a Colored Regiment," 536 (last quotation).

65. The wounds to the left arm occurred because standing in a firing line tends to present the left side of the body. Most of the men who survived amputation of the arm were discharged about six months later. Barnes, *Medical and Surgical History*, 10:727, 734, 757, 764.

66. During the summer, Gregory passed through a series of hospitals at Beaufort. He was finally discharged from the service on 5 June 1865, by reason of "anchylosis of ankle joint" resulting from the wound. By contrast, Pvt. Richard Jorman (or Jourman) of Company E was left behind, had his right leg amputated by a Confederate surgeon, and later died of "consumption." Barnes, *Medical and Surgical History*, 10:276, 12:595.

67. Nulty, *Confederate Florida*, 203; *OR* 35(1):288–90, 298, 305–6; Rawick, *American Slave*, 17:179–80 (quotation).

68. *Daily Chronicle and Sentinel*, 28 February 1864; *Peninsula*, 31 March 1864.

69. Quartermaster Returns for the 1st NCCV, Remick Papers, DU (quotation); Norton, *Army Letters*, 203–4.

70. Col. J. C. Beecher to Lt. R. M. Hall, 13 April 1864, Regimental Letter Book (first quo-

tation); Beecher to Capt. Chadwick, 16 March 1864 (second quotation); and General Order No. 11, 20 March 1864, Regimental Order Book (third quotation)—all in 35th USCT, RG 94, NARA.

71. Col. J. C. Beecher to Lt. Col. B. F. Morgan, 27 June 1864; Beecher to Capt. W. L. M. Burger, 7 July 1864, Regimental Letter Book, 35th USCT, RG 94, AGO, NARA.

72. *OR* 35(2):171–72 (quotations); Col. J. C. Beecher to Capt. Whetlock, 13 July 1864, Regimental Letter Book, 35th USCT, RG 94, NARA.

73. Wilder Diaries, 27 July 1863, p. 7a, 18 September 1863, pp. 28, 37, and 8 May 1864, p. 97—all in CU; H. R. Wirtz to ?, 29 September 1863, Personal Papers of Medical Officers and Physicians, RG 94, NARA (Mann).

74. Although evidence introduced during his court-martial indicated that De Grasse probably had a dependence on alcohol, it was also clear that some of the charges were racially motivated. Asst. Surg. John De Grasse, Proceedings of General Court-Martial, RG 153, NARA.

75. Col. J. C. Beecher to Col. C. W. Foster, 14 March 1864, Regimental Letter Book, 35th USCT, RG 94, NARA (first quotation); Keith P. Wilson, *Campfires of Freedom*, 111 (second quotation).

76. McKee, *Back "In War Times,"* 160.

77. Gordon had ordered the vessel to fire off flares if it was in trouble. He later testified that although he heard the sounds of the attack, he saw no flares and thus saw no cause for concern. Equally disturbing to the men of the 35th USCT, a larger armed vessel, the *Ottawa*, a few miles downstream, did not go to the *Columbine*'s aid even though the engagement lasted almost an hour.

78. Schmidt, *Civil War in Florida*, 107–8; *OR* 35(1):193–96.

79. Dickison, *Dickison and His Men*, 66. Both sides consistently exaggerated the numbers involved in the action.

80. Ibid., 396–98. Dickison's first report claimed that 7 officers were captured. Including the Union forces that he captured at small posts at Welaka and Fort Gates, the prisoners numbered 56. The figure of 47 captured on the *Columbine* therefore seems to have been considerably inflated.

81. Col. J. C. Beecher to Col. M. S. Littlefield, 9 June 1864, Regimental Letter Book, 35th USCT, RG 94, NARA. Beecher wanted permission for the regimental recruiting officer to enlist men at Jacksonville to fill the vacancies. But only three men were added for the entire period that Company E was in Florida, and only one other man was added to the rest of the regiment in 1864. Company E, Regimental Letter Book, ibid.

82. Another seventeen men were listed as absent because of sickness. "Returns for Company E," May 1864, Muster Rolls, 35th USCT, RG 94, NARA.

83. Redkey, *Grand Army of Black Men*, 46 (soldier in 54th Massachusetts); Norton, *Army Letters*, 210 (men of the 8th USCT); Penneman Papers, 60–61, SHC.

84. Nulty, *Confederate Florida*, 161. Nulty (pp. 210–13) records numerous anecdotes of reported atrocities.

85. *Atlanta Intelligencer*, 2 March 1864, as cited in http://extlab7.entnem.ufl.edu/olustee/letters/Hshackelford.html. (Shackelford); James Matt Jordan to Louisa, 21 February 1864, *Letters from Confederate Soldiers*, vol. 2, Georgia State Archives, as cited in http://extlab7.entnem.ufl.edu/olustee/letters/Jjordan.html (private in 27th Georgia Infantry); Coles, "'Shooting Niggers Sir,'" 75 (Virginia soldier); Nulty, *Confederate Florida*, 128 (2nd Florida Cavalry).

86. *OR* 35(1):298; Marvel, *Andersonville*, 41–43, 154–55; Coles, "'Shooting Niggers Sir,'" 78–79.

87. Goss, *Soldier's Story*, 159; McElroy, *Andersonville*, 54.

88. A number of other men were ordered dropped from the rolls and another was discharged "per G O W D." Regimental Letter Book, 35th USCT, RG 94, NARA.

89. Of course, perhaps only the strongest of the captured black soldiers even made it to Andersonville. Marvel, *Andersonville*, 154–55.

90. Ibid., 221, 282; *OR* 35(2):171 (Gordon). By November 1864 Andersonville was largely empty, but Wirz had kept the black prisoners as long as possible not only for labor details but also "per order of the secretary of war, for identification by professed owners of runaway slaves." Marvel, *Andersonville*, 221.

91. Deposition of Frank Mattox in "Gaston Davis," CWPF. This file presents a problem for researchers. Davis was captured later on the *Columbine*, not at Olustee. But in a sad twist of fate, Gaston's brother John, left behind at Olustee badly wounded, was captured and may have been the person to whom Frank Mattox actually referred.

92. "Aaron Oberman," CMSR; Depositions of Edward S. Daniels (former captain of Company E) and Starking Northcott (Northcut) in "Aaron Oberman," CMSR.

93. Since many wounds were on the left side of the body, the men were probably hit while on the firing line facing the enemy. Although a large number of the wounded Union prisoners were black, Finegan reported that among the almost two hundred prisoners who were not wounded, there were only three African Americans. *OR* 35(1):327–28.

94. Of course, if such amputations had been done, it is likely that those soldiers would have survived to leave paper evidence of their treatment.

95. At least one Union surgeon had stayed with the men in his command, as well as a number of sergeants whose commissions had arrived after they had been captured. In January 1865 a number of Union officers, including Col. William H. Noble, were confined in the provost marshal's stockade. Marvel, *Andersonville*, 112, 191, 229.

96. McElroy, *Andersonville*, 54; Coles, "'Shooting Niggers Sir,'" 81; "List of Officers," Regimental Letter Book, 35th USCT, RG 94, NARA.

97. *OR*, ser. 2, 7:198 (Gibbs); Marvel, *Andersonville*, 222; *Massachusetts Soldiers, Sailors*, 302 (quotation regarding Ladd); "List of Officers," Regimental Letter Book, 35th USCT, RG 94, NARA.

98. "Return of Company E," May 1864, Muster Rolls, ibid.

99. *OR* 35(2):15–16; Special Orders No. 6, 15 April 1864, No. 48, 24 April 1864, Regimental

Order Book (first quotation), and Col. J. C. Beecher to Capt. W. L. M. Burger, 21 July 1864, Regimental Letter Book—all in 35th USCT, RG 94, NARA; *OR* 35(2):120 (last quotation).

100. Schwartz, *A Woman Doctor's Civil War*, 65 (quotations), 77–78; *OR* 35(2):70–71.

101. *OR* 35(1):402 (Noble), 403 (Anderson); Schwartz, *A Woman Doctor's Civil War*, 81 (Marcy).

102. *OR* 35(1):408–9 (Birney: "an excellent drill"); Special Order No. 71, 14 July 1864, and Circular, 21 July 1864, Regimental Order Book, 35th USCT, RG 94, NARA; *OR* 35(1):420–21 (Birney: "these colored troops").

103. Special Order No. 188, 20 August 1864, Regimental Order Book, 35th USCT, RG 94, NARA (quotations regarding Beecher); Norton, *Army Letters*, 213, 219–21 (quotations regarding Birney).

104. Col. J. C. Beecher to Capt. W. L. M. Burger, 2 March 1865, Regimental Letter Book, 35th USCT, RG 94, NARA.

105. Perkins, "Two Years with a Colored Regiment," 537 (first quotation); Col. J. C. Beecher to Rev. Horace James, 30 August 1864, Regimental Letter Book, 35th USCT, RG 94, NARA (second quotation).

106. Col. J. C. Beecher to Lt. A. Coates, 13 July 1864, and Beecher to Capt. M. Bailey, 29 June 1864 ("ruptures"), and Regimental Descriptive Books, 35th USCT, RG 94, NARA; Berlin, Reidy, and Rowland, *Black Military Experience*, 642 (last quotation).

107. Col. J. C. Beecher to [?], 24 August 1864, Beecher to Horace James, 24 August 1864, and Beecher to Maj. F. W. Taggart, 22 July 1864, Regimental Letter Book; and Special Order No. 69, 6 July 1864, Regimental Order Book—all in 35th USCT, RG 94, NARA.

108. Norton, *Army Letters*, 220; 189. Col. J. C. Beecher to Lt. E. Dove, [August 1864], Regimental Letter Book, 35th USCT, RG 94, NARA (first two quotations); Schwartz, *A Woman Doctor's Civil War*, 67 (Ester Hawks).

109. Officers demoted for these reasons included, for example, Orderly Sgt. James Kinball ("incompetent," September 1863), Sgt. Marcus Frazier (deserted, October 1863), Sgt. Austin Sheppard ("inability to perform his duty," November 1863), Sgt. William Reilley ("incompetency and indifference," March 1864), and Sgts. Eli Barrow and Alfred Smith (both for disabilities, March 1864).

110. Special Orders No. 77, 3 August 1864, and No. 81, 27 August 1864, Regimental Order Book (quotations), and Col. J. C. Beecher to Capt. Henry McIntire, 8 September 1864, Regimental Letter Book, 35th USCT, RG 94, NARA. While in charge of pickets on Folly Island, McIntire had become drunk and, when challenged by a sentry, had cursed the enlisted man as a "damn fool." "Captain Henry McIntire," CMSR.

111. Schwartz, *A Woman Doctor's Civil War*, 76.

112. Col. J. C. Beecher to Capt. F. D. Hodge, 21 September 1864, Regimental Letter Book, 35th USCT, RG 94, NARA.

113. Schwartz, *A Woman Doctor's Civil War*, 61.

114. General Order No. 56, 29 September 1864 (first two quotations), and General Order

No. 13, 3 October 1864 ("malicious intent"), Regimental Order Book, 35th USCT, RG 94, NARA.

115. Special Orders No. 111, 3 November 1864, and No. 6, 15 March 1865; Regimental Court-Martial, 3 October, 18 November 1864—all in ibid.

116. Special Orders No. 5, 14 June 1864, No. 85, 9 September 1864 (quotation), and No. 92, 27 September 1864, Regimental Order Book, 35th USCT, RG 94, NARA.

117. Berlin, Reidy, and Rowland, *Black Military Experience*, 642.

118. *OR* 44:547; *OR* 39(3):740 (quotation); Hudson, "Confederate Victory at Grahamville," 19–20.

119. Wise, *Gate of Hell*, 215; Foote, *Civil War: . . . Red River to Appomattox*, 652.

120. *OR* 44:426, 424, 426–27 (regarding wounds); Emilio, *A Brave Black Regiment*, 250, 243 ("acting in a dazed sort of way").

121. *OR* 44:427 (quotation), 424, 856; Foote, *Civil War: . . . Red River to Appomattox*, 653; *Palmetto Herald*, 8 December 1864.

122. Emilio, *A Brave Black Regiment*, 256–60. The two men killed were Pvts. Jacob Magonly and Hardy Middleton, both of whom had joined Company D in New Bern on 22 May 1863.

123. Annual Returns of Alterations and Casualties for the Year Ending December 31, 1864, Muster Rolls and Returns (first quotation), and "List of Officers, 35th USCT," Regimental Letter Book (second quotation), 35th USCT, RG 94, NARA; Harwell and Racine, *Fiery Trail*, 82 (Osborn).

124. Annual Returns of Alterations and Casualties for the Year Ending December 31, 1864, Muster Rolls and Returns, 35th USCT, RG 94, NARA.

125. Annual Returns of Alterations and Casualties for the Year Ending December 31, 1865, ibid. (quotation); *OR* 47(1):1042–43.

CHAPTER THREE

1. *OR*, ser. 3, 3:1115.

2. Capt. Croft was then recruiting for the 35th USCT. He later accepted a transfer to the 37th USCT.

3. Berlin et al., *Destruction of Slavery*, 92.

4. For an excellent overview of the recent literature on the treatment of irregular warfare by Civil War historians, see Daniel E. Sutherland's "Sideshow No Longer."

5. Stephen V. Ash capably analyzes the factors behind the emergence of guerrillaism in *When the Yankees Came*, 38–53.

6. For the ways in which guerrilla activities led to a hardening of Federal policies articulated in General Order No. 100, see Sutherland, "Guerrilla Warfare."

7. Keith P. Wilson, *Campfires of Freedom*, 182–83; Glatthaar, *Forged in Battle*, 79; Berlin and Rowlands, *Families and Freedom*, 35–36, 39.

8. Col. Draper to Capt. George H. Johnston, 27 November 1863, LEOB, 35th USCT, RG

94, NARA. In early 1863 Wead was also incensed by the behavior of many of his officers. On 30 May, twenty-five officers had passed a petition through Wead to Gen. John Foster requesting Wead's removal from command on the grounds that he was "mentally and physically, incapable of exercising responsibilities so high and holding a trust so important." They also stated, "We consider him incompetent and unsafe as a commanding officer." The officers believed that he had obtained his commission only through political influence and the patronage of Gen. Henry W. Slocum. Wead survived and purged the 98th of ten of the offending officers—in an act that seemed to them to imitate the iron rule of Frederick the Great. Kreutzer, *Notes and Observations*, 164–66.

9. Lt. Col. F. F. Wead to Capt. Hazard Stevens, 27 November 1863, LEOB, 36th USCT, RG 94, NARA.

10. Capt. J. Ebbs to Lt. Col. Wead, 24 November 1863, ibid.

11. Col. Draper to Maj. Johnston, 1 February 1864, ibid.

12. *OR* 29(2):534. Draper's appointment by General Butler to a military commission at Fort Monroe a few days earlier had delayed his departure.

13. *OR* 29(1):484, 483.

14. Ibid., 912–13; Barrett, *Civil War*, 178.

15. *OR*, ser. 3, 3:157 (quotation); Ash, *When the Yankees Came*, 57, 63–64.

16. *OR* 29(1):910–13 (Gen. Wild quoted in his after-action report).

17. Col. Draper to Lt. [?], 23 December 1863, LEOB, 36th USCT, RG 94, NARA. Draper, it was later claimed, was offered a drink but refused, saying "that he had drank all he dared to that morning." Capt. George Proctor to Governor Andrew, 3 May 1864, Letters Received, Division of Colored Troops, V46, 1864, RG 94, NARA.

18. George Proctor, who had lost his commission because of Draper, asserted that Draper had "threatened to shoot any one of his officers who would not go in & fight the 98th." When Draper and his men reached the New Yorkers' camp, he "detailed 2nd Lieut. B. Backup & instructed him to *kill* Lt. Col. Wead by his aiming the first fire & all his company were to aim at Col. W & and kill him, this, said Col. D. I think will end the trouble." Ibid.

19. *OR* 29(1):913. The very night the soldiers arrived home, a black sentry shot and killed a white man named James Hill in Norfolk. The soldier, posted as a guard in front of the quartermaster's office, had been accosted by a group of young men who had refused to leave when ordered to do so by the sentry. The guard's shot hit Hill in the head and killed him. For critics of the black troops, such as Gen. John Foster, it was more evidence of their lack of discipline. For supporters, it was proof of the pervasive hostility toward black soldiers. *North Carolina Times*, 9 January 1864.

20. *OR* 29(1):914 (first quotation); *OR* 29(2):596 (second quotation); Moore, *Rebellion Records*, 8:304 (third quotation).

21. Ash, *When the Yankees Came*, 66, 92.

22. Yearns and Barrett, *North Carolina Civil War Documents*, 55–56.

23. Lt. Owen A. Hendrick to Col. Draper, 2 January 1864, LEOB, 36th USCT, RG 94, NARA.

24. *OR* 29(2):914–15 (Wild); *Private and Official Correspondence of . . . Butler*, 3:231–32. As late as July 1864, Butler (4:526–27) was asking for reports on the passes issued and the trade allowed by the local treasury agent on Roanoke Island.

25. *OR* 29(2):485, 562 (first quotation), 596 (second quotation).

26. Maj. Alonzo G. Draper to Governor Andrew, 28 April 1863, *Executive Letters*, vol. 102, no. 58, MA. Although Draper had little tolerance for opposition from subordinates or his peers, he was able to develop a very good relationship with senior officers like Butler.

27. Special Order No. 1, 28 January 1864, and Circular, 9 March 1864 (quotation), LEOB, 36th USCT, RG 94, NARA. The officers did not specifically complain, however, that the order, issued on 9 March, needed a longer period for compliance than 11 March.

28. General Order No. 46, Orders and Circulars, 1797–1910, entry 44, RG 94, NARA. Draper issued this last order because he found "his men insubordinate and noisy." Ibid. At the same time, he reduced to the ranks noncommissioned officers in Companies A, D, E, and F "for permitting lights to be burned in their respective tents after Taps." General Order No. 4, 14 March 1864, LEOB, 36th USCT, RG 94, NARA.

29. In mid-March reveille had been changed from 5:30 to daybreak, while dress parade was at sunset. Former slaves may have seen the irony in these hours. General Order No. 1, 1 March 1864, and General Order No. 4, 14 March 1864, LEOB, 36th USCT, RG 94, NARA.

30. Capt. George F. Allen claimed that the brigade commander had recommended him for a promotion but that Draper had prevented it by contending that he did not have the proper education.

31. General Order No. 46, 19 April 1864, Orders and Circulars, 1797–1910, entry 44, RG 94, NARA. Draper immediately filled the vacant positions, but the problem of disaffection among officers appears not to have been fully resolved. It is significant that, excluding the nine men whose commissions were revoked, the 36th USCT had many more resignations up to March 1865 (15) than either the 35th USCT (6) or the 37th USCT (4). By contrast, the 14th Reg. U.S. Colored Heavy Artillery had only one. *Official Army Register*, 164, 206–9.

32. Capt. George F. Allen et al. to Governor John Andrew, 3 May 1864, Letters Received, Division of Colored Troops, V46, 1864, RG 94, NARA.

33. Ibid.

34. Col. J. Pickett to ?, 3 May 1864, and Lt. Col. B. F. Pratt and Maj. Daniel Preston to ?, 9 May 1864, ibid. Pratt and Preston must have realized that they were placing their careers at risk, and only a few months later Maj. Preston resigned his commission. Another officer in the 36th wrote: "Col. Draper has often told me that he has had a great many rows with officers in the service & had always been successful, and that they must be careful how they meddle with *hot iron* as they might get burned." Capt. George Proctor to Governor Andrew, 4 May 1863, ibid.

35. Longacre, *Army of Amateurs*, 21.

36. Speer, *Portals to Hell*, 187.

37. *OR*, ser. 2, 6:576.

38. Speer, *Portals to Hell*, 190–91. The actual number of prisoners shot may never be known. Diaries of the POWs at Point Lookout consistently record more incidents of men being shot—at least twenty-one over a fifteen-month period—than do the official records.

39. Pierson, *Whipt'em Everytime*, 94, 98 ("too of the Rebs got kild"); Hutt Diary, 24, 25 February 1864, USAMHI.

40. *OR*, ser. 2, 7:153–54 (quotation), 177–78; Speer, *Portals to Hell*, 191.

41. Lt. John Owen to "Dear Mother," n.d., Owen Papers, MHS; *OR*, ser. 2, 6:1102. A white guard, Sgt. Edwin Young of the 2nd New Hampshire Volunteers, taunted by such claims and by a dare to shoot, did so, killing Capt. L. R. Leyton of the 2nd Kentucky Cavalry.

42. *OR*, ser. 2, 7:163–64 (first quotation); Speer, *Portals to Hell*, 188–91; *OR*, ser. 2, 7:163–64 (last two quotations).

43. Beitzell, *Point Lookout*, 35–36.

44. Tilcomb's delay in entering the camp may have been a measure of the apprehension of the Union guards in the presence of so many Southern prisoners.

45. *OR*, ser. 2, 7:164–65 (first quotation), 385 (last quotation).

46. *OR* 36(3):175 (Hoffman); *OR*, ser. 2, 7:165.

47. *OR*, ser. 2, 7:165–67, 177–78, 835 (quotation). By 23 June 1864 there were 14,000 prisoners in the actual POW camp and almost 20,000 military personnel and assorted civilians on the Point.

48. Pierson, *Whipt'em Everytime*, 101–2 (Malone); Hutt Diary, 11 March 1864, USAMHI. The soldier was probably Sony Collins, of Company K, who was "accidentally shot" and died, according to regimental records, on 12 March. Hutt may have known when the guard was shot but not when he actually died.

49. Pierson, *Whipt'em Everytime*, 101 (Malone); Regimental Descriptive Books, 36th USCT, RG 94, NARA.

50. Col. Draper to Capt. C. H. Lawrence, 7 April 1864, LEOB, ibid.

51. Col. Draper to Capt. C. H. Lawrence, 8 April 1864, ibid. The local civilian population around many army posts during the war alleged the same kinds of theft, which created hostility between citizens and soldiers. When the soldiers were black, however, measuring the causes of tensions and ill feelings becomes complicated by the racial factor. There is a danger in ignoring or exaggerating the importance of racial preconceptions.

52. Circular, 9 May 1864 (quotations), and General Order No. 10, 9 May 1864, LEOB, 36th USCT, RG 94, NARA. Sgt. Maj. Owen claimed, "We all wear our revolvers and only a word from them is enough to seal a poor rebs or conscripts death warrent." His undated letter was written before his promotion to lieutenant on 26 April 1864. John Owen to ?, [n.d.], Owen Papers, MHS.

53. Berlin et al., *Wartime Genesis of Free Labor: The Upper South*, 487–88, 501–2 (quotation,

502). The Union army implemented a new policy of confiscating Rebel-owned property on which to set up government farms to be run by the black fugitives. A lack of supplies, equipment, and livestock was a major obstacle to the farms' self-sufficiency.

54. John Owen to "Dear Mother," 28 April 1864, Owen Papers, MHS. Capt. Butler of the 5th New Hampshire also believed that the prisoners had organized gangs in the camp that would rob and kill even their own men. John Owen to ?, n.d. [early April 1864], Owen Papers, MHS.

55. There was a strong current of paternalism and a belief that basic health practices had to be enforced by the white officers. General Order No. 7, 6 April 1864, LEOB, 36th USCT, RG 94, NARA.

56. Hutt Diary, 19 May 1864, USAMHI (first quotation); General Order No. 5, 26 March 1864, LEOB, 36th USCT, RG 94, NARA (second quotation).

57. Ira Berlin, who is very critical of officers' lack of concern for black family ties, cites a number of incidents in Missouri, Kentucky, and Mississippi regiments. In one extreme case, the colonel of the 40th USCT argued that the "marital relationship is but little understood by the colored race, and, if possible still less respected." Berlin, Reidy, and Rowland, *Black Military Experience*, 659, 709, 713–19.

58. Circular, 21 May 1864, LEOB, 36th USCT, RG 94, NARA. Attempts at educational improvement were common in all of the black regiments studied here. In the case of the 36th USCT, Draper gave it a regularized, structured form.

59. *OR* 36(2):273. Sgt. Price had joined the regiment at Washington, N.C., in June 1863; at age forty-five, he was one of its oldest noncommissioned officers. Before the war he had lived in Beaufort County.

60. Ervin L. Jordan, *Black Confederates*, 275; *OR* 37(1):71–72 (Draper), 72–73. In early May, Draper had reported turning over seven thousand acres seized from Confederate landowners to the Department of Negro Affairs. Several farms had been set up on the Patuxent River, but they were "totally destitute of stock and tools." Draper hoped to use the raids to solve the problem. Berlin et al., *Wartime Genesis of Free Labor: The Upper South*, 503–4.

61. *OR* 36(3):278 (first quotation), 473, 739–40, 754; Hutt Diary, 12 June 1864, USAMHI (last quotation).

62. "General Draper's Expedition," Moore, *Rebellion Records*, 11:524; *OR* 37(1):163–64.

63. The commander of the cavalry, a Lt. Denney, was "seriously indisposed" and in his absence his troopers "behaved in rather a bad manner." Moore, *Rebellion Records*, 11:524.

64. *OR* 37(1):165–66, 164; Moore, *Rebellion Records*, 11:525. Despite Draper's criticism, Hatlinger remained with the regiment until his resignation in March 1865.

65. Hutt Diary, 17, 21 June 1864, USAMHI (quotations); *Daily Richmond Enquirer*, 7 July 1864, as cited in Ervin L. Jordan, *Black Confederates*, 132. The paper alleged that the soldiers raped the officer's wife, "Mrs. G.," 11 times and also violated 25 to 30 other women.

66. Capt. George Proctor to ?, n.d., Letters Received, Division of Colored Troops, V46, 1864, RG 94, NARA (first quotation); Moore, *Rebellion Records*, 11:525 (second quotation);

*OR* 37(1):167; Berlin et al., *Wartime Genesis of Free Labor: The Upper South*, 493. Although St. Mary's District was part of Maryland, because it contained the Union prison it was initially put under the authority of the commander of the Department of Virginia and North Carolina. After 11 November 1863 that was Gen. Butler.

67. Butler had asked for the 36th USCT on 10 May and 10 June 1864. *OR* 36(2):740.

68. Leaving Draper in charge of Point Lookout when his regiment was transferred may have been a way of responding to the complaints of his officers, while at the same time not directly challenging Butler's claim that the colonel was an excellent officer.

69. Barnes never fully recovered from the wounds he received during the Gettysburg campaign and was used by the military in noncombat roles. Although Hinks also served in limited roles while recuperating from wounds suffered at Antietam, in the summer of July 1864 the army promoted him to command a black division in the Army of the James.

70. *Private and Official Correspondence of . . . Butler*, 4:467 ("a valuable officer"); *OR* 40(2):582, 615; *OR* 40(3):6; *OR* 40(3):339 ("one of my very best officers"), 340, 422, 500.

71. *Private and Official Correspondence of . . . Butler*, 5:279. Draper also respected Butler, or at least his patronage and influence. The next year, Draper wrote Butler that he hoped "that in three years it will be my privilege to take the stump in favor of Gen. Butler's election to the Presidency." Ibid., 5:622.

72. Draper's claims to the contrary, there obviously was skepticism about the level of training that the regiment had received.

73. General Order No. 16, 5 July 1864; Circulars, 24, 29 July 1864; and General Order [no number], 24 July 1864 (quotation), LEOB, 36th USCT, RG 94, NARA.

74. General Order No. 2, 24 July 1864, ibid.

75. After Butler's retreat from Drewry's Bluff, the general had ordered vessels sunk in the channel at this point on the James River to prevent Confederate gunboats or rams from moving downstream.

76. Francis T. Miller, *Photographic History of the Civil War*, 243; *OR* 42(2):158, 1173. In November 1864 Pvt. Spenser Beasley was "killed by a Shell" at Dutch Gap. Regimental Descriptive Books, 36th USCT, RG 94, NARA.

77. West, *Lincoln's Scapegoat General*, 262, 250.

78. John David Smith, *Black Judas*, 28 (first quotation); Blackett, *Thomas Morris Chester*, 101; Regimental Descriptive Books, 36th USCT, RG 94, NARA (last quotation).

79. *OR* 42(2):417 (first quotation); Blackett, *Thomas Morris Chester*, 97 (second quotation). Hollis, a twenty-year-old native of "Whitford Co.," N.C., would be wounded again—this time by Confederates—while on picket duty at Chafin's Farm in November. Regimental Descriptive Books, 36th USCT, RG 94, NARA.

80. Capt. George F. Allen and five other officers to Governor John Andrew, 3 May 1864, Letters Received, Division of Colored Troops, V46, 1864, RG 94, NARA; Blackett, *Thomas Morris Chester*, 115. There were four soldiers named John Williams in the 36th USCT, all of

whom survived the war. There was only one James Williams, and he died of fever in Portsmouth, Va., in February 1864.

81. General Order No. 5, 25th Army Corps, 21 December 1864, Regimental Unbound Papers, 36th USCT, RG 94, NARA, as cited in Bryant, "A Model Regiment," 112–13.

82. General Order No. 5, Regimental Unbound Papers, 36th USCT, RG 94, NARA, as cited in Bryant, "A Model Regiment," 113 (first quotation); Regimental Descriptive Books, 36th USCT, RG 94, NARA (last two quotations). Pvt. Roby's name also appears variously as Raby and Raley.

83. General Order No. 5, 25th Army Corps, 21 December 1864, Regimental Unbound Papers, 36th USCT, RG 94, NARA, as cited in Bryant, "A Model Regiment," 113–14 (first quotation); Regimental Descriptive Books, 36th USCT, RG 94, NARA (second quotation).

84. Bryant, "A Model Regiment," 114; Regimental Descriptive Books, 36th USCT, RG 94, NARA; Bryant, "A Model Regiment," 114 (quotation). Thomas Morris Chester mentions at least three black soldiers from the 5th USCT who crossed into Confederate lines. One of them had been heard to say "that he was no better treated in the army than he was by his former master." Blackett, *Thomas Morris Chester*, 115, 118–19.

85. Paine's division consisted of three brigades: the First Brigade, under Col. John Holman, included the 1st, 22nd, and 37th USCT; the Second Brigade, under Col. Alonzo Draper, included the 5th, 36th, and 38th USCT; and the Third Brigade, under Col. Samuel A. Duncan, included the 4th and 6th USCT.

86. "Calvin Bowe," CWPF.

87. Sommers, *Richmond Redeemed*, 5–6, 21, 25–27; Trudeau, *Last Citadel*, 206–8 (quotation, 208).

88. Sommers, *Richmond Redeemed*, 33, 35–37; Muster Rolls of the Field and Staff, 36th USCT, RG 94, NARA. The *Official Records* put the regiment's losses at 21 killed and 5 officers and 82 men wounded, a number slightly below the regiment's records. *OR* 42(1):136, 820.

89. *OR* 42(3):100–101 (Pratt); *OR* 42(1):820 (regarding Adkins); Blackett, *Thomas Morris Chester*, 152 (regarding Gaskill); *OR* 42(1):820 (regarding Backup).

90. Scroggs Diary, USAMHI.

91. Draper subsequently found out that Simmons's real name was De Forest and that he had previously been dismissed from the army. The lieutenant was later discharged for being absent without leave. *OR* 42(1):820.

92. General Order No. 26, 16 November 1864, and Maj. Hart to Lt. Oliver Stephens, 26 November 1864, LEOB, 36th USCT, RG 94, NARA.

93. Trudeau, *Last Citadel*, 208–9.

94. Gallagher, *Fighting for the Confederacy*, 477–78.

95. *Private and Official Correspondence of . . . Butler*, 5:192.

96. John Owen to "Dearest Mother," 29 September 1864, Owen Papers, MHS; Longacre, *Army of Amateurs*, 57–58 (quotation).

97. Glatthaar, *Forged in Battle*, 277 (first quotation); Col. Draper to Surgeon in Charge, U.S. General Hospital, 4 February 1865, "Miles James," CMSR.

98. *OR* 42(1):820 (Draper); Muster Roll, 31 August–31 October 1864 (Gardner's promotion), and Special Order No. 67, 12 July 1865 (Gardner's demotion), Company I, 36th USCT, RG 94, NARA; "James Gardner," CMSR. When Gardner died in 1905, he was living in Clark's Summit, Pa., although he was buried in Calvary Crest Cemetery, Ottumwa, Iowa.

99. *OR* 42(3):101; "Samuel Gilchrist," CMSR (quotation).

100. *OR* 42(3):101 (quotation); Muster Rolls, Company E, 36th USCT, RG 94, NARA; "William Davis," CMSR.

101. Blackett, *Thomas Morris Chester*, 168 (quotation), 171. According to Thomas Morris Chester, Pratt and Hart were both "eminently popular with the men."

102. Trudeau, *Last Citadel*, 223–25, 228–30; *OR* 42(1):110, 151, 807–8, 814–17; Muster Rolls of the Field and Staff, 31 August–31 October 1864 and 31 October–28 February 1865, 36th USCT, RG 94, NARA; *OR* 42(3):399 (Weitzel); Blackett, *Thomas Morris Chester*, 175; *OR* 42(3):557; *Private and Official Correspondence of . . . Butler*, 5:279.

103. Blackett, *Thomas Morris Chester*, 195, 197, 224. Black correspondent Thomas Morris Chester claimed that picket firing and the bitter feeling associated with it were more common around Petersburg. "In front of Richmond, very unlike Petersburg, there is no firing. The pickets not infrequently, and in different ways, manifest the most cordial feelings for each other." Ibid., 228.

104. Ibid., 197; Regimental Descriptive Books, 36th USCT, RG 94, NARA.

105. Blackett, *Thomas Morris Chester*, 195–96.

106. Brig. Gen. A. Draper to J. H. Metcalf, 13 February 1865, and Brig. Gen. Rufus Ingalls to Maj. Nelson Plato, 23 February 1865 (Wild), Wild Papers, USAMHI.

107. Maj. W. H. Hart to Lt. R. W. Simpson, 5 February 1865, LEOB, 36th USCT, RG 94, NARA (quotation); Berlin, Reidy, and Rowland, *Black Military Experience*, 729–30.

108. General Order No. 32, 8 February 1865, LEOB, 36th USCT, RG 94, NARA.

109. Bernarr Cresap (*Appomattox Commander*, 137) suggests that the change was pushed by Butler "to give black troops a chance for glory as a unit."

110. Trudeau, *Last Citadel*, 378; Cresap, *Appomattox Commander*, 92, 220–21; Longacre, "Black Troops in the Army of the James," 6.

111. "Draperisms," [author unknown], April 1865, Wild Papers, USAMHI; *OR* 44(3):1211 (quotation); 199. Blackett, *Thomas Morris Chester*, 288–91, 303. Ernest Furgurson (*Ashes of Glory*, 331–32) contends that the black troops stopped before Richmond, but he appears to be referring to the city center.

112. Blackett, *Thomas Morris Chester*, 303 (correspondent); Longacre, *Army of Amateurs*, 314 (Wild); "Report of the Military Service of Edward A. Wild," Wild Papers, USAMHI; Cresap, *Appomattox Commander*, 220. Grant had apparently made the decision to remove the black soldiers when he met with Ord at City Point.

113. Blackett, *Thomas Morris Chester*, 299.

114. Gould Diary, 31 August 1865, 3 May 1865; 24 April, 2, 3, 4, 14 May 1865, USAMHI (dates follow order of text).

## CHAPTER FOUR

1. This excludes the fourth black infantry regiment and fifth black unit organized in North Carolina, the 135th USCT, which existed for only seven months (March–October 1865). The regiment "contained men from every Southern State east of the Mississippi River," primarily ex-slaves who had accompanied Sherman's troops across the Carolinas. Manarin, *Guide to Military Organizations*, 3.

2. *History of the Thirty-seventh Regiment*, 19; *Official Army Register*, 209. Chamberlain, a carriage trimmer by trade, was twenty-nine years old when he assumed command of the 3rd NCCV.

3. "Douglass James," CWPF.

4. After the capture of the Union garrison at Fort Pillow on the Mississippi River, Gen. Bedford Forrest's cavalrymen murdered dozens of captured black soldiers as well as their commanding officer, Maj. William F. Bradford. It quickly became one of the best-known atrocities of the Civil War. The most recent and by far the best analysis of the capture of Plymouth is Jordan and Thomas's "Massacre at Plymouth," reprinted in Urwin, *Black Flag over Dixie*, 153–202.

5. *History of the Thirty-seventh Regiment*, 42–49, 53–61.

6. Jordan and Thomas, "Massacre at Plymouth," 159–61.

7. Lt. Col. Chamberlain to Lt. H. W. Allen, 29 May 1864, LEOB, 37th USCT, RG 94, NARA; Jordan and Thomas, "Massacre at Plymouth," 154. Jordan and Thomas (pp. 155–57) arrive at a figure of approximately 80 recruits, half of whom belonged to the 37th USCT. On the other hand, casualty returns (*OR* 33:305) indicate that 244 "unattached recruits" were captured. It would seem that a minimum of 40 recruits were destined for the 37th USCT and possibly, if less likely, twice that number.

8. *OR* 30:287; Jordan and Thomas, "Massacre at Plymouth," 145.

9. By this time, recruiting officers for ten other black units were active in North Carolina towns, and some of their recruits may have been included in the 244 figure. *OR* 30:301, 870–71.

10. *OR* 51(2):870; *History of the Thirty-seventh Regiment*, 65; "George Burden (Berden)," CWPF (quotations).

11. There are several versions of Ward's injuries and escape. Jordan and Thomas, "Massacre at Plymouth," 172, 177.

12. Confederate officials claimed that if captured Union officers were questioned, the charges would be proved false. *OR*, ser. 2, 7:459–60, 486; Durrill, *War of Another Kind*, 206–8.

13. *OR*, ser. 2, 7:79.

14. Lt. Col. Chamberlain to Maj. R. S. Davis, 14 June 1864, LEOB, 37th USCT, RG 94, NARA; Lt. John Owen to "My Dear Aunt," 6 May 1884, Owen Papers, MHS.

15. Special Orders No. 3, 15 February 1864, and No. 10, 21 April 1864, LEOB, 37th USCT, RG 94, NARA.

16. *OR* 33:870–71 (quotation).

17. The African Brigade and a number of other regiments not brigaded but posted at Norfolk and Portsmouth were under the overall command of Gen. Wild. *OR* 33:482.

18. Ibid., 957; *OR* 31(2):16; Longacre, *Army of Amateurs*, 51 (quotation).

19. McPherson, *Battle Cry of Freedom*, 723–24.

20. Trudeau, *Like Men of War*, 216 (quotations); William Glenn Robertson, *Back Door to Richmond*, 9, 53–62; Schiller, *Bermuda Hundred Campaign*, 62–66; *OR* 36(2):20–23, 165.

21. About two weeks after the 37th USCT left Fort Powhatan, a force of about one hundred cavalrymen attacked the works but was driven off by the 10th USCT.

22. *OR* 36(2):22–23, 165.

23. Company F enrolled 24 soldiers at City Point and another half dozen at Wilson's Wharf. On 18 May, 55 men joined Company G. *History of the Thirty-seventh Regiment*, 88–91, 95–101.

24. Lt. C. Mixter to Chaplain W. A. Green, 26 May 1864, LEOB, 37th USCT, RG 94, NARA.

25. *OR* 36(2):23–24, 31, 270–71; *OR* 36(3):181–82, 205, 243. It is unclear from the records which two soldiers were captured or what their fate was.

26. *OR* 36(2):166–67. A resident of Boston, Cunningham had served in Company A, 13th Massachusetts Volunteers, before accepting a commission in the 37th USCT. Despite Hinks's criticism, Cunningham was later promoted to captain and served with the 38th USCT and the 24th U.S. Infantry before his final discharge in late 1878. *History of the Thirty-seventh Regiment*, 62; *Massachusetts Soldiers, Sailors*, 295.

27. Lt. Col. Chamberlain to Brig. Gen. George D. Raimsey, 12 May 1864, LEOB, 37th USCT, RG 94, NARA; *OR* 40(1):177. There is a danger in reading too much or too little into the following events. White regiments also had numerous discipline cases arising from differences in personal background, expectations, status, and class. However, because the officers and men in the black regiments entered the war with such different experiences and perceptions of the other, clashes between the two groups inevitably contained a racial element.

28. Lt. C. Mixter to Capt. G. A. Bailey, 11 June 1864; Mixter to Lt. A. C. Rembaugh, 4 June 1864, LEOB, 37th USCT, RG 94, NARA (quotation); *History of the Thirty-seventh Regiment*, 23, 51, 102; *Massachusetts Soldiers, Sailors*, 290. Bailey, who had been a trader in Brookline, Mass., before the war and had previously served in the 1st Massachusetts Volunteers, had been wounded twice.

29. "Recommendation Returned," 17 June 1864, LEOB, 37th USCT, RG 94, NARA. The

corporal, George Moore, was subsequently reduced to the ranks on 20 September 1864. General Order No. 25, 20 September 1864, ibid.

30. Chamberlain's attitude toward his black soldiers was reflected in his refusal, in June 1864, to have a sutler appointed to his camp, although it was standard in most regiments. Chamberlain believed that the habits of "improvidence in which these people have been brought up" would leave them less able to make the kind of prudent financial decisions that he would have expected from white troops. Keith P. Wilson, *Campfires of Freedom*, 70.

31. "Forwarded," 28 May 1864, LEOB, 37th USCT, RG 94, NARA.

32. *History of the Thirty-seventh Regiment*, 25 (commander of Company A); "William L. Benson," CWPF (private in Company E); "William P. Chase," CWPF, RG 15, NARA; *Official Army Register*, 209.

33. Lt. Col. Chamberlain to Lt. Col. Edward W. Smith, 28 October 1864, 37th USCT, RG 94, AGO, NARA. Crouse was appointed assistant surgeon in February 1864 but did not join the regiment until 26 March.

34. Gen. Robert S. Foster, commanding the Third Brigade, First Division, Twentieth Corps, needed the workers and thought that Chamberlain's black soldiers, even though they were from another division, were the logical choice. *OR* 40(2):515.

35. *OR* 40(1):215 (the private); *OR* 40(2):460 (Hinks). In fairness to the units, Hinks pointed out that three of the regiments consisted of dismounted cavalrymen who were unfamiliar with and largely untrained in infantry tactics.

36. *Private and Official Correspondence of . . . Butler*, 4:469; *OR* 40(2):488, 490 (quotations).

37. Lt. Col. Chamberlain to Capt. S. A. Carter, 28 June 1864, LEOB, 37th USCT, RG 94, NARA (first two quotations); *Private and Official Correspondence of . . . Butler*, 4:468–69; *OR* 40(2):637 (last quotation). Gen. Smith had already agreed with Butler to transfer the 37th USCT and three other black regiments to his command in return for white troops. Once the regiment received more training, it became part of Butler's force.

38. White had enlisted on 12 December 1863 as the company's first recruit. *History of the Thirty-seventh Regiment*, 103, 109.

39. Simon, *Papers of Ulysses S. Grant*, 12:67–68.

40. *History of the Thirty-seventh Regiment*, 102–24. The lone soldier from outside North Carolina as of 27 November 1864 was Thomas Johnson, who had been drafted in Company K from the District of Columbia. In January Charles Young from Norfolk enlisted, and in the next few months three more Virginians were added. Although Company K was mustered in at the same time as Company I, the former company was left in Virginia during the winter to improve its drill and efficiency. It did not rejoin the regiment until February 1865. Ibid., 125–36.

41. *OR* 40(1):265–66; *OR* 42(2):38. With so many officers of the 37th and 36th USCT drawn from Massachusetts units, friendships linked the officers of the two regiments. John Owen had previously served as sergeant major of the 36th USCT before accepting a commission in the

37th USCT. Lt. John Owen to "Dear Mother," 1864, Owen Papers, MHS; *Massachusetts Soldiers, Sailors*, 306.

42. *OR* 42(2):551–52, 554. The First Brigade was now under the command of Col. Holman. *OR* 42(2):622.

43. Lt. Col. Chamberlain to Col. John H. Holman, 20 September 1864, LEOB, 37th USCT, RG 94, NARA.

44. Longacre, *Army of Amateurs*, 211.

45. The other two brigades, led by Col. Samuel A. Duncan (4th and 6th USCT) and Col. Alonzo Draper (5th, 36th, and 38th USCT), experienced some of the toughest fighting that they would see.

46. *OR* 42(1):101; Sommers, *Richmond Redeemed*, 32, 33, 37, 147; *OR* 42(1):108–9 (quotation). By contrast, the 1st USCT suffered 21 casualties, and the 22nd USCT lost 78 men. Casualties among the other black regiments ranged from 111 to 236 troops.

47. Trudeau, *Last Citadel*, 223–24; Blackett, *Thomas Morris Chester*, 177 (quotations).

48. Longacre, *Army of Amateurs*, 228–30; Trudeau, *Last Citadel*, 229–30, 237–41.

49. *OR* 42(1):109–10; Trudeau, *Last Citadel*, 237 (quotation).

50. *OR* 42(1):815 (quotation); Trudeau, *Like Men of War*, 307. Winfield Scott's *Infantry Tactics* and William J. Hardee's *Rifle and Light Infantry Tactics* both included information on forming squares in the face of cavalry. See Griffith, *Battle Tactics*, 99, 101, 104.

51. *OR* 42(1):872; Longstreet, *From Manassas to Appomattox*, 578.

52. Longstreet, *From Manassas to Appomattox*, 578; *OR* 42(1):815, 818 (another officer of 22nd USCT).

53. Longacre, *Army of Amateurs*, 230 (regarding Weitzel); Blackett, *Thomas Morris Chester*, 177; *OR* 42(1):815; *OR* 42(3):167–70; Trudeau, *Last Citadel*, 247–48 (New Hampshire soldier); Trudeau, *Like Men of War*, 308 (officer in 5th USCT).

54. John David Smith, *Black Judas*, 31.

55. The hapless Wilkirk had been wounded in the head at Fort Harrison, suffered his fall on the retreat from the Williamsburg road, and would later injure his eyes in the fighting around Wilmington. Asst. Surg. William Craig of the 37th USCT eventually discharged him for disability in 1865. "Martin Wilkirk," CWPF.

56. Gallagher, *Fighting for the Confederacy*, 492.

57. Philip Weinmann joined the U.S. regular service as a private in 1861. He had been commissioned as captain in the 6th USCT before his promotion and transfer to the 37th USCT.

58. Special Orders No. 27, October 1864, No. 23, 4 November 1864, and No. 42, 15 November 1864, LEOB, 37th USCT, RG 94, NARA; *History of the Thirty-seventh Regiment*, 39, 55–56. Crawford was subsequently discharged on a surgeon's certificate. Reed and Harrison were later reappointed corporals. The case of Nelson and Lammerson may relate to the death of their captain, Daniel Foster, on 30 September and the appointment of Lt. George W. Singer of Company F as their new commander.

59. Capt. C. Nietzsche to Lt. Col. Chamberlain, 8 November 1864, Chamberlain to

Nietzsche, 9 November 1864, and Special Order No. 3, 14 February 1865, LEOB, 37th USCT, RG 94, NARA.

60. *History of the Thirty-seventh Regiment*, 27 (regarding Green); Lt. Col. Chamberlain to Maj. R. T. Davis, 8 July 1864, and Chaplain Green to Lt. Col. E. W. Smith, 8 November 1864 (Green's quotation), LEOB, 37th USCT, RG 94, NARA; Click, *Time Full of Trial*, 140, 142–44.

61. "John Whitfield" (T. Kelly) and "Charles Oats," CWPF.

62. On 3 December 1864 all of Butler's black troops had been combined into a single army corps, the Twenty-fifth, commanded by Gen. Weitzel, while the white troops had formed the Twenty-fourth Corps. The infantry for the first expedition to Fort Fisher consisted of Gen. Ames's division from the Twenty-fourth Corps and Paine's division from the black Twenty-fifth Corps.

63. For a perceptive summary of the personalities behind the genesis and operation of the plan, see Reed, *Combined Operations*, 324–54. The most recent account of the fall of Fort Fisher is Fonvielle, *Wilmington Campaign*. Also useful is Gragg, *Confederate Goliath*.

64. Fonvielle, *Wilmington Campaign*, 102–3 (quotation); Gragg, *Confederate Goliath*, 42. Perhaps because Grant was unconvinced that the first attack on Fort Fisher was important, the troops that he detached were not, in his eyes, among his best soldiers.

65. The two most recently raised companies of the 37th USCT, I and K, were left behind in the regimental camp at Chafin's Farm.

66. Grant's limited support convinced Porter that the powder ship was crucial to his success, but that venture was held up by a series of problems that included obtaining the quality and quantity of gunpowder needed, a decrepit ship, and bad weather.

67. It was normal for a department commander to stay with the larger part of his army, in this case the Army of the James, but either because of his enthusiasm for the project, his concerns about Weitzel's leadership, or a desire for glory, Butler decided to sail with the expedition. Fonvielle, *Wilmington Campaign*, 68–71, 96–97, 104–7.

68. Muster Rolls of the Field and Staff, 31 October–31 December 1865, 37th USCT, RG 94, NARA.

69. The ship was to carry 300 tons of gunpowder and be exploded within 450 yards of Fort Fisher. In fact, the *Louisiana* was carrying only 215 tons of powder when it exploded about 1,100 yards offshore. Moreover, the timing devices failed to function as planned, and the fire set by Rhind as he left detonated only a portion of the powder. Reed, *Combined Operations*, 338–40, 342; Fonvielle, *Wilmington Campaign*, 120–25.

70. Gragg, *Confederate Goliath*, 53 (quotation). A number of Parrott 100-pounders exploded because of faulty construction, causing significant casualties among the Union sailors.

71. Barrett, *Civil War*, 262–69; *OR* 42(1):964–70, 971–77, 980–86; Fonvielle, *Wilmington Campaign*, 153–70, 175–78; Muster Rolls of the Field and Staff, 31 October–31 December 1865, 37th USCT, RG 94, NARA.

72. Gragg, *Confederate Goliath*, 108 (Porter); *OR* 46(1):404, 46(2):16. The Twenty-third

Army Corps was also sent to Baltimore on 9 January just in case Sherman's division was not enough. Reed, *Combined Operations*, 348–49.

73. Rufus Noble to "Dear Family," 19 February 1865, Federal Soldiers Letters, SHC.

74. Trudeau, *Like Men of War*, 359 (Col. Ames); John David Smith, *Black Judas*, 32 (last quotation).

75. *OR* 46(1):423; Barrett, *Civil War*, 271–74; Reed, *Combined Operations*, 360; *OR* 46(1):394–406; Fonvielle, *Wilmington Campaign*, 218–21.

76. Fonvielle, *Wilmington Campaign*, 278–79 (first quotation, 279); Gragg, *Confederate Goliath*, 156–89; Yearns and Barrett, *North Carolina Civil War Documents*, 90.

77. Of course, Bragg would claim that the fort, given the reinforcements he had sent (but which in large part had not arrived), should have been able to hold out. He was also intimidated by the potential damage that the Federal fleet could have inflicted on Confederate attackers.

78. Gragg, *Confederate Goliath*, 213. Gen. Whiting bitterly condemned Bragg's inactivity. "I charge him with this loss; with neglect of duty," Whiting wrote a short time later while a prisoner. It is clear, however, that an attack by Bragg would not have changed the ultimate course of events. *OR* 46(1):440.

79. In many cases, the surviving military records indicate that some blacks were serving as personal servants, cooks, or musicians. For these four men, there are no records that they were not part of their regular unit. Herring was "released after taking the Oath of Allegiance June 19, 1865," and the other three had been "paroled and exchanged" several months earlier. Manarin, *North Carolina Troops*, 260, 262, 420.

80. Fonvielle, *Wilmington Campaign*, 319–23.

81. Barrett, *Civil War*, 281; *OR* 47(1):924–25; Trudeau, *Like Men of War*, 363; Fonvielle, *Wilmington Campaign*, 357–82, 396–98; Smith, *Black Judas*, 34–35.

82. Gragg, *Confederate Goliath*, 245–46 (first two quotations); Charles A. Hill to his wife, 23 February 1865, Hill Collection of Richard S. Tracy, as cited in Wood, "Port Town at War," 226–27.

83. Fonvielle, *Wilmington Campaign*, 430–33.

84. *OR* 47(1):925–26.

85. Ibid., 154.

86. Figures were compiled from *History of the Thirty-seventh Regiment*, 28–136.

87. Col. N. Goff to Col. C. W. Foster, 2 April 1865, and Maj. Weinmann to Foster, 5 August 1865, LEOB, 37th USCT, RG 94, NARA.

88. Maj. Philip Weinmann to Col. C. W. Foster, 21 September 1865, LEOB, 37th USCT, RG 94, NARA. Many privates in Company K had enlisted for only one year and were mustered out when their period of service expired. *History of the Thirty-seventh Regiment*, 128.

89. Col. N. Goff to Col. C. W. Foster, 16 March 1866, LEOB, 37th USCT, RG 94, NARA.

## CHAPTER FIVE

1. Abbott, "Massachusetts"; Glatthaar, *Forged in Battle*, 63–65. The bill excluded agents from recruiting in Arkansas, Tennessee, and Louisiana. Senator Benjamin G. Brown of Missouri had predicted that the "people of the West will feel that it is an injustice" if Eastern states used their capital to enlist Southern blacks while the West continued to send its own sons and husbands into the field. The legislation was ultimately repealed in March 1865 because of complaints about the behavior of the agents and because they were deemed to be ineffective. Bogue, *Earnest Men*, 169–73 (quotation, 173); Berlin, Reidy, and Rowland, *Black Military Experience*, 14.

2. *OR*, ser. 3, 4:484–85.

3. Governor James Y. Smith to Secretary of War Edwin Stanton, 30 August 1864, R289, 1864, Letters Received, Colored Troops Division, RG 94, NARA.

4. Muster Rolls, 22 April–31 August 1864, 14th USCHA, RG 94, NARA. The first white regiment had been authorized in May 1862 after Col. Rush Hawkins of the 9th New York Infantry had told senior officers that one could be raised "upon the assurance that they would not be called on to go out of the state." President Lincoln subsequently empowered Hawkins to begin enlisting white North Carolinians. Judkin Jay Browning, "'Little Souled Mercenaries,'" 340.

5. Muster Rolls, Company B, 22 April–31 August 1864, 14th USCHA, RG 94, NARA; Gen. U. S. Grant to Gen. B. F. Butler, 22 August 1864, in Simon, *Papers of Ulysses S. Grant*, 12:67–68.

6. Maj. Jameson to Capt. J. J. Judson, 30 August 1864, DOCLEM, 14th USCHA, RG 94, NARA.

7. *OR*, ser. 3, 4:203–4 ("bounty-brokers"), 573–74 (last quotation).

8. The "hand money" was raised because each of the towns received credit for recruits in proportion to the funds that the town collected. It was unclear from the account which person ended up with the hand money, but the implication was that it was seldom the recruit. Gordon, *War Diary*, 275.

9. Ibid., 275–76.

10. Maj. Jameson to Maj. R. S. Davis, 7 September 1864, DOCLEM, 14th USCHA, RG 94, NARA.

11. Maj. Jameson to Col. Francis, 25 August 1864, Letters Received, Colored Troops Division, RG 94, NARA.

12. Ibid.

13. Berlin, Reidy, and Rowland, *Black Military Experience*, 14; Glatthaar, *Forged in Battle*, 64–65; *OR*, ser. 3, 5:662 (number of agents and recruits); Wiley, *Southern Negroes*, 306–7; Glatthaar, *Forged in Battle*, 64–65; Berlin, Reidy, and Rowland, *Black Military Experience*, 77–78; Abbott, "Massachusetts," 209, 208 (quotation).

14. It is, of course, possible that Jameson had let some agents take credit for recruits already

in hand so those recruits could receive state bounties. The existing records, however, do not permit such a determination.

15. Regimental Muster Rolls, 14th USCHA, RG 94, NARA.

16. Maj. Jameson to Maj. R. S. Davis, 17 August 1864, and Jameson to Capt. J. A. Judson, 30 August 1864, DOCLEM, 14th USCHA, RG 94, NARA (quotations); Special Order No. 18, 25 August 1864, ibid.

17. Maj. Jameson to Maj. R. S. Davis, 17 August 1864; Jameson to Capt. J. A. Judson, 28 August 1864; and Lt. Wheaton to Judson, 5 November 1864—all in DOCLEM, 14th USCHA, RG 94, NARA. Company B had been detailed as post guard at the recruiting center in New Bern.

18. Maj. Jameson to Capt. J. A. Judson, 16 September 1864, ibid.; *OR*, ser. 3, 4:485 (quotation).

19. Maj. Jameson to Capt. J. A. Judson, 13 September 1864, DOCLEM, 14th USCHA, RG 94, NARA (quotations); Special Order No. 31, 16 September 1864, ibid.

20. Maj. Jameson to Secretary of War Stanton, 28 September 1864; Jameson to Lt. Col. Harris, 24 October 1864 (third and fourth quotations); and Jameson to Maj. Gen. Butler, 12 October 1864—all in DOCLEM, 14th USCHA, RG 94, NARA.

21. Maj. Jameson to Capt. J. A. Judson, 17 September 1864 (first quotation), and Special Order No. 33, 19 September 1864, ibid.

22. Maj. Jameson to Capt. Judson, 17 September 1864, DOCLEM, 14th USCHA, RG 94, NARA.

23. Maj. Jameson to Maj. R. S. Davis, 28 September 1864, ibid.

24. *OR* 43(2):794 (quotation); Special Order No. 26, 11 September 1864, DOCLEM, 14th USCHA, RG 94, NARA.

25. Special Orders No. 28, 13 September 1864, and No. 30, 15 September 1864, ibid.; *OR* 43(2):794 (quotation).

26. Barrett, *Civil War*, 225; Farnham and King, "'March of the Destroyer,'" 438–48.

27. Ibid., 449–52, 461–62; Thorpe, *Fifteenth Connecticut Volunteers*, 76–77 (quotation).

28. New Bern had been hit by two epidemics in less than a year, but it was yellow fever that drew most attention from contemporary writers. As Horace James explained: "During the Winter, *small pox* raged fearfully, and in the autumn, *yellow fever* swept our city with the besom of destruction. The former disease proved more fatal to the blacks, the latter to the whites." James estimated that whereas in February 1864, fifty people died of small pox per week, in October, almost that many died of yellow fever per day. James, *Annual Report of the Superintendent*, 16.

29. Special Order No. 46, 7 October 1864, DOCLEM, 14th USCHA, RG 94, NARA (quotation); Farnham and King, "'March of the Destroyer,'" 461.

30. General Order No. 4, 25 October 1864 (first quotation); Maj. Jameson to Maj. Davis, 26 October 1864; and Lt. Col. Walter S. Poor to Jameson, 4 November 1864 (second quotation), DOCLEM, 14th USCHA, RG 94, NARA.

31. Maj. Jameson to Capt. Judson, 5 November 1864, ibid.

32. Ibid. (Jameson); Thorpe, *Fifteenth Connecticut Volunteers*, 235 (Butricks). Jameson clearly had Butricks in mind when he complained that his soldiers were being "demoralized." Butricks's belief that they did not suffer from the yellow fever epidemic is revealing.

33. Morning Reports, Companies A to M, 14th USCHA, RG 94, NARA.

34. Special Order No. 34, 20 September 1864, DOCLEM, 14th USCHA, RG 94, NARA; James, *Annual Report of the Superintendent*, 42–43.

35. Estimates of the number of deaths caused by the epidemic have ranged from a few hundred to thirteen hundred. Civilian deaths are the most difficult to estimate. The most recent and exhaustive study suggests that about 300 soldiers and from 650 to 750 civilians died from the fever. Farnham and King, "'March of the Destroyer,'" 471.

36. "Cherry Wright," CWPF. Jameson had requested leave earlier so he could settle the estate of his father-in-law, George A. Otis of Boston.

37. Merrill, *Letters of William Lloyd Garrison*, 5:244, 251.

38. *Private and Official Correspondence of . . . Butler*, 5:424–25 (first quotation); Merrill, *Letters of William Lloyd Garrison*, 5:251, 257–58 (second quotation).

39. Brig. Gen. I. N. Palmer to ?, 7 February [Register of Letters] (first quotation), and Capt. Allen to Capt. Judson, 15 February 1865 (second quotation), DOCLEM, 14th USCHA, RG 94, NARA; Swint, *Dear Ones at Home*, 153; Basler, *Collected Works of Abraham Lincoln*, 8:289–90.

40. Heslin, "A Yankee Soldier," 111–12, 123, 140, 147; Poor Letters, New-York Historical Society, New York (quotation); Judkin Jay Browning, "'Little Souled Mercenaries'"; Bartlett, *Civil War in North Carolina*, 174, 208, 213.

41. Farnham and King, "'March of the Destroyer,'" 458; Thorpe, *Fifteenth Connecticut Volunteers*, 79–80 (quotations).

42. General Order No. 7, 12 November 1864; No. 8, 15 November 1864; No. 9, 15 November 1864; and No. 10, 18 November 1864—all in DOCLEM, 14th USCHA, RG 94, NARA.

43. "Chester Amieny" and "Benjamin Heston," Horner Collection, ECU; "Gordon Wiggins" and "Henry Hill" (quotation), CWPF.

44. General Order No. 12, 1 December 1864, DOCLEM, 14th USCHA, RG 94, NARA (first quotation); Lt. E. A. Edwards to Capt. Allen, 2 December 1864, DOCLEM, 14th USCHA, RG 94, NARA (second quotation).

45. "Isaac Bryant," Horner Collection, ECU; "Richard Faircloth," "Lewis Bass," "Windsor Ormond," and "Thomas Morris," CWPF.

46. "Benjamin Heston," Horner Collection, ECU; "Henry Hill," CWPF; DOCLEM, 14th USCHA, RG 94, NARA (regarding Bayman); George Taylor," CWPF. In the latter case, the pension official did not trust the lawyer working for Taylor and believed that the case had been fabricated. In one document, Taylor claimed that an inspecting officer had ordered "an old siege piece" fired, precipitating the bursting of the cannon.

47. "Simon Tyson," "William H. Moore," "Isaac Bryant," "John H. Smith," "Leary Hays,"

"Cherry Wright," "Mack Joiner," "Owen Williams," "Austin Smallwood," and "Lewis Young," CWPF.

48. "Israel Harget" and "William H. Moore," ECU.

49. Capt. J. W. Atwill to Capt. Allen, and Allen to Atwill, 27, 28 December 1864, DOCLEM, 14th USCHA, RG 94, NARA.

50. Special Order No. 15, 10 February 1865; "Endorsement," Maj. W. P. Briggs, 15 May 1865 (regarding McCabe); and Lt. Hallan to Surg. Sitler, 27 December 1864—all in ibid.

51. Simon, *Papers of Ulysses S. Grant*, 13:333; Capt. Allen to Lt. Col. T. J. Kennedy, 11 January 1865, DOCLEM, 14th USCHA, RG 94, NARA (quotation).

52. Morning Reports, Companies A to M, 14th USCHA, RG 94, NA; Capt. Allen to Lt. Col. Edward W. Smith, 11 January 1865, DOCLEM, ibid.; Heslin, "A Yankee Soldier," 112.

53. Special Order No. 23, 4 March 1865, DOCLEM; Morning Reports, Companies A to M; Special Orders No. 26, 10 March 1865, and No. 31, 17 March 1865, DOCLEM—all in 14th USCHA, RG 94, NARA.

54. Special Order No. 37, 23 March 1865, and Circular Order No. 3, 27 March 1865 (quotation), DOCLEM, ibid. The noncommissioned officers assigned to the 14th USCHA included Hendrick and Hayes plus Sgt. William H. Prescott of the 24th Massachusetts Heavy Artillery, Sgt. Nathan Hopkins of the 20th Massachusetts Heavy Artillery, and Cpls. John S. Porter and Oliver Glenn of the 24th Iowa.

55. Circular No. 5, 1 April 1865, DOCLEM, 14th USCHA, RG 94, NARA.

56. "Samuel Stone," CMSR.

57. Lt. Col. Poor to Capt. Judson, 13 April 1865, and Poor to Lt. Col. Campbell, 1, 2 May 1865, DOCLEM, 14th USCHA, RG 94, NARA.

58. "Albert Weideman," CWPF; Weymouth T. Jordan, *North Carolina Troops*, 593, 635; "William H. Hendrick" and "William H. Willey," CWPF.

## CHAPTER SIX

1. The threat of slaves deserting plantations en masse caused some owners to respond with "so-called refugeeing." Slaveowners relocated slaves to a safe refuge. Frequently the more valuable male slaves were moved, leaving their wives and children behind. Many Virginia slaves were sent to the relatively secure areas of North Carolina, while those in coastal areas were shipped to safer parts of the Piedmont. Freehling, *South vs. the South*, 143.

2. The superintendent of black refugees reported in 1864–65 that African American grocers in New Bern had annual incomes of $678; barbers were earning $675, and carpenters, $510. Even masons, seventh on the list, were making more than $400 per year. James, *Annual Report of the Superintendent*, 11–12.

3. For Wild, a settlement for the soldiers' families was both a practical and an ethical act that would stimulate recruitment. Elsewhere, others disagreed. Gen. Alonzo Thomas, recruiting in the Mississippi Valley, feared that "family problems" would hurt recruitment efforts

and informed his officers that the soldiers' dependents had "no claim on the government for rations." The widespread distress of the soldiers' wives and children, plus the uncertainty as to the government's obligations, forced the U.S. War Department to clarify its policy. In July 1864 Maj. Charles W. Foster, Bureau of Colored Troops, stated that according to the military law pertaining to black troops, there was "no provision for their families except freedom to such as owned by disloyal masters." Keith P. Wilson, *Campfires of Freedom*, 185.

4. James, *Annual Report of the Superintendent*, 41–42.

5. Colyer, *Report of the Services Rendered*, 5; Wayne K. Durrill, *War of Another Kind*, 119. Edward Stanly, the military governor of North Carolina, made clear his support for slavery and ordered the return of fugitive blacks to their former owners. Northern officers like Capt. William Hammill of the 9th New York Volunteers helped planters in the Plymouth area retain their slaves and refused aid to any freedman. Elsewhere, Durrill (pp. 104, 106, 108, 119–20) describes several incidents where Federal soldiers raped slave women. Even if the men were later punished, the physical and psychological damage to both the women and the black community had been done.

6. Colyer, *Report of the Services Rendered*, 22. Durrill (*War of Another Kind*, 132–33) describes an attempt by slaves who had escaped down the Roanoke River to return to their plantation and move valuable property and some "70 or 80 negroes," presumably friends and kin, to Plymouth. A group of planters intercepted them and opened fire. Only a few slaves made it to Union-occupied Plymouth.

7. Norris, "'The Yankees Have Been Here!,'" 6 (regarding Potter's cavalrymen); Rawick, *American Slave*, 14:79–81, 372–73; 15:227–28 (quotation, 227). The outcome of Gen. Potter's raid on Greenville, Tarboro, and Rocky Mount is one example of the black desire for freedom and the dangers involved. Three hundred newly freed men, women, and children managed to reach New Bern, but another 160 were reportedly captured and held in Kinston in the wake of the raid. Norris, "'The Yankees Have Been Here!,'" 25.

8. Pvt. Henry A. Clapp to Louise Clapp, 26 March 1863, Clapp Letter Book, TP.

9. Of course, although these men were employed by the army Quartermaster's Department, many of them complained that they were either not paid at all or not paid in a timely fashion.

10. Click, *Time Full of Trial*, 38.

11. Reilly, "Reconstruction through Regeneration," 35–36; Pvt. Henry A. Clapp to Mother, 12 February 1863, Clapp Letter Book, TP.

12. Reilly, "Reconstruction through Regeneration," 36–37 (quotation, 36).

13. Mobley, *James City*, 22 (quotation); Click, *Time Full of Trial*, 11. In addition to the refugee camps at New Bern and Roanoke, there were smaller camps at Beaufort, Carolina City, Washington, and Plymouth. Mobley, *James City*, 23.

14. Berlin, Reidy, and Rowland, *Black Military Experience*, 659; Keith P. Wilson, *Campfires of Freedom*, 183. Support for these camps also came from prejudiced Northerners who feared that displaced and endangered Southern blacks would move into Northern states. In Decem-

ber 1862 Secretary of War Edwin M. Stanton sought to reassure this element in his annual report by promising that "no colored man will leave his home in the South if protected in that home." *OR*, ser. 3, 2:912.

15. Click, *Time Full of Trial*, 2; Ash, *When the Yankees Came*, 152. For a more extensive discussion, see Gerteis, *From Contraband to Freedman*, and Powell, *New Masters*.

16. Berlin et al., *Wartime Genesis of Free Labor: The Upper South*, 42, 349 (first quotation); *North Carolina Times*, 23 January 1864 (second quotation).

17. James, *Annual Report of the Superintendent*, 6–9 (quotation, 6); Mobley, *James City*, 23–25. Because active recruiting continued in and around New Bern throughout the war, some people who had settled in the camp later became eligible for rations after sons, or perhaps husbands, volunteered late in the conflict.

18. James (*Annual Report of the Superintendent*, 4–5) claimed that about fifty blacks were working on nearby Ball Plantation, while others "hire[d] tracts of land a little way out of the towns."

19. James, *Annual Report of the Superintendent*, 10. A large number of blacks in Beaufort complained about such actions in November 1863. As a result, they wrote, they had no money to pay rents and support their families. Berlin et al., *Wartime Genesis of Free Labor: The Upper South*, 166. In 1864 there was an attempt to draft men and send them to Virginia to work on the Dutch Gap Canal.

20. "Sergeant Henry Kent," CWPF.

21. "Archibald Winn," CWPF. Harriet Winn had four children by the start of the war, but she did not indicate how many were alive in 1861 or if she had brought them to New Bern. One of these children, Thomas McCarty, was still living in 1900. It is likely that Archibald Winn was part of the group of able-bodied men taken off Roanoke Island by the government to work in New Bern.

22. In garrison towns first in the Mississippi Valley and then in the Upper South, the arrival of large numbers of dependents forced some local commanders to sanction settlements where families of the soldiers could share their rations and wages while cultivating small gardens or providing a local labor force. Other commanders, especially in the border states, did everything that they could to discourage such settlements. Berlin et al., *Wartime Genesis of Free Labor: The Upper South*, 62–63.

23. Click, *Time Full of Trial*, 12, 42.

24. *OR* 27(3):732.

25. A horrific case was reported in February 1864 at a contraband camp near Memphis. Black women, including the wives of soldiers serving elsewhere, "were herded together like cattle & soldiers went among them picking out as they might fancy here & there one to satiate lust." In the black soldiers' absence, the "wives and daughters who were left became the subjects of brutality." Keith P. Wilson, *Campfires of Freedom*, 183–84.

26. One of the more shocking cases took place at Camp Nelson, Ky., where Federal soldiers

tore down the makeshift refugee camp in late 1864 and evicted the tenants, leaving at least four hundred women and children without shelter in bitterly cold weather. Jones, *Labor of Love*, 50–51; Berlin, Reidy, and Rowland, *Black Military Experience*, 196, 269–70.

27. Colyer, *Report of the Services Rendered*, 6. Roanoke Island also differed from other contraband camps in another important way. Gen. Butler's attempt to have land purchased for the freedpeople ended when Congress gave jurisdiction over abandoned and confiscated land to the Treasury Department, but Butler was able to retain control of Roanoke Island for his Department of Negro Affairs. This spared the colony the ongoing disputes between the Treasury Department and the War Department that were prevalent in other camps. Click, *Time Full of Trial*, 156–57; Berlin, Reidy, and Rowland, *Black Military Experience*, 38.

28. James, *Annual Report of the Superintendent*, 23; Reilly, "Reconstruction through Regeneration," 37.

29. Edward A. Wild to Edward W. Kinsley, 28 July 1863, Kinsley Papers, DU; James, *Annual Report of the Superintendent*, 12–13, 23–24.

30. Byrd, "Dear Father," 70; Dix, "'And Three Rousing Cheers for the Privates,'" 76 (Pennsylvania soldier).

31. Stick, *Outer Banks of North Carolina*, 148 (first quotation); Swint, *Dear Ones at Home*, 139 (second quotation). In some military records, Sanderson is identified as having served in the 40th Massachusetts Regiment. James, *Annual Report of the Superintendent*, 23.

32. The lots were actually 40,000 square feet, not the 43,650 square feet in an actual acre. The surveyors used decimal measurements for ease of operation. James, *Annual Report of the Superintendent*, 25; Reilly, "Reconstruction through Regeneration," 41; Swint, *Dear Ones at Home*, 139; Berlin et al., *Wartime Genesis of Free Labor: The Upper South*, 161.

33. H. E. Rockwell, "The Colony at Roanoke Island," *Freedmen's Advocate* 1 (May 1864), as cited in Click, *Time Full of Trial*, 49; James, *Annual Report of the Superintendent*, 24–25.

34. Reilly, "Reconstruction through Regeneration," 45–46.

35. James, *Annual Report of the Superintendent*, 22, 24.

36. Browning, *From Cape Charles to Cape Fear*, 175, 193; Berlin et al., *Wartime Genesis of Free Labor: The Upper South*, 161–62.

37. *OR* 24(2):166, 244–45.

38. Berlin et al., *Wartime Genesis of Free Labor: The Upper South*, 162–63.

39. Clink, *Time Full of Trial*, 54–55.

40. L. B. Russell to Horace James, 1, 12 June 1863, James M. Barnard to James, 3 December 1863; L. B. Russell to James, 2 June 1863; E. D. Townsend to James, 5 December 1863; and Lt. Col. A. W. Taylor to James, 12 December 1863—all in James Papers, HC; James, *Annual Report of the Superintendent*, 43 (quotation).

41. *OR* 24(2):562, 24(1):911–13.

42. Surg. D. W. Hand to Maj. B. B. Foster, 20 January 1864, James Papers, HC.

43. Ibid.; Horace James, "The Freedmen in North Carolina," 26 January 1864, *Congre-*

*gationalist* 16 (12 February 1864): 25, as cited in Click, *Time Full of Trial*, 67 (quotations). In fact, James chose to pass over various problems facing the islanders, including the poor performance of the shad fisheries.

44. Special Order No. 113, 1 February [?] 1864, James Papers, HC (first quotation); Barrett, *Civil War*, 202–13; Jordan and Thomas, "Massacre at Plymouth," 129; *OR* 33:614 (second quotation), 619, 636, 769 (third quotation), 642 (fourth quotation).

45. Ash, *When the Yankees Came*, 168–69.

46. Rumors soon spread that captured black soldiers had been brutally treated and sometimes killed, while the black civilians had been hauled back to slavery. Jordan and Thomas, "Massacre at Plymouth," 135; James, *Annual Report of the Superintendent*, 35.

47. Swint, *Dear Ones at Home*, 138 (Chase); Elinathan Davis, "Freedmen," *American Missionary* 9 (February 1865): 25–26, as cited in Click, *Time Full of Trial*, 51; Click, *Time Full of Trial*, 92 (one missionary).

48. Col. J. B. Kinsman to Rev. Horace James, 13 February 1864, James Papers, HC; Berlin, Reidy, and Rowland, *Black Military Experience*, 729; Berlin et al., *Wartime Genesis of Free Labor: The Upper South*, 235–36; Click, *Time Full of Trial*, 127, 142–44, 167.

49. James, *Annual Report of the Superintendent*, 30.

50. Horace James to Gen. C. W. Foster, May 12, 1864, and Foster to James, May 28, 1864, Letters Received, Colored Troops Division, J79, 1864, RG 94, NARA.

51. Hood, *One Hundred Years*, 294.

52. Ibid., 290–96.

53. The men claimed that they had been paid only for January and February. The official explanation was that Gen. Weitzel had made repeated attempts to get funds from the chief engineer to pay the men working on Roanoke's fortifications but was unsuccessful.

54. Berlin et al., *Wartime Genesis of Free Labor: The Upper South*, 202–3.

55. *OR* 24(1):915.

56. James, *Annual Report of the Superintendent*, 10; Berlin et al., *Wartime Genesis of Free Labor: The Upper South*, 202–4.

57. "William L. Benson," CWPF. In military records, his surname appears variously as Bemberg, Bembury, Bember, and Bomber.

58. Several family settlements of limited success were set up around Vicksburg in the fall of 1864. Maj. George L. Stearns tried to establish one near Gallatin, Tenn., and Gen. Quincy Gillmore did the same in South Carolina. Keith P. Wilson, *Campfires of Freedom*, 191–93.

59. Reilly, "Reconstruction through Regeneration," 99.

60. Ibid., 100; H. S. Hamilton to Capt. James, 6 June 1866, James Papers, HC.

61. Reilly, "Reconstruction through Regeneration," 78–80.

62. James, *Annual Report of the Superintendent*, 55; Click, *Time Full of Trial*, 139 (last quotation).

63. Berlin et al., *Wartime Genesis of Free Labor: The Upper South*, 231–32. Because the paper

evidence of Boyle's document, located in the records of the Freedmen's Bureau, is in several fragments, it is unclear whether it constituted one petition or a series of petitions written at the same time.

64. Ibid., 232–34.

65. James ignored the fact that the boys may have been in school and that they were taken to New Bern against their parents' wishes.

66. Berlin et al., *Wartime Genesis of Free Labor: The Upper South*, 235–36.

67. Berlin, Reidy, and Rowland, *Black Military Experience*, 729–30.

68. Ibid., 727–28. The concern expressed by the petitioners that the government's goal was "to return these families to their former masters to be supported and cared for by them" was probably a direct result of James's desire to move hundreds to the mainland.

69. Click, *Time Full of Trial*, 143–44. Streeter was found guilty of fraud, "misapplication and embezzlement of public property," and "cruel treatment of the colored women under his care as Ass't. Superintendent of Negro Affairs." He was sentenced to three months' hard labor and received a $500 fine, although the punishment was subsequently reduced to just the fine after James had pleaded long and hard on Streeter's behalf. Ibid., 147–48.

70. *OR* 47(1):154 (McMurray); Click, *Time Full of Trial*, 144–45 (Holman).

71. Reilly, "Reconstruction through Regeneration," 101.

72. McFeely, *Yankee Stepfather*, 79–81.

73. Many freedpeople would have been aware of Gen. Sherman's Field Order No. 15 or Gen. Howard's Circular No. 13, both of which held out the possibility of ex-slaves receiving land. Evidence suggests that the original terms of the land turned over to the refugees were ambiguous but implied a transfer of property subject to the will of the U.S. Congress. The hope of keeping the land they presently possessed caused many freedpeople to downplay the warnings of James and Whittlesey that they would have to pay for it with the money they had earned.

74. Click, *Time Full of Trial*, 225–27; Regimental Descriptive Books, 35th USCT, 36th USCT, and 37th USCT, RG 94, NARA. The multiple ways that many names were spelled and the use of new surnames make exact linking impossible, but veterans of the 35th USCT among the petitioners included Leon Bember (Bembery), George W. Bowser (Bowzer), Benjamin Mann, Henry Martin, Riley, and Field Midget. Several other veterans from the 35th and some from the 37th USCT were also among the petitioners. The names on the two petitions were cross-tabulated with regimental records to make the links. The petitions are part of an index in Click's study of the island.

75. A black sergeant writing from Kinston described an all-too-familiar action. John G. Washington, a prosperous prewar planter living just outside of Kinston, had owned at least four hundred slaves, but "when the Union forces entered this State, he scattered them for hundreds of miles around." Redkey, *Grand Army of Black Men*, 173.

76. Berlin, Reidy, and Rowland, *Black Military Experience*, 244 (Missouri slave woman)—

for similar cases, see pp. 240–43, 245–46, 268–69, 686–88, 697; "Drew Smith," CWPF. Another case where a former owner supported a pension application was that of Pvt. Richard Faircloth, also of the 14th USCHA. "Richard Faircloth," CWPF.

77. Pension application of John Amieny (minor), Rogers Collection, ECU; Pension application of Margaret Blount, Douglas Papers, ECU.

78. Although only a few black women have been identified as having passed themselves off as men, that may be more reflective of poorer records among the USCTs and different social attitudes than it is of the actual number of black women who enlisted. At least one woman, Cathay (or Cathy) Williams, joined the all-black 38th U.S. Infantry and served for almost two years before her discharge for a disability. Blanton and Cook and Leonard argue that a majority of "army women" who enlisted as men in Civil War units were generally working-class and farm women accustomed to a hard life. To that extent, most African American women had the class background to prepare them for the hardships of army life. Blanton and Cook, *They Fought Like Demons*, 6, 23, 67, 123, 164, 55–57; Phillip Thomas Tucker, *Cathy Williams*; Leonard, *All the Daring of the Soldier*, 153–55.

79. Perkins, "Two Years with a Colored Regiment," 534.

80. Schwartz, *A Woman Doctor's Civil War*, 81, 96, 101–2, 104; Perkins, "Two Years with a Colored Regiment," 536 (quotations).

81. General Order No. 10, 21 August 1865, DOCLEM, 14th USCHA, RG 94, NARA; Keith P. Wilson, *Campfires of Freedom*, 69. For the levels of prostitution associated with both Union and Confederate armies, see James I. Robertson, *Soldiers Blue and Gray*, 90, 116–21.

82. General Order No. 9, 28 May 1865, 35th USCT, Regimental Books and Orders, RG 94, NARA; Capt. Atwell to Col. W. Poor, 17 February 1865, DOCLEM, 14th USCHA, RG 94, NARA (quotation).

83. "Eli Mariner," CWPF.

84. "Lamb Baxter," CWPF.

85. Ibid.

86. "Lewis Bass," CWPF.

87. Ibid. The 1st USCT was organized in the District of Columbia in the early summer of 1863 and was transferred to Virginia in July. During the war the regiment lost 180 enlisted men in battle or from disease, but it is not clear from existing records if Isaac Wiggins and his son were among those casualties. Dyer, *Compendium of the War*, 1721. There was an Isaac and a Daniel Lane in Company E, 1st USCT. There were also four men listed whose surname was Wiggins, but none called Isaac or Daniel.

88. Click, *Time Full of Trial*, 219.

## CHAPTER SEVEN

1. Because the War Department had decided to demobilize all of the Northern black regiments as quickly as possible, Southern black soldiers played an increasingly important role in

the occupation forces. Berlin, Reidy, and Rowland, *Black Military Experience*, 733–34; Sefton, *United States Army and Reconstruction*, 50.

2. For the symbolic role of black soldiers during Reconstruction, see Chad L. Williams, "Symbols of Freedom and Defeat."

3. In September 1865 Grant urged Secretary of War Stanton to muster out all of the black soldiers recruited in Northern states. Sefton, *United States Army and Reconstruction*, 52.

4. Lt. Col. Poor to Lt. Col. J. A. Campbell, 13 April 1865; Poor to Capt. Judson, 29 April 1865; Poor to Campbell, 1 May 1865; and Special Order No. 28, 4 May 1865—all in DOCLEM, 14th USCHA, RG 94, NARA.

5. Lt. Col. Poor to Lt. Col. J. A. Campbell, 2 May 1865, ibid.

6. Although most of the men owed money for clothing issued to them, the amounts were generally in the range of $50 to $70. Descriptive List of Deserters, Muster Rolls, 14th USCHA, RG 94, NARA.

7. Lt. Col. Poor to Capt. Goodrich, 13 July 1865, and General Order No. 9, 3 August 1865, DOCLEM, 14th USCHA, RG 94, NARA.

8. Roberta Alexander (*North Carolina Faces the Freedmen*, 130–33) argues convincingly that white acts of violence in postwar North Carolina were less often reported and punished when the alleged victims were black.

9. *OR* 47(1):57, 154; *North Carolina Times*, 24 June 1865.

10. "Charges and Specifications Preferred against 1st Lieutenant Henry Hallam," 24 May 1865, and "Endorsement," 19 July 1865, DOCLEM, 14th USCHA, RG 94, NARA. In supporting Hallam's application for leave, Poor claimed that there were seventeen officers present for duty within the District. This allowed him to include Capt. Frank Smith, who had never actually served with the regiment.

11. Special Order No. 84, 12 September 1865, DOCLEM; Special Order No. 151, 17 October 1865, Order Book, Companies A to M (regarding four freedmen); and Special Order No. 158, 1 November 1865, DOCLEM (regarding Eddins's investigation)—all in 14th USCHA, RG 94, NARA. In a number of cases, local commanders wanted to pursue the possibility of prosecuting Confederate soldiers for alleged atrocities, only to have the senior command ignore their recommendations. Coles, "'Shooting Niggers Sir,'" 83.

12. Sefton, *United States Army and Reconstruction*, 50. William L. Sharkey, provisional governor of Mississippi, also wanted "the black troops to be speedily removed," but his pleas fell on deaf ears. Chad L. Williams, "Symbols of Freedom and Defeat," 216. By the summer of 1865, Virginia was the only Confederate state that did not have black troops among the occupation forces.

13. Longacre, *Army of Amateurs*, 314 (Ord); Gould Diary, 29 April 1865, USAMHI.

14. It was suggested that Sheridan was being hustled out of town so he and Maj. Gen. George G. Meade would not have to share the same reviewing stand. Morris, *Sheridan*, 261.

15. Richter, *The Army in Texas*, 12–13, 18 (quotation); Sheridan, *Personal Memoirs*, 208–10; Morris, *Sheridan*, 261–63. Sheridan believed that it was always best to have more, not less,

force than was needed (Richter, 14). The mass desertion of the Texas soldiers with their arms and equipment was seen as a sign that they planned to renew the struggle at a later date. Cohen-Lack, "Struggle for Sovereignty," 58–59.

16. It was expected that Steele might have to deal with sizable numbers of armed and organized Confederate troops in Mexico under Gen. J. O. Shelby. Weitzel's troops, minus one brigade each at Indianola and Corpus Christi, were to support Steele. Richter, *The Army in Texas*, 17–18; *OR* 48(2):526, 622–23, 643.

17. Richter, *The Army in Texas*, 23. Although more white than black regiments were sent to Texas by the end of 1865, more than 78 percent of the white units had been mustered out.

18. The cavalry brigade of the Twenty-fifth Corps threatened mutiny when it was ordered west. Months later the men of the 48th Ohio Infantry Battalion, after serving some time in Texas, stacked their arms and demanded to be sent home. Richter, *The Army in Texas*, 25–27.

19. O'Brien, "Reconstruction in Richmond," 266–68; Robert J. Zalimas Jr., "Not in Virginia: Black Union Soldiers in Post-war Virginia," paper presented at the annual meeting of the Southern Historical Association, New Orleans, November 1995, 4–5. Ord, a conservative Democrat from Maryland with a Virginian wife, seemed much more sympathetic to Richmond's white population than to his black soldiers. At the very least, he had few concerns about sending troops he deemed inefficient to serve in Texas. *OR* 46(3):990, 1005–6.

20. Cresap, *Appomattox Commander*, 221. Halleck did not explain why troops too undisciplined to use in Virginia would be valuable for a crisis on the frontier. Simon, *Papers of Ulysses S. Grant*, 14:436, 438.

21. Maj. Gen. Godfrey Weitzel to Col. T. S. Bowers, May 16 1865, in Simon, *Papers of Ulysses S. Grant*, 15:72 (Sheridan's view, Weitzel); Joseph T. Wilson, *The Black Phalanx*, 461 (Steele's orders).

22. Frederick W. Browne, "My Service in the U.S. Colored Cavalry," *MOLLUS—Ohio*, 221–23.

23. Gould Diary, 20, 26 May 1865, USAMHI; General Order No. 50, 26 May 1865, LEOB, 36th USCT, RG 94, NARA.

24. Berlin, Reidy, and Rowland, *Black Military Experience*, 729–30.

25. Maj. Hart to Lt. Allen, 3 July 1865, LEOB, and Regimental Descriptive Books (quotations), 36th USCT, RG 94, NARA.

26. Simon, *Papers of Ulysses S. Grant*, 15:53–54, 50–51; Gould Diary, 31 May, 1–6, 14 (quotation) June 1865, USAMHI; *OR* 48(2):1140, 1142, 53:607; Glatthaar, *Forged in Battle*, 219–20.

27. Fremantle, *Three Months in the Southern States*, 8.

28. Gould Diary, 16 June 1865, USAMHI; Norton, *Army Letters*, 209; Simon, *Papers of Ulysses S. Grant*, 15:239–40 (quotation).

29. Sheridan, *Personal Memoirs*, 216–17; Cohen-Lack, "Struggle for Sovereignty," 62–63, 68. Through the 1860s and 1870s, the eastern two-thirds of Texas contained 99 percent of the state's black population. Campbell, "Grass Roots Reconstruction," 103.

30. For the quasi-race war and white attempts to maintain slavery that developed in parts of

Texas, see Smallwood, *Time of Hope, Time of Despair*, 30–35, 125–27. For the activities of the Texas Freedmen's Bureau, see Cohen-Lack, "Struggle for Sovereignty," 73–98.

31. Gould Diary, 19–22 June 1865, USAMHI; Redkey, *Grand Army of Black Men*, 198 (last quotation).

32. Maj. Hart to Maj. Ware, 2 July 1865, LEOB, 36th USCT, RG 94, NARA; Norton, *Army Letters*, 272 (last quotation).

33. Redkey, *Grand Army of Black Men*, 202 (chaplain); Glatthaar, *Forged in Battle*, 220–21; *Private and Official Correspondence of . . . Butler*, 5:671 (Weitzel).

34. At the time of the incident, at least thirteen men in the regiment had died of various diseases—scurvy, fevers, and, most frequently, chronic diarrhea.

35. Glatthaar, *Forged in Battle*, 222–24; "Dpy Clerk" to Lt. Col. D. D. Wheeler, 30 August 1865; Orders of Maj. Gen. Weitzel, 6 September 1865, Muster Rolls of the Field and Staff, 31 August–31 October 1865, 36th USCT, RG 94, NARA; "Alonzo Draper," CMSR.

36. Richter, *The Army in Texas*, 25, 28; Morris, *Sheridan*, 264; Barnett, *Touched by Fire*, 67–70. Indeed, the dramatically different attitudes toward Custer shown first during the war by the men of his Third Cavalry Brigade and then by the postwar soldiers reflect the resentment of many volunteer soldiers who were kept in the army after the summer of 1865. Leckie, *Elizabeth Bacon Custer*, 71.

37. In the second incident, a soldier denied service by a barber threatened to "blow the top of [his] head off." His commanding officer had him bucked and gagged. Richter, *The Army in Texas*, 82, 88–89.

38. Lt. Col. Hart to Lt. Col. D. D. Wheeler, 3 April 1866, LEOB, 36th USCT, RG 94, NARA.

39. Maj. Hart to Brig. Gen. E. D. Townsend, 23 September 1865, ibid.; "Benjamin Pratt," CMSR; General Orders No. 29, 26 November 1864 (first quotation), and No. 30, 27 December 1864 (last quotation), LEOB, 36th USCT, RG 94, NARA.

40. Circular, August 1865, LEOB, 36th USCT, RG 94, NARA.

41. Circular, 8 September 1865; General Orders No. 51, 15 October 1865, and No. 1, 28 February 1866; and Lt. Bacon to Capt. Hiram Allen, 23 March 1866 (quotation)—all in ibid.

42. Simon, *Papers of Ulysses S. Grant*, 16:206; Special Order No. 7, 18 August 1866, General Order No. 5, 19 August 1866, and Lt. Col. Hart to Lt. F. F. Hoyt, 10 April 1866 (quotation), LEOB, 36th USCT, RG 94, NARA; "Sergeant Richard Etheridge," CWPF; Glatthaar, *Forged in Battle*, 222–24. Although most of the regiment remained at Brazos Santiago until October 1866, Company I was stationed at Corpus Christi after 17 May, and Company G was sent to Galveston one month later. Muster Rolls of the Field and Staff, 30 April–August 1866, 36th USCT, RG 94, NARA.

43. Richter, *The Army in Texas*, 25–27. By contrast, members of the 48th Ohio Infantry Battalion mutinied because, unlike other white soldiers, including part of their former regiment, they were not being mustered out. Everyone in the unit, including the battalion commander who had been arrested for insubordination, was soon sent home with an honorable discharge.

44. Dabbs, *The French Army in Mexico*, 141. Others believed that "deserting" black soldiers would be encouraged to join the revolutionary forces under Benito Juárez.

45. Regimental Descriptive Books and Muster Rolls of the Field and Staff, 30 June–31 August 1866, 36th USCT, RG 94, NARA; Simon, *Papers of Ulysses S. Grant*, 16:206 (Sheridan). For all three North Carolina infantry regiments, almost every inspection report described discipline (except for the first months as the units were forming) as being "good."

46. Regimental Descriptive Books, 36th USCT, RG 94, NARA. By October 1866, 48 white regiments and 27 black regiments had mustered out of service in Texas. Only 5 regiments served longer in Texas than the 36th USCT. Richter, *The Army in Texas*, 26.

47. Redkey, *Grand Army of Black Men*, 203 (first two quotations); Muster Rolls of the Field and Staff, 31 August–28 October 1866, 36th USCT, RG 94, NARA; Cohen, *At Freedom's Edge*, 74–75 (Howard).

48. *OR*, ser. 3, 5:114; Sefton, *United States Army and Reconstruction*, 52; Zuczek, *State of Rebellion*, 1–6 ("people's war").

49. Rable, *But There Was No Peace*, 23–28, 84–85; Powers, *Black Charlestonians*, 75 (urban resident); Dr. B. Huger to Thomas L. Wells, 17 September 1865, in Smith, Smith, and Childs, *Mason Smith Family Letters*, 232.

50. Special Orders No. 25 (29 April 1865), No. 32 (18 May 1865), No. 34 (22 May 1865), and No. 35 (23 May 1865), Regimental Order Book, 35th USCT, RG 94, NARA; *New York Times*, 24 July 1865; Emilio, *A Brave Black Regiment*, 313. As long as there have been armies and spare time, there have been fights and brawls between different units. Fights between off-duty soldiers may occur for any number of reasons, including enjoyment of recreational violence. Although in the occupied South racial attitudes likely fueled most conflicts between white and black soldiers, racism may not explain all of them.

51. Gen. Gillmore to Maj. Gen. O. O. Howard, 2 July 1865, Letters Sent, Department of the South, RG 393, NARA, as cited in Zalimas, "Black Union Soldiers," 124; Powers, *Black Charlestonians*, 78; Zalimas, "Black Union Soldiers," 129–31.

52. Annual Returns, December 31, 1864, and December 31, 1865, Muster Rolls and Returns, and Circular, 10 June 1865, Regimental Order Book (Beecher), 35th USCT, RG 94, NARA. In July a firefight broke out between men of the 165th New York Regiment and the 21st USCT. Although senior commanders placed most of the blame on the 165th, that unit's commander, Lt. Col. G. Carr, claimed that his men had been frequently attacked by the black soldiers. Zalimas, "Black Union Soldiers," 126–30.

53. The instructional programs may also have been rooted in the belief that the 35th USCT would continue an active and difficult service for considerable time to come. General Order No. 9, 31 May 1865, Regimental Order Book, 35th USCT, RG 94, NARA; Berlin, Reidy, and Rowland, *Black Military Experience*, 734.

54. Col. J. C. Beecher to Maj. Gen. R. Saxon, 24 March 1865, Regimental Letter Book; Beecher to Col. C. W. Foster, 3 May 1865 (quotation); and Regimental Descriptive Books—all in 35th USCT, RG 94, NA.

55. General Order No. 46, 21 June 1865 (first quotation), and General Order No, 10, 6 June 1865, Regimental Order Book, and Circular, 10 June 1865 (second quotation). One gang of Confederate loyalists that swelled to eighty members in April had operated to within ten miles of Charleston and swore to "kill all the damn niggers." Saville, *The Work of Reconstruction*, 73.

56. It was understandable that Federal officials would take the possibility of guerrilla war seriously, or that they might view the activities of various outlaws as the start of a partisan struggle. Dan Sutherland, in a series of articles, has demonstrated that guerrilla warfare was waged more widely and more bitterly than most Civil War historians have acknowledged until recently. Union officials, however, had few illusions about the possibility of a bloody, protracted partisan struggle after the conventional forces had laid down their arms. The irony was that while Southern officials, late in the war, were trying to restrain partisan bands, Federal authorities had developed a hard-edged counterguerrilla policy of retaliation that it was willing to use at the start of Reconstruction. Sutherland, "Without Mercy," "Sideshow No Longer," and "Guerrilla Warfare."

57. Smith et al., *Mason Smith Family Letters*, 232 (Huger); Col. J. C. Beecher to Capt. H. White, 31 July 1865, Regimental Order Book, and "Description List, Company G," Regimental Descriptive Books (regarding Jackson), 35th USCT, RG 94, NARA; Rutledge, "Elizabeth Jamison's Tale of the War," 335. Warned that locals would attack the train and destroy his regiment, Beecher had stationed Sgt. Fred Brown and four privates in the engine. During the trip someone uncoupled the passenger cars as the train passed over a high trestle bridge, and hidden gunmen opened fire on the trapped soldiers. Brown's quick action in forcing the engineer to return and recouple the train saved the regiment from disaster. Glatthaar, *Forged in Battle*, 215–16.

58. The order, drafted with the help of Secretary of War Stanton, set aside abandoned lands on the mainland and the Sea Islands in an area south from Charleston to St. John's Island in northern Florida for the settlement and cultivation of former slaves. Marszalek, *Sherman*, 314–15.

59. Circular, 10 June 1865, Regimental Letter Book, 35th USCT, RG 94, NARA.

60. "Circular of Instructions respecting Contracts between Planters and Freedmen," ibid.

61. Special Order No. [?], 28 June 1865, Regimental Order Book, 35th USCT, RG 94, NARA.

62. Saville, *The Work of Reconstruction*, 76, 77.

63. General Orders No. 12, 19 August 1865, and No. 15, 1 September 1865, Regimental Order Book, 35th USCT, RG 94, NARA (Beecher); Smith, *Mason Smith Family Letters*, 230–31 (some white South Carolinians); Schwartz, *A Woman Doctor's Civil War*, 198 (friends of Beecher).

64. General Order No. 23, 9 October 1865, Regimental Order Book, 35th USCT, RG 94, NARA.

65. Circular, 2 December 1865, ibid.

66. Circular, 17 December 1865, ibid. (clarification); General Order No. 32, 20 December 1865, ibid. (further clarification); James C. Beecher to M. N. Rice, 7 February 1866, Letters and Reports Received relating to Freedmen and Civil Affairs, Ser. 4112, 2nd Military District, RG 393, Tt. 1, as cited in Saville, *The Work of Reconstruction*, 182.

67. Smith, *Mason Smith Family Letters*, 265–69.

68. Saville, *The Work of Reconstruction*, 83.

69. Col J. Beecher to Brig. Gen. O. H. Hart, 21 May 1866, Regimental Letter Book, 35th USCT, RG 94, NARA.

70. For the widespread belief that black soldiers would collaborate with freedmen to start an insurrection at the end of 1865, see Hahn, "'Extravagant Expectations' of Freedom," and Chad L. Williams, "Symbols of Freedom and Defeat."

71. Sefton, *United States Army and Reconstruction*, 15, 18; Schofield, *Forty-six Years in the Army*, 346; Sefton, *United States Army and Reconstruction*, 25 (first quotation); *OR* 47(3):461–63 (Schofield). Schofield objected to the suggestion that the old state constitution, amended in 1835, be followed because that document did not prevent blacks from voting.

72. McDonough, *Schofield*, 367–404.

73. Hawley had initially garrisoned the city with troops from Connecticut, New Hampshire, and New York. Wood, "Port Town at War," 233.

74. Lee, *New Hanover County*, 77–78; Boatner, *Civil War Dictionary*, 12, 387–88.

75. Maj. Weinmann to Capt. Edgerton, 27 July 1865, LEOB; Special Order No. 44, 29 July 1865, LEOB; Special Orders No. 47 and No. 48, 4 August 1865, LEOB; and Special Order No. 44, 22 June 1865, Regimental Unbound Papers—all in 37th USCT, RG 94, NARA.

76. Alexander, *North Carolina Faces the Freedmen*, 138.

77. *Wilmington Herald*, 10 July 1865; Alexander, *North Carolina Faces the Freedmen*; *History of the Thirty-seventh Regiment*, 80 (last quotation).

78. Berlin, Reidy, and Rowland, *Black Military Experience*, 738–39.

79. Muster Rolls, Companies G and D, 31 December 1864–30 June 1865, and Company B, 30 April–30 June 1865; Maj. Weinmann to Capt. Edgerton, 5 August 1865, LEOB—all in 37th USCT, RG 94, NARA. These problems seem to have been at least partially solved by August, when conditions were again rated as "good."

80. General Order No. 32, 27 March 1866, LEOB, 37th USCT, RG 94, NARA. Joseph Glatthaar (*Forged in Battle*, 221) suggests that, indeed, some officers, with an eye to their postwar lives, began to think of ways of defrauding the black soldiers of their money.

81. Gen. E. A. Wild to [?], 28 April 1864, Wild Papers, USAMHI. Chamberlain did not officially step down until 16 June 1865. Official Army Register, 209; "Forwarded," 20 October 1864, LEOB, 37th USCT, RG 94, NARA.

82. Special Order No. 146, 14 September 1865, Regimental Unbound Papers; Col. Goff to Col. Foster, 2 April 1865, and Maj. Weinmann to Foster, 5 August 1865, LEOB—all in 37th USCT, RG 94, NARA. James M. Mellon, a first lieutenant, commanded Company G and, in late August, was also given responsibility for Company I. Two weeks later, 2nd Lt. Joseph

Randall assumed command of Companies F and E. Special Orders No. 56, 28 August 1865, and No. 65, 12 September 1865, LEOB, ibid.

83. Col. Goff to Col. Foster, 2 April 1865, LEOB, ibid.; *Official Army Register*, 209.

84. Col. Goff to Col. Foster, 26 June 1865, LEOB, 37th USCT, RG 94, NARA. In some records the sergeant appears as John H. Rhodes, perhaps a result of combining one of his middle initials with his surname.

85. Berlin, Reidy, and Rowland, *Black Military Experience*, 347–48 (Ames); General Order No. 10, 1 May 1866, LEOB, 37th USCT, RG 94, NARA. 168. From January to June 1865, at least ten commissions were issued to African Americans. Glatthaar, *Forged in Battle*, 179.

86. Col. Goff to Lt. Col. J. A. Campbell, 29 May 1865, and Maj. Weinmann to Capt. Edgerton, 5 August 1865, LEOB, 37th USCT, RG 94, NARA.

87. Of course, in hindsight we realize that Reconstruction was a transition from war to peace and not truly a time of peace.

88. "James M. Mellon," CMSR, Lt. Col. Chamberlain to Maj. R. S. Davis, 14 June 1864, LEOB, and Special Order No. 110, 4 May 1866, Regimental Unbound Papers—all in 37th USCT, RG 94, NARA. *History of the Thirty-seventh Regiment*, 69. Glatthaar (*Forged in Battle*, 113–15, 222–24) outlines a number of cases of mutiny for reasons similar to those that motivated soldiers of the 37th USCT.

89. General Order No. 185, Regimental Papers, 37th USCT, RG 94, NARA.

90. Williams (whose real name was John F. Nolan) had been a second lieutenant for less than three months when the mutiny occurred. "Edward Williams," CMSR.

91. "Information Forwarded," 13 June 1864, LEOB, 37th USCT, RG 94, NARA; "Samuel D. Edgar," CMSR (quotations).

92. Capt. Farnsworth to Gen. Campbell, 23 May 1866, and Gen. Goff to [Farnsworth], 15 June 1866, Regimental Papers, 37th USCT, RG 94, NARA.

93. Sefton, *United States Army and Reconstruction*, 29–30; General Order No. 36, 8 November 1865, LEOB, 37th USCT, RG 94, NARA (quotations).

94. Simon, *Papers of Ulysses S. Grant*, 15:586–87 (memorandum); Col. Goff to Col. J. A. Campbell, 10 March 1866, LEOB, 37th USCT, RG 94, NARA; *History of the Thirty-seventh Regiment*, 83, 111, 125.

95. Gen. Goff to Col. J. A. Campbell, 30 March 1866, LEOB, 37th USCT, RG 94, NARA.

96. Lt. F. H. Moore to Col. J. A. Campbell, 5 March 1866; Maj. C. Nietzsche to Campbell, 12 March 1866; Capt. Charles F. Browne to Campbell, 12 March 1866; and Capt. S. B. Huested to Campbell, 18 February 1866, Regimental Unbound Papers—all in 37th USCT, RG 94, NARA.

97. *History of the Thirty-seventh Regiment*, 129; Simon, *Papers of Ulysses S. Grant*, 16:8–9 (quotation).

98. Lt. G. W. Singer to Maj. Weinmann, 12 January 1866, Regimental Unbound Papers (quotations); General Order No. 13, 29 June 1866; Special Orders No. 595, 30 November 1866, and No. 104, 28 February 1867—all in 37th USCT, RG 94, RG 94, NARA.

99. General Court-Martial Order No. 74, 26 May 1866, Regimental Unbound Papers, ibid.

100. Lt. J. M. Cloin to Gen. Goff, 24 August 1866, LEOB, 37th USCT, RG 94, NARA. If Howard faced a court-martial, the records have been lost.

101. *Official Army Register*, 209; *History of the Thirty-seventh Regiment*, 73. Goff, who had described Cutler as "an able and efficient officer," recommended Cutler for the promotion in March 1866. Col. Goff to Col. Foster, 16 March 1866, LEOB, 37th USCT, RG 94, NARA.

102. Maj. William A. Cutler to Gen. Campbell, 5 June 1866, LEOB; Muster Rolls of the Field and Staff, 30 June–31 August 1866; and General Order No. 39, 5 September 1866, Regimental Unbound Papers—all in 37th USCT, RG 94, NARA. Ironically, Miller had been appointed commissary sergeant only in May, after Charles Eady had been reduced to the ranks from that position. Eady had joined the regiment at Wilmington in March 1865 and had been appointed commissary sergeant in November. General Order No. 10, 1 May 1866, LEOB, ibid.

103. General Order No. 85, 8 August 1866, ibid.

104. General Order No. 19, 26 July 1866, and Gen. Goff to Hon. E. M. Stanton (quotations), 22 July 1866, ibid.

105. In March 1866 Grant had recommended to Secretary of War Stanton that black regiments be reduced, leaving, in the case of North Carolina and South Carolina, only one regiment per state. Simon, *Papers of Ulysses S. Grant*, 16:115; Alexander, *North Carolina Faces the Freedmen*, 9.

106. Special Order No. 43, 29 September 1866, and Gen. Goff to Maj. D. T. Wells, 29 September 1866, LEOB, 37th USCT, RG 94, NARA. Maj. Cutler was on leave until 7 October and Lt. Gray was not due back until 20 October. Gen. Goff to Maj. D. T. Wells, 1 October 1866, ibid.

107. Gen. Goff to Maj. D. T. Wells, 2 October 1866, Regimental Unbound Papers, 37th USCT, RG 94, NARA.

108. Maj. Cutler to Maj. D. T. Wells, 25 January 1867, LEOB, ibid.

109. Bvt. Maj. Gen. E. A. Carr to Maj. D. T. Wells, 11 February 1867, Regimental Unbound Papers, ibid.

110. Bvt. Maj. Charles Whitney to Maj. D. T. Wells, 4 February 1867, LEOB, 37th USCT, RG 94, NARA.

111. Maj. Charles H. Whitney to Maj. D. T. Wells, 11 February 1867, ibid.


CHAPTER EIGHT

1. Redkey, *Grand Army of Black Men*, 167.

2. Frederick Douglass, "Address for the Promotion of Colored Enlistments" (6 July 1863), *Douglass' Monthly*, August 1863, in Philip Foner, *Life and Writings of Frederick Douglass*, 3:365. The best study of these black veterans argues convincingly that, more than anything else, the men fought for freedom and recognition of their "manhood." Shaffer, *After the Glory*.

3. Redkey, *Grand Army of Black Men*, 173 (quotation); *History of the Thirty-seventh Regiment*, 129; "Lucas Creech, (Bond)," CWPF.

4. The most comprehensive work on black veterans, Don Shaffer's *After the Glory*, looks at issues from a national perspective. Shaffer examines the lives of 1,044 randomly sampled veterans plus those of another 200 ex-soldiers with notable postwar careers. Other works with material on Southern black veterans include Rabinowitz, *Southern Black Leaders*; Litwack and Meir, *Black Leaders in the Nineteenth Century*; Kolchin, *First Freedom*; Alexander, *North Carolina Faces the Freedmen*; and Reidy, *From Slavery to Agrarian Capitalism*. For a detailed study of black veterans in the decades after the Civil War, see Shaffer, "Marching On."

5. Logue, *To Appomattox and Beyond*, 84–85. Examples of recent scholarship on black regiments include Horstman, "The African-American's Civil War"; Versalle Fredrick Washington, "Eagles on Their Buttons: The Fifth Regiment of Infantry, United States Colored Troops in the American Civil War," published as *Eagles on Their Buttons: A Black Infantry Regiment in the Civil War*; Bryant, "A Model Regiment"; Warner, "Crossed Sabers"; Bowley, *A Boy Lieutenant*; Edward A. Miller, *Black Civil War Soldiers*; and Hutchins, "'Just Learning to Be Men.'"

6. Eric Foner, *Reconstruction*, 9; Glatthaar, *Forged in Battle*, 248, 237; Logue, *To Appomattox and Beyond*, 87. In Rhode Island, for example, the unemployment rate of black veterans was five times as high as that of black civilians (see Logue, 87).

7. This group offers the advantage of being large enough to be representative but small enough to be examined in detail. Some 5,035 recruits were officially credited to North Carolina, but recruiters from Northern states such as Massachusetts, Rhode Island, New York, and Connecticut all enlisted African Americans in North Carolina who were credited to the Northern states. See Berlin, Reidy, and Rowland, *Black Military Experience*, 12. For this study, the first step was to create a database of all soldiers in the four black regiments from the various military records, roster lists, military description books, and morning reports held at NARA. Then an ongoing sample of pension records of these veterans was incorporated into the database. The pension information comes from two different repositories. Data were selected from 195 Civil War Pension Files held at NARA and from 110 pension applications handled by black lawyer Frederick C. Douglas. The pension applications of black veterans in the New Bern area are now held in three collections at ECU's Joyner Library. The combination of information allowed for linkages and verification by the National Census of 1870 and the special Civil War veterans' census of 1890, as well as by any data appearing in printed accounts and manuscripts. It was then possible to identify veterans who had achieved success during Reconstruction. Of course, many black veterans either changed their names or had their names recorded in different ways. This, plus the paucity of extant records concerning these men, makes certain linkages very difficult.

8. Although the number of survivors amounted to about 6 or 7 percent of the state's total adult black male population, in the eastern counties where they were to be found, veterans constituted perhaps as much as 20 percent of the adult black male population.

9. The exceptions were the officers in the artillery regiment, who came from a wide range of Northern states.

10. The disease mortality rate for all African American soldiers in the Civil War was about one in seven, while the rate for white Union soldiers was one in seventeen. See Washington, "Eagles on Their Buttons," 186.

11. *OR*, ser. 3, 5:2 (first quotation); Redkey, *Grand Army of Black Men*, 202 (second quotation); Col. J. Beecher to Brig. Gen. O. H. Hart, May 21, 1866, Regimental Letter Book, 35th USCT, RG 94, NARA.

12. The best nineteenth-century census probably missed about 10 percent of the population. Moreover, the parts of society marginalized by class or ethnicity, as well as transients and young adults, constituted a disproportional segment of those undetected. In 1870 the census operated under very difficult circumstances in the Southern states, and the results reflect those problems. See Richard M. Reid, "The 1870 United States Census."

13. "Daniel Hill" and "Jeremiah Gray," CWPF.

14. "America Baum" and "Lucas Creech (Bond)," CWPF.

15. The year 1890 was selected because the Civil War veterans' census of 1890 picked up most, if not all, of the remaining veterans. See Richard M. Reid, "Residency and Black Veterans in North Carolina, 1865–1890," paper presented at the annual meeting of the Southern Historical Association, New Orleans, November 1995.

16. It was initially postulated that active military campaigning, such as that experienced by the 35th USCT, might have contributed to greater physical disability after the war. Pension records suggest, however, that the men of the 14th USCHA had as many health problems, or at least they reported as many, as the soldiers in the other regiments.

17. It is very difficult to accurately assess the number of veterans of the four regiments who were living in North Carolina at any given time. The 1870 census underenumerated blacks by probably as much as 20 percent; another significant number of veterans, perhaps also 20 percent, used at least two different names through this period. The problems of locating the North Carolina veterans in other Southern states are even greater. See Richard M. Reid, "The 1870 United States Census," 488–99.

18. The author made a random selection of from 250 to 300 soldiers mustered out from each regiment and then attempted to locate the men in the general manuscript census of 1870, as follows:

| REGIMENT | MEN MUSTERED OUT | VETERANS LOCATED IN 1870 |
| --- | --- | --- |
| 35th USCT | 278 | 105 (37.8%) |
| 36th USCT | 243 | 98 (40.3%) |
| 37th USCT | 301 | 139 (46.2%) |
| 14th USCHA | 251 | 124 (49.4%) |

19. The Civil War veterans' census of 1890 attempted to locate all Union veterans by state, giving their postal location and their former units, as follows:

| REGIMENT | MEN MUSTERED OUT | VETERANS LOCATED IN 1890 |
|---|---|---|
| 35th USCT | 881 | 134 (15.2%) |
| 36th USCT | 578 | 118 (20.4%) |
| 37th USCT | 796 | 211 (26.5%) |
| 14th USCHA | 883 | 220 (25.0%) |

20. Cohen, *At Freedom's Edge*, 69, 85, 187–97. In addition to the well-known plans to re-settle Southern blacks in Liberia, Kansas, and Indiana, labor agents recruited men in North Carolina for railroad work in other Southern states. Because in most cases only the leaders' names were recorded, it is impossible to assess accurately the number of veterans involved in each group. Of course, even the men of the 14th USCHA may have been more willing to emigrate than North Carolina blacks who did not serve in the military. In other words, the act of enlisting itself may have indicated a greater willingness to take risks.

21. Most of veterans found outside the state were located because they, or people connected to them, submitted claims to the government for pensions, bounties, or back pay.

22. "Louis Belk (alias Williams)," CWPF.

23. "Henry Clarke," CWPF.

24. "Simon McIver (alias Bostic)" and "Noah Willis," CWPF. 37. "Abram Bissel (alias Har-well, Howell)," CWPF. "George Gaylord Pension Application," Douglas Papers, ECU. East Carolina University has three manuscript collections holding veterans' pension applications handled by lawyer Frederick C. Douglas. John Jack had testified in the pension application of Noah Willis.

25. "Lucas Bond (alias Creech)," CWPF.

26. "Nicholas Clairborne" and "Nathaniel Spellman (alias Thompson)," CWPF. For the women on Roanoke Island, see Click, *Time Full of Trial*.

27. For postwar interest in the "African Dream," see Cohen, *At Freedom's Edge*, 138–67.

28. Andrews Powers, age twenty, of Martin County, had enlisted in 1863. Muster Rolls and Returns, Regimental Letter Book, 35th USCT, RG 94, NARA.

29. The 1870 census for North Carolina lists a Peter Mountain of Windsor Township, Bertie County, as having the same age and complexion as that of Pvt. Peter Mountain, Company I, 35th USCT. See "Applications for Passage," ACSP.

30. "Applications for Passage," ACSP; Almasy, *North Carolina 1890 Civil War Veterans Census*, 219. The center of recruitment was Lenoir County, home to a large number of veterans of the 14th USCHA and some from the 35th USCT. See Cohen, *At Freedom's Edge*, 176, 187–85.

31. The total is compiled from Almasy, *North Carolina 1890 Civil War Veterans Census*.

32. Work on the *North Carolina Civil War Veterans Census of 1890*, a supplementary docu-ment, began with lists from the Grand Army of the Republic and responses from newspaper inquiries; it augmented that information with thousands of letters to locate men missed by the enumerators. The census presupposed that veterans would identify themselves as such. It is possible that some black veterans living in central or western North Carolina did not wish to

be identified as former soldiers. If so, it would support the argument of a hostile climate in the northeastern counties.

33. For example, Sampson, Wayne, Nash, and Halifax counties together had provided 154 recruits to the four black regiments, chiefly after April 1864. Of these counties, only Halifax, with almost 40, had a significant number of veterans in 1890.

34. This is consistent with Donald Shaffer's (*After the Glory*, 50–51) finding that black veterans were more urbanized than other African Americans. It also explains the presence of some eighty veterans who were living in Wilmington in 1890, although few recruits had come from New Hanover County.

35. Almasy, *North Carolina 1890 Civil War Veterans Census*, 20–26; John David Smith, *Black Judas*, 36 (quotations).

36. The list of eighteen posts compiled by the Library of Congress cited the posts organized by 27 July 1871. The National Headquarters for the Sons of the Union Veterans of the Civil War has compiled the names of seventeen posts in North Carolina, including four not cited by the Library of Congress. Existing records seldom make clear if a post had white and black members or if it was segregated.

37. Stuart McConnell (*Glorious Contentment*, 213–15) has observed that by having two posts in one town, white veterans did not have to integrate their posts.

38. According to records of the Sons of Union Veterans of the Civil War (SUVCW), at least four posts were established at one time or another at Elizabeth City: Thomas F. Meagher Post 3, Harrison Phoebus Post 13, E.O.C. Ord Post 16, and Fletcher Post 20.

39. McConnell, *Glorious Contentment*, 71 (first quotation), 213–15; Blight, *Race and Reunion*, 2–5, 194; Shaffer, *After the Glory*, 7, 189; Fleche, "'Shoulder to Shoulder as Comrades Tried,'" 177–81 (second quotation, 179); Gannon, "The Won Cause," 25 (last quotation).

40. Gannon, "The Won Cause," 8 (quotation), 161–63, 166; *History of the Thirty-seventh Regiment*, 72; Fleche, "'Shoulder to Shoulder as Comrades Tried,'" 197 (Warner).

41. Reaves and Tetterton, *Strength through Struggle*, 3, 436. Lists of GAR posts place the Thomas F. Meagher Post 3 in Elizabeth City, although the most prominent black veterans at the celebration were Wilmington residents. McLaurin had served in the Union navy during the war. He later became very active in the Republican Party and represented New Hanover County in the House of Representatives from 1872 to 1874.

42. Gannon, "The Won Cause," 109.

43. George Lawrence Mabson was born in Wilmington in 1846, the mulatto son of a prominent white resident. He moved to Boston in 1854 and during the war served first in the navy and then in the 5th Massachusetts Cavalry. After the war, Mabron received a law degree from Howard University and was active in the Republican Party. Reaves and Tetterton, *Strength through Struggle*, 331–32, 431–32; *Wilmington Morning Star*, 25 January 1884.

44. Gannon, "The Won Cause," 61–64, 171.

45. Ibid., 78–79 (inspection report); "George Burden, (alias Burden)," CWPF; Gannon, "The Won Cause," 315.

46. The owning and wearing of pistols, in the face of hostile white civilians, forced Union commanders to try, unsuccessfully, to stop the practice. See General Order No. 10, 9 May 1864, Letters, Endorsements, and Order Books, 36th USCT, RG 95, NARA. The black veterans returning to Hertford County believed that they were being targeted because they had served in the Union army. See Berlin, Reidy, and Rowland, *Black Military Experience*, 801–2.

47. Evans, *Ballots and Fence Rails*, 68–73, 77, 81, 99; Reaves and Tetterton, *Strength through Struggle*, 199.

48. Reaves and Tetterton, *Strength through Struggle*, 334–35; *Wilmington Morning Star*, 10 December 1873.

49. Reilly, "Reconstruction through Regeneration," 170. Counties with the greatest recorded violence included Rutherford, Alamance, Caswell, Lincoln, Cleveland, Gaston, Mecklenburg, Guilford, Orange, Randolph, Montgomery, and Moore. See Crow, Escott, and Hatley, *African Americans in North Carolina*, 89–91.

50. Evans (*Ballots and Fence Rails*, 98–102) credits local black militia led by Union veterans for resisting white terrorists who were trying to intimidate black voters in Wilmington in 1868.

51. *New York Daily Tribune*, 19 May 1865 (quotation); Alexander, *North Carolina Faces the Freedmen*, 16; Dennett, *The South As It Is*, 148. New Bern had been the center of black recruitment, and many of the soldiers' families remained there or in James City during the war. Veterans of the 14th USCHA had begun returning to the area by December 1865.

52. Political involvement for the veterans, though difficult, would not have been impossible, especially if they had had the assistance of Republican leaders and Reconstruction officials. After all, by December 1865 hundreds of veterans from the 14th USCHA were living in the state and could have become politically active.

53. Andrews, *The South since the War*, 125. When Foster was recommended as an election registrar in 1867, he was described as "intelligent." Records of the Bureau of Refugees, Freedmen, and Abandoned Lands, RG 105, reel 32, NARA.

54. On Galloway's career, see Cecelski, "Abraham H. Galloway," 43–72, and *Waterman's Song*, chap. 7.

55. Hood, *One Hundred Years*, 292–96.

56. *Weekly North Carolina Standard* (Raleigh), October 17, 1866.

57. It is possible, given the limited information known of some of the representatives, that a few more veterans may have been elected, because names and approximate ages were similar to those of several legislators. Significantly, if these men were veterans, they chose to achieve electoral success without invoking their military past.

58. The former servants include Hawkins W. Carter, who served in the North Carolina House of Representatives (1874–80) and the North Carolina Senate (1881–83), and Isham Sweat, who was elected to the House of Representatives from Cumberland County in 1868 for one term. In addition, James H. Jones, formerly the personal servant of President Jefferson Davis, was a Raleigh alderman from 1873 to 1889.

59. Kenzer, *Enterprising Southerners*, 87.

60. Alexander, *North Carolina Faces the Freedmen*, 23–24, 84–85; Eric Foner, *Reconstruction*, 116, and *Freedom's Lawmakers*, xv–xxvi; Lowe, "Local Black Leaders"; Drago, "Georgia's First Black Voter Registrars." In the four regiments, from 7.5 to 14 percent of the men enlisted were recorded as other than "black" or "dark," and about 90 percent of all the soldiers had listed their occupation as laborer or farmer. The characteristics of the earliest recruits are described in Richard M. Reid, "Raising the African Brigade," 283–85.

61. Among the limited number of black veterans selected as registrars were Sgts. Hezekiah Foster of the 14th USCHA, John Monroe of the 35th USCT, Richard Etheridge and Frank James of the 36th USCT, and Charles Sheppherd of the 37th USCT. Because first sergeants were responsible for some paperwork, two possible reasons explain their selection. In the case of Frank Pieson, a "printer" and "late pvt. 37th USCT," who was one of the twenty-one black registrars in Ware County, or Reuben Mezell (Mazell), a teacher and late private in the 35th USCT, occupation may have been more important than service. See Registers and Reports, RG 105, NARA.

62. The "Black Second" was the creation, in 1872, of the Conservative-controlled legislature. By gerrymandering the district in such a way as to maximize the black vote here, the Conservatives hoped to emasculate black electoral strength in other districts. See Anderson, *Race and Politics*.

63. Crow, Escott, and Hatley, *African Americans in North Carolina*, 109. Although Eric Foner lists O'Hara as born in New York and removed to the West Indies as a child, George W. Reid locates his birth in the West Indies with his family moving to New York in 1850. Both agree that he was educated in New York City. See Eric Foner, *Freedom's Lawmakers*, 96–97, and George W. Reid, "Four in Black."

64. Washington, "Eagles on Their Buttons," 190.

65. By the summer of 1864, between thirty and forty troops in the 35th USCT were physically incapacitated, although Col. Beecher was having great difficulty obtaining their discharges. By the end of the year, forty-four men had been discharged for various reasons. The other three North Carolina regiments reflect the same pattern. Col. J. C. Beecher to Lt. A. Coates, 13 July 1864; Beecher to Capt. M. Bailey, June 29, 1864; and Annual Returns, December 31, 1864, Regimental Letter Book, 35th USCT, RG 95, NARA.

66. "Isaac Bryant" and "Allen Smith," CWPF.

67. "James C. Beecher," CWPF.

68. "Charles Oats," CWPF. Apparently Oats either wandered away from camp or deserted shortly before the regiment was discharged.

69. "James H. Moore" and "George Burden (alias Berden)," CWPF.

70. "Washington Newby," CWPF.

71. Shaffer, *After the Glory*, 106.

72. "Chester Amieny," CWPF.

73. "John Banks" and "Peter Downing," CWPF.

74. "Lucas Bond (alias Lewis Creech)," CWPF. Although the relevant records at Kinston had been destroyed, leaving no hard evidence of his marriage to Philis Cox, the examiner found other evidence that was persuasive.

75. James, *Annual Report of the Superintendent*, 11–12. Horace James received information from 305 blacks involved in trades and professions in the New Bern area after he had posted a request for the data. The average reported incomes were highest for grocers ($678), barbers ($675), and carpenters ($510), but average incomes also were significant for blacksmiths ($468), coopers ($418), and masons ($402).

76. On attracting white customers and the disadvantage of starting a business after the war, see Kenzer, *Enterprising Southerners*, 38–49.

77. "William Latham," CWPF.

78. By late 1864, Northern recruiting agents were offering black recruits state bounties of several hundred dollars. In 1873 a law retroactively equalized bounties for black soldiers with those of white recruits.

79. Vogel, "Redefining Reconciliation," 72; McConnell, *Glorious Contentment*, 152–53 (quotation). In 1904 Roosevelt had issued Pension Order No. 78, which defined as disabled all veterans over the age of sixty-one. In the next decade, Congress passed bills raising the pension levels and making it easier for widows to qualify for pensions (see Vogel, 85).

80. Shaffer, *After the Glory*, 126–27.

81. Mobley, *Ship Ashore*, 94–98; "Richard Etheridge," CWPF; Eric Foner, *Freedom's Lawmakers*, 68; Kenzer, *Enterprising Southerners*, 115.

82. None of the veterans, for instance, show up among the most prosperous North Carolina blacks. See Schweninger, *Black Property Owners*, 295–300.

## CONCLUSION

1. The address, "In Our Youth Our Hearts Were Touched with Fire," was delivered on 30 May 1884, at Keene, N.H., before the John Sedgwick Post of the Grand Army of the Republic. Eleven years later Holmes delivered another remarkable Memorial Day address, "The Soldier's Faith," which helped get him nominated to the U.S. Supreme Court. Posner, *The Essential Holmes*, 80–87.

2. Redkey, *Grand Army of Black Men*, 167.

3. Bruce Levine (*Confederate Emancipation*) has recently argued that the Confederate emancipation scheme was driven by military necessity, had an ulterior motive, faced extraordinary opposition from many white Southerners, and came too late to make a difference. Less than a year before, the mere discussion of arming slaves had been potentially so divisive that Jefferson Davis suppressed Gen. Patrick Cleburne's "Memorial" and swore all involved to secrecy. Although Levine is persuasive, men such as Davis supported the arming of slaves only after they had become convinced that blacks could make effective soldiers. Levine also suggests that Confederate officials grudgingly agreed to arm their slaves, in part, as a way to maintain racial

and class hegemony and to keep them in a form of peonage. See also Symonds, *Stonewall of the West*, 186–91, 194–95.

4. William Hannibal Thomas's bitterness would expand in later years as he became a vitriolic Negrophobe. John David Smith, *Black Judas*, 36, 157–61.

5. Fox, *Service of the Fifty-fifth Regiment*, 10; Gordon, *War Diary*, 275.

# BIBLIOGRAPHY

## PRIMARY SOURCES

### Manuscripts

Boston, Massachusetts
  Massachusetts Historical Society
    Edward W. Kinsley Papers
    H. H. Mitchell Papers
    James A. Munroe Papers
    John Owen Papers
Brookline, Massachusetts
  Public Library of Brookline
    Edward Augustus Wild Papers
Carlisle Barracks, Carlisle, Pennsylvania
  U.S. Army Military History Institute
    Henry Burrell Papers
    Civil War Miscellaneous Collection
    *Civil War Times Illustrated* Collection
    Lorenzo Gould Diary
    John Habberton Papers
    Charles Warren Hutt Diary
    William W. Lind Papers
    Massachusetts MOLLUS Collection
    Joseph J. Scroggs Diary
    Edward A. Wild Papers
Chapel Hill, North Carolina
  Southern Historical Collection,
        University of North Carolina
    Edmund J. Cleveland Diary
    Federal Soldiers Letters
    Eben Thomas Hale Papers

    William A. Hoke Papers
    William Penneman Papers
    Zebulon Baird Vance Papers
    Edward A. Wild Papers
Charleston, South Carolina
  South Carolina Historical Society
    Henry Orlando Marcy Papers
Durham, North Carolina
  Special Collections, William R. Perkins
        Library, Duke University
    Edward Wilkinson Kinsley Papers
    Charles H. Remick Papers
Greenville, North Carolina
  Joyner Library, East Carolina University
    Frederick C. Douglas Papers
    William H. Harper Collection
    William L. Horner Collection
    Richard E. Rogers Collection
Ithaca, New York
  Kroch Library Rare and Manuscript
        Collections, Cornell University
    Burt Green Wilder Papers
    Civil War Diaries
New Bern, North Carolina
  Tryon Palace Historic Sites and
        Gardens, Collection Branch
    Henry A. Clapp Letter Book

New York, New York
  New-York Historical Society
    Walter Stone Poor Letters
Raleigh, North Carolina
  North Carolina Department of
    Archives and History
    Alfred England Papers
Washington, D.C.
  Library of Congress
    American Colonization Society
      Papers
  National Archives and Records
    Administration
    Record Group 15
      Civil War Pension Files
    Record Group 94
      Compiled Military Service Records
      Description, Orders, Circulars,
        Letters, Endorsements, and
        Morning Report Book
      Letters, Endorsements, and Order
        Book
      Letters Received, Adjutant General's
        Office
      Letters Received, Colored Troops
        Division
      Orders and Circulars

Personal Papers of Medical Officers
  and Physicians
Personnel Files
Records of Adjutant General's
  Office
Regimental Descriptive Books
Regimental Order Books
Regimental Letter Books
Regimental Muster Rolls
Regimental Unbound Papers
Record Group 105
  Records of the Assistant Commis-
    sioner for North Carolina
  Records of the Bureau of Refugees,
    Freedmen, and Abandoned Lands,
    North Carolina
  Registers and Reports of Registrars
    Recommended for the Election
    of Delegates
Record Group 153
  Proceedings of General Courts-
    Martial, Records of the Judge
    Advocate General's Office
Worcester, Massachusetts
  Dinand Library, College of the
    Holy Cross
    Horace James Papers

## Newspapers and Periodicals

Atlanta Intelligencer
Boston Herald
Boston Journal
Daily Chronicle and Sentinel (Augusta,
  Georgia)
Free South (Columbia)
Liberator
New England Magazine
New York Daily Tribune

New York Times
North Carolina Times (New Bern)
Palmetto Herald (Port Royal)
Peninsula (Jacksonville)
Weekly North Carolina Standard (Raleigh)
Wilmington Herald
Wilmington Journal
Wilmington Morning Star

## Government Publications

*Massachusetts Soldiers, Sailors, and Marines in the Civil War.* Vol. 7. Norwood, Mass.: Norwood, 1931.

*The Medical and Surgical History of the War of the Rebellion.* Washington, D.C.: GPO, 1870–88.

*Official Army Register of the Volunteer Forces of the U.S. Army, 1861–1865.* Washington, D.C.: GPO, 1865.

*War of the Rebellion: A Compilation of the Official Records of the Union and Confederate Armies.* Washington, D.C.: GPO, 1880–1901.

## Published Primary Sources

Adams, Virginia M., ed. *On the Altar of Freedom: A Black Soldier's Civil War Letters from the Front.* Amherst: University of Massachusetts Press, 1991.

Andrews, Sidney. *The South since the War.* Boston: Ticknor and Fields, 1866.

Basler, Roy P., ed. *The Collected Works of Abraham Lincoln.* 9 vols. New Brunswick, N.J.: Rutgers University Press, 1953.

Berlin, Ira, et al., eds. *Freedom: A Documentary History of Emancipation, 1861–1867.* Ser. 1. Cambridge: Cambridge University Press, 1985–.

Berlin, Ira, Barbara J. Fields, Thavolia Glymph, Joseph P. Reidy, and Leslie S. Rowland, eds. *The Destruction of Slavery.* Ser. 1, vol. 1, of *Freedom: A Documentary History of Emancipation, 1861–1867.* Cambridge: Cambridge University Press, 1985.

Berlin, Ira, Barbara J. Fields, Steven F. Miller, Joseph P. Reidy, and Leslie S. Rowland, eds. *Free at Last: A Documentary History of Slavery, Freedom, and the Civil War.* New York: New Press, 1992.

Berlin, Ira, Thavolia Glymph, Steven F. Miller, Joseph P. Reidy, and Leslie S. Rowland, eds. *The Wartime Genesis of Free Labor: The Lower South.* Ser. 1, vol. 3, of *Freedom: A Documentary History of Emancipation, 1861–1867.* Cambridge: Cambridge University Press, 1990.

Berlin, Ira, Steven F. Miller, Joseph P. Reidy, and Leslie S. Rowland, eds. *The Wartime Genesis of Free Labor: The Upper South.* Ser. 1, vol. 2, of *Freedom: A Documentary History of Emancipation, 1861–1867.* Cambridge: Cambridge University Press, 1993.

Berlin, Ira, Joseph P. Reidy, and Leslie S. Rowland, eds. *The Black Military Experience.* Ser. 2 of *Freedom: A Documentary History of Emancipation, 1861–1867.* Cambridge: Cambridge University Press, 1982.

Berlin, Ira, and Leslie S. Rowland, eds. *Families and Freedom: A Documentary History of African-American Kinship in the Civil War Era.* New York: New Press, 1997.

Blackett, R. J. M., ed. *Thomas Morris Chester: Black Civil War Correspondent: His Dispatches From the Virginia Front.* New York: Da Capo Press, 1989.

Bowley, Freeman S. *A Boy Lieutenant: Memoirs of Freeman S. Bowley, 30th United States Colored Troops Officer*. Edited by Pia Seija Seagrave. Fredericksburg, Va.: Sergeant Kirkland's Museum and Historical Society, 1997.

Browne, Frederick W. "My Service in the U.S. Colored Cavalry." *Military Order of the Loyal Legion of the United States--Ohio*. No. 7. N.p.: Privately published, 1908.

Buck, George H. *A Brief Sketch of the Service of Company G, 40th Massachusetts Volunteers, 1862–1865*. Chelsea, Mass.: Chas. H. Pike, 1910.

Burlingame, John K. *History of the Fifth Regiment of Rhode Island Heavy Artillery*. Providence, R.I.: Snow and Farnham, 1892.

Butler, Benjamin F. *Butler's Book*. Boston: A. M. Thayer and Co., 1892.

Colyer, Vincent. *Brief Report of the Services Rendered by the Freed People to the United States Army in North Carolina*. New York: Vincent Colyer, 1864.

Denison, Rev. Frederick. *Shot and Shell: The Third Rhode Island Heavy Artillery Regiment in the Rebellion, 1861–1865*. Providence, R.I.: J. A. and R. A. Reid, 1879.

Dennett, John Richard. *The South as It Is, 1865–1866*. New York: Viking, 1965.

Derby, William P. *Bearing Arms in the Twenty-seventh Massachusetts Regiment of Volunteer Infantry during the Civil War, 1861–1865*. Boston: Wright and Potter Printing Co., 1883.

Dickison, May Elizabeth, *Dickison and His Men: Reminiscences of the War in Florida*. Louisville, Ky.: Courier-Journal, 1890.

Duncan, Russell, ed. *Blue-Eyed Child of Fortune: The Civil War Letters of Colonel Robert Gould Shaw*. Athens: University of Georgia Press, 1992.

Egan, Patrick. *A Chaplain's Experience in the Union Army*. Providence, R.I.: Published by the Society, 1893.

———. *The Florida Campaign with Light Battery C, Third Rhode Island Heavy Artillery*. Providence, R.I.: Published by the Society, 1905.

Emilio, Luis F. *A Brave Black Regiment: History of the Fifty-fourth Massachusetts Volunteer Infantry, 1863–1865*. 1891. Reprint, New York: Arno Press, 1969.

Foner, Philip. *The Life and Writings of Frederick Douglass*. New York: International Publishers, 1952–75.

Fox, Charles Barnard. *Records of the Service of the Fifty-fifth Regiment of Massachusetts Volunteer Infantry*. Cambridge, Mass.: John Wilson and Son, 1868.

Fremantle, Arthur James Lyon. *Three Months in the Southern States, April–June 1863*. New York: John Bradburn, 1864.

Gallagher, Gary W., ed. *Fighting for the Confederacy: The Personal Recollections of General Edward Porter Alexander*. Chapel Hill: University of North Carolina Press, 1989.

Gordon, George Henry. *A War Diary of Events in the War of the Great Rebellion, 1863–1865*. Boston: Houghton Mifflin, 1885.

Goss, Warren Lee. *The Soldier's Story of His Captivity at Andersonville, Belle Island, and Other Rebel Military Prisons*. Boston: Lee and Shepard, 1870.

"Corporal." [Haines, Zenas T.] *Letters from the Forty-fourth Regiment M.V.M.: A Record of the Experience of a Nine Months' Regiment in the Department of North Carolina in 1862–3.* Boston: Herald, 1863.

Harwell, Richard, and Philip N. Racine, eds. *The Fiery Trail: A Union Officer's Account of Sherman's Last Campaigns.* Knoxville: University of Tennessee Press, 1986.

*History of the Thirty-seventh Regiment U.S.C. Infantry from the Organization in the Winter of 1863 and '64 to the Present Time.* Philadelphia: King and Baird Printers, 1866.

Hodges, Thorndike D. *Personal Recollections of the War of the Rebellion.* New York: Cammondy, 1891.

Hood, Bishop J. W. *One Hundred Years of the African Methodist Episcopal Zion Church; or, The Centennial of African Methodism.* New York: Book Concern of the A.M.E. Zion Church, 1895.

James, Rev. Horace. *Annual Report of the Superintendent of Negro Affairs in North Carolina, 1864–65.* Boston: W. F. Brown, 1866.

Kreutzer, William. *Notes and Observations Made during Four Years of Service with the Ninety-eighth N.Y. Volunteers in the War of 1861.* Philadelphia: Grant, Faires, and Rogers, 1878.

Little, Henry F. W. *The Seventh Regiment New Hampshire Volunteers in the War of the Rebellion.* Concord, N.H.: Ira C. Evans, 1896.

Longstreet, James. *From Manassas to Appomattox: Memoirs of the Civil War in America.* Bloomington: Indiana University Press, 1960.

Looby, Christopher, ed. *The Complete Civil War Journal and Selected Letters of Thomas Wentworth Higginson.* Chicago: University of Chicago Press, 2000.

Mann, Albert W. *History of the Forty-fifth Regiment Massachusetts Volunteer Militia: The Cadet Regiment.* Jamaica Plain, Mass.: Brookside Print, 1908.

McElroy, John. *Andersonville: A Story of Rebel Military Prisons: Fifteen Months a Guest of the So-Called Southern Confederacy.* Toledo, Ohio: Locke, 1879.

McKee, James Harvey. *Back "In War Times": History of the 144th Regiment, New York Volunteer Infantry.* New York: Lt. Horace E. Bailey, 1903.

Merrill, Walter M. *The Letters of William Lloyd Garrison.* 6 vols. Cambridge: Harvard University Press, 1971–81.

Mobley, Joe A. *The Papers of Zebulon Baird Vance.* Raleigh: Division of Archives and History, 1995.

Moore, Frank E. *The Rebellion Records: A Diary of American Events, with Documents, Narratives, Illustrative Incidents, Poetry, Etc.* 11 vols. New York: G. P. Putnam, 1861–68.

Norton, Oliver W. *Army Letters, 1861–1865.* Dayton, Ohio: Morningside, 1990.

Palmer, Abraham J. *The History of the Forty-eighth Regiment New York State Volunteers.* Brooklyn: Veterans Association of the Regiment, 1885.

Parker, Allen, *Recollections of Slavery Times.* Worcester, Mass.: Chas. W. Burbank, 1895.

Pearce, T. H. *Diary of Captain Henry A. Chambers*. Wendell, N.C.: Broadfoot's Bookmark, 1983.

Pierson, William Whatley, Jr. *Whipt'em Everytime: The Diary of Bartlett Yancey Malone, Co. H, 6th N.C. Regiment*. Jackson, Tenn.: McCowat-Mercer, 1960.

Posner, John A., ed. *The Essential Holmes: Selections From the Letters, Speeches, Judicial Opinions, and Other Writings of Oliver Wendell Holmes, Jr.* Chicago: University of Chicago Press, 1992.

*Private and Official Correspondence of Gen. Benjamin F. Butler during the Period of the Civil War*. 5 vols. Carlisle Barracks, Pa.: Privately printed, 1917.

Redkey, Edwin S., ed. *A Grand Army of Black Men: Letters from African-American Soldiers in the Union Army, 1861–1865*. Cambridge: Cambridge University Press, 1992.

Roe, Alfred S. *The Fifth Regiment Massachusetts Volunteer Infantry in Its Three Tours of Duty, 1861, 1862–'63, 1864*. Boston: Fifth Regiment Veterans Association, 1911.

Schofield, John M. *Forty-six Years in the Army*. New York; Century, 1897.

Scott, Robert Garth, ed. *Fallen Leaves: The Civil War Letters of Major Henry Livermore Abbott*. Kent, Ohio: Kent State University Press, 1992.

Sheridan, Philip H. *Personal Memoirs of P. H. Sheridan*. Vol. 2. New York: Charles L. Webster, 1888.

Simon, John Y. *The Papers of Ulysses S. Grant*. 28 vols. Carbondale: Southern Illinois University Press, 1967–.

Singleton, William H. *Recollection of My Slavery Days*. New York: N.p., 1922.

Smith, Daniel E. Huger, Alice R. Huger Smith, and Arney R. Childs, eds. *Mason Smith Family Letters*. Columbia: University of South Carolina Press, 1950.

Smith, Rev. Edward P. *Incidents of the United States Christian Commission*. Philadelphia: B. Lippincott, 1869.

Stein, A. H. *History of the Thirty-seventh Regiment U.S.C. Infantry*. Philadelphia: King and Baird, 1866.

Stoddard, William O. *Inside the White House in War Times: Memoirs and Reports of Lincoln's Secretary* [1890]. Ed. Michael Burlingame. Lincoln: University of Nebraska Press, 2000.

Tapert, Annette, ed. *The Brothers' War: Civil War Letters to Their Loved Ones from the Blue and Gray*. New York: Vintage Books, 1988.

Thorpe, Sheldon B. *The History of the Fifteenth Connecticut Volunteers in the War for the Defense of the Union*. New Haven: Price, Lee, and Adkins, 1893.

Walkly, Stephen. *History of the Seventh Connecticut Volunteer Infantry, Hawley's Brigade, Terry's Division, Tenth Army Corps, 1861–1865*. Hartford: N.p., 1905.

Williams, George W. *A History of the Negro Troops in the War of the Rebellion, 1861–1865*. New York: Harper and Brothers, 1888.

Williams, Max R., and J. G. de Roulhac Hamilton, eds. *The Papers of William Alexander Graham*. Raleigh: North Carolina Office of Archives and History, 1973.

Wilson, Joseph T. *The Black Phalanx: A History of the Negro Soldiers of the United States in the Wars of 1775–1812, 1861–'65*. Hartford, Conn.: American Publishing Co., 1888.

Wynne, Lewis N., and Robert A. Taylor, eds. *This War So Horrible: The Civil War Diary of Hiram Smith Williams*. Tuscaloosa: University of Alabama Press, 1993.

Yacovone, Donald. *A Voice of Thunder: The Civil War Letters of George E. Stephens*. Urbana: University of Illinois Press, 1997.

Yearns, W. Buck. *The Papers of Thomas Jordan Jarvis*. Raleigh: State Department of Archives and History, 1969.

Yearns, W. Buck, and John G. Barrett, eds. *North Carolina Civil War Documents*. Chapel Hill: University of North Carolina Press, 1980.

## SELECTED SECONDARY SOURCES

### Books

Alexander, Roberta Sue. *North Carolina Faces the Freedmen: Race Relations during Presidential Reconstruction*. Durham, N.C.: Duke University Press, 1985.

Almasy, Sandra L., ed. *North Carolina 1890 Civil War Veterans Census*. Joliet, Ill.: Kensington Glen Publishers, 1990.

Anderson, Eric. *Race and Politics in North Carolina, 1872–1901: The Black Second*. Baton Rouge: Louisiana State University Press, 1981.

Armstrong, William B. *For Courageous Fighting and Confident Dying: Union Chaplains in the Civil War*. Lawrence: University Press of Kansas, 1998.

Ash, Stephen V. *When the Yankees Came: Conflict and Chaos in the Occupied South, 1861–1865*. Chapel Hill: University of North Carolina Press, 1995.

Barefoot, Daniel W. *General Robert F. Hoke: Lee's Modest Warrior*. Winston-Salem, N.C.: John F. Blair, 1996.

Barnes, Joseph K. *The Medical and Surgical History of the Civil War*. 15 vols. Wilmington, N.C.: Broadfoot Publishing Co., 1992.

Barnett, Louise. *Touched by Fire: The Life, Death, and Mystical Afterlife of George Armstrong Custer*. New York: Henry Holt and Co., 1996.

Barrett, John G., *The Civil War in North Carolina*. Chapel Hill: University of North Carolina Press, 1963.

———. *Sherman's March through the Carolinas*. Chapel Hill: University of North Carolina Press, 1956.

Beitzell, Edwin W. *Point Lookout: Prison Camp for Confederates*. St. Marys County Historical Society, 1983.

Bernstein, Iver. *The New York City Draft Riots: Their Significance for American Society and Politics in the Age of the Civil War*. New York: Oxford University Press, 1990.

Blair, William, and William Pencak, eds. *Making and Remaking Pennsylvania's Civil War.* University Park: Pennsylvania State University Press, 2001.

Blanton, DeAnne, and Lauren M. Cook. *They Fought Like Demons: Women Soldiers in the American Civil War.* Baton Rouge: Louisiana State University Press, 2002.

Blight, David W. *Race and Reunion: The Civil War in American Memory.* Cambridge: Harvard University Press, 2001.

Boatner, Mark M. *The Civil War Dictionary.* New York: D. McKay Co., 1959.

Bogue, Allan G. *The Earnest Men: Republicans of the Civil War Senate.* Ithaca, N.Y.: Cornell University Press, 1981.

Boritt, Gabor S. *Why the Confederacy Lost.* New York: Oxford University Press, 1992.

Browning, Robert M., Jr. *From Cape Charles to Cape Fear: The North Atlantic Blockading Squadron during the Civil War.* Tuscaloosa: University of Alabama Press, 1993.

Buker, George E. *Blockaders, Refugees, and Contrabands: Civil War on Florida's Gulf Coast, 1861–1865.* Tuscaloosa: University of Alabama Press, 1993.

Cecelski, David S. *The Waterman's Song: Slavery and Freedom in Maritime North Carolina.* Chapel Hill: University of North Carolina Press, 2001.

Cecelski, David S., and Timothy B. Tyson, eds. *Democracy Betrayed: The Wilmington Race Riot of 1898 and Its Legacy.* Chapel Hill: University of North Carolina Press, 1998.

Click, Patricia L. *Time Full of Trial: The Roanoke Island Freedmen's Colony, 1862–1867.* Chapel Hill: University of North Carolina Press, 2001.

Cohen, William. *At Freedom's Edge: Black Mobility and the Southern Quest for Racial Control, 1861–1915.* Baton Rouge: Louisiana State University Press, 1991.

Cornish, Dudley T. *The Sable Arm: Negro Troops in the Union Army, 1861–1865.* New York: Norton, 1966.

Cresap, Bernarr. *Appomattox Commander: The Story of General E. O. C. Ord.* New York: A. S. Barnes, 1981.

Crow, Jeffrey J., Paul D. Escott, and Flora J. Hatley. *A History of African Americans in North Carolina.* Raleigh: North Carolina Division of Archives and History, 1992.

Current, Richard Nelson, *Lincoln's Loyalists: Union Soldiers from the Confederacy.* Boston: Northeastern University Press, 1992.

———, ed. *Encyclopedia of the Confederacy.* 4 vols. New York: Simon and Schuster, 1993.

Dabbs, Jack Autrey. *The French Army in Mexico, 1861–1867.* The Hague: Mouton, 1963.

Dawley, Alan. *Class and Community: The Industrial Revolution in Lynn.* Cambridge: Harvard University Press, 1976.

Donald, David Herbert, Jean Harvey Baker, and Michael F. Holt. *The Civil War and Reconstruction.* New York: Norton, 2001.

Durrill, Wayne K. *War of Another Kind: A Southern Community in the Great Rebellion.* New York: Oxford Press, 1990.

Dyer, Frederick A. *A Compendium of the War of the Rebellion.* Vol. 3. New York: Thomas Yoseloff, 1959.

Edgerton, Robert B. *Hidden Heroism: Black Soldiers in America's Wars*. Boulder, Colo.: Westview Press, 2001.

Evans, William McKee. *Ballots and Fence Rails: Reconstruction in the Lower Cape Fear*. Chapel Hill: University of North Carolina Press, 1966.

Faler, Paul G. *Mechanics and Manufacturers in the Early Industrial Revolution: Lynn, Massachusetts, 1780–1860*. Albany: State University of New York Press, 1981.

Farber, Daniel. *Lincoln's Constitution*. Chicago: University of Chicago Press, 2003.

Fisher, Noel C. *War at Every Door: Partisan Politics and Guerrilla Violence in East Tennessee, 1860–1869*. Chapel Hill: University of North Carolina Press, 1997.

Foner, Eric. *Freedom's Lawmakers: A Directory of Black Officeholders during Reconstruction*. New York: Oxford University Press, 1993.

———. *Reconstruction: America's Unfinished Revolution*. New York: Harper and Row, 1988.

Foner, Philip S. *History of the Labor Movement in the United States*. 5 vols. New York: Industrial Publishers, 1962.

Fonvielle, Chris E. *The Wilmington Campaign: The Last Rays of Departing Hope*. Mechanicsburg, Pa.: Stackpole Books, 1997.

Foote, Shelby. *The Civil War: A Narrative, Red River to Appomattox*. New York: Random House, 1974.

Franklin, John Hope. *The Free Negro in North Carolina, 1790–1860*. 1943. Reprint, Chapel Hill: University of North Carolina Press, 1995.

Freehling, William W. *The South vs. the South: How Anti-Confederate Southerners Shaped the Course of the Civil War*. New York: Oxford University Press, 2001.

Furgurson, Ernest B. *Ashes of Glory: Richmond at War*. New York: Knopf, 1996.

Genco, James G. *Arming Michigan's Regiments, 1862–1864: A Compilation and Summary of Small Arms Issued to Michigan Troops during the Civil War*. N.p.: J. G. Genco, 1982.

Gerteis, Louis S. *From Contraband to Freedman: Federal Policy toward Southern Blacks, 1861–1865*. Westport, Conn.: Greenwood Press, 1973.

Gillett, Mary C. *The Army Medical Department, 1818–1865*. Washington, D.C.: Center of Military History, U.S. Army, 1987.

Glatthaar, Joseph T. *Forged in Battle: The Civil War Alliance of Black Soldiers and White Officers*. New York: Free Press, 1990.

Gragg, Rod. *Confederate Goliath: The Battle of Fort Fisher*. New York: HarperCollins, 1991.

Grant, Susan-Mary, and Brian Holden Reid, eds. *The American Civil War: Explorations and Reconsiderations*. New York: Pearson Education, 2000.

Griffith, Paddy. *Battle Tactics of the Civil War*. New Haven, Conn.: Yale University Press, 1987.

Grimsley, Mark. *The Hard Hand of War: Union Military Policy towards Southern Civilians, 1861–1865*. Cambridge: Cambridge University Press, 1996.

Grimsted, David. *American Mobbing, 1828–1861: Toward Civil War*. New York: Oxford University Press, 1998.

Hagy, James W. *To Take Charleston: The Civil War on Folly Island*. Charleston, W.Va.: Pictorial Histories Publication Co., 1993.

Hardy, Michael C. *The Thirty-seventh North Carolina Troops: Tar Heels in the Army of Northern Virginia*. Jefferson, N.C.: McFarland and Co., 2003.

Hattaway, Herman. *General Stephen D. Lee*. Jackson: University Press of Mississippi, 1976.

Hesseltine, William. *Lincoln and the War Governors*. New York: Knopf, 1955.

Hollandsworth, James G., Jr. *The Louisiana Native Guards: The Black Military Experience during the Civil War*. Baton Rouge: Louisiana State University Press, 1995.

Horton, James Oliver, and Lois E. Horton. *In Hope of Liberty: Culture, Community, and Protest among Northern Free Blacks, 1700–1860*. New York: Oxford University Press, 1997.

Hubbard, Charles M., ed. *Lincoln Reshapes the Presidency*. Macon, Ga.: Mercer University Press, 2003.

Inscoe, John C., and Gordon B. McKinney. *The Heart of Confederate Appalachia: Western North Carolina in the Civil War*. Chapel Hill: University of North Carolina Press, 2000.

Jones, Jacqueline. *Labor of Love, Labor of Sorrow: Black Women, Work, and Family from Slavery to the Present*. New York: Basic Books, 1985.

Jordan, Ervin L., Jr. *Black Confederates and Afro-Yankees in Civil War Virginia*. Charlottesville: University Press of Virginia, 1995.

Jordan, Weymouth T. *North Carolina Troops, 1861–1865: A Roster*. Vol. 6. Raleigh: Division of Archives and History, 1966–.

Kenzer, Robert C. *Enterprising Southerners: Black Economic Success in North Carolina, 1865–1915*. Charlottesville: University Press of Virginia, 1997.

Klingaman, William K. *Abraham Lincoln and the Road to Emancipation, 1861–1865*. New York: Viking, 2001.

Kolchin, Peter. *First Freedom: The Response of Alabama's Blacks to Emancipation and Reconstruction*. Westport, Conn.: Greenwood Press, 1975.

Kreidberg, Marvin A., and Merton G. Henry. *History of Military Mobilization in the United States Army, 1775–1945*. Westport, Conn.: Greenwood Press, 1975.

Leckie, Shirley A. *Elizabeth Custer and the Making of a Myth*. Norman: University of Oklahoma Press, 1993.

Lee, Lawrence. *New Hanover County: A Brief History*. Raleigh: North Carolina Department of Archives and History, 1977.

Leonard, Elizabeth D. *All the Daring of the Soldier: Women of the Civil War Armies*. New York: Norton, 1999.

Levine, Bruce. *Confederate Emancipation: Southern Plans to Free and Arm Slaves during the Civil War*. New York: Oxford University Press, 2006.

Litwack, Leon, and August Meir, eds. *Black Leaders in the Nineteenth Century*. Urbana: University of Illinois Press, 1988.

Logan, Rayford W., and Michael R. Winston, eds. *Dictionary of American Negro Biography*. New York: Norton, 1982.

Logue, Larry M. *To Appomattox and Beyond: The Civil War Soldier in Peace and War.* Chicago: Ivan R. Dee, 1996.

Longacre, Edward G. *Army of Amateurs: General Benjamin F. Butler and the Army of the James, 1863–1865.* Mechanicsburg, Pa.: Stackpole Books, 1997.

Magdol, Edward. *Owen Lovejoy: Abolitionist in Congress.* New Brunswick, N.J.: Rutgers University Press, 1967.

Mallison, Fred M. *The Civil War on the Outer Banks.* Jefferson, N.C.: McFarland and Co., 1998.

Manarin, Louis H., ed. *A Guide to Military Organizations and Installations, North Carolina, 1861–1865.* Raleigh: North Carolina Confederate Centennial Commission, 1961.

Manarin, Louis H., comp. *North Carolina Troops, 1861–1865: A Roster: Vol. 1, Artillery.* Raleigh: North Carolina Division of Archives and History, 1966–.

Marszalek, John F. *Sherman: A Soldier's Passion for Order.* New York: Free Press, 1993.

Marvel, William. *Andersonville: The Last Depot.* Chapel Hill: University of North Carolina Press. 1994.

———. *Burnside.* Chapel Hill: University of North Carolina Press, 1991.

McConnell, Stuart. *Glorious Contentment: The Grand Army of the Republic, 1865–1900.* Chapel Hill: University of North Carolina Press, 1992.

McDonough, James L. *Schofield: Union General in the War of the Union.* Tallahassee: Florida University State Press, 1972.

McFeely, William S. *Yankee Stepfather: General O. O. Howard and the Freedmen.* New Haven, Conn.: Yale University Press, 1968.

McPherson, James M. *Battle Cry of Freedom: The Civil War Era.* Oxford: Oxford University Press, 1988.

———. *For Cause and Comrades: Why Men Fought in the Civil War.* New York: Oxford University Press, 1997.

———. *Ordeal by Fire: The Civil War and Reconstruction.* New York: McGraw-Hill, 1982.

Miller, Edward A., Jr. *The Black Civil War Soldiers of Illinois.* Columbia: University of South Carolina Press, 1998.

———. *Lincoln's Abolitionist General: The Biography of David Hunter.* Columbia: University of South Carolina Press, 1997.

Miller, Francis T. *The Photographic History of the Civil War.* New York: Castle Books, 1957.

Miller, William J. *The Training of an Army: Camp Curtin and the North's Civil War.* Shippensburg, Pa.: White Mane, 1990.

Mitchell, Lt. Col. Joseph B. *The Badge of Gallantry: Recollections of Civil War Congressional Medal of Honor Winners.* New York: Macmillan, 1968.

Mitchell, Reid. *The Vacant Chair: The Northern Soldier Leaves Home.* New York: Oxford University Press, 1993.

Mobley, Joe A. *James City: A Black Community in North Carolina, 1863–1900.* Raleigh: North Carolina Division of Archives and History, 1981.

————. *Ship Ashore: The U.S. Lifesavers of Coastal North Carolina*. Raleigh: North Carolina Division of Archives and History, 1994.

Morris, Roy, Jr. *Sheridan: The Life and Wars of General Phil Sheridan*. New York: Crown Publishers, 1992.

Nulty, William H. *Confederate Florida: The Road to Olustee*. Tuscaloosa: University of Alabama Press, 1990.

O'Connor, Thomas H. *Civil War Boston: Home Front and Battlefield*. Boston: Northeastern University Press, 1997.

Paludan, Phillip Shaw. *The Presidency of Abraham Lincoln*. Lawrence: University of Kansas Press, 1994.

Paradis, James M. *Strike the Blow for Freedom: The 6th United States Colored Infantry in the Civil War*. Shippensburg, Pa.: White Mane Books, 1998.

Patrick, Rembert W. *The Fall of Richmond*. Baton Rouge: Louisiana State University Press, 1960.

Powell, Lawrence W. *New Masters: Northern Planters during the Civil War and Reconstruction*. New Haven, Conn.: Yale University Press, 1980.

Powers, Bernard E., Jr. *Black Charlestonians: A Social History, 1822–1885*. Fayetteville: University of Arkansas Press, 1994.

Quarles, Benjamin. *The Negro in the Civil War*. Boston: Little, Brown, 1969.

Rabinowitz, Howard N., ed. *Southern Black Leaders of the Reconstruction Era*. Urbana: University of Illinois Press, 1982.

Rable, George C. *But There Was No Peace: The Role of Violence in the Politics of Reconstruction*. Athens: University of Georgia Press, 1984.

Rawick, George P. *The American Slave: A Composite Autobiography*. 41 vols. Westport, Conn.: Greenwood Press, 1972.

Reaves, William M., and Beverley Tetterton, eds. *Strength through Struggle: The Chronology and Historical Record of the African-American Community in Wilmington, North Carolina, 1865–1950*. Wilmington: New Hanover County Public Library, 1998.

Reed, Rowena. *Combined Operations in the Civil War*. Annapolis, Md.: Naval Institute Press, 1978.

Reidy, Joseph P. *From Slavery to Agrarian Capitalism in the Cotton Plantation South: Central Georgia, 1800–1880*. Chapel Hill: University of North Carolina Press, 1992.

Reisberg, Daniel. *Cognition: Exploring the Science of the Mind*. New York: Norton, 2001.

Richter, William L. *The Army in Texas during Reconstruction, 1865–1870*. College Station: Texas A&M University Press, 1987.

Robertson, James I. *Soldiers Blue and Gray*. Columbia: University of South Carolina Press, 1988.

Robertson, William Glenn. *Back Door to Richmond: The Bermuda Hundred Campaign, April–June 1864*. Baton Rouge: Louisiana State University Press, 1991.

Robinson, Armstead L. *Bitter Fruits of Bondage: The Demise of Slavery and the Collapse of the Confederacy.* Charlottesville: University of Virginia Press, 2005.

Rugoff, Milton. *The Beechers: An American Family in the Nineteenth Century.* New York: Harper and Row, 1981.

Saville, Julie. *The Work of Reconstruction: From Slave to Wage Labor in South Carolina, 1860–1870.* Cambridge: Cambridge University Press, 1994.

Schiller, Herbert M. *The Bermuda Hundred Campaign: Operations on the South Side of the James River, Virginia, May 1864.* Dayton, Ohio: Morningside, 1988.

Schmidt, Lewis G. *The Civil War in Florida: A Military History.* Allentown, Pa.: 1989.

Schwartz, Gerald. *A Woman Doctor's Civil War: Esther Hill Hawkes' Diary.* Columbia: University of South Carolina Press, 1989.

Schweninger, Loren. *Black Property Owners in the South, 1790–1915.* Urbana: University of Illinois Press, 1990.

Sefton, James E. *The United States Army and Reconstruction.* Baton Rouge: Louisiana State University Press, 1967.

Shaffer, Donald R. *After the Glory: The Struggles of Black Civil War Veterans.* Lawrence: University Press of Kansas, 2004.

Silber, Nina. *The Romance of Reunion: Northerners and the South, 1865–1900.* Chapel Hill: University of North Carolina Press, 1993.

Smallwood, James M. *Time of Hope, Time of Despair: Black Texas during Reconstruction.* Port Washington, N.Y.: National University Publications, 1981.

Smith, John David. *Black Judas: William Hannibal Thomas and the American Negro.* Athens: University of Georgia Press, 2000.

———, ed. *Black Soldiers in Blue: African American Troops in the Civil War Era.* Chapel Hill: University of North Carolina Press, 2002.

Smith, Steven D. *Whom We Would Never More See: History and Archaeology Recover the Lives and Deaths of African American Civil War Soldiers on Folly Island, South Carolina.* Columbia: South Carolina Department of Archives and History, 1993.

Sommers, Richard J. *Richmond Redeemed: The Siege of Petersburg.* Garden City, N.Y.: Doubleday, 1981.

Speer, Lonnie R. *Portals to Hell: Military Prisons of the Civil War.* Mechanicsburg, Pa.: Stackpole Books, 1997.

Stauffer, John. *The Black Hearts of Men: Radical Abolitionists and the Transformation of Race.* Cambridge: Harvard University Press, 2002.

Stick, David. *The Outer Banks of North Carolina, 1584–1958.* Chapel Hill: University of North Carolina Press, 1958.

Swint, Henry L. *Dear Ones at Home: Letters from Contraband Camps.* Nashville, Tenn.: Vanderbilt University Press, 1966.

Symonds, Craig L. *Stonewall of the West: Patrick Cleburne and the Civil War.* Lawrence: University Press of Kansas, 1997.

Trotter, William R. *Ironclads and Columbiads: The Coast*. Winston-Salem, N.C.: J. F. Blair, 1989.

Trudeau, Noah Andre. *The Last Citadel: Petersburg, Virginia, June 1864–April 1865*. Baton Rouge: Louisiana State University Press, 1991.

―――. *Like Men of War: Black Troops in the Civil War, 1862–1865*. Boston: Little, Brown, 1998.

Tucker, Glenn. *Zeb Vance: Champion of Personal Freedom*. Indianapolis: Bobbs-Merrill, 1965.

Tucker, Phillip Thomas. *Cathy Williams: From Slave to Female Buffalo Soldier*. Mechanicsburg, Pa.: Stackpole Books, 2003.

Urwin, Gregory J. W., ed. *Black Flag over Dixie: Racial Atrocities and Reprisals in the Civil War*. Carbondale: Southern Illinois University Press, 2004.

Voegeli, V. Jacque. *Free but Not Equal: The Midwest and the Negro during the Civil War*. Chicago: University of Chicago Press, 1967.

Vorenberg, Michael. *Final Freedom: The Civil War, the Abolition of Slavery, and the Thirteenth Amendment*. Cambridge: Cambridge University Press, 2001.

Washington, Versalle Fredrick. *Eagles on Their Buttons: A Black Infantry Regiment in the Civil War*. Columbia: University of Missouri Press. 1999.

Watson, Alan D. *Wilmington, North Carolina, to 1861*. Jefferson, N.C.: McFarland and Co., 2003.

Welcher, Frank J. *The Union Army, 1861–1865: Organizations and Operations*. Bloomington: Indiana University Press, 1989, 1993.

West, Richard S. *Lincoln's Scapegoat General*. Boston: Houghton Mifflin, 1965.

Westwood, Howard C. *Black Troops, White Commanders, and Freedmen*. Carbondale: University of Southern Illinois, 1992.

Wiley, Bell I. *Southern Negroes, 1861–1865*. 1938. Reprint, New Haven, Conn.: Yale University Press, 1965.

Wilson, Keith P. *Campfires of Freedom: The Camp Life of Black Soldiers during the Civil War*. Kent, Ohio: Kent State University Press, 2002.

Wise, Stephen R. *Gate of Hell: Campaign for Charleston Harbor, 1863*. Columbia: University of South Carolina Press, 1994.

Zuczek, Richard. *State of Rebellion: Reconstruction in South Carolina*. Columbia: University of South Carolina Press, 1996.

### Articles and Essays

Abbott, Richard H. "Massachusetts and the Recruitment of Southern Negroes, 1863–1865." *Civil War History* 14 (September 1968): 197–210.

Armstrong, Warren B. "Union Chaplains and the Education of the Freedmen." *Journal of Negro History* 52 (April 1967): 104–15.

Blair, Dan. "'One Good Port': Beaufort Harbor, North Carolina, 1863–1864." *North Carolina Historical Review* 79 (2002): 301–26.

Blair, William. "The Use of Military Force to Protect the Gains of Reconstruction." *Civil War History* 51 (2005): 388–402.

Browning, Judkin Jay. "'Little Souled Mercenaries?' The Buffaloes of Eastern North Carolina in the Civil War." *North Carolina Historical Review* 77 (2000): 337–63.

Byrd, John Henry. "Dear Father." *Civil War Times Illustrated* 41 (2002): 24–27, 66–67, 70–72, 77–78.

Campbell, Randolph B. "Grass Roots Reconstruction: The Personnel of County Government in Texas, 1865–1876." *Journal of Southern History* 58 (1992): 99–116.

Cecelski, David S. "Abraham H. Galloway: Wilmington's Lost Prophet and the Rise of Black Radicalism in the American South." In Cecelski and Tyson, *Democracy Betrayed*.

Cohen-Lack, Nancy. "A Struggle for Sovereignty: National Consolidation, Emancipation and Free Labor in Texas, 1865." *Journal of Southern History* 58 (1992): 57–98.

Coles, David J. "'Shooting Niggers Sir': Confederate Mistreatment of Union Black Soldiers at the Battle of Olustee." In Urwin, *Black Flag over Dixie*.

Cook, Robert. "The Fight for Black Suffrage in the War of the Rebellion." In Grant and Reid, *American Civil War*.

Dix, Mary Seaton, ed. "'And Three Rousing Cheers for the Privates': A Diary of the 1862 Roanoke Island Expedition." *North Carolina Historical Review* 71 (1994): 62–84.

Drago, Edmund L. "Georgia's First Black Voter Registrars during Reconstruction." *Georgia Historical Quarterly* 78 (1994): 760–93.

Dyer, Brainerd. "The Treatment of Colored Union Troops by the Confederates, 1861–1865." *Journal of Negro History* 20 (July 1935): 273–86.

Farnham, Thomas J., and Francis P. King. "'The March of the Destroyer': The New Bern Yellow Fever Epidemic of 1864." *North Carolina Historical Review* 73 (1996): 438–83.

Fleche, Andre. "'Shoulder to Shoulder as Comrades Tried': Black and White Union Veterans and Civil War Memory." *Civil War History* 51 (2005): 175–201.

Goldhaber, Michael. "A Mission Unfulfilled: Freedmen's Education in North Carolina, 1865–1870." *Journal of Negro History* 77 (1992): 199–210.

Grimsley, Mark. "'A Very Long Shadow': Race, Atrocity, and the American Civil War." In Urwin, *Black Flag over Dixie*.

Hahn, Steven. "'Extravagant Expectations' of Freedom: Rumor, Political Struggle, and the Christmas Insurrection Scare of 1865 in the American South." *Past and Present* 157 (November 1997): 122–58.

Harris, William C. "Lincoln and Wartime Reconstruction in North Carolina, 1861–1863." *North Carolina Historical Review* 63 (1986): 149–68.

Heslin, James J. "A Yankee Soldier in a New York Regiment." *New-York Historical Society Quarterly* 50 (1966): 109–49.

Hewitt, Lawrence Lee. "An Ironic Route to Glory: Louisiana's Native Guards at Port Hudson." In John David Smith, *Black Soldiers in Blue*.

Hollandsworth, James G., Jr. "The Execution of White Officers from Black Units by Confederate Forces during the Civil War." In Urwin, *Black Flag over Dixie*.

Honey, Michael K. "The War within the Confederacy: White Unionists of North Carolina." *Prologue* 26 (1994): 75–93.

Hudson, Leonne M. "A Confederate Victory at Grahamville: Fighting at Honey Hill." *South Carolina Historical Magazine* 94 (1993): 19–33.

———. "Valor at Wilson's Wharf." *Civil War Times Illustrated* 37 (1998): 46–52.

Jordan, Weymouth T., and Gerald W. Thomas. "Massacre at Plymouth, April 20, 1864." *North Carolina Historical Review* 72 (1995): 126–93.

Lause, Mark A. "Turning the World Upside Down: A Portrait of Labor and Military Leader, Alonzo Granville Draper." *Labor History* 44 (2003): 189–204.

Longacre, Edward G. "Black Troops in the Army of the James, 1863–1865." *Military Affairs* 45 (1981): 1–8.

———. "Brave Radical Wild: The Contentious Career of Brigadier General Edward A. Wild." *Civil War Times Illustrated* 19 (1980): 8–19.

———. "There Will Be Many a Day before Charleston Falls: Letters of a Union Soldier on Folly Island, August 1863–August 1864." *South Carolina Historical Magazine* 85 (1984): 108–34.

Lowe, Richard. "Local Black Leaders during Reconstruction in Virginia." *Virginia Magazine of History and Biography* 103 (1995): 181–206.

Luvaas, Jay. "Burnside's Roanoke Expedition." *Civil War Times Illustrated* 7 (1968): 4–11, 43–8.

———. "The Fall of Fort Fisher." *Civil War Times Illustrated* 3 (1964): 5–9, 31–5.

McMurray, Richard. "The President's Tenth and the Battle of Olustee." *Civil War Times* 16 (1978): 12–25.

Miller, Edward A., Jr. "Garland A. White: Black Army Chaplain." *Civil War History* 43 (1997): 201–18.

Norris, David A. "'The Yankees Have Been Here!': The Story of Brig. Gen. Edward E. Potter's Raid on Greenville, Tarboro, and Rocky Mount, July 19–23, 1863." *North Carolina Historical Review* 73 (1996): 1–27.

O'Brien, John T. "Reconstruction in Richmond: White Restoration and Black Protest, April–June 1865." *Virginia Magazine of History and Biography* 89 (1981): 259–80.

Paludan, Phillip Shaw. "Lincoln and the Greeley Letter: An Exposition." In Charles M. Hubbard, ed., *Lincoln Reshapes the Presidency*. Macon, Ga.: Mercer University Press, 2003.

Perkins, Frances Beecher. "Two Years with a Colored Regiment: A Woman's Experience." *New England Magazine* 17 (January 1898).

Poole, Scott W. "Memory and the Abolitionist Heritage: Thomas Wentworth Higginson and the Uncertain Meaning of the Civil War." *Civil War History* 51 (2005): 202–17.

Redkey, Edwin S. "Black Chaplains in the Union Army." *Civil War History* 33 (1987): 331–50.

Reid, George W. "Four in Black: North Carolina's Black Congressmen, 1874–1914." *Journal of Negro History* 64(3): 229–43.

Reid, Richard M. "The 1870 United States Census and Black Underenumeration: A Test Case from North Carolina." *Histoire Sociale/Social History* 28 (1995): 487–99.

———. "Raising the African Brigade: Early Black Recruitment in Civil War North Carolina." *North Carolina Historical Review* 70 (1993): 266–301.

Rutledge, David J. "Elizabeth Jamison's Tale of the War." *South Carolina Historical Magazine* 99 (1998): 312–39.

Smith, John David. "Let Us All Be Grateful That We Have Colored Troops That Will Fight." In Smith, *Black Soldiers in Blue.*

Sommers, Richard J. "The Dutch Gap Affair: Military Atrocities and the Rights of Negro Soldiers." *Civil War History* 21 (March 1975): 51–64.

Sutherland, Daniel E. "Guerrilla Warfare, Democracy, and the Fate of the Confederacy." *Journal of Southern History* 68 (2002): 259–92.

———. "Sideshow No Longer: A Historiographical Review of the Civil War." *Civil War History* 46 (2000): 5–23.

———. "Without Mercy, and Without the Blessing of God." *North and South* (September 1998): 12–21.

Vogel, Jeffrey E. "Redefining Reconciliation: Confederate Veterans and the Southern Response to Federal Civil War Pensions." *Civil War History* 51 (2005): 67–93.

Westwood, Howard C. "Benjamin Butler's Enlistment of Black Troops in New Orleans in 1862." *Louisiana History* 26 (1985): 5–22.

———. "Captive Black Union Soldiers in Charleston--What to Do?" *Civil War History* 28 (1982): 28–44.

———. "The Causes and Consequences of a Black Soldier's Mutiny and Execution." *Civil War History* 31 (1985): 222–36.

Williams, Chad L. "Symbols of Freedom and Defeat: African American Soldiers, White Southerners, and the Christmas Insurrection Scare of 1865." *Southern Historian* 21 (2000): 40–55.

Wilson, Keith. "In the Shadow of John Brown: The Military Service of Colonels Thomas Higginson, James Montgomery, and Robert Shaw in the Department of the South." In John David Smith, *Black Soldiers in Blue.*

Zipf, Karin L. "'The WHITES Shall Rule the Land or Die': Gender, Race, and Class in North Carolina Reconstruction Politics." *Journal of Southern History* 65 (1999): 499–534.

*Theses and Dissertations*

Bryant, James Kenneth, II. "A Model Regiment: The 36th U.S. Colored Infantry in the Civil War." M.A. thesis, University of Vermont, 1996.

Buckner, Marland Everett, Jr. "Banking on Freedom: A Social History of the Beaufort Freedmen's Savings and Trust Company." M.A. thesis, University of Saskatchewan, 1992.

Gannon, Barbara A. "The Won Cause: Black and White Comradeship in the Grand Army of the Republic." Ph.D. diss., Pennsylvania State University, 2005.

Horstman, Jonathan William. "The African-American's Civil War: A History of the 1st North Carolina Colored Volunteers." M.A. thesis, Western Carolina University, 1994.

Hutchins, Shana Renee. "'Just Learning to Be Men': A History of the 35th United States Colored Troops, 1863–1877." M.A. thesis, North Carolina State University, 1999.

Kirkland, John Robert. "Federal Troops in North Carolina during Reconstruction." M.A. thesis, University of North Carolina, 1964.

Moore, Stacy Barton. "The Onset of Liberty: Triumphs and Tribulations of Eastern North Carolina Freedmen, 1862–1865." M.A. thesis, Western Carolina University, 1996.

Reilly, Stephen R. "Reconstruction through Regeneration: Horace James' Work with the Blacks for Social Reform in North Carolina, 1862–1867." Ph.D. diss., Duke University, 1983.

Schneider, Tracy Whittaker. "The Institution of Slavery in North Carolina, 1860–1865." Ph.D. diss., Duke University, 1979.

Shaffer, Donald R. "Marching On: African American Civil War Veterans in Postbellum America, 1865–1951." Ph.D. diss., University of Maryland, 1996.

Warner, John Dwight. "Crossed Sabers: A History of the Fifth Massachusetts Volunteer Cavalry: An African American Regiment in the Civil War." Ph.D. diss., Boston College, 1997.

Washington, Versalle Fredrick. "Eagles on Their Buttons: The Fifth Regiment of Infantry, United States Colored Troops in the American Civil War." Ph.D. diss., Ohio State University, 1995.

Wood, Richard Everett. "Port Town at War: Wilmington, North Carolina, 1860–1865." Ph.D. diss., Florida State University, 1976.

Zalimas, Robert J., Jr. "Black Union Soldiers in the Postwar South, 1865–1866." M.A. thesis, Arizona State University, 1993.

Zuczek, Richard M. "State of Rebellion: People's War in Reconstruction South Carolina, 1865–1877." Ph.D. diss., Ohio University, 1993.

# INDEX

Abbot, Joseph C., 178, 180–81

Abbott, Henry L., xiii

Adkins, Richard, 141

African Americans. *See* Black families of soldiers; Black noncommissioned officers; Black officers; Black recruitment; Black refugees; Black soldiers; Black veterans; Black women

African Brigade, 22, 40, 59, 153, 161, 223

*Albemarle*, CSS, 158, 198

Alcohol: excessive use of, 74–75; Draper's ban on, 124; and officers, 166–67; and whiskey rations, 209–10; illegal sale by civilians, 293–94

Alderman, Samuel, 288

Alexander, Edward Porter, 143, 173

Allen, Benjamin F., 292–93

Allen, Charles G., 62, 63, 194, 204; in charge of 1st NCCHA, 206–7; and whiskey rations, 209–10; recruiting efforts, 210–11, 212

Allen, Hiram H., 45

American Colonization Society (ACS), 25, 305

American Missionary Association, 216

Ames, Adelbert, 176–77, 178–79

Ames, John W., 179, 182, 284, 285–86, 287

Amieny, Chester, 206, 249, 317–18

Amieny, Frances. *See* Reddick, Frances

Anderson, James Patton, 100

Andersonville prison, 94–98; mortality rates, 94–95

Andrew, John A., 7, 20, 27, 43, 123, 204; recruits black regiments, 13–14, 16, 332 (n. 28)

Andrews, Nathan, 258

Andrews, Richard F., 141, 269

Andrews, Sidney, 312

Antietam, Battle of, 6

Army of Observation, 260, 266–67, 272

Army of the James, xv, 135; assault up the James, 161–64

Army of the Potomac, 23

Arnett, James, 35

Arnold, George M., 314

Arrears of Pension Act (1879), 320–21

Artis, Thomas, 138

Ash, Stephen, 114

*Atlanta*, USS, 163

Atlantic and Gulf Railroad, 78, 79

Atlantic and North Carolina Railroad, 9

Atrocities, 16; claims of, 93–94, 156–57, 159–60, 373 (n. 11)

Babbitt, James B., 62, 89

Backup, James B., 141

Bailey, George A., 165, 168, 358 (n. 28)

Banks, John, 318

Banks, Julia, 318

Banks, Nathaniel P., 17, 18, 27

Barber, Delos, 37, 89–90

Barbough, Isaac R., 72

Barbour, Mary, 218

Barnes, James, 135, 354 (n. 69)

Barrow, Lucas. *See* Bond, Lucas

Barrow, Reuben, 302

Bass, Frances, 253

Bass, Lewis, 207–8, 253

Battery Wagner (Fort Wagner), xiii, 41, 70, 72, 86, 325

Baum, America. *See* Etheridge, America

Baxter, Lamb, 251–52

Bayman, Thomas, 208

Bazaine, François-Achille, 271

Beecher, Frances. *See* Johnson, Frances

Beecher, James C., 28, 32, 54, 70, 92; background, 25; raising and training of regiment, 32–39, 71–72, 275–76; and temperance, 74–75; on leave, 75, 88; frustration with quality of weapons, 88–89; and De Grasse, 90; and Florida service, 99, 101–2, 346 (n. 81); criticism of, 104, 279; discipline of regiment, 105–6, 274; and Honey Hill, 106–8; wounded, 107; and Frances, 250; concern over behavior of freedmen, 278–80, 281; mustering out of regiment, 281, 301; mental disorder, 316–17

Beecher, Lyman, 25

Belk, Louis, 303

Belt, Louis. *See* Belk, Louis

Bemberg, Leon, 240

Benson, William L., 240

Benzoni, Charles, 248

Berdan, John. *See* Berden, John

Berden, George. *See* Burden, George

Berden, John, 157

Bicknell, Francis A., 138

Billings, Leonard Lorenzo, 24–25

Birney, David B., 139–40, 143–44, 170–71

Birney, William, 88–89, 100–101

Bissel, Abram, 304

Black, William R., 189

Black families of soldiers: problems facing, 215–16, 293; support for, 222; and white perceptions of black marriages, 243; retaliation against, 248, 324

Black noncommissioned officers, 35–36, 37–38, 44, 71, 103–4, 151, 211; demoted, 103, 104–5, 270, 348 (n. 109); clash with officers, 138–39, 165, 174; meritorious actions of, 141, 144–46, 277, 377 (n. 57); lead mounted patrols, 284

Black officers, 18; opposition to, 17–18, 27–28, 333 (n. 4); plans for, 275, 379 (n. 85); and recommendation to commission Hodges, 287

Black recruitment: early opposition to, 1–2; efforts in North Carolina, 29–33, 44–45, 163–64, 168–69, 185; and bounties, 32, 58, 188–89, 203; difficulties facing, 46–48, 55; by northern agents, 64, 188–95, 363 (n. 1); and competition for recruits, 155, 160, 189, 341 (n. 128)

Black refugees: census of, 13, 218, 220; economic opportunities, 29–30, 216, 222–23; hardships facing, 30, 217–18; and Union raids, 114, 116–17, 119, 135, 234; camps for, 131–32, 133, 220–23, 226, 367 (nn. 13, 14), 368 (nn. 22, 25, 26); support for, 216–19, 222; employment of, 218–19, 222; unpaid wages, 222, 231, 234, 242

"Black Second" Congressional District, 315, 386 (n. 62)

Black soldiers: white perceptions of, xii, xiii, 24–25, 70, 72, 83–85, 86, 111, 117, 121, 143, 297–98; army's goal of equal treatment of, 14–17, 72, 326–27; defective and used muskets, 15, 39–40, 51, 57, 82–83, 88–89, 164–65, 291, 337 (n. 66), 340 (n. 119); treatment as POWs, 16, 93–98, 156–60; unequal and irregular pay, 16–17, 103, 240, 300, 326–27, 333 (n. 33); and religion, 33–34, 152, 287; claims about poor discipline of, 39, 48, 115, 117, 201, 206–7, 260, 262; poor equipment, 39–40; live musket training, 40–41, 56, 83, 88; and use of incentives, 44–45; assigned unequal fatigue duties, 48, 56–57, 68–72, 148, 207–8, 300; conflict with officers, 50, 71, 138–39, 165, 174, 197–98, 262–63, 287–89, 292, 358 (n. 27); conflict with white troops, 57, 130–31, 273–74, 295, 376 (n. 50); desire for literacy, 73, 175, 250; re-enslaved, 95, 159; interference in recruiting, by white officers, 123; in Confederate units, 181, 362 (n. 79); and mutinies, 262–63, 269, 287–89; and elections, 289–90

Black veterans: and disabilities, 209, 315–17; and politics, 298, 311–15; adjustment of, 298–99; and employment, 299, 304, 315, 319–20; and mustering out process, 300; decisions about future, 300–301; and surname choice, 301–2, 371 (n. 74); postwar residences of, 302–7, 382 (n. 17); conflict with law, 304; and colonization, 305; and migration West, 305–6; as members of GAR, 307–10; gun ownership of, 310–11, 385 (n. 46); as office holders, 313–14; and pension officials, 316, 321–22, 365 (n. 46);

psychological adjustments of, 316–17; domestic lives of, 317–20; bounties, 320

Black women: in camp, 39, 221, 251; as wives of soldiers, 132, 222, 223, 250–53; and marriage, 223, 252–53, 317–19, 353 (n. 57); and Roanoke, 230, 232; and concern about being sent North, 240; harassed by white soldiers, 244; attached to regiment, 249, 250–51; and pensions, 252; passing as men, 372 (n. 78)

Blount, Oliver, 249

Bogle, Archibald, 86, 87, 275, 343 (n. 32); experience as prisoner, 94, 97, 98

Bond, Lucas, 302, 319

Bostic, Simon. *See* McIver, Simon

Bowen, David, 103

Boyle, Richard, 243

Bragg, Braxton, 176, 180–82, 184

Braley, Sierra F., 259

Branch, Lawrence O'Bryan, 11

Brannigan, Felix, 7

Bray, Alfred, 264

Brazos Santiago, 264, 272; description of, 265–66; conditions on, 267, 268

Briggs, W. P., 210

Bright, Daniel, 119

Brinckly, Jack, 103–4

Brook, William, 310

Brooks, Alonzo. *See* Marshall, Alonzo

Brooks, William T. H., 167

Brown, W. H. R., 25

Browne, Frederick, 262–63

Bryant, Isaac, 207, 316

Bryant, Lewis, 104

"Buffaloes," 155, 157

Bullis, William Irving, 62–63

Burden, George, 157–58, 310, 317

Bureau of Colored Troops, 8, 23

Burnside, Ambrose E., 1; North Carolina operations, 9–12, 217, 332 (n. 23); appoints Colyer, 218–19

Butler, Benjamin F., xi, xv, 3, 9, 27, 111, 170–71, 204, 238, 268; and Louisiana Native Guard, 5–6, 331 (n. 10); and contraband trade, 122–23; and resigning officers, 124–25; and Draper, 135, 147; assault on Richmond, 139–44; respect for black troops, 143, 161–62; creates medals, 144–46; and Army of the James, 150, 161–64; first Fort Fisher expedition, 177–78; and General Order No. 90, 190–91; and Northern agents, 197; concern for families of black soldiers, 232–33, 239, 247

Butricks, M. A., 202, 365 (n. 32)

Byrd, John Henry, 229

Cadwell, Charles, 271

Caffey, Soloman W., 122

Camel, Peter, 36

Cameron, Simon, 2, 4

Camp, training, 136, 167–68

Campbell, J. A., 289

Carr, Eugene A., 295

Casey, Silas, 129

Chadwick, David, 311

Chamberlain, Abial G., 53; raising and training of regiment of, 54–58, 160, 164; background, 154; report on Plymouth, 157, 159; and discipline, 165–68, 174–75, 359 (n. 30); and training camp, 167–68; assault on Richmond, 170–74; Reconstruction service, 285–86

Chance, Lofton, 258

Charleston and Savannah Railroad, 106–8

Chase, Lucy, 236

Chase, William P., 166

Cheatham, Henry Plummer, 315

Chester, Thomas Morris, 146, 171

*Chicago Times*, 7

Childs, Samuel R., 25

*Christian Recorder*, 314

*Cincinnati Colored Citizen*, 313

Clairborne, Nicholas, 304

Clapp, Henry A., 13, 14

Clark, Charles A., 36–37

Clarke, Henry, 304

Coast Division, 106–7

Cobb, Howell, xii, 325

"Coffin Island," 70

Collins, Bryant, 258

*Columbine*, USS: capture of, 91–93, 97, 98

Colyer, Vincent, 217–19

Conant, G. W. S., 120

Confederate prisoners, 126–31; shot, 126–30, 352 (nn. 38, 41, 52)

Confederate response to black troops, 16, 93–94, 126–27, 337 (n. 70); at Plymouth, 155–60; and families of soldiers, 215; in postwar service, 269–70, 273, 276–77; and Confederate decision to raise black troops, 325, 387 (n. 3)

Confirmation bias, 85–86

Connecticut units
7th Connecticut, 84
15th Connecticut Volunteers, 199–203

"Contraband of war": as defined by Butler, 3, 216

Contraband trade, 122–23, 239–40, 286

Cook, Thomas M., 142

Cooper, David, 310–11

Cornish, Dudley T., 22

Cotanch, Henry, 291, 297

Cowdry, Arthur H., 155, 169

Cox, Philis, 319

Cox, Wilson, 38

Crawford, John, 174, 360 (n. 58)

Creech, Lucas. See Bond, Lucas

Creech, Mymia, 319

Creech, Roena, 319

Crocker, Lucy, 251

Croft, James N., 32, 114, 154

Crombie, William, 63–64, 211, 341 (n. 138)

Crouse, William A., 166–67, 359 (n. 33)

Cunningham, Charles N. W., 164, 358 (n. 26)

Custer, George A., 269, 375 (n. 36)

Cutler, William A., 292–93, 294, 295

Dail, John, 241

*Daily Chronicle and Sentinel* (Augusta, Ga.), 84, 87

Daniels, Edward S., 72, 92, 95, 97, 278, 337 (n. 65)

Davis, Elinathan, 236

Davis, Gaston, 69, 95, 347 (n. 91)

Davis, Manuel, 288

Davis, Rowan. See Davis, Manuel

Davis, William, 141, 144, 146

*Dawn*, USS, 163

De Grasse, John V., 27, 33, 69, 102, 166–67; background, 25–26, 334 (nn. 22, 23);

reaction to, 29; clash with Mann, 73–74, 89; charges against, 89–91, 346 (n. 74)

Demsey, Charles, 181

Demsey, Henry, 181

Derby, William P., 29, 31–32

Desertion: of white soldiers, 84, 142, 166, 175; of black soldiers, 108, 139, 264, 292, 355 (n. 84), 376 (n. 44)

Devaux's Neck, 107–8, 109

Devens, Charles, 150–51

Dewell, Annie, 304–5

Dewell, Henry E., 304–5

Dickison, John J., 92, 346 (n. 80)

Disability Pension Act (1890), 321

Disease and illness: among officers, 49, 141, 166, 198, 205, 214, 220, 338 (n. 95); among soldiers, 69–70, 72, 76, 78–79, 101, 108, 121, 140, 146, 176, 206–7, 212, 272, 300, 382 (n. 10); yellow fever outbreak, 199–203, 364 (n. 28), 365 (n. 35); white perception of black resistance to, 200; among black refugees, 234; in Texas, 267–68, 271, 272; and psychological adjustments, 316–17

Dismal Swamp Canal, 112, 117–18

Doolittle, Oscar E., 31, 233

Doolittle, William, 102

Douglass, Frederick, 18, 297

Downing, Peter, 318–19

Doyle, J., 181

Draper, Algernon, 269

Draper, Alonzo, 42, 50, 54; background, 43; raising and training of regiment of, 44–49; and Butler, 111; character of, 111, 339 (n. 101), 351 (nn. 26, 28, 30, 34); leads raids, 112–23, 133–35; clash with Wead, 115–16, 120, 350 (n. 18); leadership style, 123–25; and resignation of company officers, 123–26; as brigade commander, 135–36, 147, 170; first into Richmond, 150–51; sends Green to Roanoke, 245; death of, 269

Drayton, Charles, 286–87

Drewry's Bluff, Battle of, 164

Drinker, R. W., 286

Duert, Henry E. See Dewell, Henry E.

Duffee, George, 103

Duncan, Samuel, 140
Dutch Gap Canal, 137, 148, 238–39, 241, 264
Dyer, Judith M., 122

Eagles, John (doctor), 322
Eagles, John S. W., 309, 310, 311, 313, 322
Ebbs, J., 115, 117
Ebon, Hardy, 137
Eddins, William H., 259–60
Edgar, Samuel, 288–89
Elliot, Willis, 176
Ellis, N. S., 189
Elmsly, James, 36, 278
Emancipation Day, 309
Emancipation Proclamation, 6–7, 13, 16
Emerson, William, 98
Emilio, Luis F., 107
Equal Rights Leagues, 312, 313
Escort, USS, 61
Etheridge, America, 302
Etheridge, Richard, 236, 322, 386 (n. 61)
Evans, Peter G., 222

Faircloth, Richard, 207
Farnsworth, John, 289
Fawn, USS, 118
Fellman, Michael, 114
Field, Bryant, 304
Field, Charles William, 147, 171
Fields, W. F., 197
Finegan, Joseph, 79
Fitz, Edward S., 238
Fitzpatrick, Thomas B. N., 54, 174–75, 339
    (n. 110)
Fleche, Andre, 308
Fletcher, G. M., 49
Foner, Eric, 298
Foreman, Brister, 117
Forrest, Nathan Bedford, xii, 357 (n. 4)
Fort Fisher: first assault on, 176–78; second
    assault on, 178–81
Fort Macon, 11
Fort Pillow, 156, 160, 357 (n. 4)
Fort Pocahontas, 162–63
Fort Powhatan, 163–64
Fort Thompson, 11
Fort Wagner. See Battery Wagner

Foster, Charles W., 27
Foster, Daniel, 170
Foster, Hezekiah, 312, 386 (n. 61)
Foster, John G., 41, 46, 47, 56, 106–7; attitude
    toward black soldiers, 112; and census,
    220; and Roanoke, 225–28, 231–32
Fox, Charles B., 327
Francis, John W., 190
Franklin, John, 207
Frazier, Marcus, 36, 348 (n. 109)
Freedmen's Bureau, 257, 266, 267, 272, 280,
    281, 286–87, 310
Free Military School, 24
Frémont, John C., xi, 3–4
Frost, Robert, 117
Furby, Peter, 117, 140
Furman, J. T., 277

Galloway, Abraham H., 30–31, 312, 314
Gannon, Barbara, 308
Gardner, James, 144, 145
Gardner, Morris, 253
Garrick, Eliza, 318–19
Garrison, William Lloyd, 25, 61, 203–4
Gary, Martin W., 172
Gaskill, Edwin C., 138, 141
Gaylord, George, 304
General Order No. 3 (1866), 291
General Order No. 7 (1865), 287
General Order No. 12 (1863), 231
General Order No. 21 (1864), 72
General Order No. 46 (1864), 124
General Order No. 90 (1864), 190–91
General Order No. 100 (1863), 119
General Order No. 143 (1863), 8
General Order No. 177 (1864), 237
General Order No. 227 (1864), 188, 189, 196
General Order No. 252 (1863), 16
George, Wallace, 308
Gibbs, George C., 97–98
Gilchrist, Samuel, 141, 144, 145–46
Gillmore, Quincy A., 41, 68, 72, 77, 274
Glatthaar, Joseph T., 40, 298–99, 316
Godette, John, 63–64
Goff, Nathan, 175, 185, 286; recommends
    Hodges for a commission, 287; and North
    Carolina elections, 290; requests new

weapons, 291; Southern criticism of, 294

Gooding, James H., 83, 342 (n. 11)

Gordon, George H., 91–92, 99–100, 191, 328, 346 (n. 77)

Gordon, W. M., 95

Goss, Warren Lee, 94, 96

Gould, Lorenzo, 151–52, 267

Grand Army of the Republic (GAR): General Reynolds Post 58, 307; J. C. Beecher Post 22, 307; J. C. Abbott Post 15, 307, 309, 310; establishment, 307, 384 (n. 36); Admiral Foote Post, 308; Major How Post, 308; Taylor Post, 308; biracial nature of, 308–9, 324, 327; Fletcher Post No 20, 309

Granger, Gordon, 261

Grant, Ulysses S., 4, 125, 135, 150, 168, 170–71; and reports of eligible recruits in New Bern, 168–69, 189–90; and Fort Fisher, 176–77, 178–79; postwar use of troops, 256, 260–62, 282, 290

Gray, Jeremiah, 141, 301

Green, John, 130

Green, William A., 155, 164, 175, 245–46, 287, 294–95

Greene, George, 37, 109

Gregg, John, 140–41

Gregory, Alexander, 138

Gregory, Henry, 87, 345 (n. 66)

Griffin, Alexander, 81

Griffin, Joel R., 121

Griffin, Larry, 131

Griffin, W., 205

Griffith, Barnes, 62, 64, 341 (n. 138)

Griggs, James H., 54

Grimes, Hull, 318

Grimsley, Mark, xiv

Guerrilla warfare, 114–17, 119–20, 134, 235, 276, 349 (n. 6), 377 (n. 56)

Gyan, Alexander, 38

Hagood, Johnson C., 182

Hale, Thomas, 29

Hall, Thomas A., 29, 91

Hallam, Henry, 259, 373 (n. 10)

Halleck, Henry W., 41, 59, 106, 179, 261–62, 374 (n. 20)

Hallowell, Norwood P., 23

Hammond, Annie, 319

Hand, D. W., 234

Hankins, Hester, 31

Hardy, Israel, 208

Harget, Israel, 206, 209

Harland, Edward, 199

Harris, George, 218

Harris, James H., 312–13, 314

Harrison, Frank, 32

Harrison, Henry, 174, 360 (n. 58)

Hart, William H., 148–49; command of 36th USCT, 146, 270; in Texas, 267–68; command style, changes in, 270–71

Hassel, Albert, 104

Hatch, John P., 106–7, 109

Hatlinger, Joseph J., 49, 134–35

Hawks, Ester Hill, 86, 99, 103, 104

Hawley, Joseph R., 284, 378 (n. 73)

Hayes, Robert B., 212

Hector, Jacob, 308

Hendrick, Owen A., 122, 165

Hendrick, William H., 211–14, 341 (n. 134)

Herring, Daniel, 181

Heston, Benjamin, 206, 208

Higginson, Thomas Wentworth, 14, 85, 334 (n. 12)

Hill, Daniel H., 61, 301

Hill, Henry, 207, 208

Hill, Warren, 196–97

Hinks, Edward W., 124, 135, 163–64, 354 (n. 69); perception of 37th USCT, 167–68

Hodges, John L. R., 287

Hodges, Thorndike, 33, 69

Hoffman, W., 47, 127–30, 133

Hoke, Robert F., 59, 155, 180–82, 198, 235

Holden, William, 290

Holeman, Henry, 292

Hollis, Silas, 138, 148, 354 (n. 79)

Holloway, Miles, 129

Holman, John H., 147, 161, 169–73, 246–47

Holmes, Oliver Wendell, 323–24, 328

Honey Hill, Battle of, 106–8

Hood, James W., 238–39, 313

Hood, John B., 143

Hooker, Edward, 133

Howard, Oliver H. P., 292–93
Howard, Oliver Otis, 245, 247, 263–64, 272
Hubbard, R. Y., 194
Huger, Benjamin, 276
Hunter, David, 4–5, 14
Hutt, Charles Warren, 126–27, 130

Ives, George W., 49

Jack, John, 304
Jackson, Jarvis, 64, 337 (n. 65), 341 (n. 140)
Jackson, William, 276
Jacksonville and Tallahassee Railroad, 99
James, Douglas, 155
James, Frank, 264, 386 (n. 61)
James, Horace: appointed superintendent of
    blacks, 220; establishes camps, 221–22;
    goals for Roanoke, 224, 228, 230, 241,
    241; and aid from North, 227, 233; re-
    ports, 231, 232; duties, 231–32; criticized
    by Hand, 234; attitude to black autonomy,
    237; supports Streeter, 237, 264, 371
    (n. 69); supports Fitz, 238–39; favors re-
    trenchment, 243
James, Miles, 129, 144–45
Jameson, Thorndike C.: background, 59–62;
    court-martialed, 64, 203–4; and Rhode
    Island bounties, 188–89; and recruiting
    expenses, 191–92; and benefits of credit-
    ing Northern states, 192; and dishonest
    recruiting agents, 195–98; role for black
    troops, 198–99; and yellow fever out-
    break, 199–203; and Poor, 201–2
Jamison, Elizabeth, 276–77
Johnson, Andrew, 247, 256, 284
Johnson, Frances, 250
Johnson, George, 87
Johnson, Jerome, 47
Johnson, Samuel, 87, 159
Johnson, Thomas, 359 (n. 40)
Johnson, Willard H., 142
Johnson, William, 44
Johnston, Joseph E., 184
Joiner, Gilbert, 164
Jones, Bill, 298
Jones, Charles A., 32
Jones, Henry, 137

Jones, Jack, 104
Jones, Rufus, 84
Jones, William, 129
Joyner, Nathan, 304
Juárez, Benito, 266

Kansas units
    1st Kansas Colored, 4
Kautz, August V., 150, 170–71
Kelly, Thomas, 176
Kenney, Edwin A., 211
Kent, Henry, 223
Kent, Mary Elizabeth, 223
Kentucky: importance to Lincoln, 3
Keyes, William, 308
Kiddoo, Joseph B., 172
Kimball, James, 35, 348 (n. 109)
Kinsley, Edward W., 25, 30–31, 102
Kirby Smith, Edmund, 260–61, 263

Ladd, James O., 88, 92, 97–98
Laird, William H., 128
Lammerson, Nicholas, 174
Lane, James H., 4, 27
Langley, Joseph G., 50
Lawson, Henry T., 205
Lee, Frank, 13
Lee, Robert E., 59, 150, 162, 171, 221, 259
Lee, Samuel Phillips, 163
Lee, William Henry Fitzhugh, 164
Lehmann, Theodore F., 245
Leisure activities, 151–52
Leonard, Andrew, 86
Lewis, John, 164
Liberator, 61, 84
Lincoln, Abraham, xi, 41, 64, 124, 203, 219;
    and black recruitment, 1–4, 6–7, 330
    (n. 3); and black POWs, 16; and Fort
    Fisher, 176
Lisk, Mark, 128–30
Littlefield, Milton Smith, 104
Lockwood, Henry H., 131–32
Logue, Larry, 298
Longstreet, James, 171
Loomis, Harlan P., 109, 278, 280
Louisiana, USS, 177–78, 361 (n. 69)
Louisiana Native Guard, 5–6, 17–18, 27, 28

Lynch, Jesse, 105
Lynn Mechanics' Association, 43

Mabson, George L., 309, 314, 384 (n. 43)
Mabson, William P., 314
Maher, Thomas P., 62, 258
Maine units
  13th Maine, 17
Malone, Bartlett, 130
Mann, Albert W., 30, 31
Mann, L., 69; clash with De Grasse, 73–74, 343
  (n. 22); and smallpox, 76–77
Manning, W. C., 86
Mansfield (doctor, 92nd New York Volun-
  teers), 46
Marcy, Henry O., 76–77, 89, 90, 91, 99–100;
  lack of sympathy for men, 102, 105; criti-
  cizes Beecher, 104
Mariner, Celia, 251
Mariner, Eli, 251
Mars, John N., 27, 34, 43, 75, 91
Marshall, Alonzo, 139
Marshall, Andrew, 165
Marston, Gilman, 132
Marvin, Hiram L., 157–60
Massachusetts Medical Society, 25
Massachusetts units
  1st Massachusetts Volunteers, 55
  2nd Massachusetts Heavy Artillery, 63, 194,
    197, 198–99, 214
  5th Dismounted Massachusetts, 135
  5th Massachusetts Cavalry, 314
  11th Massachusetts, 55
  13th Massachusetts Volunteer, 286
  14th Massachusetts, 43
  17th Massachusetts, 24, 37
  23rd Massachusetts, 24
  25th Massachusetts Volunteers, 24, 124, 220
  26th Massachusetts Volunteers, 214
  29th Massachusetts, 25
  33rd Massachusetts, 54
  40th Massachusetts Mounted, 79–80, 98
  44th Massachusetts, 29
  45th Massachusetts, 33
  54th Massachusetts, xiii, 7, 13, 68; at Olustee,
    79, 81–82, 84–85, 93, 94; reputation of,
    86; clash with white troops, 274

55th Massachusetts, 13, 14, 40, 41, 67–68,
  74, 89; move to Florida, 77–79; men con-
  victed of rape, 104
Mattick, Amos, 32
Mattox, Frank, 94, 95, 347 (n. 91)
Maximilian (emperor of Mexico), 266
McCabe, James, 210
McClellan, George B., 6, 9, 22; attitude toward
  black soldiers, 2
McConnell, Stuart, 308
McDonnell, William, 295
McDougal, Isaac, 193
McElroy, John, 94
McIntire, Henry, 103–4, 348 (n. 110)
McIver, Simon, 304
McLain, Dow, 321
McLaurin, William, 309, 385 (n. 41)
McMurray, John, 246
Means, James, 219–20
Medals of Honor, 112, 144–46
Meekins, Isaac, 248
Mellon, James M., 288
*Miami*, USS, 159
Midget, Lawrence, 137
Militia Act (1862), 4, 17, 331 (n. 7)
Miller, David, 164
Miller, Henry H., 47–48
Miller, Jackson, 157, 159
Miller, Madison, 293
Miller, Nelson, 293, 380 (n. 102)
Miller, Silas, 165–66
Monroe, John, 36, 386 (n. 61)
Montgomery, James, 79, 81–82
Moore, Isaac, 288
Moore, James H., 316–17
Moore, William, 209
Morris, Benjamin, 314
Morris, Thomas, 208
Morrow, Robert A., 202–3, 233
Moses, William E., 194, 341 (n. 138)
Mountain, Peter, 305
Mullen, Alice, 251–52
Munroe, James M., 287

Naglee, Henry M., 48
National Freedmen's Relief Association, 203,
  216

*National Tribune*, 308

Nelson, Charles, 174

Newbern, Andrew, 148

New Bern: capture of, 11, 217; economic opportunities for blacks in, 29–30, 216; Confederate attack on, 59–60; and Trent River refugee camp, 221–22

*New Bern Times*, 258

Newberry, Jacob, 94

Newborn, Allen, 302

Newby, Washington, 317

New England Freedmen's Aid Society, 216, 233

*New England Mechanic*, 43

New Hampshire units
    5th New Hampshire, 126, 132
    7th New Hampshire, 80–81; and defective muskets, 83, 344 (n. 53)

New Market Heights, Va., 140–44, 170

Newton, Allen. *See* Newborn, Allen

*New York Age*, 309

*New York Herald*, 142

*New York Times*, xii, 143, 274

New York units
    7th New York Light Artillery, 57
    67th New York, 25
    85th New York, 37
    98th New York, 45, 120
    99th New York, 62, 235
    127th New York, 274
    141st New York, 25
    144th New York, 91
    150th New York, 63
    157th New York, 91
    165th New York, 274, 376 (n. 52)

Nietzsche, Constantine, 165, 174–75

Nixon, Samuel, 310

Noble, Rufus, 179

Noble, William H., 99, 347 (n. 95)

North, James N., 47

North Atlantic Blockading Squadron, 12

North Carolina units
—black
    1st North Carolina Colored Heavy Artillery, 58; reason for establishment of, 59–60, 187; raising and training of, 61–65, 194, 199, 210–13; shortage of officers, 63–64, 194–95, 198, 211–14; redesignated 14th

USCHA, 187, 211; and nature of "heavy" artillery, 187–88; bounties, 188–89, 203; regimental strength, 194, 210–14; fatigue duties, 198–99, 206, 207–8, 212; and yellow fever outbreak, 199–203; and yellow fever deaths, 202; and possible fraud by Jameson, 203–4; move to Carolina City, 205–6, 211; tighter discipline, 206–7; hardships, 206–8; problems with alcohol, 209–10. *See also* U.S. Colored Heavy Artillery: 14th USCHA

1st North Carolina Colored Volunteers, 28; raising and training of, 32–39, 71–72; noncommissioned officers, 35–38; discipline in, 39; used weapons and equipment, 39–40, 75–76, 343 (nn. 32, 33); and musket practice, 39–41, 78–79; move to Folly Island, 41–42, 67–70; fatigue duties, 68–72, 76; and illness, 69–70, 73, 76; redesignated 35th USCT, 76. *See also* U.S. Colored Troops: 35th USCT

2nd North Carolina Colored Volunteers, 41, 111; raising and training of, 42–49, 112; shortage of officers, 44, 48–49, 51, 338 (n. 95); transferred to Virginia, 46, 112; heavy fatigue duties, 48–49, 51, 112; used weapons and equipment, 51; regimental strength, 112; takes part in raids, 112–23; and illness, 121; redesignated 36th USCT, 123; clash with white civilians, 350 (n. 19). *See also* U.S. Colored Troops: 36th USCT

3rd North Carolina Colored Volunteers, 52; recruitment and training, 53–58, 155; heavy fatigue duties, 56; clash with white soldiers, 57; bounties, 58; redesignated 37th USCT, 153; short companies, 153–54. *See also* U.S. Colored Troops: 37th USCT
—Confederate
    8th North Carolina, 9
—white
    1st North Carolina Union Volunteers, 189, 363 (n. 4)
    2nd North Carolina Union Volunteers, 62, 189, 205, 211

Northcott, Starking, 94, 96

Northern Freedmen's Aid Association, 280
Northern recruiting agents, 188–95; and fraud,
    191; historians' view of, 192–93; effec-
    tiveness, 193–94; dishonest practices,
    195–98
Nourse, Frederick A., 259, 341 (n. 138)

Oakes, B. F., 74
Oates, Charles, 176, 316–17
Oberman, Aaron, 94, 95–96
Obman, Mingo, 236
Ocean Pond. *See* Olustee, Battle of
O'Hara, James E., 315, 386 (n. 63)
Ohio units
    48th Ohio Infantry, 269, 375 (n. 43)
Olustee, Battle of, 75, 79–88, 89, 101, 105, 250,
    304, 325; casualty rates, 87
Ord, Edward O. C., 139, 149–50, 170–71;
    character of, 150; and black troops, 151,
    260–62, 374 (n. 19)
Ormond, Windsor, 208
Osborn, Thomas Ward, 108
*Ottawa*, USS, 91–92, 346 (n. 77)
Overton, William, 36
Owen, John, 128, 160, 352 (n. 52)

Paine, Charles J., xi, 136, 139–40, 143, 146, 168;
    assault on Richmond, 169–70; and Fort
    Fisher, 176–81
Palmer, Innis N., 45, 59, 63, 194, 199, 204,
    238–39
Paludan, Phillip, 114
Parker, Aaron, 46
Parker, James, 264
Patrick, Marsena R., 261
Patuxent River farm, 133, 353 (n. 60)
Paxton, Penelope, 319
Peck, John J., 46, 59, 123; as critical of recruit-
    ing activities, 160–61, 341 (n. 128); and
    refugees, 222; visits Roanoke, 232; fears
    attack on Roanoke, 235
*Peninsula* (Jacksonville, Fla.), 87
Peoples, William H., 211
"People's war," 273
Perkins, James, 94
Pettigrew, James Johnson, 202–3, 233

Phelps, John W., 5
*Philadelphia Ledger*, 84
Phillips, Sidney, 45
Pickett, George E.: attack on New Bern,
    59–60, 221–22; concern at Roanoke, 235
Pickett, Josiah, 125
Pierce, Benjamin F., 104
Pierce, Edward, 285
Plymouth: capture of, 155–60, 163
Point Lookout Prison, 111, 125, 160, 327; num-
    ber of prisoners in, 126, 127, 130, 352
    (n. 47); description of, 126–27, 132
Poole, George E., 264
Poor, Walter S.: as critical of Jameson, 201–2;
    takes command of 1st NCCHA, 203;
    background, 204–5; attitude toward black
    civilians, 205; fills 1st NCCHA, 211–14;
    denied promotion, 213, 257; and wives in
    camp, 251; and deserters, 258; handling
    officers, 259
Porter, David D.: Fort Fisher expeditions,
    176–9; attitude toward black troops, 178
Port Hudson, La., 28, 72, 325, 335 (n. 30)
Portlock, Henry, 288
Potter, Edward E., 106–7, 218, 367 (n. 7)
Powers, Alfred, 197
Powers, A. W., 305
Pratt, Benjamin F., 118, 125, 131, 135–36, 141,
    146, 263, 270
Pratt, Levi G., 71
Preston, Daniel, 125
Price, Sylvester, 133

Ransom, Matthew W., 158
Rape, 104, 105, 135, 335 (n. 34), 353 (n. 65)
Read, Abel. *See* Reed, Abraim
Reconstruction: racial violence, 255–56, 267,
    269–70, 285, 373 (n. 8), 377 (n. 55); and
    policy on use of black troops, 256–57,
    259, 260–62, 266; and killing of soldiers,
    258–59, 259–60, 276, 291, 298; and freed-
    men policy in South Carolina, 277–81
Reddick, Anderson, 159
Reddick, Frances, 249, 319
Reed, Abraim, 155, 174, 360 (n. 58)
Reed, William N., 27, 87, 89; background, 25;

in temporary command of 1st NCCV,
75–77; and Olustee, 79, 81–83; death of,
86
Regional prejudice and black soldiers, 70,
85–86, 327–28, 345 (n. 61)
Rembaugh, A. C., 165, 169
Rhind, Alexander C., 178
Rhode Island units
2nd Rhode Island Regiment, 61
5th Rhode Island Heavy Artillery, 61, 287
Rice, Marshall N., 108
Richmond and Petersburg Railroad, 162
*Richmond Examiner*, 16
Rio Grande River: and black service on frontier, 261–72
Roanoke Island: Union seizure of, 9–13, 217,
223–25; and refugees, 119; and illegal
trade, 122–23
—freedmen's colony on: establishment, 13,
216, 225–26, 369 (n. 27); arrival of refugees at, 119, 234, 235–36; and goals of
Wild, 224, 226, 228, 241; and goals of
James, 224, 228, 241, 242–43; problems
facing, 226–27, 230, 232, 234, 236–37,
242, 244–46; and fraud and abuse, 227,
239–40, 245–46; barracks in, 228–30, 234,
236; layout of, 230; and naval depot, 231;
population, 231, 232, 241–42, 245, 346;
and unpaid wages, 231, 234, 239, 242, 244,
246, 370 (n. 53); and horses and equipment for freedmen, 232, 234, 237–38;
schools and teachers in, 233, 236, 243,
345–46; overcrowding of, 234, 246; fear
of a Confederate attack on, 235; diversity
among residents of, 236, 241; and freedmen's "council," 237; and impressments
of workers, 238–39, 241; and retrenchment, 243–46; and black ownership of
property, 247–48
Robbins, Augustus, 314
Robbins, Parker, 314
Roberts, Joseph, 213
Robinson, John C., 292–93
Robinson, Jose, 138
Roby, Edward, 138
Rockwell, H. E., 230

Rodgers, Lt. Col., 196–97
Roosevelt, Theodore, 321
Rogers, Hattie, 218
Rue, George A., 312
Ruffin, Peter, 159
Rutherford, Allan, 309

Sampson, John P., 313
Sampson, Mortimer, 137
Sanderson, George O., 230, 231, 234, 239–40,
369 (n. 31)
Saunders, John, 81
Savannah and Charleston Railroad, 106
Sawyer, Hannibal, 33
Saxton, Rufus, 5, 6, 8, 280
Schofield, John M., 182, 243; Reconstruction
plan of, 282–83, 284; and elections, 290
Schools: for enlisted men, 132–33, 275; for
black refugees, 203, 219, 233; for officers,
212, 275
Scott, Henry E., 314
Scroggs, Joseph J., 142
Seagraves, George L., 49
Second Confiscation Act (1862), 4, 331 (n. 7)
Seddon, James A., xii, 16, 95
Serrell, E. N., 71
Seward, William H., 6
Seymour, Truman B., 78, 88, 93, 98, 104; and
Olustee, 79–83, 85, 344 (nn. 46, 48)
Shackelford, Henry, 84, 93
Shaffer, James R., 62
Shaw, Henry W., 9–10
Shaw, James, 99
Shaw, McKendree, 286
Shaw, Robert Gould, xiii, 23, 86
Shepherd, John F., 305
Sheppard, Austin, 36, 348 (n. 109)
Sheppard, Miles, 139, 141
Sheridan, Philip H., 179, 260–62, 271–72
Sherman, Thomas W., 4
Sherman, William T., 176, 184, 210; attitude to-
ward black soldiers, xiii; and Honey Hill,
106; provides arms to Escobedo, 266; and
Special Field Order No. 15, 277
Simmons, Edward, 117, 142
Simmons, Samuel S., 142, 355 (n. 91)

Singer, George W., 291–92
Singleton, William, 308, 310
Sisson, Henry T., 61
Sitler, Isaac W., 210
Smallwood, George, 288
Smith, Allen, 316
Smith, D. E. Huger, 280
Smith, Drew, 248–49
Smith, Frank H., 63, 373 (n. 10)
Smith, Gustavus W., 107
Smith, James, 139
Smith, James Y., 188–89
Smith, Janis, 249
Smith, John M., 45
Smith, Parker W., 207
Smith, Peter, 249
Smith, Thomas, 280
Smith, Mrs. W. Mason, 280
Smith, William F., 167
Smith, William R., 249
Special Field Order No. 15 (1865), 277, 371
    (n. 73)
Spellman, Nathaniel, 304
Stanley, David, 261
Stanly, Edward, 219, 233, 367 (n. 5)
Stanton, Edwin M., 5, 7, 8, 13, 16, 63, 127, 188,
    225, 250
Starkey, Benjamin, 64, 196–97, 341 (n. 140)
State v. Joiner (1850), 284–85
Stearns, George L., 13, 30
Steele, Frederick, 261–62
Stephens, George E., 7
Stevens, Amasa W., 237
Stevens, David, 43
Stevens, Hazard, 51
Stoddard, William, 7, 8
Stone, Henry L., 78
Stone, Samuel, 212
Stowe, Harriet Beecher, 25
Streeter, Holland, 237, 243; accused and tried
    for fraud, 245–46, 264, 371 (n. 69)
Stringham, Silas H., 9
Sugar Loaf Hill, 180, 181, 182
Sullivan, James J., 54–55
Sullivan, Michael, 138
Swails, Stephen A., 18

Tannatt, Thomas B., 123
Taylor, George, 208–9
Terry, Alfred H., 68, 78, 171, 179–82
Tew, George W., 61
Texas: postwar occupation of, 260–62, 374
    (n. 17)
Thomas, Lorenzo, 8, 22, 72, 334 (n. 12), 366
    (n. 3)
Thomas, William H., 182, 306, 325, 388 (n. 4)
Tilcomb, W. M., 129
Tilghman, Benjamin Chew, 88
Todd, Maby, 105
Trench warfare, 111, 137, 148
Trent River Settlement, 221–22
Turner, Moses, 295
Twenty-fifth Army Corps, Army of the James,
    112, 145; creation, 149–50; move to Texas,
    260–62, 264–46; claims about lack of
    discipline of, 261–62; hardships, 267–69;
    regiments discharged, 271

Ullman, Daniel, 8, 334 (n. 12)
Uncle, William, 131
Underwriter, USS, 59
Union Leagues. See Equal Rights Leagues
U.S. Army: goal of equal treatment of all
    soldiers, 15–17, 72, 326–27; early recruit-
    ment process, 19–21; training in, 21–22,
    38–39; proportion of black soldiers in,
    postwar, 271, 273, 294, 372 (n. 1), 374
    (n. 17)
U.S. Cavalry (USC)
    1st USC, 133
    2nd USC, 133
    10th USC, 303
U.S. Colored Cavalry (USCC)
    2nd USCC, 157, 262–63, 269, 314
U.S. Colored Heavy Artillery (USCHA)
    14th USCHA: rapid demobilization, 256;
        shortage of officers, 257–58; recruiting
        efforts, 257; regimental strength, 257; and
        desertion, 258; internal conflicts, 258–59;
        replaced by 37th USCT, 282; postservice
        residences, 303
U.S. Colored Troops (USCT)
    1st USCT, 117, 169–72, 182